Making the Most of Marriage

 # SOCIOLOGY SERIES
Edited by John F. Cuber

Third Edition

Making the
Most of
Marriage

Paul H. Landis

WASHINGTON STATE UNIVERSITY

Appleton - Century - Crofts

DIVISION OF MEREDITH PUBLISHING COMPANY

NEW YORK

PREFACE

The functional marriage course must take into account the contemporary stage of life on which the roles of men and women, parents and children, change so quickly. This requires the frequent revision of a text which deals extensively with the interpersonal relationships of male and female, parent and child.

The chapter organization of this edition remains the same as in the second. Internal changes in many chapters have been extensive because new research, new bibliographical materials, and new insight have pointed the way to improvement in the text as it deals with marriage at one stage or another in the life cycle of the contemporary pair.

Insight into the values, the thinking, and the struggles of youth has grown, not only by my regular teaching of the marriage course, but also by the reading of more than a thousand student autobiographies following the outline of Appendix B. The outline is retained and highly recommended because it has proved to be helpful to young people in understanding themselves and their marriageability. Those with problems rooted in the family, particularly, seem to gain self-understanding by analyzing their personalities in terms of their family background as required by the outline.

My faith in modern marriage and family as the means by which youth may attain the highest ideals in interpersonal relationships is undiminished. In fact, it has been strengthened as further world travel has permitted more extensive intercultural comparisons. The awareness of marriage problems in the United States—the intent to analyze them and to reduce their impact—is unique in the modern world. It places our culture far ahead of the many cultures in which marriage-family systems are so completely regulated by custom that they are beyond criticism. There, whatever exists in the relationship of male and female, parent and child, is unquestioned. The dead ancestral hand lies heavily on the new generation.

The very existence of functional courses and texts in marriage and family is strong testimony to the fact that in our culture we search for understanding and improvement. The seriousness with which young people seek to know what lies ahead for them in mate choice, marriage, and parenthood—their wish to know what has been learned through research that may serve them as a guide—is our best hope for improvement in marriage and parenthood.

P. H. L.

CONTENTS

FIGURES

I
INTRODUCTORY

INTRODUCTION

Marriage Has Improved

When one claims that there has been progress in any phase of human experience, he is immediately subject to challenge. He is put on the defensive and proof is demanded. This is a fair expectation. The proponent of progress is forced immediately to state the criteria by which he measures improvement, for improvement implies movement toward certain goals. Acceptance of these goals as desirable is a prerequisite to acceptance of his logic.

The goals are a more complete development of the individual person and a closer, more understanding and harmonious relationship between husbands and wives, parents and children. It is primarily by psychological measures that improvement is measured, although there are tangible evidences of progress in the area of duration of marriage and in the area of privacy and material comforts that surround the married pair and their offspring. A brief review of recent cultural trends should be convincing.

The Recent Cultural Perspective

A philosophy teacher gifted with both optimism and realism told his class, "if you wish to worship the past, don't study history too closely." This bit of advice is particularly timely in the area of marriage and the family. One need look backward only a short way to find a family that was autocratic in the treatment of children, and see woman as the great underprivileged half of our population.

Contemporary writers liken the position of woman of 50 years ago to the contemporary position of the Negro.[1] And the most unbelievable

[1] See Adrienne Koch, "Two Cheers for Equality," pp. 199-215, in Seymour M. Farber and Roger H. L. Wilson (Editors), *The Potential of Woman,* (New York: McGraw-Hill Book Co., 1963); also Paul Foley, "What Happened to Women's Rights," *Atlantic,* 243:63-65, March, 1964.

aspect of this situation to moderns is that our culture accepted this status of women as proper and right, the way things ought to be.

Now we at least hold the ideal of equality in education, in the use of the ballot, in employment, in property rights, in mate choice. We even accept the view that the right to seek political office is inherent in woman's new status, although it would still be easier for a camel to go through the eye of a needle than for a woman, no matter how gifted, to become President. Certainly a Jew or a Negro is likely to attain that goal before a woman will. But the ideal is at least on the horizon, and that is the first step.

In marriage, itself, our culture has conceded to woman in our time the right of equality in family authority, mutuality in family planning, mutuality in sexual participation. The male has been trained toward the ideal of wanting a wife with whom he can converse, consult, share intellectual exchange, and to whose judgment he can readily entrust the upbringing of his children.

These transitions in the status of woman came quickly and the gap between generations was so vast as to make older living generations feel lost and bewildered in the new world. It gave the more fixed-minded a feeling that chaos had overtaken the culture. They were sure that the male was headed for extinction and that the new woman was out to wreck the world.

The cultural trend that has made the democratic handling of children the norm of our child-training system is an immeasurable gain when contrasted against the rigid authoritarian system of the first part of the century. The goal then was that of forming routine habits seated in respect for authority. The patriarchal authority was far more powerful than intelligent. The socially sanctioned abuse of children was inherent in the culture. In fact, any other pattern was considered ruinous to the child.

The patterns of our time, with their stress on growth and development for the child, in an atmosphere of equalitarian sharing, are in such marked contrast that they represent a new earth insofar as the child-training atmosphere is concerned. Even the school system has taken a revolutionary turn in its conception of human growth and discipline.

There have been many errors in the pursuit of these new goals, but on the whole, their effect in shaping a more creative, less inhibited, more mentally healthy child is beyond question.

One can also cite as an improvement the material base of family operations. This gain is best expressed in our phrase "a home of their own." The separate family dwelling is a key to the great individuation of family members in our society. One's own separate dwelling permits the growth of the individual personality in mates and children to a degree unprecedented throughout human history.

A separate home from the beginning of marriage, a place for one's children apart from relatives and other tenants of the household, is an undreamed of advantage in much of the world and is realizable by greater numbers in our society now than ever before. The beginning of this dream itself represents a great leap forward in human aspirations. The Maces, in their *The Soviet Family,* cite this awakening dream of these apartment-crowded people. Even to have a separate apartment has long been a dream of crowded Europeans. They cannot hope for a separate house of their own or their own plot of land.

With us "the family" is not all; the individual is all. This luxury of an individual household reflects our economy of abundance and makes possible the privacy required for individual growth and development. The sterner discipline life once required has given way to luxury, privilege and the concept of the infinite worth of the individual personality. A "place of their own," a marriage unhampered by living in a joint household with elders is a dream few peoples have been able to realize as we have.

The separate family dwelling has done much to relieve the ancient in-law problem, the grandparent problem, and the aunt and uncle problem in child rearing and in husband-wife relationships. The new pair can divorce themselves from the claims of undesirable kinship about to the degree they choose. Their home is truly their castle in our day and generation.

The dependence on the great family for help in crisis has been largely replaced by social services and social security. These substitutions may seem a little cold at times, but their benefits do not carry with them the emotional costs that kinfolk often extract. Even married college students often prefer the financial struggle of independence to the parental guidance and supervision which so often accompanies any degree of economic support.

Our day of economic abundance deserves the credit for the emancipation of the family home from the traditional burdens of ancestry so deeply seated in our own history, and so omnipresent in most cultures of the world still.

The Transition to Modern Marriage

With the recent cultural trend there has been a profound shift in the purposes and objectives of American marriage over a period of a few decades, and therefore in motivations for marriage. Marriage once was primarily an economic institution and mates were chosen in considerable part for their ability to help "make a go" of the economic aspects of marriage. Both husband and wife had heavy work roles if the family was to be a success. Work and property bound them together in a life-long bond. The family was the unit of survival in the socioeconomic system. The numerous duties performed in the home and on the farm made the family relationship the primary one in every aspect of life. It is no longer so, and because it is no longer so, marriage has come to be viewed as a means for personal happiness and companionship, and not primarily as a means for status, subsistence, and blood-line continuity.

This American invention—the "love marriage"—is proving to be one of the most marketable products of our culture, as the movie spreads the gospel of dating as a means of mate choice around the world. Even the Japanese throne cast aside more than 2,600 years of tradition to permit the 1959 marriage of its prince to the girl he loved, a commoner, rather than to one of the proper status.

Still, even in the United States, domestic skills for the wife and thrift and industry for the husband are standards by which successful marriage is sometimes judged. Now, however, the success or failure of a marriage does not hinge primarily on these factors but upon the ability of husband and wife to meet each other's psychological, emotional, and companionship needs.

In 1940 an anthropologist wrote a book describing life in a town called *Plainville*. It was off the main highways, and many of the old patterns of American life were still to be found. Among his accounts of life in *Plainville* is that of the characteristic attitude of women and men toward their relationships with each other and toward marriage.

> In Plainville the husband "owes his wife a good living"; he should "be true to her," and "kind to her," he should not "meddle with the house." The wifely obligation is "to be a good helpmate." She should be a good cook, a clean housewife; "saving and not extravagant." Her "average conception" of her "wifely duties" includes also the idea, I believe, that she should "yield to her husband (sexually) without minding it too much." She should be "a good and patient mother to her children" and a "comforter" to children and husband. She should not "nag" children or husband, especially the latter. She should "tend to her business" and "not meddle with the farm" or with "money matters." Husband and wife should "advise with" each other, however, when important decisions must be made in either's economic domain, or when problems arise concerning their children. If they fail to reach a common decision, then the wife should yield to her husband's judgment. All such consultations should occur beyond earshot of the children, and are frequently held in bed. Publicly, neither husband nor wife should "look with (sexual) interest at another person," nor should they ever demonstrate affection toward each other, by word or deed.[2]

2 James West, *Plainville, U.S.A.* (New York: Columbia University Press, 1945), p. 60.

Some years ago a study compared the personal values of 250 farm and professional wives.[3] The women in the professional class stressed the importance of the recognition of individuality and of opportunity for personal development and for the growth of broad common interests; the farm women emphasized happiness, peace, comfort, security, and integrity. Only 2 percent of the farm women listed any items having to do with husband-and-wife relationships; either they did not feel free to mention them or they regarded the family as a unit in which the individual as such is relatively unimportant. The idea of individual freedom seemed to be almost nonexistent among them. The limiting of the size of families according to the level of income, considered important by the professional group, was not mentioned by the farm women. It appeared that in the farm home the *family unit* was considered of most importance; in the professional home a greater amount of emphasis was placed on *individual interests* and their expression. The emphasis these professional women placed on the personal aspects of marriage is indicative of the current trend.

In 1946 a nation-wide Gallup Poll studied the chief faults ascribed to wives and husbands by their mates. This covered 3,100 men and women and showed that farm couples found the least fault with each other.[4] A third of farm men felt that their wives had no faults. Of the total group of men polled only 8 percent felt that their wives had no faults. Not a single farmer mentioned "poor housekeeping" as a fault of his wife. There was at that time a strong carry-over in the farm family of the values of the marriage-family system that has been called by sociologists the "traditional" or "institutional" family type.

Today the personal relationship is becoming the main aspect of marriage. This has led to a new set of values and goals in marriage, as we shall see in the following chapter.

Why People Marry Today

Mating is instinctive throughout much of the animal kingdom. Even homemaking among many of the birds and animals is an instinctive or near-instinctive reaction. We know it is so because without contact with each other, each species of birds builds its own uniform and unique style of nest wherever found all over the world. They build it with a mechanical perfection that only nature can inspire.

Similarly, human beings mate because of inner drives, but marriage

[3] C. C. Woodhouse, "A Study of 250 Successful Families," *Social Forces,* 8:511-532, 1930.

[4] William A. Lydgate, "The Chief Faults of Wives—and Husbands," *Redbook,* 87:28-29, 121-122, 126, June, 1946.

itself is a social institution springing from custom rather than from biology. Mating is animal, biological in origin, but marriage and home-making, family life and all the institutions centering about them are man-made. These institutions vary from tribe to tribe and from people to people over the face of the earth—in permanence, in characteristics, in motivation, in obligations, and certainly in the material aspects of life that develop around the married pair.

The debate as to whether to remain single or to assume the respon-sibilities of marriage is one which almost everyone engages in, since few marry entirely by impulse, or even entirely by the pressure of custom. Most persons marry by choice, and understand, if they are at all wise, that in doing so they are taking on certain liabilities and handicaps as well as escaping from certain situations which are, or appear to be, undesirable.

There are, of course, still many personal and social compulsions to marry. One of the most important is the realization, as one leaves the parental home, that the only way one may feel complete again is by establishing a family of his own. Only by establishing a home can he enjoy again the pattern of living he himself experienced or longed for as a child. Only thus can life seem fully proper and adequate; only thus can he find again the intimacy, warmth, and sharing that are so much a part of the satisfactions of the socialized human being.

As has been so vividly pointed out by Levy and Munroe, one's drive to marriage begins in childhood in his own home.[5] "Marriage begins in infancy," they say. "People who have learned about family loves and hates and rivalry and emotion in their parents' homes carry these lessons into their own homes. The most perfect system fails if it does not meet the expectations formed in childhood."

Women undoubtedly feel greater social and emotional pressure to marry than do men since their upbringing is much more family-oriented. Then, too, marriage is still looked upon as their most important evidence of having attained adulthood through the competitive means of mate seeking.

Another powerful pressure to marry today is the general social expectation that, particularly in recreational affairs, people will partici-pate in pairs rather than as individuals. In the earlier agrarian economy, all age groups associated in social life, but this is rarely so in urban industrial society where all social groups are stratified by age and where pairs are the normal unit of association in adulthood. One reason the older adolescent feels a little out of place·is that it is expected that he will attend any private function with a member of the opposite sex. This

---

[5] John Levy and Ruth Munroe, *The Happy Family* (New York: Alfred A. Knopf, Inc., 1938), p. 5.

is more true of women than of men, since it is assumed that a woman will have an escort in her attendance at public and private functions.

The extent to which a person of a given age feels social pressure to marry depends a great deal on the kind of community in which he lives. The college girl of 20 with two years of school remaining will sense no social pressure to marry, rather will sense considerable pressure of parental and peer-group opinion not to marry. The girl of 18 who has left high school for a job may sense great pressure to marry.

Then, too, the social prestige of marriage in some communities is very great. In those rural communities where large numbers of young people marry in or immediately out of high school, great social pressure is exerted on girls to marry early and on parents to see them married. To be able to acquire the status of marriage and begin homemaking and childbearing is one of the highest values of the community.

Why Are We So Problem-Conscious?

If marriage value and goals have changed in the direction of greater realization for husbands and wives, parents and children; if, as this chapter contends, we have actually come nearer to the goals of greater individual development, greater personal fulfillment, more creative child development, greater mutuality in the relationships of couples and of adults and children, why all the skepticism about modern marriage, why all the fear that the new generation is headed for perdition?

Rapid culture change is never easy to accept. To knock over and plow under the ancient landmarks is always viewed with alarm by those who long for the good old days.

We have tried to point out that "the good old days" were a dream in which much was forgotten; the pleasant memories are largely fiction. Even if family culture of yesteryear had all the merits its adherents claim it would not fit our day and generation. It grew in a stern, pioneer setting and cannot be transplanted. In human history there is no going back to the simple days of a different kind of existence.

Admittedly, we are problem-conscious. Almost every woman's magazine and some magazines written for the more general public carry articles that outline and suggest help for some critical marriage problem. Divorce statistics are much quoted and the pro and con of modern sex revolution is considered.

An outsider to our culture, particularly one from the more institutionalized, custom-controlled, Asiatic cultures, where marriage adjustment is not considered to exist and where it is never discussed, might well think our marriage institution is but the ruins of some earlier state of equilibrium. Safe and relatively unchallenged by change, the joint family system of these cultures is based on the secure foundations of centuries of custom. Little wonder that they see in our nuclear marriage-family system, where so much is left to the individual choice and so little to ancestral heritage, little pattern at all.

But does any modern American think he could live under a marriage-family system so completely traditional in its orientation that he would not even dare challenge its values and goals? This is the way traditional family systems tend to be. They have no problems because the system is beyond challenge.

Canada has few divorces compared to the United States. Divorce is so taboo that in most provinces an action of Parliament is required to separate a couple from their marriage pledge. Is one to accept their low divorce rate as a certain index that they have fewer unhappy marriages than we?

Being conscious of problems, recognizing the realities of their existence, is the first step toward improvement. Traditional family systems will never improve until they become problem-conscious. This is always the first step in reform.

The fact that our society exhibits concern for the welfare of husbands and wives, parents and children represents a vast leap forward in human welfare concerns. The numerous little miseries of the pair and their children have become major social concerns in our day and generation.

We are highly problem-conscious about our marriage system, because we expect so much of it. We strive for a perfection that may be unattainable in the pair relationship and in personal happiness through marriage. Having cast aside tradition, we still pursue elusive goals, but they are not low goals, they are not the goals provided by the fate of tradition. They are the goals that reach toward lofty hopes and dreams, often too romantic, and often beyond reach, but nonetheless, high goals.

Our Divorce Rate

Admittedly our divorce rate is high. It is not the highest in the world, although one frequently reads comments to that effect.[6] It is disturbingly high. Yet, considering the values and goals of modern marriage, perhaps it is not unrealistically high.

And there is a positive side even to our statistical failure. Divorce figures are often cited to attest the failure of our marriage system. They are real indices of failure, and yet the average marriage lasts longer today than ever before.

[6] Rates are much higher in Egypt, Japan and are higher in several other countries; see *Demographic Yearbook* (New York: Statistical Office, United Nations, 1955), Table 31, pp. 734 ff.; also summarized in Paul H. Landis, *Social Problems: In Nation and World* (Philadelphia: J. B. Lippincott, 1959), pp. 430-432.

White persons in their first marriage in 1900 could expect about 30 years of married life before one partner died. Today, they may expect to live together 43 years before either dies. And the chance of a golden wedding anniversary, taking into account only the death rate, is twice as great as in 1900. It will be even longer for those now in college.

Although the divorce rate is higher than it used to be, the typical married couple live together longer than did their grandparents because of the lengthening life span. And even with the high divorce rate of today there are far fewer orphan children left than formerly, for death is less a respecter of children than is divorce (Figure 0-1). Divorce has some respect, even yet, for children.

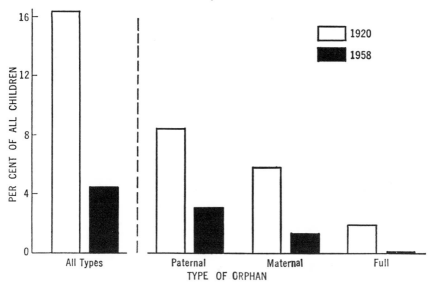

ORPHANS BY TYPE AS PERCENT OF ALL CHILDREN
UNITED STATES, 1920 AND 1958*

* Jan. 1, 1958. All basic data for both years are estimated and refer to population under age 18.

Source: Health Information Foundation. Data by L. O. Shuddle, *Social Security Bulletin*.

FIGURE 0-1————Marriage and family are safer today than ever before. Most couples live to see their children reach maturity, thus removing from the more favored populations of the world much of the age-old anxiety of untimely death of a mate and parent. The probability of a golden wedding anniversary has doubled if the couple remains together until death parts them.

TODAY'S WOMEN MARRY EARLIER, ARE WIDOWED LATER

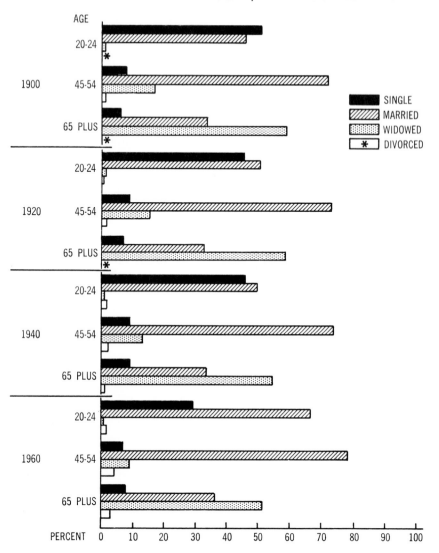

SOURCE: U. S. Department of Labor, Women's Bureau, *American Women*, Report of the President's Commission on the Status of Women, Washington, D. C., 1963, Chart 3, p. 6.

FIGURE 0-2————Early marriage and long duration of marriage are characteristic of our day. This trend gives the average couple a longer life together than at any other time in our history.

Our new, much-used reason for divorce, "mental cruelty," is indicative that marriage is no longer judged in terms of traditional value, but by the quality of the interpersonal relationship involved. Marriage is not merely a ceremony, it is a dynamic interrelationship of two individuals with personal destinies.

And even with the object lesson of failure, marriage is more popular today than ever. A greater proportion of the population in this country marry than ever before—marry younger and live together longer. Figure 0-2 shows the trend for this century. It makes strikingly clear that marriage comes much earlier and that widowhood comes much later—convincing proof of the long span of time the average couple spends together today compared to that of earlier generations.

More important than marriage statistics is the improvement of marriage in the area of interpersonal relations, in the values, goals, and realizations of the married pair. Attention is given to these areas in the following chapter.

In conclusion, modern marriage is not a failure. Its popularity indicates that it fulfills deep social and emotional needs. And the family more often sees its children to maturity without death breaking up the family than ever before in human history.

Problems

1. The modern marriage is usually expected "to meet the individual's needs for love and emotional security, status, recognition, companionship, and sex. Marriage is also sought for negative reasons—as a means of escaping certain undesirable circumstances. These needs vary in importance from one person to another, depending upon his personality and background.

   Analyze your own personality needs as best you can. Which of their various items—love, emotional security, status, recognition, companionship, sex, or negative motives—do you think will rank first in determining whom you marry? As you analyze your development why do you feel this one need is of first importance in your life?

2. Among your various personality needs, are there some which you would expect to satisfy in relationships outside of marriage? Discuss possibilities of need fulfillment through such avenues as job, friends, children, church, parents, brothers and sisters, hobbies, community activities, girls (or boys) you've previously dated, pets, etc.

3. The chapter develops the thesis that marriage has improved. Many do not

agree with this view. Present evidence to support arguments on both sides of the question.

4. Comment on the importance of separate residence as a factor in marriage and family life.

5. Explain the longer duration of marriage today, even with the higher divorce rate.

1

Values and Goals of
Modern Marriage

Marriage is a universal institution designed to provide a
stable pair relationship to assure the rearing of the helpless child, transmit wealth, and provide status. These common prerequisites of human survival are the institution's reason for existence,
but they do not encompass all values and goals of marriage. These are
added by the various cultures into which peoples are grouped. To appraise marriage, to understand its significance, even to grasp its reason
for failure, one must study it within its cultural context, for this is the
framework of human social aspirations.

Institution to Companionship

Some years ago Burgess and Locke used the "institution to
companionship" terms to describe the characteristic trend of American
marriage-family system.[1] Their conceptualization has been quite generally accepted by sociologists. It designates the radical transition from
conceiving marriage and family in terms of customary formal arrangements and traditional values to conceiving of them in terms of personal
relationships and values.

Both the old and new systems have many names, depending on their
expression in various periods of history and depending on the particular aspect of the marriage-family system being stressed.

[1] Ernest W. Burgess, Harvey J. Locke, and Mary Margaret Thomes, *The Family:
From Institution to Companionship*, Third Edition (New York: American Book Co.,
1963).

In the broadest sense, the institutional family system includes all systems in which the institution is given priority over individual inclinations and wishes. The joint family system of Asia and the affiliated family system of Latin America represent the extremes in submerging the wishes of the individual in the traditional family system. The elders dominate mate choice, provide the joint residence, and provide a joint economic security. The large family is governed by the patriarch.

The farm family of our recent past demanded less of the individual, included fewer relatives, and gave more freedom; but even so, the family and its traditions were the beginning and the end of marriage. Personal whims were not of first consideration.

Asians, viewing our current urban industrial marriage-family system, describe our marriage as the "love marriage." It is significant and surprising to them that mate choice would be left to youth, rather than being in the hands of elders, and that love rather than social status and wealth should guide mate choice.

Sociologists focusing on this aspect of our marriage system call it the romantic marriage type. This concept of marriage stresses the individual's supreme right to love and be loved in a romantic, sexual sense. This is considered the essence of supreme happiness.

In a broader framework, sociologists use the term "nuclear" family to describe the new independent family unit, consisting of the pair and their offspring. This family system has reached its most ideal form in the United States, with its high standard of living and high level of personal income. There is no need for the pooling of family funds as in the joint family, or even the pooling of family effort as in the rural economy of an earlier day. Personal insurance programs, company fringe benefits, and government security provisions liberate the individual and the pair from the economic bonds of kinship. The separate living arrangement provides the setting for the nuclear unit.

In fact, the separate abode is considered a prerequisite to independence. The pair is free to work out their relationship unhampered by close-living in-laws and rear their children with minimum interference from parents and other kinfolk.

The new stress on interpersonal relationships in marriage and family has led to the current emphasis on companionship as a major test of mate relationships. The institution is of secondary importance, romance is the lure by which mates are drawn together, but the quality of the relationship which binds it together, if it is to be durable, is companionability. Those who not only love, but who also have enough common characteristics and interests to share each other's life as companions are the ones who are destined for the happy, durable marriage.

The goals of happiness through love and companionship are very elusive ones indeed. Are they attainable? Are they significant?

The meaning of any goal is relevant to the culture in which the family functions. It is within the framework of urban industrial culture that the goals of marriage must be appraised.

Companionship As a Goal

In the United States, a man builds a house in which to spend his old age, and he sells it before the roof is on; he plants a garden and rents it just as the trees are coming into bearing; he brings a field into tillage and leaves other men to gather the crops; he embraces a profession and gives it up; he settles in a place, which he soon afterwards leaves to carry his changeable longings elsewhere.

DE TOCQUEVILLE, *Democracy in America*, 1831

Each year 35 to 40 million Americans change their residence— for some it will mean a switch to a new house or apartment close by; for others, across continent, or even an international move. The U. S. Census shows that only 35 percent of the heads of families in the nation are living in the place of their birth. Of those aged 30, 60 percent have already moved from the place of their birth. One family in 5 is living over a thousand miles from the place of the head's birth. Five million families a year move across state lines. In western states more than half were born elsewhere. College graduates are twice as likely to move as grade school educated persons.[2]

"Mobility insecurity" affects couples, small children, teenagers, and grandparents not tough enough to take it.

Mobility, and consequent anonymity, affect the typical American, particularly the urban dweller. Migration takes him, in the course of a lifetime, far from the intimate circle of his birth. This has created in the human spirit a longing for a close emotional tie such as those who lived in a world of kin and neighbors never knew. The joint family system, the close tribal unit, the integrated primary group neighborhood give the individual continuous social support. He never bears his burdens alone. His crises are shared from cradle to grave, giving his emotional life a sure anchor. He need not demand a close love-life or the compatible association of a mate in marriage, in order to guarantee a full social and emotional life.

The vast loneliness of the great city, its social isolation for the

[2] For a recent Census study of mobility see U. S. Department of Commerce, Bureau of the Census, "Mobility of Population of the United States, March 1959 to 1960," Series P-20, No. 113, January 2, 1962.

stranger, creates in the mind of man a sense of isolation and futility that has driven many persons to suicide, and others to the companionship of dogs, cats, parrots, and even to the companionship of silent, nondemonstrative pets or objects—fish, turtles, and flowers. Those most deprived of companionship even talk to these silent, unresponsive companions to hear their own voice and keep in touch with the flow of language which makes man human. A filling station operator in a neighborhood gas station recognized this problem when he said, "People come here to have someone to tell their problems to." Many a bartender feels that his place serves the same social need.

Little wonder that marriage has had to take on new meaning and that almost everyone seeks marriage today and seeks it early. The family home is a launching platform into the competitive world outside. As young people grow older and sense more keenly the impersonal character of the adult experience of our time, they understand more deeply the need to establish a close tie—one that will guarantee them not only companionship but sociability itself—stable, tangible, and ever-present sociability.

More than 35 years ago, Harvey Zorbaugh described life in the "Furnished Rooms" section of Chicago, where young people from farms and small Middle West towns landed on their arrival in the city in quest of fame and fortune.[3] Here, where the turnover of residents was very rapid and anonymity, characteristic of social life, many of the couples living together as married were not married at all. Excuses given were that they wanted to have, "someone to come home to," "someone to talk to," "someone to tell my troubles to."

Morals cannot always stand the test of the great loneliness and the feeling of being cut off from social life. Marriage is modern man's best arrangement for avoiding the solitariness of adulthood. Few men can stand a life of solitude, and even fewer women can stand it. Marriage is the institution which provides for permanent companionship. A mobile society provides no other source of enduring companionship.

Those who find marriage so miserable that they cannot endure it and seek a way out in divorce, do not survive the single state long in our society. Very soon they seek another mate, some even return to the former mate to make another try. The widowed too seek another mate in our day, when to be outside the fold of marriage is to be lonely in a sense that people are not lonely in societies with deeper ties in family and locality groups. As we shall see from data presented later (Chapter 34), the divorced are more likely to marry than are the single; the widowed also are more likely to marry than are the single of comparable age.

[3] Harvey Zorbaugh, *The Gold Coast in the Slum* (Chicago: University of Chicago Press, 1929).

The need for the companionship of a marriage partner in the industrial world cannot be written off as a superficial and spurious value. In terms of a different kind of society, it may be an unnecessary value, but not in terms of the world in which modern urban industrial man must live his life.

The anonymous life of large urban groups makes for a vast loneliness in the midst of people. Marriage is the person's best hedge against this modern disease of the metropolis. Families become scattered. Friends move or one moves away from them. In thickly populated areas people are seldom interested in their neighbors. Only the small family remains to give permanent association. The young woman of today is not likely to choose a husband by the size of his farm or the Dunn and Bradstreet rating of the business he will inherit. The perfect male nowadays is judged in terms of companionability.

It surprises some young people to learn that love in itself does not assure companionability. Companionability involves the sharing of interests, activities, values, and aspirations; love does not. One may feel a deep affection for someone many times his own age, for example, or for a person of very different interests, habits and moral standards. Companionship may be difficult if not almost impossible in such love relationships. Above all, companionship of couples today is dependent on their ability to talk things over. To be unable to communicate with a mate fully and confidentially is one of the greatest possible handicaps to marriage in the modern world.

The human being, to remain human, needs someone with whom he can interact on a continuing basis, expressing his deepest joys and fears, plans and failures, hopes and needs. The more that is known about human nature through the study of psychology and sociology, through clinical experience, even from an understanding of suicide—lonely man's last desperate resort—the more clearly it is understood that the human being who can talk frankly and freely with a confidant travels life's journey most safely.

Those who lack companionship and who have no direct way of expressing their hopes, fears, anxieties, and longing to another human being are in danger of losing their sense of personal direction, of meaning, and of rationality. Human normality is determined by the opportunity one is given for constant, meaningful communication with other persons.

A rural couple celebrating their 72nd wedding anniversary was asked how they had managed a successful marriage. The wife's answer to the question was, "We did little fussin'. We said little. Mostly we just set."

This may not be too unrepresentative of many rural marriages of yesterday. But today's couple has much greater need to communicate with each other—to fuss, to do, and above all, to talk. A marriage of silence and sitting would fall far short of success in terms of meeting the modern person's needs.

The democratic marriage relationship is the best institution provided by man for giving an atmosphere of confidence and trust in which free communication on a person-to-person level is continuously possible. Even law courts preserve this confidence by refusing to require a person to testify against his spouse. Only the companionable couple can attain a really confidential level of expression, and only they realize the most from the marriage relationship.

One of the best indices of the effect of social isolation and a sense of anonymity on personality is the suicide rate. Data for a three-year period, 1949-1951, indicate that the married are by far the least likely to suicide. Of white males, only 21 per 100,000 of those married committed suicide, compared to 80 of those divorced, 76 of those widowed, and 44 of those single. Comparable rates for the white female are 19 for divorced, 13 for widowed, 8 for the single, and 7 for the married. This is striking evidence that marriage is an insurance factor, as far as the individual's hold on his own life and the future is concerned—a vital hedge against anonymity.[4]

Happiness As a Goal

In the United States a hundred years ago happiness was not the primary concern of marriage. A person was more likely to pick a mate for qualities that wore well and to be concerned about the practical aspects of the marriage. But people also worked fourteen to sixteen hours a day in order to make a living. They struggled for the conquest of a frontier. Life was rigorous. A puritanical attitude toward all levity still carried over in the culture. Life was serious and the stake was survival itself. Pleasure seeking as such was condemned, and condemned no less in marriage than in all other aspects of life.

In our culture abundance of goods and leisure have become the lot of nearly all, and life moves in terms of a different set of values. With the increase of luxury and leisure, moderns have come to look upon happiness as a desirable goal not only for marriage but for all of life. Recreation and pleasure are considered man's just due; they are even considered rejuvenating and worthwhile—the proper rewards of work and of earned leisure.

In terms of such contemporary values, who is to say that this goal of marriage happiness is a spurious one? Most students of American marriage prefer to accept the contemporary values and hold not only that

---

[4] Metropolitan Life Insurance Company, "Mortality Lowest in Married Population," *Statistical Bulletin*, 38:5, February, 1957.

happiness in marriage is a worthy goal, but also that it represents a new and higher level of human aspiration than earlier generations dared hold.

The fact that youth can make happiness the first demand of marriage testifies to the luxury enjoyed today, both in material blessings and spiritual values. On the material side, the human spirit has been freed from the overwhelming burden of incessant work and duty. On the spiritual side, modern concepts of well-being provide a culture in which man dares dream that he can be happy. It is logical that marriage is placed at the center of this dream.

It is doubtful that humanity has ever sought a goal in marriage so difficult to realize and yet so worthy of realization as "happiness." One must grant the psychological necessity of many people compromising the ideal with the demands of reality in everyday living as man and wife, but even so, about three couples in four live out their life span without completely shattering this dream. One cannot claim that all who remain loyal to their marriage pledge fully realize happiness. But many studies[5] that have measured the happiness of married couples show that about two marriages in three are either happy or very happy.

Some critics challenge such research, saying one cannot depend on people's ratings of their own happiness or success. But some studies have used not only self-ratings, but have had friends rate the marriage too. Self-ratings and ratings by others agree.[6] This suggests that a couple knows whether or not the marriage is happy, and that the great majority of marriages that survive actually realize happiness. Three generations ago no one would have thought of asking couples whether or not their marriages were happy.

Even legal grounds for divorce today indicate how seriously the value "happiness" is accepted in the culture as the standard for marriage success. Many divorces are granted for "mental cruelty," an intangible quality but one which well expresses the opposite of happiness. The Mosaic Law recognized no such reason for dissolving marriage, nor did our nation's customs and laws of 1890. The philosophy of marriage has changed to the point where even the law recognizes that it must produce happiness or fail.

A generation or two ago, few farm couples who were considered successful in their family life manifested any affection. Some of them battled and nagged at each other chronically. The community did not worry about these marriages breaking up. The couple had land, children, and the respect of neighbors and relatives. No one expected that they would

[5] E. W. Burgess and Leonard S. Cottrell, *Predicting Success or Failure in Marriage* (Englewood Cliffs, N. J.: Prentice-Hall, Inc., 1939); Lewis M. Terman and others, *Psychological Factors in Marital Happiness* (New York: McGraw-Hill Book Co., 1938) are the best of these studies.

[6] Burgess and Cottrell, *op. cit.*, Ch. 3.

run to a lawyer simply because they did not like each other. In the good religious neighborhood, few couples acted as though they did like each other, but they had enough mutual activities to keep them occupied and interdependent. They had a farm to operate and children to raise; this was all they demanded of marriage.

Perhaps part of the impression they gave was the customary reserve of farm folks of the day in expressing affection. There was a reticence among all but the teenage group about admitting in public any interest in the opposite sex. Even the teenagers were shy about it.

Nowadays, the male admits quite openly that there is no creature on earth quite so interesting to him as woman. The once-reserved female now lets her own sex know quite frankly that the opposite sex interests her, and likely as not she acknowledges this interest to the male.

Well within the memory of some of our older citizens, boys and girls were kept on separate playgrounds for fear they would discover that there was a natural fascination of the sexes for each other. Now, from early teenage up, young people are taught to seek happiness with each other. The relationship of male and female has become the most important one in life.

Love As a Value

A few years ago a group of practicing psychologists were guests at a ministers' institute at which ministers and psychologists gave papers in turn. After three of each had spoken, it was very apparent that the psychologists were making a better case for love as a key to personality than were the ministers. There has been much recent writing of psychiatrists and clinical psychologists in which the love theme is as prominent as in the New Testament.

That love has a therapeutic effect, few can doubt today. That it is the key factor in making man's life complete and worthwhile, few question.

If this is true of mankind in general, in an industrial society love of a mate must be recognized as a supreme value for so many aspects of life have become competitive that much social experience is the very antithesis of love. The human being of our time and place on earth must find a love focus that is dependable and sure. In such a world, the "love marriage" is not merely a nice arrangement, it is a necessity.

A human being is in a dismal state indeed when he begins to feel that there is no one in the world who cares deeply about him. A person's life is most meaningful when it means a great deal to some other person or persons. This need for unqualified love is fulfilled in the normal childhood home by the parent-child relationship.

The love of a member of the opposite sex comes gradually to replace the affection parents expressed in so many forms during childhood. This new affection is not the one-sided affair parental love often is. Parents often give, expecting nothing in return. Mature love involves not only the feeling of being cared for by others, but even more important, of caring for others. It means not only wanting others to feel deeply about oneself, but also feeling a personal responsibility for their happiness.

It is through a wise marriage that one can be most fully assured of an enduring love in adulthood. The husband-wife relationship becomes for the adult the most important outlet for affection. Here, as in all human relationships, affection is found by being affectionate.

There are other kinds of close comradeship, but our society recognizes none as full, close, and complete as the marriage tie. It brings emotional security. If the marriage meets this need, it provides a place to relax and feel free from competition and assault. It is a refuge from trouble and a hiding place in a world that often brings rough treatment. In it one feels anchored. Those with a normal childhood have been trained for this kind of inner security by their childhood parental relationship. It is easy for them to find the psychological counterpart of parental affection in marriage.

Those who have not been permitted to form a close emotional attachment to parents in childhood often find it difficult to realize emotional security in marriage. But if a sense of security can be realized at all, through any human relationship, marriage is designed to bring and maintain it. One without emotional security always feels that he has a flank exposed to the enemy, that he lacks defense against his own misgivings and fears.

Marriage sometimes fails to bring emotional security. In such cases, the marriage is vitally deficient, perhaps due to emotional disturbances in the earlier parent-child relationships.

Regardless of human failures and frailties in this area, a feeling of security is required of successful marriage today. Failure to realize this is failure indeed.

Complete realization of love does much to put ego-striving in its proper place. The love-starved personality often works itself out in inordinate ambition, intolerable vanity, unreasonable demands for the service and/or respect of others. The personality that has found itself in a secure emotional relationship is mellowed and matured. The ego takes a more subdued place in the scheme of living and other people are given a larger place. It is in this sense that love, with the inherent sense of emotional security it brings, is not only the savior of the world but of the marriage relationship. It is the antidote for belligerence, conquest, conflict, competition, and self-seeking.

The late Willard Waller,[7] shrewd observer of interactions in the marriage relationship, observed that spouses going through the alienation process leading up to divorce develop overwhelming egos. The security and fullness of love is vanishing and in its place the ego emerges and makes overwhelming claims and demands. The ego-subduing love element of marriage must, in the process of divorce, be replaced by compensatory ego fictions. The mate must be blamed and the self, justified. The wife who has never written a line declares she is going to write a best seller. The husband of mediocre wealth or ability is going to become a financier or inventor. Grandiose purposes and plans represent the struggle of the personality to fill the void left by the loss of emotional security in the marriage.

With women particularly, the sense of belonging emotionally is associated with the desire to have and to give to children. The desire for motherhood, which may be in large part socially cultivated, is a normal yearning of woman as she reaches the years of maturity. She desires the full life which motherhood promises. In motherhood she sees the closest kind of human relationship and sees in it also a chance to contribute to her own future happiness and security in having children who belong to her, and to whom she belongs. Many young couples also share this feeling to the extent that it becomes a major aspiration in their lives together. This becomes one of the most purposeful aspects of their plans for marriage and for their life together.

Many, of course, cannot visualize family life this clearly in advance of marriage. Men generally have to be taught to want parenthood. Couples who seriously undertake parenthood in faith and confidence, however, do develop a deep sense of emotional security from it and thus enrich their marriage. The total family becomes the area of emotional expression and unity. The marriage relationship itself is strengthened by the extension of the bonds of affection to include children and by the joint aspirations which parents hold for them in planning their development.

In a world that too often seems filled with pessimism and gloom, children give the couple a vital stake in the future. No one who senses the world of childhood and its simple hopes can be pessimistic about the future or about man's and his own high destiny. Although these realities are often only vaguely sensed in early youth, they are a part of the reality that makes marriage and family the most basic institution of mankind and one which, when a substantial part of its goals are realized, promises the fulfillment of the greatest possible range of human emotional needs.

[7] Willard Waller, *The Old Love and the New* (New York: Horace Liveright Co., 1929).

Ego Support

Harold Summers, president of the guild of London hair-dressers declared, "modern women no longer require love—what they want and constantly seek is reassurance."[8] Freud and his followers call man's drive to excel, his "ego." Sociologists in more recent terminology have spoken merely of man's needs for status, or recognition. Counselors often refer to his need for appreciation.

Call it what we will, man's craving for recognition of his personal worth is a perpetual hunger. As has been suggested in the preceding section, love and a deep sense of belonging does much to feed the ego and put it in its proper place, but it does not annihilate it.

Social changes have radically modified the ways of satisfying ego needs. In generations past a man was known to many people in many ways. The village shoemaker was not just a shoemaker to his acquaintances—he had a name, a past, a reputation and a family connection by which he was identified. He might be thought of, for example, as gentle and honest, a good father, a steady citizen and a devout churchman, a practical joker and an all-around good fellow. Acquaintances judged him not only as a shoemaker but also as a person and a neighbor. Today the man behind the counter at the local shoe-fixery excites little interest in his many patrons. They are not concerned about his personal life or interests. They only want to know if he can fix shoes.

But man does not fit well into this impersonal and indifferent atmosphere that he has created for himself. He is no more an insensitive robot than he was in the past. The local shoe-repair man has interests, values, hobbies, abilities, and opinions about which he needs to feel proud, but who even knows of them? If he is fortunate, his wife does. From her he receives the praise, the encouragement, the constant reassurance that reminds him that he is after all an individual, that he is someone special —apart from the mass—that he is a "somebody" rather than a "nobody." This description of life does not fit all people even today, yet modern living provides relatively few with recognition in abundance. Those who make a big splash probably get more publicity and acclaim than they did in the past. With urbanization and increased vocational specialization, however, the majority of individuals are likely to feel like strangers even among their acquaintances. Without a feeling of significance, of amounting to something, many forms of personality distortion develop because the human ego must have satisfaction. Marriage today is one of the most certain ways to fulfill the need to feel significant.

8 Press release on hairdressers' convention.

Marriage must above all things help both man and wife meet the need for status and recognition. Even when there are many other channels through which ego satisfaction can be realized—and there are, particularly for the male, and for the female who can continue a career along with marriage—most persons today are much dependent on marriage for a share of their ego satisfaction.

If marriage and homemaking are a major part of her life, the demands of the wife on the spouse for ego satisfaction through her relationship with him will be great. In dating, the successful male succeeds in making a woman feel that she is the most important creature in the world because she is a woman. He makes her feel that she is beautiful, wise, comfortable to be with, understanding—that she in fact embodies all that makes life beautiful and worthwhile. If homemaking and wifehood are to be her primary role after marriage, he must continue not only to express such sentiments but to actually hold them if she is to be content and feel significant.

Because this goal is so difficult to achieve in modern marriage, the wife often feels compelled to seek outside activities as means of acquiring status and recognition. Very often she must do so or succumb to feelings of inferiority and uselessness, particularly if she is ambitious or has played vital status-giving roles prior to the marriage.

If a work outlet is blocked for the wife whose ego is suffering in marriage, she is likely to unwittingly turn her frustration toward tearing down her husband's achievements. By criticism, ignoring or belittling his own satisfaction in his own achievements, or in other ways working out her feeling of defeat she tries to draw her husband down to her own level. This is particularly true if the love bond has also weakened.

A husband too needs ego support at home. He needs a wife who appreciates his ambition and who encourages him in the realization of his aspirations. He needs to know that to her he is an important person, particularly at those times when his best efforts fail.

Finally, both men and women want in their mate someone who will command the approval and respect of others—parents, relatives, friends, colleagues at work, even strangers. And just as important, both want a mate who will bring credit, not shame and embarrassment. A proper mate draws social approval to the spouse and lends dignity and worth to the marriage motive.

An Approved Sexual Outlet

Marriage is our society's only sanctioned outlet for the natural sexual urge of man. Religion and custom sanction the joining of man and wife in the flesh as normal, natural, and moral. The married state is considered the *natural state*. Sex is a value with not only biological meaning, but also with deep social meaning.

Sex needs are real physical needs. Their mutual expression in marriage is one of the elements in the fulfillment of one's need for feeling successful, safe, and whole. In this sense of bringing personal unity, sex needs are psychological as well as physical and organic. The romantic marriage of our day, in fact, integrates the psychological and physical aspects of sex and makes them inseparable. It is in this full sense that a mate must be able to satisfy one sexually today. Prudes cannot fulfill this need, nor can the wildly unconventional who use sex merely for excitement, for adventure, or for domination.

A normal sex life is important, and in the broadest sense no personality can be fully developed without it. On the physical side, sex needs take the form of tension, irritation, hunger, etc. The male particularly is aware of his sex needs from the earliest period of adolescence. His sex hunger reaches its height during the years from twelve to twenty.

With the female, sex hunger may not be recognized as such; it more likely consists only of vague feelings, diffused tensions, and yearnings for affection rather than specific local sensation. Very often she has no localized sex sensations until they are developed through considerable sexual experience in marriage. She may never develop them at all, due to emotional or physiological blocks.

The periodicity of sex hunger, the frequency with which this need must be met by release in sexual contact varies from individual to individual. But with all normal human beings the need is there and can be completely satisfied in American society in no other way as satisfactorily as in the constancy of the marriage relationship. Once marriage is entered into it becomes the regular habitual way of bringing relief, pleasure, relaxation, comfort, and closeness to the marriage relationship.

Only in marriage does sex become a responsible act, involving for the woman the possibility of motherhood with the obligations and joys which this entails. Thus in marriage she too can participate in the sex act without feeling that she is risking the future of any child who may be born from the experience. For the man it carries the responsibilities of parenthood, with the age-long requirement that the male care for and support the female and her young, an arrangement that is as old as human history and probably predates mankind.[9]

Sex as a factor leading to marriage is probably a much more important and conscious factor for the male than the female. At least this is so if one is considering sex as physical appetite. Even those women who cannot accept sex as a pleasure generally look upon it as a means to marital security and ultimately to parenthood.

[9] Margaret Mead, *Male and Female* (New York: William Morrow & Co., Inc., 1949).

EXCESS MORTALITY OF UNMARRIED OVER
PERSONS EVER MARRIED BY SEX,
PERSONS AGED 20 AND OVER
UNITED STATES, 1963

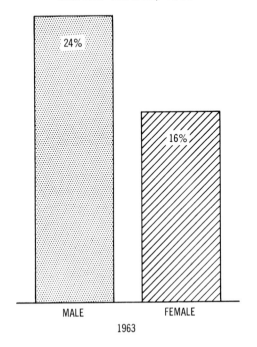

MALE   FEMALE

1963

* Adjusted to 1940 standard.

Source: Paul H. Landis.

FIGURE 1-1————The natural state of marriage is related to health and longevity. Better conditions of living, more to live for, a full expression of basic wishes all undoubtedly are factors in the greater longevity of married persons, even though biological selectivity may also operate. United Nations' data show that marriage is related to longevity everywhere, not just in the United States (*Demographic Yearbook, UN*).

It would seem, from studies of contemporary mores, that for several reasons, the married pair is capable of realizing more in this area than in any previous period of history: (1) Fear of unwanted pregnancy has been reduced. The spacing and timing of children is approaching the level of a practical science. The sexual union is now an act of pleasure, release, and mutual satisfaction, which it could never be in an atmosphere of fear and anxiety about an unwanted child. (2) Psychological impediments to mutual sharing have been greatly reduced. The taboo-ridden female, taught to be passive, felt it was a sin and shame to be sexually assertive. The young wife of today, if she is fortunate in having been given adequate sex education, looks forward to the sexual life of marriage. She views this as a form of close sharing, of appropriate sensual delight. Rather than merely catering to the male, she is an active and responsive partner. This is the ideal. (In Chapter 3 we shall indicate how difficult its realization is.)

The lowered fertility rate—confining childbearing to a short span, usually less than 10 years—and the increasing length of marriage make possible a sharing of sex life for a period of 40 years or more in the average marriage. Due to increased longevity, a couple marrying with the groom aged 21 and the bride 17 now has 42 chances in 100 of living to celebrate the Golden Wedding, whereas in 1900 their chances would have been only 19 in 100. In 1900, white persons entering marriage could expect, on the average, about 30 years of married life together before one of them died. This figure has climbed to 43 years.[10]

The typical groom of 1890 was just over twenty-six years of age at first marriage; the typical bride, twenty-two. Today, the typical groom is under twenty-three and the bride is past twenty. In 1890 the average age difference between bride and groom was four years; now it is less than three years.

If there is any advantage in marrying at all or in the "natural state" which marriage institutes—and most persons admit that there is—to be able to marry in the early twenties and give to marriage and parenthood the vigor of youth is an improvement. Think of the difference in the prospects life offers young people in the United States, where economic circumstances and custom encourage early marriage, compared to Ireland, where economic hardship and religious taboos against birth control cause more than a third of the women and almost two-thirds of the men to delay marriage past thirty years of age. Many there must postpone marriage until they have passed the childbearing age.[11]

In the United States now, about 94 percent of all women are or have been married by the end of the childbearing age.[12] This is the highest record in American history. Except for the sick and badly crippled, the

---

[10] *Family Life*, 28:10, November, 1958.

[11] The disadvantages of early marriage, particularly marriages under age 20, are discussed in Chapter 17. Infant and maternal deaths, premature births and stillbirth rates are all higher in adolescent mothers than mature women. M. F. Ashley-Montagu, *The Reproductive Development of the Female* (New York: Julian Press, Inc., 1958).

[12] U. S. Department of Commerce, Bureau of the Census, "Population Characteristics," Series P-20, No. 122, March 22, 1963, Table 1, p. 9.

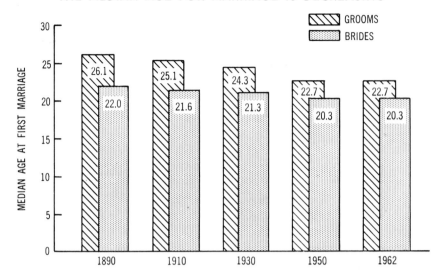

THE MEDIAN AGE FOR MARRIAGE IS DECREASING

SOURCE: U. S. Department of Commerce, Bureau of the Census, "Population Characteristics," Series P-20, No. 122, March 22, 1963, Table C.

FIGURE 1-2————Note that the difference in age of bride and groom is also
less than formerly—4 years in 1890 compared with 2.4 in 1962. Marriage age is
decreasing throughout the world, but the average is higher—24 years for
women, 27 for men—than in the United States (*Demographic Yearbook, UN*).

deformed, the emotionally warped, and the mentally defective, almost
everyone has an opportunity to marry. Even the handicapped often
marry, thanks to social security, to routine machine-powered jobs, and to
labor-saving devices in the home.

Which needs discussed—love, companionship, security recognition or
sexual satisfaction—is it most important for modern marriage to satisfy?
The answer varies from one individual to the next. Even two happily
married people may be obtaining from their marriage very different kinds
of satisfaction. A husband who is outstanding as a community citizen and
at his job may depend very little on his wife for recognition. A woman
who remains close to her old friends and family may never lean heavily
upon her husband for companionship, though she needs his love and the
feeling of security he provides her. What each individual seeks in and
demands from marriage is determined, not by custom, but by his own
personality.

Stability As a Goal

Everyone wants a lifetime tie, a dependable anchor against the vicissitudes of life. The parent family can only partially provide this anchor for the adult offspring. As one grows older, one must find this tie in marriage and in children. Although the surface manifestations would make outsiders to our social system believe that this value is not sought by the young person today, it is probably as desperately sought as anywhere. Stability is sought because it is recognized that in our kind of world, having someone always to depend on, someone with whom one can build one's life until death at last forces a separation is all-important. This atmosphere of stability is important to children who will be born to the marriage as well as to the pair themselves.

It is this value which makes marriage more than a mere mating venture; it is this which creates the family as an institution. The insecurity of our time explains in part the rush into early marriage. Youth is desperately trying to establish a sense of stability in an unstable world.

Has not modern marriage violated this standard of permanence? This is the question upon which much of the doubt and pessimism concerning present-day marriages centers.

The fact is, however, as has been implied in the introductory paragraphs of this chapter, that modern marriage is more stable than marriage of any past age in that it lasts longer. This is a statistical fact which cannot be denied. Even as late as 1890, for example, 33 marriages in each thousand in the United States were terminated each year (see Figure 1-3).

NUMBER OF MARRIAGES BROKEN

PER 1,000 ANNUALLY

BY DIVORCE, BY DEATH

PICTOGRAPH CORPORATION

FIGURE 1-3————The average marriage lasts longer today than it did in 1890 because of the decreasing death rate. In 1890, 33 marriages per thousand were terminated annually; in 1957, 27. Life expectancy permitted 30 years of married life in 1900 compared to 43 years today.

Of these marriages, 30 were terminated by death; their termination often left several orphaned children. Today, only 27 marriages per thousand are being broken each year. The proportion broken by death has been cut down to 17.5 per thousand. Divorce breaks not 3 per thousand, as then, but 9.3. In all, 6 more marriages per thousand survive today than survived in 1890.

The average community today has less than half the funerals it had in 1890.[13] Thus, even measured by this standard of stability, the human relationship of marriage is more lasting than ever before.

Today, at age 20, young people can look forward to 53 years of life. At that age, the average white female has 56 years yet to live, the male 49, colored females 51 years, colored males 47. During the first 15 years of their marriage, young people have only about 2 chances in a thousand of being separated by death.[14]

In conclusion, this chapter has stressed the shift in values of marriage during recent generations. The sturdy institution for making a living and rearing children of another day has been replaced by the modern marriage, with its hope of happiness, companionship, love, ego support, sexual loyalty, and long life together. It has come to be not only the near universal aspiration, but the actual realization of most men and women. The old institution was rigid, work-centered, custom-regulated, with well-defined roles for husband, wife, and children. The new marriage is flexible, pleasure-centered, cooperatively regulated, with loosely defined roles for husband, wife, and children.

Under the old regime, study of marriage relationships was taboo. One did not inquire into a relationship which God, biology, and custom ordained and fixed into a patterned state. Under the new regime, study of marriage is imperative. In a world of ill-defined and flexible interpersonal relationships, one must learn how to play the game or risk failure.

Problems

1. *Research exercise:* Prepare a list of expectations concerning your marriage (kind of relationship expected, kind of needs to be satisfied, kind of family life planned, number of children expected, and level of living expected).

13 During this century alone the death rate in the United States has fallen from 16 per 1000 to 9 per 1000 population. For data see Paul H. Landis, *Population Problems,* Second Edition (New York: American Book Co., 1954), Ch. 6.

14 Metropolitan Life Insurance Company, "Longevity of Industrial Population in 1957," *Statistical Bulletin,* September, 1958, Table II, p. 7.

To ensure frankness, lists should preferably be anonymous with sex of respondent indicated on the sheet. Tabulate and discuss results. Compare tabulations of men and women separately.

What do results show with regard to marriage values in this generation? Do men and women seek substantially the same goals? Far different ones? If different, are they complementary rather than contradictory? Appraise the various answers given from the standpoint of their being (a) practical, (b) realistic, (c) consistent with the expectations of the average community.

2. *Sociodrama:* A young woman is talking with her happily married sister, seeking help in deciding whether or not she should accept the marriage proposal of the night before. Her sister tries to help her decide by asking a number of questions based on contemporary values in mate selection. Their grandmother enters and adds her advice, which is largely based on the criteria of her own youth.

3. Define "anonymity." Briefly indicate why it is so characteristic of many sectors of society today and show how it affects marriage and family life.

4. Once a modern couple have married do you consider that each is obligated to "love, honor, and obey" the other for a lifetime? Explain.

5. Do you believe that sexual incompatibility, if it cannot be remedied, is justifiable grounds for divorce? Explain.

6. Read the following statement and select one of the four conclusions below which you feel best describes a realistic philosophy of marriage. Explain your choice briefly. If you believe that there is a fifth alternative, state it and defend it.

It has been said that "when you don't expect anything of your marriage you can't be disappointed." Do you believe that couples would be happier in the long run if they:

a. Expected nothing of marriage but a working arrangement for the purpose of raising a family?

b. Expected to fulfill most of their needs other than for sexual satisfactions in relationships outside of marriage?

c. Continued to expect complete need fulfillment, as most do today, but worked harder at attaining their goal?

d. Tempered their expectations with an understanding of the limitations of all human beings and all human relationships?

Selected References

ARTICLES IN BOOKS OF READINGS

Landis, Judson T., and Landis, Mary G., *Readings in Marriage and the Family* (Englewood Cliffs, N. J.: Prentice-Hall, Inc., 1952).

1. Mead, Margaret, "The Contemporary American Family as an Anthropologist Sees It," pp. 1-9.
2. Sirjamaki, John, "Cultural Configurations in the American Family," pp. 9-17.

FISHBEIN, Morris, and KENNEDY, Ruby Jo Reeves, *Modern Marriage and Family Living* (New York: Oxford University Press, Inc., 1957).

  3. BROWN, Muriel W., "Education and Family Life," pp. 17-36.

SUSSMAN, Marvin B., *Sourcebook in Marriage and Family,* Second Edition (Boston: Houghton Mifflin Co., 1963).

  4. JACO, E. Gartly, and BELKNAP, Ivan, "Is a New Family Form Emerging in the Urban Fringe?" pp. 471-476.

  5. SIRJAMAKI, John, "Cultural Configurations in the American Family," pp. 25-29.

  6. HSU, Francis, "Chinese and American Marriage Practices," pp. 21-24.

WINCH, Robert F., and others, *Selected Studies in Marriage and the Family,* Revised Edition (New York: Holt, Rinehart & Winston, Inc., 1962).

  7. JACO, E. Gartly, and BELKNAP, Ivan, "Is a·New Family Form Emerging in the Urban Fringe?" pp. 182-192.

VINCENT, Clark E., *Readings in Marriage Counseling* (New York: Thomas Y. Crowell Co., 1957).

  8. NIMKOFF, M. F., "The Family in the United States," pp. 2-12.

BECKER, Howard, and HILL, Reuben (Editors), *Family, Marriage and Parenthood,* Second Edition (Boston: D. C. Heath & Co., 1955).

  9. BECKER, Howard, "Interpreting Family Life in Context," pp. 1-49.

  10. MARTINDALE, Don, "The Variety of the Human Family," pp. 50-83.

  11. NASH, Arnold S., "Ancient Past and Living Present," pp. 84-103.

  12. KUHN, Manford Hinshaw, "American Families Today: Development and Differentiation of Types," pp. 131-168.

CAVAN, Ruth Shonle, *Marriage and the Family in the Modern World: A Book of Readings* (New York: Thomas Y. Crowell Co., 1960).

  13. BOSSARD, James H. S., "Marriage as a Status-Achieving Device," Reading 4.

  14. Metropolitan Life Insurance Company, "Increased Chances for a Golden Wedding," Reading 11.

  15. BURGESS, Ernest W., "The Changing American Family," Reading 12.

CHRISTENSEN, Harold T., *Handbook of Marriage and the Family* (Chicago: Rand McNally & Co., 1964).

  16. CAVAN, Ruth Shonle, "Subcultural Variations and Mobility," Ch. 14.

General References

BLITSTEN, Dorothy R., *The World of the Family* (New York: Random House, Inc., 1963).

CAVAN, Ruth Shonle, *American Marriage* (New York: Thomas Y. Crowell Co., 1959), Chs. 1, 2.

————, *The American Family,* Third Edition (New York: Thomas Y. Crowell Co., 1963), Parts I and II.

FARBER, Bernard, *Family: Organization and Interaction* (San Francisco: Chandler Publishing Co., 1964).

JOBERG, Gidion S., "Familial Organization in the Pre-industrial City," *Marriage and Family Living*, 18:30-36, February, 1956.

KEPHART, William M., *The Family, Society and the Individual* (Boston: Houghton Mifflin Co., 1961), Parts I and II.

KIRKPATRICK, Clifford, *The Family as Process and Institution*, Second Edition (New York: The Ronald Press Co., 1963), Ch. 6.

LANTZ, Herman R., and SNYDER, Eloise, *Marriage* (New York: John Wiley & Sons, Inc., 1962), Ch. 4.

LEMASTERS, E. E., *Modern Courtship and Marriage* (New York: The Macmillan Co., 1957), Ch. 2.

MARTINSON, Floyd M., *Marriage and the American Ideal* (New York: Dodd, Mead & Co., 1960), Chs. 3, 4.

OGBURN, W. F., and NIMKOFF, M. F., *Technology and the Changing Family* (Boston: Houghton Mifflin Co., 1955).

PETERSON, James A., *Education For Marriage*, Second Edition (New York: Charles Scribner's Sons, 1964), Ch. 1.

United Nations, *Report on the World Social Situation* (New York: United Nations, 1957)

WINCH, Robert F., *The Modern Family*, Revised Edition (Holt, Rinehart & Winston, Inc., 1963), Ch. 6.

2

Shortcomings of Modern Marriage

It would be unrealistic to ignore the weaknesses of modern marriage, particularly since the preceding pages have stressed its positive values. One can be optimistic about marriage and its potentialities and yet concede that it is far from a perfect institution. Many enter marriage with no awareness of its responsibilities and its obligations. Their expectations are impossibly romantic; problems and adjustments have no place in their dream.

Marriage is a human institution and the level of achievement is never higher than the adjustment capabilities of the two human beings involved.

Marriage Cannot Meet All Needs

No relationship can fully meet all needs of the human personality. Marriage cannot. This is suggested by research dealing with engaged and newly married couples. One hundred and twenty couples were asked the extent to which their personality needs were actually being met by their pair relationship. Here is the way the couples answered:[1]

Degree to which needs are satisfied	Men (percent)	Women (percent)
All needs	18	18
Most	12	24
Many	24	24
Half	16	16
Some	14	10
Few or none	15	8

[1] Anselm Strauss, "A Study of Three Psychological Factors Affecting Choice of a Mate," Ph.D. Thesis, University of Chicago, 1945, cited in E. W. Burgess and Paul Wallin, *Engagement and Marriage* (Philadelphia: J. B. Lippincott Co., 1953), p. 203.

Obviously, if these data are typical, many close pair relationships fall short of meeting all personality needs. Few, if any, meet all needs completely.

This study presented a group of 173 engaged or newly married men and 200 women with a check list of twenty-six needs they had hoped to find fulfilled in their pair relationship. Here are the fifteen items most often checked:[2]

[I] Wish someone to:	Men (percent)	Women (percent)
love me	36	54
confide in me	31	42
show me affection	21	38
respect my ideals	26	26
appreciate what I wish to achieve	28	24
understand my moods	23	28
help me make important decisions	15	33
stimulate my ambition	27	21
look up to	16	29
give me self-confidence	20	24
stand back of me in difficulty	16	26
appreciate me just as I am	20	21
admire my ability	19	20
make me feel I count for something	21	17
relieve my loneliness	19	19

It will be seen that in general a higher proportion of women than of men felt more needs fulfilled, particularly those in the area of love, affection, confidence, and understanding. This is an indication of a greater sense of dependence in women than in men on the marriage for love, security, and intimacy. More men than women want marriage to stimulate their ambition, indicating their need for ego support.

Failure Often Reflects High Hopes

It must be recognized as a sound principle that a person's realizations seldom exceed his aspirations. If it has been conclusively demonstrated in the preceding chapter that today couples aspire to more in marriage than they did in earlier generations, then it is easy to believe (1) that the successful realize more satisfaction in marriage than did their ancestors and (2) that many suffer defeat because they expect marriage to bring more in the way of happiness than is humanly possible.

[2] Cited in Ernest W. Burgess and Harvey J. Locke, *The Family: Institution to Companionship,* Second Edition (New York: American Book Co., 1953), p. 369.

By the same logic, it is easy to understand, too, that failure is more likely to lead to decisive action than it did in earlier generations. There is little doubt that many divorces today result from overly idealistic expectations for marriage. Many expect the humanly impossible. As English novelist Somerset Maugham has said, the American wife expects to find in her husband "a perfection English women only hope to find in their butlers." And what perfection in romantic attraction, home management, and social competence American men demand of their wives! It is doubtful that marriage has ever been asked to pass so high a test.

If a culture makes happiness the goal of marriage, it must grant the right of divorce to those who fail in its attainment. Only by this means can they be freed to seek fulfillment of their dreams in another marriage, or to return to the single state. The right of divorce is important in the new system of marriage values. It recognizes two facts: first, human judgment is fallible in mate choice, and second, those who fall in love may also fall out of love. It is known from human experience that both things happen.

Divorce is doubly serious when it represents the failure of high aspirations. But is divorce more tragic than living together in bitter conflict and dire frustration? In an earlier day, when a more stoical marriage philosophy prevailed, personal clashes brought less torture than now when marriage values are so different.

But this is not the place to discuss divorce and its meaning in the scheme of modern marriage values. That discussion will come in a later chapter (see Chapter 34). It is enough to say here that divorce is a recognized adjustment device in the modern marriage-family system—the ultimate, desperate, but sometimes necessary one. Divorce is, in fact, a part of all marriage-family institutions, historic and contemporary. In ours, its causes are related to our new marriage values.

Negative Motivations for Marriage

The positive aspects of the motivation to marriage have been stressed, for it is assumed that these are the most compelling motives which lead people into marriage, yet human motivations are rarely unmixed. Many people marry in part, or perhaps chiefly, with an avoidance motive. To cover the disgrace of pregnancy is one of the motives for marriage in our culture, perhaps for 10 to 25 percent of the population.[3]

[3] Harold T. Christensen and Hanna H. Meissner, "Studies in Child Spacing III—Premarital Pregnancy as a Factor in Divorce," *American Sociological Review,* 18:641-644, December, 1953; see also Harold T. Christensen, "Child Spacing via Record Linkage: New Data Plus a Summing up of Earlier Reports," *Marriage and Family Living,* 25:272-280, August, 1963.

In this classification are to be found many of the teenage marriages. Marriage may have been in the thoughts of one or the other or of both of the individuals concerned, but the actual precipitating event was the pregnancy.

Many youth reach the decision to marry when they do because they find the situation at home increasingly unbearable. They want greater freedom than they can have under the parental roof. They hope to find it in marriage. This probably explains in part why young people from large families and underprivileged families so often marry young. Crowded conditions of the parental home, the constant conflict with brothers, sisters and parents, the rather authoritarian patterns that of necessity prevail in such homes lead young people to choose early marriage as the better of two alternatives.[4]

Some young people marry from a sense of loneliness which has developed because of neglect or lack of affection during childhood in the parental home. They are insecure souls fleeing loneliness and seeking warmth, closeness, and affection that will shield them from the anxieties and fears of a world in which they have always felt exposed to fear, anxiety, and unearned guilt. Marriage for them is often a mistake, for these feelings are as frequently exaggerated as cured by a youthful marriage. Often they become too demanding and monopolistic of the mate and thus invite marital failure.

Some marry to cover a feeling of sex guilt. Their sex drives or acquired sex appetites, or habits, have become a constant source of guilt and anxiety. They seek marriage primarily as a sexual outlet—to sanctify desires which have plagued them from the time of earliest adolescence, sometimes even before. Some such individuals have been plagued with a sense of guilt over masturbation or other types of sexual exercise which are harmless in and of themselves, but which have proved to be harmful because of feelings of deep anxiety induced by teachings to the contrary. Others feel deeply guilty because their sexual desires, even their sensuous thoughts, seem to conflict with the teachings of their parents or the church. Others hasten into marriage to cover feelings of guilt and fear involved in a sexual relationship already begun with the future spouse.

Some marry primarily for spite, or self-justification. The loneliness, the rancor, the bitterness of a breakup are buried in a new, drastic plunge into the risky security of a hasty marriage.

Today many remarry to cure the intolerable loneliness following

[4] The author's studies indicate that all these generalizations tend to be true of the large family. See his *Teenage Adjustments in Large and Small Families*, Bulletin No. 549, April, 1954; *The Broken Home and Teenage Adjustments*, Bulletin No. 542, April, 1953, both of the Washington Agricultural Experiment Station, Pullman, Washington; see also Carol L. Stone and Paul H. Landis, "An Approach to Authority Patterns in Parent-Teenage Relationships," *Rural Sociology*, 18:233-242, September, 1953.

divorce or widowhood. They seek also to find the satisfactions which they once had and lost, or never found in a previous marriage. This statement refers to the one in five marriages which are of persons who have been widowed or divorced and who do remarry.

It is said that some people marry for pity. One finds this the theme of an occasional novel, so one must suspect that it happens in real life. The individual marries another in order to save him from some real or imagined fate, perhaps nothing more than the fate of failure to achieve marriage. One finds it hard to account for the marriage of the physically normal to the severely handicapped in terms of a motive other than that of pity, or some altruistic rather than romantic or ulterior one.

One might go on endlessly listing human motives. Probably every motive of which human beings are capable enters into one marriage or another: avoidance, fortune, prestige, or merely economic security and status seeking. Both man's negative and positive drives affect almost every decision he makes. Although one cannot say that it is wrong to marry for any of these motives, one must recognize the weakness of a marriage based on many of these motivations.

Needs Thwarted by Marriage

Very fundamental needs are fulfilled in marriage as in no other human relationship, yet marriage drastically interferes with other needs. The need to be loved, for example, often runs counter to the need for self-realization and ego satisfaction.

Certain hostilities inevitably develop when the demands of love become so great that they thwart one's desire to attain economic or vocational status and success. The shelter of marriage, which makes one feel secure, may at times interfere strongly with one's desire to be free of ties and obligations, to be foot-loose, so to speak, to venture and experiment and seek new experience. The need to be reassured and comforted is all-important at times, but at other times, when one feels more sure of oneself, a sense of self-sufficiency takes precedence. Independence replaces the need for a refuge. At such times one is ashamed of former weakness and does not want to be reminded of it.

So the changing needs of the human personality manifest themselves from day to day in the up-and-down fluctuations of moods and the adversities of the world in which we live and work. Marriage is, therefore, a constantly shifting pattern, ever new and in a certain sense never fully adequate for balancing the human being's dual need for oneness and for personal freedom. There are numerous mainsprings to human behavior and human motivation, not all of them conscious, but all of them purposeful in terms of meeting the individual's particular needs at a particular time.

Often the marriage is called upon to fulfill needs that have been thwarted in outside activities. The husband who comes home feeling uncertain or unsuccessful in his work may be in desperate need of consolation and reassurance. The mate in this case is expected to rally to the occasion when perhaps she has even greater need for reassurance herself. Yet the husband's reactions are not irrational. They are purposeful in terms of his momentary needs, even though contradictory to the self-sufficient man he may have appeared to be in the morning when he left home. The wife may have greater difficulty in accepting him as the humble child, needing comfort and strength, than as the strong man she respects and honors.

Needs are not always rational and often cannot be expressed in words, but the human organism always moves in response to them, even though they are quite contradictory from one time to another. Marriage is, therefore, a moving equilibrium in which two human personalities struggle to find fulfillment of each other's needs, with love the overall bond helping to compensate for the inevitable clashes.

Marriage is as potentially capable of creating deep hostilities, animosities, and frictions as it is of giving happiness and mutual satisfaction. Because of the high aspirations that center in it and the close and intimate demands that are made upon personality in the marriage institution, hostile tendencies are always latent in it. When they come to the surface, they can be of the most violent nature.

It is for this reason that marriage, designed to meet more human needs than is any other institution, is also capable of producing more misery, human suffering, and personal torture than any other relationship developed by man. The pair relationship has throughout history been laden with tragedy where failure has replaced success and where defeat has replaced hope. The tragedies of married life have been the favorite themes of drama and fiction, ranking second only to love itself. This kind of plot is always fascinating, for every human being can as readily identify himself with this phase of the marriage relationship, as with the comedy and glory of marriage.

It would be inappropriate, therefore, to close this chapter without this word of caution. Marriage at a distance often looks much less problem-free than it is, particularly to the young, who in the throes of happy romance lose sight of the realities of human life. This book is essentially optimistic in tone; it recognizes the high potentiality of marriage in our day, particularly for intelligent young people who seriously want a successful marriage, are well informed on all aspects of marriage, and are sufficiently aware of personality problems to know the kind of person who is likely to succeed and fail in marriage and to choose accordingly.

But marriage is not a one way street to happiness, and the pronunciation of a marriage ceremony is no guarantee that personal needs will be met. Only as marriage is entered into seriously and with the full understanding of one's own characteristics and those of the person he marries, can one venture safely and expect to realize in substantial measure the fulfillment of personality needs.

As this book develops, an attempt will be made at numerous points to differentiate between types of persons and types of background that hold high promise of success in marriage, and also to point out those types of persons and backgrounds that show comparatively little promise of success. So far, social science has no positive answers but it has hints far superior to those of folklore which have been the only guide for past generations.

Problems

1. Consider how a marriage forced by pregnancy might encounter problems not to be expected in a marriage entered into when both are ready for it.
2. Is it a sound philosophical principle that failure often represents the frustration of hopes that were too high at the beginning? Apply your answer to marriage today.
3. Do you believe that everyone who marries for money, property, or economic security is to be condemned? Why or why not?
4. *Sociodrama:* A friendless young woman marries to escape her lonely world. Her husband is a popular, out-going person whose need for companionship is satisfied by his friends and work associates. He thinks of a wife primarily in terms of her role as a housekeeper.

   Act out a situation or conversation in which the expectations of each are pictured. If possible have the husband and wife reach a new understanding of one another as a result of the conversation.
5. Have you known persons to marry for motives you would consider with suspicion? Did they succeed?
6. Have you known persons whom you considered unmarriageable? What was the basis for your conviction?

Selected References

ARTICLES IN BOOKS OF READINGS

LANDIS, Judson T., and LANDIS, Mary G., *Readings in Marriage and the Family* (Englewood Cliffs, N. J.: Prentice-Hall, Inc., 1952).

1. OGBURN, William F., "The Changing Functions of the Family," pp. 18-21.

2. LANDIS, Paul H., "The Changing Family," pp. 27-31.

SUSSMAN, Marvin B., *Sourcebook in Marriage and the Family*, Second Edition (Boston: Houghton Mifflin Co., 1963).

3. NIMKOFF, M. F., "Biological Discoveries and the Future of the Family," pp. 57-62.

BECKER, Howard, and HILL, Reuben (Editors), *Family, Marriage and Parenthood*, Second Edition (Boston: D. C. Heath & Co., 1955).

4. MALINOWSKI, Bronislaw, "Parenthood—The Basis of Social Structure," pp. 21-30.

CAVAN, Ruth Shonle, *Marriage and the Family in the Modern World: A Book of Readings* (New York: Thomas Y. Crowell Co., 1960).

5. YOUNG, Kimball, "What Strong Family Life Means to Our Society," Reading 1.

6. BURGESS, Ernest W., "The Family as a Unity of Interacting Personalities," Reading 2.

7. PANZER, Martin, "No World for a Single," Reading 5.

8. CAVAN, Ruth Shonle, "Family in the New Suburb," Reading 13.

KOENIG, Samuel, *Sociology, A Book of Readings* (Englewood Cliffs, N. J.: Prentice-Hall, Inc., 1953).

9. LEVY, John, and MUNROE, Ruth, "Why People Marry," pp. 131-135.

10. NIMKOFF, Meyer F., "Technology and the Future of the Family," Reading 14.

11. BECK, Dorothy Fahs, "The Changing Moslem Family of the Middle East," Reading 20.

General References

LEVY, John, and MUNROE, Ruth, *The Happy Family* (New York: Alfred A. Knopf, Inc., 1938).

OGBURN, W. F., and NIMKOFF, M. F., *Technology and the Changing Family* (Boston: Houghton Mifflin Co., 1955).

United Nations, *Report on the World Social Situation* (New York: United Nations, 1957).

II

MALE AND FEMALE: PREDISPOSITIONS AND ROLES

3
Male and Female: Biology

The physiological difference between the male and female originates, as do all physiological characteristics, in the chromosomes. Two of the 48 chromosomes found in the normal human will control the sex of the individual. If two chromosomes designated as X chromosomes exist in the cell, a female results; if there is one X and one Y, a male results. The appearance of the sex cell in the fertilized egg does not guarantee that the individual produced will be classified biologically, phychologically, or sociologically into the sex class which the chromosomes foretold.

The making of a male and of a female is a process involving hereditary determinants, glandular activity (including hormonal balance), and social conditioning to assure proper role identification by self and others. If either the biological or sociological sequences fail, a misfit individual results.

Genetic Classification

External genitalia are critical in sex identification. The doctor and parents are dependent upon them for the immediate classification of the newborn child into one or the other sex category. The first question of all concerned is certain to be "Is it a boy or girl?" It would hardly be appropriate for the doctor to reply, "I do not know," yet in a small proportion of cases he cannot know. The hermaphrodite is not merely a side-show attraction at the circus, where animals biologically confused in external genitalia are shown, but is a reality in medical circles. Some human beings are born without clear-cut sex distinction.[1]

[1] In cases where the sex organs themselves do not make discernible the sex of the individual, science has found a method which permits an early test of the infant to determine the hormonal make-up and thereby be relatively certain of his sex classification. This method consists of scraping cells from the inner lining of the mouth, analyzing their composition, and thereby determining the chromosomal make-up of the individual —a fairly certain index to biological maleness or femaleness. See Charles Herbert Best and Norman Burke Taylor, *Living Body: A Text in Human Physiology,* Fourth Edition (New York: Holt, Rinehart & Winston, Inc., 1958), p. 666.

Recent research indicates that the hermaphrodite (the individual who has characteristics of both sexes, and neither fully) starts out to be a distinct sex by gene determinants, but hormonal balance is not realized because of inherited malformation or prenatal injury, and the development of particular sex characteristics fails to be realized.[2]

After birth, sex rearing must be in the appropriate sex category or the individual will not be able to function in his proper sex group, even though biologically completely identified with his genital sex group. In cases where the sex organs of a newborn baby are not well differentiated (as in the hermaphrodite), the physician must decide for the parents what the sex rearing will be. (Failure of complete anatomical development may be in the external sex organs, the internal, or both. A few hermaphrodites produce both egg and sperm cells, but there is no known case where a human being has been capable of being both mother and father.)

Each embryo starts with the rudiments of sex glands in the form of genital ridges. The chromosome make-up, as we have seen, determines which will go forward in the development of the embryo, male or female. The actual development seems to be controlled by the hormones produced by the primitive gonad (undifferentiated glands) and later, it is believed by other hormones of the adrenal cortex. If the primitive gonads develop a liberal amount of male hormones (testosterone and androsterone), the direction of development is toward maleness; if they produce a sparse amount, toward femaleness. Recent research seems to suggest that all embryos could develop in the direction of femaleness if it were not for the secretion of the testes which lead embryos toward masculine development.[3]

Adult males and females carry in their genitalia marks of the opposite sex. The male carries a seam down the underside of his penis and across his scrotum which could have opened, during the embryonic stage, into the labia of the female's vagina. The female carries rudiments of the penis—the bud-like clitoris, which contains the same kind of nerve plexis as the male glans penis. Both sexes produce the same hormones but in different quantities. Even after adult development, if the hormonal balance is disturbed, modifications in the somatic structure may occur. Some women at menopause, when male sex hormones are excessive, and the imbalance is not medically corrected, tend to develop mustaches and beards. When a male is castrated the production of sex hormones is reduced and the male may develop a disposition often identified with the female in our society.

[2] Howard W. Jones, Jr. and William Wallis Scott, *Hermaphroditism, Genital Anomalies, and Related Endocrine Disorders* (Baltimore: The Williams & Wilkins Co., 1958).
[3] *Ibid.*

The Critical Period in Sex "Imprinting"

Wrong sex classification is not unalterable during the first two years of age.[4] In fact, experience shows that the sex category of a child can be changed with little disturbance until the child is two and a half years of age. Psychologists refer to certain ages in the psychological development of the individual as "critical periods." Apparently the critical period for internalizing his sex category comes prior to age two and a half: a time when he is learning language and beginning to take an interest in play with his own group. Any attempt to shift the child from one sex category to the other after this age is accompanied by increasingly severe disturbances. By age six, sex identity is for all practical purposes irreversible.

"As gender role and identity become fully differentiated, they become permanently indelible and imprinted, and subsequently, irreversible and powerful in influencing behavior as if innately preordained. . . . The evidence from hermaphroditic cases of sex assignment is that the critical period of gender imprinting is in early childhood, beginning with the onset of the mastery of language. The die is cast, pretty well, by the age of six, after which major realignment of gender role and identity is rare."[5]

Subculture Rearing

Wrong subculture rearing can apparently alter the psychological sex of any individual so much that it will be difficult for him to assume behavior suited to his biological sex. The sociological process of role indoctrination is a process so smoothly handled that it seems automatic. So effective are the means by which the male and female internalize attitudes, behavior, and expectations of their sex class that subculture identification is almost irreversible.

A girl who is brought up as a boy and treated as a boy, no matter what her genetic and hormonal structure, comes to think of herself as a boy, to act as a boy, and will, if she is allowed to develop very long in this direction, find it almost impossible to ever develop the self-attitudes of her own sex. The same is true of the boy reared as a female. Many individuals have the wrong gender identification in much or in part of their psychological orientation, even when the family and other social

[4] J. P. Scott, "Critical Periods in Behavioral Development," *Science*, 138:949-958, 1962.
[5] John Money, "Developmental Differentiation of Femininity and Masculinity Compared," in Seymour M. Farber and Roger H. L. Wilson (Editors), *The Potential of Woman* (New York: McGraw-Hill Book Co., 1963), pp. 51-65.

groups handling them fully intended that they would identify themselves psychologically and sociologically with their own sex. Studies indicate that homosexuality is due not to hormonal or hereditary difficulties, but to conditioning factors, many of which are subtle, some of which are well understood. All are on the psychological and sociological level rather than the biological.[6] Failure in gender identification manifests itself in many degrees of divergence, from transvestism (desire to dress like the opposite sex) to different degrees of latent and overt homosexuality. Even overt homosexuality varies in degree from the desire for a sex partner of one's own sex as an element of sexual variety, to an attraction to one's own sex exclusively.[7]

Gender Identity—A Delicate Balance

This brief review of interacting biological, parental, and subculture forces that enter into the making of a male or female indicates that the achievement of either sex is a highly intricate, complex process and that the maintaining of a sex distinction is a delicate balance of many factors—biological, psychological, and cultural.

The well-balanced, biologically distinct male or female is produced by heredity, proper glandular functioning, right sex classification by his group, gender identification consistent with his sex roles, and right training for role-status relationships.

The individual must be so handled that he will internalize his gender as a prerequisite of assuming the roles of the subculture of his own sex. Otherwise an individual with all male characteristics may have the psychological constitution and sexual proclivities of the female. Gender identification is likely to follow the sex rearing of the individual, no matter what his biological sex, but if it does not conform to his sex, conflict is certain to result. It is also possible that his erotic dreams, fantasies, and practices will conform to his biological sex, even when he is reared in the wrong sex group, inducing further conflict.

Hormonal composition alone will not overcome wrong sex rearing. Role training is made easy only if one is trained from the beginning for

6 A nine-year study of homosexual males by Dr. Bieber, Associate Clinical Professor of Psychiatry at New York Medical College, concludes that the roots of homosexuality are in disturbed situations in the early family relationship. In almost every case he found "a close-binding intimate" mother and/or a hostile, detached, or unrespected father, or other parental abberations. In a majority of cases he found the father hostile to the child. He concludes that a warmly supportive, constructive father neutralizes the effect of "seductive, close-binding" attempts of the mother. Summary by Robert C. Doty in *The New York Times*, Western Edition, December 27, 1963.

7 See such works as Frank S. Caprio, *Female Homosexuality* (New York: Citadel Press, 1954); Donald Webster Cory, *Homosexuality: A Cross-Cultural Approach* (New York: Julian Press, Inc., 1956).

roles in the subculture he will occupy. The general deportment of male and female, as they are shaped in their respective subcultures, takes deep roots from the standpoint of social obligation and social expectation.

Since marriage involves the interrelationships of male and female in their biological constitution, their psychological orientation, and their role conceptions, each of these areas will be explored as a basis for understanding both the preface to marriage and adjustment during marriage.

Biological Rhythms and Sequences

The female: The sexual life of the female moves sequentially, and in part rhythmically, through complex changes which have no counterpart in the male. As pointed out by Margaret Mead, "Coming to terms with the rhythms of woman's life means coming to terms with life itself."[8] The imperatives of the body are her most pressing realities.

Woman's sexual development is sometimes cataclysmic. It cannot be ignored. It must be reckoned with by society and by the marriage partner as well as by the woman herself.

The major developments are, first, the arrival of puberty with the cataclysmic event of menstruation—the primary sex-life rhythm; second, defloration, on first intercourse;[9] third, pregnancy, with its disturbance of body function and social habits;[10] fourth, childbirth—an event of great biological and sociological moment; fifth, lactation, which has profound physiological and psychological effects;[11] and sixth, menopause, or the change of life, which marks the cessation of ovulation, menstruation, and fertility, and which is accompanied by drastic glandular changes and, often, by deep emotional reactions.[12]

Defloration, pregnancy, lactation, and the menopause will be discussed later in the appropriate context. The most significant of the biological events, in terms of adjustment during a large portion of adult life, is menstruation. This marks the climax of puberty, beginning suddenly and continuing more or less without interruption, except when pregnancy takes place, for a period of almost 40 years.

The psysiological process itself has often been made a great impediment to woman. Many cultures have declared this a period of uncleanness and surrounded it with taboos. Numerous restrictions have been imposed, not only on physical activities, but also on social intercourse. Ashley-

8 Margaret Mead, *Male and Female* (New York: William Morrow & Co., Inc., 1949).
9 Considered in Chapter 12.
10 The subject of Chapter 28.
11 Discussed in Chapter 28.
12 Discussed in Chapter 33.

Montagu, anthropologist, has listed some of the common menstrual prohibitions and beliefs on which they are based.[13] Menstruating women cause flowers to wilt and wither, preserves of every sort to spoil, dough to fail to rise, seeds to become sterile, meat to decompose. In Europe women are excluded from many occupations on this account. They are not allowed to work in French perfumeries when menstruating, to pick mushrooms in commercial growing places, to tend silk worms. Rhine women are barred from handling vessels in which wine is to be fermented. They are also excluded from sugar factories.

He believes that there is some scientific basis for these prohibitions, arising from observation of the effects on living plants. Sweat secretions at this time do kill or damage certain kinds of living tissue. In some cultures anything menstruating women touch must be purified by religious ceremonials. They may be entirely barred from religious participation during menstruation, and among some primitives must even live apart during this period.

Fewer concessions to the menstrual period are made now in our culture than formerly. The use of modern sanitary protections, the daily bath, and increased standards of personal hygiene have removed the curse of "uncleanness." Modern drugs and the stress on physical activity for women have removed the taboo on activity. For a few women it remains a critically painful period. We have not quite arrived at the point where we entirely ignore the pain which sometimes accompanies the period. American women do not, as some primitives are said to do, simply rub nettles on their stomach and go about their work, using the external pain of the nettles to help them forget the internal pain.

Menstruation is an inescapable fact of woman's life from about age 13 to age 49, month in and month out, with its moods, its discomfort, its requirements for special sanitary precautions, its limits on contacts with the male. No matter what her time cycle, menstruation is part of her life, and any cessation of it is a matter of concern. If she has been involved sexually, either before marriage, in marriage, or after widowhood, its cessation may be due to pregnancy. The cessation may also be due to factors of health or emotional strain, but even so the suspicion of pregnancy is likely to be present.

The male: The male's sexual development and decline is a gradual thing without marked periods of change.[14] Prior to puberty his capacity

13 M. F. Ashley-Montagu, *Anthropology and Human Nature* (Boston: Porter Sargeant, Publishers, 1957).

14 Although the above statements are true of the general stages in the development of male and female, a more detailed tracing shows that the development of sexual maturity is not as climactic in either male or female as these obvious stages indicate. The concept "adolescent sterility" has come into the scientific literature in recent years primarily because of research among primitive peoples and among animals. It is evident

to reproduce gradually develops. Maturation of sexual capacity comes at puberty accompanied by rather marked body changes. From early adolescence on, his sexual drive gradually declines but rarely disappears until well beyond age 60, often not until the 80's, or in certain cases not until death in extreme old age. Some men when in their 90's have sired children. Men's decline is a gradual aging process which seems to affect the whole organism rather than sex characteristics as such. Nature spares women the strenuous toil of reproduction in old age. The male need not be spared. His role is primarily economic and he is often more able to provide for children after 50 than before.

There is no physical damage to the male from first sexual intercourse to mark the end of his virginity, and he has no physical responsibility for offspring other than the act of copulation itself. Copulation is an end in itself rather than a beginning, as for the female. Society places on him the responsibility for the care of the female and her helpless offspring, but this is a social obligation, not a part of nature.

The male is spared the cataclysmic cycle which characterizes the female menopause. The decline of potency and fertility in the male is a gradual and near life-long process once full maturation is reached prior to 20 years of age.

The Development of Appetites and Drives

In this field it is most difficult to separate biology from cultural conditioning. No man or woman is permitted to grow up as designed by nature. From earliest infancy, the individual's personality is subject to the molding influences of his culture until it is soon impossible to distinguish his innate from his acquired characteristics. Manifest drives and appetites are certain in most instances to reflect some degree of modification of biological forces by education.

Glandular factors: Biological forces in and of themselves are, however, decisive factors in the shaping of certain aspects of male and female personality. The profound effect of the sex glands and their hormone

---

that the boy is capable of semen ejaculations before ripe spermatozoa are produced. Menstruation begins in the girl also before ovaries are fully developed, and ova are often produced before the womb is sufficiently well developed to carry a fetus.

It has become particularly evident, from the study of primitive peoples, that among those who permit free sex play prior to marriage, pregnancy is not frequent during the early years of adolescence. In many such tribes, sex play continues uninterrupted until the girl does become pregnant and thus attests to her readiness for marriage and parenthood. In these societies it is evident that fertility rarely comes with the beginning of menstruation. Maximum fertility in the female probably is not reached until the early twenties. For a brief, nontechnical statement on this subject, see Therese Benedek, "Some Problems of Motherhood," in A. M. Krich (Editor), *Women: The Variety and Meaning of their Sexual Experience* (New York: Dell Publishing Co., Inc., 1954), Ch. 7.

secretions on the male personality, particularly on such traits as aggressiveness and courage is illustrated throughout the animal kingdom by marked change in psychology, as well as in physical build, of the animal which has had the gonads (testes) removed. The potentially courageous, sinewy, heavy-necked bull, when castrated as a calf, becomes a fat, placid, soft-tissued steer. A similar transformation is seen in the castrated rooster. Instead of a boastful, crowing cock, the capon becomes a tender-meated, passive-dispositioned creature much like the hen in temperament and tenderness of flesh.

A comparable change takes place in the human male when he is castrated at a prepubertal age. Such males (eunuchs) become pliant in disposition, fail to develop masculine secondary characteristics such as beard and body hair, become soft and girl-like in voice and flabby in muscle and sinew. Such males lose most of their interest in the opposite sex and become entirely different in psychological make-up from normal males.

Many cultures in the past have, and many still do, make much of this transformation in the male. One of the most cruel aspects of African slavery was the castration by the Arab captors of large numbers of boys to become servants in the harems of the Arab world. The crudity of the operation lead to a very high death rate. The Byzantine State based its vitality as an empire in part on the practice of the extensive employment of eunuchs in key government and military positions. Great numbers of boys were castrated for state positions. Eunuchs had no ambitious sons to place in office and could, unmotivated by nepotism, be objective in administration.[15] In the temples of Judaism, and in many other religious groups, eunuchs were used because they could possess a purity of mind unmatched by males controlled by normal glandular pressures. Eunuchs are the entertainers today at christenings and other special occasions in Pakistan and serve many other social functions as special desexed males in Oriental cultures.

The removal of both ovaries in the young female tends to produce marked changes also. The modified female, both among animals and human beings, tends to become more masculine in appearance and characteristics, indicating that these glands and their hormone secretions have a decisive effect upon the development of the female. Some women at menopause, with the decrease of female hormones and other hormonal changes, take on certain masculine characteristics such as facial hair growth and deepening of the voice. In such instances there seems to be an increase in the secretion of male hormones that are always present in the female.

[15] Herbert J. Muller, *The Loom of History* (New York: Harper & Row, Publishers, 1958), pp. 337-338.

The sex glands with their hormone secretions, in fact, determine the growth of the body itself and account for many differences in height, weight, and tissue formation of male and female.

There is undoubtedly a biological basis for man's urge to pursue and woman's passivity. Certainly these traits are widely observed among most creatures in nature. Even so, culture can blunt the male's ardor if tradition so dictates.[16] Where sexual intimacy in childhood and adolescence is a part of the culture pattern, frigidity and impotence will be rare. If too great taboos are built about sex, both male and female may lack interest. The Manus tribe, for example, looks upon copulation as a form of excretion and treats it with repugnancy and shame.[17] The birth rate in this tribe is extremely low and the tribe is on the way to extinction.

Psychosexual development: The rate of psychosexual development differs for male and female. Sex interest for the male is at its height in the teens. Masturbation and other sexual expressions are nearly universal for the young male.[18] Often the teenage girl has little or no localized sex desire and she is much less likely to masturbate.[19] Female sex interest reaches its height near the age of thirty, long after sex sensation has been localized by sexual activity. The teenage girl is interested in being coddled but in most cases is not interested in erotic expression as such. Of course, the range of difference in psychosexual interest in both male and female is very great from individual to individual. Some mature in sexual interest earlier than others. Some have very weak sex drives; others are often overwhelmed by them.

It is in the consequences of the sex act that one of the most important sex differences inheres. Women house the embryo and nurse the child. As anthropologist Margaret Mead has so dramatically stated, "Men have to learn to want to be fathers. Girls are committed in every cell of their bodies," for the mother role. Sexual intercourse for both man and woman is a matter of a few minutes, but for the man those few minutes end. For the woman, they are "laden with commitments before and commitments afterward."[20]

"Sex is the most intimate human activity."[21] It is a very private

[16] Margaret Mead, "Potency and Receptivity," in Krich, *op. cit.,* Ch. 4. Money stresses the fact that the male sex urge is hormonally regulated. *Loc. cit.*

[17] For an excellent discussion of the effect of culture patterns on sex patterns, see Margaret Mead, "Potency and Receptivity," in Krich, *op. cit.,* Ch. 4.

[18] Alfred C. Kinsey and others, *Sexual Behavior in the Human Female* (Philadelphia: W. B. Saunders Co., 1953), p. 126.

[19] Kinsey and his co-workers found in their studies of thousands of males and females that at age 22, 40 percent of females had never experienced a sexual orgasm, whereas 80 percent of the boys had experienced an orgasm by 15 years of age, and 98 percent by 18 years of age.

[20] Margaret Mead, "Introduction," in Krich, *op. cit.*

[21] *Ibid.,* Editor's preface.

activity, yet in its consequences it is of great public importance. This is particularly true for women. Women, from early adolescence and throughout adulthood, are much more concerned with their bodies and their personal appearance than are most men. It is their biological function to attract the male and bind him to the responsibilities of parenthood. Men are much more concerned with affairs and activities external to themselves than with their own bodies and feelings. These are, in part, matters of conditioning in American culture, but probably not entirely so.

Cultural adaptations to biology: One of the most penetrating analyses of basic organic differences between male and female as factors in their respective sexual training and behavior is that by Frank K. Shuttleworth.[22] The essence of Shuttleworth's view is that male and female are conditioned differently sexually because they are so basically different in their biological make-up, as far as genital aspects of biology are concerned. Differences in conditioning begin in infancy and continue through childhood and adolescence. At least five biological differences lead to the differences in conditioning.

First, the female is a childbearer and has the mammary equipment for nursing. This Shuttleworth states as a fact, but he does not elaborate on the significance of it.

The *second* major biological difference is the greater height, weight, and physical prowess of the male, which Shuttleworth feels practically all societies make a great deal of. He believes that sex aggressiveness is part of this total pattern of the male's superiority in physical build and energy.

The *third* fact, of which he makes a great deal, is the erectile penis, which, being external, is exposed from earliest childhood to stimulation from bedding, clothes, and later from self-manipulation. The male infant has frequent erections. These continue throughout childhood and friction brings gratifying response. Thus, there is a profound difference between the baby boy and the baby girl, as well as between the male and female child and adolescent. The boy is aware of this organ and of the sensation which it brings. He develops genital responsiveness very early and cultivates it through maturity.

The females have no such awareness, because of the different formation of the sex organs themselves. The first sexual arousal of the male comes early; Kinsey suspects between the ages of six and eight.[23] The first sexual arousal in the female comes later, usually between eight and

22 Frank K. Shuttleworth, "A Biosocial and Developmental Theory of Male and Female Sexuality," *Marriage and Family Living,* 21:163-170, May, 1959.

23 Alfred C. Kinsey and others, *Sexual Behavior in the Human Male* (Philadelphia: W. B. Saunders Co., 1948).

thirteen.[24] This difference, Shuttleworth believes, is due in a substantial part to the difference in the physical make-up of the sex organs themselves, the accessibility of the male organs and the inaccessibility of the female organs to stimulation. There is, therefore, a constant development of sexual interest on the part of the male. In later childhood, masturbation begins. It usually is learned from other boys; but if it is not, the boy learns it by himself. Girls do not masturbate in nearly as high a proportion of cases; and when they learn, it is often from boys, rarely from other girls. Very few learn from self-discovery.

Nature has prepared the male for instant readiness. His desires are easily aroused by a wide range of psychic stimulation. This is nature's way of preparing him for the sex act, for his part in reproduction depends upon his readiness to take the initiative when the opportunity is offered.[25] To fail to be able to respond to opportunity is one of the greatest threats to his masculinity.

The Kinsey[26] researchers find, for example, that although male and female are alike in their ability to experience sensation of an erotic nature in various parts of the body and that there is no difference in the time male and female require to reach orgasm, once the sex act has begun, there are striking differences in the kind of phychological stimuli to which the two sexes respond and, therefore, in psychological preparation for the sex act.

They studied men's and women's reactions to a list of psychological phenomena: seeing the body of the other sex, seeing the other's sex organs, viewing one's own body, erotic art, motion pictures, etc. In all, 33 different types of psychological stimuli were presented and the male was found to respond to 29 of the 33 items more fully and more quickly than did the female. In one they were equal. The only three items to which the female responded more readily were motion pictures, reading romantic literature, and being bitten. Differences on these three items were not great.

The male progresses in sexual development by learning more effective ways of erotic stimulation, until he eventually reaches the ultimate satisfaction of sexual intercourse. His sex life begins in the nonerotic

24 Alfred C. Kinsey and others, *Sexual Behavior in the Human Female* (Philadelphia: W. B. Saunders Co., 1953).

25 *Ibid.* Numerous studies have indicated that the male is much more aggressive in sexual matters than the female. For an excellent summary of studies dealing with the premarital period for both high school and college groups, see the summary made by Warren Breed, "Sex, Class and Socialization in Dating," *Marriage and Family Living*, 18:137-144, May, 1956.

26 Alfred C. Kinsey and others, *Sexual Behavior in the Human Female* (Philadelphia: W. B. Saunders Co., 1953, pp. 687-689.

masturbation at ages three to five. It recedes, and then reaches another peak at six or seven years of age when it again subsides. Responsiveness to sex talk reaches its peak in boys of ten to eleven years of age, and then this interest declines. Homosexual responsiveness reaches its crest at around twelve. Masturbation regularly reaches its peak at about fifteen, after which come responsiveness to female nudity, day-dreaming, dancing, and so on. Nocturnal dreams seem to increase up to the late teens or early twenties. Petting experiences are more common in the twenties. And finally, of course, the male experiences the more perfect means of sexual arousal and orgasm that comes from sexual intercourse.

By contrast, Shuttleworth finds that the sexual development of the female is a slow gradual learning process, encouraged by the male. Most of what women know about practice in the area of sex is taught them by men. In many tribes, initiation of girls to sex experience is by older men, men experienced in the arts of stimulating female interest.

The *fourth* major biological difference is that in orgastic response. In males it is an easy inherent reaction; with females it is not. Males are more often rewarded than are females. In nature there is nothing in female reproductive physiology that requires an orgasm. The ancestors of the male who cannot reach an orgasm are long since extinct, since to reach an orgasm is a part of the reproductive act with the male. Shuttleworth believes that few females in the animal world respond to orgasm— that there are probably human females who are biologically incapable of orgasm. Universally, males respond to an orgasm in very much the same way. It is a part of their natural response. The variation in females is from none to multiple orgasms.

The *fifth* biological factor which Shuttleworth stresses as explaining the differences in sexuality of male and female is seminal fluid. He presents extensive evidence, recalculating some of the Kinsey data for various groups of males and females, to show that one of the major reasons for the male's constant and persistent sexuality is the build-up of sexual fluids. The method for stimulating the discharge will vary by social class, by education, by religion, and other environmental factors, but the regularity of the discharge is more or less constant throughout all social groups, by age level. The frequency of discharge will depend on the particular male. It may be in the form of a nocturnal emission; it may be induced by masturbation, by homosexual contacts, petting, or by heterosexual intercourse. But the regularity of the male seminal discharge is an incontrovertible fact. Whether the man is married or unmarried these discharges take place.

Comparison with the female shows there is no such regularity of orgasmic frequency. Shuttleworth believes the difference in male and female is due to the constant build-up of the seminal fluid in the male organs. He presents strong evidence to the effect that the frequency of the outlet for the male is governed by the production of seminal fluids and not by sociocultural factors. Religion seems to be one of the most effective sublimating factors, for there are actually fewer total outlets among the religious than the nonreligious. The nonreligious less often find an outlet in nocturnal dreams than the religious.

Shuttleworth does not feel that the five factors discussed are the only biological ones which may be of importance in male and female differences in sex behavior. He does present a very strong case for the fact that some of them are of tremendous importance in understanding the difference in the sexual development and sexual expression of males and females.

Confirming evidence of male persistent sexuality is found in studies of male sex activity. The Kinsey research group report that men who are divorced continue to have about the same number of sexual outlets as during marriage, and most of the outlets involve heterosexual coitus.[27] Goode finds that although the folk conception of a divorced woman is that she is a "loose woman," divorced women may cease sexual activity altogether and most are much less active sexually than they were in marriage.[28]

Female Receptivity

The actual rhythm of sexuality throughout nature is pretty much determined by the female and her seasons, although in some species the male's sex interest and potency also is seasonal. Her seasons, in turn, are determined by the period of ovulation and the consequent flow of hormones and genital secretions which increase her excitation and attract and excite the male, challenging him to win or overpower her. His is normally the problem of pursuit.

In human beings, where the sex act, because of romantic connotations, becomes conditioned by psychological and esthetic considerations, biological rhythms are for the most part lost and sex stimulation becomes associated with tenderness, wooing, manipulation of the erotic areas of the body by fond caresses, and other such types of excitation which operate on the automatic nervous system.[29]

Among humans, the woman may become an active, rather than merely a passive participant in the sexual act. The pattern will vary according

27 Alfred C. Kinsey and others, *Sexual Behavior in the Human Male* (Philadelphia: W. B. Saunders Co., 1948), pp. 294-296.

28 William J. Goode, *After Divorce* (New York: Free Press of Glencoe, Inc., 1956).

29 For a discussion of the estrus period (period of receptivity) see Chapter 24.

to the culture. Even so, the female is generally the less active partner in initiating as well as in performing the sex act.

Women's sexual role is much easier than that of the male, for she can be merely a passive partner and accomplish what nature intends for her to accomplish. All she has to do is avoid blocking the male's advance. Her big problem is not to struggle with her sexual drives and try to control them, as does the male, but rather to make herself so attractive that she will interest the male and assure his readiness to perform the act of fertilization when social circumstances make this appropriate.

The female learns to value many other rewards apart from sex, and modifies any natural period of receptivity she has by these other rewards. All that receptivity requires is softening and relaxing of her body. She needs none of the readiness which must be sustained by the male. She can easily fit into the sex pattern of the culture by mere compliance, "balancing the mood of the moment against the mood of tomorrow, and fitting her receptivity into the whole pattern of a relationship."[30]

For most women, the mere physical act of sex is an inadequate expression of love. The woman demands a much broader sense of completion, since sex for her involves a range of feminine roles, the climax of which is motherhood. From the earlier childhood she is taught the risks of sex. She knows the penalty of the ill-advised sex relationship.[31] She develops a modesty based on fear of what sex can cost her unless she manages it wisely or confines it to the type of relationship with the male that gives her maximum security. Often she even carries this reserve over into marriage, for the ceremony does not have the magic power to remove many of her built-in inhibitions.

The fending off of the male's advances is in part a reaction of the female to a fear of pregnancy. This is no less true in marriage than outside marriage. Pregnancy for the female is always costly—personally and socially. It involves much cost in terms of time and pursuit of personal interests, and drastically affects her social status, both inside and outside marriage. Moreover, family standard of living, as well as the advance of civilization itself in terms of improvement in conditions of life, is dependent on the control of her fertility. She is much more aware of this problem than is the male, who becomes lost in the momentary satisfaction of the sex act itself. It is women the world over who try to limit offspring, who destroy unborn infants, who practice infanticide if custom or personal wishes so dictate; and it is women who pioneer the family limitation movements by crusading for and adopting practices of birth control.

The female has much greater tolerance both for sexual excesses and for sexual deprivation than does the male. In general, she has sex more

---

[30] Mead, in Krich, *op. cit.*, p. 16.
[31] *Ibid.*

under volitional control. Havelock Ellis long ago observed the tolerance of women for sexual excesses.[32] Kinsey has shown their greater variability over the male in sexual activity and has also indicated that many married women do not suffer from the sudden termination of a regular sex life.[33] The male does.

Male Potency

Sexual potency is the key to masculinity in most cultures. Destroy it and the male's confidence and assurance goes. The male's satisfaction is derived from activity; the female's from receptivity. The male is easily distracted from one erotic object to another; the female is not. He devotes a great deal of energy in sexual pursuit and performance. In nature, and to a more covert extent in human society, this leads to roaming, aggression, assertiveness, and the defense of territorial rights and sexual property. The glandular-impelled differences even show up in the higher death rate from accident of male than female children.

Margaret Mead has pointed out that a civilization that goes too far in denying the male sexual spontaneity will destroy itself, since the male's performance is dependent on his spontaneity.[34] Female ardor is unimportant in race survival, provided she will yield to the male's advances for the sake of motherhood.

The Practical Problem of Sex Drives

Basic differences in potency and receptivity are one of the troublesome aspects of dating relationships. The female adolescent can rarely fully understand and appreciate the male. Surveys of high school girls indicate that they consider him "sex-driven." This may be a shocking discovery but there is a natural basis for it. The college male is no different.

The male identifies his sex drive with localized glandular tensions. Culture teaches him to sublimate and control, yet he constantly seeks more satisfactory sexual outlets. To elevate sexual attraction to the level of romantic love, the goal of our marriage system, requires the suppression and sublimation of the male's physical desires.

The female without sexual experience, by contrast, is less likely to be

[32] Havelock Ellis, *Man and Woman: A Study of Secondary Sexual Characteristics,* Fifth Edition (New York: Charles Scribner's Sons, 1915).

[33] Alfred C. Kinsey and others, *Sexual Behavior in the Human Female* (Philadelphia: W. B. Saunders Co., 1953).

[34] Margaret Mead, *Male and Female* (New York: William Morrow & Co., Inc., 1949).

aware of localized sexual tensions and of desire. She tends to be romantic by nature, her love impulses being more diffused and less identified with sex drives.

Much misunderstanding between the sexes in dating is due to the fact that they do not comprehend or accept the differences in the way they view the natural sequence of steps following sex attraction. For women, there are generally three steps: (1) friendship, (2) respect and love, and (3) sexual intercourse.[35] Most men can skip the middle step. A man is attracted to a "sexy" woman physically even though he does not love her. A woman may be sexually attracted to a man by physical qualities but more likely senses sexual attraction after she respects him and is to some extent in love with him.

With a woman, friendships grow into love relationships. Men often claim "love at first sight." When lightly claimed, this is a man's approach for sexual exploitation without any love being involved at all. When serious, some authorities believe that love at first sight, without previous friendship having been established, is indicative of a pathological state— "symptomatic of profound disorder in the love life."[36]

The female is more cautious in yielding to sex attraction at each step, since at the end of the consummated love relationship, for her there is always the likelihood of pregnancy, with the biological and social obligations which this entails. This is why the female generally requires a permanent relationship before yielding completely to the sexual demands of the male.

In conclusion, male and female anatomical sex differences appear during embryonic growth. Glandular and hormone developments at puberty bring with them other marked sex-differentiating characteristics. These unique attributes of male and female, although often greatly modified by culture, still affect male and female emotional and social growth decisively.

The softer flesh and more gentle disposition of the female, her different emotional and social reactions are, in part, attributable to the role for which nature has designed her—that of caring for and nursing the young. So also the aggressive, prowling disposition of the male is, in part, glandularly induced, although the culture may either thwart or encourage these tendencies. The differences in certain psychological and psycho-

[35] This observation was made by Ralph Eckert in lectures in The University of California Family Life Education Workshop in 1949.

[36] Willard Waller and Reuben Hill, *The Family* (New York: Holt, Rinehart & Winston, Inc., 1951), p. 200.

sexual responses of male and female also relate to the part each plays in nature. Man is gifted with sexual preparedness. For the female, in cultures where the source of life is known, readiness usually involves some foresight with regard to the social consequences of the act.

Male and female are biological complements to each other, each being equally important to the process of reproduction and yet far different in specific capacities and functions. The female is handicapped by the menstrual cycle, by the burden of carrying the young, and by all the responsibiliites which center around these functions. The male bears none of these burdens, but in most cultures he has to bear the economic burden of supporting the female and her helpless young.

One can make too much of biological differences in male and female, as history indicates so clearly. In the relationships of men and women today, social roles are probably more decisive to the success of dating and marriage.

Problems

1. Do you feel that this chapter gives too much weight to biological factors in male-female development? Explain.
2. Do you feel that women still suffer discrimination in our culture because of their so-called infirmities?
3. Discuss the importance of male-female biological differences in drives as they bear on marriage relationships.
4. *Research exercise:* Poll members of the class or some other student group on (a) color preferences, (b) favorite recreation, (c) favorite hobby (other items may be added). Tabulate results for men and women separately. Analyze, discuss and point up significance of findings.

   Are innate or conditioned factors involved? What differences are probably attributable to peculiarities of American culture? How do certain differences bear on the relationships between men and women?
5. Custom is still somewhat opposed to women occupying certain positions and playing certain roles: high governmental posts, the ministry, executive positions in business, campaigning in politics, practicing law, etc. (a) Tell why the customs came into being. (b) Describe assets or liabilities women possess for these roles.

Selected References

ARTICLES IN BOOKS OF READINGS

KRICH, A. M. (Editor), *Women: The Variety and Meaning of Their Sexual Experience* (New York: Dell Publishing Co., Inc., 1954).

1. MEAD, Margaret, "Introduction," pp. 9-24.
2. MEAD, Margaret, "Potency and Receptivity," pp. 111-135.

FISHBEIN, Morris, and KENNEDY, Ruby Jo Reeves, *Modern Marriage and Family Living* (New York: Oxford University Press, Inc., 1957).

3. SEWARD, Georgene H., "Sex and the Social Order," pp. 87-99.
4. MANWILLER, Charles E., "Sex Education and the Child," pp. 476-483.

CAVAN, Ruth Shonle, *Marriage and the Family in the Modern World: A Book of Readings* (New York: Thomas Y. Crowell Co., 1960).

5. SYMONDS, Percival M., "Difference in Attitude Toward Love and Sex," Reading 25.

General References

FARRIS, Edmund J., *Human Ovulation and Fertility* (Philadelphia: J. B. Lippincott Co., 1956).

JAY, Phyllis C., "The Female Primate," pp. 3-13; MACCOBY, Eleanor E., "Woman's Intellect," pp. 24-39; OVERSTREET, Edmund W., "Biological Make-up of Woman," pp. 13-23; "Research on the Nature of Woman" (Panel Discussion), pp. 40-50; all in Seymour M. FARBER and Roger H. L. WILSON (Editors) *The Potential of Woman* (New York: McGraw-Hill Book Co., 1963).

MEAD, Margaret, *Male and Female* (New York: William Morrow & Co., Inc., 1949).

SHUTTLEWORTH, Frank K., "A Biosocial and Developmental Theory of Male and Female Sexuality," *Marriage and Family Living*, 21:163-170, May, 1959.

4

Male and Female: Physical
and Emotional Strength

In a world where the male has almost always been the favored sex, it has been easy to take for granted presumed superiorities of the male and inferiorities of the female. A scientific-minded age probes more deeply to try to learn what men and women are really capable of—physically, psychologically, temperamentally. It is not always possible to detach innate factors from those grafted on by male and female subcultures, but complete isolation of these factors would serve only a theoretical purpose, not the practical functional one which is the concern of this book.

Differences in Physical Strength and Stamina

Male and female architectures are obviously quite different. But what is the significance of these differences? Do they add up to an all-around male superiority in physique as tradition suggests by labeling women "the weaker sex," or has folklore distorted the facts on this as on other issues?

Although the female is less muscular than the male and falls short in tests of brute strength, she is more durable and has greater resistance to fatigue. She can stand more suffering and go longer without sleep. At every age of life from birth to old age, the death rate of the male exceeds that of the female (see Figure 4-1). Even prenatal deaths of males exceed those of females, more males being stillborn. Nature offsets this in part by a sex ratio at birth which, in most countries, runs from about 105 to 106 male births to each 100 female births (105.7 in the United States). The

AGE-SPECIFIC DEATH RATES OF MALES AND FEMALES, UNITED STATES, 1962

(DEATHS PER 1,000 MIDYEAR POPULATION)

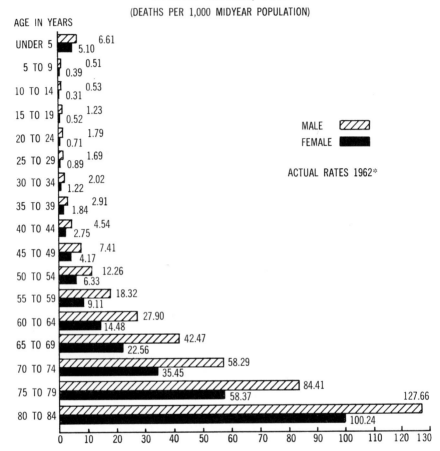

* Based on death statistics obtained from the National Center for Health Statistics, U. S. Public Health Service.

SOURCE: U. S. Department of Commerce, Bureau of the Census, "Projections of the Population of the U. S. by Age and Sex: 1964-1985," *Current Population Reports*, Series P-25, No. 286, July, 1964.

FIGURE 4-1————At all age periods, the male death rate far exceeds that of the female. During the teens and early twenties it is more than twice as high. It is almost twice as high in the years 50 to 70.

higher general mortality rate and war together explain why men are in the minority in all of the older nations and why with the cessation of immigration from other lands (long-distance migrations are always dominated by males) they have recently become so in the United States.[1]

Women's operative rate runs 46 per thousand compared to 38 per thousand for men. Rates run about the same for the common ailments like the removal of the tonsils, adenoids, and appendix. Surgery on the genital organs is four times as frequent on women as men, but hernia operations are five times as frequent on men as on women.[2]

Women have minor illnesses more often than men. Before the days of psychosomatic medicine these were known as "female complaints." But women survive them. They do have a much more complicated glandular make-up to reckon with than do men. Much can go wrong with the female urogenital mechanism because it is so complicated. In advanced societies, where diagnosis and treatment prolong life, few women get through the life span without serious difficulty in connection with menstruation or childbirth, and many undergo operations involving some part of the reproductive mechanism. Males rarely have difficulty in this part of their anatomy except for the enlargement of the prostate gland in later life. No doubt another reason for women's most frequent complaints is that they get more of a hearing in social intercourse—their operations certainly bring more social acclaim than do those of men. Men, at least in American culture, get no credit for their frailties. Women are getting less credit for them than in an earlier day when their role in society was a more passive one.

Even so, the differential in length of life is increasing rather than decreasing. In 1926, white males in the United States averaged 57 years, females 59.6, a difference of 2.6 years; in 1955, white males averaged 67.3 years, females 73.6, a difference of 6.3 years.[3] By 1975, the Social Security Administration predicts a life span of 71 years for the male, 77 years for the female.

Women's greater longevity may be in part due to the fact that they visit doctors more, even aside from calls related to childbirth, and that they are able to take better care of themselves, not so often being under the pressure of a scheduled job as are men.[4]

[1] For a comprehensive discussion of this topic, see Paul H. Landis, *Population Problems: A Cultural Interpretation*, Second Edition (New York: American Book Co., 1954), Ch. 4.

[2] Data reported by Dr. Morris Fishbein of the American Medical Association in "Medical News of the Month," *McCall's*, September, 1960, p. 66.

[3] Metropolitan Life Insurance Company, "Sex Differences in Mortality Increasing," *Statistical Bulletin*, 58:1-4, September, 1957.

[4] For a discussion of various aspects of this problem see a statement by George Bugbee, President, Health Information Foundation, 6:6, December, 1957.

In our culture, men are more definitely committed to the work world than are women. A man's ego satisfaction is found there; he measures his success by the achievements of work and by the advancements in his work position. The warning to the aspiring executive sometimes given is "promotions can kill you." This is indicative of the high pressure which may be inherent in great success in the work world.

The extent to which men are committed to the work world is partly a matter of culture, rather than biology, particularly to heavy manual work. In peasant economies and primitive cultures, women often are thought to be as fit for hard labor as men; in some, even more fit. Ethel M. Albert reports that she was advised in Central Africa that: "Everybody knows that men are not suited to heavy work, that women are stronger and better workers. Men drink too much and do not eat enough to keep up their strength; they are more tense and travel about too much to develop the habits and the muscles needed for sustained work on farms."[5]

Woman is physically awkward, by man's standards. But man is thinking of the way he throws a baseball. If a graceful man were forced to unfasten a back-buttoning garment, as women often must, he would soon learn how awkward he is. The male reaches over his shoulders to skin off a sweater; the female, around her ribs. He pulls his gloves on from the front; she, from the back of her hands. He doubles his fingernails into his upturned palm to look at them; she turns her palms down and straightens her fingers to look at the fingernails. He strikes a match toward him; she, away from her. He carries books hooked in a hanging hand. She cradles them on her stomach. He is hinged for certain movements; she, for others.[6] Different, but unequal only if one prefers one style of movement to the other.

In our day when many industrial jobs take nimble fingers, employers have long since learned that many women have physical skills unequaled by many men. Employers sometimes pay women less than men, but this is a survival of custom rather than a denial of equality in ability to produce.

Historical Performance

The male's greatest claim to superior natural endowment over the female is the record of history. The chronicle of humanity's long past is studded almost exclusively with the accomplishments of the male. Even

[5] Ethel M. Albert, "The Roles of Women: Question of Values," in Seymour H. Farber and Roger H. L. Wilson (Editors), *The Potential of Woman* (New York: McGraw-Hill Book Co., 1963), pp. 105-115.

[6] For photographs of these various actions, see Leslie Lieber, "Double Standard in Actions!" *This Week*, March 14, 1954, pp. 14-15.

those women who achieved enduring fame generally did so by influencing the activities of men rather than by achievements of their own. Yet history shows that now and then a woman has demonstrated her genius by supreme accomplishment, showing that the genes of greatness have not gone entirely to the male.

What the worshipers of precedent forget in making historical comparisons of male-female accomplishment is that accomplishment is no less a product of opportunity than of genetic inheritance. Few cultures have allowed the female to assume what they considered a creative role; practically all cultures have placed the male in this role. The infrequent references to women in history probably proves little except that women in most cultures have been excluded from all but the subservient or domestic activities of the group.

Psychological Differences

Among the first comparative scientific studies of male and female were those of the anthropologists and psychologists which compared brain weight, reaction time, and sensory acuity of the sexes. The brain-weight test favored the male—more grams of brain, therefore more brain capacity. By such simple logic was the die cast in favor of male superiority.

It remained for the recently devised intelligence test, and the competitive situations provided by coeducation to banish this bit of poorly conceived logic from the halls of science. The notion that men have superior innate ability as a gift of nature seems so absurd now that few would even attempt to argue the case, yet the proof on which the modern notion of equal ability of the sexes rests is little more than fifty years old. It is not surprising that many still act as though they did not believe women were equal in mental ability to men.

In certain sensory abilities there are slight differences between the sexes. Women, at least as trained in our culture, are generally better co-ordinated in speech. They rarely stutter. Men inherit a sensory defect which women carry in the genes, but pass on in body characteristics chiefly to the male, namely color blindness.

Watts finds that the male tends to "spotlight" knowledge, whereas women tend to "floodlight" it. The female senses a variety of things simultaneously.[7] He finds that our culture tends to specialize in and reward the spotlight kind of performance.

Margaret Mead believes that the work cycle of the females in most

[7] Alan Watts, "The Woman in Man," in Farber and Wilson, *op. cit.*, pp. 79-86.

cultures tends to be adapted to the rhythm of her biological nature.[8] Not all cultures do adapt their work cycle to the natural rhythms of the female, that is, to the rhythm of the monthly cycle and the cycle of pregnancy, nursing, and so on, although it is more convenient if they do so. Man is under no limitations of this kind.

She finds evidence that the man tends to work by spurts of great effort, and that the spurt-rest pattern of the male may be related to his endocrine system. Women tend to work at a more constant pace, although Mead cites cultures in which women also work at a spurt-rest cycle. Women have greater capacity for monotonous, repetitive work and bear up under it with less psychological expense.

In the area of interests there are measurable evidences of significant psychological differences between male and female.

Eleanor E. Maccoby, Stanford University psychologist, reports that girls early develop greater interest in people than boys and are more concerned about what people think of them. They are more conforming and more influenced by the opinions of others.[9]

Years earlier other Stanford psychologists, after months of study in this field, and after covering more than forty of the best researches made by scientists in different fields, reported:

> Women are consistently more intimate and personal than men. They are strongly interested in persons and spend more time and thought on people and personalities than men do. Excellent studies of young children show that girls very early are more interested in relationships with others, while boys are more interested in material things.[10]

This gives a scientific basis for women's greater tendency to gossip and men's greater interest in material gain.

Studies made by eavesdropping show that women talk mostly about personal things—other people, their friends, themselves, or their feelings and loves; men more often talk about activities—politics, business matters, sports, their sexual exploits, and their accomplishments.

Dr. Theodor Reik, Director of the New York Society for Psychoanalytical Psychology, has observed that a woman is rarely separated from her husband or lover in her thoughts and inner emotions, even when at work. They do not like impersonal work; they want to be working for someone—husband, boss, child, community, or they may want to impress a man through their work. Men are always trying to produce an effect;

---

[8] Margaret Mead, *Male and Female* (New York: William Morrow and Co., Inc., 1949), Ch. 8.

[9] Farber and Wilson, *op. cit.*, pp. 24-39.

[10] Winifred Johnson and Lewis M. Terman, "Some Highlights in the Literature of Psychology of Sex Differences Published Since 1920," *Journal of Psychology*, 9:327 ff., 1940.

they want to change the world. For the woman the nicest words are, "I love you," for the man, "I am proud of you."[11]

A woman will express herself in terms of how she felt on a certain occasion; a man, in terms of what he said, did, or at least thought. Characteristic female reactions might be "I was embarrassed to death," or "I could have died, I was so humiliated." But in talking about a similar situation, the man boasts, "I told the guy to shut up or I'd knock his teeth down his throat."

If the conversation turns to generalized traits of human nature—like selfishness, greed, obstreperousness, or goodness, for that matter, the woman immediately says to herself, and maybe to others, too, "Am I like that?" She personalizes generalizations about people. A man shifts the generalization to someone else who fits the picture. "That's old Jake Sampson to a 'T'," he says. It never occurs to him that he might be that way himself.

Women are more frequent readers of fiction, for they identify themselves with characters and situations much more readily and completely than do men. If asked to criticize a bit of fiction, a woman appraises situations in terms of how she has acted or thinks she would act under similar circumstances. A man is more likely to rationalize his criticism in terms of principles and universals rather than his own experience.

A man must always be careful in making any criticism of women in the presence of wife or sweetheart for she immediately feels that his abstract criticism is really meant for her. A man, on the other hand, may fail to get the point when a woman's criticism, aimed at "men," is really meant for him. Likely as not he recognizes that men are that way, but is equally sure that he does not share these imperfections of his sex. His ego is too well fortified to be punctured by so dull a weapon.

A male, in meeting others, tries to influence them by his conversation and behavior. The female is more often interested in making an impression on them by her appearance.

Women are seldom as direct in stating what they think as are men. For instance, if a man doesn't like what another does, he is likely to tell him so, and have it out in the open. A woman is more likely to tell someone other than the offender, thus approaching the issue indirectly. Of course, she hopes her remarks will eventually get around to the right party without her receiving the blame for them.

Men are more inclined to be competitive, to outdo others, to achieve success and fortune. Women are more interested in getting along with people, although this pattern is changing because of coeducation and women's work experience.

[11] Theodor Reik, *Sex in Man and Woman* (New York: Farrar, Straus & Co., Inc., 1960).

Research on college dating shows that the bright coed will often deliberately "act dumb" to keep from outdoing her less brilliant date. Of course, a part of this is a woman's sense of the practical in human relations. In this, as in so many of her relationships with the male she must masquerade.

Men and women differ decidedly in the kind of psychological stimuli to which they respond. How much of this is conditioning by the culture and how much is innate difference is debatable, but whatever the original cause, this decidedly affects the ability to respond in various situations.

Emotional Differences

Romantic inclinations: There is little doubt that the inhibiting of sexual impulses has much to do with romantic feeling. In American culture, at least, perhaps in most cultures of the world, women have more cultural inhibitions imposed upon them in the matter of sexual expression than do men. This, undoubtedly, explains in part why women are much more romantic in temperament and outlook than are men, why their sex impulses more often take on the character of fantasy, daydreaming, and other forms of covert erotic expression which are in themselves often more satisfying than the physical sex experience itself.

This tends to enrich her erotic life and to bring to her a more diffused sexual sensation than that of the male, who approaches sex more directly. It has been proposed by some psychologists that such a diffused development of love may actually, in the case of some women, interfere with physical expression of love or make the physical expression seem much less important when it is experienced than is the enriched sexual fantasy. The expression of erotic love may more readily, in the case of women, perhaps also lead to a degree of narcissism, or self-love, which expresses itself in adoration of the body, excessive pride in personal appearance, and general self-absorption as a substitute for sexual love.

It is possible that the female finds it more easy to develop masochistic traits than does the male. The male is the active, aggressive partner in the sexual relationship. The female by nature is the passive partner, and these psychological traits may more readily be converted into a masochistic self-torture, which carried to an extreme becomes a perversion. A masochistic personality tends to develop if the father is cruel with the girl or employs overly stern discipline and physical punishment (see Chapter 6). The tendency of the female to psychologically identify with the male and feel herself a part of him and his activities, which is a natural part of so many cultures, creates a psychological climate which makes it easier for her to develop a self-suffering complex than it is for the male.

Deutsch has suggested that women who commit suicide because of the break-up of a love affair often do not do it because they are suffering from a loss of the love object but because of narcissistic injury to their ego.[12]

The connection between woman's sexual and emotional life is far different from that of the male. Nature has provided him with an insistent and easily aroused desire, and it may be quite emotion-free in the broader sense of love's connotation. He is vulnerable if his readiness fails him. The woman's problem is that of attracting the male she wants as a mate. Her role is that of surrender but surrender has a price, she wants sex identified with love.

When cultures choose to make the female highly aggressive, as among the Zuni Indians, stories of fear of the wedding night are about grooms, not brides. In polygynous cultures of the world the universal quest is for an aphrodisiac to bolster the male's prowess in sexual performance.

The premenstrual syndrome: The emotional life of the female must be reckoned with in part because of her biological rhythms, which may be reflected in moods. The temperament cycle of the female tends to affect her energy and sociability during the twenty-eight day menstrual cycle. The first peak period is shortly after the menstrual flow, the second is near the mid-period at about the time of ovulation, and the third is just before the onset of the menstrual flow, when there is a rise in basal metabolism rate. Each of these energy periods are found to be associated with secretions from the ovaries which are evidenced by increased work performance of women.[13] Generally speaking, during the upbuilding of the uterine wall following menstruation, there is a period of great activity, vitality, and sociability. This is known as the estrogen phase of the menstrual cycle. It is climaxed by a slight rise in temperature near the time the ovum is released. After ovulation, the progesterone phase begins and the woman is more likely to be moody and suffer some tension. Her tensions increase as the time of menstruation approaches, although just before menstruation there is an upturn in physical energy due to a rise in the basal metabolism rate.[14]

Tension may express itself in various moods and in various antisocial reactions. Some women fall into a deep depressive mood prior to menstruation. The whole world looks black and hopeless. Some become so depressed as to be almost suicidal for a short period during this time of the month. Others snap at those about them, becoming so hostile as to be almost impossible to get along with. Roommate, husband, or other

[12] Helene Deutsch, *The Psychology of Women, a Psycho-analytical Interpretation* (New York: Grune & Stratton, Inc., 1944), p. 198.

[13] Edmund J. Farris, *Human Ovulation and Fertility* (Philadelphia: J. B. Lippincott Co., 1956).

[14] *Ibid.*

close associates need to beware. Later they regret this antisocial behavior, but at the time they seem to be hardly able to control it.

The subject of premenstrual tensions has received much study by gynecologists, internists, and psychiatrists, since they have been concerned with the "premenstrual syndrome." The majority of women have some elements of the syndrome.[15]

Morton found 80 percent of 249 women prisoners had elements of the premenstrual syndrome.[16] Eichner found 70 percent of nurses had symptoms.[17] Several other studies show 30 to 75 percent. Pennington found 95 percent of 1,000 high school and college students had symptoms.[18] Proportions showing symptoms depend on symptoms described by interviewers.

Most symptoms appear in the premenstrual week; some women have emotional symptoms at the beginning of menstruation, a few at the mid-menstrual period, and a few past the midpoint. Early in the new menstrual phase relief from tension comes to most, although some experience physical and emotional stress in the first quarter of menstruation.[19]

W. R. Cooke[20] reported that most crimes of a group studied in Paris were committed during the premenstrual period. J. H. Morton and colleagues report that at New York State Farm for women prisoners 62 percent of crimes of violence occurred during the premenstrual week, 17 percent during menstruation.[21]

The most common theory is that premenstrual tension is due to low progesterone and to high levels of unantagonized estrogen. The estrogen-progesterone ratio seems to be most disturbed at this time in those with symptoms. The premenstrual syndrome is more severe in women with neurotic constitutions.[22] It is also more severe, Cook found, among women who have a fear of becoming pregnant.

Frequency of symptoms as reported in several studies dealing with the premenstrual period are seen in Table 4-1. Note that headache is the most common experience reported by various groups. Fatigue, depression, and irritability are often reported, as is swelling and tenderness of breasts.

---

15 Irwin N. Perr, "Medical, Psychiatric, and Legal Aspects of Premenstrual Tension," *American Journal of Psychiatry,* 115:211-219, September, 1958.

16 *Ibid.*

17 E. Eichner, "Premenstrual Tension Syndrome," an address reported in Perr, *op. cit.*

18 V. M. Pennington, *Journal of American Medical Association,* June, 1957.

19 Judson T. Landis' study gives attention to all four quarters, rather than the fourth only. Most studies have been concerned with the premenstrual phase. See Table 4-1 for source.

20 W. R. Cooke, *American Journal of Obstetrics and Gynecology,* 49:457, 1945.

21 J. H. Morton, *American Journal of Obstetrics and Gynecology,* 65:1182, 1953.

22 The probable effect of the menstrual cycle on sexual desire is discussed in Chapter 24.

TABLE 4-1————Symptoms found in the premenstrual syndrome*

	Greene and Dalton† PATIENTS (*Percent*)	Rees‡ PATIENTS (*Percent*)	Eichner and Waltner§ NORMAL SUBJECTS (*Percent*)	Eichner and Waltner‖ PATIENTS (*Percent*)	Landis¶ 181 COLLEGE GIRLS (*Percent*)
Headache	69.5	63	—	—	33
Nausea	29.7	37	—	—	10
Lethargy (fatigue)	13.1	63	59	—	44
Rheumatism	16.7	—	—	—	—
Vertigo (dizziness)	10.6	—	—	—	—
Depression	6.0	80	62	—	48
Irritability	6.0	100	51	—	43
Edema (congestion)	6.0	73	32	72	—
Rhinorrhea (excessive mucous secretions from nose)	7.2	—	—	—	—
Mastalgia (swelling or tenderness of breasts)	2.4	63	69	—	44
Tension	—	100	—	—	—
Emotional lability (inability to concentrate, etc.)	—	—	—	56	39
Anxiety	—	73	—	—	36
Insomnia	—	40	—	—	—
Pruritus (itching and skin eruptions)	—	40	—	—	58
Marked thirst	—	20	—	—	—
Physical discomfort (chills, cramps, etc.)	—	—	—	58	23

* Adapted from Irwin N. Perr, "Medical, Psychiatric, and Legal Aspects of Premenstrual Tensions," *American Journal of Psychiatry*, 115:211-219, September, 1958, with additions.

† R. Greene and K. Dalton: *British Medical Journal*, 1:1007, 1953.

‡ L. Rees: *British Medical Journal*, 1:1014, 1953.

§ E. Eichner and C. Waltner: *Medical Times*, 83:771, August, 1955.

‖ E. Eichner, "Premenstrual Tension Syndrome," Presentation at N.Y.S. Academy of General Practice, October, 1957.

¶ Judson T. Landis, "Physical and Mental-Emotional Changes Accompanying the Menstrual Cycle," *Research Studies of the State College of Washington*, 25:155-162, June, 1957.

Temperament: Because of women's unique biological constitution, as well as by unique cultural conditioning, there may be truth in the folk conception of the female as being more highly keyed, more sensitive, and more gifted with those emotions which lead to protective behavior of the infant and child. Women may be more intuitive. They no doubt are less ego-centered, live less in bold and courageous action than does the male in most cultures. They may be vain, but not as ruthlessly ambitious as the male.

Although business and industrial experience have tended to lead to greater control, crying remains a part of the female subculture. It is strictly taboo for the adult male of American culture (this is not so of the Latin cultures, where crying as an expression of joy or sorrow is much more acceptable). The American male is not as stoical as the native Indian but he is very stoical compared to the female when it comes to expressing emotions.

These subtle emotional differences are the theme of many works of fiction and of some scientific literature. These supposed traits, and many like them, may be myth or may be reality, but it is known that a feeling of need for security, emotional and economic, is very strong in women of our culture. Whether innate or learned, or a combination of both, is not known.

Stanford psychologists[23] found that women are more temperamental, for the female glandular system is much more complicated than is that of the male. Women are given to up-and-down moods during the monthly cycle of glandular functioning and during pregnancy. Their moods exceed the temperamental deviations of the male. Women are also more given to tears than are men. These traits are, in part, culturally determined, of course. Cry, they do, but when real emotional problems arise, women have more toughness than do men. During World War II, they stood the strain of air raids better than men.

Built-in shockproofing: Although women have more emotional problems, or at least are more aware of their problems, it is men who most often get ulcers. Even during the teen years, girls are much more aware of problems and tensions in the parental home and in their social relationships generally than are boys.[24] Tradition holds that women fret and worry more than men throughout life, but only about a third as many of them take their anxiety seriously enough to commit suicide.

Even so, far more women than men attempt suicide in the United States. Whether they do not have the courage to do it effectively, use the wrong tools, or for some other reasons of a more subtle nature fail, is a

23 Winifred Johnson and Lewis M. Terman, "Some Highlights in the Literature of Psychological Sex Differences Published Since 1920," *Journal of Psychology*, 9:327 ff., 1940.

24 See, for example, Table 10 in Paul H. Landis and Carol L. Stone, *The Relationship of Parental Authority to Teenage Adjustment* (Pullman, Wash.: Washington Agricultural Experiment Station, 1952), Bulletin No. 538.

TABLE 4-2————Suicide deaths and suicide death rate by sex, color, and means of suicide, United States, 1960-1962*

| MEANS OF INJURY | WHITE | | NONWHITE | |
	Males	Females	Males	Females
Suicide—Total				
Average annual number	13,812	4,458	745	218
Rate per 100,000	17.5	5.5	9.1	2.4
Percent	100.0	100.0	100.0	100.0
Poisoning	19.3	40.7	10.6	24.0
Hanging and strangulation	16.8	15.5	17.0	17.0
Firearms and explosives	54.7	25.3	52.7	25.9
Other	9.2	18.5	19.7	33.1

* SOURCE: Metropolitan Life Insurance Company, *Statistical Bulletin*, 45:8-9, July, 1964. Data from reports of U. S. Division of Vital Statistics.

Observe that three times as many males as females commit suicide among whites; almost four times as many males as females commit suicide among nonwhites, where the suicide rates is much lower than it is for whites. Women, however, attempt suicide more often. Do you see a possible explanation for the sex difference in success of means used? Are there other reasons?

matter of speculation.[25] It is very probable that many do not seriously wish to kill themselves. They may use suicide as an attention-getting device, to spite someone, to get publicity, or for other such reasons, and plan the act, perhaps subconsciously, so they will be discovered before it is fatal.[26]

Men and women fall victim to nervous breakdowns and mental illness in about equal numbers, but women are more likely to respond to psychological treatment and to recover.[27] It seems very probable that men, being disciplined in ignoring pain and discomfort, and being taught to be tough, neglect nervous problems longer than women do and reach the clinician after the disease is much further advanced. Women express their feelings more than men; therefore, men may get in a much worse emotional state before they or others recognize it.[28] Our culture denies

[25] Women, rather than using firearms, usually use poison or overdoses of drugs which in prescribed quantities are not dangerous. Lack of familiarity with firearms is a factor, but also their desire not to disfigure themselves for the funeral. These and many other aspects of suicide are discussed in Paul H. Landis, *Social Problems: Unfulfilled Welfare Aspirations of Nation and World* (Philadelphia: J. B. Lippincott Co., 1959), Ch. 10.

[26] Being more social than men, they are more likely to be discovered than men by a roommate or friend, in case of slow-acting methods of suicide.

[27] Amram Scheinfeld, *Women and Men* (New York: Harcourt, Brace & Co., 1943).

[28] The male has more emotional instability at ten than at any other age. The male generally is the stoical sex according to Carle C. Zimmerman and Lucius F. Cervantes, *Marriage and the Family* (Chicago: Henry Regnery Co., 1956).

men the safety valve of tears, tantrums, and other such releases permitted in the female subculture.

Male and female differences in temperament, emotions, and physical strength and stamina are not all a matter of folk myth. Some differences do exist and they are important to man and wife relationships. In some respects women are the stronger sex, in others, men. Their strengths and weaknesses may complement each other, but cultures do not always take advantages of differences in defining male and female roles. In the area of emotional differences, the female biological constitution may be a major factor.

Problems

1. Discuss the proposition, "Custom, rather than native endowment, is probably responsible for the fact that men hold more positions of authority in our society."
2. Women are frequently credited with having a greater capacity for "spiritual love" than do men. Explain the probable basis for this belief. Do you think it is justified?
3. Do you believe men and women differ in any or all the following traits: mental superiority, reasoning ability, emotional stability, quick thinking, sense of humor, ability with figures, practical common sense, sensitivity, sympathy, efficiency in work, submissiveness, stubbornness? Those who believe in differences should offer proof for their view. Note whether each sex always considers the opposite sex deficient.
4. Philip Wylie has written a book entitled *The Disappearance* in which he alternately describes our country suddenly left peopled only by women, and then, only by men. He speculates about governmental changes, social changes, even changes in war and international behavior.
   Make your own statement on such a world as you visualize it.
5. Is it true that studies have proven that there are practically no native differences between men and women other than those of anatomy? Explain and illustrate.
6. For what reason have women traditionally been referred to as the "weaker sex"? Upon what grounds might it accurately be said that women are the "stronger sex"? Read Ashley-Montagu below for a point of view.

Selected References

ARTICLES IN BOOKS OF READINGS

KRICH, A. M. (Editor), *Women: The Variety and Meaning of Their Sexual Experience* (New York: Dell Publishing Co., Inc., 1954).

1. DEUTSCH, Helene, "Prepuberty in Woman," pp. 71-95.
CAVAN, Ruth Shonle, *Marriage and the Family in the Modern World: A Book of Readings* (New York: Thomas Y. Crowell Co., 1960).
2. GREENBERG, Selig, "Why Women Live Longer Than Men," Reading 23.

General References

ASHLEY-MONTAGU, M. F., *The Natural Superiority of Women* (New York: Lancer Books, Inc., 1953).

LANDIS, Judson T., "Physical and Mental-Emotional Changes Accompanying the Menstrual Cycle," *Research Studies of the State College of Washington,* 25: 155-162, June, 1957, p. 160.

MEAD, Margaret, *Male and Female* (New York: William Morrow & Co., Inc., 1949).

OVERSTREET, Edmund W., "Biological Make-up of Woman," in Seymour M. FARBER, and Roger H. L. WILSON (Editors), *The Potential of Woman* (New York: McGraw-Hill Book Co., 1963), pp. 13-23.

PERR, Irwin N., "Medical, Psychiatric, and Legal Aspects of Premenstrual Tension," *American Journal of Psychiatry,* 115:211-219, September, 1958.

————, "Sex Differences in Mortality Increasing," *Statistical Bulletin,* 58:4, September, 1957.

WALLER, Willard and HILL, Reuben, *The Family* (New York: Holt, Rinehart & Winston, Inc., 1951), Part 3.

5

The Sex-Identification
Process

Cultures do amazing things to human beings by virtue of
sex assignment. What is appropriate for the female in
one culture may be strictly masculine in another culture, and vice versa.
Granted clear-cut biological differentiation, the male and female are
cultural products and a great deal of socialization is required to form
the appropriate male and female personality. In every known society,
male and female subcultures are different, and an individual growing
up in one subculture is never quite at home in the other, no matter what
the biological sex category is. The boy becomes a man by participating
in the male subculture and imitating males; the girl becomes a woman
by living in the female subculture and imitating females.

One of the major problems of any society is the development of the
personality of male and female in such a way that the majority of individuals will become identified in psychological orientation and social
interests with the roles and expectations of their own sex. This is done
so automatically that society is not particularly aware of the conditioning process and rarely is the individual aware that the process is going
on. The person has usually forgotten, by adulthood, the steps by which
he or she was inducted into the sex roles of male or female.

It is only when the training process goes astray that its striking significance is made apparent, and often it does go astray, for in spite of the
best efforts of society to condition the female toward female attitudes
and expectations and the male toward masculine patterns, many failures
result.

On the genital level, failure to develop sex identification leads, as we
have seen, to homosexuality. On the social level, such failure produces

women who identify primarily with the male role, have male interests, and feel frustrated in living by the female life patterns; and it produces males whose social training has been such that they identify in their secret wishes and often in their external behavior with the opposite sex.

The Genital Stage of Sex Identification

Very early in childhood the striking fact of genital sex differences impresses itself upon the child. How early this comes depends greatly on whether or not the children are allowed to see each other and parents in the nude. If so, within the first two or three years of life, consciousness of male-female genital differences dawns on the child. It is possible that the significance becomes apparent to the girl at an earlier age and presents a greater challenge to her, leading to questions and a need for explanation. The small child lives in an environment of absorbing mysteries which challenge his investigation. By investigating, he learns. Body differences are such a mystery. It is a fortunate child whose parents, recognizing the critical but at the same time random and incidental character of the child's interest, allow free and unemotional exploration.

Probably few parents—or, for that matter, few adults—are capable of true objectivity in this area. Children sheltered in infancy from the knowledge of sex differences may become aware of body structure only after starting school. Many modern nursery schools do not segregate the sexes for toilet use. Teachers of young children have themselves been taught the great importance of handling the innumerable curiosities of their small charges with naturalness, honesty, and without shock. The teachers can help the "delayed learner" to catch up, but the school situation, no matter how enlightened, cannot adequately substitute for enlightened parents.

Freudian psychologists have emphasized *penis envy* as a factor in female inferiority. This presumably develops when the young girl first observes that the young male has an external organ which she lacks. This makes her feel deficient and is the beginning of her feeling of inferiority to the male. In more severe cases penis envy leads to what is described as *genital trauma*. This in turn, according to the Freudian view, tends to build up female passivity in the sexual relationship.

Deutsch points out that young children envy anything the other child possesses and that penis envy, therefore, is normal and more or less inevitable.[1] She points out that many girls claim they once had a penis and

---

[1] Helene Deutsch, *The Psychology of Women, a Psycho-analytical Interpretation* (New York: Grune & Stratton, Inc., 1944), pp. 234 ff.

lost it. Other young girls, seeing a boy's penis, may try to take it away from him. Penis envy, therefore, is the same kind of envy that arises from the possession by another of any kind of property.

It is possible that the girl feels something is lacking in her body when she first becomes aware of the male difference. Whether or not her awareness develops psychological significance depends largely on the way in which it is handled. If parents explain frankly and honestly and without any sense of shock, "Yes, a boy does have more on the outside, but you have much more in the inside. You can be a mother. A boy never can," she is usually able to accept the difference without being psychologically scarred. A fact of life has been established that takes on no more significance than difference of hair color or any other physical trait. If the parents are shocked at this query or shocked when the girl, first observing the male organ, touches it and asks questions, if they hush her and shame her, the difference may become of vital psychological significance.

It is possible, too, that the necessary differences in toilet training of the boy and girl may have a psychological impact on sex identification. The girl may envy the boy's standing position in urination. The expanding use of standing facilities for both sexes, as is evidence in some modern schools as well as in other public buildings, may well mark the beginning of a decline of cultural difference here. Other cultures—those in Asia, for example—have long experience in identical toilet posture for the sexes. In Asia this is a half-standing, half-sitting posture and it seems to bear no relationship to the development of sex identification in this part of the world.

Finally, one may well question whether observing the sex organs themselves is for the child any more surprising, or shocking, or any more a part of awareness of sex identification than observing the length of hair on the head or observing the mother's breasts. The adult who registers shock in connection with the child's observation of genital differences assumes that the child is equally shocked. Of course, if the child's first knowledge of genital differences comes from observing another child, then the problem is unique in that the child of the opposite sex shows no other differences in physical form.

The Oedipus Complex

Freud saw sex identification as a deeply complex, incestuous struggle. He coined the term *Oedipus complex* to describe it, taking the name from a famous Greek myth. The infant Oedipus was exposed to die in the ancient Greek fashion of disposing of a child who did not appear to be strong at birth. A shepherd found the boy and adopted him. He grew to manhood and became king of a state rival to that of his father. Later, he conquered his father's kingdom and killed his father, not knowing it was his father. Becoming king on his father's throne, he married the queen mother, his own mother, and, had four children by her. Eventually the truth became known. His mother-wife killed herself and Oedipus tore out his own eyes in guilt.

Freud used this Greek myth to symbolize what he thought was the love attachment between mother and son, an attachment which the child, when he reaches the age of social insight, has to fight and destroy within himself.

The *Electra complex,* based on another Greek myth—the story of Electra's love for her father—involves the same mechanism of love and guilt in the relationship between daughter and father.

Freud carried these concepts over into the theory of "parent image" in heterosexual love. The male and female child, he held, are attracted to the person who represents the parent of the opposite sex—the boy to the image of his mother, the girl to the image of her father.

To begin with, both sexes love the mother because she satisfies their needs. They resent the father because he is regarded as a rival for the mother's affections. The development of the male Oedipus complex begins with the boy's incestuous craving for the mother and his growing resentment toward the father which brings him into conflict with his parents, especially the father. He imagines that his dominant rival is going to harm him, and his fears may actually be confirmed by threats from a resentful and punitive father. He is afraid that his jealous father will remove his genital organs because they are the source of his lustful feelings. Fear of castration or, as Freud called it, *castration anxiety,* induces a repression of the sexual desire for the mother and hostility toward the father. Castration anxiety also helps to bring about an identification of the boy with his father. By identifying with the father, the boy also gains some vicarious satisfaction for his sexual impulses toward the mother. At the same time, his dangerous erotic feeling for the mother is converted into harmless tender affection for her. Whether considering Freudian or other approaches to sex-identification problems, it is important to remember that psychosexual development takes place below the level of conscious thought. One does not recall these feelings because they are always repressed into the subconscious.

The sequence of events in the development and dissolution of the female Oedipus complex (the Electra complex) is more involved. According to Freud, when the girl discovers that a boy possesses a protruding sex organ and she has only a cavity, she can have varying reactions of disappointment. It is a traumatic discovery for her and has several important consequences. She holds her mother responsible for her castrated condition and transfers her love to the father because he has the valued organ which she aspires to share with him. However, her love for the father, and for other men as well, is mixed with a feeling of envy because they possess something she lacks. Penis envy is the female counterpart of castration anxiety, and collectively they are called the *castration complex*. She imagines that she has lost something valuable, whereas the boy is afraid he is going to lose it.

Unlike the boy's Oedipus complex, which is repressed or otherwise changed by castration anxiety, the girl's Oedipus complex tends to persist although it undergoes some modification due to the realistic barriers that prevent her from gratifying her sexual desire for the father. But it does not fall under the strong repression that the boy's does. These differences in the nature of the Oedipus and castration complexes are the basis for many psychological differences between the sexes.

These Freudian conceptions of the complexities of sex identification may or may not have a basis in reality, but to read intelligently one must understand them, for these conceptions are a part of the heritage of psychoanalytic theory.

Social Pressures in Sex Identification

The social pressures to insure proper sex identification actually begin prenatally. First of all, males and females are labeled with different names. These names are usually tentatively selected before the birth of the child. Second, a layette is planned with a difference of color for boy and girl. Thus, the social stamp of approval is put on sex identification from the very outset.

In infancy and early childhood, the attitudes that a boy has toward his father and mother are very much the same as those felt by a girl. The very small child has little, if any, conception of his own sexual characteristics and has had few opportunities to learn from those around him how he does or should differ from the opposite sex.

As he grows, however, he begins to think of himself as a member of a particular sex. This association begins as he observes the opposite sex and becomes aware of his own dissimilarities and physical characteristics. As was pointed out earlier, it is important that this identification of physical sex differences come early, and that questions be answered fully and naturally. The child's curiosity must be satisfied about not only what the differences are, both inside and outside the body, but why they are important.

This simple set of facts may seem far from an important issue in the development of the child's capacity to love, yet the answers, and even more the atmosphere in which they are given, are of very great importance. Sex attitudes will throughout his lifetime play a vital part in his love relationships. To give him the factual background for understanding will make for normal and natural development of sex values and attitudes.

If the child of two or three does not begin definitely to move toward identification with his own sex, parents make deliberate attempts to push him in that direction. The boy who has a primary interest in dolls, dressing-up, and other feminine interests is cautiously pushed toward cowboy gunplay and other masculine pastimes. To encourage him, the parents buy a special costume or toys for masculine activities.

Similarly, the girl who is too absorbed in masculine types of play is steered toward feminine interests, encouraged to imitate her mother, provided with dolls and equipment for baby care so that she can practice the accustomed roles of motherhood.

Usually, by the age of four, often even earlier, the affection a child feels toward members of both sexes is strongly colored by his own identification with one sex. A boy feels tender love and dependence upon his mother, but if he has lived around a domineering and demanding father, he may also treat his mother with what he considers proper male condescension. He feels a strong attachment to members of his own sex but is careful to display his feelings only in a very masculine manner. From about eight to twelve or fourteen years of age he thinks of girls as sissyish and in his attempt to be the complete man, scorns not only the activities and ways of women, but women themselves. He teases and fights his sister and her friends.

This period of rebellion against the opposite sex makes identification with his own sex more complete. It does not, however, kill interest in the opposite sex. The very fact that the sexes wish to fight and tease each other indicates that the interest is still there, even though at this period, negatively defined.

Girls similarly have their periods of having no interest in boys, detesting them, looking down on them, considering them uncouth and unfit for companionship. This stage of intense identification with one's own sex seems to be a part of normal psychological growth.

The occasional instances of love affairs among preadolescents has little to do with any real affection toward age mates of the opposite sex. The eight- or ten-year-old girl (or boy) who admits to being in love with some pal generally does so in order to further imitate grown-up behavior. Any strong attachment felt by a child of this age toward members of the opposite sex is more likely to be directed toward an adult—a girl may fall in love with a movie star the age of her father, a teacher, or her own father. The general rule is, however, that until late childhood or early adolescence, the strongest attraction is to members of one's own sex.

The Adolescent's Preoccupation with His Body

The growing boy takes increasing interest in the penis and the satisfaction which results from its manipulation. In spite of certain prohibitions, fears, and a sense of guilt that may center around it, the penis becomes a source of great sensous enjoyment and a symbol of manhood.

This development is so important in the life of the male that Freud saw masturbation guilt being converted in the mind of the adolescent boy to a *castration fear*. This castration fear, Freud felt, reflects the high evaluation the boy is beginning to place upon his genital organs. This Freud defined as the *phallic phase* in the boy's sexual development.

Much of the adolescent male's preoccupation with role identification at this period has to do with physical prowess in all areas: capacity for sexual expression (usually through masturbation), testing muscles in games of skill, flexing muscles and comparing them with pals, testing himself in feats of daring, torture, or endurance. He has come to see maleness as physical toughness and endurance.

Harlow's studies with monkeys showed that the young male more often initiates rough-and-tumble play and more often engages in copulatory play, indicating that these inclinations in the human male may have a strong natural base.[2]

The female becomes extremely preoccupied with her body and its care during the period of adolescence, since with the maturing of sexual functions her body becomes her stock in trade in mate seeking and in realizing the deepest interest of human life, that of childbearing. This interest in the body is not, except in exaggerated cases, narcissistic in character; it is a normal interest which accompanies social awakening and a budding interest in the opposite sex.

The technique of attraction is, of course, greatly stimulated by those cultural values which encourage attractiveness and display and by the informal training in the art of being alluring. Cosmetics culture is largely female: scents, style, powders and paints are much more her speciality than a male's speciality. Here again Harlow finds a parallel in the behavior of monkeys, where the play of the young females involves a great deal of mutual grooming. Even throughout her adult life, the next most time-consuming activity of the female monkey after motherhood is mutually relaxed grooming.[3]

---

[2] Harry Harlow, "The Nature of Love," *American Psychologist*, 13:673-685, 1958.
[3] Phyllis C. Jay, "The Female Primate," in Seymour M. Farber and Roger H. L. Wilson (Editors), *The Potential of Woman* (New York: McGraw-Hill Book Co., 1963), pp. 3-12.

That culture plays a profound part in developing feminine techniques, for example, is definitely shown in regional comparisons within the United States. Historically, the Southern girl was trained well in the art of flirting. In the Far West, where women were scarce and men competed for them, the development of these characteristics was at a minimum. In fact, women could be independent and unconcerned and still succeed in attracting a man. The culture of the West, therefore, neglected the development of the mate-attracting traits in the female.

It is during adolescence that direction in sex-role identification becomes most pronounced. With the coming of puberty, the society insists on greater separateness, greater role identification with one's own sex. Most societies have provided rites of passage designed to impress deeply upon the young adolescent his maleness or femaleness. The male in primitive societies may be put through torturous initiation ceremonies to test his capacity for suffering. When he has demonstrated by suffering that he is worthy to be a man, he is accepted as such. Girls in these cultures are often isolated for the initiation rites of puberty. They may be taught about sex, marriage, and the roles of womanhood. This period may involve sex initiation and modifications in hair or dress, even body mutilations. For example, among the Kikuyu of East Africa, there is circumcision for the male and clitoridotomy (the cutting off of the clitoris) for the female. In some tribes sex initiation may involve the splitting of a labia for the girl. It may also involve, for both male and female, extensive scarification of the body, modification of hair style, and other such ritualistic procedures.

In modern society less attention is given to initiation rites. In certain social circles, coming-out parties are in order; in the school program, there is often a break between junior high and senior high school at this period, but sex identification by elaborate ceremony scarcely exists.

There are, however, at this stage some marked psychological transitions symbolic of sex identification of the period. Some psychologists feel that all adolescents at this time become homosexual in their attachments, with many homosexual activities actually being engaged in.[4] On the emotional level one observes many evidences of such behavior; the close pal relation of boys with boys and girls with girls, the small intensely loyal clique groups and other such phenomena are near universal. The constant association between these pals, their lengthy conversations on the telephone when absent from each other, their frequent desire to spend nights together are indicative of the deeply emotional loyalties which are characteristic of this period.

With girls custom permits a considerable amount of physical expression without casting suspicion of homosexuality; putting arms around

[4] Ralph Eckert, *Sex Attitudes in the Home* (New York: Association Press, 1957).

each other and hugging and kissing each other are common behavior. For boys, such overt expressions are less common, but there is the close intimate palship and sometimes mutual masturbation and other sex activities.

The psychology of this transition seems to be that of the young person, becoming emancipated from the emotional ties of childhood, tends to cast his parents aside, except at times when he feels abandoned by friends. He desperately seeks a love orientation outside the immediate family. The transition toward attachment to members of the opposite sex seems to be too great for the average adolescent, so he transfers intense, extra-familial loyalty to his own sex and only gradually does he emerge from this period into true heterosexual relationships. Some never get beyond the homosexual stage. Their love life becomes fixated there. Those who move into heterosexual love eventually move into marriage and complete the full cycle of sex identification by taking on the roles of father and mother.

Formal Training for the Male Role

As long ago as the turn of the century a majority of men, particularly in urban occupations, spent most of their waking hours away from home. Twelve- and fourteen-hour working days were not uncommon. Men had little if any time to spend in recreation or with their wives and children. As a result parenthood required of men little preparation.

Today a seven- or eight-hour working day and a five-day work-week are standard practice. The future holds promise of even more free time. But what is being done to prepare young men in the use of this leisure? They find themselves in the midst of a wife's domain for long weekends, or sharing busy evening hours. Many feel awkward and out of place; some feel guilty about not helping but embarrassed at the very thought of domestic tasks. All too many are bored and completely unprepared to enjoy this new opportunity for sharing in family life.

E. E. LeMasters has shown that for most young fathers, fatherhood is a crisis of real significance, partly because of the male having no conception of what it involves.[5] Other studies have indicated that marriage is more disillusioning for the male than the female, because the male is untrained in the responsibilities he is undertaking. Child expert, Dr. Benjamin Spock, has commented on the lack of training of the young

[5] E. E. LeMasters, "Parenthood as a Crisis," *Marriage and Family Living*, 19:352-355, 1957.

male for the parenthood role and the need of such training.[6] In fact, the male's preparation for adult sex roles in the romantic, companionship type of family arrangement we have come to accept is at many points inadequate.

Here the school and home can do much to remedy the situation by providing boys with early and enjoyable contacts with the domestic side of life. Instead of being kidded or shamed for showing an enthusiasm in domestic tasks and interests, the boy should be encouraged. The adolescent boy's interests should not all be channeled into vocational preparation; some should be channeled toward home, family, and parenthood.

The task involved in preparing boys for home life today has negative as well as positive aspects. It necessitates the unlearning of many traditional concepts of "how a man should be." Boys should be helped to give up adolescent gang concepts which teach the superiority of the male and require a show of indifference or hostility to pursuits generally followed by girls.

Boys need to be helped to accept the new status of women. Those who have grown up in homes patterned along patriarchal lines are ill-prepared for life with a self-respecting, assertive, and fully self-confident woman. The values of the new type of marital relationship are not beyond the scope of classroom discussion, and neither is it fair to assume that boys are "naturally" not interested in such matters. Where boys are allowed to indicate subjects in which they are interested without the threat of shame from their contemporaries, marriage and other interpersonal relationships rank high on their lists.[7]

Young men should demand of themselves not only toleration but a full appreciation of the ambitious and well-trained college woman. College men particularly must learn to accept women as equals. They must learn to expect as much of their wives in the way of accomplishment as of themselves—not only expect it but, what is more important, accept it. This is a very hard thing for most men to do.

The late Richard Neuberger, United States Senator from Oregon, was formerly a member of the state legislature. His wife was elected to the same legislative body. In a magazine article he told of the time when he first accepted her as an equal and came to respect her as a person of real competence, rather than as "just" a wife, a companion, and the

[6] In an *Associated Press Release*, New York, October 15, 1958. This research has been further verified by Everett D. Dyer, "Parenthood as Crisis: A Re-study," *Marriage and Family Living*, 25:196-201, May, 1963.

[7] A group of teenage boys, when asked what interests they would most like to consider in discussion groups, listed dating, courtship, and marriage above other interests like hobbies, current events, etc.

mother of his children. An important bill was before the house and Mrs. Neuberger was to speak on it. He confessed taking her aside and coaching her carefully in what to say. She was new in the legislature; he, in the typical masculine manner, knew all the ropes, or so he thought. His wife thanked him generously, but having a mind of her own and ideas of her own, she went ahead and prepared her own talk. It proved to be more effective than the attack he had planned and he had to admit this, even to himself. Mr. Neuberger no longer regarded his wife with condescending tolerance but respected her as an equal.

College men should stop deceiving themselves and recognize that women are their intellectual equals. In fact, because a more select group of women than men go to college, college women generally average a little higher scholastically than do the men. The man who can accept this fact will marry a wife who will be a true partner.

One of the traditional aspects of male role preparation has been the conditioning of the male sex in the direction of sex exploration. Many fathers in the older generation encouraged their boys to visit a prostitute as a proper initiation to sex life. Even now some boys visit prostitutes in their early teens as a way of proving their manhood. Often they do so on dares, usually in groups, none of the boys really having intended to go. Sometimes older boys take younger boys.

From his study of a small number of cases, Kirkendall believes that it is a male group experience through which the boys are trying to achieve a group purpose.[8] It results often from trying to prove that they are grown-up, daredevil, and worldly-wise. Curiosity about how a prostitute operates is also a factor in their going. For the most part, the sex experience is unsatisfactory. Often they are unable to carry out the sex act because of fear.

In an earlier day, when the male sexual role was one of conquest and dominance, when the wife was supposed to be passive, this kind of training may have had some place. Today, in the setting of the romantic marriage bond, where mutuality is the goal of marriage adjustment, such training is inappropriate.

Even though the criticism directed at the training of the American male for adult family roles is well merited, it is only fair to state that his role preparation for family life is much more adequate than that of the male in many other cultures. For example, it is doubtful that the British male ever feels really at home in the family in the sense that the American male does. His training is for administrative duty. His discipline in the boys' school, often away from home, is under the stern master. It is

8 Lester A. Kirkendall, "Why Teen-age Boys Visit Prostitutes." A paper before the 1959 meeting of the Pacific Northwest Conference on Family Relations, Seattle, Washington.

designed to make him immune to many of the personal sentiments, interests, and pleasures of our culture. As an adult, he feels more at home in the office, the club, the army, and the pub than in the domestic scene.

Formal Training for the Female Role

When the domestic role was the culturally predestined one, the forming of personality in women was clear-cut. A woman knew her place and her roles and was trained for them. Only the rebellious and unconventional felt thwarted because the defined roles were so completely institutionalized. Here is a comment, made a century and a half ago, on the direction the education of women should take.

> The profession of ladies, to which the bent of their instruction should be turned, is that of daughters, wives, mothers, and mistresses of families. They should be therefore trained with a view to these several conditions, and be furnished with a stock of ideas, and principles, and qualifications and habits, ready to be applied and appropriated as occasion arises. . . . An early habitual restraint is peculiarly important to the future character and happiness of women. They should, when very young, be inured to contradictions. . . . They should be led to distrust their own judgment; they should learn not to murmur at expostulation; but should be accustomed to expect and endure opposition. It is a lesson with which the world will not fail to furnish them. . . . It is of the last importance to their happiness in life that they should early acquire a submissive temper and a forbearing spirit.[9]

One cannot deny that the role of the woman who chooses to marry and devote herself, for a period of twenty years or more, to housekeeping and child rearing is vastly different from the roles of the woman who will spend all her active years in a career role similar to that of the male. The difference involves attitudes and values as well as roles.

Since the day feminism came to full flower, women have been trained for a dual role, or rather increasingly for a role in the competitive educational and work world, with the traditional family role kept in the background.

After her years of competition with men in school and at work, many an intelligent and ambitious woman has found the role of wife and mother most frustrating. Many of the most competent and competitive women have found themselves ill-prepared psychologically and emotionally for the maternal role, and even awkward in its routine demands.

The conflict of her two roles is one of the most serious dilemmas in the life of modern woman and of modern education. The problem has

[9] Hannah More, *Strictures on the Modern System of Female Education* (Boston: J. Loring, 1883), Vol. I, pp. 61, 81-82.

become the concern of educators, some of whom cry for a return to family-oriented education for women, but there is no going back. Women today must be adequately prepared psychologically as well as technologically to play both parts in life.[10] Industrial society is here to stay. Women must come to share much of the same freedom of choice men have in marriage. They must be able to go on satisfying their productive and creative urges without seriously interfering with their roles as wives and mothers.

Parents and educators alike need to reexamine many of their practices in the formal and informal education of girls in our society. One of the results of such an examination would be the discovery that much of a girl's education is not, after all, as well rounded as many think, nor as well rounded as her future life demands.

In the schools, for example, vocational specialization is highly emphasized. Even at the high school level a girl may concentrate almost all of her time on commercial subjects or on home economics. Problems result because in adult life she must attempt to play several roles, not just the one for which she has been prepared by this narrowly-focused curriculum. The young woman who comes out of the public school system an expert stenographer may discover, upon marrying, that she not only has few of the skills which home economics would have given her, but also that she holds few of the values desirable in a homemaker.

Studies have indicated that in the diversified curriculum of the modern high school there is a great difference in the prestige attached to the different programs of study.[11] Girls who qualify for the "college preparatory courses" look down upon those who are in the "commercial program" or the "home economics program." They soon begin to feel that only by concentrating in the academic subjects can they "rate high" with their classmates and teachers.

These values undoubtedly carry over into adult life. The girl who looked down upon the study of homemaking as a student is likely to look down upon the job of homemaking as a wife. Her years of study and training in an academic or professional field and the values she absorbed in the process make it difficult for her to give up her professional life for marriage, or if she does so, difficult for her to subordinate her career values to those of homemaking. Meal planning, household management, child care, which would have been challenging and absorbing jobs had

---

[10] For a good statement of the dilemma and possible solution, see Lynn White, Jr., *Educating Our Daughters* (New York: Harper & Bros., 1950); see also Terry Ferrer, "Rosemary Park: New President of Barnard," *Saturday Review*, April 20, 1963, pp. 66-68.

[11] These value differences are stressed in various of the "social class" studies; also in August B. Hollingshead, *Elmtown's Youth* (New York: John Wiley & Sons, Inc., 1949).

she learned to value them, become instead the dull routine of married life. Bitterness, marital frustration, boredom, and discord are the common symptoms of disappointment.

This situation is very common and yet it could be largely eliminated by the recognition upon the part of educators that although most of their graduating girls will have vocational aspiration an even larger percentage will be required to attend to the business of homemaking. There is need not only for greater emphasis upon the arts and skills of home management and child care but also for a more convincing presentation of the values and satisfactions of these tasks. Women need to learn again that there is dignity and social value in making a house a healthy, happy place to live. They need to be reminded that raising well-adjusted children is a more difficult and socially valuable task than efficiently operating an office or industrial machine.

This does not mean that all girls must be put into the home economics curriculum. It does mean, however, that along with vocational or academic courses, every girl should receive some effective preparation for the parts she will probably play as a wife and mother.

Parents too can do more in preparing girls to accept their dual-role existence in adulthood. Much of the intimate, firsthand knowledge of home life can be taught by mothers and fathers more effectively than by the school. Through a system of sharing the responsibilities of homemaking with their sons and daughters, parents can give them an invaluable apprenticeship in the jobs they will one day assume. In so doing they can also prepare them psychologically for the acceptance of these responsibilities.

In far too many homes young people are either coerced into doing a certain number of "horrible chores" around the house each day or else they are excused completely on the grounds that they would only be underfoot. What is needed is the development of a feeling of family loyalty and responsibility which makes "cooperation" rather than "obligation" the theme of housework. This means that young people get credit as well as duties. It means they must be allowed to share in the planning as well as in the work. It means that they get their share of the enjoyable tasks—buying household items, driving the family into town, planning furniture arrangements, cooking a special meal—as well as routine jobs such as dishwashing, dusting, lawn mowing.

The attitudes that a young woman has toward her role as mother and housewife generally reflect rather accurately the attitudes of her own parents and the degree to which she was accepted as a full member and working partner in her childhood home.

LeMasters' study showed that young mothers had no conception of what they were getting into with their first child.[12] For them, parenthood constituted a real crisis and demanded many attitude changes that women trained to anticipate the role of motherhood would have found less drastic. Such a situation is uncalled for in a culture which takes up so much of a young person's time in training him, presumably, to meet life's situations.

Mature Sex Roles

For those in whom the process of identification with their own sex-group roles has been adequate, moving into adult roles is relatively easy. These roles are motherhood for the woman and fatherhood for the man.

Motherhood, Margaret Mead[13] found, requires very little encouragement from civilization. Fatherhood, on the other hand, is a social invention and requires a lot of cultural conditioning. It consists, essentially, in the tie between male and female based on the economic arrangement of the male providing for the female and her young. Among primates, to some extent, the male shares in the protection of the young, but only among human beings does the male share food with the female and her young as a consistent practice. This is a practice found in all cultures. Although the female may do much of the actual raising of the food, men do the things that are considered to be most essential to the economic survival of the group.

Since the dawn of history this practice has marked the relationship between man and woman. Margaret Mead[14] believes that the marriage system predates the knowledge that there is a relationship between the man's part in the sex act and offspring. The marriage system may be closely related to the willingness of the female to grant sex favors in return for food and protection. "In every known human society," she finds, men learn as they grow up that to be a full member of society they must "provide food for some female and her young."[15] However, this does not necessarily mean that a man cares for a wife—he may have to care for his sister instead.

She points out that in all societies there are some tramps, ne'er-do-wells, and recluses who refuse to accept the burden of fatherhood. There are also culturally accepted ways in which a man may avoid the social

12 E. E. LeMasters, "Parenthood as a Crisis," *Marriage and Family Living*, 19:352-355, 1957.

13 Margaret Mead, *Male and Female* (New York: William Morrow & Co., Inc., 1949).

14 *Ibid.*

15 *Ibid.*

obligation. He may join the priesthood, or monastic orders, or the Buddhist priesthood in Burma, or join the army or navy. For women, on the other hand, motherhood is so natural that only complicated social arrangements can break it down entirely.[16]

Margaret Mead also points out that under certain conditions human society may raise the status of the single woman so high that women will strangle their children with their own hands. She also points out that illegitimacy may be such a shame in the culture that women resort to abortion or give their children away secretly. But these are the rare exceptions to the general rule of a mother nurturing and protecting her child.

In conclusion, sex itself is physical, but becoming a male or female in behavior and aspirations is a complicated social process. It moves so smoothly in the average case that little attention is given to formal training, yet failure of the individual to learn the role behavior of his own sex is failure indeed.

Problems

1. Are you aware of any of the training that entered into your conception of your sex role?
2. What do you think of Freud's views in the area of sex identification?
3. Do you willingly and naturally accept most of the roles assigned your sex in our culture?
4. Contrast male and female adolescent interests.
5. Do you agree that the key male role in our society is that of provider for women and children?
6. Contrast two cultures in their shaping of males or females: British, German, American, Latin, or take cases from Margaret Mead, *Male and Female.*
7. Compare developmental play of male and female monkeys.

Selected References

ARTICLES IN BOOKS OF READINGS

Winch, Robert F., and others, *Selected Studies in Marriage and the Family,* Revised Edition (New York: Holt, Rinehart & Winston, Inc., 1962).

16 *Ibid.*

1. BRIM, Orville G., Jr., "Family Structure and Sex Role Learning by Children: A Further Analysis of Helen Koch's Data," pp. 275-290.
2. BARRY, Herbert, III, and others, "A Cross-Cultural Survey of Some Sex Differences in Socialization," pp. 267-274.

COSER, Rose Laub, *The Family: Its Structure and Functions* (New York: St Martin's Press, 1964).
3. SLATER, Philip E., "Parental Role Differentiation," pp. 350-369.

General References

ECKERT, Ralph, *Sex Attitudes in the Home* (New York: Association Press, 1957).

HARLOW, Harry, "The Nature of Love," *American Psychologist,* 13:673-685, 1958.

JAY, Phyllis C., "The Female Primate," in Seymour M. FARBER and Roger H. L. WILSON (Editors), *The Potential of Woman* (New York: McGraw-Hill Book Co., 1963), pp. 3-12.

SCOTT, J. P., "Critical Periods in Behavioral Development," *Science,* 138:949-958, November 30, 1962.

ZUK, G. H., "Sex—Appropriate Behavior in Adolescence," *Journal of Genetic Psychology,* 93:15-32, September, 1958.

6
Female Roles in Transition

The most profound change in woman's life in our day and place is that the culture requires a radical shift in roles throughout her lifetime. She is not born to fill a place, but to adjust her life periodically to new roles.

In school she is the equal of the male, competing with him in the classroom and sharing with him in extracurricular activities. She moves into the work world as a temporary worker to remain there until children come. For most, motherhood brings a radical change. She retires temporarily from the work role to become submerged in the lives of husband and small children. The old, ego-satisfying roles are lost, competitive achievements are abandoned.

But motherhood is also a temporary period. Childbearing is confined to a span of a half dozen years. Perhaps soon, perhaps not for 15 to 20 years, she moves back into the work world where she will stay until retirement age forces her back to the home. She is "only a wife" again. This state is terminated in widowhood in the later years.

The problem of woman's roles in this day in history is that they are not and cannot be structured by tradition, and yet no culture can shed the persistent past, which so often affects the emotions of the person, even if not his overt behavior.

Roles in Historical Perspective

Throughout much of history, female infants have been unwanted. This is so today in much of the world. The male child, it has been assumed, brings advantages to his family; the female, disadvantages. Female infanticide as a way of reducing girls in the family has been common. For a wife to bear sons is to be honorable in the eyes of the husband and his relatives and to rise in status in the community. Having daughters only, in some societies, is sufficient grounds for divorce. Thus the wife's honor has often been equated with her ability to produce sons.

Even American culture is not completely free from the traditional preference for a male child. A study of 380 university students revealed a strong preference for the male child, both among the male and female students.[1] Asked if they would prefer a boy or girl if they had only one child, 92 percent of the male students and 66 percent of the female students, making a total of more than three-fourths of both sexes, would prefer a boy. The results were not quite so extreme in expressing a preference that the first child be a male, yet almost 62 percent of the men and 59 percent of the women expressed preference for a boy. Only 4 percent of the males and 6 percent of the females preferred a girl first. The rest of the group expressed no preference. The Jewish students showed a greater preference for a male child as the first child than other religious groups. Almost as great a number of Catholics indicated a preference for a male child. Fewer Protestant students stressed a desire for a male child as the first child.

The authors of the study raise the question of whether there is as much equalitarian philosophy in American life as we usually hold, when even the college population shows little evidence of accepting the girl on the same basis as the boy. The authors also speculate as to whether or not we can expect couples to treat the male and female children equally under such a value system. They also raise the question of what might happen when it becomes possible to control the sex of the child.

The subservience of the female to the male, the denial to her of common rights and privileges, her lack of place in the esteem of both men and women, and even of children, has been and is so commonplace that only violent social revolution can revise her status in any particular social order. In many cultures it is still appropriate for her to be the hod carrier, the water carrier, and the tiller of the field, in addition to her domestic tasks and her function as mother.

Much stress is placed on the freedom gained by American women, yet evidence of deep prejudices survives. For example, a recent Gallup poll compared prejudice against women in the political area with religious discriminations.

Would you vote for a qualified:	Yes (percent)
Catholic	84
Jew	77
Woman	55
(of men 58)	
(of women 51)	

[1] Simon Dinitz, Russell R. Dynez, and Alfred C. Clarke, "Preferences for Male or Female Children: Traditional or Affectional?" *Marriage and Family Living*, 16:128-130, May, 1954.

Foley observed that women hold very few key places in either elective or appointive offices in government. This is only partly because of a lack of interest.[2]

American Woman—The Symbol of Freedom

Even with these limitations, the American woman has become the symbol of the new woman of our day throughout the world, thanks to the wide advertising of her freedom, her attractiveness, and her daring as displayed by Hollywood. Most Scandinavian women have more sex equality than women of the United States, but it is less well advertised and in certain respects perhaps less accepted by the male there than are women's rights and prerogatives in the United States.[3]

The gospel of Hollywood and the world travel of American women are certainly factors in the world-wide revolution in women's roles and statuses of our day. In all but the most isolated regions of the globe, their struggle for liberations is not only challenging old social structures, but is also bringing modifications in marriage patterns, child rearing, political systems, work roles, and standards of living.[4] Take for example Africa, the last great continent to feel the immense impact of urban industrial civilization and its attendant patterns. In East Africa women have always been chattles by Western standards. They are sold by their fathers to prospective husbands for the standard medium of exchange, cattle or goats. Thousands of one-time bush families are now residents of great modern cities where they have cash incomes. The men now buy their wives with cash, sometimes on the installment plan. If they are delinquent in their payments, the father repossesses the daughter for resale. As the woman moves into the urban labor market she wonders why she should any longer be sold and bought by father and husband. She can earn her living and be independent of both. If she loses her job, sex can be sold in the marketplace, with more choice involved than in the customary marriage.[5]

In the Moslem world, where purdah and the harem have secluded women and protected men from the competition of women, the shackles of centuries are being broken—violently in some places, gradually in

2 Paul Foley, "Whatever Happened to Women's Rights," *Atlantic*, 243:63-65, March, 1964.

3 *Social Sweden* (Stockholm: Social Welfare Board, 1953). Bruce Gould, Editor of the *Ladies Home Journal*, is reported to have concluded after a visit to England, "In England I would rather be a man, a horse, or a dog, or a woman, in that order. In America I think the order would be reversed."

4 United Nations, *Report on the World Social Situation, Part II* (New York: United Nations, 1957).

5 *Ibid.*

others, but there is everywhere in Moslem culture the beginning of the revolution in sex statuses.[6] The tent of purdah goes, then the confining harem (walled-in home in which wife and older daughters stay isolated from men outside the immediate family), and soon the courageous and privileged few are on the public platform and in the halls of state. So too in India, where motherhood has been part of the symbol of woman's inequality, and where her status has been won by bearing sons, the shackles are falling off. Some of the most modern-minded Indian delegates to the United Nations and some of the most progressive members of the Indian Parliament are women. They are among the most aggressive leaders in challenging women's age-old subservience to the automatic operation of the laws of human fertility. Planned parenthood is state policy in India, as it is not in the United States or European countries.

Even in the conservative Latin American culture of Puerto Rico, Hill reports change in mate-seeking practices which would indicate a change in sex roles.[7] The American ideal of free mate choice is being accepted increasingly by the new generation, but parents, who have been accustomed to the institutional system of choosing mates for children, still hold the veto power over the young people's choice.

The sweeping changes in sex roles and the consequent changes in the relationships of men and women around the world constitute one of the great revolutions of our day. American women, being directly and indirectly responsible for this in considerable part, have achieved a level of equality which, though inadequate still, seems liberal indeed compared to that found in much of the world. What has been the price? Will others have to pay it?[8] What has she yet to realize? Where have her attainments put her in her relationships with men? with children? in her own conception of herself?

The Culture-Concept Approach

The relationships of men and women are culturally defined. Since the development of the "culture concept" in sociology and its use in interpreting human behavior over the past forty years, it has become

[6] Dorothy Fahs Beck, "The Changing Moslem Family in the Middle East," *Marriage and Family Living*, 19:340-347, 1957.

[7] Reuben Hill, "Courtship in Puerto Rico: An Institution in Transition," *Marriage and Family Living*, 17:26-35, February, 1955.

[8] This problem cannot be handled adequately here. For a more adequate treatment see Paul H. Landis, *Social Problems: Unfulfilled Welfare Aspirations in Nation and World* (Philadelphia: J. B. Lippincott Co., 1959), Ch. 15. Other aspects of the problem of sex roles have also been covered in Paul H. Landis, *Social Control*, Revised Edition (Philadelphia: J. B. Lippincott Co., 1956), Ch. 9, and Paul H. Landis, *Introductory Sociology* (New York: The Ronald Press Co., 1958), Ch. 17.

increasingly apparent that a culture can create almost anything in the way of social relationships. The customary behavior of men and women of one culture may be contradicted by their customary behavior in another. Manners and morals are relative to the cultural history of the group. Informed people no longer assume that behavior of men and women is dictated by "nature" as it was once thought to be. Culture is the final umpire of appropriate behavior.

The Social Structure—Role-Status Orientation

Another sociological concept of great importance in understanding the relationships of men and women is "social structure." Briefly, the social structure is the framework of statuses characterizing any given social system. Social structures, like manners and morals, differ greatly from one group to another. Roles that bring high status in one social structure may bring a much different rating in another.

In all social structures certain social statuses are ascribed to large groups. The status of the female in the broadest sense is in this category, as are several of her more specific statuses, such as, for example, the single girl, the virgin, the young married woman, the mother, the grandmother. These are all statuses which are usually ascribed by custom within any given social structure.

Likewise, the male has certain statuses which are more or less universal within his group and are ascribed to all men, regardless of their particular achievements: the baby, the boy, the teenager, the young male, the father, the grandfather.

In highly advanced societies, social structures become extremely intricate. In open-class societies, like our own, so many statuses are achieved rather than ascribed by custom, as in caste social structures, that the complexities of social status are almost beyond the comprehension of an outsider. In a society with many achieved statuses, the complex variety of roles performed by each sex, the overlapping roles of male and female, and other such problems are always present. It is with the complexity of these achieved roles that we are particularly concerned as we try to analyze the relationship of men and women in contemporary American culture.

Customary Roles vs. Expected Roles of Women

Customary roles are learned largely from the family. It is through the attitudes, expectations, and habits formed in the family that a young person gets his basic training in role attitudes and role expectations, both for his own sex and for the opposite sex. In our time these customary roles are often in direct contradiction to the expected roles of the peer group.

The peer group is for the most part oriented toward new attitudes and new expectations for both sexes. The high school and university experience of today's youth has probably been the main influence in the creation of new role expectations in America. The interaction of boys and girls in school situations, where they function for the most part as equals, has tended, in the course of three generations, to break down much of the customary role expectations of the past. From this teen-group culture has emerged a new concept of equality such as feminists of an earlier day could never have conceived. More and more young men and women are participating in similar kinds of recreation, intellectual endeavors, and even in similar vices. Here, in playing up to the role expectations of their peers, they tend to part company with the role expectations of the family group.

It is at this point that much of the conflict between the generations has come.[9] Parents of the succeeding generations have seen their daughters moving into types of role behavior foreign to their concept of the role of the lady and the woman. They have registered shock as the daughter has taken on new role behavior considered appropriate for her in the urban industrial community. To many parents her informality of dress, her companionship with the male, her ignoring of the impediments of female biology have been symbols not merely of an emancipated generation, but of a wayward generation.

Role Conflicts—The Female Dilemma

In the life of each sensitive woman today, there is likely to be a great deal of confusion in her concept of her role due to her exposure to conflicting value systems. Part of her concept of what her role ought to be is parent indoctrinated and, therefore, internalized. Since her peer-group concept of what her role should be is often so contradictory, she feels guilt in responding to peer-group pressures. Yet, in the early adolescent years, the pressure of the peer group has supreme meaning to her. If she cannot measure up with her peer group, she has lost her closest and most vital tie, the one which binds her to her generation. Therefore, she is likely to play roles consistent with peer group expectations. This, in turn, often brings her into open conflict with her parents, and she is forced to rationalize her concept of how a girl "ought to behave" and how she must behave to get along in her group.

[9] The U. S. passed the crisis in this area prior to World War II. Japan is the best example of this revolution since World War II.

Her role concept is extended as she becomes acquainted with male friends and dates and later moves into betrothal and marriage. Often she finds that her husband's concept of the female role fails to coincide with any of her previous concepts; neither that of her parents, her peers, or that which she has personally evolved through conflict and compromise. She often finds herself resisting role concepts that her husband gathered in his own family from observing his own mother or sisters, or from roles that he has observed from association with other young women during the dating period. Since any woman, to have a successful marriage, must try to reproduce in her personality some semblance of her husband's image of what a woman should be, she must yet again try to recast her values, her philosophy, and her behavior to fit new role concepts.

Many men cannot seem to reconcile the traditional roles of women —those of mother and housekeeper—with the very diversified roles which wives claim for themselves.

Children often cannot reconcile the various activities of their mother with the concept of motherhood they see represented in the homes of some of their own playmates. Although most married women work at some time during their marriage, and the work role seems to be a well-established practice, a study[10] of eighth- and twelfth-grade children showed that boys were more often opposed to their future wives working than the girls were opposed to working.

If those close to a wife and mother do not see eye to eye with her regarding her own role expectations, she will probably internalize their standards to some extent. As a consequence, she may feel considerable guilt and anxiety and build within herself the feeling that she is neglecting her children, her husband, or her household duties. Yet, at the same time she must, to satisfy herself, continue to play her roles in the larger world, for she knows from previous experience that if she drops these roles she is less than the person she must be to retain her self-respect and to feel herself productive, useful, and significant.

It may well be that the mother-in-law will have a part in the wife's role conflict. This influence may come in the form of direct criticism from the mother-in-law or through her husband who wants her to be like his mother. Many a wife is forced, in facing the realities of marriage adjustment, to modify her behavior for no better reason than that it must fit her husband's concept, or his mother's concept, of what her role as a wife should be.

Finally, in the broader circles of the community, she must face new roles defined in the particular segment of the community where she is active. In industry, appropriate role conceptions are demanded. They

---

[10] Raymond Payne, "Adolescent's Attitudes toward the Working Wife," *Marriage and Family Living*, 18:345-348, November, 1956.

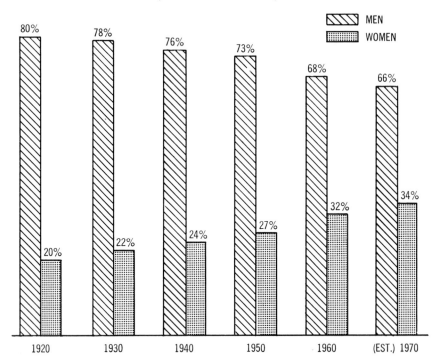

EVERY THIRD WORKER IS A WOMAN
(PERCENT OF ALL WORKERS)

SOURCE: U. S. Department of Labor, Women's Bureau, *American Women*, Report of the President's Commission on the Status of Women, Washington, D. C., 1963, Chart 10, p. 28.

FIGURE 6-1————Of the new roles for women, none is more important than the work role which takes them outside the home and family circle. Increasingly women have entered the field of gainful employment. This modern trend brings with it both new freedom and new responsibility.

represent not only work-role situations, but also interest-group activities of which she must become a part.

There is always, of course, the ultimate dilemma, "What do I do if I do not get a chance to marry at all?" A college girl expressed it in this way, "I have a double set of life goals; one set is for if I get married, the other if I remain single."

In all aspects of woman's life, we see evidence of the stress which choice brings. With it comes emotional confusion induced by confused role expectations. Unequal pressures of various participant groups constantly challenge her internalized role conceptions.

The fact that social roles are so numerous and so much a matter of individual decision means that they are no longer stereotyped by the culture and, therefore, every woman is running a complicated maze of choice. This the sociologist sees as a primary reason why neuroses are so common among modern women.

Experiments with animals show that neurotic behavior is the natural result of presenting the individual with so many choices that he is driven to distraction by repeated frustration. The best example is the simple psychological experiment of a rat in a maze. If the maze is relatively simple, with only few alternate pathways to the cheese, he enters into problem-solving with enthusiasm and vigor and after a few trips down blind alleys soon learns his way to the fragrant cheese and satisfies his hunger. Complicate this maze by a hundred alternatives and soon you have a rat approaching the point of nervous exhaustion. He gives up the quest and settles down into a corner completely distraught with feelings of anxiety, frustration, and defeat. He may tremble in helplessness at his own feelings of pain and tension. Add to this complicated maze several blind alleys in which an electric shock is added to intensify fear, frustration, and anxiety, and one builds up the pattern of neurosis even more quickly.

The life of contemporary women have many parallels. The responsibilities of role choice are so great, the risks of failure and frustration so numerous, the pain of being thought out of order in one social circle or another for attempting various ventures is so severe that anxiety, fear, and tension may readily result.

Marya Mannes in a discussion panel on the roles of modern woman commented most wisely, "I believe whatever decisions one makes, one pays for. Therefore, there is such a thing as complete acceptance of choice but no such thing as finite and complete fulfillment. We make a mistake in thinking, Will I be happy if I do this or that? We cannot be entirely happy all the time, and conflict, in a creative woman, often makes for pain and difficulty along with its joys. We must accept a degree of unhappiness, which I think is a natural condition of man."[11]

An Appraisal of Women's Roles

This analysis of the female dilemma may seem pessimistic. It is not so intended, nor is it intended to suggest that we return to the former customary roles for women. Women could not go back to their former position, even if it were more satisfying, which it most probably

[11] Marya Mannes, "The Problem of Creative Women," in Seymour M. Farber and Roger H. L. Wilson (Editors), *The Potential of Woman* (New York: Mc Graw-Hill Book Co., 1963), pp. 153-154.

would not be. The modern industrial world has left no place for the kind of secure, family-absorbed woman of previous generations. Today women, as well as men, must function as individuals and must, through performing significant roles outside the family, achieve their own distinct social status.

The experience of modern woman has many parallels to the experience of the adolescent. In shifting from the age of childhood, the period of economic dependency, moral irresponsibility, and parental guidance, the adolescent goes through a time of struggle in learning to make choices for himself. He is often torn by choices of vocation, mate selection, and moral behavior. We, therefore, think of adolescence as a period of great strain, imposed by the necessities of choice in an individualistic society. But a person must go through this to become an adult, and by going through a period of society-imposed choice, he becomes a much more independent, useful, and individualistic person than he could otherwise be.

American women are gradually moving into a period, not only of greater freedom and greater choice, but of greater self-assurance. The more fully their new roles come to be accepted by themselves and by men, the less tension and frustration there will be, and the more nearly will men and women be able to function as full equals in society.

With all her new freedom, the female still faces many of the discriminations long common to her sex. In wages and in occupational rank, she is still generally subservient to the male. In dating and in marital choice, the initiative is still his. In sex matters her unequal status is most blatantly obvious. The siring of a child out of wedlock by the male brings little personal or social guilt. The conception of a child by an unmarried female is still looked upon as one of the most serious of moral offenses. Society gives the woman and the child little protection or sympathy. The double standard obviously remains at the point where it hurts most.

Women are not now considered an inferior group, looked down upon by men, treated as subjects, humored, and used, as once they were, but at times men still like to think of women in the traditional way. Many men want their wives to be ornaments and clinging vines, even those men who expect their wives to support them. They miss the honor and respect that were once considered their inherent right. Today the male must earn these from his wife and children as well as from his male associates. In most cases, however, men are becoming aware of the more-than-compensating advantages that equality has brought. They want the strength, support, intelligent direction, advice, and companionship that only this modern woman can provide.

The threat to the male ego has been great and many men still cannot take it. Yet the trend is in the direction of greater equality in sex roles, and both men and women are growing in their understanding of each other under the new philosophy.

In the old-fashioned marriage, the successful wife was generally a shrewd student of the male personality, for most of her wishes had to be realized by manipulating him indirectly. By indirection and subtlety she acquired whatever prestige and advantage she held in the household and in the pair relationship.

Today, women need be much less subtle. They approach men on a different level. Most take their equality for granted and, therefore, assume that flattery and cunning are beneath them.

The Cultural Handicap to Female Role Adjustment

The customary roles defined for a particular group may ease the transition through various phases of the life cycle, or make them unnecessarily difficult. It appears that in the United States the culture has tended to create difficult periods of adjustment for the female. The first critical stage comes when she moves from her adolescent beauty in the late teens into mature womanhood. This transition has been analyzed by Sirjamaki, who sees the woman's highest point in status in the United States at the college-age period.[12] Then, as never again, she is the center of attraction—the envied coed, the beauty queen, spending her time in dressing-up, dating, and dancing. In this, our culture contrasts decidedly with most other cultures in which the highest status role for women is motherhood. Supreme ego gratification prior to assuming mature roles may well leave a young woman feeling let down as she takes over mature roles.

Where the girl reaches her climax in social status prior to marriage, as in our culture, the marriage is often blamed for the eclipse in popularity which would have come in any case with increasing age and more limited social circulation. For the popular college girl, particularly, the quiet and unspectacular role of housewife is a striking and often unsatisfactory contrast. The ego suffers and she may feel rebellious against the limitations family and motherhood have imposed upon her. Many neuroses originate here. Popular articles lead one to believe that the campus beauty queen does not often prove to be the contented, happy, satisfied housewife. It must be recognized, however, that few reach the beauty-queen level of ego satisfaction in the teens.

American culture defines the male peak role much more realistically. He does not achieve his maximum point of recognition and respect until

[12] John Sirjamaki, "Cultural Configurations in The American Family," *American Journal of Sociology*, 53:464-470, 1948.

he is somewhere in his thirties and has won it by social placement through occupational achievement and by home and family.

The status peak for both sexes, when contrasted with other societies comes strikingly early. Elsewhere, it is more usual for the aged—regarded, to use A. G. Keller's phrase, as "repositories of wisdom"—to be most revered of all age groups. Where elders are so revered, they have a secure place in the bosom of their families. Where their wisdom is regarded as the outmoded folk wisdom of yesterday, they frequently must spend their last years outside the family in loneliness.

Finally, the "empty nest" crisis for the devoted mother marks the beginning of her loneliness. With the loss of her children, her most vital role of her mid-years goes. Grandmothers are suspect in our culture if they interfere with the relationships of husbands and wives or if they so much as hint how young Johnny should be brought up. The loss of work at retirement sends the aging male and female into eclipse. No longer can they manipulate others or expect to be respected for their know-how. Youth in a technological age soon outstrips the wisdom of experience, which in other cultures has made the old wise.

Emancipation by Work Roles

No doubt the most influential factor in the emancipation of women, aside from education, has been their entry into the work world. Two wars produced the man-power shortages which drew women into the labor market. Once there, they stayed, and by staying, brought about revolutionary changes in home administration, in the male-female relationship, and the role conception.

Work roles are of profound significance to role interaction of husbands and wives today. Women work not only prior to marriage, but early in the marriage, and then typically enter the labor market again after a period of childbearing. Childbearing is over for most at about the age of 28. When the mother is 34, the youngest child is in school, so the mother enters the labor market again. A third of all married women work and they are still working as grandmothers. Half of the group of married women over 40 are working. In fact, as many grandmothers are working as are teenagers (see Figure 6-2).

For the most part, married women do not work for economic reasons primarily, but rather to fulfill other wishes which homemaking leaves unsatisfied. As much as 40 percent of their earnings is likely to go for taxes.[13] If there are dependent children, the cost of child care and house-

[13] For a comprehensive view in this area see the report of a Columbia University Symposium, *Work in the Lives of Married Women* (New York: Columbia University Press, 1958).

PROFILE OF WOMEN WORKERS

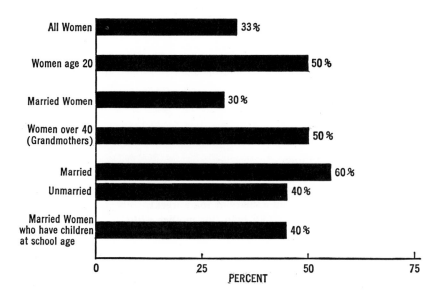

SOURCE: *Work in the Lives of Married Women* (New York: Columbia University Press, 1958).

FIGURE 6-2————It will be seen that as high a proportion of women over 40 are working as of women age 20, and a larger percent of married than of single women work. Even of women with children of school age, 40 percent work.

hold help takes substantial sums. Transportation, special clothes, and other incidentals reduce the margin of profit (see Table 6-1).

Employment outside the home brings social contacts, a chance to use skills and capabilities, a sense of work satisfaction, a chance to dress up, a real need for beauty-parlor care, and numerous other satisfactions. Work also gives life a satisfying routine which the housewife sometimes lacks in an age of household technology. It also brings status and independence.[14]

For many it brings a routine which insures them against the neurosis of a purposeless existence. Dr. Nadina Kavinoky, gynecologist and former president of the National Council on Family Relations, once said, "Much of the neurosis among American women would vanish if they had to leave for the office every morning at 8:00 a. m." Psychiatrists in London prior to World War II had a large case load afflicted with what they

[14] *Ibid.*

called "suburban neurosis." Most of it vanished when war work drew women into group-shared activity in a common cause.

TABLE 6-1————Gross versus net income of the working mother*

Job-related expenses as estimated by Budget Standard Service of the Community Council of Greater New York.

EXPENDITURE	WEEKLY COST
Lunch	$ 4.75
Transportation to work	3.00
Union dues	.80
Additional clothing	2.55
Additional personal care	.40
Additional laundry	1.15
Social Security tax (on a salary of $65 a week)	2.35
Child care and household help (for mother with young children)	30.00
Taxes (state and federal)	5.00 to 10.00
	$50.00 to $55.00
Actual net gain to family for $65 per week salary	$10.00 to $15.00

* Reported in *The Family Life Coordinator*, Vol. 8, April, 1963, p. 53.

One can scarcely conceive of all the social and psychological implications of the developing work role of American women. It has brought them great freedom, for only those able to earn and support themselves can have any real freedom of choice. Marriage is optional now, as is divorce, for the threat of dependency in the absence of male support has been greatly reduced.

Some men take a patronizing view of their wives working. "Let the little woman amuse herself," is their attitude. A common difficulty created by women's entrance into the work world is the psychological effect it has upon some husbands. When wives become seriously interested in their own jobs they are thrown into competition with their husbands on two counts: (1) their husbands feel they are losing their wives' love and devotion and (2) they fear their wives may beat them at their own game. Few men of an earlier generation could stand this kind of competition.[15] Men are becoming accustomed to it today. Yet no one enjoys being outdistanced by another person and it is particularly difficult for the American male to maintain his self-respect while being outdistanced by his wife. There is also a social attitude to contend with, particularly in

[15] The above points are discussed in John Levy and Ruth Munroe, *The Happy Family* (New York: Alfred A. Knopf, Inc., 1938).

smaller rural communities; a man who cannot support his wife adequately is often ranked as a failure in such communities. Some husbands fear, and others actually sense, the development in their wives of assertive, individualistic, aggressive traits.

On the positive side, the work role of women has increased their insight into a man's life and problems. There is some evidence that successful work experience prior to marriage is favorable to success in marriage.[16] No doubt the insight gained into work roles is a factor. The new work roles have increased woman's incentive to acquire an education, with the privileges and breadth of experience which this brings. Competition in the classroom has increased men's respect for women and their capabilities as even their competition in the work world could not have done.

Male prejudice against women's activities outside the home has decreased, although one must grant that each new venture of women has been marked by initial sneers and vulgar suspicions. The latest major work role undertaken by women is in the military. Although this country has not permitted women to fight alongside men, as some nations involved in World War II did, and had no need for women in an underground force, women were taken into the armed forces for special duties in offices, hospitals, etc.

For this venture, they were not accorded the same patriotic respect as service men, or credited with a motive of sincerity. It was assumed by many that the only women who joined were those of questionable character seeking male association. Certainly in many quarters their morals were questioned and their characters suspected. So it has always been when women have ventured beyond the accustomed roles of the social order. Virginia Gildersleeve, speaking of the Waves, said, "If the Navy could possibly have used dogs, ducks, or monkeys, certainly the older admirals would probably have preferred them to women."

Contrary to what one might expect, the wide-scale entry of women into the world of work has served as an incentive rather than a barrier to early marriage. As the work world has opened to younger women, regardless of their marital status, the economic handicap to early marriage has been largely removed. By the careful use of contraception and by their both entering the work world, young people may marry immediately after high school or college and suffer relatively little hardship in their level of living. They may even, in fact, marry and continue in school, each working part time and during summer vacations, or if the wife seeks no further schooling, she may work and see her husband through college or graduate school.

[16] Ernest W. Burgess and Leonard S. Cottrell, *Predicting Success or Failure in Marriage* (Englewood Cliffs, N. J.: Prentice-Hall, Inc., 1939), pp. 398-401.

In all these respects, therefore, the entry of women into the work world has been an incentive to early marriage, and to marriage in general. Once again, as in an agrarian society, a wife can be an economic asset rather than an economic liability.

The major occupational field for women today is clerical (see Figure 6-3). (At one time the main occupational outlet was the "operatives"—mostly manufacturing.) Service work (protective services, waitresses, cooks, etc.) ranks second in women's occupations. Operatives are now third and

MAJOR OCCUPATION GROUPS OF EMPLOYED MARRIED WOMEN, HUSBAND PRESENT, APRIL 1947 AND MARCH 1963*

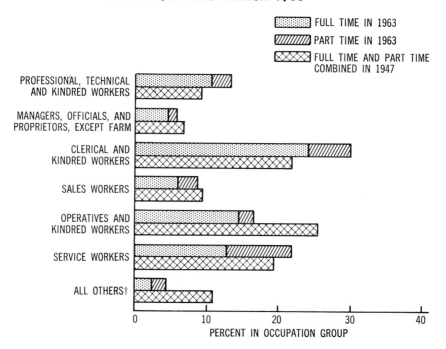

* Data for the 2 years are not strictly comparable because of changes in estimating procedures, and inclusion of Alaska and Hawaii in 1963.
† Includes craftsmen, farmers, and laborers.

SOURCE: "Special Labor Force Report," No. 40. Reprinted from *Monthly Labor Review,* Reprint No. 2433, February, 1964, p. 151.

FIGURE 6-3

the professions rank fourth. Of the professional group, 40 percent are teachers and 23 percent nurses.[17]

In March, 1963, 34 percent of all married women living with their husbands in the same household were in the labor force. The percentage of those in the labor force was greatest among those with the most education and smallest among those with the least education. For example, of those with less than five years of schooling, 20 percent were in the labor force; of those with grade school training, 27 percent; of the high school trained, 35 percent; of the college graduates, 50 percent.

An increasing proportion of all women is found in the labor force. Table 6-2 compares the percentage of women workers in all age groups in 1950 with the percentage in 1962. It will be seen that in all age groups but one (14-17), women workers are on the increase. Note particularly the marked increase in the proportion of women in the ages above 45 who have entered the labor market.

TABLE 6-2————Increase in proportion of women in various age groups who worked in 1950 and 1962*

AGE	PERCENT OF FEMALE CIVILIAN NONINSTITUTIONAL POPULA- TION WHO WORKED DURING	
	1962	*1950*
Total, 14 years and over	46.5	41.1
14 to 17 years	32.5	33.3
18 and 19 years	67.2	61.6
20 to 24 years	63.3	58.7
25 to 34 years	47.5	43.7
35 to 44 years	53.2	47.2
45 to 54 years	59.6	44.9
55 to 64 years	46.3	32.3
65 years and over	14.3	11.8

* "Special Labor Force Report," No. 40. Reprinted from *Monthly Labor Review*, Reprint No. 2433, February, 1964.

Although more single and married women are working than ever before, the fact remains that women are more marriage-minded than career-minded in role expectations. This is clearly demonstrated in a study by Lemar T. Empey at Washington State University, where he found that 8 out of 10 college women preferred marriage to a career, if

[17] "Special Labor Force Report," No. 40. Reprinted from *Monthly Labor Review*, Reprint No. 2433, February, 1964.

it came to an alternate choice; only 8 percent actually preferred a career; the remainder were uncertain.[18] The sample dealt with over a thousand high school girls and over 400 undergraduate women at Washington State University.

MOST WOMEN WHO WORK ARE MARRIED

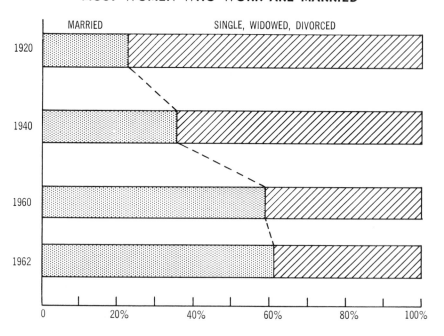

SOURCE: U. S. Department of Labor, Women's Bureau, *American Women,* Report of the President's Commission on the Status of Women, Washington, D. C., 1963, Chart 11, p. 29.

FIGURE 6-4————During the venturesome early days of women in the work world it was the unmarried career women who sought gainful employment. To-day over 60 percent of the female working force is married. Then, the career vs. marriage dilemma was one for the unmarried girl. Now, working out a marriage in which roles of homemaking and working are synchronized is a lifelong problem for an increasing number of women.

Significantly, in this study Empey found that high school girls are more likely to look upon work as a pleasant activity than are boys. The differences, however, were slight. Approximately three-fourths of each group looked upon the work world as a pleasant one.

[18] Lemar T. Empey, "Role Expectations of Young Women Regarding Marriage and a Career," *Marriage and Family Living,* 20:152-155, May, 1958.

The Career Dilemma

The career dilemma is much less a reality now than it was a few generations ago when feminism was at its height. Women then were demanding a new status in the work world and daring souls, defying all tradition, achieved it. They usually did so at the cost of marriage. At that time, less than half of the graduates of women's colleges married, as did less than three-fourths of the women graduates of the coeducational college. For a woman to get married was assumed to be a waste of college training.

With college education becoming more nearly universal, these attitudes have changed decidedly. Although the career dilemma is no longer what it once was, the facts are that college women must still weigh the alternatives in deciding whether to marry, when to marry, and what to do about a career. It is known that each year's delay reduces the probability of a woman's marrying (see Figure 17-2). It is also known that college women in general have greater difficulty in marrying than do noncollege women. A special table (Table 6-3) developed by the Bureau of Labor Statistics shows the marital status of women 35 to 44, by education. Fewer of the college graduates than any other educational grouping are or have been married.

TABLE 6-3————Educational attainment of women 35 to 44 years old, by marital status, March, 1962 (numbers in thousands)[19]

YEARS OF SCHOOL COMPLETED	MARITAL STATUS				
	Total	*Single*	*Married (husband present)*	*Other*	*Percent ever married*
Elementary school					
less than 5	399	37	263	99	90.7
5 to 7	829	36	631	162	95.7
8	1,326	57	1,086	183	95.7
High school					
1 to 3	2,463	88	2,042	333	96.4
4	5,160	238	4,495	427	95.4
College					
1 to 3	1,314	56	1,134	124	95.7
4	903	100	741	62	88.9

[19] Prepared by U. S. Department of Labor, Bureau of Labor Statistics, September, 1964.

Women with the greatest amount of education show the lowest marriage rate. Is it that those who fail to find a mate pursue education as a compensation, or do they seek through education to guarantee their economic future should they fail to marry? Is their failure in achieving marriage due to deliberately putting off marriage commitment, or did they in the process of schooling lose their technique of mate attraction? Or is the deficiency in the male who fears an equal or superior woman?

Does college tend to select a less marriageable type? Do the restraint and discipline of education make a woman less attractive? Or is it merely that the years creep up on women during college? Perhaps all these things are important.

Paul Popenoe, founder of the American Institute of Family Relations in Los Angeles, who has counseled many spinsters in the high educational brackets, warns the college woman that she should not neglect the development of her romantic interests. Most men are not interested in the college degree itself but in the warmth and humanness of the girl they marry.[20] He also believes that men still want wives who will bolster their egos rather than detract from them. He feels that the highly competitive woman is not particularly attractive to the American male.

A college girl, in her autobiography, senses a trend in her own personality development unfavorable to marriage. She writes:

> I have enjoyed college tremendously ever since I arrived. I can literally feel myself changing, and I honestly believe the changes are all for the better. I'm neater and much more considerate since I share a dorm room, rather than having a room of my own. I've got a quicker, clearer mind, and much more self-assurance since I've been subjected to the brisk discussions of many of my classes.
>
> Still, in the back of my mind there is a growing uncertainty as to what all this will mean in my future. Even today, after only a few months of college, I know that I would be less acceptable to most fellows as a wife than when I first came. I'm too opinionated, too independent and ambitious. I have the terrible feeling that after four years I could never play the part of the self-effacing, hero-worshipping wife that most men want.

There may be some carry-over of tradition in the resistance of men to the intellectual woman, and certainly there is much injustice in it. But there is some evidence that those who drive hardest toward a career, and who become most ambitiously motivated along vocational lines, are not particularly marriageable persons.[21] Such women may be quite content

[20] Paul Popenoe, "Where Are the Marriageable Men?" *Social Forces*, 14:257-262, December, 1935.

[21] Evelyn Ellis, "Social-Psychological Correlates of Upward Social Mobility Among Unmarried Career Women," *American Sociological Review*, 17:558-563, October, 1952.

without marriage and should not let the usual values that prevail among women interfere with their becoming the socially useful and creative persons they should be. There are, no doubt, some women for whom marriage should be secondary in our culture. Certainly, the generations can be replaced without all women participating in childbearing. It would be unfortunate, however, if a large portion of the inherently talented and capable should fail to replace themselves in the next generations.

To college women, the choice of career or marriage often comes, not as a major theoretical decision, but as a personal choice whether or not they should accept a good opportunity to marry before finishing college.

EDUCATION AND EARNING POWER GO TOGETHER

(MEDIAN INCOME OF WOMEN, 1961)

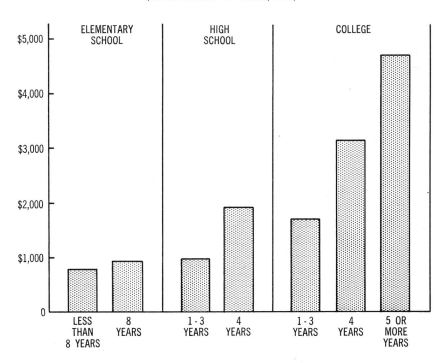

SOURCE: U. S. Department of Labor, Women's Bureau, *American Women*, Report of the President's Commission on the Status of Women, Washington, D. C., 1963, Chart 20, p. 68.

FIGURE 6-5————Education is an economic elevator for women as it is for men. (For income of men by schooling see Figure 27-1.)

There is no one answer to this question. Some women are more strongly motivated than others toward academic and vocational achievement, and they could not possibly find happiness in terminating college for marriage. For them, marriage would represent more an "end" than a "beginning." Others, in spite of parental pressure, should at this point marry, even though it costs them their college degree. Ruth Reed, in her book *The Single Woman,* has shown that the reason some single women missed the boat was that either they or their parents placed too high a value on finishing college. Looking back on their decision, they have regretted that they did not marry, for no other satisfactory proposal for marriage came.

The woman who wishes to marry must be realistic on this point, in spite of the prevailing values of the college campus. After college graduation there are comparatively few opportunities to meet marriageable men on an intimate and long-time basis. But in our day the choice need not be "either, or," for marriage need not represent the termination of a girl's opportunity for schooling.

Whether a girl continues her college education or terminates a college course prior to graduation seems to be in part a matter of social-class background, according to Christensen.[22] The girl from the more privileged home is inclined to rate marriage above graduation, if the right opportunity for marriage comes along; whereas the girl from a family that is fighting its way up the social scale is more likely to pursue her college course to the end, even at the risk of losing a marriage opportunity.

Girls need not feel that the marriage-career dilemma is a major problem. It is not, given an understanding husband and adequate cooperation within the family. With this help, it is increasingly possible for women to have both career and marriage. Children must have affection and care, but this does not mean that the able and talented mother must spend all her time with the children. With help in the home she often can carry on her career with only short interruptions. Moreover, she can often start her career before marriage, have it during marriage before children come, and with the increased length of life continue it after the children are in school, even if she drops out completely during the period when her children are small. The small family of today—two or three children born close together—takes up only about twenty years of the mother's life.

A change of attitudes in this area will go a long way toward correcting frustrations in marriage centering around problems of parenthood.

[22] Harold T. Christensen and Marilynn Swihart, "Postgraduation Role Preferences of Senior Women in College, *Marriage and Family Living,* 18:52-57, February, 1956.

At the present time the constant confinement of the mother to the care of the young child is most trying, particularly to the college woman.

The child is a definite threat to the individualistic roles, goals, and ambitions of the educated wife. Childbearing tends to isolate her from her role as an independent woman. In a sense, childbearing itself becomes a humiliating concession to biological forces which automatically limit her chances of realizing the social and economic goals she has been conditioned to desire.

In all previous societies, children were an inevitable part of marriage. To fortify woman's role as childbearer a whole series of precepts was built up about a mother's duty and obligation to her children. Children fitted into this conception of life organization. If there were too many, one accepted them as the gift of an all-wise Providence. Today, it is not uncommon for women to bear children whom they actually do not love.

Women's Feelings Concerning Their Role

Margaret Mead is a proponent of the view that not only do women consider their role superior to that of men, but that men do also.[23] No man can ever attain the sense of reality which his childhood conception of the role of motherhood has given him. Men must, therefore, be given work roles, and the culture defines these roles as superior to fortify his ego and make him think that his life is worthwhile. Only in this manner can he gain a sense of "irreversible achievement" which his childhood knowledge has taught him women have by motherhood. Only as men can be allowed to surpass women in some work sphere can they be made to feel important.

Cultures, on the other hand, have to work very hard to make women want anything more than motherhood to make life full for them. Most societies, in fact, find in motherhood the model for the mystic, the artist, and the saint.

As Mary Beard has clearly pointed out in her *On Understanding Women,* women, throughout history, have assumed the "chief responsibility for the continuance and care of life."[24] This activity of womanhood in the affairs of human life she considers one of the strongest forces in history. Women are often the main influence in the destinies of men and nations. She sees in the force of women the power behind the rise and development of civilization itself: cooking, weaving, spinning, gardening, doctoring, and providing the comforts and conveniences, as well as the

[23] Margaret Mead, *Male and Female* (New York: William Morrow & Co., Inc.).

[24] Mary R. Beard, *On Understanding Women* (New York: Longmans, Green & Co., Inc., 1931), p. 513.

decorative arts, are part of the growth of civilization that relates to her function of caring for the life created.

She sees women lifting their male companions above the beasts, above the level of sex impulse and nature comforts, to the level of the civilized human being. She sees women transforming social forms and building cultures, and through them building men into responsible creatures. The manufacture and distribution of commodities to produce comforts have become the major activity of mankind due to woman's quest for greater safety and convenience in maintaining life. Mary Beard also points out that throughout history, even when woman's place was very low, again and again a woman emerges, managing empires, great estates, or playing the decisive role in influencing great men.

This has been the history of civilization and of women until the present stage, when the conflict between state and family has become of major concern. She concludes that if the femininism of the older generation, which won the freedom that women now enjoy, passes, real femininity will emerge. Yet women will still be the center of man's life, as man is the center of woman's life.

Historians and anthropologists have been less prone to commit women to an inferior status than have people of the current generation generally. Robert Briffault, many years ago, wrote a three-volume treatise entitled *The Mothers,* in which he saw motherhood at the core of civilization and the matriarchy as the key to human authority from the beginning of time.

Currently, Ashley-Montagu depicts woman as the stronger sex and describes her supremacy in practically every area of critical importance.[25]

Frazer in his *Golden Bough* mythology highlights the theme of women and of life; sex and reproduction are made the key to all life and the basic fact of all civilizations.[26]

Such views are in direct contradiction to the inferiority-complex views of Alfred Adler and his followers who have stressed the concept, *masculine protest.*[27] According to this view, there is a secret wish in women to have been born men. Adler, a Viennese psychoanalyst, in developing the concept of inferiority feelings, identified power with masculinity and weakness with femininity. Inferiority was created with the unmanliness of femininity, the compensation for which he called the *masculine protest.* Overcompensation, he believed, is indulged in by both men and women when they feel inadequate and inferior.

Research seems to give little support to this view, although the

[25] M. F. Ashley-Montagu, *The Natural Superiority of Women* (New York: The Macmillan Co., 1953).

[26] James Frazer, *The Golden Bough* (New York: The Macmillan Co., 1926).

[27] *Individual Psychology of Alfred Adler,* Edited and Annotated by Heinz L. Ansbacher and Rowena R. Ansbacher (New York: Basic Books, Inc., Publishers, 1956).

amount of protest may well be related to the degree of equality already existing. A poll suggests that women have less rebellion against their role here than in Canada, where they have somewhat less equality. Elmo Roper, in a poll conducted for *Fortune* magazine, asked men and women in Canada and the United States this question, "If you could be born over again, would you rather be a man or a woman?"

The answers showed that men are more often satisfied with their role than are women. A fourth of the women in the United States and well over a fourth in Canada would rather have been men. Only a small percentage of men would have chosen to be women. From this, one would expect women in the United States, and women in Canada even more, to enter further into fields of traditional male activity.

Here are the percentages of men and women choosing the male and female roles as preferable.

	Male role is preferable (percent)	Female role is preferable (percent)	No preference (percent)	Undecided (percent)
United States:				
Men think	92	3	2	3
Women think	25	66	2	7
Canada:				
Men think	80	6	9	5
Women think	29	60	8	3

Opinion News, Vol. VIII, No. 13, National Opinion Research Center, University of Denver, June 24, 1947.

The generally favorable attitude of both men and women toward the male role is, no doubt, entirely a matter of training, much of it unwittingly given. It slips out in our attitudes, as with the father who, when playing with his little girl, very injudiciously remarks, "I wish you were a boy; then we could do more things together."[28]

Roper asked his respondents who had an easier life, men or women. Almost half the men thought the women did and 41 percent of the women thought the men did. Asked which had the more interesting time, only a fourth of the men thought the women did, but over a third of the women thought men did. The devout follower of Adler would no doubt say that the superior appraisal of the male role here by both men and women is an expression of the "masculine urge," the inner drive of all human beings to be masculine.

As long as women get less pay than men for the same work, one need

[28] I am indebted to Lester A. Kirkendall, Professor of Family Life Education at Oregon State College, for this example.

not resort to quite such imaginative concepts to find a logical explanation. Even the college woman cannot expect to earn a salary or wage equivalent to her male competitor's. She, too, may end up in a high-status occupational bracket and will get better pay than her sister who skips college, but she will fall far short of the earnings she would have enjoyed by virtue of being a male.[29] Even in the United States Civil Service, where one might expect equal treatment, few women are in the higher income levels (see Figure 6-6). This no doubt reflects in part her inferior training

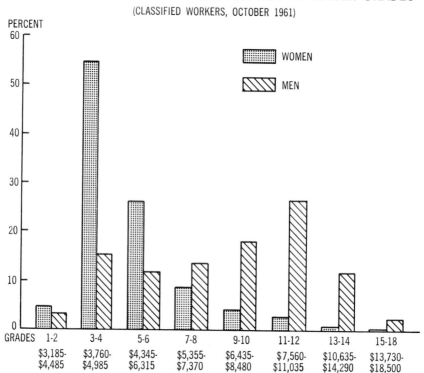

MOST WOMEN IN FEDERAL SERVICE ARE IN LOWER GRADES

(CLASSIFIED WORKERS, OCTOBER 1961)

Source: U. S. Department of Labor, Women's Bureau, *American Women*, Report of the President's Commission on the Status of Women, Washington, D. C., 1963, Chart 12, p. 31.

FIGURE 6-6————Civil Service workers in federal employ by grades and income, 1961.

[29] See Ernest Havermann and Patricia Salter West, *They Went to College* (New York: Harcourt Brace & Co., 1952); Paul H. Landis, "The Dollar Value of an Education," *National Education Association Journal*, 38:366-368, May, 1949; Paul H. Landis, *The Territorial and Occupational Mobility of Washington Youth* (Pullman, Wash.: Washington Agricultural Experiment Station, 1944), Bulletin No. 449.

and her lack of dedication to a career, but even in comparable activities she is to be found in the lower pay bracket (see Figure 6-7).

HOURLY PAY IN RETAIL TRADE

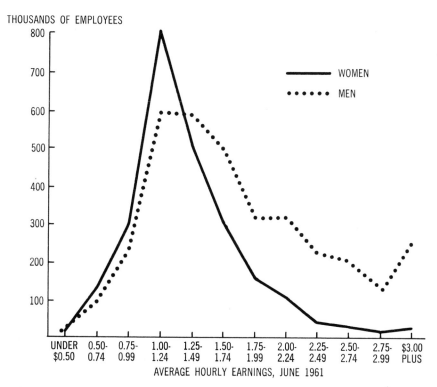

SOURCE: U. S. Department of Labor, Women's Bureau, *American Women,* Report of the President's Commission on the Status of Women, Washington, D. C., 1963, Chart 14, p. 39.

FIGURE 6-7————Women usually face discriminatory pay scales in the labor market. This is a picture of earnings of men and women in retail trade.

She achieves as high a record as her brother in college, but while she is doing so, she lessens her chances of marriage by comparison with her sister who stops short of college. The male's chances of marriage are not diminished by education. But more of this later on.

Many privileges in all societies have been reserved for the male. Among our forebears, the saloon and other places of conviviality were for men only. Today, in our society, the teenage boy in the family has far greater liberty than the girl, even in the more democratically inclined families (See Table 6-4).[30]

TABLE 6-4————Percentage of teenagers living under democratic, intermediate, and authoritarian family patterns, classified by parental residence and by sex*

| | | | FAMILY ADMINISTRATIVE PATTERN | | |
Place of residence	Sex	Number of cases	Demo-cratic	Inter-mediate	Authori-tarian
Farm	boys	562	38.1	39.3	22.6
	girls	606	21.6	55.4	23.0
Town	boys	429	45.7	38.5	15.8
	girls	654	22.2	57.7	20.2
Cities—2,500-9,999	boys	308	40.3	40.3	19.4
	girls	355	22.2	55.2	22.6
Cities—10,000-50,000	boys	317	40.4	35.3	24.3
	girls	448	23.6	54.1	22.3
Cities—150,000 and over	boys	285	37.5	40.0	22.5
	girls	345	22.1	54.8	23.1

* No matter in what area they live, fewer girls than boys are accorded democratic treatment in the family today. Data are for 4,310 high school seniors. Landis and Stone, *op. cit.*

These few examples serve to indicate that the female role is still in several respects the socially less desirable one from the standpoint of many practical considerations.

In seeking to acquire the privileges of the male, without giving up those of the female, the modern woman quite often finds herself in a confusing and contradictory situation. Even those men who are least resentful of woman's inroads into the male domain resent the fact that many such women still insist upon the special treatment, the flattery, undue politeness, and deference accorded women in their former more ornamental role. As one man insisted in a moment of outrage at his female co-worker: "If you insist on acting like a man, then I insist on treating you like one!"

The consequences of this dual existence are often more than superficially disturbing. The women themselves suffer as much or more than

30 Paul H. Landis and Carol L. Stone, *The Relationship of Authority Pattern to Teenage Adjustments* (Pullman, Wash.: Washington Agricultural Experiment Station, 1952), Bulletin No. 538; also Carol L. Stone and Paul H. Landis, "An Approach to Authority Patterns in Parent-Teenage Relationships," *Rural Sociology*, 18:233-242, September, 1953.

their bewildered husbands or co-workers as they attempt to be both "sexlessly modern" and "traditionally feminine" in their daily lives. The head-long clashes and incessant contradiction of these two roles result in an emotional and even philosophical turmoil that leaves many a modern woman little of the inner tranquility and self-assurance of her feminine ancestors.

This emergence of conflicting roles is relatively new in American society—much more recent in fact than is generally realized. Women have had the ballot only since 1920, with the passage of the nineteenth amendment to the Constitution. American universities have operated on a co-educational basis for little more than a hundred years. The work world has only gradually opened to women.

There is now much confusion, even in the housekeeping and home-making role. Women are sticklers for tradition in this area more than are men. When 932 engaged couples were asked whether or not they expected the wife to keep house alone, or whether the husband would help, or whether or not they would have a maid, only 12.5 percent of the men indicated that the wife should keep house alone; over two-thirds of the women expected that she would. Seventy-two percent of the men indicated that she would keep house with his help; only 48 percent of the women thought so. Clearly, these men were more willing for equality in the domestic role than were the women.

Because sex roles are no longer distinct, women and men are now competitive as they never were before, and competition is known to be one of the most vicious enemies of successful dating, marriage, and family life. One expects intimacy, sharing, and a boost to his ego rather than the competition of his mate. Much difficulty arises from the fact that a couple cannot agree as to what is the accepted role for man and wife in our time. There is also the conflict over aspirations and life goals, particularly when those of one mate seem to interfere with those of the other.

Personal Realizations of Women in Life and Marriage Today

A woman today may find satisfaction, not only in the marriage relationship itself, but in numerous activities outside the home—both avocational and vocational. In a rural world, historically, there was little chance for expression of the personality except through domestic channels, which have always been frustrating to a certain proportion of women, even when they were trained to expect this as their role in life.

In an earlier day, marriage was for woman a necessity. She had few other choices; in fact, practically no other choice at all, if she was to be secure in life and have a respected place. Today, marriage is a choice for woman and the kind of marriage she will have is also her choice. She assumes that she has a right to expect much more outside of marriage, and along with marriage, than her great-grandmother even dared to dream of. She is a full person in a sense that women have never been before. One only has to take a glimpse at the underdeveloped areas of the world to see how near the level of the beast has been the lot of the married woman. In many countries of the world today she helps to pull the plow, along with the oxen.

American women have never been that low in the estimation of men or of the social order, but still their lot of an earlier day would shock the modern woman if she stopped to realize even for a moment how far greater are her privileges.

Finally, on the strictly material side, we have gotten away from the necessity for long hours of work, which always grinds down the human spirit, and which has historically borne most heavily on the spirit of women. Women's work in the old-fashioned family was literally never done. Solomon's description of the good wife was of a woman who rises long before dawn to take up her spinning and who continues her work far into the night after the children and husband have retired. This has been the picture of the married woman's life from ancient times until very recently.

The woman of today, even in rural areas, has become something of a lady of leisure, with freedom to venture outside the home and refresh herself by daily contacts and diversions that make her a better wife and a better mother. She has a chance to enjoy marriage because she enjoys life in a way wives of previous generations could not possibly do.

She is an asset to her husband and offers him much more in the way of being an interesting and worthwhile person than she could have done in an age of greater seclusion. This does not mean that happiness comes to all without price even now. No material circumstances and no change in human philosophy can insure happiness to all in marriage, but the stage is set for a marriage of happiness today more than ever before.

Modern Woman's Failure

Women seem to be quite as vocal as men in pointing to areas where modern woman has failed in role-status attainments. Margaret Mead, in lectures to college audiences, has criticized American women because they no longer want to be wives, but only mothers.[31] European

---

[31] "Student Marriages: Good or Bad," *U. S. News and World Report,* June 6, 1960.

women, she points out, want to be wives. She feels that American culture is caught in an "extreme reproductive cycle," which may be a threat to national survival. Even men have been drawn very much into the inner circle of caring for children. Early dating, early mating, early parenthood threatens individual development. She points to the verdict of history, suggesting that no civilization has survived which allowed men to get "too close to children." They must be free to venture, to explore, to invent.

We have more young people in school, and more women college graduates per capita than any nation on earth, yet the proportion of women entering the professions and other creative work endeavors is much less than a generation ago. The National Manpower Commission concludes that only one in 300 women capable of earning a Ph.D. gets one. Only 11 percent of all Ph.D. degrees are granted to women.

Much is written today of the lack of evidence of the serious ambition of American women. Few are found in medicine, law, and other such exacting professions. The contrast is often made between our output of trained women in medicine and that of countries with far fewer proportions of women privileged by the opportunity of college and university training. The Soviet Union is heavily staffed with women doctors, some 76 percent of the 350,000 doctors being women.[32] In many European countries a third or more of practicing physicians are women.

This is explained by what has been called the "marriage blackout," by which is meant that a young woman's vision stops at the point of marriage. Here she loses sight of herself "as an individual human being."[33] Part of the reason is that she is still clinging to the false idea that she must choose between marriage and career.

Women are stampeded into marriage here, Foley believes, more than in any other enlightened society, by the social stigma which attaches to the unmarried. The motto becomes, "Marry as early as possible without appearing to be frantic, and try for the best prospect of suburban prosperity and security."[34]

There is increasing opinion by critics to the effect that women should "perfect themselves as human beings," that this is the only road to happiness and often is the surest way to a really successful life and marriage.

Marya Mannes, discussing the problems of creative women, comments, "The United States is plunged into an orgy of domesticity and

[32] Paul Foley, "Whatever Happened to Women's Rights?" *Atlantic*, 243:63-65, March, 1964.
[33] *Ibid*.
[34] *Ibid*.

childbearing."[35] Britain, Scandinavia, and Russia, by contrast, are pushing more and more women into intellectual attainments. She feels that in the United States there are "hidden pursuaders . . . cultural forces telling a woman it is unladylike to use her mind."

While Mannes states the presumption that women throughout history have found their fulfillment in motherhood, she asks whether many women in our society with its alternatives would not have been happier and had a greater sense of fulfillment as doctors, mathematicians, etc. She feels that our culture should recognize that procreation is a luxury today, not a necessity for all. She believes that mass media must recognize that many women are not satisfied with domestic roles, and that we must no longer stifle the creativity of the girl of great capacity by making her feel that creativity is unfeminine. She says that "the identity of women as human beings is as essential to them as their identity as wife and mother."

Betty Friedan has perhaps received more attention for her views than any contemporary writer and lecturer—whether permanent or passing, it is too early to know.[36] She feels women have slid back from the feminist achievements of an earlier day and become involved in the "feminine mystique," which identifies fulfillment with motherhood. As a result, she finds them unhappy and disenchanted.

Friedan feels that the talented woman must make a genuine commitment, not just to a job for a job's sake, not just to community busy-work, but to a job she can take seriously as part of a life plan, "work in which she can grow as part of society."

Rosemary Park, Barnard President, believes that the woman's college is still necessary for women today, for it is so difficult for a woman to develop a "sense of independent individuality." In the background of a girl's mind lurks the traditional thought "that someone will take care of her, that some man will come along and give the answer."[37]

"Most of you," Park says, "will probably live to be 100. If you want to keep from being a stuffy old bore for forty years, that is, between sixty and 100, then you've got to learn something now. . . . To be young and feminine at sixteen is no achievement. To be a respected person at sixty is."

This long-run failure of women is often expressed in both learned opinion and in research findings. Too early and too complete commitment to motherhood without an awareness of the long-term perspective

[35] Marya Mannes, "The Problems of Creative Women," in Farber and Wilson, op. cit., pp. 116-130.

[36] Betty Friedan, The Feminine Mystique (New York: Dell Publishing Co., Inc., 1963).

[37] Terry Ferrer, "Rosemary Park: New President of Barnard," Saturday Review, April 20, 1963, pp. 66-68.

of life is often tragic to marriage, to parenthood, and to every following phase of the life cycle. Only the purposeful individual can survive happily the later phases of the life cycle in our day of increasing longevity.[38]

Finally, we know that the woman who has enthusiastic interests in work and creativity is not handicapped for marriage or parenthood. Those with a purpose other than marriage make good in marriage and family life. Long ago Burgess and Cottrell found a high correlation between educational achievement and marriage success (see Table 6-5).[39] Contemporary studies show that women who prior to marriage and childbearing were "most taken up and bound to their jobs are the ones who are most enthusiastic and committed as mothers when they do have children."[40]

TABLE 6-5————Marriage adjustment scores at different educational levels*

| | MARITAL ADJUSTMENT SCORE | | | |
Wife's educational level	Very low	Low	High	Very high
Graduate work	0.0	4.6	38.7	56.5
College	9.2	18.9	22.9	48.9
High school	14.4	16.3	32.2	37.1
Grades only	33.3	25.9	25.9	14.8

*Ernest W. Burgess and Leonard S. Cottrell, *Predicting Success or Failure in Marriage* (Englewood Cliffs, N. J.: Prentice-Hall, Inc., 1939), p. 271.

Serious commitment to intellectual pursuits, to a profession or other career may well be indicative of prospective success in marriage and parenthood. Psychologists describe this process as "feeding from one facility to another."

Problems

1. Outline the lifetime shifts characteristic of woman's roles in our culture today.
2. Men: Present your views on the proposition below which you are willing to defend:
   a. "I would rather marry an 'old fashioned' girl because . . ."
   b. "The 'modern' girl, in my opinion, makes a more ideal wife because . . ."

[38] Several papers in Farber and Wilson, *op. cit.*, discuss this problem; see also Lawrence E. Dennis (Editor), *Education and a Woman's Life*, Proceedings of the Itasca Conference on the Continuing Education of Women, American Council on Education, Washington, D. C., 1963.

[39] Burgess and Cottrell, *op. cit.*

[40] Eleanor E. Maccoby in a discussion, in Farber and Wilson, *op. cit.*, p. 45.

3. Women: Present your views on the proposition below which you can conscientiously defend:

   a. "The men of yesterday were a different and better breed than their modern counterparts. I would rather marry the kind of man who lived about _____ than a modern man because . . ."

   b. "Men have changed but mostly for the better. I'd prefer to marry a 'modern' man because . . ."

4. Discuss the implications of points of view expressed in activities 2 and 3. Do you think a young person's view on these alternative questions reflects primarily (a) his upbringing, (b) his experience with the opposite sex, or (c) other factors.

5. Describe several areas in which the line of demarcation between male and female roles seems to be disappearing.

6. Can you name roles that are still primarily one-sex roles?

7. Which sex seems to be changing the most in terms of traditional roles? What do you think accounts for this situation? Do you approve?

8. In what occupations and activities will you find women who have moved further away from the traditional female role?

9. In what occupations and activities will you find men who are most determined to live up to the traditional concept of the "masculine role"? In what occupations and activities is one most likely to find men who have adopted some traditionally feminine interests and activities?

10. Do you think that the differences in the social roles of the male and female will continue to diminish? Explain.

11. Briefly describe the situation to which the author referred in speaking of "the modern dilemma" in male-female social roles.

12. What is meant by the expression "women's career dilemma"? In what way may it be said that the dilemma is a less serious one today than it was a generation or so ago?

Selected References

ARTICLES IN BOOKS OF READINGS

LANDIS, Judson T., and LANDIS, Mary G., *Readings in Marriage and the Family* (Englewood Cliffs, N. J.: Prentice-Hall, Inc., 1952).

1. SIRJAMAKI, John, "Cultural Configurations in the American Family," pp. 9-17.

2. KOMAROVSKY, Mirra, "Cultural Contradictions and Sex Roles," pp. 375-383.

3. WALLIN, Paul, "Cultural Contradictions and Sex Roles: A Repeat Study," pp. 384-386.

4. KIRKPATRICK, Clifford, "Inconsistency in Marriage Roles and Marriage Conflict," pp. 386-392.

FISHBEIN, Morris, and KENNEDY, Ruby Jo Reeves, *Modern Marriage and Family Living* (New York: Oxford University Press, Inc., 1957).

5. MUDD, Emily Hartshorne, "Women's Conflicting Values in Relation to Marriage Adjustment," pp. 262-274.
6. KOMAROVSKY, Mirra, "Working Wives and Mothers," pp. 275-287.

SUSSMAN, Marvin B., *Sourcebook in Marriage and the Family*, Second Edition (Boston: Houghton Mifflin Co., 1963).

7. MALINOWSKI, Bronislaw, "Parenthood—The Basis of Social Structure," pp. 40-47.
8. LINTON, Ralph, "Women in the Family," pp. 167-172.
9. RAINWATER, Lee, and others, "The Inner Life and Outer World of the Workingman's Wife," pp. 173-185.

WINCH, Robert F., and others, *Selected Studies in Marriage and the Family*, Revised Edition (New York: Holt, Rinehart & Winston, Inc., 1962).

10. SUGIMOTO, Etsu Inagaki, "Old Love and New," pp. 437-438.
11. WHYTE, William H., Jr., "The Wife Problem," pp. 111-125.
12. KOMAROVSKY, Mirra, "Cultural Contradictions and Sex Roles," pp. 126-132.

CAVAN, Ruth Shonle, *Marriage and the Family in the Modern World: A Book of Readings* (New York: Thomas Y. Crowell Co., 1960).

13. Metropolitan Life Insurance Company, "The American Wife," Reading 8.
14. DUFFIN, B. Keith, "Career as a Lifetime Choice," Reading 52.
15. GLICK, Paul C., and MILLER, Herman P., "The Importance of College Education in Career Success," Reading 53.
16. VINCENT, Clark E., "Helping the College Woman Choose Her Role," Reading 55.
17. *Changing Times, the Kiplinger Magazine,* "Should Mother Take a Job or Stay Home with the Kids?" Reading 56.
18. KENT, Druzilla C., "Women as the Country's Major Labor Reserve," Reading 57.

COSER, Rose Laub, *The Family: Its Structure and Functions* (New York: St Martin's Press, Inc., 1964).

19. WATT, Ian, "The New Woman: Samuel Richardson's Pamela," pp. 267-289.
20. KAMAROVSKY, Mirra, "Functional Analysis of Sex Roles," pp. 290-305.

General References

AXELSON, Leland J., "The Marital Adjustment and Marital Role Definitions of Husbands of Working and Non-working Wives," *Marriage and Family Living*, 25:189-195, May, 1963.

CUSSLER, Margaret, *The Woman Executive* (New York: Harcourt, Brace & World, Inc., 1958).

DENNIS, Lawrence E. (Editor), *Education and a Woman's Life,* Proceedings of the Itasca Conference on the Continuing Education of Women, American Council on Education, Washington, D. C., 1963.

FARBER, Seymour M., and WILSON, Roger H. L. (Editors), *The Potential of Woman* (New York: McGraw-Hill Book Co., 1963). This is a symposium. See particularly Part Three, "The Roles of Woman."

FOOTE, Nelson N., "New Roles for Men and Women," *Marriage and Family Living*, 23:325-329, November, 1961.

GRUENBERG, Sidonie M., and KRECH, Hilda Sidney, *The Many Lives of Modern Women: A Guide to Happiness in Her Complex Role* (New York: Doubleday and Co., Inc., 1952).

Harper's Magazine, Special Supplement on contemporary woman, October, 1962.

HEER, David M., "Dominance and the Working Wife," *Social Forces*, 36:341-347, May, 1958.

HOFFMAN, Lois Wladis, "Effects of the Employment of Mothers on Parental Power Relations and the Division of Household Tasks," *Marriage and Family Living*, 22:27-35, February, 1960.

KAMMEYER, Kenneth, "The Feminine Role: An Analysis in Attitude Consistency," *Marriage and Family Living*, 26:295-305, August, 1964.

KIRKPATRICK, Clifford, *The Family as Process and Institution*, Second Edition (New York: The Ronald Press Co., 1963), Chs. 7, 17.

LANDIS, Paul H., *Introductory Sociology* (New York: The Ronald Press Co., 1958), Ch. 17.

————, *Social Control*, Revised Edition (Philadelphia: J. B. Lippincott Co., 1956), Ch. 9.

————, *Social Problems: Unfulfilled Welfare Aspirations in Nation and World* (Philadelphia: J. B. Lippincott Co., 1959), Ch. 15.

LeMASTERS, E. E., *Modern Courtship and Marriage* (New York: The Macmillan Co., 1957), Chs. 21, 23.

LEOPOLD, Alice K., "The Family Woman's Expanding Role," *Marriage and Family Living*, 20:278-283, August, 1958.

MEAD, Margaret, *Male and Female* (New York: William Morrow & Co., Inc., 1949), Ch. 2.

MYERS, George C., "Labor Force Participation of Suburban Mothers," *Marriage and Family Living*, 26:306-311, August, 1964.

NYE, F. Ivan, and HOFFMAN, Lois Wladis (Editors), *The Employed Mother in America* (Chicago: Rand McNally & Co., 1963).

RIESMAN, David, "Permissiveness and Sex Roles," *Marriage and Family Living*, 12:211-217, August, 1959.

SCHEINFELD, Amram, *Women and Men* (New York: Harcourt, Brace and Co., Inc., 1943).

U.S. Department of Labor, Women's Bureau, *American Women*, Report of the President's Commission on the Status of Women, Washington, D. C., 1963.

WHITE, Lynn, Jr., *Educating Our Daughters* (New York: Harper and Bros., 1950).

7

Male Roles in Transition

In any social structure there must be some complementation and coordination in male-female roles. Therefore, we must assume that the shift in women's roles in America has involved a radical change in men's roles. To the extent that women have gained privilege, men have had to change attitudes and expectations or suffer considerable loss of self-esteem. Woman's crusade to seek equality with men strikes at the core of the male's ego strength, the tradition of inherent masculine superiority. When woman assumes that she can play any role which man can play, he must either accept that premise, fight it and retain his dominance, or reach some kind of workable compromise.

Conflicting Expectations in Male Role Behavior

The male has maintained throughout the centuries a pattern of more nearly uniform role behavior than has the female. Yet he has not escaped, in this age, the pressure to conform to new roles. Modifications of behavior, which have been strenuous, embarrassing, and sometimes disastrous to him have been necessary. No doubt the male would have preferred to remain in his traditional role as patriarch of his family, as master of his household, and as guardian of the family property. This role, so long given community support and so long unchallenged, has had to be sacrificed in part to the newer values of the equalitarian marriage and the democratic household.

The wife has, often in spite of his protests, moved into the work world. He has thus had to share the provider role. He has also had to give up his position as custodian of family wealth as the wife has come to share in the spending. Lynn White, Jr., President of Mill's College, declares that many young husbands who not many years ago would have been ashamed of their wives working, now boast about the economic prowess of the little woman. He points out that this represents a definite mutation of the male's ego.[1]

The husband has come to recognize his wife's equality and sometimes her superiority as she has become more educated and more aggressive in community affairs. With her increased knowledge of child training and psychology she has educated him in the belief that children have rights equal to his own and that the fullest development of the child's personality is achieved, not by authoritarian methods, but by the counseling, developmental approach.

The big deficiency in men's training, White says, is their lack of preparation for the role of parenthood and family life. Women are much more adequately prepared for this role. Man's training ignores this reality of their adulthood. Husbands are often forced to admit it.

The Domesticated Male

The old model of family life, which has gone out of style, held that the male was the thinker and doer, the female his less gifted helpmate. Women wanted marriage; men were drawn into it. In the new regime both boys and girls want marriage, and they both want children. Family life has come to be meaningful to both sexes.

In the broadest sense, the American male is more domesticated than in any previous period of American history. On the frontier, the masculine virtues were valued far above refinements. The strength of a man's arm and his physical performance in field and forest had survival value, and because they did, such qualities were rated highly in the culture. The virtues of brute strength and accomplishment have always been rated highly where man is pitted against nature. These values still survive, particularly in the logging and mill towns of our West, and to some extent in all of rural America.

In direct contrast to these traditionally masculine values are the so-called effeminate characteristics of the urban male today. Some attribute the increasing effeminacy of the male to childhood training. Because of the long daily absence of the father from the suburban home, the training of the child is left largely to the mother. Added to this has been the decrease of the number of male teachers in grade schools with the consequence that the training of the child in the formative years in the schoolroom has usually been carried out by women. Those who criticize this trend feel that the effeminate development of the male personality makes for softness and is a disadvantage to national survival.

[1] Lynn White, Jr., "The Changing Context of Women's Education," *Marriage and Family Living*, 17:293, November, 1955.

One may challenge this criticism on two counts: first, is it true? and second, are these effeminate characteristics in the male undesirable? The writer believes that there is a trend toward more effeminate character development of the male. The maternal supervision of home and schoolroom may be important factors. Perhaps even more important, however, is the shift in dominant values in the American culture itself. Human brawn, generally speaking, has long since been replaced by horsepower, kilowatt power, and machine and atomic power. Today, a refinement of perception, a delicacy of touch, and a fine coordination are generally of more value than the strong hand, arm, or back. The brute strength of the frontier is no longer worshiped because it is no longer needed. Development along different lines would seem, therefore, to be more appropriate to the life men live now.

Male Roles

Ashley-Montagu seems to have no fear of the effeminization of the male. He believes that the culturally induced, so-called masculine qualities of "self-assertiveness, aggressiveness, and bluntness" are not the qualities that build the kind of world we want. He sees love, sympathy, compassion, and the "desire to conserve," predominantly feminine qualities as our culture rates them, as the key virtues in human survival. He believes the failure of humanity to achieve greater happiness on earth is very much due to the fact that women have been denied the opportunity for "active participation in the government of human affairs."[2]

He would also so organize the work world as to permit men greater time for fatherhood, reducing the work day of fathers with young children to four hours a day with no pay cut and supplementing income with family allowances to help with the economic burden of child care.[3]

In the rural family gatherings of a few generations ago, the men ate, then went outside to smoke, talk, look over the livestock, or hunt. Not one of the men would have dared suggest helping the women with the dishes or helping supervise the feeding of the babies. The men ate first, then the children, and finally the women; and, after all that, the women settled down for an afternoon of dishwashing and packing up the things to go home. The big holiday gatherings were not vacations for women, except that they had a chance to visit and exchange notes on housekeeping and child rearing. In an urban gathering of young couples today, the men often help with the cooking and dishes, or even take these duties

2 M. F. Ashley-Montagu, *Education and Human Relations* (New York: Grove Press, Inc., 1958), p. 170.
3 *Ibid.*, Ch. 10.

over completely. This shift in roles is accepted and it is profound in terms of the degree of sharing it has made psychologically possible.

This sharing of the domestic role is not merely a public display reserved for special occasions. In many homes, it is a daily routine in which the father changes diapers, takes the baby out for a stroll, puts the children to bed, and even helps with the cooking, dishes, and washing. The disappearance of the sharp line of demarcation between male and female functions, as far as home activities are concerned, has been only one of a great many changes in the relationships between men and women during the last few decades.

The extent to which this role sharing has gone is strikingly shown in a study by Theodore B. Johannis, Jr.[4] of the University of Oregon. Data comparing activities of 543 fathers, collected from tenth-grade students in Tampa, Florida, in 1953, are presented in Table 7-1. The percentages of middle- and lower-class fathers who participate in the 18 tasks listed is shown. The first three tasks may have been a part of the male role for a long time, but the others have been traditional female activities. Some men have taken over many tasks and even more men share them. Men seem to balk at the ironing. Only one in 200 middle-class males irons and only one in a hundred of the lower-class males. Caring for the yard is the most often shared task in the list.

The new part of the wife in breadwinning is not the only factor bringing about this shift of roles in the American home. In rural America, the man's work outside was never done. The wife often had to share in it, even though the husband never thought of sharing in her domestic tasks. Today the family lives in an apartment or in a small house. The amount of work a man has to do outside has been greatly reduced, and in small communities where he lives near his work, the amount of leisure time he has from work has greatly increased. He has the time to share the burdens of domestic life.

Another factor has been the disappearance of the servant class from American society. The growth of industrial and service occupations has given untrained girls from working-class homes an opportunity to enter occupations of higher status and higher pay than the domestic positions which they have traditionally taken. Other factors have been a decrease in need for domestic help with the trend toward smaller homes and the increase in labor-saving devices in the home. These devices may have helped to attract the man to cooperation in homemaking tasks. There is considerable satisfaction for the mechanically inclined male in using an electric dishwasher, an automatic washing machine, and other such equipment.

[4] Based on data presented in a paper before the Research Section, National Council on Family Relations, Oakland, California, July 9, 1954.

TABLE 7-1————Percent of 202 middle-class and 341 lower-class fathers in Tampa, Florida, who usually do alone or who share with other family members household tasks listed*

Task	PERCENT OF MIDDLE-CLASS FATHERS WHO USUALLY:		PERCENT OF LOWER-CLASS FATHERS WHO USUALLY:	
	Do	Share	Do	Share
1. Fix broken things (for example, electrical appliances, toys)	54	20	55	29
2. Lock up at night	39	29	33	30
3. Take care of yard	11	34	14	38
4. Take care of garbage and trash	15	11	21	14
5. Pick up and put away clothes	0	19	3	16
6. Get breakfast	5	13	2	7
7. Set breakfast table	4	7	1	8
8. Get day's main meal	0.5	5	3	7
9. Do dishes for day's main meal	2	4	1	5
10. Do family wash	0.5	4	1	6
11. Clear breakfast table	1.5	4	1.5	4
12. Clear table for day's main meal	1.5	3	1	4
13. Clean and dust	0	1.5	1	5
14. Make beds	0.5	2	1	4
15. Set table for day's main meal	1	1	0.5	4
16. Do breakfast dishes	1.5	1	1	3
17. Mend family's clothes	0.0	2	2	1.5
18. Do ironing	0.0	1.5	1	3

* Theodore B. Johannis, Jr., based on data presented in a paper before the Research Section, National Council on Family Relations, Oakland, California, July 9, 1954.

Most profound of all has been the change in the value systems of the male. In an earlier day, and to an extent in more isolated rural areas today, all of the arts and all things domestic were defined as effeminate and shunned by the male. The boy talented in music could expect the scorn of his father, maybe even of his mother, and certainly of other boys and adults of the community, if he indulged this talent. As vocations, all of the arts—drama, sculpture, painting, even writing and scholarship—were looked upon as effeminate. Few males aspired in these directions.

No boy dared dream of these kinds of accomplishments and expect to be accepted in his neighborhood.

Thomas Wolfe, one of the greatest of the American novelists, who grew up in Asheville, North Carolina, describes in his book *Look Homeward, Angel* the disappointment he was to his parents and to his father, particularly, when he chose to write. His father thought his gifted son should go into law.

Many boys hesitate, even now, to indulge their desire to cook. That activity, perhaps especially in rural cultures, has traditionally been effeminate. In urban life, the arts are more often considered as natural to the masculine temperament as to the feminine. In radio, stage, and screen, in sculpture, writing, and music, and also in cooking, the doors are as open to men as to women, and the roles are as readily accepted by men as by women.

Finally, with the entrance of women into numerous vocations, it is not impossible for the male and female roles to be reversed in the field of parenthood itself. There are a few families in which the mother is a driving, ambitious person, and in which the father has actually taken over the maternal role insofar as his becoming the emotional center of the household is concerned. In such cases, the father actually mothers the children, giving them the affection and intimate attention which children require. While these instances are rare and perhaps not yet fully approved by the culture, they do represent the extreme to which the male role has been modified and can be modified in our day.

The twentieth-century democratization of the American home has played a significant part in refashioning the domestic role of men. This new pattern of family life encourages the maximum involvement of the father and husband in family affairs. Thus not only do modern wives demand greater involvement on the part of their husbands and not only do modern occupations allow time for this greater domestic involvement, but, most important of all, the modern male actually seeks this involvement for his own satisfaction.

When marriage and family relationships are based upon companionship rather than upon economic considerations and rigidly patterned institutional roles, the male is found to seek the company of his wife and children more than in the past. The husband who, for example, bathes the children while his wife washes the evening's dishes, does so not only out of a sense of obligation or because of his wife's insistence. He enjoys this opportunity to play with his youngsters and to feel that he is contributing to their daily care and development. By reducing the number of his wife's after-dinner tasks he also insures their maximum number of hours together as a couple.

An occasional cartoon still features the aproned, bedraggled, domesticated husband, but such cartoons are becoming fewer and less popular. The apron, the dustpan, the dishcloth, and diaper pins are symbols of his new domesticity, it is true; but today we are coming to realize that they may also be symbols of a deeper and more satisfying family life than men have ever had before.

Even the child-training function, traditionally considered a female one, is shared by the male today. Johannis' study of father roles with an urban sample taken in Tampa, Florida, in 1953 shows this strikingly (Table 7-2).

TABLE 7-2————Percent of 202 middle-class and 341 lower-class fathers in Tampa, Florida, who usually assume or share child-training functions listed*

Task	Middle-class fathers (percent)	Lower-class fathers (percent)
1. Teach the children right from wrong and how the family expects them to behave	82	79
2. Teach the children facts, skills, and how to do things	80	75
3. Punish the children when they do something wrong	76	76
4. Tell the children what time to come in at night	73	70
5. See that the children have fun	68	67
6. Help the children choose what they will do when they finish school	65	58
7. See that the children have good table manners	50	47
8. See that the children go to bed on time	40	49
9. See that the children do their homework	44	40
10. Help the children with their schoolwork	49	35
11. Care for the children when they are sick	35	38
12. See that the children get to school or work on time	32	25
13. Get the children up on time in the morning	28	20
14. See that the children eat the right foods	19	19
15. See that the childhen wear the right clothes	3	7
16. See that the children get washed and dressed	5	5

* Johannis, *op. cit.*

The first three items may always have been largely in the male's hands in the rural society which is the American heritage. If so, these data indicate that they have carried over into urban life. But fathers share the responsibilities of training in many other phases of behavior, as these data show.[5]

5 *Ibid.*

Strain in Contemporary Male Roles

Helen Hacker[6] sees that the masculine role has been greatly modified by the new role demands of the female, and somewhat to the male's disadvantage. She finds, first, that many of the role demands of an earlier period still exist and may have been increased by the numerous status pressures now centering around the traditional role of bread winner. Second, she feels that the male may suffer from feelings of inadequacy because of the uncertainty and ambiguity of his role expectations. She finds that he is particularly confused about his own masculinity. It is sometimes hard to know what is masculine today, and what kinds of masculinity will be accepted. Finally, she finds that there are problems in adapting male roles to the new freedoms and responsibilities of women.

Hacker feels particularly that man's status as a lover has been challenged. Man's evaluation of himself from time immemorial has been supported by his dominance in the sex act. Historically this has been an almost unilateral male expression. Today his sex prowess is being determined more and more by his ability to evoke a full sexual response from the female. The new sexual emancipation of women has in a definite way been a threat to this key aspect of his masculinity. She believes male ego adequacy is dependent on sexual success. The female's is not. A woman can have status and not live up to any of the standards of femininity. A man cannot be a man without living up to standards of masculinity. A woman can be unfeminine and still be important as a person. To use Hacker's phraseology, "there is a neuter category for women, but not for men." She sees increasing homosexuality as part of the flight of men from the stigma of their inadequate relationship with women.

She sees the male's position in society being challenged in many subtle ways. Women are concerned with survival; men with honor, but man's honor in many areas is now subject to question.

Do Unique Male Roles Exist?

We have stressed the fact that there has been forced change in male roles in modern culture so that they may be more in harmony with the changing roles of women. Do distinct male roles still persist? There is little doubt that the strong, domineering, aggressive, pugnacious male of frontier days has been modified, just as the gentle, passive, submissive female has become a character of yesteryear. Yet there is little

6 Helen Meyer Hacker, "The New Burdens of Masculinity," *Marriage and Family Living*, 19:227-233, August, 1957.

doubt that men are still trained to be more worldly, more materialistic, and more success-minded. Men still seem to be more politically and community oriented than women and to find less support in religion and virtue. Although their interests in domestic tasks and activities have greatly increased, although they are more aware of the psychological and social needs of their children, they are still less gentle in disposition, less family-centered, and certainly less domestically oriented than are women.

Strength, courage, the ignoring of minor infirmities, are still values of the male subculture, not the significant values they were and are in agrarian culture, but still genuine values. Men still rate themselves and each other more in terms of efficiency, competence, material success, and prowess in sports and in sex than in terms of beauty, refinement, virtue, and goodness. It is probable that the average man still rates leisure below work, and luxury below the tools of productivity.

It appears also that woman expects many of these traits in man even though she has encroached on all his prerogatives. Many women still want the male to be strong when the test comes; many wish at times to feel dependent. They want to be treated as an equal; they do not wish to be dominated ruthlessly, pushed around, made subservient and made to feel lower in status, but they still admire and feel more safe with a strong male if college class discussions are indicative of her attitudes. If these assumptions are correct, men still have to display some of the traditional elements of courage and roughness to meet the expectation of the female subculture.

These expectations of masculinity have not spared the male a certain amount of conflict and anxiety. In a strictly male-dominated culture he did not have to be careful in drawing the line on his dominance. If he overstepped, the woman was not likely to challenge him. Today, even those elements of masculinity approved by the female must be displayed with discretion. How masculine he must be in order to win and hold her depends on the particular woman and her conception of the male's place in the family relationship. He risks being the offender in the delicate balance of role relationships, but she is more likely to be the one to take issue and to decide when he has overstepped his bounds. Women take the initiative in most of the divorce actions today.[7]

Even the timing of the sex act itself, traditionally controlled by the male, has to some extent been taken out of his control in modern culture. The female who was trained to a passive role in the marriage bed and taught that to be assertive was to be vulgar never put him on trial. Today, the female may also take the initiative in the sexual relationship, and she may properly recognize her needs as the equivalent of his own. He is often put on trial and may be found wanting.

[7] Discussed with support of data in a later chapter.

Deceptive Symbols of the Female's Sharing Roles

Prior to any marriage, the average young woman is likely to display considerably more interest in performing joint roles on a sharing basis than she will be willing or able to continue after the marriage is concluded. The great emphasis on companionship, today a value which serious couples rate above love as a basis for mate choice,[8] has led the young woman to go all out in being a pal in the man's world. She has adopted the short haicut and donned slacks; she goes hiking, hunting, skiing, hot-rodding, and fishing. Many of her clothes have become more utilitarian, less delicate, and less alluring. She has adopted the male's manner of speech, even his strong language. She may sometimes share his broad humor; she patronizes the tavern; she smokes. Her liberties in the area of sublimated sex behavior are very broad, catering to males' recognized sex needs.

In her youth the gun, fishing rod, skis, golf clubs, and other paraphernalia of the rugged outdoor type are indicative to the male that she shows the same eagerness for speed, blood, and gore as he. She has become a worker beside him and is perhaps more likely than he to lay by a nest egg for establishing a home. Thus she proves to him that she is a real companion and that this companionship is likely to cost him nothing. He retains the traditional statuses; enjoys the traditional recreational forms, and she is a real pal to him, undemanding, enthusiastic, making him feel that life is complete.

It would be unfair to claim that all of this is part of the deceptive technique of the female in winning her man. Many modern young women thoroughly enjoy these activities, but many who participate in them do so as part of the necessary game for capturing the kind of male they want. After marriage, however, the requirements of home and family will most likely make this type of mutual role participation difficult, if not impossible, except on rare occasions. Then the male finds that he must seek other companionship, usually of his own sex. At the same time he will find himself drawn more tightly into the inner circle of the family. The role demands of the female, so unapparent prior to marriage, may become very great. Whether they are greater where the palship has been establishd prior to marriage is a matter of speculation. Certainly much of the after-marriage palship must be in relation to domestic activities, yard- and home-centered.

The male may find also that most of his pal relationships, rather than being in the field, on the golf course, or in a boat, are at social functions,

8 Ernest Burgess and Paul Wallin, *Engagement and Marriage* (Philadelphia: J. B. Lippincott Co., 1953).

church, PTA, and other institutionalized relationships which are more carefully structured, and which may or may not be pleasing to him, depending on his own inclinations. One suspects that today many males who have been very much outdoor oriented, or sports oriented, once they are married become oriented toward domestic activities and family-centered institutional activities to a point they never dreamed possible. If they make the adjustment readily, there may be a definite gain to the family. If they make this transition with resentment, feeling they have sacrificed their roles and liberties as men, or feel they have been denied the right to function in the male subculture, it may create issues that are quite disastrous to the marriage.[9] The same thing may apply to a woman who feels she has been denied her right to work, or other role activities.

The adjustments required after marriage are undoubtedly related to the degree of honest understanding that couples have of their respective expectations in these areas.

This analysis is presented, not primarily in a criticism of women or in justification of men, but rather as an effort to clarify premarital role expectations that may not always be honest and straightforward.

The Strain of Harmonizing Roles

The strain put upon a wife in meeting role expectations of her husband and his family, in adapting to the demands of his work schedule, in moving to the location of his work, etc., are the most severe adjustments made. Women bear the brunt of marriage adjustment. But there is a case for the male's problem which seems to be of increasing significance. The crux lies in his taking a wife from the college, school, or work situation in which she has established roles and statutes which are precious to her, and which she may in one way or another project on him. With most women today, entering marriage from either the work or school situation has become a near universal situation.

To make the problem concrete and illustrate how the role shift of the female impinges on the man marrying her, we take the situation of the boss who marries his secretary. In the office her role as secretary has been well defined. He gives her orders, makes the decisions. She does his secretarial work, buys small items from petty cash, keeps a list of his appointments and reminds him when they come due. She controls the coming of persons for interviews and conferences. She is his confidante in many important business decisions. Then they marry. Is he still her boss or does he now become her equal? Who is to give the orders? Who decides the coming of guests? Who handles the money?

9 Charles W. Hobart, "Disillusionment in Marriage and Romanticism," *Marriage and Family Living*, 20:156-162, May, 1958.

What about the role changes of the boss? He has been used to pressing the buzzer or switching on the intercommunication system and having a woman appear to do all his office chores. She has been a pleasant person, always neatly dressed and properly made up in the appropriate cosmetics. She has treated all his business as confidential. She has been willing to stay overtime and sacrifice her own interests for his at times when work was pressing. He has learned to shift all routine to her, to depend on her for his memory work.

Now he is her husband rather than her boss. There is no buzzer or intercommunication system. He makes his own telephone calls and shares the home work by answering some of the calls coming into the home. He shares money matters with his wife, and likely as not is expected to help her with the home chores and baby care. More often than not, she rather than he makes the social engagements in which they will spend their leisure time. In the office he says without fear of contradiction: "Tell them I'm not in. It's too nice a day not to be on the golf course." Does he tell her that at home now and go unchallenged?

This example shows how marriage roles differ from many other roles in everyday life, and how impossible it is today to handle roles of husbands and wives by custom. They have to be worked out by each couple for themselves. A good secretary may or may not be a good wife, and a good boss may be a wretched husband—will be if he tries to demand of a wife the same kind of loyalty, obedience, and sacrifice he expects of a private secretary. Secretaries like to work for the big boss who manipulates men, materials and money on a large scale, but wives don't like to be manipulated.

Protected Male Domains

Several years ago when smoking was becoming common among women, an anthropologist predicted that cigarette smoking would soon become a strictly feminine pastime; that once the female took up the practice, it would no longer be appropriate for men to smoke cigarettes. He was basing his judgment on the tendency of all cultures to assign certain practices to one sex or the other. He apparently failed to take into account either that the cigarette habit is very hard to break or that we are approaching a time when men do not resent encroachment on their cherished prerogatives; for men have not given up the smoking of cigarettes with the growth in cigarette smoking by women.

When women can take over men's vices and men still do not drop them, does any protected reserve of male prerogative remain? LeMasters contends that there is still a tavern society that is basically the male world, that there are many male organizations that constitute the male-club society from which the female is excluded; the Elks Club, the Moose, the Masons, the American Legion and other veterans' organizations, some athletic clubs, some luncheon clubs, some hunting clubs are a unique part of this male society.[10]

Expense-account society is a male world which women, and particularly wives, rarely share. A survey by the Dartnell Corporation shows that the typical top-layer businessman travels some 30,000 miles on 19 trips, with 54 days away from home per year. Louis Harris and Associates estimate than 86 of every 100 airline trips are business trips. The corporation bill may run as high as four million for travel; many companies have a bill running a million or more dollars.[11]

While there are men who really hate travel, and some who refuse jobs with extensive travel, these jobs do carry status. Travel itself is a status symbol. Many who enjoy it, picture its dismal aspects to their wives, telling them of the boredom and loss of sleep. To the home-bound wife the romance of it, the adventure, the breadth of experience, may inspire envy. Often too, it is the basis of suspicion and distrust as she reads of the call-girl society of business travel. Few companies are willing or able to pay the cost of travel for the wife, and even if they could, the wife with young children is not free to join her husband in the expense-account world.

Much of the business world is a male society. There is undoubtedly much in the world of the man that most women do not understand and do not want to understand. The operation of the stock and commodity markets, the phenomenon of inflation, or the significance of interest, are matters much less likely to concern her than the male. There is also a world of mechanics, with the torsion bars, the gear ratio, and a thousand other details of mechanical precision that are to date primarily male interests. It is not that women do not have the capacity to understand these refinements of technology, merely that their interests are more likely to be devoted to other matters.

Bossard has pointed out that sex distinctions are apparent in the very vocabulary that survives in the male and female subculture.[12] The male uses a language of stronger terms, while the female uses her own more gentle adjectives. For example, the adjective "lovely" is used extensively

10 E. E. LeMasters, *Modern Courtship and Marriage* (New York: The Macmillan Co., 1957).

11 For a discussion of this male world see *This Week*, May, 1964, pp. 14-16. For an earlier study see William H. Whyte, Jr., "The Wives of Management," *Fortune*, 44:86 ff., October, 1951; and his "Corporation and the Wife," *Fortune*, 44:109 ff., November, 1951.

12 James H. S. Bossard, "Private Worlds of Men and Women," *Family Life*, 18:1-3, October, 1955.

by women, rarely by men. The stock phrases of men and women differ, as well as the subjects they discuss. The child grows up learning the appropriate phraseology of his subculture.

In conclusion, the male's once lofty position has not gone unchallenged in this day of approaching sex equality. His authority, his sexual prerogatives, his favored roles have all been challenged, and he has gradually become domesticated as the male of the frontier could never have been. He is perhaps as a consequence more closely drawn into the intimate family circle of women and children than ever before.

Problems

1. Do you feel that men in America are becoming more effeminate? Is this equally true of all sections, or is it an urban phenomenon? Is it as true of one region as another.
2. If you consider that men are becoming more effeminate, how do you explain this and what are some of the risks, if any?
3. Do you agree that at times most women want their man to be the strong commanding type whom they can look up to?
4. Occasionally one sees a very strong female type married to a very flexible and spineless male. Do you think there is a tendency for the stronger female to seek the weaker male in marriage?
5. Momism is sometimes referred to as a curse of American society. Appraise this view.
6. Do you agree that there is considerable confusion in male roles today? Illustrate.

Selected References

ARTICLES IN BOOKS OF READINGS

SUSSMAN, Marvin B., *Sourcebook in Marriage and the Family,* Second Edition (Boston: Houghton Mifflin Co., 1963).
    1. KOMAROVSKY, Mirra, "Functional Analysis of Sex Roles," pp. 125-132.
KRICH, A. M. (Editor), *Men: The Variety and Meaning of Their Sexual Experience* (New York: Dell Publishing Co., Inc., 1954).
    2. BENEDEK, Therese, "The Meaning of Fatherhood," Ch. 7.
CAVAN, Ruth Shonle, *Marriage and the Family in the Modern World: A Book of Readings* (New York: Thomas Y. Crowell Co., 1960).

3. Metropolitan Life Insurance Company, "The American Husband," Reading 7.
4. GLICK, Paul C., and MILLER, Herman P., "The Importance of College Education in Career Success," Reading 53.
5. DUFFIN, B. Keith, "Career as a Lifetime Choice," Reading 52.
6. Dun and Bradstreet, "Executive Staff and Distaff: A Wives' Eye View," Reading 54.

WINCH, Robert F., and others, *Selected Studies in Marriage and the Family*, Revised Edition (New York: Holt, Rinehart & Winston, Inc., 1962).

7. HENRY, William E., "The Business Executive: A Study in the Psycho-dynamics of Social Role," pp. 103-110.
8. WHYTE, William H., Jr., "The Wife Problem," pp. 111-125.
9. *The Daily Northwestern*, "The Problem of Pants," p. 133.

General References

ASHLEY-MONTAGU, M. F., *Education and Human Relations* (New York: Grove Press, Inc., 1958).

FARBER, Seymour M., and WILSON, Roger H. L. (Editors), *The Potential of Woman* (New York: McGraw-Hill Book Co., 1963). This is a symposium. Part Five deals with "The Male Revolt."

FOOTE, Nelson N., "New Roles for Men and Women," *Marriage and Family Living*, 23:325-329, November, 1961.

HACKER, Helen Meyer, "The New Burdens of Masculinity," *Marriage and Family Living*, 12:227-233, August, 1957.

HOFFMAN, Lois Wladis, "Effects of the Employment of Mothers on the Power Relations and the Division of Household Tasks," *Marriage and Family Living*, 22:27-35, February, 1960.

LANDIS, Judson T., "A Re-examination of the Role of the Father as an Index of Family Integration," *Marriage and Family Living*, 24:122-128, May, 1962.

LANDIS, Paul H., *Social Problems: Unfulfilled Welfare Aspirations in Nation and World* (Philadelphia: J. B. Lippincott Co., 1959), Ch. 15.

LEMASTERS, E. E., *Modern Courtship and Marriage* (New York: The Macmillan Co., 1957), Chs. 22, 23.

LYNN, David B., "The Husband-Father Role in the Family," *Marriage and Family Living*, 23:295-296, August, 1961.

RIESMAN, David, "Permissiveness and Sex Roles," *Marriage and Family Living*, 12:211-217, August, 1959.

Work in the Lives of Married Women, A Symposium, Columbia University (New York: Columbia University Press, 1958).

8

Unsolved Problems in
Role Behavior

The cultural approach to social life leaves little room for
biological determinism in the area of human social behavior. While nature may better prepare men for some roles and women
for others, most roles can be reversed by culture. Margaret Mead, for
example, in her anthropological studies of sex and temperament among
the primitive Mundugumor and Tchambuli women, found that the men
were the submissive, fearful, nervous ones; the women the virile, aggressive, domineering sex.[1] In their training from childhood, boys and girls
were taught to play roles which are the opposite of the sex roles of our
culture and most other cultures, indicating that personality traits of men
and women have grown, in part at least, out of the roles which society
expects each sex to play.

We must assume that men and women will continue to work out
their role relationships through the process of social interaction with no
appeal to innate predisposition or cultural tradition. A new age demands
new patterns of behavior.

The Ego Struggle in Role Conflict

Perhaps the greatest ego struggle in the relationships of husbands and wives, growing out of the new roles of women, lies in the area
of work. Prior to marriage, girls become fond of having a pay check of
their own; they learn to spend in ways which men consider unimportant.

[1] Margaret Mead, *Sex and Temperament in Three Primitive Societies* (New York:
McGraw-Hill Book Co., 1935), p. 119.

The superiority of the male role has lain primarily in his ability to earn and to control spending. His status is threatened when he can no longer control income—and he no longer can do so if the wife has money of her own. This became apparent in Great Britain when the family allowance was introduced. The lower-class male had always dominated by virtue of the pay check. When the family allowance was introduced, payments were made to the wife directly in order to help guarantee that children's needs would be met first. These lower-class women began to assert them- selves in new ways, to demand greater independence, and to make it clear to their husbands that they no longer ruled the roost unchallenged.[2]

One must recognize that in some relationships between husbands and wives, role reversal provides mutual insight. But if rivalry results, there is a serious threat to the marriage relationship. Margaret Mead is con- vinced that the male's ego strength has largely depended upon his posi- tion as supporter of the family, and that therefore cultures have defined certain work roles as of first importance and have denied to women the right to perform them.[3]

The Power Struggle

Blood and Hamblin have studied the effect of the wife's work- ing on the power structure of the American family.[4] Although they found evidence of her greater feeling of equality because of her work, the working wife seems to have little more effect on the power structure as evidenced in decision-making than does the nonworking wife. It was found that 45 percent of the working wives' suggestions in the home were adopted compared to 43 percent of those of the nonworking wives. The median amount of housework performed by husbands whose wives worked was 25 percent, while the husbands of nonworking wives per- formed 15 percent. Working wives wanted their husbands to do more housework, and the researchers believed that work sharing was a matter of cooperation rather than a shift in roles involving the power structure of the marriage.

Perhaps the most striking finding of this study is the great degree of equalitarian behavior in both decision-making roles and work roles. It may well be that the power struggle has passed for the average American family. If so, this means that wives as well as husbands are recognizing the responsibility that is inseparable from power. Wives as well as hus- bands must face the consequences of their decisions. Equality, in other

2 So marriage counselors in London advised the study group led by the author.
3 Margaret Mead, *Male and Female* (New York: William Morrow & Co., Inc., 1949).
4 Robert O. Blood, Jr., and Robert L. Hamblin, "The Effect of the Wife's Employ- ment on the Family Power Structure, *Social Forces*, 36:247-252, May, 1958.

words, has its price. There may well be in many marriages, also, the knowledge that to misuse power is to threaten the love relationship, perhaps the marriage itself.

Certainly if the power struggle has ceased in the more privileged classes in the United States, it has not done so in most cultures of the world. The great power struggle for equalitarian roles is only in its beginning. The right to work and the right to spend are key issues, as they have been in the evolution of equalitarian roles in this country.

Environmental Pressures

Lynn White, whose experiences as president of Mills College —a woman's college in California—makes his views significant, states that the suburb has created a new type of family life which is neither rural nor urban as it relates to men's and women's roles. This new family is definitely white-collar and leisurized. Both inside and outside the home, there is convergence of interest of the male and female. Husbands have been brought into the home as never before, and women have been drawn out into the work world in order to make marriage possible and to make family life more satisfactory in terms of material possessions.

The work world now embraces many jobs which do not require brute strength and which women can satisfactorily perform. The shortened workday permits the husband to enter family life in a way that has never been possible before. Men and women dress more alike and act more alike; White believes they actually feel more alike. The "crucible" of this new alchemy is the suburban home which represents the key both to living and recreation.

White cites *Sunset Magazine* as indicative of this new suburban trend. This magazine is devoted to home and outside yard activities, and White concludes that "men and women are turning to marriage and larger families, to the home and its industries, to counteract the loneliness of this age."

With this new type of role interchange, White feels that the big problem of education is not women's education but men's. He feels that authorities in men's colleges still work under the assumption that men are going to live celibate lives. Men students may feel a need for orientation toward family life. When Radcliffe girls were offered a course in child psychology at Harvard, more men than women enrolled. Whether this was a genuine interest in child psychology or in meeting Radcliffe girls one does not know.

Ashley-Montagu, seeing the development of love in children as the great challenge both to parenthood and to teaching, feels that we should quit teaching women as though they were going to be men. We should proceed on the assumption that they are going to be mothers, and train all women first of all for motherhood. This is the way to the improvement of humanity.

The second phase of their training should be in the direction of "social participation" so that they will not merely be "second-class or third-rate men," or an inferior group, but complete persons with rights, privileges, and obligations in the community. Being a good mother and wife, he sees, as the greatest service a woman can perform in her society. When the raising of children is largely completed, she then has many useful years ahead in which to contribute creatively to other activities.[5]

With the leisure and material comfort that modern life has brought to the family, White feels the big problem now is not one of staying alive, but of wanting to live. This he feels calls for emphasis on things of the spirit so that the modern family will not be destroyed by idleness and boredom.[6]

Role Conflicts Inevitable

One of the most certain aspects of the relationship of men and women today, both before and after marriage, is that of role conflict. Such conflict is inevitable because of the different perspectives on roles which men and women hold for themselves and for each other.

The values of the female subculture today are very much in conflict. The residual values of an earlier age persist in the home training of a girl, yet the school curriculum, especially the college curriculum, treats the girl much the same as it treats the man insofar as goal expectations are concerned. The possible exception is the curriculum in home economics. Moreover, there is little, if any, direct training of the male in role expectations with regard to the female. The man may expect of his wife the same role behavior as his mother practiced. In fact, this will probably be the strongest conditioning element in his upbringing, as far as attitudes toward the roles of his wife are concerned. Yet, neither husband nor wife may be able in marriage to follow out their own concept of what their role should be. The force of circumstances bears very heavily on roles in urban industrial society. Here a high standard of living, high pressure of advertising, and the needs of a comfortable home often compel a type of role behavior on the part of the woman, particularly in the work world, which is foreign both to her and her husband's expectations.

5 M. F. Ashley-Montagu, *Education and Human Relations* (New York: Grove Press, Inc., 1958), see especially Ch. 10.

6 Lynn White, Jr., "The Changing Context of Women's Education," *Marriage and Family Living*, 17:291-295, November, 1955.

One sees this among college couples. Consider, for example, one young couple who came from a fairly high standard of living and had two children while in college. In order to maintain what they considered a decent way of life, the wife had to obtain a job. Without her husband's knowledge, she became a carhop waitress in a local establishment. When the husband found out he was so embarrassed at the threat to their status that he tried to get her to quit. Failing in this, he went to the manager of the establishment and asked him to fire his wife. It was some weeks before his wife found out that her husband had tried to get her fired. She was very much upset. Her comment was, "What if I had been fired, and not known the real reason." It created a rift which will heal only with the passage of time.

Among college wives one sees many contradictions between role expectations and the actual roles circumstances demand. Couples put up with this situation with the rationalization that "when we are done with college we'll really live!"

A description of one of the worst cases of "couple conflict" that has come to the writer's attention is quoted here because it represents many aspects of the interaction between husband and wife involving differing role concepts, differences of equality, and differences even in the feelings of romance—the husband using his college contacts to sharpen his appreciation of the opposite sex.

> I have found many problems as a result of my working. I do feel intellectually on a lower level than my husband. There is no time to read and study things of interest to me that would help me. Although this may not bother some people it does bother me a great deal. Our social life is nil. No time, always studying. We have few friends and they are in my husband's field only. I object to this greatly and would like to join University Dames where there is a cross section, so to speak, of various fields, but my husband just wants me to be interested in Veterinarians' Wives, a very narrow group. No time for just relaxing, knitting, sewing, etc., unless housework suffers and my husband objects to that most strongly. Insecurity. I sometimes feel my husband could have just married me to help him through school.
>
> Working poses another problem. It tires me so that when I have to go home and work some more (housework) it's enough to drive me out of my mind. Rush, rush all the time. I'm nervous and cranky as a result and give my husband a very bad time.
>
> Another problem—there is not as much time for personal appearance as there was before we were married and my husband does so appreciate the opposite sex and how much more attractive they (women students) are.[7]

[7] I am indebted for this example to Mr. Joe Perry, who interviewed a group of working girls on the campus of Washington State University as a part of a seminar project.

Role conflict may lie in the fact that the wife actually wants to go to school and regrets the fact that she is married and working for the sole purpose of making it possible for her husband to finish his education. She may feel that her work life actually decreases her attractiveness and holding power over her husband. She recognizes the chief place of the husband as a breadwinner, but has a very difficult time sublimating her own desire for an education. Often entering into these feelings is a fear that the husband will outgrow her or find someone more attractive.

Other wives resent deeply the fact that, while they work themselves to fatigue daily, the husband does not help adequately with the housework or even assume the amount of financial responsibility which he should. Perry pointed out, after personal interviews with 18 working wives, that college couples tend to subordinate many goals to that of finishing school and live in the hope that most of their role conflicts will disappear once they are out of school.[8] While he admits schooling often aggravates role conflicts, creating difficulties which might not appear under other circumstances, Perry feels couples may be too optimistic about a change in role conflicts and role expectations after school.

They do have one consoling factor while in school, however. Other couples are also having role conflicts.

The writer suspects that the worst role conflicts in husband-wife relations are to be found among couples both of whom have already obtained a college degree. Robert Coughland, writing on "The Changing Roles in Modern Marriage" for *Life* magazine, describes what he found in the suburbs as the "suburban syndrome."[9] Here the wife who worked before marriage, or who was otherwise very active, finds her married life one of boredom. She has been educated and conditioned toward a stimulating type of work and intellectual activity which carries prestige and ego satisfaction. She marries and finds herself in the psychologically degrading position of being "just a housewife." Coughland feels that many intelligent married couples confined to a small home or apartment with children needing constant care and with little money for servants or luxuries, face the problem of a morbid wife whose emotional condition may actually be bordering on depression.

The writer encountered this same situation in leading a study group in London. The group was advised by a psychiatrist that, prior to the World War II London bombings, the greatest case load the practicing London psychiatrist had was what came to be termed "suburban neurosis." The bombings and war brought the chance for wives to work for money or in the social services. Women then felt themselves a part of the ongoing world and the case load in this category was reduced to nothing.

8 *Ibid.*
9 *Life*, Vol. 47, December 24, 1956.

This experience is contrary to the long-held assumption by sociologists that the working wife had more problems than the nonworking wife. It appears now, however, in certain levels of American society at least, or perhaps rather on certain levels of education, that the nonworking wife shows just as many problems, mostly of a psychological nature, as does the working wife.[10] This leaves out of the discussion the problems of the children of working mothers. At this point our interest is in role conflicts of husbands and wives rather than in problems of children, which will be handled elsewhere.

One of the best descriptions of role behavior of the wife in the highly complex and stratified structure of the large industrial community is given by sociologist Whyte, working for *Fortune* magazine. Whyte analyzed this role behavior and its relationship to the status hierarchy in the industrial community. The good executive wife, according to Whyte,[11] is not a fixer, meddler, climber, or one who pushes a husband around, but rather a stabilizer who makes the home a place where the lonely and the overworked executive may relax. At the same time, she must be a gregarious social operator and be able to put people at ease. Several unwritten rules apply to her conduct. She (1) doesn't talk shop or gossip with the girls, (2) doesn't invite superiors in rank until after they have made the first bid, (3) keeps away from the office, (4) avoids getting chummy with wives of men her husband may soon pass in the climb, (5) isn't disagreeable to company people she meets—you never know . . . , (6) is attractive, (7) is a phone pal of her husband's secretary, (8) never gets tight at a company party, (9) isn't too good. She keeps up with the Joneses, but doesn't too obviously get ahead. Getting ahead must be timed exquisitely in connection with her husband's advancement.

It is pointed out that if the husband moves up faster than his age group, the wife is almost forced to move into a higher-class residential community, because he so completely controls the destiny of the lives and families of her former intimates that she no longer feels at home with them or they with her.

Family possessions are a symbol of rank. One does not get a grand piano until one "is ready for it" in terms of the husband's place in the managerial hierarchy. Automobiles, particularly, are symbols of one's place in the system. One moves cautiously from one model to the next

---

[10] See, for example, Harvey J. Locke and Muriel Mackeprang, "Marital Adjustment and the Employed Wife," *American Journal of Sociology*, 54:556-558, May, 1949; see also, Ivan Nye, "Employment Status of Mothers and Marital Conflict, Permanence, and Happiness," *Social Problems*, 6:260-267, Winter, 1959; see also F. Ivan Nye and Lois Wladis Hoffman (Editors), *The Employed Mother in America* (Chicago: Rand McNally & Co., 1963).

[11] William H. Whyte, Jr., "The Wives of Management," *Fortune*, 44:86, October, 1951; and his "Corporation and the Wife," *Fortune*, 44:109, November, 1951.

higher, leaving the luxury cars for the president and members of the board.

Whyte finds that the corporation does not object to a climbing executive getting a divorce, apparently assuming that he will choose a new wife more sympathetic to his position, work, and new status in the corporation hierarchy.

The Unsolved Sex-Ratio Problem

Seldom, in a world of wars and migrations, are sex ratios even. Uneven sex ratios call for modifications in behavior to increase bargaining power of the surplus sex. Figure 8-1 shows the recent trend in sex ratio by age. The great excess of females is in the older age bracket, because of the higher death rate of the male. But the data show males falling below the 100 level even in the early marriageable ages. The sex ratio is more uneven for nonwhites than for whites, there being a greater shortage of males. For example, in the age group 15 to 24, July 1, 1963, there were 99.2 white males per 100 females, among nonwhites there were only 95.4 males per 100 females. In the age group 25 to 44, the white ratio was 96.8 males per 100 females, for nonwhite 87.1 per 100.[12]

Since males tend to marry downward in age, a more precise measure of the marriagable age ratios of male and female must take this into account. Jacobson[13] has compared the ratios for males aged 20-25 to females aged 18-23. He gets the following ratios of males per 100 females:

Year	Males (20-25) per 100 Females (18-23)
1890	96
1900	96
1910	101
1920	96
1930	93
1940	96
1950	102
1960	98
1965	92

This comparison shows that we are now more short of males for females in the most marriageable age group than ever before, to be precise, eight males short per 100 females.

12 U. S. Department of Commerce, Bureau of the Census, Series P-25, No. 276.
13 Paul H. Jacobson, *American Marriage and Divorce* (New York: Holt, Rinehart & Winston, Inc., 1959), p. 33.

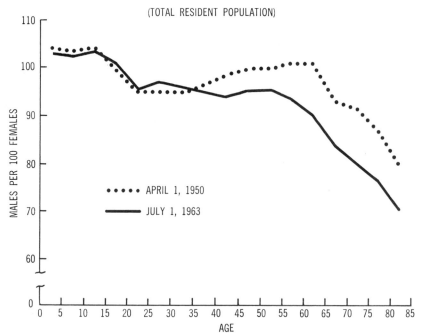

SEX RATIO (MALES PER 100 FEMALES)
OF THE POPULATION BY AGE,
UNITED STATES, 1963 AND 1950

(TOTAL RESIDENT POPULATION)

•••• APRIL 1, 1950

———— JULY 1, 1963

SOURCE: U. S. Department of Commerce, Bureau of the Census, "Estimates of the Population of the United States, by Age, Color, and Sex, July 1, 1963," Series P-25, No. 276, November 19, 1963, pp. 4-5.

FIGURE 8-1————Observe that although an excess of males is born, by the dating-marriage age, there is a deficiency. In the 15-24 age group, there are only 98.7 males per 100 females. By the 25-44 age group there are only 95.7 males per 100 females, a deficiency of more than 4 per 100. Among whites the ratio is less extreme than among nonwhites. Even larger is the problem of unequal sex distribution by type of community.

Migration greatly exaggerates sex-ratio differences in particular localities. Farm and small-town girls flock to the cities in higher proportions than do young men. This leaves both farm and small-town areas short of women of marriageable age, with the situation being more extreme in the farm and ranch areas. Large urban areas tend to have a great excess of women of marriageable age. The extent of the unbalance depends on the dominant occupational character of the city. Washington, D.C., for example, with its large clerical and professional force, is heavily female. Some industrial cities are less imbalanced; particularly those with heavy industries. In all cities, the sexes tend to segregate somewhat by occupation.

With the decrease in their bargaining power, a certain proportion of women tend to become more aggressive in mate seeking. They become more willing to use sex as a bargaining device in attracting and holding the male, and in trying to secure a favorable marriage. The uneven sex ratio is also a threat to the stability of marriage.

No doubt the uneven sex ratio has tended to develop greater aggressiveness on the part of the average urban female than existed in the more chivalrous rural culture of another day, in which women were taught to be modest and meek and to play the passive role in their relationships with the opposite sex. One must, of course, grant that there has always been a certain proportion of women who assumed the role of the aggressor in mate seeking, where the occasion seemed to demand it. We must also grant that the majority of women, even today in urban areas, still play a passive role.

The increase in the illegitimate birth rate[14] in this country, however, is suggestive that women are, in certain instances at least, using sex as a bargaining resource for marriage, particularly women in urban areas where illegitimacy rates are highest. In this respect, they may be approaching, by degree, standards of women in Northern Europe and Scandinavia where births out of wedlock run as high as 10 percent of all births.

If the sex-ratio situation should become critical, it is very probable that the more individualistic American women would come to demand artificial insemination, with the rights of motherhood out of wedlock by artificial inseminating being accorded full respectability. At present, it would seem that this day is some years ahead.

In Europe, after both world wars, polygamy was considered as a solution for the millions of women without prospects of marriage and legitimate motherhood. It was not adopted, but the uneven sex ratio did undoubtedly have an effect on the morals of women, as evidenced by the easy shift to respectable out-of-wedlock motherhood so widespread during the Hitler regime.[15]

14 The illegitimate birth rate increased by 80 percent during World War II and the postwar years. One cannot attribute too much of this to the sex ratio. The great increase was among girls of seventeen or younger. See Paul H. Landis, *Social Problems* (Philadelphia: J. B. Lippincott Co., 1959), p. 413. The number of reported illegitimate births increased from 150,300 in 1952 to 245,100 in 1962. The greatest increase was in the age group 25-29; see U. S. Department of Health, Education, and Welfare, "Illegitimacy and Dependency," Reprinted from *Indicators*, Washington, D. C., September, 1963.

15 Margaret Mead reports "it is said that the sex ratio in Germany after World War I may have been one of the factors which defeated the Weimar Republic and

In examining the changes that have occurred and are occurring in male and female roles, several questions inevitably come to mind. First of all, what does the future hold? Will the distinction between the parts played by men and women continue to fade until only those biologically determined remain? Second, since the merging of sex roles is conducive to greater equality, and therefore desirable in a democratic society, what can be done to facilitate the transition?

Must Role Differences Persist?

Even with the very decided trend toward merging of male and female roles and personalities during a half century, the significance of sex roles is still of vast importance. In the taboo field, our abhorrence of homosexuality and our legal inhumanity toward the homosexual are indicative of how important we consider the dividing line between the sexes. A man born with, or trained into, excessively effeminate traits has a rough time in our culture, as does the very masculinely inclined female.

The case of the effeminate American youth who submitted to months of painful surgery at the hands of a Danish physician in order to change his sex role attracted worldwide attention and interest. It was of no less interest in the United States than in countries where the gulf separating the sexes is far wider. Tragic, indeed, is the person who for some reason cannot fit the male-female subculture patterns of his culture.

The division of labor between men and women and the work roles of husband and wife vary greatly from society to society, but everywhere boys are brought up to know that they are expected to help provide for a woman and her children as part of their adult role.

This conditioning in itself affects personality patterns of male and female as they train for and take up their respective roles, and is a fact of life that cannot be fully evaded even in our machine age. As long as the institution of the family persists as society's approved relationship for conceiving and rearing children, it is likely that work roles and to some extent domestic and social roles will tend to differ between the sexes. If, however, state institutions continue to develop around child rearing—taking the child at an early age and keeping him for longer periods of time—distinctions between the roles of husband and wife can be expected to grow less clear. And if the educated woman and her husband can accept parenthood as a temporary but highly rewarding role, much frustration may be avoided.

---

gave rise to the Nazi Party. Jobs were given to the older men. This left young men unable to compete with older men for women's favors." Margaret Mead, *Male and Female* (New York: William Morrow & Co., Inc., 1949), p. 151.

Institutional Prerequisites to Sex Equality

Sex equality, on a biological level, is a matter with which society cannot deal. Some of the inherent differences in the sexual make-up of men and women have been discussed (Chapter 3). These will always be present. The matter of role development and personality formation, however, is to a large extent culturally determined. In this area society can bring about more sex equality than has been realized to date. Some allowance will always have to be made for biological differences, but many of the purely social differences can be obliterated in any society which sets out to do so. It is interesting, therefore, to speculate on some of the institutional prerequisites that are necessary for genuine equality in the social roles of men and women.

To attain genuine sex equality, certain conditions must exist in the culture which make the freedom of woman a possibility, not merely an ideal. Some conditions essential to this are: (1) economic equality, (2) social institutions which free the mother from complete subservience to the needs of the young child, (3) equal freedom with the male to participate in the sex act, (4) equal right of marital choice, and equal right in dissolving the marriage.

There may be other more debatable conditions—for example, the right to motherhood outside marriage if the culture insists that males choose the mates. Many women who would be excellent mothers are now denied motherhood. This condition could be corrected today by permitting single women to adopt children, or by artificial insemination. Sweden under certain circumstances does permit adoption by an unmarried mother. The right of artificial insemination outside of marriage, so far as the writer knows, does not exist anywhere.

Let us consider the four essential factors in sex equality and see to what extent they have been, or can be, realized in our society.

1. EQUAL ECONOMIC OPPORTUNITY

Equal economic opportunity means that women should receive the same pay as men for the same work in any occupational field they wish to enter. In order to make this possible, numerous adjustments are required in the culture. Sweden, where the employment of women is extensive, has achieved a high level of equality in this area. There has been no poverty in Sweden since at least 1890; there are no slums in Stockholm, and both men and women can obtain a job at equal rates of pay. For women to have equal opportunity for employment, the culture must take into consideration the fact of motherhood and its penalties. Before this can be a reality, various adjustments must be made in social institutions. This has been done in Sweden and some of the other Scandinavian countries by various devices—such as stopping work and receiving half pay some weeks before confinement, and continuing this throughout confinement and for a period of weeks afterward. The reduction in pay is offset by some sort of birth allowance. This birth allowance may be in cash, or, as in Sweden, the layette and various other items for the child may be provided. This latter arrangement presupposes that the state will pay some sort of family wage or family allowance and thus take into account the economic load of another child. In Sweden, as in most democratic countries of the world except our own, this is done by a family allowance which is paid by the government for each child from birth to sixteen years of age. Ordinarily this allowance is paid to the mother. In some countries, Canada for one, it is paid monthly—$6 to $8 per child, depending on age, from birth to age sixteen. In other countries, the allowance is paid on a quarterly basis.

For the mother, there must be assurance that when her confinement is over, her job will be waiting. Mothers have this assurance in Sweden and in the other Scandinavian countries. There must also be some sort of community system of medical care. This may take the form of state medicine, maternity insurance, or general insurance for medical-hospital care. Only in this way can serious economic anxieties be removed from the field of childbirth for the working mother.

Equal opportunity, not only for the mother but for any couple with children, can be assured only by some sort of public recognition of the burden of child rearing. The family allowance is one form of assistance. There are others.

Throughout much of Europe and Scandinavia, priority in public housing quarters and in cooperative housing units is based on a point system which takes into consideration the number of children in the family. In some countries, private homes for families with children are exempt from taxation for a long period of years after construction. These measures take into account the economic responsibilities of childbearing in a competitive economy where wages and salaries are the prevailing means of support. Only by such devices can the married worker have children without being penalized economically. To summarize, in competitive industrial societies there can be no economic equality except as parenthood is taken into account by some sort of allowance for children, and as supplemental institutions shift the load of child care from the individual worker to the social group.

In the United States, for example, we have the very difficult situation of couples trying to rear families on incomes that are the same as those of childless people. The childless people may live in luxury, but the couple with children may live in relative poverty. This has been demonstrated again and again. The Census data in the accompanying chart gives the picture as of 1957 in the United States (Figure 8-2).

CHILDREN AND INCOME

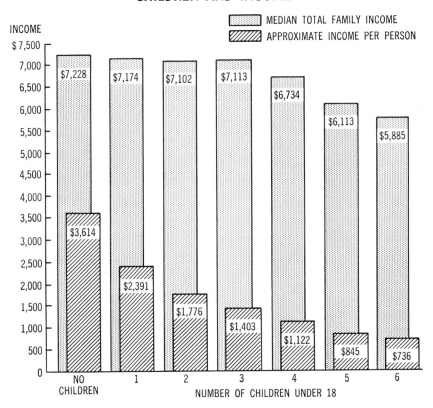

SOURCE: U. S. Department of Commerce, Bureau of the Census, "Income of Families and Persons in the United States, 1962," *Current Population Reports, Consumer Income,* Series P-60, No. 41, October 21, 1963, Table 5, p. 28.

FIGURE 8-2————The larger the family, the smaller the pieces into which the economic pie must be cut. Couples without children have an average per capita income of $3,614. Add a child and that average drops to $2,391 per capita. Add six children and it drops to $736 per capita.

It is certainly clear that the more children there are in a family, the smaller are the pieces into which the economic pie is cut. Labor leaders in the United States have fought a family allowance such as practically all industrialized countries now have. They want to see the wages of every worker raised to the point where families with children will have enough. The theory is commendable but illogical, for regardless of how high the level of living, those with small families or no children can still indulge in luxuries which the large family cannot aspire to. The situation of gross inequality would still prevail.[16]

2. FREEING THE MOTHER FROM SUBSERVIENCE TO THE CHILD'S NEEDS

The greatest handicap to sex equality in the United States and, for many of the more intelligent women, the most frustrating aspect of their marriage experience is the mother's constant subservience to the demands of the young child. The average working mother, if she is interested in employment, and particularly if she is career-minded, cannot be content with dropping her career to become a housekeeper and child's nurse.

In order to free the working mother and particularly the career-minded mother from these demands and still make it possible for her to have children, numerous adjustments are required in the culture. Our culture has not made these adjustments. We have, through the nursery school and kindergarten, freed part of the mother's time. During the war we made ambitious beginnings with nurseries for child care. These, however, were privately sponsored and required a cash payment by the mother, so that only the more prosperous mothers could afford them. There was then and there is now extensive neglect of children of working mothers.

Again one can cite Sweden and Denmark as countries which have provided at least some of the social institutions that help emancipate the working mother from the child.[17] In these countries large apartment houses, some exclusively for working couples or for unmarried mothers, with home service for the care of children and for the care of living quarters is provided. Some of these housing projects are cooperative; some are privately supported. For low-income groups the services are subsidized by the state or municipality—even the building itself is subsidized.

These housing units have nurseries which are open from six in the morning till eight at night. Here young children are given the best care by trained nurses and yet may spend the night with their families. For

[16] Few, if any, family allowance schemes or other subsidies in any nation are sufficient to completely equalize the burden of people having children with that of people having no children. The financial demands of parenthood are probably more nearly met in France than any other country.

[17] *Social Sweden* (Stockholm: Social Welfare Board, 1953).

every age group these units have summer play schools, after-school play schools, and provisions for an after-school snack, homework study, work-rooms, shops, sewing rooms, kitchens, libraries, art rooms, recreation rooms. Each group through the teens can be occupied creatively and under supervision until the mother and father return from work. In this way children are given constant care by professionals during the period when mothers and fathers are required to work.

That these institutions are effective in helping to socialize the child and in making him feel a part of the social system is evidenced by the fact that in Copenhagen, for example, a city of a million people, there are only a dozen or so court cases dealing with juvenile delinquents in a year's time. These compare with the thousands of cases that appear before the juvenile courts in the average American metropolitan community.

To have genuine sex equality, it must be generally recognized that motherhood is a worthwhile activity and an end in itself entirely apart from other work. This requires that the mother have help available through the community, help which will permit her to obtain some free-dom from the home, perhaps an annual vacation whether she can afford it or not, and other benefits.

In Sweden, couples who cannot afford baby-sitters may turn their children over to professionals without expense to themselves and with small expense to others, for an evening a week. Mothers who need it are given at municipal expense a two-week holiday completely apart from husband and children. The children are usually sent to camps.

While these measures are helpful in relieving mothers from the con-stant strain of caring for young children, their psychological importance probably far exceeds their physical benefit. These measures recognize that homemaking and motherhood are vocations of social importance, and grant them the same social status as other vocations.

3. EQUAL RIGHT TO PARTICIPATE IN THE SEX ACT

The double standard has long prevailed in our society and in many others. It assumes that the male has sex prerogatives which the female cannot share. Sex equality assumes that both man and woman have equal right to participate in the sex act and are free to do so with equal pro-tections and with equal safety. This is a hard goal to realize, and there has been practically no attempts to achieve it in American culture.

In the Scandinavian countries, steps have been taken which go a long way toward guaranteeing the equal freedom of male and female in the sex act. These steps involve financial protection of the woman and her child if premarital or extramarital relationships result in pregnancy, and also provide for equal status of both mother and child with women having children in wedlock.[18]

This discussion should not be interpreted as meaning that the writer recommends more extensive premarital and extramarital sex relations in our society. The point of the argument is that women should have whatever rights men have in this respect. If the culture taboos premarital or extramarital sex relations, they should be equally taboo for men and women. If the culture permits them, sex relationships should be equally accessible to women and men. Only so, can equality be a reality in this area.

This is one area in which the goal of equality is extremely difficult to realize, even with the Swedish type of financial protection mentioned. Men have, in most societies, been extremely jealous of women's sexual activity with others both premarital and extramarital. Where the male carries the economic load of supporting a woman and her child, he wishes to be certain that the child supported is really his own. Time only can tell what the new age of perfect control of conception will bring in the way of change.

4. EQUAL RIGHT OF MARITAL CHOICE AND OF DIVORCE

The choice of whether to marry or not to marry must belong to women, as to men, if there is to be genuine equality. For women, the choice has long been an economic one. In America today the woman who does not wish to marry can support herself on an approximately equal level with the male. We have achieved equality here.

Equal rights of divorce is also essential to sex equality. Perhaps we have achieved this, at least to some degree, although alimony in many cases is unjust to the male. So, also, are breach-of-promise suits, which have no place in a world of genuine sex equality.

Formalities Are Not Enough

It is obvious that some of the devices which have been developed in Scandinavian countries are essential for providing the formal framework in which equality can be a social reality. Without these devices, or similar devices, many realities of sex equality must remain in the field of theory. Sex equality requires the support of numerous social institutions, and many of them we do not have in the American social system.

[18] More information on these programs is presented in Chapter 20; also see *Social Sweden* (Stockholm: Social Welfare Board, 1953).

On the other hand, it must be recognized that formal devices alone are not enough. Value systems are the final test. Can women recognize themselves as equals, and are they willing to pay the price that choice and initiative require of an independent person?

And, too, there must be psychological attitudes on the part of the male recognizing this equality and accepting it in all situations and relationships. Any culture which creates the institutions making possible sex equality has already gone a long way in developing the necessary attitudes and values.

So far our culture is very deficient in respect to these attitudes. Our women are more ready for equality in most areas than are our men. Studies of attitudes toward women working show that women are more ready and willing to work than are men to have them work. This is even true of the new generation, as evidenced by a Michigan study where thousands of young people were asked to state their opinion on women working.[19]

Some Major Cultural Modifications Needed

The longevity of modern woman, combined with the fact that childbearing and child rearing are limited to so short a span of her life, creates problems of life-long adjustments. Millions of women become grandmothers by age 45.[20] Even before that age their major task of rearing children has been completed, and the school and other community institutions have taken over most of the load. Large numbers must move into the work world or feel that their lives are filled with frustrated uselessness and boredom.

Many have lost contact with the work world during the child-rearing period, yet they constitute a skill reserve of immense dimensions. Often they can, by very brief retraining programs, enter the work world, or enter it on a higher level then if such training were impossible. Often women who had specialities in college or even in the work world prior to childbearing, have, due to their experience as mothers, developed new interests or values and wish the kind of training which will help them move in the direction of these new interests.

A survey[21] of 15-year alumnae, showed that after this span of years following graduation, a third were employed and five out of six were

[19] *Youth and the World of Work* (East Lansing: Social Research Service, Michigan State College, 1949).

[20] Nelson N. Foote, "New Roles for Men and Women," *Marriage and Family Living*, 23:325-329, November, 1961.

[21] Esther Peterson, "The Impact of Education," in Seymour M. Farber and Roger H. L. Wilson (Editors), *The Potential of Woman* (New York: McGraw-Hill Book Co., 1963), pp. 188-198.

either seeking positions or thinking of doing so. Many wanted to go into teaching, having learned as mothers how great the need for better teachers is. Many of those with teaching aspirations had not considered becoming teachers when they were in college. Many were interested in preschool teaching, feeling that a great need for competence exists at that level of teaching.

It is apparent that many of these women at mid-life are anxious to go in the direction of acute social need, provided that the opportunity for training and for work are open to them. It may be assumed that there would not only be a social gain if short courses for retraining would make the fulfillment of their aspirations possible, but that these women would get greater psychological and financial reward by being upgraded in their work. It is not expecting too much to hope that as happy, creatively useful persons they would also be better wives.

It may well be that propaganda campaigns aimed at employers, calling their attention to this competent reserve of labor, will be needed. It has been estimated that in the labor force of 1970, 56 million will be men, 29 million, women. In this labor force, 10 million will be professional persons as compared to only 7.5 million in 1960 (see Figure 8-3).

It is apparent that in the training of all women from the beginning we need a program that will feature "flexibility and adjustment to change." The life cycle is becoming quite definitely marked by a series of steps which most women will follow:

1. coeducational schooling
2. a brief work-world experience
3. home and family
4. return to work world (preferably after short retraining course)
5. retirement and return to domesticity

In conclusion, the great complexity of social roles is the dominant aspect of relationships between the sexes in modern times. That numerous problems are involved in this complexity of roles, and in the lack of precise definition of roles, is self-evident. This situation is indirectly at the base of most marriage problems.

On the other hand, the very fact that men and women are highly individualistic in the development of their personalities and are capable of so many diverse roles—most of them interchangeable between the sexes —has provided a basis for a new level of understanding, communication, and companionability. The marriage which can cast aside the traditional concept of role differences holds promise of an equality such as marriages of an earlier generation never achieved. In marriage today, there

PERCENT OF WOMEN WORKERS OVER 45 IS RISING

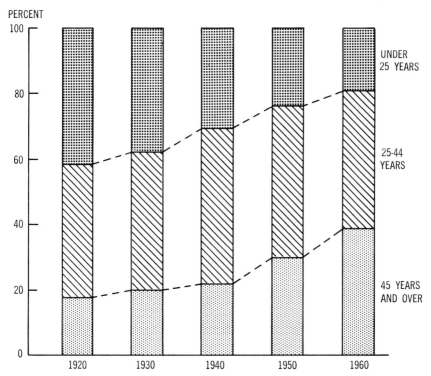

SOURCE: U. S. Department of Labor, Women's Bureau, *American Women*, Report of the President's Commission on the Status of Women, Washington, D. C., 1963, Chart 4, p. 11.

FIGURE 8-3————The increase in the number of older women who work reflects a great need for effective retraining programs for housewives finished with child rearing, who still have many years to give to work-world activities.

can be a genuine sharing in nearly every aspect of life. This makes marriage itself a far richer experience than was possible under the old regime, and makes parenthood a shared joy such as it probably rarely was in the patriarchal family.

Modern woman's life involves a series of major role shifts in the course of a lifetime. If the latter half of her life is to be fulfilling and useful, she must be broadly trained in youth, and then after the brief period of child rearing, return to the work world or to other meaningful activities, this often after a period of brush-up in school or of retraining to enter occupational activities that are different from those she aspired to while in school.

Problems

1. *Sociodrama:* A husband has just come home from work, tired, hungry, and in need of a little sympathy after a difficult and frustrating day. He finds no dinner, an untidy house and a wife who has spent her afternoon electioneering for a friend. The husband's first line is an angry one:

    "What kind of a wife are you? Women didn't used to be like this!"

    The wife answers indignantly:

    "You're right; times have changed and so have women!"

    Go on from there to show how confusion and disagreement in role behavior can be at the bottom of marital conflict.

2. *Research exercise:* Poll a student group on the following (other questions dealing with roles may be added if desired); (a) favorite work, (b) greatest ambition, (c) what I want to be at age 50. Tabulate and analyze results by sex. Are marked differences apparent in the roles of men and women? Do they reflect cultural conditioning or biological inclination primarily? If differences appear in life patterns of men and women, do they seem to be supplementary rather than contradictory? What implications do they suggest for the relationships between men and women of this generation?

3. It is sometimes asserted that the more choices we have, the more problems we have. If this is true would you say that the young woman of today has greater or fewer problems than young women of the past?

4. List several choices a young unmarried woman might consider that were never open to women of several generations past.

5. Think about the merging that has already taken place and is taking place in male-female roles. Now do a little speculative thinking about the future if this merging continues. Elaborate on such topics as the following:

    a. "The man of the future . . ."

    b. "The woman of the future . . ."

    c. "The marriage of the future . . ."

6. If you feel that there is a need for greater sex equality in the United States, prepare a program fulfilling this need. Your program should include any institutions or legislation which could help to bring about the desired reforms.

Selected References

ARTICLES IN BOOKS OF READINGS

CAVAN, Ruth Shonle, *Marriage and the Family in a Modern World: A Book of Readings* (New York: Thomas Y. Crowell Co., 1960).
1. American Institute of Family Relations, "The Private Worlds of Men and Women," Reading 24.

SUSSMAN, Marvin B., *Sourcebook in Marriage and the Family,* Second Edition (Boston: Houghton Mifflin Co., 1963).

2. RAINWATER, Lee, and others, "The Inner Life and Outer World of the Workingman's Wife," pp. 173-185.

3. HOFFMAN, Lois Wladis, "The Effect of Maternal Employment on the Child," pp. 241-247.

GOODE, William J., *Readings in the Family and Society* (Englewood Cliffs, N. J.: Prentice-Hall, Inc., 1964).

4. HEER, David M., "Dominance and the Working Wife," pp. 115-123.

General References

BLOOD, Robert O., Jr., and HAMBLIN, Robert L., "The Effect of the Wife's Employment on the Family Power Structure," *Social Forces,* 36:247-252, May, 1958.

CAVAN, Ruth Shonle, *American Marriage* (New York: Thomas Y. Crowell Co., 1959), Ch. 16.

DENNIS, Lawrence E. (Editor), *Education and a Woman's Life,* Proceedings of the Itasca Conference on the Continuing Education of Women, American Council on Education, Washington, D. C., 1963.

DINITZ, Simon, DYNEZ, Russell R., and CLARKE, Alfred C.,"Preferences for Male or Female Children: Traditional or Affectional?" *Marriage and Family Living,* 16:128-130, May, 1954.

FOOTE, Nelson, N., "New Roles for Men and Women," *Marriage and Family Living,* 23:325-329, November, 1961.

GRUENBERG, Sidonie M., and KRECH, Hilda Sidney, *The Many Lives of Modern Women: A Guide to Happiness in Her Complex Role* (New York: Doubleday & Co., Inc., 1953).

HACKER, Helen Meyer, "The New Burdens of Masculinity," *Marriage and Family Living,* 12:227-233, August, 1957.

HUNT, Morton M., "The Direction of Feminine Evolution," pp. 255-272, in Seymour M. FARBER and Roger H. L. WILSON (Editors), *The Potential of Woman* (New York: McGraw-Hill Book Co., 1963).

KAMMEYER, Kenneth, "The Feminine Role: An Analysis in Attitude Consistency," *Marriage and Family Living,* 26:295-305, August, 1964.

KIRKPATRICK, Clifford, *The Family* (New York: The Ronald Press Co., 1963), Chs. 7, 17.

LANDIS, Paul H., *Introductory Sociology* (New York: The Ronald Press Co., 1958), Ch. 17.

LEMASTERS, E. E., "Parenthood as a Crisis," *Marriage and Family Living,* 19:352-355, November, 1957.

LEOPOLD, Alice K., "The Family Woman's Expanding Role," *Marriage and Family Living,* 20:278-282, August, 1958.

MEAD, Margaret, *Male and Female* (New York: William Morrow & Co., Inc., 1949), Ch. 9.

MYERS, George C., "Labor Force Participation of Suburban Mothers," *Marriage and Family Living,* 26:306-311, August, 1964.

NYE, F. Ivan, and HOFFMAN, Lois Wladis (Editors), *The Employed Mother in America* (Chicago: Rand McNally & Co., 1963).

U.S. Department of Labor, Women's Bureau, *American Women,* Report of the President's Commission on the Status of Women, Washington, D. C., 1963.

WHITE, Lynn, Jr., "The Changing Context of Women's Education," *Marriage and Family Living,* 17:291-295, November, 1955.

————, *Educating Our Daughters* (New York: Harper & Bros., 1950).

III

THE PREFACE TO MATE CHOICE

9
Foundations of Love

Love, man's finest social experience, his most perfect emotional reaction, seems to be triggered by a very simple mechanism at its outset, the mechanism of physical warmth and comfort. Food is incidental to this comfort, in that the child is usually held next to the warm body of the mother when given food. Studies by Harry F. Harlow, President of the American Psychological Association, leave little doubt that it is the warm, comfort-giving, body-to-body contact that actually triggers the emotion of love, and with it the feeling of security and safety.[1]

He experimented with newborn monkeys, providing an unheated wire mother for one group and an electric-light-bulb-heated, cloth-covered, sponge-rubber mother for another—a mother soft, warm, and tender. Each substitute mother performed the nursing function. The contact with the heated-cloth mother proved to be the one that built the affectional response. This also proved to be the contact to which the young monkeys fled when fear-producing stimuli were introduced. The older the monkeys became, the more they fled to this warm substitute mother for comfort. Evidence of some psychosomatic development was indicated where monkeys had only the wire substitute mother.

Harlow concludes that the main factor in the emotional development is the infant-mother body contact, rather than the nursing contact as such.

Built-in Security Through Mother Love

The length of these warm contacts, and their certainty probably has much to do with the feeling of security which the person has as he faces the colder situations life brings. Anthropologists and psycholo-

[1] Harry F. Harlow, "The Nature of Love," *The American Psychologist,* 13:673-685, December, 1958.

gists have commented on the great security of children reared under certain types of child-rearing practices.

Here is LeBarre's appraisal of child rearing among American Indians and the resultant effect on personality:

> There was an old army man in the 1890's, James Mooney, who was involved in the Sioux wars—The Battle of Wounded Knee and Custer's Last Stand— who from a lifetime of experience with various Indian tribes, came to the kind of understanding that I think is essential to the issue.
>
> "The Sioux," he says, "are direct and manly, the Cheyenne high-spirited and keenly sensitive, the Arapaho generous and accommodating, the Comanche practical and businesslike."
>
> And the reason clearly is that the Sioux, the Cheyenne, the Arapaho, and the Comanche have different ways of bringing up their children. . . .
>
> In the most primitive groups, because of their pediatric backwardness and lack of Frigidaires, a child is ignorantly suckled a minimum of two or three years—and, worst of all, he is fed whenever he is hungry, in a hopelessly un-scheduled fashion! (Some American Indians are permitted an occasional visit to the breast even up to the age of five.) Is the dignity, the inexpungable security, the settled self-judgment and self-possession of such American Indians a surprise to us, then? I have known American Indians whom the threat of the atomic bomb itself would not disorganize; upon knowing the worst of all imaginable situations, they would continue to adjust to them. I know one American Indian who conducted himself through the terrors of a modern war with a really distinguished aplomb. We would mistakenly call it courage —for him it was something to be taken for granted like his own manhood; he simply lacked these reservoirs of neurotic anxiety which flood us in stress situations. He lacked the culturally defined guilts that would lead him irrationally to anticipate punishment; he had not experienced the frustrations and hence did not have the hostilities to project and to be persecuted by as neurotic fears; he had not had his childhood ego systematically attacked and traumatized so that he had any doubt of his ability to cope with any current situation. . . .
>
> The really serious thing is the kinds of human being we make, and the ways in which we go about making them. The child, we say easily, is the father of the individual man. But more than that, in the larger sense, the child is the father of all future mankind.[2]

With the human infant, it is not long before the warmth of body contact becomes associated with other stimuli that broaden the base of love—the voice, the smile, the caress by the mother are all a part of the broadening process. Then comes play with the mother and other members of the family—the father, sister, brother, grandparent, and others.

---

[2] Weston LeBarre, "Wanted: A Pattern for Modern Man," *Mental Hygiene*, 33:2-8, April, 1949.

Others enter into this circle as the infant develops the ability to smile and thus respond to attention. The association of safety and well-being with the mother gradually spreads out to include "people." At this early stage in his development the child is already learning that love and happiness are associated with the interdependence of individuals. He is developing a physical concept of love. For him, there is nothing complex in the manifestation of affection—it amounts to nothing more than physical comfort, gentle voices, and warm caresses.

The Heartbeat and Security

The rhythmic sound of the mother's heartbeat seems to be a factor in the emotional security of the infant, apparently helping to allay its fear of abandonment. Dr. Lee Salk, clinical psychologist, found that infants in a nursery with recorded heartbeats transmitted to them cried less and showed greater depth and regularity in breathing and less restlessness than the control group.[3] He also observed that mothers, whether left- or right-handed, usually cradle babies in their left arm with the baby's head held tightly to the chest wall near the heart.

With the infant, ease of feeding and depth of sleep are the evidences of security. Dr. Salk found that babies who had trouble getting to sleep were helped by the recorded heartbeat. In the experimental group exposed to the heartbeat, 70 percent gained weight. In the control group not exposed to it, only 33 percent gained weight on the same amount of milk. Salk has developed a mechanical heart which is used in hospital nurseries to provide the heartbeat.

The Denial of Love

There are instances in which to describe the absence of a value often taken for granted is to make more strikingly clear its supreme importance. This is so with love. The following example is true, even though extreme. This, along with various sociological examples of feral children,[4] demonstrates, by a negative approach, how essential love is to the development of a child into a human being. Here is a summary of a filmed study by Dr. René A. Spitz, an American psychiatrist, of children

[3] Paul Popenoe, "Close to the Mother's Heart," *Family Life,* 21:1-2, May, 1961.

[4] Feral means "wild." Several children denied human association have been studied extensively. The most famous of these is Casper Hauser. For a study of this case and many others, see any introductory sociology text. Some of these are presented in Paul H. Landis, *Introductory Sociology* (New York: The Ronald Press Co., 1958), pp. 138-139.

in a South American orphan home who were almost completely denied love and the close human association love implies:

> Foundling Home was an excellent institution from the standpoint of hygiene. The food was varied, adequate, and carefully prepared; no person whose clothes and hands were not sterilized could approach the babies. A well-trained staff of physicians and many consulting specialists checked daily on the infants' health. This institution harbored babies from birth to the sixth year. Up to the fourth month the infants in this institution developed well, even better than the average of a family child. The average baby up to four months in this institution was a month ahead of its age level.
>
> From the fourth month on, however, this picture changed radically. The developmental level of these children dropped more and more until at the end of the first year the average child of Foundling Home was alarmingly retarded. A 12-months-old child in Foundling Home showed the picture of an 8-months-old child.
>
> What happened to bring about this change in the developmental picture of the 69 children in Foundling Home, without any exception? All the conditions of hygiene were identical for younger and older children. There was only one factor which had changed. The presence of the mother. The practice in Foundling Home was that mothers brought in their children at birth and stayed with them until the end of their fifth month. They took care of them and breasted them. After this time the mothers had to leave the institution. Trained nurses took over the care of the children. However, the financial provisions of the institution provided only one nurse for 12-15 children. Therefore infants in Foundling Home from their fifth month on had only a twelfth or a fifteenth part of a mother. Their emotional interchange with human beings was drastically reduced, their response to it was drastic deterioration.
>
> Unfortunately the limited duration of my stay in the country in which the institution was situated did not permit me to follow these children after their first year. An assistant I trained during my stay was entrusted with the follow-up. Although these data seem superficial they are revealing.
>
> The most striking result of this study was that 27 children of those observed originally had died. This is really an alarming figure considering the utmost precautions which were taken in regard to hygiene. It seems that in spite of good food and meticulous medical care these children had too little energy left to resist minor and major ailments.
>
> Besides the 27 children who died, some other children could not be accounted for, as they were adopted, placed in other institutions or simply lost from sight. My assistant had only the opportunity to observe 21 children who ranged from 2½-4½ years. These children were all undersized and underweight. Only 3 of these 21 children had the normal weight of a 2-year-old and only 2 attained the length normal at this age. Their mental performance was no better. Of these 21 children, of whom the youngest was 2½ years old, only 5 could walk unassisted, only one had a vocabulary of a dozen words and only one, a 4½-year-old, used sentences. On the other hand, 8 of these

21 children could neither stand nor walk, 6 could not talk at all and 11 were limited to the use of 2 words. Even this superficial sketch reveals these children as ranging from mental debility to idiocy.

Psychotherapeutic intervention was tried in a few cases by other investigators to abolish or at least to mitigate the consequences of such early institutional care. The result was nil. The damage inflicted to the children's systems seems irreversible.

This tragic consequence of deprivation of the mother represents not only a theoretical challenge to the scientist who investigates the dynamics of early childhood, but also an important challenge to anyone concerned with the future of a nation, with the future of the world. . . .

Presence or absence of the mother is the to be or not to be for the development of the baby. If a society wants to guarantee the health of its young generation and with that its own survival it has to guarantee an average amount of motherly love to the average child.[5]

This is a striking picture of the meaning of love, and its denial presents in this instance a stark picture of the destruction of personality, and in many instances of life itself.

The mother is the key person with whom all love experience begins. As Spitz[6] concluded from his research with infants, "During the first year of life it is the mother, or her substitute, who transmits literally every experience to the infant. Consequently, barring starvation, disease or actual physical injury, no other factor is capable of so influencing the child's development in every field as its relations to its mother."

Tragic Results from Emotional Crippling

The more psychologists and sociologists study the human personality, the more apparent it becomes that any severe denial of love is costly, particularly where this denial is by the mother. And those denied must find substitutes if they are to reach any practical degree of social adjustment.

The sexually delinquent girl, the homosexual individual, the juvenile delinquent, the insecure individual who is a likely candidate for the mental institution or for suicide, the potential alcoholic and the drug addict, the poor marriage risks—the majority of all these types are persons who have been afflicted by a denial of love. The degree of denial is in a general way related to the seriousness of their deficiency in social relation-

5 René A. Spitz, "The Importance of Mother-Child Relationship During the First Year of Life," published by the Washington Society for Mental Hygiene and the Graduate School of Social Work, University of Washington (Seattle, 1947). Based on a series of film lectures presented in Seattle, June 15-17, 1947.

6 René A. Spitz, "The Role of Ecological Factors in Emotional Development in Infancy," *Child Development*, 20:145-155, 1949.

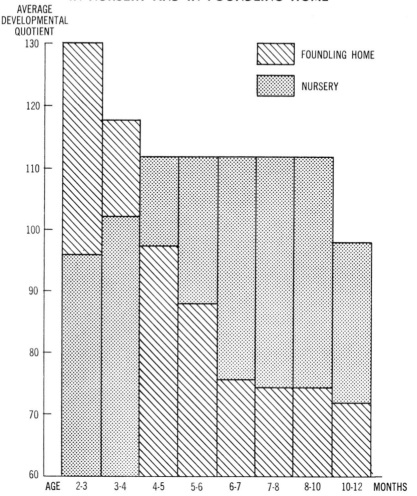

DEVELOPMENTAL RATES OF INFANTS
IN NURSERY AND IN FOUNDLING HOME

AVERAGE
DEVELOPMENTAL
QUOTIENT

FOUNDLING HOME

NURSERY

AGE 2-3 3-4 4-5 5-6 6-7 7-8 8-10 10-12 MONTHS

SOURCE: René A. Spitz, "The Role of Ecological Factors in Emotional Development in Infancy," *Child Development*, 20:145-155, 1949.

FIGURE 9-1————A comparison of development of 239 children in a nursery home (mothers present) with 91 children in an orphan home (mothers absent after the first three months and nurses overworked.) Observe that the orphaned children developed even better than the nursery children during the months their mothers were present; after that, development was at a proportionately de-creasing rate. In the end, serious physical and mental deterioration set in with the orphaned group (see Figure 9-2). The absence of emotional interchange with a mother or mother substitute was the critical factor.

TWO-YEAR MORTALITY RATE OF CHILDREN
IN THE ORPHAN HOME

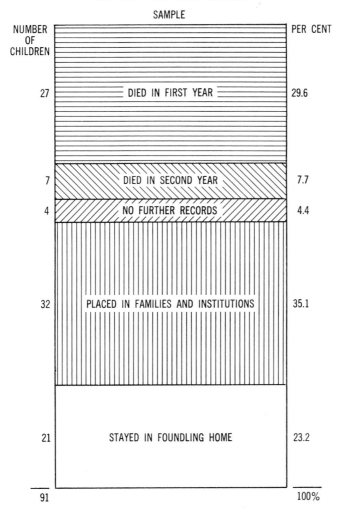

SAMPLE

NUMBER OF CHILDREN		PER CENT
27	DIED IN FIRST YEAR	29.6
7	DIED IN SECOND YEAR	7.7
4	NO FURTHER RECORDS	4.4
32	PLACED IN FAMILIES AND INSTITUTIONS	35.1
21	STAYED IN FOUNDLING HOME	23.2
91		100%

SOURCE: René A. Spitz, "The Role of Ecological Factors in Emotional Development in Infancy," *Child Development*, 20:145-155, 1949.

FIGURE 9-2————Emotional starvation not only led to retarded development, but also to physical deterioration. Thirty-seven percent died. With two exceptions, those who survived the emotional starvation behaved like "agitated or apathetic idiots." Two-year-olds never learned to speak, walk, or feed themselves. In the nursery group of 239 who had normal loving, not a single child was lost through death.

ships. Many of their errant ventures are in a quest of love, or are compensations to gain recognition and ego satisfaction to balance their lack of love.

Research shows that the home atmosphere, the relationship of parents to each other and to the child is the key factor in juvenile delinquency. A long-time study of delinquent children, following them into adult life, indicates that where the home situation is lacking in warmth and harmony, community efforts, social-work programs, and counseling show little results in improvement. Denial of love as a disciplinary device seems to help produce a personality prone to suicide.[7]

But if this is the true story of human growth, how do so many survive who seem to have been greatly denied love? Fortunately there are parent substitutes in many families, and in social groups, outside the immediate family. Many a love-denied child has found love in the close tie with the motherly parent of a pal. Others have found it in an older brother or sister who has been the real emotional parent. In primary groups there are neighbors, relatives, aunts, uncles, and above all grandparents, whose capacity to love is often very great indeed. In the growing years beyond childhood, buddies, pals, and army units may have great emotional meaning. And always there is the possibility of pets, some of which are very demonstrative of affection, dogs particularly and horses, even cats to a point, and with the small child, the warm blankets is a comforting substitute when there is a feeling of denied love.

In the teaching of marriage, it has been the practice of the writer to require autobiographies of the students based on the outline which appears in the appendix. Every semester in every class there are papers from those who clearly recognize in themselves an impaired capacity to love. Their experience can be classified into two types: (1) impairment because of a lack of affection between child and parents, usually the mother—their lack results from emotional rejection, the child's capacity to love not having been developed causing much hostility in the personality—and (2) a denial due to folk cultures—in these cases young people come from families, usually immigrant families or stern rural families, in which the tradition of covering up affection is strongly ingrained. In these families there is often deep loyalty between family

---

[7] William McCord, *Origins of Crime* (New York: Columbia University Press, 1959). This is a report of the Cambridge-Somerville Youth Study begun in the early 1930's with 650 boys—a delinquent group of 325 and a matched control group. The one was subject to all the reform efforts which money and social-work knowledge could provide. Reform for the most part failed utterly, yet it was probably the most intensive and costly ever attempted in this country. For an analysis of the relationship between love frustration, guilt, and suicide see Andrew F. Henry and James F. Short, *Suicide and Homicide* (Glencoe, Ill.: Free Press, 1954).

members, but there is no affectional expression of this loyalty, and therefore young people feel crippled in not being able to express affection overtly.

Slocum, studying 2,500 high school upperclassmen in Washington state, asked about the affectional patterns in their immediate family. Of the boys, 23 percent classed their families as unaffectionate; of the girls, 30 percent. Girls apparently are more aware of the emotional climate than are boys. At the other extreme, 27 percent of the boys and 33 percent of the girls classified their families as affectionate. The remaining group said that their families were sometimes affectionate, sometimes not.[8]

The Father in Love Development

The broadening of the range of love is brought about in part by the father and his contacts with the growing child. In this the mother has a part in encouraging sharing of the child, his comfort giving (like that inherent in bathing and changing the diapers), and his play with the father. Thus the mother helps provide the opportunities for emotional growth which will not come if she remains monopolistic of the child. The child becomes accustomed to the larger physique, the rougher touch, the deeper voice of the male.

If the father remains a stranger or primarily a disciplinarian in the minds of his children it is easy to understand why boys may develop distorted concepts of the role of the male in family and society, and undesirable attitudes about the relationship of man and wife.

Judson T. Landis,[9] studying family patterns, finds closeness to the father predictive of positive family values. The Cambridge-Somerville youth study showed poor relationships of fathers to boys to be highly predictive of criminality.[10] "Warm fathers and passive fathers produced very few criminals. Paternal absence, cruelty, or neglect, however, tended to produce criminals in the majority of boys."

Girls are also affected by the role their father plays. Attitudes can vary from love to hatred and defiance, depending on the relationship established. Whether or not a girl can love the opposite sex is very much affected by her concept of how men act as determined by her relationship with her father. A father has it in his power to develop in the daughter the capacity to love or to hate his sex.

---

8 Walter L. Slocum, *Family Culture Patterns and Adolescent Behavior* (Pullman, Wash.: Washington Agricultural Experiment Station, October, 1963), Bulletin No. 648.

9 Judson T. Landis, "A Re-examination of the Role of the Father as an Index of Family Integration," *Marriage and Family Living*, 24:122-128, May, 1962.

10 McCord, *op. cit.*

Childhood Love Acquires New Dimensions

During the first two or three years of life, the child understands and expresses love almost exclusively in terms of physical manifestations. At this stage in the development of the capacity for love, the parents' attitude toward the infant's bodily eliminations is considered by some authorities to be critical.[11] If his physical eliminations lead to disgust or to punishment on the part of the mother, it is believed that the capacity to love may be damaged. Bowel and bladder voiding should be accepted with praise on the part of the mother, as it is the first experience of the child in giving. Its control should be left until later and should never be handled by authoritarian means. The more love and affection are denied the small child, the more likely that voluntary control of bowel and bladder will be delayed far into childhood.

As the child grows, his range of association widens and so also do the stimuli which evoke the love response. He watches the play of his brothers and sisters and their friends; gradually, he takes part in their play himself. He begins to include giggles, laughter, loud but happy voices, rough treatment, and occasional bruises in his concept of affection interaction. He learns that the funny-faced frown and the playful spank of his mother are just as loving as her kiss or gentle hug, but in a different way. He is learning of companionship, a nonphysical kind of love.

Less is known about the ultimate effect of the rough-and-tumble play of childhood on love development in humans than in monkeys. Harlow's studies[12] show clearly that if monkeys are denied such play with their age mates, they never develop normal adult sex and parental patterns. In childhood the male monkey more often initiates play than does the female, and he is the aggressor in rough-and-tumble play. As age increases, his activity often takes the form of copulatory play. The female's role is more persistently in the direction of grooming playmates.

Placed in individual cages, with no chance for play with age mates,

---

[11] See Erik H. Erickson, *Childhood and Society* (New York: W. W. Norton and Co., Inc., 1950) for a full discussion of problems in this area of child development. To many such Freudian views seem fanciful. Freud believed that the child passes through a series of dynamically differentiated stages during the first five years of life which are decisive for the formation of personality. The *oral stage* is the first stage of development and lasts for about a year, during which time the mouth is the principal region of dynamic activity. The *anal stage* follows, during the second year when toilet training is usually initiated. During this period the child has his first decisive experience with the external regulation of an impulse. He has to learn to postpone the pleasure that comes from relieving his anal tensions. Depending upon the particular method of toilet training used by the mother and her feelings concerning defecation, the consequences of this training, according to the fanciful Freudian view, may have far-reaching effects upon the formation of specific traits and values such as stinginess or generosity.

[12] Harlow, *op. cit.*

monkeys in the experimental situation fail to develop normal sexual patterns upon maturity. Neither sex is able to master the copulatory act even under the tutelage of an experienced mate. A few of the females did become pregnant with experienced males, but proved very inept mothers, as likely to crush and kill their babies on the floor as to pick them up gently. Similar defects from isolated rearing were observed with young chimpanzees. These defects in sexual and parental behavior do not appear if the monkeys are allowed spontaneous play for at least 20 minutes per day.

One cannot assume that the same defects in personality result with the human child, but Money[13] has raised the question as to whether suppression of play, particularly childhood sexual play, among children may adversely affect sexual development in adulthood.[14]

We do know that in the case of the human child, only-child rearing is a definite liability to normal love development. The only child has more dating problems, less often feels secure in dating relationships, less often marries, and when he marries is less often successful in marriage itself than are sibling-reared children. How much of these love deficiencies are the product of lack of contact with age mates and how much a product of other factors in the only-child situation is unknown.[15] In many only-child families sufficient contact with other children is no doubt provided to offset serious damage.

From the time a child is able to toddle alone across the lawn toward a neighbor or a group of children at play, the wise parent has stepped aside and let the youngster begin the development of new relationships. Encouraging him in the formation of friendship throughout childhood and adolescence; helping him develop loyalties to his friends as well as to his family; understanding that as he forms closer ties outside the family, the family ties themselves are bound to loosen some—all are important ways in which normal parents help their youngster in the normal process of emotional growth.

The physical love beginning in infancy, the companionship love beginning in childhood, are both important aspects of the love later given and sought in marriage.[16] A childhood barren of these important experiences in affection does little to prepare individuals for marriage and

13 John Money, "Developmental Differentiation of Feminity and Masculinity Compared," in Farber and Wilson, op. cit., pp. 51-65.

14 Some sexual play takes place in the experience of most children even in our inhibited culture. See William R. Reevy, "Child Sexuality," Encyclopedia of Sexual Behavior (New York: Hawthorn Books, Inc., 1961).

15 More attention to the only-child problem and to bibliography on this subject is given in Chapter 29.

16 Ian D. Suttie, in The Origins of Love and Hate (New York: Julian Press, Inc., 1952) has stressed the need for companionship rather than sex as the basic element in love.

family happiness in later years. When a child is born unwanted or grows up in a family that has no time or inclination to love and play with him, his attitude toward people is likely to be suspicious, overly demanding, or one of fear and utter dependence. He has difficulty in dating and in building the attitudes, relationships, and ties that lead to an affectional relationship. In the worst cases, he finds it impossible to do so.

When these first experiences in love have been happy ones, the infant develops into a child who can easily accept new people—first pals and grown-up friends, then teachers, scoutmasters, and complete strangers. He looks upon the world with trust because he has no cause to fear it. The exact importance of the early months of life to later happiness has never been accurately appraised, but all of the evidence indicates that a child born into a loving devoted family goes into marriage with a better chance for happiness than a child whose first steps were taken in an impersonal, unloving world. In most families, certainly in the ideal family, love is given as easily as companionship and as naturally as food, clothing, and shelter. It is not something which a child must demand or even earn. It is his birthright. This is why most human beings develop with considerable capacity to love and be loved.

Direction Is Needed for Wholesome Emotional Development

Brothers and sisters, parents, teacher, friends, and even casual acquaintances all play an important part in helping or hindering an individual in the growth of his capacity to love. Older brothers and sisters as well as friends and acquaintances of both sexes are frequently responsible for the attitudes and behavior a young person develops toward the opposite sex. A boy whose older brother, or whose pals, brag of their feminine conquests is apt to develop attitudes of exploitation toward feminine companions. Tenderness, respect, and selflessness—characteristics commonly associated with the concept "true love"—are neither natural nor inevitable in themselves. There is much in the upbringing of the average male to make him less than he ought to be as a lover. Usually, some girl, by imposing restraint and requiring affection, teaches him to love intimately, if as an adult he is to love in a true sense at all.

A child who, by formal or informal learning, has picked up attitudes of disrespect or condescension toward the opposite sex, cannot be expected to make an about-face when the time comes for his own engagement and marriage. Conditioned attitudes, whether good or bad, are deep-grained and pervasive. They affect one's capacity to love and be loved.

Developments at Puberty

The physiological changes of puberty make interest in the opposite sex take on new dimensions. But most young people do not immediately become interested in the game of pursuit of the opposite sex. In fact, the transfer of the primary core of love from parents to a member of the opposite sex seems to be too great to be made in one step. Close attachment to a member or members of their own sex is the usual thing for both adolescent boys and girls. This transition stage is sometimes referred to as the homosexual stage.

There comes a time when the young person begins to show an increased interest in age mates of the opposite sex. This occurs somewhat earlier among girls than among boys, but even within one sex the age of budding interest in the opposite sex varies considerably.

Actually, there is no way of knowing how much of the awakening is due to physical maturation and how much is a consequence of social customs. Both operate. In some communities and among certain social classes, young people are expected to begin dating early; in others, they are expected to wait until they are older. The conformity of the young teenager to the customs and expectations of his group suggests that the part nature plays in determining when love begins is only one aspect of the total situation.

Regardless of the basic motivations for this transfer of affection from one sex to the other, the transition does take place in all but a small minority of young people. When it does, most adolescents are able to move on with relative ease into heterosexual love. When there is a fixation of interest on the parents or on a member of one's own sex, the development of heterosexual interests is blocked.

The growth of affection in the adolescent in the contemporary family is made possible by cooperation, fairness of discipline, and democratic management of the family.[17] The father, particularly, seems to have much to do with the adolescent girl's attitudes toward the opposite sex and her capacity to love in a normal way. The father in a very real sense becomes for her a symbol of men.[18]

Problems of Transfer of Love Objects

Even when a young person is eager to and completely capable of a growing interest and attraction to the opposite sex, problems frequently arise to complicate the process. Some young people, because of

[17] Walter L. Slocum and Carol L. Stone, "Factors Associated with Family Affectional Patterns," *The Coordinator*, 7:21-23, December, 1958.

[18] Ralph Eckert, *Sex Attitudes in the Home* (New York: Association Press, 1956).

acquired attitudes, have been habituated to depreciating the opposite sex and find it difficult to reverse themselves. After all, it is hard to admit, even to oneself, that the little girl who only yesterday was scorned, now seems both beautiful and interesting.

Some adolescents have grown up in such a tightly knit family circle that they find it new and awkward to form relationships with other young people.

At this stage in emotional growth one of the most common stumbling blocks is raised, not by the young people themselves, but by one or both of their parents. Well-meaning fathers and mothers, in their attempts to protect their children, frequently stand in the way of the normal development of their sons and daughters. In some instances they set up rules and regulations around their youngsters' social life and dating that make normal interaction with the opposite sex virtually impossible. In other cases they use ridicule, shame, or an appeal to family loyalty and affection to hold their teenagers back. In either case, they only complicate and delay a process which must begin before normal heterosexual love can be cultivated.

Some parents meet this period in their teenagers' lives awkwardly because they have exaggerated notions of the dangers involved; others, because they know too little about the part they can and should play in helping their youngsters safely to the next stage. Some parents get panicky because they are made suddenly aware of broad areas in child training that they never bothered with; they are uncertain of what the results of their neglect will be. In some instances the parents are thus awakened to the fact that their child or children are almost grown. They think ahead to the years of loneliness that await them when the children are gone, and they hope that by delaying the social development—the dating interests of their children—they can hold them back for a little while longer.

Parents who set up harsh or unnecessary restrictions at this point seldom accomplish the results they desire. The youngster whom they hope to hold is more often driven to open rebellion. The parent-child ties, instead of being strengthened, are often irreparably broken by the youngster in anger and disgust. This may drive the child to seek love desperately, often through sex experience.

At this point the wise parents realize that in order to keep their children—their love, respect, obedience—they must give a greater measure of freedom and self-direction. This is a time when counsel may be welcomed by the young person, but dictates and commands are despised.

The mature parent ceases directing the life of the young person and gives him experience in making his own decisions and suffering the consequences of his own mistakes. He even stands by at times and sees his teenager take risks which may not be safe. This is a part of the upbringing of children in our time when a great deal of independence and self-reliance is required of them as they grow into adulthood. Unwise and experimental love affairs may be a part of this venturing in a quest to replace the lost affection for parents.

During adolescence, young people normally grow progressively more independent of parents and home. Most of their waking hours are spent in the outside world. Most of their favorite activities and keenest interests are shared, not with mother and father, but with age mates. Their life becomes almost completely absorbed in the teen group. Their need to feel loved and to love in return is as strong as ever, yet custom and circumstances are carrying them ever farther from the parents. One of the most common phrases by which the girl expresses her attitude toward her mother is, "Oh, but you wouldn't understand." Boys are less likely to say it, but they feel this way also. Their confidant is their close friend, and not adults.

As the strong childhood attachment to his parents weakens, the teenager revolts against his parents and may consider the family old-fashioned. He finds it necessary to defy the traditions of the parents and start life on his own, with different aspirations and more distant goals than his parents ever dreamed of having. This is a necessary step in attaining freedom from the emotional attachments of the family. While parents sometimes look with alarm and fear at the spirit of rebellion which often characterizes the teenager, the wise parent will look upon this with favor as long as it doesn't get completely out of bounds. This rebellion increases his need for a strong attachment to the teen group and intensifies his need for love of the opposite sex to replace the strong parental love that no longer seems appropriate.

The young person who cannot go through this period of revolt is seldom able to break his ties with the parental home and establish a home of his own. To fail to make this break is to remain so attached to parents that marriage becomes difficult, if not impossible. When the adolescent emerges from this stage of rebellion, his childhood affection and devotion to his parents, his blind worship of them as the only people in his life, is gradually replaced by mature respect and affection. He looks on them, then, as equals rather than as authoritarian superiors.

Once family ties begin to weaken—as they must and should—they can never be completely restored. The older adolescent in college or on a job may feel an ever-growing need for the kind of love he used to feel at home, but if he is healthy and growing in maturity, he realizes that he must seek it elsewhere and not attempt to return to the past. Marriage begins to loom ahead as the chief means for satisfying this need.

It may well be that only after marriage will the child be sufficiently mature to view life as an adult. Then the parents are seen in a different light. The young person begins to see that the parents were not as far out of step as he thought.

Elements of Love

Love seems to be one of those topics about which people with the most experience have the least to say. In the earlier stages of dating, the young teenager asks himself and his friends the serious, and to him all-important question, "How do I know it's love?" He assumes, if it is love, that all other aspects of the relationship naturally fall into line. After more experience and when he has become more mature, he asks rather, "Is love enough?"

Writers and scientists still have not given up in their efforts to define the stage or emotion called love. But more and more they are content to speak of various kinds of love rather than seek a single, all-inclusive definition. The crush a thirteen-year-old has on a teacher or movie star, for example, is thought by some to be an important first experience in real love. The attraction this youngster will one day feel for her husband can most certainly be called love but will probably be less moving than the crush. The ties that will one day bind her to her own children, that already unite her to her parents, brothers and sisters, and closest friends are also love. None of these loves are the same; yet they are all love.

What have the experts to say on this subject? Love, according to the late Havelock Ellis, famed English sexologist, "is a synthesis of sex and friendship." He was obviously restricting the concept of love to the relatively mature relationship of a man and woman who have known one another long enough to become friends as well as lovers.

Sociologist Willard Waller, a follower and interpreter of Freud, considered that love involves idealization. This implies, first, imputing desirable qualities to a person lacking them; second, exaggerating their proportion when they are present; and, third, denying the existence or minimizing the extent of unfavorable qualities.

Waller was obviously thinking of love in the narrowest sense possible, or equating it to what is generally referred to as "blind love" and restricting it to the initial stage of a relationship in which physical attraction is the primary bond.

Paul Popenoe, founder of the American Institute of Family Relations in Los Angeles, in his newspaper column entitled "Making the Most of Marriage," examined the subject somewhat more thoroughly. He suggested that love is the satisfaction of the personality needs of each by the other.

Popenoe broadened the concept so that it might include the mother-child love relationship or the love that close comrades feel toward one another. Still, there are loves—important loves—that this definition does not cover. In many instances, for example, the most passionate or sincere of loves are not returned but flow unheeded or even unknown from one individual to the unresponsive object of his affection.

Although no single definition of love can cover all of its minute details and variations, it does seem that each of the various kinds of love has two basic elements in common.

First, there is in every love relationship, whether it is one-sided or returned in kind, a basic element, *attraction*. People may speak of "platonic love," "pure love," or "spiritual love," but the fact is that one cannot feel love for an individual whom one finds repugnant. It is important to point out, however, that love need not be the outgrowth of beauty. The element of attraction operates in the shared love of child and parent, the love of close comrades, and the unspoken love of child for teacher or movie hero, as well as in the love relationship of boy and girl or man and woman.

The second element common to all love relationships is that of need satisfaction. A love which does not bring satisfaction to the lover—call it happiness if you will—is not love at all. The folk phrases, "tormented love," "painful love," and many other variations on this theme would seem to contradict this and romantically inclined suitors at times feel called upon to insist that: "I've never been so miserable in my life as I've been since falling in love with you."

While some love relationships are accompanied by problems and many others create difficult situations, it is not love, but the situations themselves, which produce the torment or misery. Love, in and of itself, is capable of producing only happiness, satisfaction, and joy.

In this connection one is reminded of such instances as the unrequited love of the American poet Emily Dickinson or the undying devotion of many a Sunday-supplement wife to her uncouth, unloving, and usually brutal mate. "Doesn't this prove," one is tempted to ask, "that some love can bring nothing but sadness?"

The unromantic but realistic fact is that the individual who continues such a love is getting great satisfaction of a type which few normal people seek. While this strange relationship is not common enough to warrant detailed consideration here, it is worthwhile to note that the kind of satisfaction each person seeks in love is determined by his own special needs and the values given him by his conditioning. A girl who has lived under a harsh or brutal father may not be able to respect and love a kind man. She may actually be capable of loving only a brutal man and may love him most deeply after he has given her a beating. The love life of a person can actually be, and in the past often has been, so formed.

The book and film, *The Quiet Man*, depicted well how such a process of conditioning is elevated to the level of national custom in a locality of Ireland.

Psychological studies of "critical periods" in development orientation of young animals show that "imprinting" during critical periods need not be accomplished by pleasant association; the only requirement is that the time be right in the cycle of development of the individual and that the emotional association be strong. During the imprinting period, hunger, fear, pain, and loneliness are effective just as are love, comfort, food, and other pleasant stimuli. Whatever the stimuli, it becomes self-enforcing after the critical period is past, and in time becomes irreversible. Scott, commenting on the implications of this research for human beings, states that this may explain why neglected children often have "strong affection for cruel and abusive parents."[19]

One may speculate a step further and guess that children who develop such a love orientation beyond the irreversible point could love only an abusive mate. Observation of human cultures leads one to believe that the female is more easily turned in the direction of a masochistic orientation of love than is the male.

The person who willingly suffers, who is only happy as another person's slave, or who remains devoted to a nagging wife or brutal husband does so because it brings a masochistic happiness and satisfaction. In this sense, all kinds of love are fundamentally "selfish." Although love often causes an individual to give up many things, it is selfish because, as Dr. Anna K. Daniels has pointed out, in the very act of sacrificing for a loved one the lover obtains "a tremendous amount of ego satisfaction."[20]

Most of the elaborate definitions involving long lists of things one must feel or do before he can be sure "it's love," might best be forgotten. Even in narrowing the area down to encompass only the love of man and woman, one finds many strange variations and contradictions in patterns of affection. In the following chapter we will look more closely at romantic love to discover some of its characteristics.

Problems

1. Describe briefly the reaction of your own parents to your early ventures in love. Did they seem eager or reluctant to help you transfer your affections outside the family circle? What effect did their reactions or expressed attitudes have on you?

[19] J. P. Scott, "Critical Periods in Behavioral Development," *Science,* 138:949-958, November 30, 1962.

[20] Anna K. Daniels, *Five Kinds of Love for Mature Women* (Englewood Cliffs, N. J.: Prentice-Hall, Inc., 1953).

2. Develop a comprehensive definition of love.
3. Suppose for a moment that you are a parent keenly aware of the loathing most people feel toward homosexuals. You observe that your twelve-year-old daughter is very much attracted to another girl in the neighborhood, carries her picture in her wallet, talks about her, imitates her, and prefers her company to that of any other person. As a parent would you:
   a. Forbid her to associate with the girl?
   b. Arrange for a medical examination?
   c. Seek psychiatric aid?
   d. Try to interest her in dating boys?
   e. Encourage the relationship?
   f. Warn her about the dangers of the relationship?
   g. Recognize it as a transient phase of development?
4. Explain your choice of alternatives in terms of the material presented in the chapter.
5. Which alternative represents the worst possible course you could follow? Why?
6. *Sociodrama:* A man and woman visit a family relations counselor and explain that try as they may to make their home a joyful place and themselves, interesting, their adolescent children (aged 15 and 17) seem bored with them and eager to be out with their friends most of the time.

   Present the drama so that it emphasizes the attitudes of the parents as well as the explanation and advice given by the counselor.
7. The "movie magazine" craze is often thought of as a normal part of an adolescent girl's development toward mature love. Do you consider this belief justified on the basis of the facts presented in this chapter? What is it about these magazines that appeals?
8. Upon what grounds is it often argued that the first few years of life greatly affect the success or failure of many marriages?
9. State your views on each of the following propositions:
   a. Custom has provided that marriage should occur sometime during the age period of 18 to 22 because this is the time when the emotion called love begins to manifest itself.
   b. The most unselfish appearing lovers (those who willingly suffer in order that their mates can be happy) may be shown to be fundamentally selfish.
   c. Nature has devised a scheme whereby individuals grow normally from one stage of love to the next. It is therefore undesirable for the school or parent to interfere with the affectional development of the youngster.
10. Select and defend one alternative. Children brought up in orphanages:
    a. Are probably incapable of adjusting to marriage since they have not known parental love.
    b. Are likely to be unusually successful in adjusting to marriage because it provides them with an intimate relationship such as they have not previously known.
    c. Will probably have a more difficult time adjusting to marriage than children from a happy home.

Selected References

ARTICLES IN BOOKS OF READINGS

BECKER, Howard, and HILL, Reuben (Editors), *Family, Marriage and Parenthood,* Second Edition (Boston: D. C. Heath & Co., 1955).

   1. BAIN, Read, "Producing Marriageable Personalities," pp. 169-205.

CAVAN, Ruth Shonle, *Marriage and the Family in the Modern World: A Book of Readings* (New York: Thomas Y. Crowell Co., 1960).

   2. PRESCOTT, Daniel A., "Role of Love in Human Development," Reading 35.

   3. SYMONDS, Percival M., "Expression of Love;" Reading 37.

COSER, Rose Laub, *The Family: Its Structure and Functions* (New York: St Martin's Press, 1964).

   4. GOODE, William, "The Theoretical Importance of Love," pp. 202-219.

   5. SPITZ, René A., "Hospitalism," pp. 399-425.

   6. DAVIS, Kingsley, "Isolated Children," pp. 394-398.

CHRISTENSEN, Harold T., *Handbook of Marriage and the Family* (Chicago: Rand McNally & Co., 1964).

   7. DAGER, Edward Z., "Socialization and Personality Development," Ch. 18.

GOODE, William J., *Readings on the Family and Society* (Englewood Cliffs, N. J.: Prentice-Hall, Inc., 1964).

   8. CARPENTER, C. R., "Social Relations of the Gibbon," pp. 2-6.

   9. HARLOW, Harry F., and HARLOW, Margaret K., "Social Deprivation in Monkeys," pp. 7-10.

General References

BEE, Lawrence S., *Marriage and Family Relations* (New York: Harper & Row, Publishers, 1959), Ch. 6.

BLANTON, Smiley, *Love or Perish* (New York: Simon and Schuster, Inc., 1955).

CAVAN, Ruth Shonle, *The American Family* (New York: Thomas Y. Crowell Co., 1953), Ch. 15.

DANIELS, Anna K., *Five Kinds of Love for Mature Women* (Englewood Cliffs, N. J.: Prentice-Hall, Inc., 1953).

HARLOW, Harry F., "The Nature of Love," *The American Psychologist,* 13:673-685, December, 1958.

MARTINSON, Floyd M., *Marriage and the American Ideal* (New York: Dodd, Mead & Co., 1960), Chs. 7-8.

MEAD, Margaret, *Male and Female* (New York: William Morrow & Co., Inc., 1949).

ORLANSKY, H., "Infant Care and Personality," *Psychological Bulletin,* 462:1-48, 1949.

Scott, J. P., "Critical Periods in Behavioral Development," *Science,* 138:949-958, November 30, 1962.

Sewell, William H., "Infant Training and the Personality of the Child," *American Journal of Sociology,* 58:150-159, September, 1952.

Suttie, Ian D., *The Origins of Love and Hate* (New York: Julian Press, Inc., 1952).

10
Romantic Love

> Man's love is of man's life a thing apart,
> 'Tis woman's whole existence; man may range
> The court, camp, church, the vessel, and the mart,
> Sword, gown, gain, glory, offer in exchange
> Pride, fame, ambition, to fill up his heart,
> And few there are whom these cannot estrange;
> Men have all these resources, we but one,
> To love again, and be again undone.
>
> LORD BYRON

In the United States, romantic love is one of the major concerns, if not the main one, of the teen years, and interest in it scarcely ceases with the twentieth birthday. Throughout most of the Asiatic world, on the other hand, romance is not considered a significant part of relationships between men and women. This has been true since ancient times. Sensuous desire is known and looked upon as a kind of human madness.[1] People in many cultures have considered romantic love a sign of weakness and have ridiculed the person who yielded to it, rather than glorified it in poetry, fiction, screen, and in adolescent experience.

Since our culture has staked so much on romantic love, each individual of necessity does so. He acquires his values as naturally as though these values were in the nature of things, and meant to be. But love is a trait that must be cultivated in human nature, and the patterns of romantic love, too, are formed by custom. Even the key points of allure are culturally defined. Whether this be the trim ankle or the hidden ear lobe depends on what culture has defined as romantic.

[1] Oswald Schwarz, in A. M. Krich, Editor, *Women: The Variety and Meaning of Their Sexual Experience* (New York: Dell Publishing Co., Inc., 1954), p. 290.

In recent years romantic love, or affection, to use a somewhat less controversial term, has become an interest of physical and social scientists. As a consequence, some of the facts of love are being learned, and these facts in themselves are as fascinating as the age-old fables. A scientific understanding of love promises to make this subject more important, rather than less important in everyday thinking, for the evidence so far indicates that love is not the sudden indefinable disease of adolescence, but a life-long emotion which begins to manifest itself in the earliest days of life and which persists as a personal need throughout life. To understand romantic love in its various ramifications, and in the diverse ways it manifests itself in different persons, one must begin at the beginning.

Sometime during later childhood or early adolescence, most young people become aware of their first real love affair. The object of affection may be the boy or girl next door, but it is just as likely to be an older acquaintance—a movie star, a teacher, or a friend's big sister or brother. This seems to be the beginning step—at first awkward and sometimes amusing (to adults)—on the road to romance and marriage. Before this first big crush, boys and girls are unaware of the kind of feeling that will eventually lead to the altar.

Actually, the beginnings precede this awakening by many years. As we have seen, in reality, children begin almost in infancy preparing for the day when each will look at some one person and say, "This is the one I've been waiting for." Many very young children, in fact, talk about marrying their mother or father. The love they feel and demonstrate for their parents and sisters and brothers is related to the love they will later feel for some member of the opposite sex. The relationship a child has with his father and mother, as was implied earlier, plays an important part in determining the happiness and success he will one day find in dating and marriage. The kind of life and the daily experiences he shares with his brothers, sisters, and childhood friends also play a part in preparing him for adult love and marriage.

Sex Attraction

The love which an individual feels for some member of the opposite sex has both of the elements described in the preceding chapter, attraction and personal satisfaction. In addition to these, it always has at least one more element—sexual interest. It may have many other aspects —it should have if it is to lead to marriage—but it always has sex attraction.

Some individuals feel called upon to deny the existence of a sexual attraction in their relationship with a member of the other sex. One college girl insisted, blushingly, even on her wedding day, that "It's his mind, his ability, and his wonderful sensitivity that I'm marrying; sex just doesn't enter it!" The blush gave her away.

Even in our enlightened age there are many girls and some young men who think of sex, or think they *should* think of sex, as something unclean, unimportant, or somehow beneath the dignity of "nice people." But mating must occur in order to propagate the species, and a good measure of sexual desire has been included in the make-up of mankind. To deny that sex is important to love between the sexes is to argue uselessly against an obvious fact.

Sexual attraction should not be the only foundation upon which a marriage is founded. It *need not be* the most important motivation for marriage, but it certainly *should be* an important part of the mutual attraction and interest two young people feel for one another before they consider marriage.

This list of additional elements which may enter into the love of man and woman is endless. The happiest love affairs are those including such qualities as respect, admiration, the desire to please, to protect, to share, and to assist. Many other qualities may characterize a relationship. Sympathy, even pity, is occasionally an important part of love. The desire to dominate or to be dominated is also common. The desire to have children may be uppermost, or the desire to have money, status, adventure, or security.

In a sense, one has no right to condemn any of these motives or elements in love. When they are sincere, they represent nothing more than the manifestations of an individual's personality needs. The only thing that can justifiably be said against the more selfish motives is that they less often produce mutually satisfying love affairs and seldom lead, in themselves, to successful marriages.

Numerous writers have described components of sexual love in various language—the language of poets, of scientists, of philosophers, of lovers. Like life itself, love is most difficult to put into words.

The great English philosopher, Herbert Spencer, in his *Principles of Psychology,* classified love of man and woman for each other into nine distinct elements as follows:

1. physical sex impulses
2. feeling for beauty
3. affection
4. admiration and respect
5. desire for approbation
6. self-esteem
7. proprietary feeling
8. extended liberty of action from the absence of personal barriers
9. exaltation of the sympathies

Sexual Desire As a Factor in Romantic Love

Walter R. Stokes, M.D., marriage counselor, has said, "The only sound motive for a happy marriage is being overwhelmingly in love on a frankly sexual basis, centering about physical desire."[2] Had Dr. Stokes stopped at that point many an infatuated young couple would have had excellent ammunition in battling down paternal opposition to a youthful marriage. But Stokes went on to add that fundamental though sex is, "there is much more to a good marriage."

Sex alone is hunger—raw animal appetite. Love is a combination of sexual desire with all the other impulses that go into the highest type of association between the sexes. Love is a synthesis of friendship, tenderness, self-surrender, altruism, kindness, loyalty, self-sacrifice, and, in fact, of all the finer traits of human nature combined with the feeling of sexual need.

In sexual desire, the ego motive is dominant, the desire to conquer and force to surrender, or to be conquered and to surrender. The physical appetite is animal; love is social in the finest sense. Sex need is the basis for reproduction; it is Nature's way of assuring that passion will lead to fertility and from fertility to the reproduction of the species. Physical desire is concerned with no more distant goal than this.

Love is social, humanized, institutionalized, and becomes the basis in one way or another for almost every activity of the human being. It is, in fact, the basis for human society itself. Love is sexual desire idealized, controlled, and made to conform to social living. Physical appetite is self-centered. Love is other-centered. Physical appetite is craving for physical satisfaction, physical release; love is a craving for an intimate sharing with another.

The most significant aspect of sexual love, from a human standpoint, is that it becomes socially purposeful as it is harnessed and directed by human culture. Sexual need is the biological motive for marriage. As love expands in the personality, it brings with it a sense of shared obligation to the mate and to offspring. This provides the social basis for the loyalty of marriage and for the permanence of family life as expressed in the care of dependent children.

An exceptional few rush into marriage with little more than an overwhelming desire for one another and, years later, are still utterly in love. Motion pictures and popular fiction would have us believe that the experience of these few is very common. Part of it is; most of it is not. Many people do marry, particularly during wars, solely on the basis of sexual attraction, but these marriages are seldom successful over a period

[2] Quoted by A. K. Davis in *Coronet*.

of time. Either new and more lasting reasons for love are soon discovered or the marriage falls apart. Men and women are so constituted biologically that, demanding though their sexual desires are, they are quickly satisfied. Once an individual has obtained sexual satisfaction, his partner must be much more than beautiful or desirable to hold his continued interest.

If a man or woman were willing to negotiate a marriage in which the sole function was to satisfy the other sexually, physical attraction might be an adequate ground for marriage. Few humans would be interested in such a limited relationship. They literally want to share their lover's life. To do so, they must have much more to offer and must look for much more in return.

There is no shortcut to a lasting love. There is no way to know a person well without taking the time to get really acquainted, and there is no way of loving a person completely without first getting to know him. The existence of strong sexual attraction does not diminish the importance of shared interests, values, and expectations. Neither does it guarantee their existence.

While love may not be blind, it is most certainly often blinding. The man or woman who mistakes physical attraction for complete love frequently does so because of a sincere, though inaccurate, conception of what a complete love is like.

The Psychological Advantages of Romance

Havelock Ellis defined romantic love as the synthesis of sex and friendship. The female is so constituted that, unless conditioned otherwise, sexual attraction, respect, and deep friendship tend to give her a love feeling that is diffused throughout her body, something far more than a localized sexual need. With the male, sex attraction tends to create localized sensations which are no more diffuse and meaningful than a desire for the sex act itself. In the male, sex is specific, local, glandular. The synthesis of sex attraction through love and friendship, where it involves restraint of sex expression in the form of coitus over a period of time, seems to have the effect of diffusing love feeling much more widely in the male, sublimating sex desire, sanctifying it, making it a thing of supreme importance in the personality, preparing the male for the ultimate unifying of the pair in the sex act when marriage is consummated.

It is a sound psychological principle that the more interpersonal love becomes, the more a matter of mutual interest and sharing, the more sublimated in character, the more it grows in personality. A tribe of Plains Indians discovered this to their great satisfaction. The young bride was wooed for weeks after marriage before the sex act was consummated.

Warriors often talked with nostalgia of the first weeks of marriage when they would lie awake all night "quietly talking to their young wives."[3] Some tribes developed the chastity-blanket as an encouragement to restraint, and perhaps as a way of birth control. Couples were expected to seek the pierced blanket from the chief, since sexual intercourse required use of the blanket.

Ernest Van den Haag, analyzing the cultural prerequisites to the growth of romantic love concludes:

> When sexual objects are easily and guiltlessly accessible, in a society that does not object to promiscuity, romantic love seldom prospers. For example, in imperial Rome it was rare and in Tahiti, unknown. And love is unlikely to arouse the heart of someone brought up in a harem, where the idea of uniqueness has a hard time. Love flowers best in a monogamous environment morally opposed to unrestrained sex, and interested in cultivating individual experience. . . .[4]

If there is any truth in this view, the restrained dating relationship and the restrained engagement which stop sex activity prior to the consummation of the sex act would seem to be the logical preparation for the romantic type of marriage-family system developed in our culture. It is significant that, to date, studies show that chastity prior to marriage is the best preparation for successful marriage. The subtle psychological factors discussed above may well be important here.

The Course of Love

Some people think of love—real love—as a white-hot flame that is destined to burn steadily until the very end. Others feel sure that even the greatest of loves are destined to die as two people live together and share the cares of everyday life.

The idea that one "falls" in love is widespread. This concept of American culture probably carries over from the day when love was looked upon as something instinctive and inevitable, something that swept one off his feet against his wishes and carried him into a blind and blissful state from which there was no return. The more informed young person of today recognizes this as an idea out of which good fiction plots are made, but one which has little likeness to the more durable relationships of modern life.

[3] Margaret Mead, *Male and Female* (New York: William Morrow & Co., Inc., 1949).
[4] Ernest Van den Haag, "Love and Marriage," in Rose Laub Coser, Editor, *The Family: Its Structure and Functions* (New York: St Martin's Press, Inc., 1964), pp. 192-202.

While a person may suddenly be swept off his feet once in his lifetime, most individuals are more wary the second time and control their emotions until they are surely channeled toward a person who has the traits, attitudes, and life aspirations which make the relationship appear to be safe.

The idea that love is a fate from which one cannot escape is held by comparatively few informed young people and by none of those who have had variety in dating experience. Such persons know that an enduring love must be something that is cultivated, and that the soil in which it is grown must be appropriate. It usually begins with friendship which continues until respect and admiration develop. Only then may the emotions be given free play.

Ralph Eckert, teacher and counselor, has stressed the view that a young person should expect to grow in love, putting aside the notion of falling in love as a phenomenon of immaturity.[5]

Love is rarely an unmixed emotion. It has underlying it the negative emotions—hostility and hatred—which always tend to resist the involvements of love. It is an up-and-down affair in most pair relationships. In fact, it is often very complicated. It is not always a thing of excitement and discovery. It is certainly not always a thing of novelty. There are long periods when the thrill is absent and life takes on prosaic routines. Love becomes what people make it by constant interchange through communication and contact of personalities with each other.

Love does not stand still, neither does it continue on the same level nor at the same intensity for a lifetime, but this does not mean that all loves are destined to die. The normal course of love may be compared to a wave. The successful loves surge upward; the unsuccessful affairs fall away. Regardless of their ultimate outcome, most loves begin alike with a strong attraction involving physical awareness between the partners. This initial attraction may characterize the couple's first meeting or it may come after months or even years of casual contact. In either case, no real heterosexual love may be said to exist until some feeling of sexual attraction has been aroused.

From this point on, the affair may move to a quick conclusion or develop very slowly. In instances where physical attraction alone unites a couple, the spiral generally begins a rather early downward course. The highest point of love in such an affair is either at the beginning or soon after. With increased knowledge of one another, the attraction lessens and the interest subsides.

Unfortunately, many marriages take place before the course of the

5 Ralph G. Eckert in lectures at the University of California at Los Angeles, Summer Workshop in Family Life Education, 1948.

spiral has been revealed. In other instances, couples decide to marry in spite of the fact that they are each aware of a slackening interest in one another. One disillusioned young bride described the logic of such a marriage in this way:

> Ken and I were madly in love for about three months. We were together almost constantly and found it difficult to keep from getting too involved physically. We necked quite a bit, I guess you'd say, but both of us wanted to avoid doing anything wrong.
>
> When we began to quarrel and disagree and get on one another's nerves, we thought it was probably due to the fact that we both were constantly restraining ourselves. We decided that if we would hurry up and get married all of our tensions would be relieved and we could easily save our dying friendship.
>
> That's what we did and for the first two months everything was grand. Now we've discovered that the quarrels we had amounted to more than we thought they did. Marriage is no solution to an affair that is dying.

Other affairs begin with an immediate upward curve. Initially, they may grow very rapidly. As the couple discover more and more reasons for loving one another, the love itself grows in intensity. If the affair continues into a happy marriage, their love may continue its upward curve for a lifetime, although seldom if ever at its initial pace. When the first few years of mutual discovery have passed, the love spiral develops more slowly. Each event or situation that brings the couple together, or gives them a new understanding or appreciation of the other, causes their love to grow, but new events and new insights are likely to decrease in number as the years pass by.

Not every love affairs ends in marriage. Love can only grow with increased acquaintance, but at any point in this process of "getting acquainted," what one person learns about the other may cause him to cease to love.

An important point, too seldom mentioned in the literature in this field, is that the longer one loves, the more difficult it is to cease loving. In the early days of an affair even a minor crisis will often bring its termination. After years of growing affection, however, most love affairs can withstand tremendous difficulties. Seldom would a young bride or groom continue a marriage in which the mate was even once unfaithful. Yet among middle-aged couples many a husband or wife waits patiently, still loving, for the unfaithful mate to outgrow an illicit attraction. This does not necessarily mean that love has lost any of its meaning to the older couple. In some instances it testifies to an even greater and deeper love than the younger couple have yet discovered.

The Test of Love

What then is the test of real love? At what point has a love matured sufficiently to warrant marriage?

Popenoe[6] has listed five factors that characterize the well-rounded attitude toward love:

1. biological impulse leading to sex attraction
2. tenderness and affection
3. comradeship
4. a developing desire for children
5. a desire for economic interdependence

When only one or two of these attitudes characterize a romance, it is doubtful that the couple is ready for marriage. Biological impulse, tenderness, and affection may come early in an affair; but real comradeship, the desire for a family, and economic interdependence generally develop only as a result of long and mutually satisfying acquaintance.

Popenoe has also devised a scorecard test that he has found "goes a long way toward determining whether the basic and most essential elements of real love are present." The scorecard is designed as a series of questions one should ask concerning the other person. The questions may easily be reworded to apply to oneself, however, and they are equally effective in revealing the intensity and maturity of one's own state of affections:

1. He seems to take pride in you and wants to show you off, to introduce you to his friends and relatives.
2. He tries, when you are in a group with him, consistently but inconspicuously to put you in a favorable light.
3. His plans seem to keep organizing themselves around you as well as around his own personal ambitions.
4. He seems to defer to your judgment and give full weight to your views.
5. He is eager to share his experiences with you.
6. He shows respect and consideration for your family and friends.
7. He seems eager for your success and the fulfillment of your own plans and ambitions.
8. He seems to find intellectual as well as emotional stimulus in association with you.
9. He acts as though he really wants to love you—that he is not doing so against his better judgment.
10. He gives you to understand that he wants children.

6 Paul Popenoe, *Marriage, Before and After* (New York: Funk & Wagnalls Co., Inc., 1953), Ch. 3.

Analyzing their love affairs in terms of factors such as Popenoe suggests in these questions will convince many young people that, exciting though their loves may be, not all affairs can or should lead in the direction of marriage. Love relationships that are terminated short of marriage need not be looked upon as unfortunate experiences nor as failures. Since each new relationship can contribute something to the personal development of both parties, we might even safely say it is fortunate that few first loves are so successful as to be last loves.

The Cycle of the Unsuccessful Love Affair

Most events that enter man's experience have their ups and downs. All are familiar with the business cycle, with its booms and depressions. Even one's mood has ups and downs.

Love affairs, also move in a cycle. The pace will differ from person to person, and with the same person in different affairs. Kirkpatrick and Caplow[7] plotted the cycle of love affairs with a group of University of Minnesota students. The 455 students (141 men and 314 women) were given a sheet of graphs and asked to check the one which pictured best the ups and downs of their emotions during the courtship period. They were given four additional graphs to check which indicated the trend of their love feelings after breaking up. In case none of these graphs fitted his case, the student was asked to draw a chart which did (see Figure 10–1).

The group plotted their total 582 love affairs by this means. Most students' loves followed the steady up-and-down pattern, with no radical fluctuations; that is, the love rose to a climax, from which it fell in an uninterrupted line. Only a few went through a whole series of ups and downs. A gradual rise to the point of love, followed after a longer or shorter period of time by a steady decline would seem to be the pattern for most couples who fail to continue in love.

On breaking up, some couples (15 percent) rise to a new height of idealized love (Graph A) after which decline takes place. (Historically, many inexperienced lovers failed to return to earth, if one is to take fiction and biography seriously. The idealized love and phantom lover continued to live on, making interest in further loves impossible. Most college young people seem to be able to avoid this.)

Graph B is a pattern of complete indifference after the breakup. Over half of these college loves ended this way. Graph C is a pattern in which indifference turns to positive dislike (10-13 percent ended so). Graph

7 Clifford Kirkpatrick and Theodore Caplow, "Emotional Trends in the Courtship Experience of College Students as Expressed by Graphs, with some Observations on Methodological Implications," *American Sociological Review*, 5:619-626, October, 1945.

EMOTIONAL TRENDS IN BROKEN LOVE
AFFAIRS OF COLLEGE STUDENTS

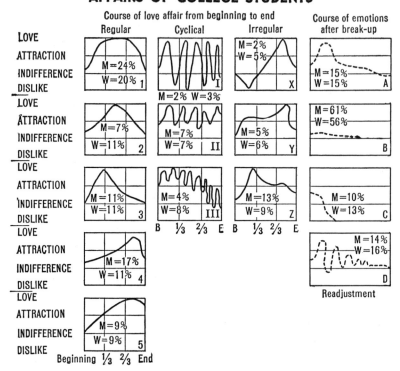

SOURCE: Clifford Kirkpatrick and Theodore Caplow, "Emotional Trends in the Court-ship Experience of College Students as Expressed by Graphs, with Some Observations on Methodological Implications," *American Sociological Review*, 5:619-626, October, 1945.

FIGURE 10-1————Graphs presented to students to represent ups and downs of their broken love affairs. Percentages indicate proportion of men (M) and women (W) selecting each graph. The regular graphs (left column 1-5) were selected by most students. Most often selected was number 1—attraction to a period of love, followed by a gradual cooling off to indifference. About 15 percent followed the up-and-down fluctuations of hot and cold love represented in the cyclical charts (second column I-III). Less than 20 percent selected the irregular patterns of charts in column three (X-Z). The graphs in the column at the right represent their ways of getting over a love affair. Well over half picked B to represent their experience—one of indifference. Of both men and women, 15 percent experienced an after flare-up of love, as in graph A; about the same proportion, the hot and cold fluctuations of D. A few experienced a strong dislike of the former lover, as in C.

D is a pattern of repeated, but gradually weakening flare-ups of love (15 percent of students checked this pattern). In all, 90 percent of these student love affairs terminated in what the researcher considered a normal pattern. In a later chapter, breaking of the engagement and its consequences will carry the study of this aspect of the love experience further.

The writer has collected data in graph form of several thousand love affairs of college students over the past ten years. They follow patterns similar to the typical ones described in the chart. Occasionally one finds, as in the cowboy movie, a relationship in which the initial contact is one of hostility, rather than attraction. "I couldn't stand him when I was introduced to him. I thought he was the most obnoxious, egotistical person I had ever met." But later the miracle of attraction takes place, then love, and in some cases even marriage.

The Control of Romantic Love

Most cultures have distrusted romantic love. The reasons have been many. Where the institutional family structure is in existence, romance tends to create many awkward relationships. In the institutional family system, marriages are for social status, for guaranteeing the family inheritance, and improving economic status. People with this conception of marriage cannot let romantic love interfere with parental arrangement. Therefore, they tend to laugh at romantic love or consider it shameful and transmit this idea in the culture.

After marriage, romantic love is distrusted in the joint family. Through romantic love, parents lose first place in their children's affection. In patri-local family systems, where the husband brings the wife into the family home, the mother and sister try to outdo the wife in holding the son's and brother's affections and attention. At the same time the wife's parents, particularly the mother, constantly try to prejudice their daughter against her husband so that they can hold first place in their daughter's life.

Most cultures also put numerous impediments in the way of romantic love prior to marriage. They may require marriage between relatives, usually cousins. They may employ child betrothal, often bringing the engaged into the home as a servant long before the marriage is consummated. They may limit betrothal to persons in a certain social position or class. Segregation of the sexes, precluding secret romances among the young; the veil; the harem; selection of mates by parents or other elders; stressing the value of chastity before marriage; and many other such devices have been and are a part of folk cultures, one important purpose being to control the romantic impulse and keep it from disturbing customary arrangements.[8]

While we have come to recognize romantic love as a legitimate basis for mate selection, we have had to face the reality that romantic love is not enough. One of the chief advantages of marriage courses has been to help young people discount romantic love as an independent value and force them to check it against some of the realities of human experience. Research in the field of marriage and the family has been concentrated largely on the problem of trying to determine the kind of background factors and social-emotional traits which help or hinder success in marriage. By presenting young people with this factually derived information, which, although tentative, far exceeds folklore in authority, teenagers are helped to temper romantic expectations with realistic ones. It is not unusual for such teaching to break up existing romances, and to cause young people to appraise future relationships in other than romantic terms. The marriage counseling clinic is another device that has emerged in answer to the needs of our modern urban-industrial culture in which total strangers often meet and date with resulting romances that may get out of hand. These clinics are available for helping young people critically appraise each other before marriage. The inquiring couple usually face a battery of tests that appraise their emotional, background, and personality factors. The clinician then tries to give them some objective awareness as to their likelihood of success or failure in marriage.

Those who study marriage and the family have learned to consider romance as only one of various prerequisites for mate selection. They realize that some of the most fabulous romances end in the most tragic marriages. The film *This Charming Couple* presents a wonderful romance. The man is a dreamer, an interesting classroom lecturer, a bohemian by disposition. He is sophisticated, profligate, his economic values are unrealistic. The girl in the pair is the systematic, thrifty, conventional secretary whose life must be ordered according to plan, whose future must be made economically secure and framed in a familiar nitch of people with familiar patterns. The romance is out of this world. Their very differences fascinate the couple and make their moments together moments of supreme joy. Their marriage, however, is tragic, for they have no basis whatever for a life of similar habits, expectations, and plans.

Many a romance between the American GI and the foreign girl reaches a romantic peak which is impossible to couples of similar backgrounds. The girl's spoken accent is sexually attractive to the man and charms him, but, making a marriage with one of vastly different cultural

---

[8] For an excellent analysis of this problem see William J. Goode, "The Theoretical Importance of Love," *American Sociological Review*, 24:38-47, February, 1959.

background is quite a different matter from romance. Romance often flourishes brilliantly across racial lines. Many persons have a deep sexual affinity for members of a race of a different skin color. Their hearts flutter, their imaginations run rampant, they feel a compelling sexual urge— being drawn to the member of the contrasting race with an almost hypnotic fascination. This is ground for wonderful romance, not necessarily for a successful marriage.

One might go on with examples to show that romance is not enough, nevertheless, the American marriage without some romance would be dull indeed. Older cultures have recognized this for centuries and have often reserved romance for the mistress, not for the wife, thus ensuring family stability. Wifehood and motherhood are recognized as institutions, not merely as flighty emotional experiences. They are symbolic of the persistent, systematic, demanding routine aspect of life.

In trying to combine romance and marriage in the marriage-family system, Americans have made some gains, but these can only be realized as realities of married life are projected into the romance.

Romantic Love as a Basis for Marriage

One of the exciting and yet dangerous aspects of the romantic love situation is the influence of what psychologists characterize as "halo effect." By halo effect the psychologist means the assessing of personality entirely in terms of some particular trait. Given one or several attractive traits, the personality is wholly accepted on the basis of these traits. Or, conversely, given one or several unattractive traits, the personality is wholly rejected on the basis of these traits.

Halo effect operates in the love relationship more than in any other social relationship. Sex attraction and the appeal of certain superficially valuable "dating skills" provide a brilliant halo that obscures all other personal qualities. They symbolize to the attracted partner the ultimate of everything that is desirable. If the love is not pursued to the point where the halo can be penetrated, permitting a reasonable appraisal of the romanticized one's true capacities, the risk is great indeed. This is a hazard of marriages that occur without an adequate period of acquaintance. Disillusionment following marriage is an inevitable consequence of marriages that have occurred in the glow of the halo effect.

Margaret Mead, with the comprehensive view of the anthropologist, sees the American concept of romance as a factor in marriage instability.[9] After marriage, in our culture, even casual flirtation is considered a

[9] Margaret Mead, *Male and Female* (New York: William Morrow & Co., Inc., 1949), pp. 64-65.

threat. In cultures where marriage is a permanent institutional relationship, however, as in Europe, flirtations and even heated extramarital affairs are not serious threats to the marriage. In our marriage system romance is put to the test after marriage as well as before.

Even if Mead is right in assuming that our romantic marriage leads to too much temperature-taking after marriage, the essential elements of the romantic mate-choice system are likely to continue in our way of life—with, perhaps, some tempering by other values.

Actually, it appears that romance, as a method of mate selection, is on the wane in the United States, although much on the increase in some other countries. In Japan, where for centuries mate selection has been by proxy and go-betweens, romantic love matches are greatly on the increase, and there, where society is in transition between old and new philosophies of marriage, a Supreme Court Justice has estimated that marriages made by parents and go-betweens end in divorce four to five times as often as "love matches."

Sociologists, Burgess and Wallin, studying 1,000 engaged couples in the United States, express the belief that romantic love is on the decline in the United States as a major factor in mate choice, and that an increased emphasis on companionship and compatibility are in evidence.[10] They find that 12 percent of men and 15 percent of women even go so far as to think that it is all right to marry a person when not in love with him.[11]

One suspects that a reason for the emergence of this view is the emphasis upon romance and thrill seeking during the dating period. Many young people learn during this period that highly excited romance is often a temporary thing, so that when they settle down to selecting a mate, they are more interested in the enduring qualities that can survive in a day-to-day relationship. This means ability to get along together in social and recreational life; ability to make plans together for children, family, and for an economic future.

There probably is more realism in mate seeking today, at least among the more intelligent groups of the population, than there was a generation ago. Of course, college professors in the field of marriage and family like to think that they have played a part in this, in that for more than two decades the emphasis in marriage education through books, magazine articles, and lectures has stressed the desirability of realism. But one must grant that if professors thought love was all that mattered, there would be no reason for their writing books and articles on marriage or

[10] Ernest W. Burgess and Paul Wallin, *Engagement and Marriage* (Philadelphia: J. B. Lippincott Co., 1953), p. vii.
[11] *Ibid*, pp. 393-395.

teaching about marriage. Nature would handle the job of mating and marriage.

In summary, love means different things to different people and the definition any one person gives to love tells us more about that person than it does about love itself. The very young inexperienced person thinks of love in narrow, absolute, and highly romantic terms. The unhappy or incomplete person thinks of love in terms of his own personality needs. The individual who knows love best feels least capable of offering a simple all-inclusive definition of the term.

Love in its broadest sense includes the love of parents for their children and of children for their parents, relatives, and dearest friends. It includes the love of comrades, aged people, and secret one-sided love. It even includes the love that the very wise may feel for all humanity. Love may partake strongly of companionship, it may grow out of admiration, and be characterized by submission and devotion. Love may grow out of pity, or insecurity, and it may involve domination, selfishness, and even cruelty.

Loves of all kinds, however, have two basic elements in common. First, there must be a strong feeling of attraction to the love object. One cannot love another individual whom one finds genuinely unattractive. Second, love of every kind brings satisfaction to the lover. The joy of a love either far outweighs the unhappiness it sometimes brings or else the individual who is "miserably in love" actually enjoys his state of misery.

In addition to the above qualities, all love affairs which involve members of the two sexes have a sexual aspect, too. There may be strong overtones of intellectual respect or spiritual companionship which strengthen the relationship, but sexual attractiveness remains basic to the love of man for woman and woman for man.

In this love relationship the element of self-satisfaction is most clearly operative. Parents, relatives, and even many friends are just "inherited," but when it comes to finding a love, or loves, among the opposite sex, pure self-interest seems to take over. Consciously or otherwise, people seek dates, and later, mates, who have personality traits that compliment their own and that seem to promise the fulfillment of their own deepest needs.

Understanding these personal needs, and evaluating potential mates in terms of them, may sound unromantic, but such considerations add up to common sense and successful marriage. Evaluating one's own traits, one's general maturity and readiness for marriage, is an equally important task as one begins to think seriously of marrying.

This does not mean that it is wrong to "get serious" more than once. Close relationships with the opposite sex can get out of hand and lead to problems, but they also have many beneficial effects in personality development. And, contrary to popular belief, the breakup of an affair is not often the disastrous experience it once was thought to be. In recent studies of college students, only a small minority reported actual traumatic experiences resulting from broken love affairs. In most instances, love faded gradually and undramatically into indifference and the once-loved one was rather quickly forgotten.[12]

Problems

1. Draw curves of your various love affairs. What kind of up-and-down pattern do they show? Are they all similar in trend? Do all move at the same speed? Can you mark the relationship or act that brought about the termination of former love affairs?

2. As a group project, devise what you believe to be an adequate test of love. With one person at the blackboard as recorder, have members of the class suggest behavior, attitudes, etc., which an individual should expect of himself or his loved one before concluding "this is love." For example:
   a. "I am physically attracted to him or her."
   b. "I am proud to have my family and friends meet him or her."

3. Make three criticisms of the dating customs of your campus or community. Briefly describe how these shortcomings could best be remedied by individual or community action.

4. Have the class divide into sections for an informal discussion concerning the most desirable function of dating. Have one group support dating as "preparation for marriage"; have the other defend dating as "a form of amusement." At the end of the discussion decide as a group whether the two interpretations seem irreconcilable or not.

5. Do library research on the dating or mate-choice customs of other countries and report.

6. Pick the three items which rate highest with you. In asking for or accepting a date I am most interested in someone who:
   a. Is good looking.
   b. Is popular among individuals of my sex.
   c. Is courteous.
   d. "Rates high" on campus or in the community.
   e. Is modest and unassuming.
   f. Shares my religious and cultural background.
   g. Would live up to my parents' standards.
   h. Enjoys a good time and isn't too prudish.

[12] Discussed more fully in Chapter 19.

What does your choice suggest with regard to (*a*) your background? (*b*) the kind of marriage you are likely to have? Does the consensus of male and female students differ? If so, discuss the significance of this fact.

7. The dean of women in a small coeducational college described the following situation to a gathering of the dormitory house-mothers. She did so in order to get their suggestions for improving the situation. Read her description and consider possible action that could be taken:

"Girls on our campus outnumber boys almost two to one. Competition among the young women for the available dates is intense and of an alarming character. Girls from the finest homes seem to lose all of their respect for propriety, modesty, and fair play; those who do not, are left dateless.

"The mode of dress on the campus is changing from that of traditional college simplicity to one of open suggestiveness. Drinking and petting are becoming the rule instead of the exception on off-campus dates. Girls are willing to risk open criticism and poor grades by cutting class in order to keep coke dates with the fellows.

"Girls who came to our college seriously concerned about an education seem to have lost their heads in this mad scramble for male attention.

"One's first inclination is to 'crack down.' We have seen that done on many campuses. I came here to speak to you, hoping that we might avoid this by immediate action of a more positive and constructive nature."

Selected References

ARTICLES IN BOOKS OF READINGS

BECKER, Howard, and HILL, Reuben (Editors), *Family, Marriage and Parenthood,* Second Edition (Boston: D. C. Heath & Co., 1955).
    1. FOLSOM, Joseph K., "Steps in Love and Courtship," pp. 206-245.
WINCH, Robert F., and others, *Selected Studies in Marriage and the Family,* Revised Edition (New York: Holt, Rinehart & Winston, Inc., 1962).
    2. BEIGEL, Hugo G., "Love: Courtly, Romantic and Modern," pp. 510-517.
    3. GOODE, William J., "The Theoretical Importance of Love," pp. 455-470.
FISHBEIN, Morris, and KENNEDY, Ruby Jo Reeves, *Modern Marriage and Family Living* (New York: Oxford University Press, Inc., 1957).
    4. BOWMAN, Henry A., "The Diagnosis of Love," pp. 132-143.
LANDIS, Judson T., and LANDIS, Mary G., *Readings in Marriage and the Family* (Englewood Cliffs, N. J.: Prentice-Hall, Inc., 1952).
    5. KIRKPATRICK, Clifford, and CAPLOW, Theodore, "Courtship in a Group of Minnesota Students," pp. 79-90.
    6. TRUXAL, Andrew G., and MERRILL, Francis E., "The Family and Romantic Love," pp. 108-113.
COSER, Rose Laub, *The Family: Its Structure and Functions* (New York: St Martin's Press, Inc., 1964).
    7. GOODE, William J., "The Theoretical Importance of Love," pp. 202-219.

SUSSMAN, Mervin B., *Sourcebook in Marriage and the Family,* Second Edition (Boston: Houghton Mifflin Co., 1963).
    8. BEIGEL, Hugo G., "Romantic Love," pp. 86-93.
KRICH, A. M., (Editor), *Women: The Variety and Meaning of their Sexual Experience* (New York: Dell Publishing Co., Inc., 1954).
    9. SCHWARZ, Oswald, "On Love," pp. 286-311.
CAVAN, Ruth Shonle, *Marriage and the Family in the Modern World: A Book of Readings* (New York: Thomas Y. Crowell Co., 1960).
    10. FOOTE, Nelson N., "Love," Reading 36.
    11. HORTON, Donald, "The Dialogue of Courtship in Popular Songs," Reading 38.
CHRISTENSEN, Harold T., *Handbook of Marriage and the Family* (Chicago: Rand McNally & Co., 1964).
    12. BURCHINAL, Lee G., "The Premarital Dyad and Love Involvement," Ch. 16.

General References

BURGESS, Ernest W., and WALLIN, Paul, *Engagement and Marriage* (Philadelphia: J. B. Lippincott Co., 1953), Ch. 7.
CAVAN, Ruth Shonle, *American Marriage* (New York: Thomas Y. Crowell Co., 1959), Ch. 6.
GOODE, William J., "The Theoretical Importance of Love," *American Sociological Review,* 24:38-47, February, 1959.
GOODENOUGH, Ruth, "Dating and Security," *Understanding the Child,* 26:59-60, January, 1957.
HOBART, Charles W., "Disillusionment in Marriage and Romanticism," *Marriage and Family Living,* 20:156-162, May, 1958.
KEPHART, William M., *The Family Society and the Individual* (Boston: Houghton Mifflin Co., 1961), Ch. 11.
KIRKPATRICK, Clifford, and CAPLOW, Theodore, "Emotional Trends in the Courtship Experience of College Students as Expressed by Graphs, with Some Observations on Methodological Implications," *American Sociological Review,* 5:619-626, October, 1945.
MARTINSON, Floyd M., *Marriage and the American Ideal* (New York: Dodd, Mead & Co., 1960), Chs. 9-11.
MERRILL, Frances E., *Courtship and Marriage,* Revised Edition (New York: Holt, Rinehart & Winston, Inc., 1959), Ch. 3.
WALLER, Willard, and HILL, Reuben, *The Family* (New York: Holt, Rinehart & Winston, Inc., 1951), Ch. 7.

11

The Dating Game

Dating is an American invention, and it is proving to be one of the more diffusable inventions of our civilization. It is being borrowed widely throughout the world wherever American films and American soldiers are to be found. The older generations abroad mistrust it; the young like it. So it is spreading with tremendous rapidity in countries like Japan, our most conscious imitator, and to a lesser extent in many parts of the world.

Whether we are doing the world an injustice in providing such a pattern only history will tell. Certainly it is a daring thing to trust mate choice to the impulse of youth. In mate choice society risks its most cherished values—family status, which is a precious social heritage; its property, for property is transmitted through family inheritance; family name, which is its method of biological survival through the centuries. These values have, in most societies, been jealously guarded. Historically, it was assumed they could not be trusted to the judgment of youth, certainly not to youth guided by the elusive quality we call romance. Elders have of necessity, or so they thought, arranged marriages of their young people, and have in most cultures created devices of isolation and taboo designed to make romance impossible prior to the wedding night, when couples meet face to face and are alone for the first time.

Perhaps one can blame the American frontier for too much, but certainly it was responsible for banishing caste lines. A man on the frontier came to be measured by his performance; woman, by her ability to hold her own in meeting the challenge of an untamed environment. The tradition of established English and European society offered few status patterns that assured survival in frontier culture. A person survived or perished by his wits and endurance. His status was achieved, not prescribed by the social position of his ancestors. Geneologies tended to be forgotten and mates chosen on the basis of performance rather than social position. And in a nation of abundant resources, the need to pass on an inheritance was minimized as compared with cultures where generations of family effort were required to accumulate any property at all.

A direct contrast is seen in India and Pakistan, where parent-arranged marriages have been the pattern for centuries. A Ph.D. candidate at Washington State University explained that his degree would be worth $3,000 to him in a marriage bargain when he returned to Pakistan. An Indian student for the Ph.D. said his would be worth even more to his family in bargaining for a wife.

Here are advertisements clipped from the "Matrimonial" column of a New Delhi metropolitan newspaper. These are young people for the most part whose relatives have died, and who have no one to negotiate for them, but some are liberated young people who assert their right of mate choice. Note that status, education, and/or earning capacities are included in qualifications:

MATRIMONIAL

An Advanced, Beautiful, Educated, well-versed, Maharashtrian girl 21 and engineer 25, invite confidential details from similar cultured parties, view matrimony. . . .

Educated, Good Charactered, healthy Christian of good family 35-40 for a cultured, talented lady. Those drawing 5 and above need apply. Correspondence confidential, view matrimonial. . . .

Gujarati Double Graduate Respectable Bania youth doing business invites correspondence from beautiful, cultured girls or their parents, view matrimony. . . .

Wanted A Youngman Of Liberal views, educated and well settled in life for a highly accomplished and cultured girl of 23 B.A. (Hons.); only daughter of a Gazetted Officer, belonging to Maharashtrian, Brahmin community, holding high position outside Bombay State. . . .

To the influence of the frontier as a factor in breaking class barriers and institutionalized marriage forms we must add the growth of urban industrial culture and of a mobile population—all developments that have made dating, as a way of getting acquainted, a necessary innovation in mate choice. In a society in which young people leave the family nest to go to college or to seek their future in a distant state or city, parents and other elders are in no position to choose for their young people.

Add to this the rapid upward climb made possible in a land of opportunity, where education and occupational achievement tend to raise the new generation above their parents in schooling and vocational level, and one has a situation in which the new generation distrusts the elder's ability to choose and in which the elders often as not feel incompetent to do so. The elders sense that their sons and daughters have already outdistanced them in knowledge, even if not in the practical judgment that age alone can ripen.

These are some of the cultural and social factors that have led to the pattern of dating in our society, a pattern of increasing interest. Young people are dating earlier and the proportion of the teen group dating seems to be increasing. Also, dating is increasingly accepted by adults.

Youth, influenced by movies, becomes skilled in the technique of lovemaking. The automobile has provided privacy—a quality lacking in most other cultures—for only here in America can many teenagers have a car to use. Dating has become an important pastime of the adolescent years—an experience of thrills, hurts, confidences, and betrayals—through which the age group becomes seasoned in experience with the opposite sex.

Because of the dating pattern of mate choice and the romantic emphasis of teenage social life, love (in this narrow sense) has become a national problem. It is certainly one of the greatest personal problems of high school and college social life. The girl's counselor at both levels of schooling spends much of her time listening to the woes of the brokenhearted. Many a long session involving high school or college teenage peers is spent in analyzing "love" mates and "love" experiences. The relationships between men and women are the primary concern of the girl previous to marriage, and not a minor concern of men, although certainly girls major in this concern more than do men.

From "Keeping Company" to Dating

In the horse-and-buggy days, "keeping company" was standard practice. Dating as it is now known was not a part of the accepted pattern of life. Taking a girl home from church was almost the equivalent of being pinned or engaged today. The reason was that everyone knew everyone else, their families, their reputations, their economic status, their character. When young people "walked out" together, they already knew a great deal about one another. Intentions could be and were more or less serious from the beginning. A boy and girl seen together more than once were assumed to be "courting." The community so regarded them, as did competing young men or women.

Dating is a social engagement between two people for the sake of the date itself, and without marital intentions.

Dating has evolved as the natural and logical product of the anonymity, urbanization, individualism, secularization, and the emancipation of young women from chaperonage that has gradually come to characterize American society. As the nation's population shifted from farms and small towns to large cities, the earlier customs defining boy-girl relations broke down. Courtship patterns of the past were built around a relationship involving two people who had known one another more or less intimately for years—usually since childhood. There are today few city residents who have known their neighbors and friends very long.

While many of the transplanted families tried to maintain what they considered the "high standards" of their rural past, this usually meant isolation and loneliness for the young people of the family. After all, a girl in a large city who was forbidden to go out with anyone she had not known for years, usually found that, in effect, this meant she did not go out at all.

Traditions of mate seeking were not so ingrained and sacrosanct as to withstand the numerous contacts of teenagers in the modern city. Gradually, the rules and regulations in most families relaxed, and newly acquainted young men and women began building together new codes of behavior and new concepts of right and wrong to govern their associations with one another. Somehow they had to get acquainted, and, since conditions did not allow for the growth of familiarity through inevitable day-to-day relationships, a more casual type of initial relationship was demanded. Thus dating—a means of getting better acquainted, of looking one another over, and of indicating interest but with no strings attached—has gradually become the rule.

The family has ceased to be the center of life for the young person. Dating received a further impetus as high schools and colleges brought together increasingly large groups of young people of the same age. The daily association of young people in curricular and extracurricular activities in coeducational high schools and colleges made dating the central activity of social life for this age period, and hence, also, the key to much of happiness or disappointment.

It is possible for a person to date through high school and/or college without ever having any serious intention to select a mate. Although potentially any date may develop to the point of serious interest, dating as such is now a part of the normal social activity of young people. By dating, they size up members of the opposite sex and extend their close acquaintance with them long before they have any intention of choosing a partner for marriage. It is in this setting, nonetheless, that romantic love has become exaggerated out of all normal proportions, as viewed historically and as viewed by most other peoples in the world.

Dating Under Attack

European college women have a low opinion of American dating. One finds the same attitude among foreign students here, at least until they become used to the customs of American college campuses.

They think American young people must be a promiscuous lot since they date so freely, kiss, and engage in other forms of physical intimacy after only casual acquaintance. The Europeans expect these contacts only after a considerable period of "walking out" and often only with the person whom they expect to marry. They see dating as a strenuous competitive game in which the American girl is trying to secure as many men as possible at the same time. This, they suppose, is her only way to become popular. They assume that such a girl has to resort to all kinds of tricks to keep the male coming back for more dates. While she is doing this, she isn't sure of her relationship with any one man. European women feel that such a relationship is too uncertain to be interesting.[1]

The European male, from his observations of love making in American movies, and from his noting the sex emphasis of advertising and love stories in American magazines, is quite sure that the American female is ready, on the most casual acquaintance, to participate in full sexual relationships with any male she finds attractive. It is likely that if an American youth of a hundred years ago were suddenly to reappear, his first conclusion would be quite similar. The close association of the sexes sanctioned in dating circles today were in his day reserved for the final stages of going together or for marriage itself.

But it has not been the superficial observer alone who has challenged dating. Those who have made a study of marriage and the family have attacked it on scientific grounds.

The late Willard Waller[2] introduced into American thinking the idea that dating is a competitive game, engaged in primarily for status, rather than serving any useful function in the mate-selection process. He found that on the college campus it means thrill seeking and adventure. He saw dating as a game of trying to win favors without becoming involved emotionally oneself. He saw in it men and women trying to associate on an intimate basis, without either one breaking down and losing control. He felt the least emotionally involved member manipulated the situation, with the most involved being the likely victim of exploitation.

---

[1] For a scathing criticism of American women, and particularly of coeds, by a French woman who spent three years in high school and college teaching in the United States see Christie Rieuf, "Praying Mantises," *Atlas*, 1:40-45, April, 1961.

[2] See Willard Waller, "The Dating and Rating Complex," *American Sociological Review*, 2:727-734, 1937. His theories are also discussed in Willard Waller and Reuben Hill, *The Family*, Revised Edition (New York: Holt, Rinehart & Winston, Inc., 1951).

The male, he found, has his line, and the female her wiles, and each tries to win the other without being won. He observed that the man who rated highest on the campus had plenty of money, a car, good clothes, and fraternity membership. The experienced college man was one with a "good line," smooth manners, good appearance, and the ability to dance well. With the girls, the keynote was "nothing succeeds like success." Women who rated best were those who managed to be seen at the right place with the right men, who had a "good line," good clothes, and skill in dancing. However, an appearance of propriety with respect to drinking and unconventional behavior was also important. Waller felt that students "extend themselves enormously" in order to meet the qualifications of the campus standards for dating according to these varied and yet fairly well understood norms.

Waller saw in these values much that is contradictory to success in marriage. He felt that these spurious considerations tended to distract a student's attention from the kind of values that contribute most to lasting marital success. The whole dating pattern, he believed, was built upon competition and materialistic display—two values that have only a negative association with happiness and adjustment in marriage.

He held that this dating-rating game has no relationship to serious mate seeking, and he felt that the entire activity tends to indicate a decay of the moral structure centering around family behavior; that the objective is largely one of physiological sensation and tension relief. He believed that dating, with its necking and petting, should be regarded as a game rather than as having any serious relationship to courtship. He also felt that the risk of emotional injury resulting from dating is great. He believed that when a person shifts from casual dating to the serious matter of courtship, an entirely new set of values and behavior patterns are required; that, in fact, there is a distinct break between the one type of experience and the other.

Even though he considered that many of the dating practices have no positive relationship to marriage, and may actually detract from marriageability, he did grant that, in some cases, courtship does follow. However, he felt that the thrill-seeking experiences of dating were better training for future thrill seeking than for marriage. He believed that dating developed the habit of dalliance in the personality, that is, of deliberately stalling the development of any close emotional relationship which might lead to courtship and marriage.

Sociologists have taught the Waller theories for more than thirty years, have discussed them, and have subjected them to research. The controversy still goes on and evidence increases.

Authors of a more recent and extensive study of dating practice among students in three Midwestern and two Western coeducational colleges, find that dating involves considerable rating on the college campus.[3] They feel that the acceptance or rejection of a date is definitely related to the status aspect of the situation. Dating being regarded as an event, with no direct relationship to marriage, it can be treated entirely as a matter of gaining status, if a person so desires to use it. These authors find that fraternities, sororities, and other organizations play a decided part in dating on the college campus, and that their social events require or encourage dating. Jessie Bernard has described fraternities and sororities in coeducational schools as "in large part dating and courting institutions."[4]

Rogers and Havens, at Iowa State, find rating enters decidedly into dating.[5] Eleven undergraduate judges rated major residence groups as to prestige. Data show that prestige classes entered into all phases of mate selection from casual dating up to mate choice itself. Students date, become pinned, become engaged, and marry within their own prestige class. They conclude further that, "Waller's hypothesis that prestige rating governs casual campus dating but not more serious mate selection is not substantiated to any great degree by present findings. Instead, these findings indicate that students follow prestige lines at all stages in the mate-selection process."

A Wisconsin University study finds that, in general, fraternity men tend to marry sorority women.[6] The above researchers find that in these intimate groups on the campus, rating takes place, too. A fraternity man, for example, is generally given a higher rating than a nonfraternity man; sorority girls rate higher than nonsorority girls. Different statuses may be assigned to different fraternal groups, as to different offices or positions on the campus. This rating affects personal relationships in that a couple often is as much aware of the impression they are going to make on others as they are of the impression they are going to make upon each other. Campus queens and similar competitive contests based upon feminine beauty or feminine form enter into this rating complex.

This study, however, found no basis for the theory that dating develops a habitual pattern of dalliance—that is, putting off close relationships with the view to deferring marriage. It showed no evidence that men and women in their dating relationships try purposely to avoid the growth of emoitonal bonds which might lead to love and marriage.[7]

[3] Ernest W. Burgess and Paul Wallin, *Engagement and Marriage* (Philadelphia: J. B. Lippincott Co., 1953).

[4] Jessie Bernard, *American Community Behavior* (New York: The Dryden Press, Inc., 1949), p. 394.

[5] Everett M. Rogers and A. Eugene Havens, "Prestige Rating and Mate Selection on a College Campus," *Marriage and Family Living*, 22:55-59, February, 1960.

[6] T. C. McCormick and A. P. Sundal, "Age at Marriage and Mate Selection," *American Sociological Review*, 16:37-48, February, 1951.

[7] *Ibid.*

There was no consistent tendency for an individual's later dating relationships to be longer or closer than his earlier ones. In fact, if anything, some of the earlier relationships for men tended to be longer than some of the later ones. Women seemed to report the opposite, later relationships tending to be somewhat more permanent. In over a fourth of their early dating relationships, both men and women had discussed the possibility of marriage.

Herman[8] believes he finds some evidence that there is dalliance in the dating pattern on college campuses. While many couples are oriented toward marriage in their heavy dating, others are definitely dallient in their attitudes.

Dating is dalliance to the extent that it is uncommitted association. There is no obligation to repeat the date, or to give the slightest consideration to marriage. What is done on a date is without future irrevocable committments. The dating continues only so long as each finds it interesting and each other's behavior satisfactory. Moreover the very attitude of putting off serious committments may develop a habit of dalliance which is hard to overcome. As a college senior age 26 said, "I have put off being serious so long for the sake of my education, now that I am ready for marriage, I can't overcome the habit of looking for faults and magnifying them in prospective mates."

A study of young men and women at Pomona College sought to learn the reasons why these students did not become seriously interested in the young man or woman they dated.[9] The three reasons most often given by 300 young women for not becoming seriously interested in any of the more than 1,100 young men whom they had dated were that the men: (1) were self-centered, (2) were weak, dependent, or had no ambition, (3) represented cultural and family differences.

A hundred young men gave the following as their three most important reasons for not becoming seriously interested in any of the over 350 young women whom they had dated: (1) the women were shallow, weak, or the clinging-vine type, (2) they were self-centered, or (3) they represented cultural and family differences.

Robert O. Blood,[10] sociologist at the University of Michigan, made the Waller rating hypothesis the subject of a special study, using a group of University of Michigan students. He also made comparisons of his findings with data from two other institutions. He found very little support for the Waller thesis. Although students were found to be aware

8 Robert D. Herman, "The Going Steady Complex: A Re-examination," *Marriage and Family Living*, 27:36-40, February, 1955.

9 Ray E. Baber, *Marriage and Family*, Revised Edition (New York: McGraw-Hill Book Co., 1953), pp. 130-133.

10 Robert O. Blood, Jr., "A Retest of Waller's Rating Complex," *Marriage and Family Living*, 17:141-147, February, 1955.

of most of the items in the Waller thesis, such as fancy clothes, fraternity-sorority membership, a "good line," great popularity, money, etc., they rated them much lower than many other factors in their dating behavior and in their evaluation of dating partners. Blood found that "more than half of Waller's items failed to be chosen by a majority of Michigan students and, therefore, do not constitute norms for this campus as a whole in 1953."

He finds little support for Waller's idea that a student has to change to an entirely different type of behavior when he shifts from casual dating to serious dating.

No doubt a major factor in the decline of the college "rating" system is the product of profound changes in values in American youth culture. The college population has long since ceased to be upper class or even upper middle class. The base of selection has broadened to include the lower middle class and even a sprinkling of the lower class as scholarships have been made more numerous. Competence rather than pedigree tends to be the criterion of worth as both high school and college students become more serious about scholastic matters. Competition for college entrance, and for survival once enrolled, has tended to develop seriousness of purpose in the student. The decline in the prestige of fraternity houses, along with the stress on integration, have brought added pressure in the direction of equalitarian values. They carry less snob appeal than in earlier generations. In many quarters, their value system has been made suspect. Some campuses have dared to ask the question of whether or not such class-conscious groups should be permitted in a democratic social order, and some campuses have already outlawed them.

The Values in Contemporary Campus Dating

Blood has tried to arrive at the values which college young people hold uppermost in their evaluating of a date. A group of 95 men and 134 women, a cross-sectional sample of the undergraduate students at the University of Michigan, was presented with a check list of 37 items pertaining to dating values.[11] They were asked to check values for both casual dates and for serious dates. The table below lists the six items that were selected by almost all men and women students for both casual and serious dates.

[11] This summary and the tables are taken from a mimeographed report presented by Robert O. Blood before the Groves Conference on Marriage and the Family, at Purdue University, April 30, 1954. See his "Uniformities and Diversities in Campus Dating Preferences," *Marriage and Family Living*, 18:37-45, February, 1956.

TABLE 11-1————Items selected with substantially unanimous approval of University of Michigan students as elements in the campus rating complex for both sexes and as qualities preferred in casual and serious dates

| | PERCENT OF RESPONDENTS CHOOSING ITEM | | | |
Item	*Campus Rating Complex*		*Personal Preferences*	
	for women	for men	casual dates	serious dates
1. Is pleasant and cheerful	100.0	97.8	97.9	99.4
2. Has a sense of humor	91.6	97.8	96.8	98.7
3. Is a good sport	93.7	97.8	94.5	98.9
4. Is natural	93.7	96.3	95.5	100.0
5. Is considerate	95.8	99.3	96.6	100.0
6. Is neat in appearance	100.0	97.8	98.2	99.4

Blood doubts that, in the light of this evidence, Waller's contention that casual dating is unfavorably related to mate selection is valid; in fact, he doubts that it has any application to contemporary college students.

In November, 1950, The *Purdue Opinion Poll for Young People* studied 8,000 high school students scattered throughout the United States. While conditions will vary in different localities, this is the best picture at present on just how high school young people rate various traits in dating. They checked the following seven traits as of first importance in making or accepting a date.[12]

1. is physically and mentally fit
2. is dependable, can be trusted
3. takes pride in personal appearance and manners
4. is clean in speech and action
5. has pleasant disposition and sense of humor
6. is considerate of me and others
7. acts his own age, is not childish

Both boys and girls were pretty well agreed that these are the things that count most in a date. There is little evidence here of rating being of major importance among the younger set.

A study of unmarried students in the University of Colorado showed the traits these young people rated highest in characterizing a good mate.

———
[12] The findings reported here are from Harold T. Christensen's analysis of a stratified sample of 2,500 cases drawn from the above sample and published in his "Dating Behavior as Evaluated by High School Students," *American Journal of Sociology*, 57:580-586, May, 1952.

Both men and women rated companionability as the most important characteristic of a good date and a good mate. Men and women differed somewhat in certain values. Men rated physical appearance fairly high, whereas women rated social graces higher than looks.[13]

In Defense of Dating

Most sociologists contend that dating is a necessary and important part of the mate-selection process in modern society. They believe that it fulfills the function of sexual selection; that it is a normal stimulus to maturation; and finally, that it involves a chain of "allure and pursuit, by means of which the prospective mates are ultimately carried on toward biological union."[14]

It is quite logical to believe that some kind of dating is necessary to the development of the judgment and pair interaction that is at the root of real objectivity in mate selection. Since few people can marry a playmate from the old home town, dating is the modern way of bridging this gap. It is the only way of bringing potential mates, their pasts and their values, under scrutiny before any serious intentions are declared.

Those who have dated more than one person have a chance to compare and to learn some of the usual behavior patterns of members of the opposite sex. They learn to distinguish between those whose personalities seem to promise a durable compatibility and those whose personalities obviously do not. Dating is an exploratory experience through which young people learn. It no doubt contributes to the development of the ability to feel at ease with the opposite sex and the love play sanctioned in dating may well be an important factor in the development of a normal heterosexual orientation in the psychosexual area.

In the United States, where nearly all young people have so many superficial and transient contacts, there is no other way to get acquainted with members of the opposite sex and to discover their ways of acting and thinking. If marriages are to be based on compatibility, young people must learn to size up members of the opposite sex in all aspects of their personalities.

In most circles today, therefore, it is considered desirable that young people "circulate," rather than "go steady" from the beginning, until they find a relationship that will satisfy both their temperamental and intellectual tastes. It is even considered that some variety of dating

[13] Eleanor Smith and J. H. Greenberg Monane, "Courtship Values in a Youth Sample," *American Sociological Review*, 18:635-640, December, 1953.
[14] Niles Carpenter, "Courtship Practice in Contemporary Social Change in America," *The Annals of the American Academy of Political and Social Sciences*, 160:38-44, 1932, presents a representative statement of this view.

experience is favorable to ultimate mate choice. The girl who is considered desirable as a date by a number of fellows is presumed to be the one most likely to be sought after in marriage. Dating teaches that there is no "one and only" by predestination. After normal experience in dating, the average young person comes to appreciate the fact that there are certain individuals with whom he could not possibly be happy, and that there are certain individuals with whom he could live happily. He may even discover that the more normal and adjustable he is, the greater the range of persons whom he could marry and with whom he could be content.

Awkward as this dating business may seem to outsiders, it appears to be the only method open to a highly individualistic society. It puts much more moral responsibility on young people than they have ordinarily been trusted with. It burdens them with the momentous choice of a life partner, yet this is a choice which young people in an individualistic society such as ours prefer to retain.

In summary, it has been observed that dating is not merely a game, as some authorities have claimed, but a necessary adaptation of our age. One cannot deny that dating has its rating aspect,[15] but human beings enter into few social relationships that are completely free of this. Possibly dating-rating may find its worst expression among fraternal groups, which in themselves have some snob appeal, but the evidence seems to indicate that, by and large, young people pick and choose dates for substantial qualities rater than for status alone.

Those who are inclined to discount dating solely on its rating aspects will do well to remember that courtship in the more staid period of an earlier day had its rating aspects, too. Marrying for connections, for dowries, for a share in the quarter section of land down the road, are as old as human nature. In many cultures rating is still a very much institutionalized part of the mate-selection-marriage pattern, and is given precedence over young people's romantic inclinations.

Problems

1. We have emphasized that there is no "one and only" and that a successful marriage is primarily a matter of mutual adjustment. Therefore, dating to

[15] Another approach to the status aspects of dating has been that of the social class theorists who are interested in the extent to which lines of social stratifications are held. This is quite a different problem. August B. Hollingshead, for example, has shown that dating is usually within the same social class. See his *Elmtown's Youth* (New York: John Wiley & Sons, Inc., 1949), pp. 211 ff.

find the "right mate" is a valuable preface to mate selection. Do you agree with this view?

2. Discuss the pro and con of the proposition: "Where competition for dates is intense but the group's codes of dating behavior are high, the competition may actually be a constructive force in personality development."

3. Discuss the Waller thesis on dating and present research evidence to support or refute it.

4. Poll the class on the five traits they most desire in a date. Tabulate results and compare responses of men and women. Do the standards held by the group appear to be spurious and superficial or genuine and durable? Do preferred traits mentioned seem to be of the kind on which a sound mate choice could be made? Are the values of men or women the more sound?

5. Discuss the extent to which girls on your campus feel they must play the role of temptress or coquette in dating. What effect does this have on their personal adjustment? The views of both men and women should be sought on this problem.

6. Do you consider that the girl or fellow of college age who dates a great number of persons, but refuses to go steady, is probably emotionally unstable and in need of personal counseling? Discuss the pros and cons of this question.

7. Is petting considered necessary or at least desirable for successful dating on your campus?

Selected References

ARTICLES IN BOOKS OF READINGS

WINCH, Robert F., and others, *Selected Studies in Marriage and the Family*, Revised Edition (New York: Holt, Rinehart & Winston, Inc., 1962).
   1. WALLACE, Karl Miles, "An Experiment in Scientific Matchmaking," pp. 532-542.
   2. WINCH, Robert F., "The Function of Dating in Middle-Class America," pp. 506-508.

LANDIS, Judson T., and LANDIS, Mary G., *Readings in Marriage and the Family* (Englewood Cliffs, N. J.: Prentice-Hall, Inc., 1952).
   3. WALLER, Willard, "The Rating and Dating Complex," pp. 60-65.

CAVAN, Ruth Shonle, *Marriage and the Family in the Modern World: A Book of Readings* (New York: Thomas Y. Crowell Co., 1960).
   4. KTSANES, Thomas, and KTSANES, Virginia, "Do 'Opposites Attract' or Does 'Like Marry Like'?" Reading 29.

CHRISTENSEN, Harold T., *Handbook of Marriage and the Family* (Chicago: Rand McNally & Co., 1964).
   5. BURCHINAL, Lee G., "The Premarital Dyad and Love Involvement," Ch. 16.

General References

BEE, Lawrence S., *Marriage and Family Relations* (New York: Harper & Row, Publishers, 1959), Ch. 7.

BLOOD, Robert O., Jr., "International Dating Experiences of American Woman Students," *Marriage and Family Living*, 24:129-136, May, 1962.

————, "Uniformities and Diversities in Campus Dating Preferences," *Marriage and Family Living*, 18:37-45, February, 1956.

BREED, Warren, "Sex Class and Socialization in Dating," *Marriage and Family Living*, 18:137-144, May, 1956.

BURGESS, Ernest W., and WALLIN, Paul, *Engagement and Marriage* (Philadelphia: J. B. Lippincott Co., 1953), Ch. 3.

CAVAN, Ruth Shonle, *The American Family* (New York: Thomas Y. Crowell Co., 1953), Ch. 12.

————, *American Marriage* (New York: Thomas Y. Crowell Co., 1959), Chs. 4, 5.

CHRISTENSEN, Harold T., "Dating Behavior as Evaluated by High School Students," *American Journal of Sociology*, 57:580-586, May, 1952.

DUVALL, Evelyn M., and HILL, Reuben, *Being Married* (New York: Association Press, 1960), Chs. 7, 8.

HOBART, Charles W., "Emancipation From Parents and Courtship in Adolescents," *Pacific Sociological Review*, 6:258, October, 1958.

KIRKPATRICK, Clifford, *The Family as Process and Institution*, Second Edition (New York: The Ronald Press Co., 1963), Ch. 12.

WALLER, Willard, "The Dating and Rating Complex," *American Sociological Review*, 2:727-734, 1937.

————, and HILL, Reuben, *The Family* (New York: Holt, Rinehart & Winston, Inc., 1951), Part 3.

12

Sex Roles and Sex Codes in Dating

The American dating pattern is one in which favors are exchanged between the sexes. Although it is not a strictly commodity-oriented activity, there is something of this element present in dating in that values are exchanged. The male invests money and time. He expects sex pleasure in return. It is a matter of degree as to how much sex pleasure will be expected and how much will be given.

Probably the greatest parental concern, where daughters are involved, is sex conduct in dating. And as the girl gets older, this proves to be the area of greatest conflict between mother and daughter. Bell and Burkle[1] found it so in the relationship of mothers with daughters from age 20 on, in a college sample. Mother-daughter views clash as do their ideals of conduct.

The part each sex plays in dating and the way the other sex reacts to the role played determines the nature of the game, its interest and outcome. What is known about male and female roles in dating?

The *Purdue Opinion Poll for Young People* data previously cited[2] throws considerable light on sex roles in dating in the early teen period. Girls viewing the boy's role in dating felt that boys are usually more careless and thoughtless, less inhibited, more disrespectful, sex-driven, and loud. Boys criticized girls for being "less natural and more touchy, money-minded, unresponsive, childish, and flighty."

[1] Robert R. Bell and Jack V. Burkle, "Mother and Daughter Attitudes to Premarital Sex Behavior," *Marriage and Family Living*, 23:390-393, November, 1961.

[2] A. J. Drucker, Harold T. Christensen, and H. H. Remmers, "Some Background Factors in Socio-Sexual Modernism," *Marriage and Family Living*, 14:334-337, November, 1952.

When it came to placing blame for lack of success in dating, boys were much more likely to blame the girls than to blame themselves or other boys. Girls were more likely to feel that some other girl was a competitor, thus hindering the success of the date.

Male Initiative

Both boys and girls of the high school group confessed that they very often feel "shy, self-conscious, or ill-at-ease" when dating. This is probably why almost half the boys and a little more than a fourth of the girls thought girls should take more initiative in making dates. This question and some other important questions of the poll are shown below, with the percentage of boys and girls answering yes.

	PERCENT ANSWERING YES	
Do you believe that:	*Boys*	*Girls*
It would be a good thing if girls could be as free as boys in asking for dates?	48	27
It would be a good thing if girls would pay half the expenses of dates?	29	21
It is all right for a couple to kiss on the first date?	51	33
Intimate petting should be delayed until after marriage?	31	66
Sexual immorality is any more wrong for girls than for boys?	27	36

As one looks this list over, he sees reasons why young people often differ as to what should be done on a date. In asking for a date, and in money matters, the boys are much more willing to have the girls share equally with them than the girls are to do it. In matters of intimate relations, the girls claim stricter standards than do the boys.

Viewing sex roles in dating at the college level, college men and women approach dating from divergent viewpoints.[3] The college man looks upon dating as a form of entertainment by which he postpones marriage until he is established in a career. The college woman is interested in dating as a means of securing a partner from the freshman year on. Men who do not date avoid it because they are not interested in it. Women who fail to date ordinarily have no opportunity to date. Women rarely choose not to date; men do choose not to date.

In college situations, dating often involves an event, not merely a personal relationship. College dating also involves certain codes that are

---

[3] Ernest W. Burgess and Paul Wallin, *Engagement and Marriage* (Philadelphia: J. B. Lippincott Co., 1953), pp. 63-109.

more or less standardized on the campus, in addition to whatever personal codes the individual may have. Such group codes offer considerable moral protection to the girl in the dating of relative strangers on the college campus.

The chief problem in dating is the sex problem. Anything from a goodnight kiss to necking, light and heavy petting, or in some cases even sexual intercourse may be involved. Men take the aggressive role; women appraise it in terms of whether or not it is accompanied by affection. The girl is more likely to "draw the line" than the boy. Girls are more interested in the moral reputation of the men they date than are boys in the moral reputation of the girls they date. Fear of acquiring a bad reputation acts as a factor in sexual restraint on the girl's part.

Contemporary researchers find only a limited amount of the sexual exploitation on the college campus such as Waller said existed. They feel that public opinion generally operates as a check on exploitation in spite of the heterogeneity of the modern student body.[4]

In dating, the double standard still holds sway in economic and in sexual matters. Money is a definite handicap to the man's dating; sex a risk of the woman's dating.

The distinction in sex roles in dating, however, is beginning to disappear, with women taking more initiative and encouraging "Dutch treat"—even at times paying the expense of the recreation.[5] Women enter into planning the date more than formerly, too. Possibly there is also a relaxing of the double standard of morality. If this is so it is because women's codes are relaxing. All these points are debated issues. One study which compares dating practices through three generations, finds no evidence of any change in the matter of men paying the bills and giving most of the gifts.[6] In Scandinavian cultures the practice is one of sharing costs.[7]

In sexual matters, it is still assumed that the male will be the aggressor and that the female will set the standards. The usual, and perhaps natural tendency of the male, is to see how far the female will go. The girl is more restrained because she fears society's unsympathetic condemnation of premarital pregnancy, and because of her awareness of her role as a potential mother.

Some people believe that the male's tendency to take sexual initia-

[4] Ibid., p. 88.

[5] John F. Cuber, "Changing Courtship Customs," The Annals of the American Academy of Political and Social Science, 229:31-34, 1943.

[6] Marvin R. Koller, "Some Changes in Courtship Behavior in Three Generations of Ohio Women," American Sociological Review, 16:366-370, 1951.

[7] William Simenson and Gilbert Geis, "Courtship Patterns of Norwegian Students and American University Students," Marriage and Family Living, 18:334-338, November, 1956.

tive, and the female's role of being seductive and alluring, rather than aggressive, have their roots in biological evolution.[8] These characteristic male-female traits are in evidence in many animal species. Those who hold this theory believe that the female is unnatural when she tries to assume initiative, and becomes aggressive. They believe such a woman hinders her cause in dating and marriage.

Whether man and the beast are analogous, and whether or not sex roles are entirely a matter of shaping the personality by culture patterns, are questions that can be debated endlessly and perhaps with little value. The writer has already (Chapter 3) expressed a preference for the view that biology is at least a factor. Whatever the cause, the male-female roles are still definitely typed in American culture and affect the reaction of the sexes to particular approaches. In large cities where the sex ratio, from the standpoint of mate choice, is greatly in the male's favor, the female not only has become more aggressive, but is expected to be. In rural areas, where men are in the majority and where the traditional attitudes toward the female still persist, the aggressiveness of the urban female would be spurned.

Physical Contact in Dating Success

In dating, the question of how far to go in physical contact is a matter of considerable importance to women. Playing the passive role in dating as they do by custom, having dates represents for them a kind of competitive achievement. Being able to hold the interest of the male is a constant problem. Sex plays a part in this.

Waller[9] believed that girls in competitive situations, particularly where males are in the minority, have to compromise on sexual morality in order to keep the male from breaking up the relationship.

One hundred and forty-one young men and 258 young women at the University of Minnesota[10] were asked this question: "Did you give in on important moral or theoretical issues for fear of losing him or her?" Eighty-one percent of the women denied ever having done so. Sixteen percent said they did occasionally; only 3 percent said they often did. Two-thirds of the men said they never did; 28 percent said, occasionally; 4.5 percent, often.

Girls who indulge in close forms of physical intimacy rationalize that

[8] See, for example, Paul Popenoe, "Mate Selection," *American Sociological Review*, 2:635-643, 1937.

[9] Willard Waller, "The Dating and Rating Complex," *American Sociological Review*, 2:727-734, 1937.

[10] Clifford Kirkpatrick and Theodore Caplow, "Courtship in a Group of Minnesota Students," *American Journal of Sociology*, 51:114-125, 1945.

only if they do so can they have dates. Girls holding the opposite view, however, seem to be correct. Studies of attitudes on college campuses over a period of more than ten years show that most college students do not believe moral compromise necessary for popularity. One may be sure that many students are speaking from experience.

A study of the attitudes of 364 students at Cornell in 1941 showed 94 percent did not consider that "a girl must pet on dates to be popular." In 1947, 2,000 students at Michigan State were asked the same question, and in 1952, 450 students at the University of California. At Michigan State, 77 percent of the men and 94 percent of the women said, "No." At California, 82 percent of the men and 92 percent of the women said, "No." Very few at any school answered, "Yes." A number were undecided.[11]

LeMasters[12] is skeptical of such research. He believes girls reply in the negative, for to reply otherwise would reflect on their confidence in their other charms. Also the "no" reply fits the mores better. Boys also say "no"—otherwise it would appear they cannot rise above sex desire in their dating relationships. Men want girls with sex appeal. LeMasters believes it is the unusual girl who can be popular without the use of such devices of sex attraction.

Although most young people state that petting is not a factor in holding a member of the opposite sex, its practice is more general now than at the beginning of the century, as are other forms of intimate sexual contact.[13] This is due partly to social sanction, and partly to cultivated interest in sexual excitement by some persons with extensive dating experience. One suspects, too, that it is an indication of an effort on the part of many girls to prove to themselves that they are adequate, not frigid, etc. So much is made of sex in contemporary culture, and the average male's drives are so specific and intense, that many girls feel inadequate. They fear their lack of specific sexual feelings and want to play a compensating part, not knowing that most women in their teens have little or no recognizable sexual desire. The nature of woman's sex drive is discussed more fully later (Chapters 23 and 24).

There is much current literature about "sex on the college campus." Authors of varying degrees of competence, under highly marketable titles, present their views. Few substantiate their opinions concerning a great

---

[11] These studies, the first by Rockwood and Ford, the others by Judson T. Landis, are graphically summarized in Judson T. Landis and Mary Landis, *Building a Successful Marriage,* Third Edition (Englewood Cliffs, N. J.: Prentice-Hall, Inc., 1958), pp. 85-90.

[12] E. E. LeMasters, *Modern Courtship and Marriage* (New York: The Macmillan Co., 1958), pp. 192-193.

[13] Alfred Kinsey and his colleagues find it so. See Alfred C. Kinsey and others, *Sexual Behavior in the Human Female* (Philadelphia: W. B. Saunders Co., 1953).

increase in premarital sexual intercourse. Pressure for interdormitory visiting on some campuses has added fuel to their suspicions of the breakdown of sexual morality.

There is no doubt that young people are more aggressive in wanting sex left in their own personal control, unregulated by administrative authority. There may be some increase in premarital sexual intercourse as confidence in birth control increases. No evidence has been accumulated by reliable researchers to demonstrate a widespread breakdown in sexual morality on the college campus. It is very likely that there is still a stricter code of sex morals there than in any other large sector of young people of similar age in society outside the campus.

Ehrmann's extensive study of college behavior, with particular attention to sex behavior, finds that physical contact in dating tends to go through certain stages with increasing degrees of intimacy. The male usually initiates; the female usually determines the limits. The male with extensive dating experience tends to be the one with most experiences in erotic behavior. For the "female, sexual expression is primarily and profoundly related to being in love and to going steady."[14]

Technical virginity is the norm of the middle more educated classes. It is less so of the lower social classes and lower educational group. Data of the Kinsey research team[15] strongly suggest that necking, petting, and masturbation are sublimating devices, primarily of the middle-class group, which help this group to delay coitus and marriage for the attainment of goals realizable through a college education.[16] Girls enforce the limitations on sex, which stop short of coitus, but the middle-class male believes in this standard, too, since he expects conformity to it of the girl he becomes serious about. Even heavy petting seems to be primarily a substitute for sexual intercourse, rather than a stimulus to it.[17] It permits sexual excitement of a high degree without defloration.

The significance of defloration in our society, as in all societies which consider it of significance, is largely cultural, for the biological process itself is, in the case of most women, a minor incident. In some cases, where the hymen is extremely heavy, it may be broken only with diffi-

[14] Winston Ehrmann, *Premarital Dating Behavior* (New York: Henry Holt and Company, 1959).

[15] Alfred C. Kinsey and others, *Sexual Behavior in the Human Male* (Philadelphia: W. B. Saunders Co., 1948), pp. 343 ff. Alfred C. Kinsey and others, *Sexual Behavior in the Human Female* (Philadelphia: W. B. Saunders Co., 1953), pp. 233-234; see also Margaret Mead, *Male and Female* (New York: William Morrow & Co., Inc., 1949), pp. 209-291; also Eugene J. Kanin and David H. Howard, "Postmarital Consequences of Premarital Sex Adjustments," *American Sociological Review*, 23:556-562, October, 1948.

[16] *Ibid.*

[17] So the Kinsey group data suggest.

culty, and may even require surgical attention, but in most instances it is very easily broken.

The social aspect is serious. Our culture, like many others, makes the hymen a symbol of virtue and judges morality by its presence or absence. This means that defloration under unapproved circumstances can be a major crisis in the life of a woman. In some cultures, the absence of the hymen is taken as absolute evidence that he girl has lost her virginity through sexual intercourse. In such cultures it is a major tragedy, often of lifelong importance, for no man will think of marrying the woman who is not a virgin. This philosophy has been very prominent for the upper classes in Latin cultures, in Pakistan, India, and in many other societies as well as in some primitive tribes.

Modern medical science has revealed that a broken hymen is not necessarily proof of loss of virginity. Some girls have practically no hymen at birth. In others it has been injured in infancy and early childhood, so that practically no hymen remains, or perhaps none at all. The hymen may be accidentally broken by the very athletic girl in various play activity; it may be destroyed through masturbation; it is stretched or broken by internal medical treatment and by routine monthly use of tampons— a "sanitary" development of modern science which is nearly universally established in certain age-educational-cultural groupings. In some environments, however, presence or absence of the hymen is still of great social significance.

Balance in Dating Interactions

Cultivating emotional responsiveness while maintaining standards of morality is the chief problem of modern dating. Many primitive societies permit unrestrained sex play previous to marriage. Other cultures condone or even encourage pregnancy before marriage. In these cultures, the female becomes a more desirable mate if she can show her suitors that she is capable of pregnancy.

American culture still places a high value on chastity. Most young men who initiate sexual relations with their dates prefer to marry girls who have never compromised their own standards. At the same time, those girls and young women who participate in intimate premarital relations seldom do so as a matter of principle or preference. More likely, they succumb to momentary excitement, or they yield to men they respect, or they have a mistaken notion of "what a girl must do to hold her man." Few do so because of an overwhelming desire.

In our society the whole business of boy-girl relations is complicated for some young people by this contradiction between values and behavior.

The girl or boy who gets off to a good start in interpersonal relations, who have an outgoing personality, who makes friends easily and shares many interests and activities with age mates is seldom faced by the problem. The unsuccessful boy or girl, on the other hand—the one who wants friends but doesn't know how to make them, who wants dates but feels that he or she has little to offer—generally stumbles into this dilemma at one time or another. The problem is not just "what others will think," but also what the promiscuous individual thinks of himself. An individual cannot long live happily believing one way and behaving in another way.

With emotionally insecure young people, the love-sex element in dating is particularly risky. Having no deep anchor in parental love, the dating game becomes a substitute for the love these young people missed as children and do not receive at home.

But even the emotionally secure youth today runs a considerable risk of becoming prematurely involved in an emotionally exaggerated relationship. The intense loneliness and uncertainty produced by living in a highly mobile, ever-changing group, drives many young people to desperate lengths to find a sense of permanency. In our chaotic modern world, it is inevitable that some adolescents will reach out to members of the opposite sex for the security and sense of belonging that emotional involvement seems to promise. Some of the most striking examples of this are to be noted among soldiers, who, in times of war, quite seriously propose marriage to girls whom they have known for as little as half a day, or for only an evening.

In novel circumstances and situations of psychosocial isolation, deep affection for a member of the opposite sex is likely to be used as a device for restoring self-assurance, and for protecting oneself against the apparent hostility and coldness of the world. For such an individual, love comes to stand for success in social adjustments.[18]

In the long run, certain attitudes on the part of the male or female do more than anything else to insure the success or failure of their dating relationship. The double standard in sex matters is a relatively insignificant factor, for example, as compared to the more general attitude of the individual toward members of the opposite sex.

Many men still cannot genuinely accept women as equals. This is bound to affect their behavior in dating situations. It is also true that many women do not as yet accept themselves as the equals of men. Some

[18] For a discussion of some of these psychological problems see Karen Horney, *The Neurotic Personality of Our Time* (New York: W. W. Norton & Co., Inc., 1937), pp. 286-287; also J. K. Folsom, *The Family and Democratic Society,* Revised Edition (New York: John Wiley & Sons, Inc., 1948).

intelligent women feel that in order to succeed on a date they must play down their intelligence and competence, lest they overshadow the male ego and in that way threaten his loyalty to them. There is no doubt some carryover in the male of the days of chivalry. Some want the female to be a clinging vine. The male likes to be admired and to have his ego flattered. Some college girls actually do play down their intelligence, skills, and competence as persons, in their dating relationships.[19]

It is doubtful that such tactics, however, can in the long run win or hold a man. Almost any man, in the final analysis, respects a woman for being what she is, without pretense. Trying to hide what one is in interests, temperament, and abilities can later bring trouble and misunderstanding.

Paul Popenoe, marriage counselor and founder of the American Institute of Family Relations in Los Angeles, reproduced in his newspaper column a letter from a girl who said, "I'm getting tired of acting inferior to my dates in order to hold them."

Popenoe's reply was "They're probably getting more tired of it than you are."

The dating situation is one of changing sex roles, and in an area of locally defined—often campus-defined—custom. Although certain sex roles in dating are fairly well-defined, all are subject to challenge.

Male and Female Sex Codes in Casual and Serious Dating

One of the great complications of dating—and perhaps this is the fascination of it—is that men and women approach their dates not only with different conceptions of what their roles should be, but also with different conceptions of what the opposite sex expects their role to be. Nowhere is this more evident than in the area of sex behavior. Blood's students at the University of Michigan were asked to indicate from a check list their perceptions of what the opposite sex expected of a date. They were also asked to check their own ideas of traits a good date should possess.[20]

In Table 12-1, the left-hand column shows the percentage of women checking a particular item as their idea of what men want when they take a woman out on a casual date. In the right-hand column appear college

---

[19] Paul Wallin, "Cultural Contradictions and Sex Roles: A Repeat Study," *American Sociological Review*, 15:288-293, 1950.

[20] Robert O. Blood, Jr., "Uniformities and Diversities in Campus Dating Preferences," *Marriage and the Family*, 18:37-45, February, 1956.

men's actual preferences. Most college women think popularity with the opposite sex is an essential. Little more than half the men think so. About two-thirds of the women are inclined to think that reputation concerning physical contacts (questions 3, 4, 5) has a decided bearing on being a desirable date. Men are much less particular about a woman's reputation on these matters than women think.

TABLE 12-1————Significant discrepancies between the female rating complex at the University of Michigan as perceived by women students and the actual dating preferences of men students*

	PERCENT OF RESPONDENTS CHOOSING ITEM	
Female characteristic	Women's perceptions	Men's casual dating preferences
1. Is popular with the opposite sex	86.6	54.7
2. Has a car or access to a car	2.2	11.6
3. Doesn't have a reputation for necking	62.3	29.7
4. Doesn't have a reputation for petting	68.9	38.9
5. Is willing to pet on occasion	29.1	58.9
6. Is willing to join in a group	97.0	82.1
7. Is a well-rounded person	91.8	81.1
8. Is a good listener	97.0	87.4

* Differences between percentages are considered statistically significant when the probability of their occurring by chance in a sample of this size is not greater than .05.

The following table (Table 12-2) reverses the situation and men show what they think women want in a date (left column). The right column shows what women actually want. Men rate a car much more highly than women, as they do also fraternity membership, activities, money, clothes, visits to popular places, skill in dancing, and looks. Here again differences in sex codes of men and women are in striking contrast, with women discounting a man for the kind of sex behavior men think women expect of them. It is little wonder that the sex problem has become the most critical one in modern dating relationships. It must continue to be so as long as attitudes of men and women are so far apart.

It is often stated that young people's attitudes toward intimate contacts during dating depends on whether or not the relationship has reached the serious and steady stage of going together. Strong support is found for this view in the responses of University of Michigan students. Men, as tradition holds, impose much higher sex behavior standards on the girl they are seriously interested in than on the girl they take on a

TABLE 12-2————Significant discrepancies between the male rating complex at the University of Michigan as perceived by men students and the actual dating preferences of women students

	PERCENT OF RESPONDENTS CHOOSING ITEM	
Male characteristic	Men's perceptions	Women's casual dating preferences
1. Is popular with the opposite sex	77.9	61.2
2. Has a car or access to a car	57.9	11.2
3. Doesn't have a reputation for necking	44.2	70.9
4. Doesn't have a reputation for petting	50.0	78.4
5. Is willing to pet on occasion	53.3	8.2
6. Is willing to neck on occasion	74.7	34.3
7. Is affectionate	77.7	54.5
8. Belongs to a fraternity	50.5	11.9
9. Is prominent in activities	49.5	17.2
10. Has plenty of money	34.7	6.7
11. Has plenty of clothes	20.0	4.5
12. Has polished manners	81.1	68.7
13. Dates popular students only	12.6	3.7
14. Goes to popular places	77.9	38.8
15. Knows how to dance well	76.6	49.3
16. Is good looking	86.2	61.2
17. Is willing to drink socially	50.0	32.8
18. Is natural	90.5	98.5

casual date. Here are the men's responses to two key questions dealing with sexual contacts in dating:

	Prefer on casual dates (percent)	Prefer on serious dates (percent)
Doesn't have a reputation for petting	39	75
Doesn't have a reputation for necking	35	67

Almost twice as many men prefer the woman who is free with intimate behavior on casual dates as prefer the woman who is free with intimate behavior on serious dates.

Most women, by contrast, want their intimate contacts confined to serious dates. Here are college women's responses to two key questions:

	Prefer on casual dates (percent)	Prefer on serious dates (percent)
Is willing to neck on occasion	34	68
Is willing to pet on occasion	8	32

Hewitt, also, finds that young people are much more selective about a marriage partner than they are about a date.[21] Things they consider crucial in the selecting of a marriage partner, they consider as relatively unimportant concerning the date. For marriage they want companionability, which requires a mate who is well-mannered, emotionally mature, affectionate, thrifty, and who has a sense of humor.

Hewitt's study of young men and women at Ball State Teacher's College shows also that men and women have rather serious misconceptions regarding what the other sex wants in certain areas.[22] In the areas of physical attractiveness, being affectionate, and sexual conventionality, there is considerable disagreement in what men and women want in future mates. In traits like having a car, men enormously overrate what they think women want. In the matter of sexual conventionality men very much underrate what women want, since women are great sticklers for conventionality. In the area of ambition and being sensible about money, both men and women rate these traits as very important for themselves but underrate them in the opposite sex. On the matter of rating socially, both men and women depreciate this trait for themselves but are unable to give the other sex credit for not thinking it important.

The Male Line

The sexually aggressive male has numerous techniques for turning the date into a sexually complete experience. The physical technique of lovemaking may be no more important than the verbalized attempts in achieving his goal. The girl must not only know where to draw the line, in terms of point of termination of necking or petting activities, but also must know what weight to give to words in terms of their motivations as persuasive techniques. Here briefly are some of the verbal tactics employed in sexual exploitation:

Technique	*Verbalization*
The domineering or threatening	"Do you think I'll spend my time and money and not . . ."
Big shot	"I've got plenty of girls who will."
Love at first sight	"No girl has ever affected me as you do."
Pity	"I'm so tense."
Injured	"But you've led me on, and now, . . ."
Shame	"Don't you have any feelings?"
Abnormal	"You're a cold cucumber."

[21] Lester E. Hewitt, "Student Perception of Traits Desired in Themselves as Dating and Marriage Partners," *Marriage and Family Living*, 20:344-349, November, 1958.
[22] *Ibid.*

Logic   "It's good experience, etc., . . ."
Universality   "Kinsey found . . ."
Authority   "Kirkendall believes . . ."
Restrained, calculating   No love-making, until girl breaks, then
                                         moves in for the kill.

Drinking and Sex in Dating

Drinking is one of the problems of modern dating. A comprehensive study[23] of the drinking habits of 5,000 American college women and 10,000 American college men in 27 colleges scattered throughout the country indicates very clearly that college is not to be blamed for the drinking habits of very many young men and women. An overwhelming majority of college young people who use liquor, used it before they came to college. It was a pattern in their homes; it was imbedded in the customs of their families. The study shows that those who drink tend to associate largely with those who drink. It shows that drinking increases with the amount of income and that almost as much drinking to excess results from the use of beer as from stronger liquors. Comparatively few college men or women drink to the point of becoming drunk.

In clarifying the effect of drinking on dates, this study is inconclusive. While the authors recognize the folk belief that alcohol stimulates sex activity, breaks down inhibitions, and facilitates intimate contact in dating, they find that there is a counteracting tendency also; that young men who are tempted to drink to excess often restrain themselves for fear that they will be involved in violence, and that young women who fear they will drink to excess often restrain themselves sexually in drinking situations for fear of the pregnancy and reputation risks involved. They find that few students attribute school problems, encounters with the law, accidents, or social difficulties to their drinking. Six percent of the students who drink, however, already show tendencies toward alcoholism.

The study shows that 17 percent of men and 10 percent of women have considerable anxiety about their drinking, apparently fearing its consequences on their lives. For the most part, this group was made up of the heavy drinkers. The study also shows that drinking has greatly increased in recent generations.

Rather than alcohol being a stimulant, the authors of the study, after a review of medical research, conclude that it has a depressant effect,

[23] The study is published as one of the Yale Center of Alcohol Studies publications, and is by Robert Straus and Selden D. Bacon, *Drinking in College* (New Haven: Yale University Press, 1953).

bringing loss of sensitivity, reducing speed of reaction, and tending to cause loss of control. They find also that it tends to reduce discrimination.

All of these effects would seem to be points against the use of alcohol in dating situations in which one has any serious intentions toward mate selection. In making a choice of a life mate, the maximum perception and discrimination are desirable.

Problems

1. *Research exercise:* Poll the class with the following brief questionnaire (other questions may be added if desired). Indicate your sex but do not give your name.

    a. I have on occasion drunk while on a date. _____ yes

       _____ no

    b. I did so—because I enjoy drinking _____.

       —because I wanted to fit in with the others _____.

    c. I believe drinking among students on the campus is—common _____.

       —uncommon _____.

    d. I believe a girl who won't "neck" a little on a casual date is too prudish. _____ yes

       _____ no

    e. My feeling is "you're only young once," so if you can have some sexual thrills without running much of a risk I say go ahead. _____ yes

       _____ no

    f. I would resist heavy petting because I know it would

       —displease my parents _____.

       —be unfair to my future mate _____.

       —leave me with less self-respect _____.

       —soon "get around" and spoil my reputation _____.

    Compare results for men and women. Discuss the significance of findings to marriage and family life.

2. The following statement was made by a popular college senior who, by the way, did not drink. Analyze it and discuss its merits:

    "The reason so many of us get in trouble about drinking is that drinking is always associated in our minds with 'being adult' but 'moderation' is a virtue we cannot understand. I believe that if drinking were permitted during adolescence as is smoking, it would soon loose its mysterious appeal. Girls who want to should be able to learn to prepare a decent cocktail in college as well as a full-course dinner. Fellows who want to drink on their date should have access to decent cocktail lounges where moderation and propriety are the rule; this would make secretive drinking unnecessary and unexciting."

3. A college sophomore girl is urging her friend to accept a double date with a fellow who has a reputation for drinking and petting. Present both arguments, as each girl sees them, in a convincing manner.

4. Discuss dating regulations on your campus. Are they:
   a. Reasonable?
   b. Too lax?
   c. Outmoded?
   d. Overly authoritarian?
5. When young people of high school or college age begin to drink on dates or in mixed groups of their age mates, do you consider that they are trying to make a bid for status in their group's eyes, or to imitate Hollywood, or what are they trying to do?
6. The male animal in most species, and in most human societies, is the aggressor in male-female relationships. Do you consider that it would be against nature's design, and therefore undesirable, to encourage female initiative in dating and courtship behavior, or is this merely a matter of modifying customs? Discuss.

Selected References

ARTICLES IN BOOKS OF READINGS

WINCH, Robert F., and others, *Selected Studies in Marriage and the Family,* Revised Edition (New York: Holt, Rinehart & Winston, Inc., 1962).
1. DAVIS, Allison, "Class Differences in Sexual and Aggressive Behavior Among Adolescents," pp. 352-355.

VINCENT, Clark E., *Readings in Marriage Counseling* (New York: Thomas Y. Crowell Co., 1957).
2. KIRKENDALL, Lester A., "A Viewpoint on the Premarital Sex Problem," pp. 117-126.

FISHBEIN, Morris, and KENNEDY, Ruby Jo Reeves, *Modern Marriage and Family Living* (New York: Oxford University Press, Inc., 1957).
3. STEPHENS, Anna O., "Premarital Sex Relationships," Revised by Morris Fishbein, pp. 158-166.

LANDIS, Judson T., and LANDIS, Mary G., *Readings in Marriage and the Family* (Englewood Cliffs, N. J.: Prentice-Hall, Inc., 1952).
4. MURDOCK, George P., "Sexual Behavior, What Is Acceptable? A Comparative Anthropological Approach," pp. 403-408.
5. WOODWARD, Luther E., "Viewpoint of the Mental Hygienist," pp. 408-412.
6. KIRKENDALL, Lester A., "Sound Attitudes Toward Sex," pp. 419-427.

CAVAN, Ruth Shonle, *Marriage and the Family in the Modern World: A Book of Readings* (New York: Thomas Y. Crowell Co., 1960).
7. PRINCE, Alfred J., and SHIPMAN, Gordon, "Attitudes of College Students Toward Premarital Sex Experience," Reading 39.
8. KIRKENDALL, Lester A., "Premarital Sex Relations: The Problem and Its Implications," Reading 40.

CHRISTENSEN, Harold T., *Handbook of Marriage and the Family* (Chicago: Rand McNally & Co., 1964).

9. EHRMANN, Winston, "Marital and Nonmarital Sexual Behavior," Ch. 15.

General References

BELL, Robert R., and BURKLE, Jack V., "Mother and Daughter Attitudes to Premarital Sexual Behavior," *Marriage and Family Living*, 23:390-393, November, 1962.

BURGESS, Ernest W., and WALLIN, Paul, *Engagement and Marriage* (Philadelphia: J. B. Lippincott Co., 1953), Chs. 4, 11, 12.

CAVAN, Ruth Shonle, *American Marriage* (New York: Thomas Y. Crowell Co., 1959), Ch. 10.

DEDMAN, Jean, "The Relationship Between Religious Attitude and Attitude Toward Premarital Sex Relations," *Marriage and Family Living*, 21:171-176, March, 1959.

DRUCKER, A. J., CHRISTENSEN, Harold T., and REMMERS, H. H., "Some Background Factors in Socio-Sexual Modernism," *Marriage and Family Living*, 14:334-337, November, 1952.

EHRMANN, Winston, *Premarital Dating Behavior* (New York: Henry Holt and Co., 1959).

KANIN, Eugene J., and HOWARD, David H., "Postmarital Consequences of Premarital Sex Adjustments," *American Sociological Review*, 23:556-562, October, 1948.

KINSEY, Alfred C., and others, *Sexual Behavior of the Human Female* (Philadelphia: W. B. Saunders Co., 1953).

KIRKPATRICK, Clifford, *The Family As Process and Institution*, Second Edition (New York: The Ronald Press Co., 1963), Ch. 14.

KOLLER, Marvin R., "Some Changes in Courtship Behavior in Three Generations of Ohio Women," *American Sociological Review*, 16:366-370, 1951.

LEMASTERS, E. E., *Modern Courtship and Marriage* (New York: The Macmillan Co., 1957), Ch. 9.

POFFENBERGER, Thomas, and others, "Premarital Sexual Behavior: A Symposium," *Marriage and Family Living*, 24:254-278, August, 1962.

STRAUS, Robert, and BACON, Selden D., *Drinking in College* (New Haven: Yale University Press, 1953).

13

Personality Ratings of Those Who Do and Do Not Date

In any competitive game or activity some must lose. The penalty the loser pays has made many people wish to do away with competition entirely. Educators, religious thinkers, reformers, as well as revolutionary political leaders have dreamed of a beautiful but unrealistic life in which all competition has been done away with, and in which every man's and every woman's sense of personal worth is unthreatened by the superior success of rivals.

Whether or not such a life would be interesting to mankind is perhaps debatable. Surely it has seldom been achieved, and where a seemingly noncompetitive order has been found among primitives, the culture has not been noted for its achievements or for its high standard of living or aspiration. Nonetheless, one cannot dismiss lightly the effect of failure in competition on the individual who fails. Dating is competitive. Failure here is real failure.

There is considerable evidence that young people from the more privileged homes, where opportunity for social growth generally exists, are the ones who tend to date earlier, to date a greater number of persons, and tend to avoid extensive steady dating. They also tend to defer marriage longer for the sake of education.[1]

Early dating and going steady is found to be typical of those who are American in heritage, who are above average in education and are from small families of relatively high socioeconomic status. Soon many revert to playing the field. Late dating is more typical of those of foreign heritage, lower in education, and from large families. These go steady quickly after starting dating and tend to stay with it.

[1] See Samuel H. Lowrie, "Early and Late Dating: Some Conditions Associated with Time," *Marriage and Family Living*, 23:284-291, August, 1961; also *Purdue Opinion Poll for Young People*, 15:4a, February, 1956.

Judson T. Landis,[2] studying 3,000 college students, related their dating history in junior high, high school, and college to happiness of the parents' marriage. Those from happy homes formed friendships more readily in early adolescence, developed more active and confident dating patterns, had a more favorable self-evaluation of their personalities, and had greater confidence in their likelihood of making a successful marriage

The *Purdue Opinion Poll for Young People* showed that almost half of the high school boys and 39 percent of the girls in their sample of 8,000 had rarely or never dated (Figure 13-1). This included, of course, the whole age range from freshman to senior year. A study of college young people[3] showed that 31 percent of the men and 20 percent of the women had not yet begun dating at age seventeen.

Here then is a statistical picture of the nondating group. If this were all a matter of personal choice, the statistics might have little significance. However, the girl who fails to obtain dates and, later, proposals of marriage, suffers one of the unfortunate by-products of our highly romantic conception of marriage. She is likely to feel that she has lost out in the most important competition of a woman's world, and she will probably feel defeated and frustrated. Although this is primarily a woman's problem, some men also are crowded out in the competitive process.

Winch has tried to appraise the factors that relate to dating behavior.[4] This study showed that a favorable attitude on the part of parents helped to determine early dating; that young men and women of higher socioeconomic status tended to date more than those of low status; that better-looking men and women dated more persons and more frequently than those who were less attractive. Appearance and money may be almost as important to the dating behavior of the younger adolescent boy as to the girl.

Dating As a Step in Psychological Weaning from the Family

Ceremonial rites (rites of passage) marking the transition from childhood, or adolescence, to manhood have been extensively practiced among primitive peoples. Such initiations for boys often take the form of

2 Judson T. Landis, "Dating Maturation of Children from Happy and Unhappy Marriages," *Marriage and Family Living*, 25:351-353, August, 1963.

3 Ernest W. Burgess and Paul Wallin, *Engagement and Marriage* (Philadelphia: J. B. Lippincott Co., 1953), p. 119.

4 R. F. Winch, "Interrelations Between Certain Social Background and Parent-Son Factors in a Study of Courtship Among College Men," *American Sociological Review*, 11:333 ff., 1946; also R. F. Winch, "Courtship of College Women," *American Journal of Sociology*, 55:269-278, 1949.

SELDOM DATE
HIGH SCHOOL STUDENTS

PICTOGRAPH CORPORATION

DID NOT BEGIN DATING BY AGE 17
COLLEGE STUDENTS*

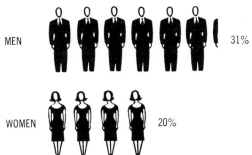

PICTOGRAPH CORPORATION

* 1,223 college students.

Source: Ernest W. Burgess and Paul Wallin, *Engagement and Marriage* (Philadelphia: J. B. Lippincott Co., 1953). Reproduced by permission of the publisher.

FIGURE 13-1————Dating is a highly selective institution.

ordeals testing a youth's capacity to suffer. In many societies the period of puberty is spent in isolation from parents in special shelters or camps. In these bachelor quarters the boys are initiated into the roles and philosophies of adulthood in their community, and are taught their new relationship to women, to work, and to children. Girls in similar camps are in the custody of wise old women who teach them what it means to grow up and become mothers and administrators of tribal households.

There are no such formal rites in American culture unless coming-out parties, mixed social gatherings, dances, etc., could qualify. These functions unquestionably help to push young people out of the family nest. More significant, however, is the sanction of informal dating relationships which permit the growth of heterosexual attachments.

The roots of emotional life are in the family. They remain there throughout childhood, the parents and siblings being the natural center of emotional attachment. During adolescence there must be a gradual shift of this attachment from the family focus to members of the opposite sex. The ultimate attainment of emotional maturity depends in large part, as was suggested in an earlier chapter, upon the effectiveness with which the adolescent succeeds in making this transfer of his deeper emotional attachments to a member of the opposite sex. Those who fail to make the transfer and who remain permanently "tied to the mother's apron strings," or too much attached to the father, or to a brother or sister, fail to achieve the kind of emotional maturity that is necessary for establishing a new, independent family.

Dating is not absolutely necessary to this weaning process, but it does seem to provide a normal and natural shift to heterosexual emotional alignment outside the family.

Dating, with its close personal ties, is a factor in developing the psychosexual nature of the individual, particularly today when concrete expressions of emotion are expected. Kissing and necking when they express genuine emotion, become overt steps in a young person's emotional transfer from the family circle. The stimulation such contacts provide often represent a desirable preliminary to the growth of natural heterosexual interests. The way is paved for a normal responsive approach to members of the opposite sex. Without dating, the young person lacks this experience and is to that extent retarded in emotional development.

Comparative Personality Ratings of Those Who Do and Do Not Date

Since preoccupation with dating and with its related activities and interests is unquestionably characteristic of today's adolescent world, one might logically expect to find those who do not date seriously deficient in personality development and in general adjustment. Is this the case? Is there any significant relationship between dating and all-around adjustment?

Nimkoff and Wood's study of dating and courtship among Bucknell University students found only a slight relationship between dating and social and emotional adjustment. In fact, those who did not date had almost as high adjustment scores on the *Bell Adjustment Inventory* as did those who dated.[5]

There was a slight but significant difference in personality. Those who never dated were more retiring and had some tendency toward emotional maladjustment. The best adjustment was found among those who started going steady during the senior high school years. Excessive dating was related to only moderate emotional adjustment, and was also related to social aggressiveness. This study, of course, does not answer the question whether dating itself is conducive to adjustment or whether people merely feel maladjusted because they do not date.

A study of the dating habits of 500 students in coeducational colleges showed that very early pairing-off may be a serious emotional handicap.[6] This study showed that those who started going steady in grade school or in junior high school were in great danger of having emotional maladjustments later than were those who deferred going steady until senior high school or college, when marriage could be seriously considered. Of course, there is no way of knowing whether this going steady at an early age is cause or effect. The maladjustment may already be there, and the early steady emotional attachment may be an expression of it, rather than the reverse.

Burgess and Wallin's study of college students[7] found that those who do not date may suffer slightly from defects in personality, that they sometimes are less well adjusted emotionally, and sometimes exhibit a lack of skill in social relations. On the other hand, students often do not date because of preoccupation with other interests, sometimes athletic, sometimes intellectual. It was found that those who willingly forgo dating usually find more or less satisfactory compensation for this lack in their own personalities.

This study finds that girls are more aware of the positive effect of dating on their personality development than are boys. Since girls take the passive role in dating, success in dating tends to replace an inferiority feeling with self-assurance. Both sexes, this study reports, tend to feel that dating has a bearing on a young person's ability to size up prospective mates in terms of temperament, interests, ideals, and general compatibility. On the negative side, students felt that dating is a competitive game and that those who most need dating from the standpoint of personality development are largely excluded.

There is a tendency toward superficiality in dating relationships

5 Meyer F. Nimkoff and Arthur L. Wood, "Courtship and Personality," *American Journal of Sociology*, 53:263-269, 1948.

6 *Ibid.*

7 Ernest W. Burgess and Paul Wallin, *Engagement and Marriage* (Philadelphia: J. B. Lippincott Co., 1953), pp. 121-126 ff.

which may result in a selfish, highly competitive, aggressive type of boy-girl relationship. Such a relationship ignores many human qualities and kindnesses that perhaps are less often apparent in those who play this game than in those who are excluded from it. The girl who cannot date is left out of many, if not most, of the important social activities of the campus. This is cruel and in many cases extremely unjust, since the evidence seems to indicate that there is about as much character and ability among those who do not date as among those who do. The non-daters frequently lack only the more superficial flashy qualities that are so important in obtaining college dates.

In the case of the girl, particularly, being without dates intensifies her feeling of inferiority and of being left out. The experience of being left out seems to be cumulative, in that if a girl does not get started dating early in her college career, it likely means that her chances decline progressively with each year in college. Soon she will begin to doubt her social competence and ask herself chronically, "What's wrong with me?"

A Reappraisal of Dating

In summarizing what they observed about college dating, Burgess and Wallin conclude that the good-night kiss is usually reserved for the second or third date, necking for the keeping-company stage—that is, going steady or being pinned. Petting is reserved for engagement, and sexual intrecourse for marriage. In the holding of this not-too-definite line, the study finds, the coed herself is usually primarily responsible. The college male, while he has respect for these standards, especially in the one he hopes to marry, is quite willing to violate them at almost all stages in the sequence. He is inclined to be interested in sexual satisfaction as an end in itself, and can readily divorce it from affection as such.

Burgess and Wallin conclude that dating has become a highly individuated phenomenon and an area in which a personal sense of responsibility determines what is done and is not done. They find dating to be one of the few remaining areas where American life is characterized by "unbridled competition and individualism."[8] Though dating may appear to be democratic, actually a large number of young people are excluded from it; and on a college campus, particularly, it takes on many aspects of status seeking, superficiality, and social immaturity.

After this rather lengthy review of fact, theory, and opinion concerning dating, it is necessary to reappraise this new social institution of American culture and to arrive at a tentative answer as to whether dating is merely a new game for young people—an activity to be enjoyed for

8 *Ibid.,* p. 109.

its own sake—or whether it is a social invention having some important relationship to mate selection and marriage in the modern world. Certainly it is an interesting game, one of the most interesting of the teen years. The evidence points to the fact that dating also serves an important purpose in preparing the way for mate choice and marriage.

First, dating offers a means whereby modern youths may form intimate friendships with members of the opposite sex. In the relatively impersonal climate of today's city, male-female relations of a companionship nature are not easy to initiate outside of the dating relationship. The urban world is not like the small town or rural community of the past where the number of one's friends was limited only by the size of one's town, and where friendships with all were the result of having grown up together from childhood. Today, dating has become the substitute for many of yesterday's inevitable and informal contacts.

Second, dating serves the very necessary function of preparing young people for marriage. It does this in several ways: (1) It provides opportunities for youth to meet and develop a closer acquaintance with a number of potential mates. (2) It allows young people to study character and personality types which will help them in judging the potential compatibility of their final choice. (3) By bringing couples together under a variety of circumstances, it provides actual experience for each in adjusting to and getting along with members of the opposite sex.

Third, dating seems actually to contribute to the personality development of the individuals involved. Dating is a highly competitive activity, and one in which most young people want desperately to succeed. While some youths may turn to compensative behavior—elaborate spending, conspicuous dress, or sex play—the majority rely upon the cultivation of their own personalities to insure dating success. Dating may thus be thought of as an intense type of motivation for self-improvement—a type of motivation seldom provided in the family, by the school, or even in relationships with one's own sex. With dating experience, many young people begin to see the importance of being a fine person, rather than merely expecting somehow to find the right mate.

Finally, dating makes an important contribution to the general ideological maturation of the individual. During the course of the average period of attraction in which two people will date one another there are many opportunities for more or less serious discussions of ideas, ideals, and expectations. As a matter of fact, it is only as a result of such discussions that most dating relationships finally break up or reach a point of real seriousness. By talking over their values, their convictions, their life plans, young people come to see just how much they do or do not have to offer one another. The desirable outcome of these discussions is not so much what one young person learns about the other, but what each one learns about himself. Through discussions of this type, young people come face to face, perhaps for the first time, with their own lifetime accumulation of attitudes, values, and ideals. In voicing them, defending them, comparing them, they learn many things about themselves and hereby achieve ideological integration. By providing for the crystallization of his values, dating helps a young person to develop a coherent and conscious philosophy of life.

Improving Dating

While dating contributes significantly, in each of the ways outlined, to the development of the individual, one need not conclude that dating as it exists today is without fault or beyond criticism. No system of mate selection has ever been perfect. Some of the studies reported in this discussion indicate that those who could profit most by dating are most often denied its advantages. Other studies note that while dating does benefit the individual in several important ways it affects him detrimentally in other ways.

No cure-all can be offered to remedy the defects of modern dating. Dating practices differ from one section of the country to another and from one socioeconomic stratum of the population to another. A far more formidable barrier to reform, however, is the fact that dating attitudes are but a part of a vastly more complicated network of attitudes and behavior. A young man who thinks of his dates in terms of sexual exploitation needs more than a "sound talking to." He needs help in completely revising his attitudes in such comprehensive areas as moral and social responsibility. He probably also carries with him inaccurate or outmoded attitudes relative to male and female roles. The college girl who would not dream of dating a nonfraternity man, or a man without a car, is suffering from more than a case of adolescent snobbishness. She is reflecting the attitudes which, no doubt, characterized her childhood home. She is carrying into action the ideals which she observed in the behavior of her parents and friends.

Basic changes in dating practices depend upon equally basic changes in the attitudes and ideals of many American families. As long as some families are motivated by social climbing, and overextend themselves financially in order to equal or surpass the Joneses, as long as they are given to excessive and unregulated competition, one cannot expect the dating behavior of their young people to reflect healthier or more constructive aims.

This does not mean that the situation is hopeless. As a matter of fact, there is increasing evidence that many of the basic attitudes which affect dating behavior are in the process of changing. The higher standard of living of the working class, and the more extensive educational opportunities now open to all, are breaking down many of the barriers that have traditionally separated young people of different economic groups. Class lines are ignored in many high school and college situations.

Within the framework of existing attitudes much is being done and can yet be done to help young people improve their dating practices and beliefs. The last few years have witnessed the introduction of many different courses on the high school and college level that are aimed at helping students succeed in interpersonal relations. The introduction of sociology courses, sex education and family life education courses on the high school level, and the growing popularity of the social sciences and marriage and family relations courses on the college level are but a few of the encouraging developments in this area.

Textbooks are by no means the only literature dedicated to constructive changes in this field. Magazines and popular books offer the interested reader a variety of authoritative articles on such topics as how to choose a date, how to be popular, how to get along with your friends, etc.

Schools, parent groups, churches, and service organizations have also shown an increased interest in providing guidance and community resources that will help young people have more enjoyable and more understanding relationships with the opposite sex. Schools and churches particularly have abandoned their traditional attitude of hostility or indifference to the dating interests of their young people. There are now church recreational centers, Y.W.C.A.- and Y.M.C.A.-sponsored get-togethers, school-supervised dances, clubs, and community activity centers. These all reflect the growing desire on the part of adult community members to help young people to a happy, profitable adolescence and to prepare them for successful marriage and community membership.

Burgess and Wallin conclude that since dating is young people's own invention, they must find the cure for its problems, and suggest an increase in activities in which boys and girls can associate together in groups rather than as pairs. They see hope, particularly, in group gatherings where young people having specialized interests will be drawn together.[9]

The importance of this suggestion is confirmed by Kirkpatrick and Caplow's study at the University of Minnesota.[10] Fifty percent of college students there felt that opportunities to meet members of the opposite sex were inadequate. Almost three-fourths of college men felt that when they did meet girls, they were of the wrong kind.

9 *Ibid.*
10 See Clifford Kirkpatrick and Theodore Caplow, "Courtship in a Group of Minnesota Students," *American Sociological Review,* 51:114-123, 1945.

Science to the Aid of Dating

There are few areas in which science fails to offer a better guide than that of folklore and custom. Can it contribute to dating?

The use of the card sorter was widely popularized in a national television series some years ago in which Univac was used to match selected couples and give them a send-off on a paid dating spree. With scientific interest, Karl Wallace started a dating service some years ago designed to do with the card sorter what the "lonely hearts" clubs of the cities have long done and still do with differing degrees of skill and reliability.

Wallace's first venture, with his wife as associate, was to found a service to provide research data for a doctor's thesis. After graduation, he ran a dating service as a vocation. His results have been published in the book, *Love Is More Than Luck.*[11]

Introduction services operate under considerable suspicion from public authorities and from prospective patrons as well. There is fear that such institutions will be used exploitively, or for ulterior motives, and there is the reticence to trust such personal matters as dating contacts to an impersonal organization, operating for a profit. There is also likely to be the suspicion that anyone met through such a service might well be less than a desirable date and prospective mate.

Wallace found that those who register are in the older-age groups. The sex ratio of registrants is dominantly male, particularly in the younger-age group. Wallace's registrants were almost four men to one woman in the age group under 35. In the group above 55, there were more women than men.

No doubt, for the lonely in our impersonal society of the great cities, legitimate means of contact and introduction, such as that by Wallace, should be developed. Many countries have such services and with social approval. We have cited the matrimonial ads of daily newspapers in India (see Chapter 11). England for more than a hundred years has published *The Matrimonial Post and Fashionable Marriage Advertiser* where a person may announce the type of mate being sought and list his or her own personal characteristics.[12]

The anonymity of the modern college campus would seem to make campus-wide introduction service using card-sorting matching techniques desirable. Certainly it would bring together those of like interests and

---

[11] The Karl Wallace Foundation has a history of a reliable scientific approach in the operation of an Introduction Service. (270 S. Alexandria Ave., Los Angeles.) See also the analytical report on his work in Karl Wallace, "An Experiment in Scientific Matchmaking," *Marriage and Family Living*, 21:342-348, November, 1959.

[12] Joseph K. Folsum, "British Family Welfare," *Marriage and Family Living*, 7:25, 1945.

aspirations much more readily than random dating. No doubt it would widen the opportunities of many girls for dating suitable men.

Students at Iowa State University of Science and Technology held a "computer dance." Each student answered some 120 questions dealing with travel, the arts, current events, sports, attitudes toward dating, marriage, religion, politics, and education. They also answered other questions dealing with an evaluation of their own personalities. For the dance each girl was given a number and each boy was given three numbers representing the first, second, and third most compatible date for him. The dance was pronounced the best mixer ever.[13]

Discriminating Taste in Mate Choice

Outsiders looking in on the American dating system might well think that any young person has numerous opportunities in mate choice. Yet this seems not to be so. Apparently even those who date very extensively become so discriminating in taste or judgment that they find few whom they can marry. One may well question whether their judgment is always wise, but it seems to be a fact that with all the random dating our society of anonymity permits, no person has a multitude of acquaintances from whom he could select a person whom he would consider a suitable mate.

Karl Wallace has reviewed studies in this field over a period of some 25 years.[14] Few men and women meet and become acquainted with more than three or four persons whom they could consider suitable mates. And few women receive more than two or three proposals of marriage. The conclusion of even those who have dated very widely is that there are few persons in one's dating experience who could be considered really eligible.

From the background of these previous studies and from his own experience in operating a dating service, Wallace concludes that the problem of finding a suitable mate is most serious for the American middle class. This is because their moral code eliminates many of the methods of meeting mates used by the lower class and because they are more demanding in mate choice. He lists nine factors that limit their mate choice:

1. Conservative attitudes toward methods of meeting mates. They tend to taboo efforts to meet suitable persons, "wait for the right person to come

---

[13] Reported in *Time*, October 25, 1963, p. 102.

[14] Karl Wallace, "Factors Hindering Mate Selection," *Social Forces*, 44:317-329, May-June, 1960.

along." Wallace finds that marriages more often result from the type of secondary contacts tabooed by the middle classes than in approved contacts.

2. The cultural emphasis on beauty and sex. These values are especially prominent in the values of the male. They hinder many in finding a suitable mate.

3. The unbalanced sex ratio in various localities (see p. 150 for discussion and data on this problem).

4. Social stratification and segmentation. Class, race, and religious differences tend to act as barriers.

5. Urbanization. Its complexities make the finding of a suitable mate extremely difficult because of isolation and anonymity.

6. Sex differences in attitudes and expectations which make it difficult to meet on common ground.

7. Our competitive courtship system which tends to award the aggressive, dominant, and ambitious type and to overrun the quiet, reserved, unsocial person.

8. The widowed and divorced, of whom there are 13 million, encounter special problems.

9. Hereditary differences in glandular activity, I.Q., in health and energy, in height, weight, etc., not to mention disfiguring defects. For example, the woman who is 5 feet 10 inches tall will likely exclude 90 percent of the men she meets from her list of eligibles.

This list of hindrances in our society suggests that the practical problem of meeting a suitable mate is not solved merely by meeting or by dating a number of people of the right age at random.

In conclusion, dating is not merely a game, but a necessary adaptation of mate-selection practice to the needs of a mobile society. With the casual contacts brought about by the mobility of an urban-industrial society, comparative strangers meet and associate under varying circumstances. Dating has become a means of getting acquainted. It can be and often is conducive to social development and psychological and emotional emancipation from the parental family. It provides a liberal education in the appraisal of and adjustment to members of the opposite sex.

Many improvements are needed to extend this experience to greater numbers of young people and to check some of the more vicious competitive aspects of dating practice.

Problems

1. A college counselor was deeply concerned when a sophomore girl said that she refrained from dating because, "My parents have spent so much of their life's time and energy on me, that the least I can do is spend my evenings with them." Do you believe the counselor's concern was justified? Do you believe the counselor should have encouraged the girl in her filial devotion? What would you have said to such a girl?

2. A popular song of long ago began, "Tie Me to Your Apron Strings Again, I Know There's Room for Me Back on Your Knee." What is the figurative meaning of the song? What do you believe accounts for the existence of such a sentiment among some adults? Should the elderly parents of such an adult be commended on having made themselves so indispensable?

3. Does dating affect the following personal characteristics and if so how? (a) self-confidence, (b) better grooming, (c) poise, (d) broad-mindedness, (e) social know-how, (f) conversational ability, (g) charm, (h) manners

4. In your opinion, are these traits superficial qualities or are they important in life and worthy of cultivating?

5. Discuss the following possible solutions to the dating problem:
   a. Establish teenage "date bureaus" and try to locate escorts for every dateless girl, as well as dates for every shy or unpopular boy.
   b. Run "date clinics" in which young people are taught personal and social techniques for dating.
   c. Establish clubs that bring the sexes together informally so that they can get acquainted.
   d. Plan activities for both sexes in which talent, personality, good humor, etc., take precedence over beauty or attractive clothing.
   e. Plan group discussions that seek to analyze the community's dating standards.

6. Which of these courses of action do you believe would have the most beneficial effects?

7. Which course of action do you most disapprove of? Why?

8. What other concrete action might be taken?

General References

BAIN, Read, "Making Normal People," *Marriage and Family Living*, 16:27-31, February, 1954.

CAVAN, Ruth Shonle, *The American Family*, Third Edition (New York: Thomas Y. Crowell Co., 1963), Chs. 11-13.

KIRKPATRICK, Clifford, and CAPLOW, Theodore, "Courtship in a Group of Minnesota Students," *American Sociological Review*, 51:114-125, 1955.

MEAD, Margaret, *Male and Female* (New York: William Morrow & Co., Inc., 1949), Ch. 22.

NIMKOFF, Meyer F. and WOOD, Arthur L., "Courtship and Personality," *American Journal of Sociology,* 53:263-278, 1949.

WALLER, Willard, and HILL, Reuben, *The Family* (New York: Holt, Rinehart & Winston, Inc., 1951), Part 3.

WINCH, R. F., "Interrelations Between Certain Social Background and Parent-Son Factors in a Study of Courtship Among College Men," *American Sociological Review,* 11:333 ff., 1946; also WINCH, R. F., "Courtship of College Women," *American Journal of Sociology,* 55:269-278, 1949.

IV
MATE CHOICE

14

Mate Selection:
By Impulse or Insight?

Throughout human history the principle of "preferential mating" has operated.[1] Incest taboos usually bar kinsmen, although in some cultures certain kinfolk are eligible. Brother and sister marriages have been the rule for certain royalty as in ancient Hawaii, Egypt, and among the Incas. Cousin marriages are not unknown in the United States and have been common in the Arab world.

In many cultures there are age, race, caste, religion, and nationality factors which can bar marriage. Even democratic society has not entirely eliminated them. We are less inhibited in mate choices than most historic or contemporary peoples, in that customary barriers have fallen; but choice has become personal and to know when the right mate has appeared would, at times, be advantageous.

It would be fortunate indeed if some genius could develop a color chart or statistical device by which couples who find their dating becoming serious would know at once whether or not they were suited to pursue each other into the painful but pleasant depths of romantic involvement.

In this area, women's insight is greater than men's. A study of marriage failures showed 70 percent of the husbands whose marriages failed felt very confident the marriage would succeed; only 48 percent of the

[1] Linton C. Freeman, "Marriage without Love: Mate-selection in Non-western Societies," in Robert F. Winch, Robert McGinnis, and Herbert R. Barringer, *Selected Studies in Marriage and the Family* (New York: Holt, Rinehart & Winston, Inc., 1962), pp. 439-455; also Russell Middleton, "A Deviant Case: Brother-Sister and Father-Daughter Marriage in Ancient Egypt," in Rose Laub Coser, *The Family: Its Structure and Functions* (New York: St. Martin's Press, Inc., 1964), pp. 92-94.

wives felt this way.[2] Even the girl's family and her best friends are better prophets than the boy's family and his best friends.[3]

No social scientist has quite reached the goal of precise forecasting of success or failure. Some of those most willing to venture a step beyond science and use its meager findings as a clue, already use simple statistical devices to measure and match personalities for dating and marrying couples.[4] Better results are reported than those obtained only by common-sense advice.

Most marriage clinics, like guidance clinics and vocational placement clinics, now use some kind of measuring devices which give couples a tentative profile of their temperaments and personalities, and interpret findings as they relate to marriageability. Most young people, however, do not have access to such services and many would not take advantage of them if they did. They must trust romance as their guide or be content with the opinions of friends, family, or some other personal confidant, even though statistical norms could be more helpful.

Not all persons are marriageable. If the unmarriageable could be eliminated, marriage would be a safer institution. Many other persons— and these cause much difficulty—are marginal in marriageability. Unfortunately, datability and marriageability are not synonymous. A person may seem very interesting on a short-time acquaintance, but become intolerable as a long-time companion. On the other hand, many people who have little or no opportunity to date are very marriageable persons. So the winnowing process goes on, not always logically, and certainly with much error in judgment, as the rate of marriage failures shows.

Mate selection is now looked upon as a process, not just an event.

2 Ernest W. Burgess and Paul Wallin, *Engagement and Marriage* (Philadelphia: J. B. Lippincott Co., 1953), p. 563.

3 *Ibid.*, pp. 565-566.

4 Clifford Adams in his book *How to Pick a Mate* (New York: E. P. Dutton & Co., Inc., 1946), published a list of traits on which both men and women should check themselves; also other traits by which a couple in love could match their personalities by totaling up the score. Many of his traits are from the Burgess-Cottrell *Marriage Prediction Scale*, which itself was a tentative measurement device for predicting marriage adjustment. For many years Dr. Paul Popenoe and his colleagues in the American Institute of Family Relations in Los Angeles have used Roswell Johnson's *Temperament Test* as a means of helping a person to understand himself and as a guide to his marriageability. Both Adams and Popenoe report very favorable results from the use of these instruments, supplemented by premarital counseling and medical advice. How much of their success in guidance is due to the measurement devices and how much to the intangible aspects of the counseling experience is unknown. Burgess and Cottrell, as a consequence of their pioneer research, *Predicting Success or Failure in Marriage* (Englewood Cliffs, N. J.: Prentice-Hall, Inc., 1939), developed a marriage prediction scale which has had wide usage in various modified forms. Karl Wallace, a Ph.D. in Sociology, has attempted to put dating on a scientific basis with his Introduction Service (The Karl Wallace Foundation, 270 South Alexandria, Los Angeles). He uses punch cards and statistically matches persons for introduction. See his book, *Love Is More Than Luck* (New York: Wilfred Funk, Inc., 1957).

Often it is a very complicated process extending over ten years or more. Beginning with casual dates, the couple gradually shifts to going steady. This going steady, or being pinned, while it has some of the elements of a preliminary engagement may be nothing more or less than being able to depend on a date for particular functions. Eventually each young person is expected to use whatever judgment and insight he has and make a choice of someone with whom he thinks he can have a lasting, compatible, and even inspiring life.

In movie-made romance, impulse is assumed to be a safe and infallible guide. Few intelligent young people, particularly those who have had some variety in steady dating, can believe in impulse as a safe guide. They know from experience that one must be alert to the long-term values in the man-woman relationship. Unless they get completely carried away with physical desire, young couples know that differences in ideas and values, aspirations and life goals are basic in determining the success or failure of marriage.

On college campuses, young people are very much aware of these long-term values when they begin to face the serious business of mate selection. For example, a group of students were asked to rate eighteen factors in order of importance in mate selection. Both men and women put "dependable character" first. They rated emotional stability and maturity second. Pleasing disposition was rated third. Mutual love and attraction was fourth on the list, showing that this group was well aware that love is not all that matters. Here are some other traits in the order in which they were listed: good health, desire for home and children, refinement, neatness, ambition and industriousness, good cook and housekeeper, chastity, education and general intelligence, sociability, similar religious background, good looks, similar educational background, favorable social status or rating, good financial prospects, similar political background.[5]

Engaged men and women rate compatibility and common interests much higher as factors conducive to success in marriage than either love or sex as such.[6]

During the last twenty-five years, sociologists and psychologists have directed a great deal of research to the problem of sorting out the marriageable and unmarriageable on the basis of personality traits, social background, developmental history, parental relationships and other such factors. This research has also called attention to the problem of matching—that is, of learning what kinds of people can safely marry. For

[5] Reuben Hill, "Campus Values in Mate Selection," *Journal of Home Economics*, 37:557 ff., November, 1945.

[6] Ernest W. Burgess and Paul Wallin, *Engagement and Marriage* (Philadelphia: J. B. Lippincott Co., 1953), p. 412.

example, is there anything to the notion that like backgrounds, like temperaments, like religion are desirable? Or is variety truly the spice of life?

Research has tried to throw light on the problems that young people most often face in their mate-selecting quandries. Since experience is the only safe guide, research has atempted to bring together the exprinces of hundreds of persons (on some problems, of thousands of persons) who, successfully or otherwise, have run the gauntlet of mate selection. Although the experiences of a multitude could never give an infallible answer to anyone, they can at least clarify the nature of the mate-selecting problems.

Is There an Ideal Mate?

This question takes many forms. In the dreamy days of adolescent love young people are likely to feel that their love is heaven sent, that they were created for each other. The idea that there is somewhere in the universe a "one and only" for everyone is deeply rooted in fiction and tradition. But in our time, due probably to the dating custom, this idea is fast losing ground.

A more practical view is that the well-adjusted person can marry any one of a number of people and be happy, whereas the maladjusted, unhappy person can be successfully married to no one.[7] This view emphasizes the thought that one can make oneself into the "right" person. It agrees with marriage counselors and students of marriage who know that one finds in marriage only what he takes into it. Marriage has no magic power to make people over. Happy and successful persons make successful marriages. The number of people they could successfully team up with is great.

This does not mean that the well-adjusted person could make a go of marriage with anyone; far from it. He too, of course, must choose wisely, but the circle from which he can choose is wide. The person with defects in temperament and personality is more limited in choice as well as in his prospects for a happy marriage.

While the view that no one is predestined for any specific member of the opposite sex is generally accepted today, young people nonetheless have some concept of the traits and qualities they want their mate to have. A study of college young people shows[8] that almost a third of the

---

[7] Proposed in lectures by Ralph Eckert, in charge of parent education at the University of Connecticut, who has had many years of experience working with young people in high schools and colleges.

[8] Ernest W. Burgess and Paul Wallin, *Engagement and Marriage* (Philadelphia: J. B. Lippincott Co., 1953), p. 188.

men and almost a fourth of the women are very conscious of the characteristics of their ideal mate. Almost equal numbers have a vague consciousness of such ideals. Very, very few are entirely without any awareness of what their ideal mate should be like.

Research has attempted to define the ideal mate in terms of general background. Here are the ten factors in the background of a person which will tell most about his marriageability.[9]

1. superior happiness of parents
2. childhood happiness
3. lack of conflict with mother
4. home discipline that was firm, not harsh
5. strong attachment to mother
6. strong attachment to father
7. lack of conflict with father
8. parental frankness about matters of sex
9. infrequency and mildness of childhood punishment
10. premarital attitude toward sex that was free from disgust or aversion

Any person who possesses all ten of these is a much better than average risk in marriage.

It will be seen at a glance that all of these important background factors indicating favorable marriage prospects have to do with interpersonal relationships in early home life, with the example the parents have provided, and with the attitudes and training they have passed along to their children. Of all the factors listed, happiness of parents' marriage and one's own childhood happiness are most deterministic (they go together). This was indicated not only by the research cited above but is further confirmed by several additional studies.[10] Few children from unhappy homes make happy marriages.

Marriage happiness runs in families; so does unhappiness and divorce. One judge of a divorce court, addressing an audience, felt this so strongly that he said, "I sometimes think divorce is hereditary." Heredity, of course, is not the primary seat of the problem. The vital factor is rather the pattern of adjustment set in the home. But marital unhappiness and divorce do, nonetheless, run in families. Parents who are happy, well mated, and who settle problems together, establish a pattern of adjustment that children learn and carry into their own homes. Families

9 Lewis M. Terman and others, *Psychological Factors in Marital Happiness* (New York: McGraw-Hill Book Co., 1938), pp. 366-367. This study analyzed the background factors in the happiness and unhappiness of 792 married couples.

10 Ernest W. Burgess and Leonard S. Cottrell, *Predicting Success or Failure in Marriage* (Englewood Cliffs, N. J.: Prentice-Hall, Inc., 1939), pp. 101 ff. Deals with 526 marriages. Paul Popenoe and Donna Wicks, "Marital Happiness in Two Generations," *Mental Hygiene*, 21:218-223, 1937. Deals with 4,000 marriages. Judson T. Landis has found that divorce tends to run in families. For a summary of data see Chapter 34.

characterized by constant bickering between parents and brothers and sisters also set a pattern that children are likely to imitate in their association with each other and carry over into their relationship as husbands or wives. Families which are unhappy, in which husband and wife are dissatisfied with each other, in which there is pessimism and gloom, pass these traits on in the habits and attitudes of their children. This, in turn, complicates the job young people face in establishing and maintaining a happy home and a desirable place for rearing their own offspring.

Close relationships between child and parent are shown to be favorable to marriage.[11] Yet we all know about the boy who cannot fall in love with a girl without a feeling of guilt about forsaking his mother. And there are the girls, too, who can't possibly leave home because father and mother need them. Too strong a family attachment takes on the character of fixation and makes marriage impossible. This is one of the most important reasons why otherwise normal people do not marry. (This problem is discussed in Chapter 29 dealing with individuals who fail to marry.) Good relationships with parents must be within the normal range of emotional attachment, which means that the young person, when the time comes for mate choice, must be capable of making the chosen member of the opposite sex the first person in his affections.

Theories of Mate Choice

Sociologists and psychologists have propounded various theories of mate choice, some dealing with more obvious environmental factors, others with subtle and largely unconscious forces in the personality.

Value theory: Robert H. Coombs has expounded a "value theory" of mate choice which he feels incorporates most other theories, or at least explains the factors which make them a reality. Briefly, he holds that each person possesses a value system which consciously or unconsciously guides him in mate selection.[12]

Propinquity theory: Considerable study has centered around the idea of propinquity as a major factor in mate choice. The theory originally was applied to those living in the same general neighborhood. Some would now include those who go to school together or who work together.

11 This was shown, not only by Terman and others, but also by Burgess and Cottrell, *op. cit.,* pp. 341-349.

12 Robert H. Coombs, "A Value Theory of Mate Selection," *Family Life Coordinator,* 10:51-54, July, 1961; also Robert H. Coombs, "Reinforcement of Values in the Parental Home is a Factor in Mate Selection," *Marriage and Family Living,* 24:155-157, May, 1962.

This theory states that people must and usually do meet each other by some form of daily association—same neighborhood, school, church, or office. To stress propinquity and engage in extensive proof, as has been so often done, would seem to be an elaboration of the obvious.

Parental image theory: Freudian in origin, this theory holds that the child tends to develop a deep affection for the parent of the opposite sex: boy for his mother, girl for her father. In certain instances, the tie may be between a brother and sister or other sibling. In the mate chosen the youth sees the image of this childhood attachment. This puts mate choice largely on a level below consciousness.

The theory has not been well substantiated. To accept it at face value would be to make the study of mate choice largely meaningless, for it would remove choice largely from the voluntary level, assigning it to the predestination of childhood parental attachments.

Coombs concludes that since the parents are the agents of socialization, the parents and child hold similar values. This becomes the basis for choice of a mate who has characteristics and values similar to those of the parents.

Strauss[13] finds little similarity per se, but he concludes that parents do influence choice in that if the child has shared meaningful relationships with parent, he wishes to find similar traits in the mate; if hostile relationships with parents have persisted, he seeks different traits in the mate.

Complementary needs theory: The theory of complementary needs has been propounded by Winch and given some testing, but it lacks objective support. It assumes that the individual seeks out a mate to complement his own personality.

All students of the family accept the view that wish fulfillment is the main motive for marriage. Folk knowledge too takes this for granted. But Winch introduced the theory to explain why a particular person picks the mate he does. He holds that "in mate selection the need-pattern of each spouse will be complementary rather than similar to the need-pattern of the other spouse."[14] It is as though the mate is chosen to match out weaknesses of one's own personality. In these deep psychological needs, opposites tend to attract, thus complementing the self.

Although this theory is a challenging one, and Winch found some support for it with a small sample, other researchers have failed to confirm it. In fact, the preponderance of evidence to date leads to the

13 Anslem Strauss, "The Influence of Parent-Image upon Marital Choice," *American Sociological Review*, 11:554-559, October, 1946.
14 Robert F. Winch, *Mate Selection: A Study of Complementary Needs* (New York: Harper & Row, Publishers, 1958).

conclusion that the theory has no foundation in human behavior.[15] Quite to the contrary, couples want to satisfy similar needs in each other.[16]

Homogamy theory: This theory is concerned with whether or not a person in mate seeking chooses one with similar or different (heterogamous) economic, racial, religious characteristics. In general, we know that like marries like, particularly in general social characteristics, and that the more homogamous pair, in general social characteristics, gets along best in marriage. Similarity in church background, education, economic background, social class,[17] age, race, moral and religious background is important. Even the divorced and the widowed tend to marry their kind.[18] It is in this general area that most fruitful sociological research has centered.

"Ideal mate" theory: This last theory assumes that the individual has some more or less tangible idea of the perfect mate for him. Coombs would hold that one's conception of an ideal mate for oneself is within the framework of one's value constructs.

Personality Factors in Mate Selection

A person with dating experience learns that some personalities clash, while others supplement each other, making for a feeling of completeness. The "battle of the sexes" is a frequently heard phrase and has some meaning, yet antagonism cannot be the rule of successful pair relationships. Some couples may profit from a flare-up once in a while. In temperament and disposition couples need not be alike, but they must supplement each other, giving a sense of need fulfillment.

It has even been found[19] that the extrovert may successfully marry the introvert, but this does not mean that all extroverts will be satisfied with introverts as mates. More often the socially minded marry those who

---

[15] Charles E. Bowerman and Barbara R. Day, "A Test of the Theory of Complementary Needs as Applied to Couples during Courtship," *American Sociological Review,* 21:602-605, 1956; also James A. Shellenberg and Lawrence S. Bee, "A Reexamination of the Theory of Complementary Needs in Mate Selection," *Marriage and Family Living,* 22:227-232, 1960.

[16] See data from Anselm Strauss' Ph.D. thesis in this area, summarized in E. W. Burgess, Harvey J. Locke, and Mary Margaret Thomes, *The Family,* Third Edition (New York: American Book Co., 1963), p. 261.

[17] See, for example, August B. Hollingshead, *Elmtown's Youth* (New York: John Wiley & Sons, Inc., 1949), p. 211.

[18] Charles E. Bowerman, "Assortative Mating by Previous Marital Status, Seattle, 1939-1946," *American Sociological Review,* 18:170-177, April, 1953; also T. C. McCormick and A. P. Sundal, "Age at Marriage and Mate Selection," *American Sociological Review,* 16:37-48, February, 1951. Jerold S. Heiss and Michael Gordon, "Need Patterns and Mutual Satisfaction of Dating and Engaged Couples," *Marriage and Family Living,* 26:337-338, August, 1964.

[19] Terman and others, *op. cit.,* pp. 125 ff.

are highly social. One person may find a sense of security and the satisfaction of emotional needs in a person of like temperament; another may find his own personality filled out by someone quite his opposite in temperament.

One person may need a mate to lean upon while another needs to feel that he or she is the tower of strength in any relationship. One person needs the center of the stage and wants to marry an admirer rather than a competitor; another feels more secure when he or she can stay in the background and bask in the mate's accomplishments. Stories once painted every perfect wife as a clinging vine and every perfect husband as a daring and strong-willed protector. Today we realize that no such simple definition of the "perfect mate" is possible and that the perfect mate for one person might be all wrong for another.

Most men, in persistent traditional patterns, prefer to be the strong member of the household. Probably most women like them to be. Women of dependent disposition must marry this kind of man in order to be happy. The sensitive, insecure, cautious man may need a maternal type of wife whose capacity for comfort and sympathy are inexhaustible. This man will often marry a woman considerably older than himself. A high-strung person may need a placid mate, or he may want one with whom to race through life at full speed ahead. Two strong-willed persons may make a match, but will most likely clash head on before the engagement is over. Then one must recognize the other as dominant and give some ground, or they may go ahead agreeing to disagree in certain compartments of their lives. The chances are they may be happier with more yielding partners, although even here rules are hard to make.

Personality tests help some people in understanding themselves and their prospective mate. Counselors' advice, based on test results, is often even more helpful. There is, however, no substitute for an extended period of going steady, followed by an engagement of at least six months, to test compatibility of personality types in real-life situations. In the early days of going steady, couples are on their good behavior. It is only after long acquaintance that the put-on self is laid aside and the real self begins to show. When this stage is reached, the couple who really want to know will learn whether or not their personalities clash or supplement each other, for the type of adjustments that emerge will be symptomatic of future adjustments in marriage.

But are there certain personality types to be avoided in marriage?

This is an oft-raised question, and quite a legitimate one, for certainly there are unmarriageable types. Moreover, men generally detest certain traits in women and wish to avoid them, just as women detest certain traits in men and wish to avoid them. Possession of some of the traits discussed in the remainder of this chapter does not necessarily bar one's way to marriage but may hinder it, just as it may hinder the development of a steady relationship leading to engagement. Admittedly, some of the traits discussed here are speculative, and the list is incomplete. Certain traits that work out badly in marriage are discussed in Chapter 23 and traits that often put one in the spinster and bachelor column are discussed in some detail in Chapter 32.

Personality Types That Have Difficulty in Marriage

It is always a little risky to classify personality types into categories on the basis of specific behavior patterns. Yet it is by such shorthand conceptualization that all of us size people up in everyday life. Moreover, science becomes meaningful as it conceptualizes into type categories.

Research, practical experience, and a knowledge of human interrelations suggest that persons who approach the extreme in the behavior patterns outlined below will make difficult, if not impossible, mates.

THE OVERLY POSSESSIVE

1. *Male:* Jealous and demanding, he seeks to reassure himself of his own importance by complete domination of another person. He considers his jealousy a tribute to his lady's charms; actually, it is only a testimony to his own sense of insecurity. In marriage he is likely to allow his mate little in the way of a life of her own; he will demand that he and his interests be the unqualified focus of her entire life, and he will consider her attention to her own interests to be a rejection of himself.

2. *Female:* Clinging and dependent, or motherly and demanding, she may play the part of the helpless little girl or the "mother-knows-best" little dictator. In either case she is sure that she and the marriage itself should be the chief, if not the only, reasons for her husband's existence. She is jealous, sometimes secretly and often openly, of every other aspect of his life—his job, his male companions, his parents and family, and above all else, any feminine acquaintances. In marriage she finds a limitless number of reasons for keeping him tied to his home, and is able to convince herself that this is all he wants and that her demands are for his sake, not hers.

THE CONTINUALLY DISSATISFIED

1. *Male:* This type is overly ambitious for goals he can only vaguely define. He hurries from one job to another, one community to another,

or from one set of values to another, hoping to find "the perfect solution" rather than working constructively toward some selected and highly valued goal.

2. *Female:* She holds marital and social expectations that only a wealthy prince charming could hope to satisfy. With the help of motion pictures and novels, or of a frustrated parent, she has developed unrealistic life expectations which she prefers to call "idealistic." The fact is that life will probably never measure up to the picture in her mind. She will continue to nag, drive, or complain regardless of what advancements are made, for she has no worldly-attainable goal in mind.

THE TEMPERAMENTAL

1. *Male:* Moody and self-centered, he finds himself and his ever-changing outlook the most interesting subject for thought as well as conversation. The impositions he allows himself to make upon others he excuses by his own complexity and superiority. In marriage, he is likely to expect his wife to be nurse, mother, and constant admirer, giving little thought to what his wife may need from him.

2. *Female:* Dramatic and unconventional, she seldom has the qualities that wear well in marriage. She sees life as a drama and people as her audience. The routines of housework and child care rest heavily upon her shoulders.

THE "SUPERIOR"

1. *Male:* He knows a little bit about a lot of things and sparkles in every conversation as long as it remains on a superficial level. He is admired and even feared for his wit because he doesn't mind turning its sharp edge against even his closest friends. This aggressive exterior is often a convenient shell which protects a frightened and uncertain self. He is largely bluff, and if his bluff is called and his shell broken, he frequently never recovers. He is a poor risk for marriage for his chances of never being outdone are few. The wife is likely to end up pampering and humoring a bitter and frustrated man.

2. *Female:* Her determination to be a tremendous success at everything—career-wise and socially, as well as in the role of wife and mother —usually suggests that she is overcompensating for some deeply felt inadequacies. Like all other relationships, she is apt to view marriage in terms of competition rather than cooperation. Her husband, her friends, even her children are seen as threats to her own status. She almost inevitably ends up blaming marriage and family for the fact that she never reached her real goals.

THE OVERLY METICULOUS

1. *Male:* Faultless in dress and in his personal habits, he cannot tolerate carelessness or indifference in others. Frequently, he is the man who has been a bachelor for a number of years or the young husband whose mother was "perfect" at everything. In either case, a more happy-go-lucky person has litle chance of pleasing him. Whenever he faces personal problems and frustrations, his standards seem to go higher and his demands increase.

2. *Female:* Her germ-proof, dustless, perfectly kept house, her spotless children, her faultless menus are frequently the result of a deep sense of failure in other areas of life. The girl who feels unsuccessful in social relationships or who resents or fears the intimate sexual side of marriage is likely to concentrate all her time and energies into the routine of housework. Some of these habits of cleanliness take on the characteristics of fetishes. She will deeply resent the fact that her husband expects more of her.

THE FLIRT

1. *Male:* Always the "ladies' man," he enjoys feminine companionship and shuns his own sex. He is charming, flattering, and considered quite a "catch." This frequently indicates a lack of real masculinity and emotional maturity. His incessant preoccupation with the other sex is meant to reassure himself and others that he is very much the male. Since most of his attitude is put on, he is apt to be a complete failure in the real emotional and sexual involvements demanded of a happy marriage.

2. *Female:* Attracting a man—any man—is a game she never tires of playing. Usually attractive and overly clothes conscious, she seldom takes well to the unglamorous aspects of family life. The consequences of her flirtations may never be serious but she will be a constant source of anxiety and embarrassment to her uncertain husband. As she begins to lose her youth, she is a likely candidate for infidelity, for only by feeling attractive, sought after, and involved can she escape the oppressive knowledge that she is growing old.

Some Indices of Emotional Abnormality

A college sophomore recently insisted that along with every premarital physical examination there should be a psychological examination as well. "In what sense," she argued, "can physical defects be considered half so important as whether or not the fellow is a psychotic or neurotic?"

In answering her question, another student, after mentioning the time and expense that would be involved, concluded: "Anyway, if you've gone with a fellow long enough to marry him, you've probably had plenty of chances of discovering for yourself whether or not he is normal, neurotic, psychotic, or just plain maladjusted."

Which of the two students was most nearly correct? Are psychiatric or psychological profiles needed in order to judge the normality of a potential mate or is common sense an adequate tool for this purpose?

In the first place, although neither law nor custom requires their use, psychological test results are available to many young people in school, community, and marriage clinics. The couple who are seriously interested in impersonally compiled data on themselves and one another can easily take advantage of these resources. Many do, and it is safe to say that most marriages could profit, not alone by the data so obtained, but also by the attitude that would make such information of interest.

On the other side of the picture, however, is the fact that serious dating itself can and should provide sound information in most cases, if couples are alert and aware of what to look for. If tests were able to indicate selfishness, egotism, or brutality, many young couples would merely conclude that the tests were all wrong. Experience itself is usually the most effective teacher. Still, few individuals are capable of looking analytically into their lovers' minds and emotions. How are they to discover psychological faults and frailties?

The fact is that neurotic or psychotic tendencies can seldom be kept completely hidden from one with a knowledge of common symptoms. Problems of a less serious nature are even harder to camouflage. In his or her daily associations with other people, the maladjusted individual almost invariably reveals his inner deficiencies in the form of social inadequacies. It may take an expert to define and treat the problem, but the symptoms themselves are usually painfully obvious. This does not mean that they are likely to be revealed during the first date or during the first dozen dates. Even the most seriously disturbed are often capable of putting on a front for a while. But—and here rests one of the chief arguments in favor of a prolonged acquaintance and engagement period—the informality and the familiarity that characterizes every affair after a few months invites both parties to relax and be themselves. It is at this time that both begin to reveal their personalities freely.

A great deal is known about the common outward manifestations of severe personality problems. Here are some of the social characteristics that may be telltale signs of personal inadequacies in their mild form on the more common level of maladjustment.

SOCIAL MANIFESTATIONS OF COMMON NEUROTIC TENDENCIES

1. Shows fear and anxiety when faced with a new or unusual social situation that holds no real threat; expresses an unprovoked sense of guilt which seems to have no reason at all for asserting itself.
2. Experiences frequent instances of emotion and excitement which are more intense than the situation calls for or which are not appropriate to the situation; is given to frequent hysterical laughter or tears or general excitement that seems unwarranted.
3. Has phobias; shows fear or unwarranted disgust toward certain objects, situations, or ideas to which people do not ordinarily so react.
4. Is ritual ridden; daily life is unnaturally patterned around the exacting performance of specific tasks in a specific way.
5. Has uncontrollable impulses—suddenly felt desires to do particular things regardless of consequences.
6. Has obsession with state of health—a hypochondrial concern about his own health, frequently accompanied by a limitless number of complaints, the area of pain shifting frequently.
7. Has deep moods of depression often accompanied by unwarranted feelings of guilt.

SOCIAL MANIFESTATIONS OF COMMON MALADJUSTMENT PROBLEMS

1. Shows extreme shyness, submissiveness, and inability to relax in presence of others.
2. Shows hostility and antagonism toward others, toward society, the government, various forms of authority, or just the world in general.
3. Expresses suspicion and extreme scepticism concerning new people, new ideas, and new values.
4. Makes a conspicuous display in clothing, possessions, finances, etc., in order to impress others—even strangers.
5. Shows arrogance and an attitude of condescension around even long-time acquaintances.
6. Is given to boisterous, loud behavior regardless of the mood or purpose of the group in which he finds himself.
7. Is preoccupied with sex or sex-linked subjects or shows a strong aversion to sex.
8. Has insatiable yearning for excitement and adventure and inability to enjoy quiet times or more subtle forms of pleasure.
9. Makes tactless and embarrassing public displays of affection for friends of either or both sexes.
10. Is given to lying or distorting facts in order to put himself and his accomplishments in a more favorable light.

11. Shows overeagerness to please everyone, even strangers, by doing their bidding, agreeing with their opinions, etc.
12. Shows extreme dependence and desire to have everything settled and unchanging.

The neurotic symptoms listed here are likely to seriously hinder marriageability, particularly if they tend toward the extreme in their expression. (The most extreme cases, of course, are already in institutions for the mentally ill.) Such symptoms should never be ignored in mate selection. Their cure usually requires some form of psychological therapy.

Maladjusted persons having traits such as the ones listed above, unless the traits are extremely pronounced, are not in most instances unmarriageable. They are less marriageable, however, and require a more tolerant and sympathetic mate than persons who are well adjusted. The number of persons with whom they could live successfully in marriage is greatly limited.

In applying the above lists to one's problems of mate selection, it must always be kept in mind that the types and traits mentioned are found in some measure in all individuals. Persons who possess them in more than usual degree are the ones to be wary of in mate selection. It is among such persons that a very high degree of marriage failure is to be found. Modern marriage makes exacting demands and those who lack emotional maturity and facility in social adjustment have difficulty in meeting its demands.

Premarital Counseling—An Aid to Mate Choice

Most marriage-counseling clinics have provisions for premarital counseling, as has been indicated. A part of the counseling is the giving of tests which reflect marriage fitness and which also help match pairs for compatibility. Although most young people seem to prefer the dictates of their own emotions, there is little doubt that a more general use of premarital counseling would improve mate choice.

In summary, impulse, that vague romantic "something" that promises to guide one to a one-and-only, has been found by both social scientists and disillusioned couples to be a very poor guide to successful mate selection. Modern young people are discovering for themselves (and by reading of the experiences of others) that finding the right mate is more often a long process than a sudden event. Very rarely does a person suddenly find the right mate. More likely he decides very gradually, over a period of months or years—knowing what he does about himself, his likes and dislikes, his habits, ideas, values, and life plans—that this or that kind of individual offers him the greatest promise of marital happiness and compatibility.

As young people of today shake themselves free of the romantic misconceptions of yesterday, they turn increasingly to the counsel of those who have made marriage and family living the focus of their study and interest. From these sources youth learns that marriageability can, in a sense, be measured and that there are data available to help them analyze both themselves and their potential mates as marriage risks.

This new attitude of levelheaded thoughtfulness may appear to take some of the romance out of mate selection. The fact is, however, that this course can do much to put romance into marriage. Whirlwind affairs, in which physical attraction is supreme, may bring months of excitement and dreams of bliss. It is the well-planned affairs, however, in which young people get acquainted and established in companionability before they marry, that are more likely to bring the years of marital happiness and compatibility all seek.

Problems

1. Recently the Master of Ceremonies of a radio quiz show asked a female participant how she met her husband. She answered, "I was brought up very strictly and although I dated a number of young men, none of them ever lived up to my high standards. I was thirty-two and on vacation in New York when I finally met the right one. It was just as I knew it would be. A friend introduced me to this fellow and after one date we were sure that we were meant for each other. We got married immediately and we haven't been unhappy for a moment since then."

    "How long ago was that?" the Master of Ceremonies asked in amazement.

    "Last month," the woman replied. "We're on our honeymoon."

    In your opinion is this woman one of the rare few to find her ideal mate? Was there anything in her statement to suggest that the future may be less rosy?

2. In the light of evidence in the chapter studied, would you say similarity of background is generally more significant in marriage success than similarity of temperament? Discuss.

3. Try to type men and women whom you feel should never get married.

4. After hearing the following statement from a young bride-to-be, a marriage counselor urged the young couple to either postpone their marriage for a while or else to consider continued counseling after the marriage should take place. Read the statement and decide whether or not the counselor's requests seem justified. What do you think were his reasons for urging a delay?

"I think I'll make Ted a pretty good wife because I'm not sloppy and unstrung like so many girls I know. I like to get up at exactly 6:45. In fact, I always get up then. It upsets me until I'm almost ill if I have to stay in bed later for some reason.

"The first thing I do is make my bed. That takes about twelve minutes, because I like it perfect. If I see a wrinkle or a crooked sheet it bothers me all morning. Then I wash my hands and face and scrub my fingernails with a disinfectant soap.

"There won't be any germs in our house! I rinse the plates and cups off too and I rub each spoon and fork with a clean napkin. I'm just that way with everything. It takes all my time but it pays off. I'm healthy and strong and I'm determined to keep my Ted healthy too."

5. Hillsdale is a relatively small Midwestern community of conservative, deeply religious farmers. The citizenry pride themselves on their German ancestry, their independence of the outside world, and their refusal to be influenced by newcomers, new ideas, or new gadgets and machines.

Richard Flanders, a socially prominent New Yorker, inherited a large farm equipment store in an adjoining county and moved there with his wife and children. The Flanders family, accustomed to the social whirl of a large city, were bored with rural life and amused by the religious and social customs of the community.

Young Dorothy Flanders, age 19, for want of something better to do, joined the Hillsdale Church and the group of young people her age. She was attractive, well dressed, and an experienced hand at competitive dating.

For several months she amused herself by collecting marriage proposals from the young men of her group, but on Christmas morning she shocked her family by announcing that she had been married the night before. Her groom was a handsome young man who would one day inherit a small but prosperous farm. He was quiet, reserved, rather shy, and undecided as to whether he should wait to inherit the farm or prepare instead for the ministry.

Analyze this situation in terms of the following questions:

a. How could the two have considered marrying in the first place?
b. What facts seem to indicate that the marriage was an unwise one?
c. How would you rate their chances for marital success?
d. What could be done to improve their chances for marital success?

Selected References

ARTICLES IN BOOKS OF READINGS

BECKER, Howard, and HILL, Reuben (Editors), *Family, Marriage and Parenthood,* Second Edition (Boston: D. C. Heath & Co., 1955).
   1. KUHN, Manford Hinshaw, "How Mates Are Sorted," pp. 246-275.
WINCH, Robert F., and others, *Selected Studies in Marriage and the Family,* Revised Edition (New York: Holt, Rinehart & Winston, Inc., 1962).

2. GLICK, Paul C., and LANDAU, Emanuel, "Age as a Factor in Marriage," pp. 622-626.
3. KOLLER, Marvin R., "Residential and Occupational Propinquity," pp. 472-476.
4. HOLLINGSHEAD, August B., "Cultural Factors in the Selection of Marriage Mates," pp. 477-488.

FISHBEIN, Morris, and KENNEDY, Ruby Jo Reeves, *Modern Marriage and Family Living* (New York: Oxford University Press, Inc., 1957).

5. BURGESS, Ernest W., "The Wise Choice of a Mate," pp. 117-131.

LANDIS, Judson T., and LANDIS, Mary G., *Readings in Marriage and the Family* (Englewood Cliffs, N. J.: Prentice-Hall, Inc., 1952).

6. STRAUSS, Anselm, "The Influence of Parent-Images upon Marital Choice," pp. 99-106.

SUSSMAN, Marvin B., *Sourcebook in Marriage and the Family,* Second Edition (Boston: Houghton Mifflin Co., 1963).

7. HOLLINGSHEAD, August B., "Cultural Factors in the Selection of Marriage Mates," pp. 101-108.
8. STRAUSS, Anselm, "The Ideal and the Chosen Mate," pp. 120-124.

GOODE, William J., *Readings on the Family and Society* (Englewood Cliffs, N. J.: Prentice-Hall, Inc., 1964).

9. KERCKHOFF, Alan C., and DAVIS, Keith E., "Value Consensus and Need Complementarity in Mate Selection," pp. 83-89.

General References

BABER, Ray E., *Marriage and the Family,* Second Edition (New York: McGraw-Hill Book Co., 1953), Ch. 4.

BOWMAN, Henry A., *Marriage for Moderns,* Fourth Edition (McGraw-Hill Book Co., 1960), Ch. 7.

BURGESS, Ernest W., LOCKE, Harvey J., and THOMES, Mary Margaret, *The Family,* Third Edition (New York: American Book Co., 1963), Ch. 12.

——, and WALLIN, Paul, *Engagement and Marriage* (Philadelphia: J. B. Lippincott Co., 1953), Ch. 6.

CAVAN, Ruth Shonle, *American Marriage* (New York: Thomas Y. Crowell Co., 1959), Ch. 7.

CLARKE, Alfred C., "Residential Propinquity as a Factor in Mate Selection," *American Sociological Review,* 17:17-22, February, 1952.

HEWITT, Lester E., "Student Perception of Traits Desired in Themselves as Dating and Marriage Partners," *Marriage and Family Living,* 20:344-349, November, 1958.

LEMASTERS, E. E., *Modern Courtship and Marriage* (New York: The Macmillan Co., 1957), Chs. 4-8.

SIRJAMAKI, John, *The American Family in the Twentieth Century* (Cambridge: Harvard University Press, 1953), Ch. 4.

SNYDER, Eloise C., "Attitudes: A Study of Homogamy and Marital Selectivity," *Marriage and Family Living*, 26: 332-335, August, 1964.

WALLACE, Karl, *Love Is More than Luck* (New York: Funk & Wagnalls Co., Inc., 1957).

WALLER, Willard, and HILL, Reuben, *The Family* (New York: Holt, Rinehart & Winston, Inc., 1951), Part 3.

WINCH, Robert F., "The Theory of Complementary Needs in Mate Selection: An Analytical Descriptive Study," *American Sociological Review*, 19:241-249, June, 1954.

15

Religion in Mate Choice

In a nation of mixed religious background, growing religious tolerance, and increasing secular orientation of education, the problem of interfaith marriages is one of profound importance to the separate survival of minority religious groups. In the case of the Jew, it is a question of the survival of the Jew as an ethnic group and a "separate people."[1] The emphasis of all religious groups on separateness, the marriage of people with like faith, runs counter to the strong emphasis on integration in the culture of our time. Young people of all faiths, with increased education in secular schools rather than in academies and church colleges, are becoming considerably sophisticated in matters of mate choice where religion is concerned. They are increasingly inclined to defy church edicts and admonitions in their mate choice. These very attitudes over the course of time may well make the religious issue less important than it has been historically and than it has been shown to be in researches to date.

The Catholic Ecumenical Council has dared raise the issue of abandoning the marriage pledge required of the marriage pair of mixed religion. Even so, the mixed religious marriage will continue to have its unique problems, perhaps less severe than in a day when church integration barriers were more imposing than now; but because of the very tolerance which exists among the new generation, the numbers crossing the major religious barriers will greatly increase.

The Statistical Picture

In 1958 the Census Bureau published, for the first time, a nationwide picture of the extent of mixed marriages involving the three major religious groups in America—Protestant, Roman Catholic, and

[1] Thomas B. Morgan, "The Vanishing American Jew," *Look*, 5:41-45, May, 1964.

Jewish.[2] Data are for all persons 14 years old and over, and cover 36,576,000 couples. Here is the situation as reported:

Like Religion

Both Protestant	24,604,000
Both Roman Catholic	8,361,000
Both Jewish	1,258,000

Mixed Religion

Protestant-Roman Catholic	2,255,000
Protestant-Jewish	57,000
Roman Catholic-Jewish	41,000
	2,353,000

Proportionately, Catholics suffer most from interreligious marriages, over a fifth (21.2 percent) marry Protestants, and a few (0.4 percent) marry Jews. A detailed breakdown of the extent of mixed marriages is presented in Figure 15-1. Of all marriages in the three major religious bodies, 6.4 percent were mixed.

While these data suggest that the intermarriage problem is of significant dimensions, sample studies indicate that the actual number of persons crossing the major interfaith barriers in marriage is about twice as high as shown by the Census data. Many abandon their church before or after the ceremony. Although they are of different faiths in background, the difference has vanished as a statistical fact. The authorities of the U. S. Census Bureau have expressed the view that Census enumerators may have in some cases overlooked the fact that the husband and wife might be of different religions. Convincing studies have shown that the Jewish-Gentile marriages in the nation have been running about 13 percent.[3] Sample studies of Catholic marriages, although less extensive in scope, suggest that those of Catholic background cross the line in 35 to 50 percent of cases. Jesuit sociologist, John L. Thomas of St. Louis University, places the figures at almost half of all marriages, if the invalid (those not sanctioned by the church) are added to the valid interfaith Catholic marriages.[4]

These data may accurately represent the approximate ratio of outgroup marriages among the different major faiths, but in all cases, the number of those marrying out is approximately twice as high as shown.

[2] U. S. Department of Commerce, Bureau of the Census, "Religion Reported by the Civilian Population of the United States, March, 1957," *Current Population Reports: Population Characteristics*, Series P-20, No. 79, February 2, 1958.

[3] Erich Rosenthal, *Studies of Jewish Intermarriage in the United States*, Vol. 64, *American Jewish Year Book*, 1963. (Also in a reprint pamphlet.)

[4] John L. Thomas, *The American Catholic Family* (Englewood Cliffs, N. J.: Prentice-Hall, Inc., 1956).

INGROUP AND OUTGROUP MARRIAGES
IN THE UNITED STATES, 1957
(All Civilian Population. 36,576,000 Marriages)

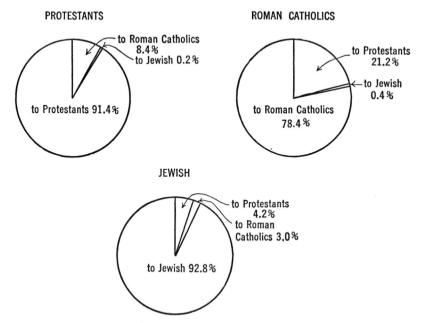

Source: U. S. Department of Commerce, Bureau of the Census, "Religion Reported by the Civilian Population of the United States, March, 1957," *Current Population Reports: Population Characteristics*, Series P-20, No. 79, February 2, 1958.

FIGURE 15-1————A high proportion of Catholics in our dominantly Protestant country marry outside their faith. In such marriages the Catholic Church dictates the terms; but how successfully in the long run of the marriage? Actual rate of people marrying out of their faith may run twice as high as shown here.

Locke and his colleagues have proposed the thesis that, other things being equal, interfaith marriages will increase as the minority group decreases in ratio to the total population.[5] But in this area other things are never equal. The Jewish group is the smaller ratio group but maintains an in-group loyalty unmatched by the Catholic group.

In considering the problem of mixed religious marriages, one generally thinks only of those alliances which involve members of the three major religious faiths in America—Protestant, Catholic, and Jewish. In

[5] Harvey J. Locke, George Sabagh, and Mary Margaret Thomes, "Interfaith Marriages," *Social Problems*, 4:329-333, April, 1957.

reality, the situation is even more complicated. Within the Protestant group, there are over 200 denominations, many of them differing radically from the others in values and beliefs, as well as in restrictions placed on the behavior of their adherents.

There are no legal barriers to marriage across religious lines, yet most church groups advise against it. The Catholic group places important restrictions on interfaith marriages, and the Orthodox Jewish group prohibits it altogether. Still, studies show that approximately half of college students would cross these major religious barriers in marriage if other aspects of the relationship were satisfactory.[6] Gordon[7] studied attitudes of 5,407 college students in some forty colleges and universities of the nation. He found 37 percent of non-Jews would marry Jews; 56 percent of non-Catholics would marry Catholics. In the total sample, half did not favor marriage to a person of another religion.

Almost half of husbands in interfaith marriage studied by Prince[8] would be willing for their children to enter such a marriage, and well over a third of wives would be willing. Less than a fourth of husbands and wives were negative on this subject. This would indicate that the effect of interfaith marriage is cumulative through the generations that do intermarry.

Why Religion Is So Important to Marriage Adjustment

Judson T. Landis[9] found a very positive association between religiousness and success of marriage. Those reporting no faith showed a high rate of marriage failure. These findings are consistent with findings of sociologists over a period of some thirty years.[10]

Rockwell Smith,[11] an astute churchman, has observed that religion

[6] The initial study by Ray E. Baber asked, "All other things being satisfactory, would you marry a person with a different religious faith (Catholic, Jewish, Protestant) than your own?" He received replies from 642 students in New York University. Ray E. Baber, *Marriage and the Family*, Second Edition (New York: McGraw-Hill Book Co., 1953), p. 119. Judson T. Landis repeated the question to 2,000 Michigan State students in 1947 and to 1,600 students in 11 colleges in 1952. See Judson T. Landis and Mary Landis, *Building a Successful Marriage*, Fourth Edition (Englewood Cliffs, N. J.: Prentice-Hall, Inc., 1963), Ch. 13.

[7] Albert L. Gordon, *Intermarriage*, (Boston: Beacon Press, 1964), Ch. 2.

[8] Alfred J. Prince, "A Study of 194 Cross-Religion Marriages," *The Family Life Coordinator*, 9:3-7, January, 1962.

[9] Judson T. Landis, "Religiousness, Family Relationships and Family Values in Protestant, Catholic and Jewish Families," *Marriage and Family Living*, 22:241-247, November, 1960.

[10] Carle C. Zimmerman and Lucius F. Cervantes, *Successful American Families*, (New York: Pageant Press, Inc., 1960).

[11] Rockwell Smith in Howard Becker and Reuben Hill, *Family, Marriage and Parenthood*, Revised Edition (Boston: D. C. Heath & Co., 1954), Ch. 20.

is a very great socializing factor. During the dating period, young people are so completely wrapped up in each other and so completely satisfied emotionally in their lives together that they tend to overlook the place of religion and church activities in their lives. However, when they settle down after the honeymoon to the adjustments of marriage and community life, they again want to establish the social ties which have been most meaningful to them. Each then naturally wishes to turn to his own church and the church group he has found congenial.

If the couple are of the same religious faith, this building of the marriage into the larger fellowship of the church group is made easy and natural. If, however, they have different religious backgrounds, a great handicap faces them as they try to build church relationships. Instead of being able to participate naturally in the same kind of religious exercise in the community, there is a tendency to compete for church loyalty. The couple constantly find a block in the way of their joint participation in any kind of religious activity.

It is often only after marriage that the couple begin to realize, too, how deeply embedded are the philosophies of life and standards of behavior that form a part of any religious faith. A person who has had his life and goals oriented around the goals and aspirations that are the essence of his faith finds religion more deeply significant in his life than he has realized. Often the person who has been quite casual in his religious attitudes has more deeply seated religious values than he is aware of until these values come into direct opposition to the values of a person he loves, but whose core of religious philosophy is quite different.

It is, of course, particularly shocking for the person whose life is built around religious values to realize after marriage that the person whom he has married is entirely without religious orientation and holds none of the concepts and values which make life meaningful to him.

These facts are probably the basis of the findings of sociological research which indicate that, where couples are not matched in religious background, their church participation usually decreases after the marriage. Many couples probably find this the only way to peace. Even though it may not bring satisfaction, it may at least help to reduce tensions. For example, Zimmerman and Cervantes found that about half the Catholic men they studied who were involved in mixed marriages ended by abandoning their faith.[12]

The real issue comes, of course, when children enter the family and the question arises as to whether or not to train them religiously, and if so, in what religion. Religious differences can no longer be avoided. It is then, most frequently, that the problem of religious differences becomes something besides a theoretical question between two individuals. How a

12 Zimmerman and Cervantes, *op. cit.*

child's faith shall be directed and his life values established are certain to be of deep concern to parents. With this background, let us consider the findings of research.

Persons with and without Religious Connections

Religion and family have a great deal in common in basic ideology, at least in the Western world where Jewish-Christian tradition, founded in the Old and New Testaments, prevails. In this tradition God is the father, and at many points the relationship of both Christian and Jew to deity is like that of child to parent. Much more basic than these analogies of scripture, however, are the ideologies of religion itself— love, self-sacrifice, putting others' needs before one's own, loyalty, self-forgetfulness, faith, and a sense of the high destiny of man. These religious virtues are the virtues that make marriage work.

Whatever the reasons, it is an established fact that those without religious affiliation are a greater marriage risk than those with acknowledged religion, and that the risk of failure in the marriages of the former is even greater than in some combinations of marriages that cross religious lines. Even in Michigan, a state where divorce rates are relatively low, and among a parental group which could be expected to be more conservative on matters of divorce than the general population, it was found that 18 percent of marriages in which neither parent had religious affiliations had ended in divorce as compared to 14 percent of mixed Protestant-Catholic marriages.[13] Of those in which the wife was a church member and the husband not, 16 percent ended in divorce.

A study[14] of mixed marriages among parents of over 6,500 school children in Spokane, Washington, where the tradition of easy divorce prevails, found that 24 percent of the marriages studied ended in divorce when the couple was without religion as compared to a 17.4-percent failure in mixed-religion marriages. A study of parents of 13,528 Maryland youths found a divorce rate of 17 percent in homes without religion compared to 15 percent for mixed marriages.[15]

Zimmerman and Cervantes[16] report that in marriages where one has religious affiliation and the other does not, the divorce, desertion, and delinquency rate of children are generally twice as high as in marriages in which both are affiliated with a religious group. Where both of the

[13] Judson T. Landis and Mary G. Landis, *op. cit.*, pp. 197-202.

[14] H. Ashley Weeks, "Differential Divorce Rates by Occupation," *Social Forces,* 21:336 ff., March, 1943.

[15] Howard M. Bell, *Youth Tell Their Story* (Washington, D. C.: American Youth Commission, American Council on Education, 1938).

[16] Zimmerman and Cervantes, *op. cit.*

pair are without religion, the chances of divorce, desertion and of child delinquency are four times as high as where there is religious affiliation.

Other studies have indicated that religious training makes a significant contribution to marriage success and happiness. Both men and women with strict religious training have been found to have higher happiness scores in marriage than those whose training was rated "considerable to none."[17] Those with many years of Sunday School training also have been found to make a better adjustment to marriage than those with little or no training.[18]

Not only is religious training significant, but also whether or not a couple remains actively associated with some church organization is statistically important. Even as early as the engagement period, church attendance has been found to be a factor in the success or failure of the relationship. One study[19] found that more than half of the engagements in which the girl attended church more regularly than the boy were finally broken. This was also true of engagements in which neither had religious affiliations. Fewer engagements were broken among those couples who attended church once a month or more.

This association with a church, which contributes to success in engagement, is equally significant in marriage. Higher marital happiness scores were registered by couples who, after marriage, continued attending church regularly.[20] It has been found, too, that striking differences in marriage adjustment are associated with the cicumstances under which a couple marries. Those who are married in a church or parsonage generally enjoyed a more successful marriage than those who took their vows outside a church before a civil officer.[21] This, of course, does not mean that the ceremony and the minister in themselves exert a lasting influence upon the fate of the marriage. It is, rather, further evidence that those with serious religious connections are more marriageable than others, since those who take their religion seriously more often choose to be married with religious sanction.

All the evidence, therefore, adds up to the effect that a religious background is an asset to marriage, or to state it negatively, that those without religion are less likely to succeed in engagement and marriage.

Religions vary greatly, however, in their contribution to marital happiness. The degree of authoritarianism in religion seems to have some

17 Lewis M. Terman and others, *Psychological Factors in Marital Happiness* (New York: McGraw-Hill Book Co., 1938).

18 Ernest W. Burgess and Leonard S. Cottrell, *Predicting Success or Failure in Marriage* (Englewood Cliffs, N. J.: Prentice-Hall, Inc., 1939), pp. 392 ff.

19 Ernest W. Burgess and Paul Wallin, *Engagement and Marriage* (Philadelphia: J. B. Lippincott Co., 1953), pp. 290-291.

20 Burgess and Cottrell, *op. cit.,* p. 393.

21 *Ibid,* pp. 394, 417.

relationship. Chesser's study in Great Britain of over 6,000 marriages indicates that the highest proportion of happy childhoods and happy parental marriages were found among the nonconformists, that is, the Protestants, rather than in the Church of England group. The lowest degree of happiness was among those with no religion. Jews were very close to second in producing the lowest proportion of happy marriages.[22] Roman Catholics had the highest proportion of unhappy marriages and unhappy childhoods and highest rate of premarital intercourse.

The Church-Attendance Issue

The religious issue for many couples is in reality a church attendance issue. The husband's workweek is time structured, often to the extent of commanding some of his leisure time. This and community activities may schedule most of his weekdays. Sunday is his free day and he wishes its time unstructured by any institution. It is the one day when he feels he should have a right to do as he pleases. He may even feel that the free use of this day for relaxation and esthetic enjoyment is the essence of religion itself. To the wife, on the other hand, the Sunday routine of Sunday School and church represents the one certain time in the week when she can dress up, have social contacts outside the home with the family as a unit, and can be seen in the company of her husband. She is likely to find the church service relaxing and stimulating entirely aside from the religious context, since it is a marked variation from her regular weekday routine.

The church today is more vital to women in another nonreligious sense. Much of the social activity of the church is in women's groups, as is much of its service-directed activity, both local and worldwide. The church offers women many leadership roles—for many housewives their only such opportunity. Participation in church-going may be essential to obtaining and retaining leadership roles in many of these less formal activities of the church, and to many wives this is of great importance. They could go to church alone, but their position is strengthened if their husbands are beside them.

Protestant-Catholic Combinations

The alliance of Protestant with Catholic represents one of the most common problem-producing marital combinations in our country. Many interfaith affairs no doubt develop out of dating which was never meant to be serious. The young people become attached to each other

[22] Eustace Chesser and others, *The Sexual, Marital, and Family Relationship of the English Woman* (New York: Roy Publishers, Inc., 1957).

before differences take on significance. Still, when one considers the problems and prohibitions involved, one cannot help feeling surprise at the extent of Catholic-Protestant involvements in courtship. One study,[23] at the University of Minnesota, showed that one-fifth of the affairs among Protestants were with non-Protestants. Among Catholic women, almost two-thirds were with non-Catholics.

The Catholic group, in most communities, is in the minority and consequently under some pressure to cross religious lines in order to find suitable mates. In fact, more than a fourth of all Catholic youths in the United States have ecclesiastical marriages to non-Catholics.[24] This takes no account of those Catholics who forsake the church in marriage outside their religion. The highest rate of mixed marriages is among those with higher education and with high socioeconomic status.

What is the ultimate outcome of the Protestant-Catholic combination? First, one must recognize the obstacles if the relationship terminates in marriage and the Catholic member is to avoid excommunication. The Protestant member of the pair is expected to attend a series of several lessons by the priest, during which he is indoctrinated in the Catholic point of view and given instructions concerning the way children born to the marriage are to be reared. He must, if the marriage is to be sanctioned, sign a contract that the child will be reared in the Catholic Church, that he will not interfere with the mate's religious practice, that he will respect the Catholic principle not to practice birth control, and that they will be married only by the Catholic priest. The marriage is a sacrament, considered of God and therefore indissoluble. The non-Catholic need not become a Catholic. Here is the contract:

ANTE-NUPTIAL AGREEMENT

To Be Signed by Applicants for Dispensation from Impediment of
Mixed Religion or Disparity of Cult.

Non-Catholic Party

I, the undersigned_____ of _____,
not a member of the Catholic Church, desiring to contract marriage with
_____ of _____, who is a member of the
Catholic Church, propose to do so with the understanding that the marriage
bond thus contracted can be broken only by death.

And thereupon in consideration of such marriage, I, the said _____
_____ do hereby covenant, promise, and agree to and with

23 Clifford Kirkpatrick and Theodore Caplow, "Courtship in a Group of Minnesota Students," *American Journal of Sociology*, 51:114-125, September, 1945.

24 John L. Thomas, "The Factor of Religion in Selection of Marriage Mates," *American Sociological Review*, 16:487-491, August, 1951.

the said _____ that he (she), the said _____
shall be permitted the free exercise of religion according to the Catholic faith
without hindrance or adverse comment and that all the children of either sex
born of such marriage, shall be baptized and educated only in the faith and
according to the teachings of the Roman Catholic Church, even if the said
_____ shall die first.

I hereby promise that no other marriage ceremony than that by the Catholic
priest shall take place.

I furthermore realize the holiness of the use of marriage according to the
teaching of the Catholic Church which condemns birth control and similar
abuses of marriage. I shall have due respect for the religious principles and
convictions of my Catholic partner.

Witness my hand this _____ day of _____ 19_____
at _____ in the County of _____, and State of _____
Signed in the presence of
Rev._____   _____
                                          Signature of Non-Catholic

Catholic Party

I, the undersigned _____ a member of the Catholic
Church, of _____ Parish, _____, wishing to
contract marriage with _____, a non-Catholic, hereby
solemnly promise to have all the children of either sex born of this marriage,
baptized and reared only in the Catholic faith.

Furthermore, I promise that no other marriage ceremony than that by the
Catholic priest shall take place.

I also realize my obligation in conscience to practice my religion faithfully
and prudently to endeavor by prayer, good example and the reception of the
Sacraments, to induce my life partner to investigate seriously the teachings of the
Catholic Church in the hope that such investigation may lead to conversion.

Witness my hand this _____ day of _____ 19_____ at _____
_____ in the County of _____, and State of _____
Signed in the presence of
Rev._____   _____
                                          Signature of Catholic

A day or so before the marriage ceremony, a parent of the non-
Catholic is summoned before the priest, and without prior knowledge
concerning the questions to be asked, is required to give his oath before
the priest that the answers are true. Among the several questions asked
are usually questions dealing with whether or not the young people to
be married have discussed birth control and the indissolubility of marriage with him.

If these seem like hard requirements, it must be remembered that the
Catholic Church is positive in its advice against members entering into a
marriage with non-Catholics. The Catholic Church does not want inter-

faith marriages because they tend to weaken not only religion, but marriage itself.

Neither do Protestant denominations want mixed marriages, though they do not generally oppose them by formal requirements or rigid prohibitions. This being the case, the Catholic view dominates any Protestant-Catholic marriage with reference to five fundamental points: (1) birth control, (2) wedding ceremony, (3) nature of marriage (sacred *vs.* civil), (4) permissibility of divorce, (5) and most important of all to the long-run adjustments of marriage, the training of children likely to be born to the union.

Mixed Marriages—High-Risk Marriages

Engagements of couples with different religions are more fragile than of those with the same religion.[25] Marriages between Protestants and Catholics are far more likely to end in divorce than marriages within either faith.

The divorce rates of the mixed group in most cases run three to four times as high as for Catholic marriages and about twice as high as for Protestant marriages. Notice the divorce rates in interfaith marriages below:

Marriage combination	STUDY I* Bell, Maryland 13,528 couples	STUDY II† Weeks, Spokane, Wash. 6,548 couples	STUDY III‡ Landis, Michigan 4,108 couples
Both Catholic	6.4	3.8	4.4
Both Protestant	6.8	10.0	6.0
Mixed, Protestant-Catholic	15.2	17.4	14.1
Catholic father- Protestant mother	—	—	20.6

* Bell, *op. cit.*, p. 154, † Weeks, *op. cit.*, p. 336, ‡ Landis and Landis, *op. cit.*, p. 154.

When one pauses to consider the stand taken by the Catholic Church against divorce, he can well appreciate the inner turmoil and marital conflict to which these figures testify. The Catholic cannot get a divorce and remain a Catholic. For every Catholic who resorts to divorce there are no doubt many more who suffer great difficulty in the marriage rather than take the forbidden step.

Judson T. Landis[26] has suggested that the high divorce rate of the Catholic husband-Protestant wife combination may be due to the initiative that Protestant wives generally take in the matter of divorce, an

[25] Burgess and Wallin, *op. cit.*, Fig. 36, p. 290.
[26] Landis and Landis, *op. cit.*, pp. 202-203.

initiative which the Catholic wife cannot exercise in the other combination. It may, however, be more than a technical issue. There is reason to believe that such a combination could lead to a maximum number of marital problems. Child training, for example, is generally a wife's function, but when the father is the devout Catholic in a mixed marriage, the job of religious training falls largely upon his shoulders. When, as must often be the case, he has neither the time nor the ability to assume this function, serious family problems seem likely to result, particularly if he blames the wife for her failure to qualify as his substitute.

Zimmerman and Cervantes, studying 40,000 urban families with children, found divorce rates three times as high in mixed Protestant-Catholic marriages as in those of like faith.[27] The State of Iowa collects data on religious affiliation of marrying couples. These data, analyzed extensively by Burchinal and Chancellor, present sociological data of major significance to the problem of marriage stability of interfaith unions.[28] These studies show clearly that the mixed marriage has a shorter duration and also that the marriages of unaffiliated persons are much shorter in duration than those with church connections (see Table 15–1). Length of duration of marriages prior to divorce, they found, is

TABLE 15-1————Percent of marriages surviving in the state of Iowa by religious affiliation*

Spousal religious affiliation type	Marital survival rate
Homogamous Catholic	96.2
Presbyterian-non-Catholic	94.6
Homogamous Lutheran	94.1
Lutheran-non-Catholic	93.0
Methodist-non-Catholic	92.9
Homogamous Methodist	91.4
Homogamous Presbyterian	91.0
Catholic-Lutheran	90.5
Baptist-non-Catholic	90.0
Catholic-Presbyterian	89.8
Homogamous Baptist	89.8
Catholic-Methodist	83.8
Catholic-Baptist	81.6
Homogamous-unaffiliated Protestant	35.0
Catholic-unaffiliated Protestant	28.7

* Adapted from Burchinal and Chancellor, op. cit., Table 5, p. 758.

27 Carl C. Zimmerman and Lucius F. Cervantes, *Successful American Families* (New York: Pageant Press, Inc., 1960).
28 Lee G. Burchinal and Loren E. Chancellor, "Survival Rates Among Religiously Homogamous and Interreligious Marriages," *Agricultural and Home Economics Experiment Station Research Bulletin 512*, December, 1962.

also related to age when married and to social status, older age and higher social status leading to longer duration of marriage.

It is among the nominal (unaffiliated) Protestants that the rate of marriage failure is extremely high. This study also found the rate of failure higher in Catholic-Protestant unions where the Catholic member was the husband.

Zimmerman and Cervantes found the failure rate of Jewish-Gentile marriages very high, much higher than that for any other combination.[29]

Weighing the Religious Issue in Advance

In spite of the probable difficulties of the Protestant-Catholic marriage, many are willing to face the risks. Those Protestants and Catholics who have serious thought of such a marriage owe it to their future to weigh several issues, all of which should be agreed upon before marriage is contemplated. Here are some of the questions that are pertinent:

1. Can one of us adopt the other's religion?
2. If not, can we be happy going to one church or the other, or will we each go alone to our own church?
3. Will one or both of us break with the church altogether?
4. If we agree to keep our church attachments, what will we do about birth control, observance of special religious days, or eating customs?
5. What about benevolences?
6. How will our parents and friends accept the match?
7. How will our children be reared? In which faith, or in no faith at all?
8. If in the Catholic faith, can the Protestant member fully accept church supervision of the training of his child?
9. Can we stand the pressure of devout parents or grandparents, or representatives of our churches, who will bring pressure to have the children reared in their own faith?
10. In case of emancipation from religious connections, are we strong enough to stand alone when the crises of life overtake us in marriage, or will we, as so many do, revert back to the security, certainty, and faith of our childhood religion? This question is particularly pertinent for the Catholic-reared member.

The Child-Training Issue

Some years ago, case studies of Protestant-Catholic marriages showed that half the conflicts in such marriages were over religion, often centering around how the children would be trained.[30] Conflicts over the

[29] Zimmerman and Cervantes, *op. cit.*

[30] Ray E. Baber, "A Study of 325 Mixed Marriages," *American Sociological Review*, 2:705-716, October, 1937.

religious issue were about as numerous among those couples who were both rather indifferent in religion as among the devout.

Since the training of the children is the greatest troublemaker in the cross-religion marriage, Landis' research tried to find a statistical answer to child training and related questions by following mixed marriages into the second generation.[31]

It was found that among the over 4,000 parents of the college young people studied, over a third of one religion or the other had forsaken their faith to follow the faith of the other spouse. This change of faith usually took place before marriage, although in some cases it came later. Among those who did not change their faith, it was found that half of the children had been reared in the Protestant faith, 45 percent in the Catholic faith, and 5 percent in no faith at all. Obviously the pledge taken by all Catholics to raise their children in the faith is not easily followed. Thomas reports a loss to the Catholic group of 40 percent.[32] The Church seems justified in being wary of the cross-religion marriage.

Landis showed further that in these homes young people are subjected to various religious training programs. In more than a third of the cases, the mother took all the responsibility. In most of the other cases, the child was exposed to both faiths, sometimes by one parent, sometimes by both. In a few cases, he actually was taken to both churches in turn. These college students, looking at the mixed marriages of their parents, were inclined to feel that in general it had been a serious handicap in their home lives.

Prince, studying a small sample, found that the tendency was for the couple to raise the child in the faith of the mother, but with the likelihood that in the case of the two minority religious groups, training was likely to be in this faith.[33] Nationwide data for the Jewish group suggest that Judaism is losing about 70 percent of the children born to the mixed-faith couple. They may not be reared in the Protestant or the Catholic faith in many of these cases, but they are not reared in the Jewish faith.[34]

Zimmerman and Cervantes indicate that in nine thousand mixed marriages they studied, six out of ten children in the Catholic-Protestant mixed marriage end up rejecting all religion.[35]

There are also scattered data which suggest that the birth rate of the mixed marriage may tend to run lower than that in the marriage of like

---

[31] Landis and Landis, op. cit., Ch. 13 and Baber, op. cit., also studied this problem with a small sample.

[32] John L. Thomas, The American Catholic Family (Englewood Cliffs, N. J.: Prentice-Hall, Inc., 1956).

[33] Alfred J. Prince, op. cit.

[34] Erich Rosenthal, op. cit.

[35] Zimmerman and Cervantes, op. cit.

faith.[36] This seems particularly true in the case of the Jew. Whether it is the mixed marriage that is responsible or whether both the mixed marriage and the low birth rate are indicative of emancipation from tradition might well be asked.

Jewish-Gentile Marriages

An early study showed that comparatively few young people of Jewish origin dated outside their religious group—slightly more than a fourth of Jewish male and only 15 percent of Jewish female college students at the University of Minnesota.[37] Jewish-Gentile marriages are not as frequent as Catholic-Protestant ones. This results in part from religious observances, but it probably also reflects an attitude of anti-Semitism, which in most communities is a live prejudice.

About 13 percent of Jewish marriages are interfaith.[38] Studies of Jewish-Gentile intermarriage show that in most cases the marriage is between a Jewish man and a Gentile woman; comparatively few are between Jewish women and Gentile men. When such marriages do take place, they are between reformed or liberal Jews. Orthodox Judaism does not permit Jewish-Gentile marriages except in cases where the Gentile has been converted to the Jewish religion. The more liberal and reformed Jewish group, which is now in the majority in the United States, has no absolute prohibition against intermarriage, but does discourage it.[39]

There is a very close family supervision over the dating of Jewish young people, particularly of the Jewish girl. Any dating between Jews and Gentiles is seriously frowned upon by the Jewish group.[40]

The real difficulty with the Jewish-Gentile marriage of the religiously emancipated Jew is that more differences than those of religion are involved. Judaism is a culture in and of itself, as is Christianity, not merely a religion. The Jewish world is a world of customs dating back through the centuries. Jews differ from Christians in observing a different day of

36 *Ibid.*; also Thomas B. Morgan, *op. cit.*; also Zimmerman and Cervantes, *op. cit.*
37 Kirkpatrick and Caplow, *op. cit.*
38 This is the figure reported by Rosenthal, *op. cit.*; see also Ruby Jo Reeves Kennedy, "Single or Triple Melting Pot?: Intermarriage Trends in New Haven, 1870-1950," *American Journal of Sociology*, 57:56 ff., January, 1952.
39 J. S. Slotkin, "Jewish-Gentile Intermarriages in Chicago," *American Sociological Review*, 7:34-39, February, 1942, classifies various Jewish types entering into Gentile marriages: the emancipated (most numerous), the rebellious, marginal, adventurous, promiscuous, and disorganized were the types found in his study of 183 cases of intermarriage in Chicago.
40 Milton L. Barron, "The Incidence of Jewish Intermarriage in Europe and America," *American Sociological Review*, 11:12 ff., February, 1946.

rest, different religious holidays, different foods, and in numerous other ways. Not many young people reared in the Jewish culture can entirely forsake it, and few Gentiles reared outside this world can completely accept it.

One of the major handicaps in the Jewish-Gentile marriage has been that in approximately half the cases, one or the other or both families reject the new son or daughter.[41] A second handicap is the prejudice against Jews exhibited in many circles. The Gentile in this marriage must face anti-Semitic prejudice against himself and his children.

In an early study of cross-religion marriages, it was found[42] that in the Jewish-Gentile cross, the Jewish religion was usually passed on to the children, both in the marriage of Jews to Protestants and to Catholics. This study, like others, found that the difficulty over training children was foremost in the interfaith marriage and that conflicts are about as frequent over this issue in marriage where couples are not seriously religious as where they are.

With the current trend toward integration of racial, ethnic, and religious groups, interfaith marriages of Jews are greatly on the increase. With increased education at the higher levels in secular universities, this trend will likely continue. Greater tolerance is extant in the culture everywhere. No doubt many of the problems of the Jewish-Gentile marriage today are less severe than in marriages studied in the past. It may well be that greater acceptance of the couple by families joined by such marriages prevails. If not now, certainly this would seem to be the trend of the future.

Before Jewish-Gentile dating relationships become very serious, young people should ask themselves all the questions listed for the Catholic-Protestant combination and should visit each other's communities and homes and get a firsthand insight into the difference between the two cultural worlds. Certainly before marriage they should visit each other's homes and establish understanding relationships with each other's families. It is often easy, when young people live far away from their own relatives, to forget how important religious differences can be when one joins two family lines in marriage. In these days of detached, urban dating it is easy to forget that one marries, not only a person, but also a family. The Jewish family is a very closely knit group, and even though the Jewish young person may emancipate himself from his religion, he rarely emancipates himself completely from his family and its influences.

41 J. S. Slotkin, "Adjustment in Jewish-Gentile Intermarriages," *Social Forces*, 21:226-230, December, 1942.

42 Ray E. Baber "A Study of 325 Mixed Marriages," *American Sociological Review*, 2:705-716, October, 1937.

Interdenominational Marriages

Prince,[43] in his study of cross-religion marriages, included 52 marriages between different Protestant denominations. Although the sample is too small to justify wide generalization, two findings are strongly suggestive of outcome. (1) A very high percentage classed their marriage in the "entirely satisfied" or "very much satisfied" group compared to the interfaith marriages. (2) Only 19 percent retained their own separate denomination, compared to 55 percent of the interfaith group who retained their separate faith. In two-thirds of the cases the husband or wife adopted the other's faith. In 11.5 percent of the cases the couple adopted another denomination differing from the former loyalties of either.

If this research should receive further confirmation one would be justified in the conclusion that interdenominational marriages usually do not terminate the couple's adherence to some Protestant body, and generally the religious difference is not a major barrier to the marriage.

Burchinal and Chancellor calculated survival rates of interdenominational marriages and found them generally quite high (refer again to Table 15–1 p. 289).[44] They were, however, dealing with the more standard denominations, rather than fringe revivalistic groups. It is probable that these groups do not too often marry into the more conservative denominations with large memberships. The highest rate of failure was among the nominal (unaffiliated) Protestants.

Such marriages may be very hard on church membership in particular denominations. Bossard and Letts[45] have studied the problem of intermarriage by Lutherans, a rather conservative liturgically oriented group, through contacts with pastors. It was found that twice as many women as men married outside their church. Although Lutherans are generally very loyal to their church, where they entered mixed marriages there was a loss of somewhere between 17 to 25 percent to the Lutheran group.

One suspects that young people who are loyal to very orthodox or revivalistic religious groups would find themselves quite out of harmony with those who are members of the more formalistic or ritualistic churches. The formal and ritualistic group, too, is far different from the extremely modern fringe. Between such denominations, there is a vast difference in the level of religious appeal, esthetic appreciation, and emo-

---

[43] Prince, *op. cit.*
[44] Burchinal and Chancellor, *op. cit.,* p. 758.
[45] James H. S. Bossard and Harold C. Letts, "Mixed Marriages Involving Lutherans —A Research Report," *Marriage and Family Living,* 18:308-310, November, 1956.

RELIGION REPORTED BY PERSONS
14 YEARS OLD AND OVER:
CIVILIAN POPULATION, MARCH, 1957

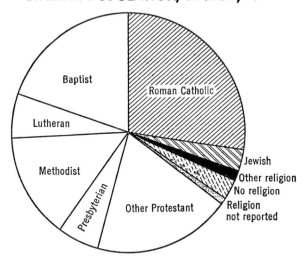

	Number	Percent
Total, 14 years and over	119,333,000	100.0
Protestant	78,952,000	66.2
Baptist	23,525,000	19.7
Lutheran	8,417,000	7.1
Methodist	16,676,000	14.0
Presbyterian	6,656,000	5.6
Other Protestant	23,678,000	19.8
Roman Catholic	30,669,000	25.7
Jewish	3,868,000	3.2
Other religion	1,545,000	1.3
No religion	3,195,000	2.7
Religion not reported	1,104,000	0.9

SOURCE: U. S. Department of Commerce, Bureau of the Census, "Religion Reported by the Civilian Population of the United States, March, 1957," *Current Population Reports: Population Characteristics*, Series P-20, No. 79, February 2, 1958.

FIGURE 15-2————Beside the major religious bodies there are some 200 Protestant denominations. The membership of the larger bodies is shown here.

tional outlet. There is also often involved a radically different philosophy of life and a difference of socioeconomic class.

While such differences may not be as great as Protestant-Catholic differences, for example, they are great enough to be grounds for caution. The dating period should be made to bring the couple, deliberately, into close relationships with the religious philosophy, the church, and the family of both young people. The liberal-minded person can generally feel little tolerance for the person who is extremely dogmatic or narrow in religious philosophy; it is often equally difficult for the one reared in a strict religious environment to liberalize his philosophy of life and religion.

The sum of evidence to date would seem to be that interdenominational marriage probably leads to a considerable shifting of denominational allegiance, but does not seem to be a major handicap to marriage success or survival. Certainly the evidence is strong that church membership in and of itself is important to marriage success; that merely claiming to be Protestant or Catholic without practicing the faith is related to a high degree of marriage failure.

It is important that a young person who is a loyal member of a church think twice before marrying someone who has no interest in church and church affairs. The person with religious attitudes and church loyalties has had this slant toward life built into his or her personality for some twenty years before marriage. His particular values, attitudes, and aspirations are too deeply ingrained to be easily discarded or ignored. The Landis study[46] previously cited makes it clear that marriages between those who are loyal to a religious system and those who are not, are relatively hazardous from the standpoint of success and permanence.

In conclusion, it may be said that while religious differences account for many marital problems, religion itself is a powerful asset in making marriage succeed. Individuals with similar religious backgrounds, values, and opinions have a good chance to succeed in marriage. Even those who embark upon the uncertain path of an interfaith marriage have a better chance than the couple without religious convictions.

One may well wonder why this is so. Religious values are, in essence, the values that make for a well-adjusted personality, mature living, and emotional equanimity. The highest virtues of most religions are: meekness, kindness and consideration for others, helpfulness, self-sacrifice, putting off immediate sensuous satisfaction for the sake of more distant goals, sacrifice of the temporal for the spiritual, the placing of ideals

---

[46] Landis and Landis, *op. cit.*

above ambitions, the placing of goodness above material gain, and many other such core human values. Persons who are able to hold and to live by these positive values in large measure cannot but be well-adjusted, forward-looking, peace-loving individuals.

Those who are truly religious possess the traits out of which good human adjustment and good family living spring. They have the values which make parenthood not merely an obligation, but a high achievement, not merely a duty, but a virtue, not merely a biological exercise, but a spiritual achievement.

It must, therefore, be expected that those who have captured the essence of religious virtues and who have learned how to apply them in social relationships, will be good prospects for marriage. This does not mean, of course, that people without church affiliations never possess any of these virtues—they may. On the other hand, there is greater likelihood of a person's having them if he belongs to church groups in which these values and aspirations are taught and practiced.

The problems which interfaith marriages encounter are not, as one might suspect, primarily the result of constant clashes in religious discussions. They are more frequently the outcome of differences over child training and over general values in life. Religion has an influence over far more than the spiritual life of its adherents. Major religious groups teach widely differing attitudes and value systems as well as beliefs. Young people are more often able to change their beliefs than the accompanying attitudes and values.

Problems

1. *Sociodrama:* A young man, religiously indifferent rather than agnostic or atheistic, has just proposed to a girl of serious religious faith. She refuses his proposal. The play begins with her refusal. Bring out her explanations, present his arguments, and include in the play their final decision.
2. Name several attitudes characteristic of a religious person which would be assets to him in marriage adjustment.
3. Would you say that a Protestant minister who advises young people against marrying either Catholics or Jews is probably prejudiced and intolerant?
4. Think of the ways in which children born to a marriage magnify the problems of an interfaith marriage. How would you handle the religious training of a child of an interfaith marriage?
   a. Let the father decide?
   b. Let the mother decide?
   c. Have some respected outsider decide?
   d. Try to combine the dogma of both faiths?

   e. Expose him to both faiths and let him decide for himself when he is
       old enough?

   f. Expose him to neither faith and let him decide in later years?

   g. Choose some other alternative?

5. In your opinion, what accounts for the greater degree of marriage failure
   among people without religious affiliation?

6. Catholic, Jewish, and Protestant faiths all share the same fundamental
   ethical codes. What, then, accounts for the many problems that confront
   marriages of mixed religion?

7. In most American homes is it the husband or the wife who assumes the
   religious leadership of the family? How would you explain this fact?

8. When individuals of different religious faiths decide to marry but maintain
   their separate beliefs, is there any justification for an intensive study by
   each of the faith of the other?

9. It has been said that the problems that arise out of interdenominational
   marriages often reflect differences in socioeconomic background rather than
   in religious belief. Does this statement make sense?

10. Is there anything that the churches could do to help make interfaith and
    interdenominational marriages more common and more successful? Do you
    believe that the churches should or should not make such an attempt? Why
    or why not?

11. Ask a marriage counselor or a family relations counselor, or a minister,
    priest, or rabbi to describe one or more actual instances of interfaith or
    interdenominational marriages. Ask the speaker to note specifically the
    kinds of problems reported by the couple or couples, the solutions sought,
    and whether or not their problems were solved.

Selected References

ARTICLES IN BOOKS OF READINGS

BECKER, Howard, and HILL, Reuben (Editors), *Family, Marriage and Parenthood,* Second Edition (Boston: D. C. Heath & Co., 1955).

   1. SMITH, Rockwell G., "Religion in Family Life," pp. 596-615.

KLING, Samuel G., and KLING, Esther B., *The Marriage Reader* (New York: The
Vanguard Press, Inc., 1947).

   2. BOWMAN, Henry A., "Mixed Marriage," pp. 53-89.

FISHBEIN, Morris, and KENNEDY, Ruby Jo Reeves, *Modern Marriage and Family
Living* (New York: Oxford University Press, Inc., 1957).

   3. BARRON, Milton L., "Race, Religion, and Nationality in Mate Selection,"
      pp. 60-73.

LANDIS, Judson T., and LANDIS, Mary G., *Readings in Marriage and the Family*
(Englewood Cliffs, N. J.: Prentice-Hall, Inc., 1952).

   4. LANDIS, Judson T., "Marriages of Mixed and Non-Mixed Religious
      Faith," pp. 203-210.

Sussman, Marvin B., *Sourcebook in Marriage and the Family*, Second Edition (Boston: Houghton Mifflin Co., 1963).

5. Thomas, John L., "The Factor of Religion in the Selection of Marriage Mates," pp. 108-112.

6. Vincent, Clark E., "Interfaith Marriages: Problem or Symptom?" pp. 349-358.

Cavan, Ruth Shonle, *Marriage and the Family in the Modern World: A Book of Readings* (New York: Thomas Y. Crowell Co., 1960).

7. Prince, Alfred J., "Attitudes of College Students toward Inter-Faith Marriage," Reading 60.

8. Pike, James A., "The Problems of Mixed Marriage—and the Solution," Reading 61.

General References

Baber, Ray E., *Marriage and The Family*, Second Edition (New York: McGraw-Hill Book Co., 1953), Ch. 5.

Barron, Milton L., "The Incidence of Jewish Intermarriage in Europe and America," *American Sociological Review*, 11:12 ff., February, 1946.

Bossard, James H. S., and Letts, Harold C., "Mixed Marriages Involving Lutherans—A Research Report," *Marriage and Family Living*, 18:308-310, November, 1956.

Bowman, Henry A., *Marriage for Moderns*, Fourth Edition (New York: McGraw-Hill Book Co., 1960), Ch. 8.

Burchinal, Lee G., "Membership Groups and Attitudes toward Cross-Religious Dating," *Marriage and Family Living*, 22:248-253, August, 1960.

————, and Chancellor, Loren E., "Survival Rates Among Religiously Homogamous and Interreligious Marriages," *Agricultural and Home Economics Experiment Station Research Bulletin 512*, December, 1962.

Burgess, Ernest W., and Wallin, Paul, *Engagement and Marriage* (Philadelphia: J. B. Lippincott Co., 1953), Ch. 6.

Cavan, Ruth Shonle, *American Marriage* (New York: Thomas Y. Crowell Co., 1959), Ch. 8.

Christensen, Harold T., *Marriage Analysis*, Revised Edition (New York: The Ronald Press Co., 1958), Ch. 8.

Duvall, Evelyn M., and Hill, Reuben, *When You Marry*, Revised Edition (Boston: D. C. Heath & Co., 1953), Ch. 19.

Gordon, Albert L., *Intermarriage* (Boston: Beacon Press, 1964).

Heiss, Jerold S., "Interfaith Marriage and Marital Outcome," *Marriage and Family Living*, 23:228-233, August, 1961.

Jacobson, Paul H., *American Marriage and Divorce* (New York: Holt, Rinehart & Winston, Inc., 1959).

Kane, John J., *Marriage and the Family: A Catholic Approach* (New York: Henry Holt and Co., Inc., 1952), Ch. 8.

KENNEDY, Ruby Jo Reeves, "Single or Triple Melting Pot?: Intermarriage Trends in New Haven, 1870-1950," *American Journal of Sociology*, 57:56 ff., January, 1952.

LANDIS, Judson T., and LANDIS, Mary G., *Building a Successful Marriage*, Fourth Edition (Englewood Cliffs, N. J.: Prentice-Hall, Inc., 1963), Chs. 13, 19.

LOCKE, Harvey J., SABAGH, George, and THOMES, Mary Margaret, "Interfaith Marriages," *Social Problems*, 4:329-333, April, 1957.

ROSENTHAL, Erich, "Studies in Jewish Intermarriage in the United States," *American Jewish Year Book*, Vol. 64, 1963.

SAMENFINK, J. Anthony, "A Study of Some Aspects of Marital Behavior as Related to Religious Control," *Marriage and Family Living*, 20:163-169, May, 1958.

SLOTKIN, J. S., "Adjustment in Jewish-Gentile Intermarriages," *Social Forces*, 27:216-230, December, 1942.

————, "Jewish-Gentile Intermarriages in Chicago," *American Sociological Review*, 7:34-39, February, 1942.

THOMAS, John L., *The American Catholic Family* (Englewood Cliffs, N. J.: Prentice-Hall, Inc., 1956).

————, "The Factor of Religion in the Selection of Marriage Mates," *American Sociological Review*, 16:487-491, August, 1951.

ZIMMERMAN, Carle C., and CERVANTES, Lucius F., *Successful American Families* (New York: Pageant Press, Inc., 1950).

16
Interracial and
Intercultural Marriages

Of the gaps in social distance that separate various
groups in American society, and particularly in mar-
riage, the one between race is by far the greatest. Gordon,[1] in his study
of student attitudes in forty colleges and universities, obtained the reaction of 5,407 students to the question of intercultural marriage for themselves. Here is the way he classifies their answers:

Do not favor marriage to person of:	Percent
another color	91
another religion	50
another educational group	31
another nationality	16
a different economic class	13

Would find it easiest to marry a person with:	Percent
economic differences	64
nationality differences	58
educational differences	39
religious differences	27
color differences	6

We have just entered a new era in race relations. It remains to be
seen whether the great gap that has existed here will remain. The racists
of the deep South presume that it will not. They have said much of the

---

[1] Albert L. Gordon, *Intermarriage* (Boston: Beacon Press, 1964), Ch. 2.

coming "mongrelization" of the white race once the Negro is accepted as equal. They prefer to overlook the fact that the races have been in the process of "mongrelization" since the beginnings of slavery, with the illicit sexual contacts that have prevailed.[2] Few pure Negroes remain. Historically the mongrelization has been that of the Negro, since most sexual contact has been between the white male and the Negro female. The resulting child goes with the mother and is considered Negro. It is the mongrelization involving the Negro male and the white female that racists obviously consider a threat to racial purity.

The sociological fact is that wherever social distance between groups exists, whether it be the product of religion, nationality, economics, race, or other biological or cultural variables, once the process of integration and assimilation gets under way, amalgamation also begins. The ultimate step in integration is intermarriage.

As with all cases of conflicts involved in social distance, once affairs reach the point where intermarriage is considered, the hostilities which create problems are already vanishing.

Intercultural Factors

Although race is one of the most complicated factors to be dealt with in mate selection today, it is by no means the only important one. Other factors have been found to have a bearing on the success and failure of marriage—nationality and previous marriage experience, for example. There are still other factors which may or may not have so much bearing on the outcome of marriage, but which young people wonder about, like differences in the amount of schooling of man and wife, differences in age, and differences in economic background and standard of living in the parental homes. What does research show that will help one arrive at an objective and mature judgment here?

Obviously, some of these factors are of increasing importance; others of less importance than in an earlier day. Marriages crossing nationality lines in the United States are on the decrease as we are ceasing to be the melting pot of European nations, but the new problem here is the marriage of thousands of service men to foreign brides while the former are stationed abroad. Differences in education of men and women are not so great as in a day when it was considered inappropriate for women to go to college. In many parts of the country there is nearly universal high school education. Economic lines tend to be obscured during the high school and college dating years and one suspects that an increasing proportion of marriages are between young people from families which have quite different levels of living.

2 *Ibid.*, p. 222.

Another problem of increasing proportions today is that of marriages between those without and those with previous marital experience. Not many years ago, marriage to a divorced person was a rare occurrence. Today, one in every five marriages involves a person with previous marital experience. Some of the remarried persons have been widowed by death, but even more have been widowed by the failure of the previous marriage. How heavily should one weigh a previous failure in considering marriage to a secondhand mate?

Certainly the effect of such differences in background and experience may be expected to have a bearing on the success or failure of marriage, and therefore merits study.

Interracial Marriages

Integration factors: What we know from research on the problems of the interracial marriage is probably already obsolete knowledge due to the change in temper of the American racial climate. Laws forbidding intermarriage of the races are still prevalent, but are already being challenged and revoked.[3] Whether challenged or not, they will increasingly be ignored, if they remain on the statute books.

Increasingly the race crossings will be among the educated who work together on the college campus and fight together in the crusade for equality. The Peace Corps, too, brings many interracial contacts of youth. These social forces will bring a respectability to interracial marriage they have not had previously. The general climate of opinion will also be increasingly tolerant toward the children of the mixed marriages, so that this will no longer be so great an anxiety-provoking factor in the experience of those who brave the color line in marriage.

Those who are shocked to anticipate the increase in interracial marriages will do well to remember that throughout the course of human history the races have mixed. One need not travel widely over the face of the earth to be convinced of this fact. The racial crossing between all branches of the human race is fertile.

College campuses are becoming more cosmopolitan yearly. Any observer of campus life is aware that already the taboos against white girls dating those of other races are breaking down, particularly where the dark-skinned male is from another country. Often marriages of this type mean marrying up into the aristocracy of the country from which the male student comes. This gives such marriages respectability. The next step is for dating and intermarriage to be less selective.

Research guides: Adams' early study of interracial marriage in Hawaii, where there is no caste-color line, showed that marriage problems

3 *Ibid.*

were more a matter of cultural norms and sex roles than of social pressures affecting the marriage from the community standpoint.[4] The native-
stock (Polynesian) Hawaiian woman marrying a Chinese or a white man
of good character moved up in standard of living—chairs, tables, beds,
dishes, etc.—and took pride in adopting the husband's way of life for
herself and her children. In general these husbands are better providers
than the native island males. The marriages in general did well.

In rare cases where the native male married a non-Polynesian female,
marriages often turned out to be unsatisfactory. This male's standards of
industry fell far below those of the Chinese or the white and the wife
became intolerant of his easy-going ways and his lack of responsibility
as a provider. These wives were, moreover, not willing to assume the
customary tasks of the Polynesian wife.

Thus we have interracial-international marriages involving the same
strains turning out differently depending on which combination of male
and female are involved. The problem proves not to be racial, but rather
one of subcultural differences, primarily in role expectations of male and
female. This principle may well have wide applications in international
and interracial cross-marriages everywhere.

One other principle discovered by Adams was that the degree of disorganization of the particular group or groups involved in marriages
across race and nationality lines was a key factor in the divorce rate.
Groups going through a rapid period of reacculturation not only crossed
the line in marriage more often, but also had very high divorce rates, both
with in-race and cross-race marriages.[5] This behavior was particularly
characteristic of such groups as Filipinos, Koreans, and Puerto Ricans.
Japanese and Chinese tended to remain loyal to their culture and to
marry outside very little. Those who did break with their race and culture
group had a high divorce rate.

Since World War II there has been opportunity to observe intermarriage, both of nationality groups involving the same racial strain and of
interracial groups. For example, in the year 1946 alone there were 1,600
Air Force marriages to German girls, and thousands had married English
girls. By the end of 1955, the American Embassy reported that there had
been over 20,000 marriages of GI's to Japanese women. This was in spite
of the fact that for a considerable part of the occupation period the Army
forbade marriages with Japanese girls.

While comprehensive research is lacking, a few special studies throw
some light on interracial marriage, particularly with the Japanese. Joseph

[4] Ronanzo Adams, *Interracial Marriage in Hawaii* (New York: The Macmillan Co.,
1937); see particularly Ch. 5.
[5] *Ibid.;* see particularly Ch. 16.

Grant,[6] writer for the Associate Press, reports an interview study of 224 wives from Europe and the Far East by University of Hawaii sociologist, Yukiko Kimura. All of these women had married Hawaiian men and lived in Hawaii five years or more. Two out of ten considered themselves unhappy, wishing they had not come to Hawaii. Another three out of ten said they probably would not have married their husbands if they had it to do over again, thus making half who would not repeat their marriage. The largest percentage of unhappy women were Japanese who married "Nisei" husbands, that is, American men of Japanese ancestry.

The happiest marriages in this study were Japanese girls married to Caucasian husbands. The second most happy group were Europeans married to "Nisei." Three-fourths of these European girls would marry their husbands again.

Apparently the main difficulty with the Japanese girl marrying the "Nisei" is in-law troubles. The husband's family demands that the wife conform to Japanese old-world patterns. They expect her to work hard and be obedient. The modern Japanese girls do not wish to follow these patterns because most of them are from Japanese cities which have already been very much westernized.

It appears that the Japanese-American marriage in the United States since World War II has, for the most part, not fared too badly. The Schnepp and Masoko study of 40 couples indicates that the marriages have on the whole done very well.[7] Strauss' study in Chicago, based on interviews with 30 men and 15 women in American-Japanese marriages, indicates that in many respects marriage adjustment is eased by the combination of Japanese and American sex roles and marriage values.[8]

In a very comprehensive analysis of the cultural and social interactional factors involved in the Japanese-American marriages, Strauss concludes that one cannot arrive at the easy conclusion that interracial marriages are necessarily doomed to destruction or even that they present unusually great problems of adjustment.

Such cultural values as the lack of vocational aspirations of the wife, the absence of strong institutional loyalties, even the lack of strong loyalty to the religious institutions of her nation, an attitude of acceptance of the American standard of living (which is far superior on every level to anything she has known), and the acceptance of the husband as he is, rather than pushing him to improve himself, all favor the Japanese wife. The Japanese philosophy of the girl shifting her allegiance to the

[6] *Honolulu Star Bulletin,* June 27, 1957.

[7] Gerald Schnepp, Yui Schnepp, and Agnes Masoko, "Cultural and Marital Adjustment of Japanese War Brides," *American Journal of Sociology,* 61:48-50, July, 1955.

[8] Anselm L. Strauss, "Strain and Harmony in American-Japanese War Bride Marriages," *Marriage and Family Living,* 16:99-106, May, 1954.

husband's family when she leaves her home in marriage also helps her in making the adjustment to a new way of life.

Scoring happiness at 100 for very happy marriages, Baber's early study of 48 interracial marriages between whites and members of the black and yellow races rated their happiness at only 62, a score much lower than those of interfaith and mixed-nationality marriages. One-third of the couples had no children, although none of them had been married for less than three years, and the median period of marriage was ten years. Undoubtedly some of this group had refrained from having children because they did not want children born into an environment of discrimination and trouble. And there was no way to know how large a proportion of such interracial marriages had already failed.[9]

Pavela[10] made a study of 95 Negro-white marriages in Indiana, where such intermarriages have been illegal since 1852 and where it has been illegal for a person to marry such couples. Of these, 69 were Negro men with white wives, 26 were white men with Negro brides. He found couples more often entered marriage with a previous divorce and were older than average at the time of marriage. There was no evidence of the Negro male marrying down in occupational and social status, as is often assumed. Most were middle class. Few were married in a religious ceremony.

Pavela concludes, "It would appear that . . . interracial marriage occurs between persons who are, by and large, economically, educationally, and culturally equal and who have a strong emotional attachment, be it rationalization or real. The external pressures faced by the interracial couples are often great but certainly do not appear to be overwhelming."

He goes on to explain that with most couples, the children were still young and the real crises of adjustment may have lain ahead.

The child's problem: Gordon, after his comprehensive study of interrmarriage, concludes that the chances of failure of an interracial marriage is greater than of an interfaith marriage.[11] Interracial marriages lack the social support which interfaith marriages have. Mass public opinion is opposed to the former. He goes on to comment about the fruit of such unions in these terms:

> The children born of Negro-white marriages in the United States are, I believe, among the most socially unfortunate persons in all the world if they seek or expect acceptance by the white community in America. . . . They

---

[9] Ray E. Baber, "A Study of 325 Mixed Marriages," *American Sociological Review*, 2:705-716, October, 1937.

[10] Todd H. Pavela, "An Exploratory Study of Negro-White Intermarriage in Indiana," Chicago Urban League, 1958-1959.

[11] Gorden, *op. cit.*, p. 348-349.

must find their roots in the Negro community or remain unaccepted and unacceptable to the white community.[12]

He finds unanimity of agreement among Negro-white parents in their thinking that the teenage period for their youngsters would be the most trying period of their lives, because of the taboos on interdating. He then raises the question of whether a couple in love have any moral right to create such problems for their children.

The long term view, of course, is that such problems would vanish if complete tolerance prevailed; but Gordon is no doubt right in his appraisal of the current situation and that it will not soon vanish from our society.

Both the law and the weight of public opinion in American society stand in the way of intermarriage for certain groups. Yet the crossing of ethnic and racial lines goes on. For some people there seems to be a fascination in unlike skin color which cultural taboos are insufficient to control. Stories are always afloat about the exotic flavor of interracial sexual ventures, and these encourage race crossing outside wedlock wherever peoples of different skin color inhabit the same territory.

There is no reason, from the hereditary standpoint, why race lines should not be crossed in marriage. There is even some indication that a kind of hybrid vigor results where pure strains are crossed, as is found in hybrid strains of plants and animals. In countries where race crossing is approved by custom there is no objection to intermarriage. Interracial marriages have taken on special significance in the United States only because of race prejudice, which expresses itself in segregation and discrimination. Prejudice is particularly severe against individuals crossing racial lines to marry and the child of mixed blood is in many situations accepted by neither racial group. Color prejudice is a social reality and no amount of idealism or faith on the part of young people in love can make it possible for them to evade this fact.

It must be expected, however, that as America plays a leading part in world leadership, more and more of her young men are going to have the opportunity to marry girls of different racial and nationality strains while stationed abroad. Such marriages are often entered into from loneliness and during periods of great sex hunger. It is not likely that choices made at such times will be based on clear judgment and objectivity. There is often an inclination on the part of the youth to forget that his foreign wife will be expected to fit into a world entirely new and strange to her when he returns home. The transition is so great that few foreign women can be expected to make it without great difficulty and without consider-

[12] *Ibid.*, p. 333-334.

able tolerance on the part of the husband and his family. The cultural differences here add to the racial difference.

Differences in Education

It is a well-established fact that most marriages are between those of similar education and intelligence.[13] This is to be expected in a country where everyone spends most of his dating years in school and associates for the most part with those of similar educational experience and achievement. High schools and colleges are sometimes humorously referred to as match-making factories, which they are and should be.

Studies of college students indicate that girls prefer to marry men above themselves in education, while men generally prefer women their equals in education and intelligence. Two studies in particular[14] have sought to discover just what educational requirements or preferences young people hold regarding prospective mates. Men, it was found, are generally willing to marry someone having less education or intelligence than they possess. Women are less willing to accept such a match although in the latter of the two studies referred to, more than twice as many women (42 percent as opposed to only 18 percent in this first study) indicated that they would be willing to marry someone with less intelligence or education than themselves, other things being equal. This would indicate that women are much less demanding on the matter of education than they once were. This, in turn, probably reflects the great increase in opportunities for married women to earn and maintain the standard of living they choose. The majority, however, still want a husband at least their equal in education and ability. This results in part, no doubt, from practical considerations, but much of it merely reflects traditional American conceptions of the perfect mate.

On education, findings indicate that only 1 percent of the girls studied preferred husbands with less education, 18 percent wanted equal education, and 81 percent preferred husbands with superior educational

[13] The problem of assortative mating by education and for ability is dealt with in the following: Paul Popenoe, "Mate Selection," *American Sociological Review*, 2:735-743, October, 1937; Lewis M. Terman and others, *Psychological Factors in Marital Happiness* (New York: McGraw-Hill Book Co., 1938), pp. 189 ff.; William S. Bernard, "Student Attitudes on Marriage and the Family," *American Sociological Review*, 3:354-361, June, 1938; Ray E. Baber, *Marriage and the Family*, Revised Edition (New York: McGraw-Hill Book Co., 1953), pp. 126-127; D. U. Mather, "The Courtship Ideals of High School Students," *Sociology and Social Research*, 19:169, 1934-35; Paul H. Landis and Katherine H. Day, "Education as a Factor in Mate Selection," *American Sociological Review*, 10:558-560, August, 1954.

[14] Ray E. Baber, *Marriage and the Family*, Revised Edition (New York: McGraw-Hill Book Co., 1953), p. 119; Judson T. Landis and Mary G. Landis, *Building a Successful Marriage*, Second Edition (Englewood Cliffs, N. J.: Prentice-Hall, Inc., 1953), p. 84.

attainment.[15] Nine percent of the men wanted their wives to have more education and 9 percent less, 82 percent the same.

When it comes to actually selecting a mate, women come nearer to realizing their education ideal than do men. This is explained in part by the fact that more men than women reach the higher levels in education. It may also indicate that men attach much less significance to this trait in their wives than do women in their husbands. In many instances, one suspects a young man actually in the marriage market discovers he does not want a wife who is his educational and intellectual equal.

Figure 16-1 shows the proportion of college young people marrying those who were educationally higher, equal to, and lower than themselves.

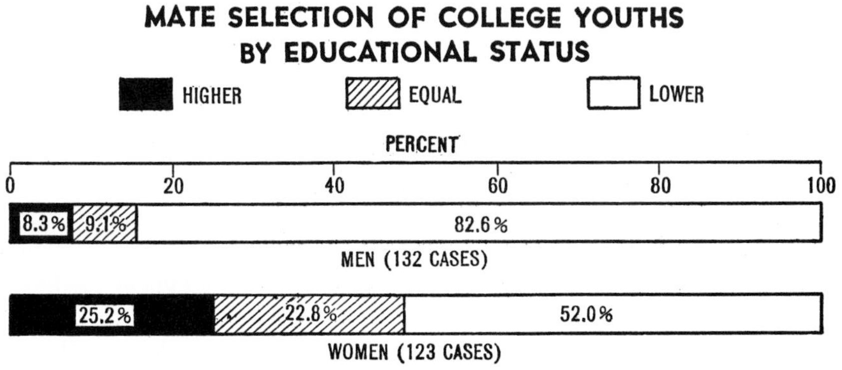

MATE SELECTION OF COLLEGE YOUTHS BY EDUCATIONAL STATUS

SOURCE: Paul H. Landis and Katherine H. Day, "Education as a Factor in Mate Selection," *American Sociological Review*, 10:558-560, August, 1954.

FIGURE 16-1————Most college men married below their level of education; very few married higher. Almost half of all college women married equal to or above their educational level—over a fourth above.

Most college men married below themselves in educational status, but half the women succeeded in marrying educational equals. The further a young person went in college, the more likely he was to marry a person with some college training. Of those who graduated from college, 80 percent married persons with some college training.

The desire of women to marry up and the practice of men to marry down probably reflects basic differences in motivation of the sexes in mate selection. The male, who is by custom the breadwinner, is usually judged by a woman, at least in part, by his ability to offer security and con-

15 Landis and Landis, *op. cit.*, p. 84.

stancy of income. Since education has a direct bearing on economic success,[16] a good education has become a trait greatly to be desired in a husband. Moreover, the male has more to do with establishing and maintaining the general social status of the family, which is determined in our society by such factors as income, occupation, and standard of living. The young woman who can associate herself by marriage with a person of higher education and training is bargaining for a better standard of living than she could expect as a result of her own training and skills.

The man, on the other hand, in facing the problem of mate selection, is likely to consider criteria other than education of prime importance. Men are not particularly attracted to women with college diplomas or other evidence of intellectual prowess. Attractiveness and feminine charm rate high in our culture, and their importance is constantly reaffirmed by pin-up girls, Miss America contests, and other symbols of the cult of beauty.[17]

The belief in the intellectual superiority of the male has so long been a part of American thinking that few men, and for that matter few women, are comfortable in a relationship where the female is obviously the more outstanding. A marriage having this relationship frequently brings feelings of resentment, inadequacy, and frustration to the husband. Few men wish to have their position of authority in the family threatened by the superior educational qualifications of their wives. Popenoe believes the educated man wants a wife who will flatter his ego.[18] Women reared in the popular tradition wish to feel that their husbands actually are superior persons to whom they may look up. Although one might think college women different in these attitudes, numerous class discussions with upper division classes has convinced the writer that college women hold this view also.

That this pattern of assortative mating is deeply rooted is suggested by findings that women who marry above themselves in education are more likely to be happy in marriage than those who marry below themselves.[19] In other words, the pattern is so well established that acting contrary to it increases the danger of maladjustment in marriage. With men, lack of education in the spouse is not so important to happiness.

Finally, education itself seems to be an asset to marriage—the more

[16] Paul H. Landis, "The Dollar Value of an Education," *Journal of the National Education Association,* 38:366-368, May, 1949; also Ernest Havermann and Patricia Salter West, *They Went to College* (New York: Harcourt, Brace & Co., 1952). Figure 23-1, p. 460, shows the relationship between occupation and marital happiness.

[17] Various check lists show clearly that young men rate good looks more highly than do young women in mate selection.

[18] Paul Popenoe, "Where Are the Marriageable Men?" *Social Forces,* 14:257-262, December, 1935.

[19] Terman and others, *op. cit.,* p. 191.

educated person being more often successful in the venture. This may be, of course, because education tends to delay marriage until a person reaches adult attitudes on matters of desirable mate selection. It may also be because education extends the range of dating and gives young people varied associations. Perhaps those with more education develop superior problem-solving techniques. Certainly the way a couple approaches problems in their marriage is of prime importance to its success. Whatever the reason, the relationship exists. Marriages of college-educated couples turn out far better than does the average marriage. (For convincing data turn to Figure 23-1, p. 460, showing marriage happiness by occupation.)

In summary, the evidence favors the view that a similar amount of schooling is desirable for marriage partners, and that if there is a difference in the amount of education, it is better for the husband to be the one with more education than the wife.[20] Even so, these differences are much less significant to marriage adjustment than religious and racial differences.

Age Differences

Today, the average age difference between young people in marriage is three years, with the husband being the older. The average bride is twenty, the average groom is twenty-three. (Refer again to Figure 1-2, p. 30.) Seventy years ago the average age difference was four years, the average bride being twenty-two and the groom, twenty-six. About 90 percent of college girls today want their husbands to be older than themselves. Three-fourths of college men want their wives to be younger.[21]

Studies of marital adjustment indicate that similar age is desirable although age is one of the least significant of differences to be investigated by various researches. There is meager evidence to the effect that the age difference should be either slight or considerable and it is not too consistent.[22] Young people within three or four years of each other in age belong to the same generation and have more in common. Other things being equal, they should find marriage adjustment easier.

When marriage age differs by eight to ten years or more, the relationship frequently takes on the character of a father-daughter relationship when the man is older, and a mother-son relationship when the woman is the older. Some such marriages do achieve great happiness, but it is possible that such marriages are entered into only when the persons involved prefer the parent-child relationship to a relationship of equality.

[20] *Ibid.*
[21] Data from Baber, *op. cit.*, and Landis and Landis, *op. cit.*, p. 84.
[22] Terman and others, *op. cit.*, p. 184, make the most comparisons on the various aspects of this problem.

That is, such marriages may be selective according to particular personality types.

Certain obvious difficulties are inherent in these marriages. If the wife is considerably older, the couple's ability to have children may be greatly decreased; if the husband is decidedly older, the wife is almost certain of a long period of widowhood. If the husband is older by a period of many years, this widowhood may well come while she still has dependent children.

Differences in Economic Background

Fiction and fairy tale have woven many a plot around the Cinderella-type prince-and-pauper marriage. Such stories have most meaning when they come out of a social system which is strongly stratified by class distinctions. The open-class system of the United States teaches that every man can be a king and attempts to ignore economic lines. This philosophy is encouraged by territorial mobility, which helps one shed his past, and by the prevailing belief in social climbing, which tends to obliterate class lines.

The lower-class girl, class theorists find, is the victim of the sexual exploitation of the upper-class boy when she is his date. If this is true, one might well ask whether it is the lower-class girl who is a victim of the upper-class boy, or whether the lower-class girl is exploiting the boy's financial and status resources. Kinsey[23] finds that lower-class girls are no more accessible sexually than upper- or middle-class girls. Each seems to participate in premarital intercourse in about the same proportion of cases. Kinsey does not, however, go into the matter of whether the joint participants in the sex acts are of the same social strata.

Although many studies have shown a tendency to date and marry within similar socioeconomic classes, lines are by no means rigidly drawn; in fact, they are very indistinct. Where differences in economic backgrounds are great, certain difficulties may logically be anticipated. Fellows and girls alike who consider marriage into different social backgrounds or into families with very different ways of life must expect to overcome certain handicaps and make difficult adjustments in order to find happiness in marriage.

It is easier for a man to marry down the economic ladder than for a woman to do so. The man is not criticized too severely for picking a girl who comes from a lower social, economic, or educational level. If a woman is beautiful, he is excused, often envied, even though she falls

23 Alfred C. Kinsey and others, *Sexual Behavior in the Human Female* (Philadelphia: W. B. Saunders Co., 1953).

short in many other qualities. At the same time, many social groups are critical of the woman who marries a socially, economically, or educationally inferior man. This is not particularly because she is giving up a higher standard of living. Actually, the criticism such a woman draws upon herself results from a complex of social attitudes and traditions. First, she is bucking custom—tradition says each woman should find someone to care for her and protect her, someone to give her all of the things she "deserves." It is popularly believed, too, that one's choice of a mate is a reflection upon one's self. The first question which is likely to enter the minds of her friends is, "Couldn't she do any better than that?" Finally, marrying "down" instead of "up" is quite generally taken as an admission of personal or social inadequacy.

The average girl can adjust more easily to a higher than to a lower standard of living. There is always some risk in marriage when the young wife is accustomed to a much higher level of living than her new mate can provide, although few girls should expect to start on the level their parents have attained by middle age. Only an unusual girl from a wealthy home can face low-income living, even in her own home. The man who marries under these circumstances owes it to his own future happiness, as well as to that of his fiancée, to make clear that he cannot hope to maintain the level of living to which she is accustomed.

If the wife, in order to maintain her past standard of living, begins to depend on her family as a source of living or to obtain accustomed luxuries and recreation, this becomes a source of embarrassment to her husband, whom society expects to provide for her.

Sometimes parental assistance comes because the wife's family want to save their daughter from hardships or presumed hardships. They cannot stand to have her going without things they themselves have, things she has been used to in her childhood home. In fact, they are even unwilling to have her go through the struggles that they themselves went through happily and profitably as a young couple. Parents with these feelings are inclined to buy expensive gifts for the daughter in order that she may have some of the things they want her to have. This may become embarrassing to her husband and a source of serious conflict.

Remarriage: What Are the Risks?

In our time, 22 percent of all marriages are remarriages. Three-fourths of these marriages involve a divorced bride or groom. The other fourth are widowed persons. In the younger age group, most of those eligible for remarriage are divorced persons (see Figure 34-7).

Are second tries of divorced persons successful enough to justify the risk? This is becoming a serious consideration to an increasing number of people. Divorce, widowhood, and remarriage are discussed more fully in separate chapters, but these problems cannot be ignored in considering dating and mate selection among the previously unmarried.

The older girl in the city is particularly likely to face this question, for of the men approaching thirty—the group to which she is most attracted—there are few single ones who are really marriageable.[24] The crop in this group has been picked over, and the maladjusted ones rejected again and again. A widower or divorced man may seem to be a much better marriage prospect. Even college students are not as strongly opposed to marrying divorced persons as some might expect. Judson T. Landis[25] has asked large numbers of college students in twelve universities, and at two different periods of time, the question, "All other factors being satisfactory, would you marry a person who has been divorced?" In both studies, it was found that 48 percent of the college women would do so; 54 and 56 percent, respectively, of the college men.

What are the odds? Census data show that the rate of failure in second and subsequent marriages is much higher than in the first marriage. The divorced man is a 50 percent higher risk than the single man and the divorced woman is a somewhat higher risk still.[26] Divorce rates increase with increase in the number of remarriages.[27]

Thomas P. Monahan,[28] studying divorce statistics for Iowa during the years 1953 to 1955, found the rate to be 16.6 per hundred marriages for those in their first marriage. Where one had been divorced the rate jumped to 36.6 per hundred marriages.

Why remarriages sometimes succeed and sometimes fail has not been made the subject of extensive study. One suspects that success frequently results from the fact that the person learns something by the first experience, gaining maturity and insight into himself, or gaining knowledge of the opposite sex. In other cases, perhaps the second marriage is entered into more realistically, and mate selection itself made more on the basis of reason, and less on the basis of unrealistic expectations. In many cases, no doubt, the divorced person who succeeds after remarriage is one who

24 This problem of "marriageability" is discussed at length in Chapter 29.

25 Judson T. Landis and Mary G. Landis, *op. cit.*, p. 84.

26 U. S. Department of Commerce, Bureau of the Census, *Marital Status, Number of Times Married, and Duration of Present Marital Status: April, 1948*, Series P-20, No. 23, March 4, 1949. Turn to page 717 of this text for a summary of statistical data or see Paul H. Landis, "Sequential Marriage," *Journal of Home Economics*, 42:625-628, November, 1951, for an analysis of the Census data; see also Paul H. Jacobson, *American Marriage and Divorce* (New York: Holt, Rinehart & Winston, Inc., 1959), Chs. 5 and 6.

27 Thomas P. Monahan, "How Stable Are Remarriages," *American Sociological Review*, 58:280-298, November, 1952.

28 Thomas P. Monahan, "The Changing Nature and Instability of Remarriage," *Eugenics Quarterly*, 5:73-85, June, 1958.

was from the beginning good marriage material himself, but was married to someone who was a poor risk. In a second choice of mates, he avoided the mistake of picking an unmarriageable person, or one who was difficult to live with. Sometimes, no doubt, the incident or incidents which led to the divorce were the kind that could have been avoided by a more mature and far-seeing person. He enters marriage the second time with greater caution and more understanding of what is important in a relationship between husband and wife.

The higher proportion of failures in remarriages than in first marriages is no doubt explained in part by the fact that a person may be less tolerant of difficulties in marriage the second time than the first, since his horror of divorce is probably already tempered somewhat by having gone through the experience. There is always the chance that the person who has been divorced once is a relatively unmarriageable type, or at least a difficult marriage type. There is also the possibility that the divorced person is one who customarily runs away from problems, rather than facing and solving them. If this is the case, he will probably resort to divorce again when serious problems arise.

Since divorced people tend to marry divorced people, probably because of their similarity of experience background, the likelihood is doubled that one or the other may be a person of questionable marriageability.

The person marrying for the first time and considering marrying someone who has been divorced needs to be particularly alert in evaluating the personality and adjustability of the intended mate. Such a person, statistically speaking, is a greater risk than the person who has not been married. The divorced woman is a slightly greater risk than the divorced man.

For a more extensive discussion of the various aspects of divorce and remarriage, and the data on which the conclusions above are based, turn to Chapter 34.

In summary, it has been observed that, in addition to religious considerations, differences in race, nationality, education and ability, age, economic background, and previous marital experience all figure significantly in marriage failures. In each of these areas there are, of course, many instances of marriages that succeed, but the risks, statistically speaking, in some areas of difference are relatively high; in others, low. Religious, racial, and marked nationality differences bring high risks in marriage. Educational differences and differences in ability are not so significant except where they are very great; age differences are not of much significance. Economic background takes on most significance when the woman comes from a distinctly higher level of living than the man she marries. Failure in a previous marriage is a high risk factor, and repeated failure, particularly so.

Awareness of these facts, if they are applied at the early stages of dating, can often guide young people away from unnecessary problems and appreciably simplify the task of mate selection.

Problems

1. *Sociodrama:* The honeymoon is over, figuratively as well as literally, and a wealthy, well-educated, young woman and her husband of humble background and little education are trying to plan their leisure hours together.
2. Charles and Katherine are graduate college students in a northern university. They have known each other since early high school days and are familiar with one another's values, ideals, and ambitions. They are both from wealthy families, both plan to be chemists, and both tend to be introverts with little interest in or need of outside friendships.

    After five years of dating during which their attachment has steadily grown, Charles finally broached the subject of marriage, though none too courageously, for Charles is a Negro and Katherine is Irish by descent. In your opinion should Katherine:
    a. Refuse outright?
    b. Talk the matter over with her parents and minister?
    c. Consent?
    d. Consent but plan to move to another country?
    e. Consent but insist that they have no children?
    f. Delay her consent until she has discovered whether or not Charles would be accepted by her friends, parents, and community?
    g. Consent and plan to identify herself with his family and friends if they will accept her?
3. What might account for the attraction many girls feel for men ten to thirty years their senior? What might be the advantages in such a marriage? What are the disadvantages?
4. If there is a foreign war bride in your community ask her to describe some of the adjustments demanded by an international or interracial marriage.
5. "Marriage," they say, "is a private affair." Why, then, should an individual hesitate to marry someone of another race whom he sincerely loves?
6. In what way do children complicate the adjustments of interracial marriages?
7. Do you believe that encouraging interracial marriages among those who are unprejudiced would tend to reduce interracial hatred and intolerance in general?
8. Marie is from a patriotic French family. Otto was a German pilot in World War II. They both live in the United States now. They have lost their

accents and few people could tell from looking at them that they are not of the same nationality. In what way, then, might nationality stand in the way of their achieving marital happiness?

9. What arguments can you think of in favor of marriages in which the wife is a few years older than her husband? What might the disadvantages be?

10. What age relationship between husband and wife do you consider ideal? Why?

11. A wealthy young man has proposed to a friend of yours from a lower-class home. Would your advice be:
    a. "Jump at the chance. This is every girl's dream."
    b. "His background of wealth doesn't make any difference in America, so don't let that influence you."
    c. "Don't marry him; you could never be happy together."
    d. Some other advice.

12. "Experience," they say, "is the best teacher." Does this mean that the marriage experience of a divorced or widowed person promises greater happiness than marriage to a previously unmarried person?

13. In our society, tradition favors a woman's marrying above rather than below her economic station in life. In your opinion, has the time come to do away with this practice as outmoded? Justify your answer.

14. What do you believe accounts for the fact that men generally prefer wives of equal or slightly less education than themselves?

15. Do you believe that the responsibilities of caring for a home, financial management, and child rearing make a college-educated woman a better wife?

16. What educational relationship do you believe ideal for husband and wife? Why?

17. The Duke of Windsor's story (in his book, *A King's Story*) is one of the great romances of history involving those of very different background. Discuss and appraise the former king's choice.

Selected References

ARTICLES IN BOOKS OF READINGS

FISHBEIN, Morris, and KENNEDY, Ruby Jo Reeves, *Modern Marriage and Family Living* (New York: Oxford University Press, Inc., 1957).
　　1. BARRON, Milton L., "Race, Religion, and Nationality in Mate Selection," pp. 60-73.

LANDIS, Judson T., and LANDIS, Mary G., *Readings in Marriage and the Family* (Englewood Cliffs, N. J.: Prentice-Hall, Inc., 1952).
　　2. BABER, Ray E., "A Study of 48 Inter-racial Marriages," pp. 210-214.

WINCH, Robert F., and others, *Selected Studies in Marriage and the Family*, Revised Edition (New York: Holt, Rinehart & Winston, Inc., 1962).
　　3. GOLDEN, Joseph, "Social Control of Negro-White Intermarriage," pp. 496-501.

General References

ADAMS, Ronanzo, *Interracial Marriage in Hawaii* (New York: The Macmillan Co., 1937).

BERNARD, Jessie, *American Family Behavior* (New York: Harper and Brothers, 1942), "Sib Relationships," Ch. 13.

BURGESS, Ernest W., and WALLIN, Paul, *Engagement and Marriage* (Philadelphia: J. B. Lippincott Co., 1953), Ch. 6.

CAVAN, Ruth Shonle, *American Marriage* (New York: Thomas Y. Crowell Co., 1959), Ch. 8.

FARBER, Bernard, *Family-Organization and Interaction* (San Francisco: Chandler Publishing Co., 1964), Ch. 5.

GOLDEN, Joseph, "Patterns of Negro-White Intermarriage," *American Sociological Review,* 19:144-147, April, 1954.

GORDON, Albert L., *Inter-Marriage* (Boston: Beacon Press, 1964).

HAVERMANN, Ernest, and WEST, Patricia Salter, *They Went to College* (New York: Harcourt, Brace & Co., 1952).

LANTZ, Herman R., and SNYDER, Eloise C., *Marriage* (New York: John Wiley & Sons, Inc., 1962), Ch. 10.

MERRILL, Francis E., *Courtship and Marriage,* Revised Edition (New York: Holt, Rinehart & Winston, Inc., 1959), Part 1.

MONAHAN, Thomas P., "How Stable Are Remarriages?" *American Sociological Review,* 58:280-298, November, 1952.

SCHNEPP, Gerald, SCHNEPP, Yui, and MASOKO, Agnes, "Cultural and Marital Adjustment of Japanese War Brides," *American Journal of Sociology,* 61:48-50, July, 1955.

STRAUSS, Anselm L., "Strain and Harmony in American-Japanese War Bride Marriages," *Marriage and Family Living,* 16:99-106, May, 1954.

WALLER, Willard, and HILL, Reuben, *The Family* (New York: Holt, Rinehart & Winston, Inc., 1951), Part 3.

17
Readiness for Marriage

In the old days, most marriages took place in the spring before the busy days of harvest. This placed the first off-spring in the late winter, so that neither the honeymoon nor the birth would interfere too greatly with the demands of making a living. In this institutionalized marriage-family arrangement, the practical considerations outweighed the interpersonal in this as in other things. But now, when the interpersonal relationship is the key to the life-long relationship, the emotional climate involving "readiness" is the important thing, not the seasons. Readiness is a complex matter indeed.

One author has said ironically that it is a good idea nowadays to marry young and thus assure oneself of a congenial college roommate.[1] The increasing trend toward early marriage is not confined to college, however. It seems to be a trend in high school, and outside school altogether. Those who work in the marriage area are increasingly skeptical that readiness for marriage comes as early as the ceremony in the case of the younger pair, who seldom have much conception of what they are getting into.

Readiness for marriage admittedly cannot be measured by chronological age, yet it is certainly not entirely divorced from chronological age. It is difficult to acquire a mature perspective on life without attaining the experience that comes with the years.

Certainly success in marriage is in part a matter of readiness in the broad sense of having reached the age at which one can accept and carry the obligations marriage involves. Levy and Munroe[2] believe that emotional readiness for marriage is much more important than any particular

---

[1] E. J. Kiefer, in *The Saturday Evening Post.*
[2] John Levy and Ruth Munroe, *The Happy Family* (New York: Alfred A. Knopf, Inc., 1938), p. 43.

personality traits. They believe that persons who have the proper mental attitude toward marriage can work out a way of life together and make a good adjustment to life, just as such people do in a field of work which may not be the most ideal from the standpoint of their interests and needs.

This view considers that "when to marry" is the real question and that this is answered in terms of one's own development. It holds that acceptance of the marriage relationship is the big thing—to be able honestly to accept and practice the words, "to love, honor, and cherish, for better or for worse, till death do us part." It holds that a husband and wife can have a lot of conflicts and face many problems, but if they have this attitude of certainty toward their marriage, they can work the other problems out to a solution. They feel that an experimental approach to marriage is a sure signpost to Reno.

There is a great deal of truth in this view. There is a finality about marriage, and only those persons should marry who have reached the time when marriage is more important to them than anything else. One's age at marriage, his preparation, the particular time in world affairs, the stage of one's career development, one's achieved state of social, emotional, and economic maturity—all have a bearing on marriage readiness.

Age for Marriage

It is a commonly held folk belief that early marriages are likely to work out well, because of the adjustability of youth. The more mature person is pictured as habit-ridden and unalterably fixed in his ways. This notion may have had substance in the fixed relations of agrarian societies. In a rapidly changing society it is very likely that the person who has acquired a greater degree of maturity and greater breadth of experience is more adjustable than the teenager with his limited horizon and circumscribed existence. The experiences of leaving home, changing communities, meeting and working with strangers, and planning one's life seldom come before the late teens or early twenties. These experiences might be expected to contribute appreciably to one's adjustability.

It is known that along with the trend toward younger marriages there has been a marked increase in the divorce rate. Whether or not the two are in any way interdependent is, of course, a matter of speculation. Youthful marriages are certainly not the only cause for divorce today, and whether or not marriages end in divorce should not be the only criterion for determining to what extent all marriages have succeeded or failed. We must also be concerned with the degree of happiness attained by those marriages which last.

Glick, studying Census data, finds divorce of those married before age 18 almost three times as high as of those marrying between 22-24.[3]

Christine H. Hillman analyzed inquiries in an advice column in a newspaper. She found that 66 percent of these inquiries came from married individuals and that 72 percent of the inquiries of the people who were or had been married were from those who had married before their 18th birthday. The median age of first marriages of these people was 16.8 years.[4]

There is convincing evidence from various research relative to the connection between age of marriage and general marital success. One such study of an upper-middle-class group of more than 500 couples compared adjustments of individuals in various age groups.[5] It was found that the likelihood of good adjustment for women between the ages of 16 and 30 years increased steadily with later marriage (see Figure 17-1). Among the cases studied, more than twice as many women nearing 30 were found to have made a good marital adjustment as had women marrying under 18.

What about men? Here again the evidence indicates that in a general way the more mature individual has the best chance to succeed in matrimony. Men who married before the age of twenty-two stood considerable chance of poor adjustment. Those who married between twenty-eight and thirty took the least risk. However, men who married after thirty were found to make good adjustments less frequently. This probably indicates, not that men become less marriageable as they pass thirty, but merely that by this age the crop has been pretty well picked over and those with the best potentialities have already been selected.

These findings are consistent with other research on this subject and suggest that marriage for the girl under 18 and the boy under 20 is subject to much higher risk than marriage above these ages. Actually, however, the data on this matter are very incomplete. The above study, like most others in this area, was concerned primarily with middle-class city dwellers of better-than-average education. It is known that farm youth, particularly girls, tend to marry earlier than those in urban occupational groups. It is not known, however, whether early marriage in farm communities has the same disadvantages as in the groups studied. Certainly it is a fact that if girls in farming areas did not marry early, few farm men would have wives, for in the average farming and small-

3 Paul C. Glick, *American Families* (New York: John Wiley & Sons, Inc., 1957), Table 72, p. 112; see also Paul H. Jacobson, *American Marriage and Divorce* (New York: Holt, Rinehart & Winston, Inc., 1959).

4 Christine H. Hillman, "An Advice Column's Challenge for Family-life Education," *Marriage and Family Living*, 16:51-54, February, 1954.

5 Ernest W. Burgess and Leonard S. Cottrell, *Predicting Success or Failure in Marriage* (Englewood Cliffs, N. J.: Prentice-Hall, Inc., 1939), pp. 115-117.

RELATION OF MARRIAGE AGE AND MARITAL HAPPINESS

HUSBAND

AGE AT MARRIAGE	POOR ADJUSTMENT	FAIR ADJUSTMENT	GOOD ADJUSTMENT
19-21 ★	38.5%	32.7%	28.8%
22-24	17.3%	33.9%	48.8%
25-27	24.6%	29.5%	45.9%
28-30	18.8%	20.3%	60.9%
31 AND OVER	28.8%	24.2%	47%

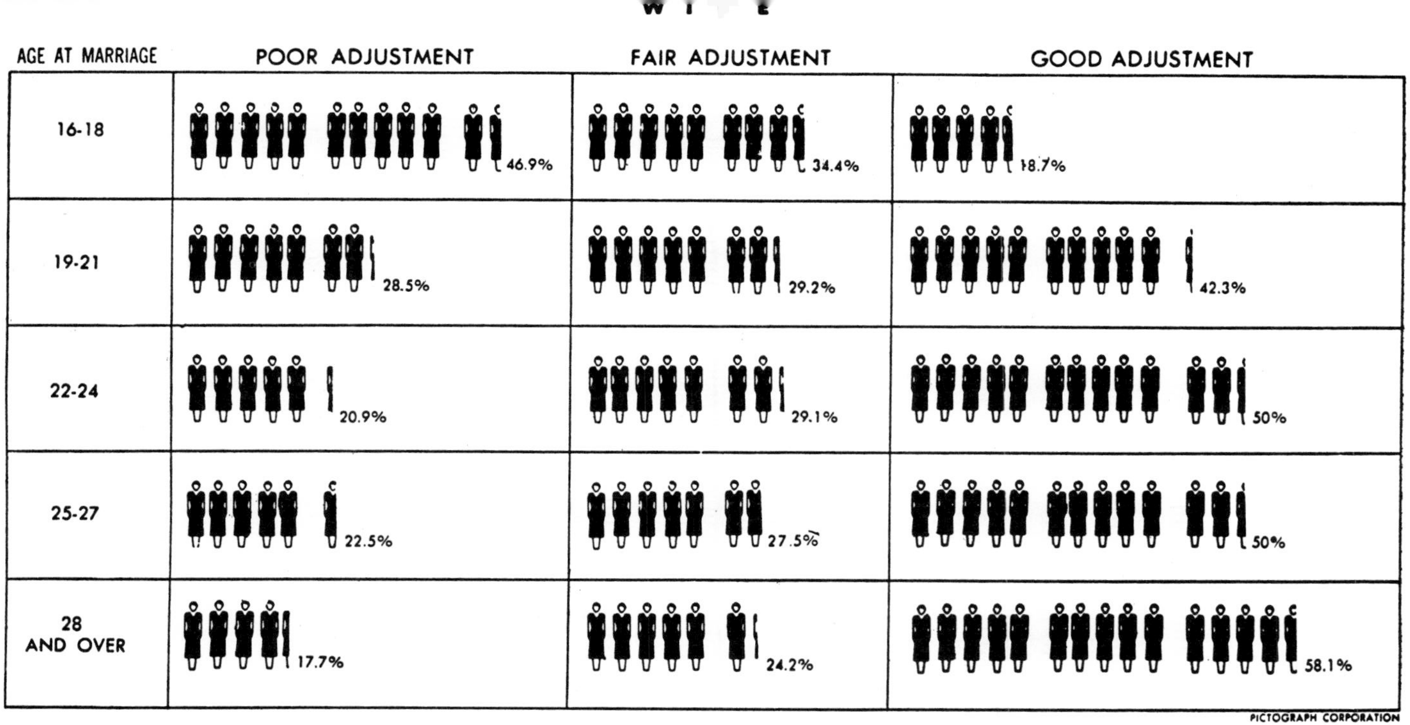

AGE AT MARRIAGE	POOR ADJUSTMENT	FAIR ADJUSTMENT	GOOD ADJUSTMENT
16-18	46.9%	34.4%	18.7%
19-21	28.5%	29.2%	42.3%
22-24	20.9%	29.1%	50%
25-27	22.5%	27.5%	50%
28 AND OVER	17.7%	24.2%	58.1%

PICTOGRAPH CORPORATION

SOURCE: Based on data from Ernest W. Burgess and Leonard S. Cottrell, *Predicting Success or Failure in Marriage* (Copyright 1939, by Prentice-Hall, Inc., New York). Reproduced by permission of the publisher.

FIGURE 17-1————Almost one-half of the wives who married under 19 made poor adjustments in marriage; few made good adjustments. Husbands who married under 21 stood considerable chance of poor adjustment. Data are for middle-class, urban couples. We do not know whether the same relationship holds for rural couples.

town community, those girls who do not marry during or immediately after high school generally leave for college or migrate to a larger town or city to find work.[6] Having left the small community, few go back to marry, so that sex ratios in the rural farm population are heavily weighted on the male side.[7]

No comparable studies dealing with age of marriage and its success are available for the laboring classes either. It is known that they, too, marry younger than the more prosperous and more educated group. For this group, however, there is some indirect evidence that early marriage may be unfavorable to happiness.

The happiness ratings of various occupational groups have been compared.[8] One study employed, as a measure of happiness, ratings by close acquaintances of the couple. It was found that among the laboring classes generally there was a high proportion of unhappy marriages. Early marriage may be a factor, although one cannot be sure that it is the important one (see Figure 23-1).

Divorce rates are much higher among marriages that occur at an early age. Some studies in this area deal with all socioeconomic classes, providing further evidence of a relationship between age of marriage and its outcome.[9] Burchinal and Chancellor,[10] studying marriages that ended in divorce, found that when both were 19 or under, the marriages lasted only half as long as when they were 20 or older. Where the husband was of low occupational status, duration of the marriage prior to divorce was also briefer than when he was of high occupational status. Age of marriage and occupational status are inevitably related since training is a prerequisite to high occupational status.

Marriage today requires many adjustments and great adaptability. It is probable that these traits are not well developed in most girls until near

6 Many boys migrate, too, but girls leave earlier and a higher proportion of them leave. For a comprehensive study of this problem and data, see Paul H. Landis, *Rural Life in Process,* Second Edition (New York: McGraw-Hill Book Co., 1948), Ch. 14.

7 In 1950 there were 114 males per 100 females in the age group 20 to 24 in the rural farm population.

8 Richard Lang, Ph.D. thesis at the University of Chicago, reported in Burgess and Cottrell, *op. cit.*

9 Harvey J. Locke found that a relatively high proportion of divorced women in a group studied in Indiana had married before age 18; and of divorced men, before age 21; see his *Predicting Adjustment in Marriage: A Comparison of a Divorced and Happily Married Group* (New York: Henry Holt & Co., Inc., 1951), pp. 101-102. Judson T. Landis, studying 1,051 marriages, found a divorce rate of 14.3 percent where both married under 20. The rate dropped consistently to 2.3 percent where both were over 30. Judson T. Landis and Mary G. Landis, *Building a Successful Marriage,* Fourth Edition (Englewood Cliffs, N. J.: Prentice-Hall, Inc., 1963), pp. 127-131.

10 Lee G. Burchinal and Loren E. Chancellor, "Survival Rates Among Religiously Homogamous and Interreligious Marriages," *Agricultural Experiment Station Research Bulletin 512,* December, 1962.

the age of twenty and in most boys until they are about twenty-two. Or perhaps younger couples have not reached the time in life when marriage can continue to be their most important concern. There are, of course, marked variations, some individuals being precocious and others greatly delayed in development. Some of the practical considerations by which maturity can be tested are discussed in the remaining sections of this chapter, for it must be recognized that age at best is merely an index of the general period in life when young people in our culture are customarily expected to assume certain roles.

The question of age for marriage becomes one of maturity, not just of years. But what kind of maturity is basic to marriage success and how is it to be measured?

Chronological Age vs. Marital Maturity

It is quite generally recognized in this age of psychological measurements that chronological age is only a very rough measure of one's level of maturity. It is not even generally accurate to say that a given person is either more mature or less mature than his age indicates. The situation is much more complex, for he is likely to be both. The individual is like a tree with many limbs, each growing at its own separate rate. Thus the physically matured person may actually be younger than he looks and his social, intellectual, and emotional maturity each in turn may be at very different levels of development.

This, of course, greatly complicates the issue of age for marriage. Unfortunately, there seems to be no single factor which might be called "marital maturity." If such a thing as marital maturity does exist, it consists of general maturation in a number of different areas of growth. Maturity in the following fields is an absolute minimum for success in marriage.

1. *Physical maturity:* a body sufficiently developed to perform the normal functions of adult life, including work responsibilities and the biological functions of reproduction and child care. The human female is not fully ready for the reproductive function until long after puberty. Adolescent sterility has long been noted by anthropologists observing primitives who have no taboos on sexual intercourse among adolescents. Full fertility and biological capability of producing sound offspring is not reached, on the average, until the early twenties. Ashley-Montagu's studies show a high rate of infant and maternal mortality among adolescent mothers, and a high rate of premature births, miscarriages, and stillbirths.[11]

11 M. F. Ashley-Montagu, *The Reproductive Development of the Female* (New York: Julian Press, Inc., 1958).

2. *Vocational maturity:* having a reasonable plan for providing for one's dependents; a plan which takes into account *(a)* one's abilities, training, and interests, *(b)* the welfare of one's dependents, *(c)* available and potential job opportunities, and *(d)* provision for the ultimate realization of other values such as travel, free time, promotions, independence, etc., or such of these as will be required to make one reasonably content.

3. *Moral maturity:* having a code by which one may live with self-respect and with the respect of one's mate and members of the community; this code should take into consideration the demands of society as well as one's own values and sense of responsibility. Moral maturity requires that a person assume responsibility for his acts, rather than expecting parents to be responsible as they were during his childhood.

4. *Emotional maturity:* one's readiness to transfer attachments away from parental family and engage without reservation in the heterosexual and interdependent relationship of marriage.

5. *Social maturity:* one's readiness to accept the status and responsibilities demanded of adults in the community. This implies a willingness and readiness to accept children and make them truly welcomed members of the family.

These five areas of maturity leave some phases of life almost untouched—such as the intellectual and religious development and the possession of significant life plans. These additional areas are ones in which maturity is a great asset to marriage. We know, however, that growth in these fields may be and often is a life-long process and that in many successful marriages young couples develop together in these important areas of living.

Emotional Maturity

Of the five areas briefly discussed, one of the most often mentioned but least understood is that of "emotional maturity." This concept appears again and again in the literature on marriage and family life and is frequently referred to as the most significant psychological index to one's marriageability. Yet the concept "emotional maturity" has little meaning to the average student uninoculated with psychological terminology. The phrase implies that the person who possesses emotional maturity has reached a level in development where he can react to life situations in a fully social way. The person who does not possess emotional maturity reacts in various devious ways, all purposeful in terms of satisfying his needs, but unsatisfactory from the standpoint of adequate social behavior—therefore, not satisfactory for most marriage partners. A few such people may be successful if they find exactly the right mate.

Others cannot make the grade in marriage at all, particularly not in a democratic marriage.

The effects of emotional immaturity upon a marriage can easily be imagined. The immature mate is unable to assume his proper share of the responsibilities that marriage implies. This inability may manifest itself in sexual inadequacy, in the day-to-day demands of marital companionship, or in a failure to adjust to the normal and unromantic routines of marriage and adult life.

How can one recognize the emotional immaturity in oneself or in a prospective mate and avoid an unfortunate, or even disastrous marriage?

Here is a list of traits which frequently betray the emotionally immature. The individual:

1. Is overly eager to form a binding relationship—may want to go steady, become engaged, or marry very early hoping to find security and thus escape the uncertainty of more casual social relationships.
2. Wants marriage without children—fears having to share the affections and loyalties of his mate or is unready to accept the responsibilities which parenthood implies.
3. Treats opposite sex with condescension—may realize marriage is desirable biologically or socially, but is unready to accept it on any other than his own terms.
4. Is inordinately interested in sex—may behave or converse in such a way as to keep relationship focused on sexual level without the development of other interests because he has not as yet developed a mature desire for complete emotional involvement.
5. Wants marriage but appears indifferent or hostile to physical contacts—may be seeking in marriage a parent substitute rather than a sexual partner or may have been taught to consider sex as vulgar or sinful.
6. Is jealous—because of his own feelings of inadequacy may see any interest of his intended mate in others as a rejection of himself.
7. Demands constant tokens and reassurances of love—because of his own uncertainty or because he has not as yet developed a two-sided conception of devotion involving "giving" as well as "receiving."
8. Wants marriage but is unwilling to declare independence from parents—may want to live with or near parents or to have parental advice in all plans and decisions, either because he is still too involved emotionally with his parents or because he is mistrustful of his own ability to succeed independently of them.
9. Is overly submissive, dependent, or unopinionated—may suffer from feelings of inferiority and unworthiness or may seek in mate a parent substitute, someone to "lean upon" rather than "stand beside."
10. Holds highly romantic conceptions of marriage and the opposite sex—may expect Hollywood version of courtship and marriage because he has not as yet passed emotional adolescence.

Emotional maturity, while it cannot insure marital success, does seem to be prerequisite to marriage readiness. More than chronological maturity, it seems to be the real criterion for judging the best "age for matrimony." This factor, like the four other areas of maturity discussed, all have to do with an individual's personal characteristics as they affect the timing of marriage. There are other considerations of a more general nature that are equally important in determining when one can or should marry. Financial plans, educational expectations, prospects of military service, and vocational plans are factors which also have a vital bearing on early marriage.

Early Marriage and Money Problems

Rightly or wrongly, custom today favors the financial independence of young people from their parents at the time that they marry. This is more true now than in most periods of history. Dowries have disappeared with romantic mate choice. With self-employment being the rule today, the young person cannot too often enter farming or business with the parent, as was once so common. This is a great handicap to early marriages. While some couples seem to be able to take financial help from parents and not be embarrassed by it, most are too individualistic and independent-minded to be able to do so even if the parents can afford the financial outlay. Part of the reason is because they fear that "he who pays the piper calls the tune." And that is a real danger to the new marriage.[12]

How secure financially should one be before taking the step of marriage? Financial security is an elusive thing. An "exact" answer to this question is impossible. Sometimes people who have the most money feel and act the least secure. For example, young people from families with the highest incomes delay marriage longer and have fewer children than those from lower-income homes. Farm owners marry later and have fewer children than farm laborers and farm renters, yet they have more income. Most young couples expect to pay their way today by one or both working. The general acceptance of women in the work world has helped make early marriage possible. Abundant work opportunities of recent decades probably explain in considerable part the increasingly youthful

12 Judson T. Landis found this to be so in studying campus marriages at Michigan State after World War II. Parents who helped pay the bills wanted to give advice too; see Judson T. Landis and Mary G. Landis, *op. cit.*, Ch. 10. Marvin B. Sussman and Lee Burchinal, "Parental Aid to Married Children: Implications for Family Functioning," *Marriage and Family Living*, 24:320-332, November, 1962, pictures the flow of family income toward the children early in marriage; later in life the children may help the parents.

age of those who marry, for during the last twenty years any boy or girl in the middle teens could begin working.

In the last analysis whether a couple has money enough on which to marry is a question of their standards, values, ideals, and expectations. Some are willing to face the struggle of life together with a meager income when they are in their teens or early twenties. These couples marry without money, both work, and live in furnished quarters or buy furniture on time contracts. Others want to begin married life with all the comforts and luxuries their parents enjoy after a lifetime of work, denial, thrift, and saving. These are the two extremes. When potential income is enough to permit living apart from relatives, one can reasonably marry, so far as economic aspects are concerned. If both are willing to work, this goal may be reached as soon as education is complete, in some instances even before. If plans for college also enter the picture, however, early marriage raises special problems.

Should One Marry While in College?

With the declining average age of those who marry, this is a question of increasing importance to many young people. Marriage has become the style with college students since the days following World War II when married veterans literally flooded campuses across the country.

Some research has thrown light on problems of marriage adjustment of college students, and on success of married couples in their studies. In essence they have shown that marriage while in college is a satisfactory venture, both from the standpoint of scholastic achievement and marriage adjustment as such.

A Wisconsin study, for example, showed that even couples with children made better than average grades.[13] The divorce rate during the first few years of college marriages is lower than among educated people generally. Judson T. Landis' study[14] of 544 couples at Michigan State College in 1947 indicated that not only do these married students have a better grade average than the unmarried group, but that they have a greater sense of security and feel more settled. The men queried felt that a wife was a help rather than a hindrance in their college life. Of these couples, 95 percent gave themselves a rating of happy or very happy in appraising their marriage.

Some husbands were critical of the wife's interest in having more

13 Svend Reimer, "Married Students Are Good Students," *Marriage and Family Living*, 9:11-12, February, 1947.

14 Judson T. Landis and Mary G. Landis, *op. cit.*, pp. 114-116.

social life than the husband could take time for, but on the whole, college marriages were considered successful.

Lawrence L. Falk studied 40 married and 40 single students, comparing their grades and finding no difference. Those who married while in school kept the same grade level or improved.[15]

Christensen and Philbrick's study at Purdue University in 1950 asked student couples whether or not, knowing what they knew now, they would marry again while in school.[16] Three-fourths said they would marry while in college if they had it to do over again. A fourth of the group felt that the difficulties of making a living, of finding housing, and of doing satisfactory college work offered too great handicaps. The researchers, however, suggest the probability that some of these gave external factors as rationalizations, that in many of these instances the marriage itself was one which had little hope of surviving because of deep psychological problems. (Lower happiness ratings were in evidence in the group that would have deferred marriage because of college.)

It must be remembered that most of these studies are of an older-than-average college group and that most of the marriages were government subsidized, so that economic worries were greatly reduced. While many sociologists, the author among them, believe that it would be wise social policy to subsidize the marriage of able and socially mature college students, such a program does not exist. This means that nonveterans are on their own when they marry, unless they can work out and willingly accept some sort of subsidy or loan from parents.

Obviously, then, the advisability of marriage where husband or wife or both are still in school depends largely upon the financial arrangement and prospects. If funds are in prospect, there must be a willingness for complete economic cooperation. This often involves the wife working and helping to carry the load of support for the household. It involves the husband sharing household duties and absorbing part of the normal female role in housekeeping and child care.

Finally, with early marriage, there must be a willingness to take into account the likelihood of children. There must be willingness to assume parental duties should children come.

One of the possible eugenic benefits to the nation of college postwar marriages was that the birth rate of the college group increased. This, however, often created personal problems that college couples did not always anticipate. The Michigan State study showed that two-

---

[15] Lawrence L. Falk, "A Comparative Study of Problems of Married and Single Students," *Marriage and Family Living*, 26:207-208, May, 1964.

[16] Harold T. Christensen and Robert E. Philbrick, "Family-size as a Factor of Marital Adjustment of College Students," *American Sociological Review*, 17:306-312, June, 1952.

thirds of the pregnancies among this group had not been planned; one-third admitted carelessness; the other third had done everything possible to avoid pregnancy. Clearly, a college couple marrying must take into account the possibility, or even the probability, of having children.[17]

Christensen and Philbrick found similar results in a study of student-couple pregnancies at Purdue involving 346 couples.[18] This study further reports that children proved to be a serious handicap to college performance, taking time, making study difficult, requiring loss of sleep, and as they got older wanting to play with the parents when parents got home from school or work.

Johannis reports that two-thirds of the parent couples he studied in Oregon felt that children brought difficult problems for the student marriage—crowding, high-rent costs, problems of getting baby sitters and paying for them, and lack of play space for children.[19]

If a student cannot face these handicaps he should delay marriage, or realize that the gateway to his chosen work or profession may be closed. To enter the professions, for example, requires not only college, but graduate school, law school, or medical school in addition. This means that a man who wishes to enter a profession will be in school until he is twenty-five years old or older. Unless he has a source of income, or unless his wife is qualified, able, and willing to work and support him, marriage and especially children are usually obstacles until schooling has been completed.

Kingsley Davis, in satirical vein, has made some very destructive comments about the early-marriage trend in the United States, with reference to the college group particularly.[20] He points out that it tends to destroy the ambition of women, since they are becoming increasingly content to enter marriage and bear children without other contribution to society of a significant sort. Thus they sacrifice professional and creative aspirations and fail to make a contribution to the labor force as, for example, they do in Russia where there are many women engineers and doctors. He feels that we are seeing a strong return to primitivism in the behavior of women. Too many women have abandoned ambition and sacrificed careers to their college-attending husbands.

The American girl seems too eager to enter into marriage as soon as she reaches approximate physical maturity. Many women sacrifice their future status as effective wives by cutting off their training while helping their husbands through school. Davis feels that often they cheat them-

---

17 Judson T. Landis and Mary G. Landis, *op. cit.*, pp. 150-151.

18 Christensen and Philbrick, *op. cit.*

19 Theodore B. Johannis, "The Marital Adjustment of a Sample of Married College Students," *The Coordinator*, 4:4, June, 1956.

20 Kingsley Davis, "The Early Marriage Trend," *What's New*, summarized in *WSC News*, 7:3, October, 1958.

selves out of the reward of high status in marriage and also risk their marriage, as the husband outgrows them in training and sophistication.

He suggests that the early-marriage rate tends to make young people, particularly girls, dawdle through school. They have little motivation to pursue academic interests seriously. He sees the young married generation becoming a generation of spongers, depending on parents to put up the money for school, for down-payment on a house, for doctor and hospital bills when the baby comes, for loans to buy the automobile or other luxuries.

Appraising the Cultural Trend

Margaret Mead, in lectures on college campuses, has expressed concern over the trend toward early marriages which threatens intellectual development and makes earning a living take precedence over scholarly achievement.[21] Unlike European society, where men of great ambition were encouraged to put off family responsibility, youth in our society are pushed into it. This, she believes, tends to deny them the chance to explore, challenge, venture. She fears men can no longer be expected to strive for great achievement when they must give priority to earning a living and caring for babies. Babies have "engrossed women for a thousand years, and it now looks as if they were going to engross men, too." She goes on to ask the question whether anyone will have time for "statesmanship, art, science, exploration of outer space?"

No society can have both men and women devoting their time to infants. This makes for a "settled, security-loving, unadventurous people." This she views as serious in an age when countries like the Soviet Union and China have women as well as men striving for great achievement, feeling that the future belongs to them and is worth sacrificing for.

"If we retire into a kind of fur-lined domesticity, in which everyone is concerned with his own little family and his own little house, I think it is going to curtail seriously the contribution that we can make as a nation to the development of civilization on this planet."

Problems of the too Early College Marriage

As the age of marriages is pushed downward, many young people marry immediately out of high school and come to the college campus married. As an increasing number of freshmen, sophomores, and juniors marry (in addition to the older age group on which most past

[21] These ideas have been published by Margaret Mead in *U. S. News and World Report,* June 6, 1960.

studies of college marriages have been made), one may anticipate an increasing number of problems created by the college marriage, both economic and those involving personal interaction in other fields. Certainly the young person coming to college already married, or who marries during the first two years of college, cuts himself off from much of the teenage social life which is such a vital part of the college experience. His chances for leadership are undoubtedly greatly reduced, as well as his chance for developing special talents such as are demanded in the numerous extracurricular activities of the campus.

It is true that he has a compensating social life among married young people which may replace some of these disadvantages. Yet class discussions in marriage problems courses lead one to think that the average college young person feels it would be a decided loss to have been married during the early years of college, entirely aside from the economic hardship that is likely to be faced. There is also, of course, the practical problem of the great risk of pregnancy before the educational career is terminated. Those who already have children on coming to college have an unusually heavy economic burden, unless they have been out for a long period of time and have accumulated essential financial resources before entering college.

There is danger of the husband outgrowing the wife if she drops out of school to support him, or to become a homemaker, and thus isolates herself from many of the social experiences which would, for a single woman, bring a great deal of growth during these late teen years.[22] The husband may outgrow the wife in training and sophistication and he may reach the time in college or later when he feels the need for a more worldly (in the broadest sense) woman to share his role as a professional or business man and to influence his career as the wife he has now outgrown never could.

Whyte, studying wives of management for *Fortune* magazine, learned that in the managerial hierarchy industry does not object to a man getting a divorce, for it is felt he will choose a woman more compatible to the aims of the corporation when he chooses again.[23] Industry recognizes that perhaps one of the main reasons why men on the climb get a divorce is because their wives did not climb with them.

Undoubtedly this is one of the realities of the growth experience of college men whose wives take a subservient role in becoming the breadwinner or homemaker, thus providing the opportunity for the husband to grow while slighting their own growth.

[22] Lester A. Kirkendall finds this a real risk in his "Married Undergraduates on the Campus: An Appraisal," *The Coordinator*, 5:2, December, 1956.
[23] William H. Whyte, Jr., "The Wives of Management," *Fortune,* 44:86 ff., October, 1951; also his "Corporation and the Wife," *Fortune,* 44:109 ff., November, 1951.

With the younger couples, constantly pressed by financial need, the opportunities to develop the romantic aspect of their life together are limited indeed. The happy carefree recreation periods common to college dating are not available to the married couple if one or both are spending much of their spare time working, and when not working are involved in trying to catch up on studies. Even their sex life may be less than it ought to be because of fatigue and nervous tension. Everyone needs recreation and periods of relaxation. And yet, some young couples are so weighted down by the constant demands made on their time and energy that they have practically no time to enjoy activities together. There is great risk that such couples will become bored with life and with each other. Even the common devices for relaxation that are part of a normal home may be lacking in their crowded quarters. The wife cannot enjoy the radio while doing housework, or while resting in the evening, because the husband must study. The couple probably won't have television, but even if they do it is certain to interfere with one or the other's study period.

The college campus probably offers more protection from sideline romances than do work situations in the world outside. Yet a wife may gain a distinct impression that her husband considers the girls he associates with in the classroom and in the college student union building, very attractive. It is not unusual for him to roam during her pregnancy and the campus offers ready opportunity. On the college campus there is likely to be more criticism of disloyalty than in the average industrial or other work situation, but extramarital ventures are not uncommon.

Colleges and universities could do a great deal to improve the circumstances in which college marriages operate. Ready availability of nursery schools and kindergartens and child-care centers would do a lot to ease the burden of couples with children. Such facilities are particularly needed if the wife works. But even if she does not, they are needed on occasion to provide her with an opportunity to get out of the home and to escape its confining routine.

More comprehensive medical care programs, better housing, counseling services, child-guidance clinics, and other such facilities would be proper steps in the recognition of college marriage and its needs.

Cynics would no doubt say that the more we provide for the needs of the college marriage, the more we encourage the college marriage, and certainly we do not want to encourage it. This is a two-sided question. Whether improving the conditions would encourage couples is doubtful. It is likely that those seriously set on marriage tend to ignore the conditions. Such facilities could help provide an environment in which college marriages would involve less hardship and in which couples who do encounter serious difficulties in their marriage, or with their family problems, might be given help.

Although the average college campus still lacks most of the institutions it needs to cope with student-family needs, a study at Iowa State College shows that in this institution there are not less than 20 wives' auxiliaries providing social outlets for married students. Baby-sitting services and special youth groups have also appeared.[24]

Research at Washington State University shows that marriages are one of the main reasons for academic mortality among women.[25] Judson T. Landis found it so among high school students in California.[26]

High School Marriages

There is no consistent policy from state to state on the high school marriage. Judson T. Landis made an extensive study in California and finds policies even differ with school administrators from school district to school district.[27] Although a New Mexico study showed that high school students who married were usually removed from school, this was not the general system found by Landis in California. Ranging from the rural to the metropolitan, he obtained data on married students in 205 high schools which enrolled over 100,000 students.

Landis finds a high drop-out rate among girls who are married, but for the most part these drop-outs were voluntary. In general, the attitudes of school administrations were contradictory regarding the married high school student, particularly the girl. Most California principals, unlike those of New Mexico, did not encourage withdrawal from school. The married students were generally treated more leniently with regard to school attendance. Only a small proportion said they treated married students exactly as they treated other students. About one-third had a talk with the married students, often including parents. Most have no plans for changing policy with regard to married students. In all, 178 principals considered married students to be a problem in the *school.* Eighty of them thought married students discussed marital sex experiences with unmarried students. A few thought married students were a generally bad influence. In all, 111 principals thought that married students were a problem in the *classroom,* 144 did not find them so.

---

[24] Everett M. Rogers, "Married Student and Extracurricular College Culture," *Marriage and Family Living,* 21:119, May, 1959.

[25] Walter L. Slocum, *Academic Mortality at the State College of Washington* (Pullman, Wash.: State College of Washington, 1956).

[26] Judson T. Landis, "Attitudes and Policies Concerning Marriages Among High School Students," *Marriage and Family Living,* 18:128-136, May, 1956.

[27] *Ibid.*

One of the risks of the married schoolgirl is pregnancy. What practices exist in handling the pregnant girl? The majority, 103 principals, indicated that they brought pressures for the girl to withdraw as soon as the pregnancy was apparent. Only 38 thought no action was necessary because the girl would drop out anyway; 29 reported they had no policy at all; 28 indicated the girl could attend as long as she desired to attend.

A few principals considered that the married students were an asset. Some felt that they were more dependable and stable, more industrious, that they made a contribution to such courses as family life and homemaking. Some felt that their more mature attitude helped stabilize the general student attitude. Landis concluded that the general evidence seems to be that high school principals and teachers have not thought through, or planned, for the problem of high school marriages, yet in these school systems, 2.4 percent of the sophomore girls, 4 percent of the junior girls, and 5.7 percent of the senior girls had married. In all, over 2,000 girls and 220 boys were married.[28]

June Marcum Henton[29] reported no significant differences in dating behavior, sex information, and ideas concerning acceptable age of marriage between schools permitting married students and those barring them. She concludes that restrictive policies serve no useful purpose.

The Census reported in 1954 that 4.8 percent of girls 14-17 years of age were married and .04 percent of high school boys.[30] Yet Census data on young people in school for the fall of 1957 show that only 0.2 percent of boys and 0.7 percent of girls were married.

Time reports such a rapid increase in marriage in Dallas, Texas, schools that the Parent-Teachers Association recommended to the school board that married students be denied extracurricular activities.[31] A second recommendation was that the board establish separate schools for married students. The school board voted against segregated schools for married students.

We have already discussed the biological unreadiness of the average teenage girl for parenthood as evidenced by the high death rate of mothers and children in the age group, and the high rate of spontaneous abortions and stillbirths among them (see footnote 11, p. 29).

28 *Ibid.*

29 June Marcum Henton, "The Effect of Married High-School Students on Their Unmarried Classmates," *Marriage and Family Living*, 26:87-88, February, 1964.

30 U. S. Department of Commerce, Bureau of the Census, "Marital Status and Family Status," *Current Population Reports, Population Characteristics, April, 1954,* Series P-20, No. 56, March 18, 1955. U. S. Department of Commerce, Bureau of the Census, "School Enrollment, October, 1957," *Current Population Reports, Population Characteristics,* Series P-20, No. 80, February 13, 1958.

31 *Time,* May 25, 1959, p. 70.

The Lengthening Shadows of Spinsterhood or Bachelorhood

The career woman of yesterday is a vanishing specimen. Today most women do not have to make the choice of career or marriage, as their sisters did in the early days of the feminist movement. Then, a woman working outside the home was so unusual that only a few daring women took the bold step. The career woman was looked upon as one who had decided that success in the work world was more important than marriage and family and, therefore, chose not to marry.

Today, practically all girls expect to engage in gainful employment, some for a short time before marriage and some for a year or so after marriage, until children are born. Other girls consider that life will never be complete unless they have a job or a professional or business career. Yet most of this career-minded group today want and plan marriage and family, too. They expect to carry on both together. Even so, the timing of marriage is still a factor in vocational plans.

The woman who would enter a career must delay marriage ordinarily until the major part, if not all, of her schooling is completed. A very strong career drive is a handicap to early marriage for both men and women but particularly for women.[32]

College women who find it desirable to delay marriage in order to train for and establish themselves in highly specialized business and professional careers increase the risk of not marrying. Age alone is a severe handicap in finding a mate. By the time a woman reaches thirty, for example, her chances of marriage are little more than fifty-fifty. After forty-five the chances fall to one in ten (see Figure 17-2).

Why? The discipline and competitiveness that may characterize such a woman after a long period of schooling and business activity are in complete contradiction to those qualities most men regard as attractive in a mate. But there are several other handicaps, too. The young men she knew as a girl are already married. The professions into which women most often go—school teaching, social work, library work, and nursing—are, for the most part, one-sex occupations, which means that there are few opportunities to meet marriageable men.

These women are further handicapped by the fact that men their own age are usually more attracted to younger women. By the time a man is thirty-five he usually marries, not a woman of thirty-two, but rather a woman in her late twenties. Likewise, a man in his late twenties is more

[32] R. F. Winch, "Courtship of College Women," *American Journal of Sociology,* 55:269-278, 1949.

CHANCES OF MARRIAGE FOR SINGLE WOMEN

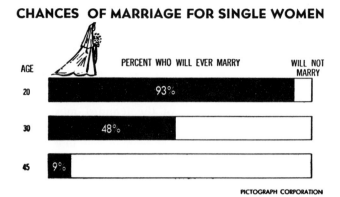

SOURCE: U. S. Department of Commerce, Bureau of the Census.

FIGURE 17-2————To remain single till 30 reduces marriage chances by half; till 45, to about one in ten.

likely to marry a girl in her middle or early twenties than one near his own age. This means that the professional woman in her late twenties must seek a partner among men approximately thirty-five years of age. Most men who are interested in or suited to family life are already married before they reach that age. A woman in her late twenties or early thirties is likely to find her best chance to marry among widowers and divorced men. There are some very desirable marriage partners among this group, but divorced men are a 50-percent greater risk, as far as marriage success is concerned, than men entering their first marriage.[33]

These facts are important not only to those young women who wish to delay marriage to pursue a business or professional career, but to those who for other personal reasons delay marriage until well into the twenties. Among this group are those who want to enjoy a relatively long period of freedom prior to settling down to the responsibilities of a home. Some want to earn enough to travel, thinking that after marriage they may never have an opportunity to satisfy this desire. Marriage seems so final to many girls; in fact, it means the end of many liberties that their education and experience have caused them to consider highly desirable. For a time at least the girl may place more value on these liberties than on marriage. In some cases in which the girl does not feel this way, her parents may.

Girls sometimes delay marriage primarily because they are cautious

[33] Paul H. Landis, "Sequential Marriage," *Journal of Home Economics*, 42:625-628, October, 1950. Data are presented in Chapter 34, pp. 717-721.

rather than because of a desire to achieve another goal in life. They want to be sure they have reached an age when they know what kind of husband they want. They may want the security of a career to fall back on if their marriage should fail or if untimely death should take their husband.

All of these are worthy motives and each must decide for herself whether the goals she seeks to realize before marriage are important enough to justify the risk of finding herself at an age and in a work situation where establishing close friendships with the opposite sex is difficult.

Today, practically all women desire to marry. The data presented show that the further a girl goes into the late twenties or early thirties, the greater her likelihood of not finding a marriage partner. For many, the goals they wish to realize before marriage make the risk worthwhile; for others, delay seems to be unwise.

The average girl who, by choice or by circumstance, delays marriage into the thirties is almost certain to feel an increasing anxiety about her ultimate marriage. This anxiety is in part a product of the role a woman must play in being passive—always waiting for an invitation—and in part it is a product of the community's expectation that a girl will marry some time in her early twenties.

In spite of women's advancement in education, approaching equality in many occupations, and opportunities for work in numerous new vocational outlets, most women still value romance above all other things in life. For this reason, few women put romance entirely out of their thinking. They are likely to pursue their work with a double purpose; one eye is on the job and its possibilities, while the other eye scans every likely opportunity for romance.

Delayed Marriage—A Man's Problem Too

The college man at the close of his education has to face certain problems with respect to the time he wishes to marry. Although he is already well past the age when he might reasonably marry, he is likely to endure economic hardship if he marries immediately. If he is entering a profession, he will have a relatively low income for a period of several years. He may, in the face of these economic handicaps, choose to delay marriage. If he delays marriage itself but becomes engaged, there is the difficult problem of living as an engaged person for a long period of time. He may, on the other hand, decide to remain a bachelor, delaying any serious interest in engagement and marriage until such time as he becomes established in his profession and has sufficient income to support the home and family that he desires. There is some danger in this case that he may lose all interest in romantic attachments and fail to marry.

The young man preparing for a profession, like the young woman, should associate with the opposite sex and keep alive his interest in dating. The same applies to the young man who delays marriage because of military service and to the young man in a farming area where marriageable women are scarce.

These persons must make a special effort to go where young women are to be found, and to keep friendships with those they have met and known. Age alone is not as great a handicap to a man as to a woman in making a marriage, but it can become so if he isolates himself, is critical of the opposite sex, and fails to develop a warm and appreciative nature that makes him attractive as a person.

The young farmer in isolated sections is still the most likely candidate for bachelorhood, and this situation has not been helped by consolidated schools. Now even the rural school teacher (usually a woman) no longer comes to the outlying community. His best chance of marriage comes in high school or college. If he delays beyond that, the young farmer should force himself to keep up his contacts in his town or city church and in social groups where he will have an opportunity to meet and become acquainted with young women. The farm community has very few unmarried women in their twenties.

In conclusion, because all people seek to realize various goals in life, and because some of them can be realized only by delaying or sacrificing others, one must often choose among them. Marriage promises to fulfill several basic wishes, but other wishes may have to be sacrificed if one marries too soon. Work is for many girls a satisfying and creative experience which they want before marriage. Some young people want freedom to earn and spend as they please, to travel, to date widely and make new friends, to strive for economic security. For them these wishes must be satisfied before assuming the obligations of the family life. But there are situations in life where one must master his fate by choosing the one alternative that is most meaningful, for as the old saying goes, "one can't have his cake and eat it too."

Between the choices youth create for themselves, and those which are forced upon them by military service, the places they live and work, and other such circumstances, finding a satisfactory marriage partner and ultimately realizing a satisfactory marriage may be something of a problem.

Individuals considering early marriage should be aware of the fact that when they marry they are assuming the responsibilities of grown men and women. These responsibilities, once taken, cannot be put aside again for the freedom and independence of childhood and early youth.

Young persons contemplating marriage should ask themselves the following questions:

1. Are we ready to give up the status, the special care, treatment, and advantages of childhood?
2. Are we ready for the responsibilities of adulthood—earning and saving and building a home together?
3. Can we stand on our own feet and be independent of our parents?
4. Are we ready to assume the responsibilities of parenthood, with the exacting routine which the care of children requires?

In the final analysis, one's own answer to the question of when he should marry is determined by the wishes he expects to satisfy in life. Early marriage will assure the immediate realization of some goals, but it may well make the realization of others virtually impossible. Good questions to ask oneself in thinking about an early marriage are:

1. How many of the other goals which I wish to achieve in life must be forgotten or delayed by my marrying now?
2. How important are these goals to me?
3. Will I be content if my marriage should make the attaining of any or all of these goals impossible?

Much unhappiness is caused by not being able to reach the goals we have set for ourselves. Early marriage can be a serious handicap in attaining some goals—among the most important of which are finding the job one wants and attaining economic security. Yet marriage is, in the final analysis, an all-important step at the right stage in life. To pass it by lightly or delay it unreasonably is neither wise nor satisfying. Whatever decision one makes should be a thoughtful one for its significance is bound to be far-reaching.

Readiness for marriage, in the sense that one is able to commit himself to it finally and without regret, is the key to timing. Those who have such an attitude will not be easily turned from their purpose to make marriage a success regardless of obstacles encountered after marriage.

Problems

1. In the light of evidence studied so far in this course, do you feel it is better for a girl to marry a little too young rather than take the risk of not having a chance to marry when she is older?
2. What are your views on the desirability or undesirability of college marriages? Consider your answer from the following standpoints: economics (for ex-

ample, would you feel it right for the wife to carry the econmic burden until the husband is through school?) parenthood, the change in recreational life and freedom involved, studies, risk to completing education, and other problems you foresee. Would you be willing to marry while in college?

3. Beth and Keith are juniors in college. They have dated since their freshman year and have been engaged for over a year and a half. They are quite certain of their compatibility but have serious doubts about advisability of marriage. Beth has one more year to complete her education and Keith must continue for at least another six years before he is prepared for his vocation. He cannot hope to support a wife and home until his education is completed, and since his family is already contributing financially to his education he can expect little more financial aid from them. Beth feels that it would be a mistake to delay marriage for six years, at which time both would be twenty-six years old. What would be your advice?
   a. Wait the full six years?
   b. Marry now and get as much financial help from both families as possible?
   c. Marry now but delay parenthood for the six years?
   d. Postpone marriage until Beth's graduation and plan to have her support the family?
   e. Other advice.

4. *Sociodrama:* A high school senior girl is wondering about the desirability of marrying her twenty-year-old fiancé before he is drafted. She discusses the problem with an older girl whose husband is overseas.

5. Which area or areas of maturity do you consider most essential as prerequisites to marriage?
   a. Physical maturity—a fully developed body.
   b. Intellectual maturity—a fully developed mind.
   c. Emotional maturity—understanding and perspective with reference to own feelings.
   d. Vocational maturity—definite vocational goals.
   e. Spiritual maturity—a fully developed and satifying philosophy of life.
   Discuss the importance of the kind or kinds of maturity you think most essential.

6. Here are three individuals, *A, B,* and *C,* from whom you are to select a marriage partner. None of them is ideal. Choose the one with that combination of traits you consider most important.
   A is—
      physically immature
      intellectually very mature
      spiritually mature
      emotionally immature
   B is—
      physically very mature
      intellectually immature
      vocationally mature
      spiritually immature
      emotionally mature

C is—
physically mature
intellectually immature
vocationally immature
spiritually mature
emotionally very mature

7. Discuss the experiences you have had since high school graduation which have affected your values and tastes in mate selection. Answer such questions as:

   a. Is your "ideal" mate today different from the ideal you held during high school days?

   b. Has your attitude toward having children changed?

   c. What specific experiences have contributed most to any change or maturation you observe?

8. *Research exercise:* Poll the class on the ideal age at which a man and a woman should marry. Tabulate results and make a four-way comparison: men's view of ideal age for man and for woman, women's view of ideal age for woman and for man. If differences are found try to explain them in terms of *(a)* economic factors, *(b)* customs, *(c)* sex interests, *(d)* maturity, and any other factors that may seem important.

9. *Sociodrama:* A mother tries to discourage her nineteen-year-old daughter from marrying a man twenty years her senior.

Selected References

ARTICLES IN BOOKS OF READINGS

Landis, Judson T., and Landis, Mary G., *Readings in Marriage and the Family* (Englewood Cliffs, N. J.: Prentice-Hall, Inc., 1952).

1. Popenoe, Paul, "A Study of 738 Elopements," pp. 127-132.

Cavan, Ruth Shonle, *Marriage and the Family in the Modern World: A Book of Readings* (New York: Thomas Y. Crowell Co., 1960).

2. Ellis, Albert, and David, Lester, "Should Men Marry Older Women?" Reading 30.

3. Christensen, Harold T., "Why All These Young Marriages?" Reading 43.

4. Hoeflin, Ruth, "When Shall We Marry?" Reading 44.

5. Kirkendall, Lester A., "Married Undergraduates on the Campus: An Appraisal," Reading 45.

6. Bunting, Marion, "Why I Am Glad I Didn't Marry While in College," Reading 46.

7. Marchand, Jean, and Langford, Louise, "Adjustments of Married Students," Reading 47.

8. Frank, Lawrence K., "Housing for Married Students," Reading 48.

Winch, Robert F., and others, *Selected Studies in Marriage and the Family,* Revised Edition (New York: Holt, Rinehart & Winston, Inc., 1962).
   9. Glick, Paul C., "Stability of Marriage in Relation to Age of Marriage," pp. 622-626.

General References

Bowman, Henry A., *Marriage for Moderns,* Fourth Edition (New York: McGraw-Hill Book Co., 1960), Ch. 4.

Burgess, Ernest W., and Wallin, Paul, *Engagement and Marriage* (Philadelphia: J. B. Lippincott Co., 1953), Ch. 4.

Cavan, Ruth Shonle, *American Marriage* (New York: Thomas Y. Crowell Co., 1959), Ch. 3, co-authored by David M. Fulcomer.

Christensen, Harold T., and Philbrick, Robert E., "Family Size as a Factor of Marital Adjustment of College Students," *American Sociological Review,* 17:306-312, June, 1952.

Duvall, Evelyn, and Hill, Reuben, *Being Married* (New York: Association Press, 1960), Ch. 5.

Ellis, Evelyn, "Social Psychological Correlates of Upward Social Mobility Among Unmarried Career Women," *American Sociological Review,* 17:558-563, October, 1952.

Farber, Bernard, *Family: Organization and Interaction* (San Francisco: Chandler Publishing Co., 1964), Ch. 5.

Glick, Paul C., *American Families* (New York: John Wiley & Sons, Inc., 1957), Table 72, p. 112.

————, and Carter, Hugh, "Marriage Patterns and Educational Level," *American Sociological Review,* 23:294-300, June, 1958.

Klemer, Richard H., "Factors of Personality and Experience Which Differentiate Single from Married Women," *Marriage and Family Living,* 16:41-44, February, 1954.

Koos, Earl Lomon, *Marriage* (New York: Holt, Rinehart & Winston, Inc., 1953), Ch. 21.

LeMasters, E. E., *Modern Courtship and Marriage* (New York: The Macmillan Co., 1957), Ch. 10.

Levy, John, and Munroe, Ruth, *The Happy Family* (New York: Alfred A. Knopf, Inc., 1938).

Reed, Ruth, *The Single Woman* (New York: The Macmillan Co., 1942).

Samenfink, J. Anthony, and Milliken, Robert I., "Marital Status and Academic Success: A - Reconsideration," *Marriage and Family Living,* 23:226-227, August, 1961.

Wallace, Gerald R., "High Schools and Married Students—Are They Compatible?" *Marriage and Family Living,* 24:295-296, August, 1962.

18

Engagement: The Testing Ground

The various steps leading up to marriage today are much less clearly marked than in an earlier generation when each couple proceeded along a familiar and conventional path from keeping company to engagement and then marriage.

Today, serious interest in social relationships with the opposite sex generally begins to be manifested in the early teens. From then until marriage a number of steps ordinarily follow in sequence. Some young people skip most of them, jumping from first acquaintance into marriage; others go through each stage and even add a few of their own. In either case, while there is a general pattern that most people follow, there are many variations and exceptions, and no one is surprised or disturbed to hear of a completely unique pattern.

The Natural History of a Modern Mate Choice

There are a number of social devices and material symbols by which young people indicate, first, their interest and, later, their attachment to each other. These indications are meant not only to please and reassure one another, but also to signify to friends and competitors the stage reached in the development of the relationship.

Young people of high school and college age, for example, recognize a few standard procedures for "getting started" with another person. Comments of interest and approval are generally made to a mutual friend on the assumption that the comments will soon reach the ears of the admired one. When this is impossible or ineffective, there are more direct approaches: glances which, as one college freshman described them, "are supposed to literally ooze with meaning and emotion"; attempts to increase the number of informal contacts (joining the same groups and clubs, signing up for the same classes, attending the same events); anonymous and, later, signed notes (still very common at the junior and senior high school level); and, finally, if all else fails, outright confessions of interest and direct requests for a first date.

During the initial stages of the relationship present-day custom frowns on too intense a display of interest, particularly on the part of the female. Both are supposed to feel free to continue dating others. An early display of possessiveness or jealousy on the part of the male is usually resented. When these traits are displayed by the girl first, the relationship is almost immediately doomed.[1] Being too eager is considered an indication of poor taste or a lack of self-confidence. Even when both parties are mutually and intensely attracted, most teenagers attempt to cover up the fact during the "get-acquainted" period.

If, after a number of dates, interest and attraction has continued to grow, everything can change, providing the male always takes the initiative in advancing to a new stage in the relationship. At no time before actual marriage does custom approve of the girl admitting to stronger or deeper feelings than the boy, or of the girl speaking of these feelings first.

This is unrealistic and often a severe handicap to both, but folklore has it that the male is the eager suitor and the female the reluctant uncertain party who must be won. Mate choice is, in this sense, a drama involving two main characters and a host of minor ones. Each knows the other's part and the role is to be played in the expected way. At the same time, both players are conscious that the parts are not completely adequate for expressing themselves. Until engagement or even marriage breaks down these barriers, it is difficult for many couples to be completely sure of the full meaning of their relationship to each other.

After the real or assumed "casual interest" of the first stage has passed there is some hurry in indicating a more definite relationship. Most young women assume that after a reasonable length of time (ranging anywhere from a month to a year of regular dating) the relationship should either cease entirely or pass on to a more serious (or, at least, more definite) stage of interest. When the young man does not make the appropriate overtures, the girl generally feels bound to begin the "terminating" steps, although frequently she does so only for pride's sake. When the male does not seem eager for a more definite commitment, it is frequently his

[1] For a study of this subject see H. K. Moore, "Why Men Drop Women," and "Why Women Drop Men," summarized in *Family Life*, 11:4 ff., August, 1951, and 11:4 ff., November, 1951, respectively.

way of signaling to the girl that she should "begin to lose interest in him, quickly!" When the girl does not take the hint, the male is allowed to become somewhat less gallant and simply "drop" her.

The young man who is eager, or at least willing, to continue the relationship beyond casual dating generally indicates his interest by offering to the girl one of the accepted symbols of attachment. He may begin by seeking to exchange rings or pins in junior high or during the senior high school years. The custom of "pinning," which undoubtedly originated in fraternity-sorority circles, has become the usual procedure among college students, and is now more or less universal even on the high school level.

Fraternity-sorority pins, rings, athletic sweaters, charm bracelets, or some other tangible symbols are exchanged between the couple. The exact meaning of this depends somewhat on the couple's age. In the younger set, it means that they are going steady. With the college group, it seems to mean more than this, although the meaning may not be too well defined even there. Most students, no doubt, consider it something of a promise of engagement, if all goes well. The ring exchange, which comes later, is taken much more seriously, although studies of college students show that on the college campus even the pinning has much more significance for the girl than for the boy. (At California, 80 percent of the girls considered a pinned person as "engaged to be engaged," but only 63 percent of the men so regarded it.)[2] Among those who consider the exchange of pins synonymous with engagement, women also outnumber men. (At Michigan State, 44 percent of the women so regarded it as compared to 27 percent of the men.)[3]

If the pin does not mean engagement then a ring (or an explanation) must soon be forthcoming or again the girl is expected to begin the termination of the relationship. Even if the man must engineer the motivating circumstances (such as attempting to be seen with another girl or consciously hurting his girl's feelings), it is nevertheless considered the right—the gallant—thing for him to wait for the girl to offer to return his pin.

The ring, among all symbols, is the one which carries with it the most specific meaning. It stands for engagement and the engagement in turn implies marriage plans (although often of only the vaguest nature). We know today that even the ring is not a final binding promise, for a fairly high proportion of relationships are terminated even after this most

---

[2] Judson T. Landis has studied this problem extensively among college students on the Michigan State University campus and the University of California campus. See Judson T. Landis and Mary G. Landis, *Building a Successful Marriage,* Fourth Edition (Englewood Cliffs, N. J.: Prentice-Hall, Inc., 1963), pp. 227-228.

[3] *Ibid.* This study was made five years earlier than the California study. It is possible that the trend in colleges is toward taking pinning less seriously.

formal of all commitments. Even the ring itself must often be followed with continued symbols of dedication, flowers, gifts, etc.

The engagement which drags on too long is supposed to arouse the girl's suspicions. When discussions of marriage plans are not willingly initiated by the male, the girl is supposed to think seriously of offering to return his ring.

Ideally, engagement implies the selection of some particular person of the opposite sex with whom one begins to associate on the assumption that this person will be one's husband or wife. As this closer association takes place, each begins to appraise the other in terms of his or her future role as husband or wife. The couple try to merge their personalities into a unity by interweaving their interests, aspirations, and plans.

There is little doubt that each stage of greater commitment is more meaningful to women than to men. All the symbols are more precious and women tend to give these symbols more meaning. In a real sense they represent a victory in the highly competitive game of attracting a mate. Each symbol inspires envy and brings appreciative comment from friends of her sex. It is, therefore, given to women to announce steps in their success.

The male is more likely to keep the commitment private. This is consistent with this reticence to commit himself in the first place. Male friends, when they learn, are likely to jibe him for having been "hooked." In a sense his commitments to the fair sex represent defeat in the battle of the sexes as viewed through the eyes of the male subculture.

How and Where Persons Become Engaged

The various steps which enter into mate selection today make it less easy than formerly for a couple to know when they actually are engaged. The old-fashioned method (which, of course, is no doubt mostly fiction) of the boy kneeling before the girl while she sat on the parlor sofa certainly was a different kind of engagement arrangement than that of today. Undoubtedly, it is the college group now that goes through the greatest number of steps in becoming engaged. While a definite date can be set for the formal announcement, few couples are completely clear on just when both agreed they were ready for such a relationship.

The picture of a suitor humbly asking for the girl's hand in marriage is probably also only a myth. Today, in any case, it is reserved for jokes and cartoons. With the free give-and-take that characterizes the conversations of modern youth, it is likely that hints of marriage and questions about the possibility of marriage come up quite early in the serious stages of most relationships. In many instances there is probably no formal proposal as such; there merely comes a point in the discussions when both recognize the interests and intentions of the other.

The idea of the woman having absolutely no initiative in these discussions and of her hiding her wishes until the man has come completely out in the open with a blunt request to marry is also probably more characteristic of an earlier generation than of this one. How much initiative the woman takes often depends upon the bashfulness and hesitancy of the man. She rarely, if ever, actually proposes, but one suspects that the woman who seeks marriage is quick to follow up any hints or awkward leads which the timid man may drop.

In an earlier day, parental consent entered into whether or not a couple became engaged. Today, the home and parents have pretty much disappeared from the picture. Several years ago a study of the locales in which engagements were likely to take place showed that the most important place was the automobile, not the family parlor, and that about as many engagements are made on the street, in parks, restaurants, or other public places as in the home.[4] In vacation places, resorts, trains, on ships, at dinner parties and dances, engagements are entered into. The family, as well as the family parlor, have come to play a diminished part in determining when and whom a young person will marry. What chance does the family have to participate in these functions with the youth who may be a thousand miles or more away attending college, or on a job? This is much too migratory an age for family participation in such experiences of youth.

How soon do couples get engaged after their first date together? Not much recent information is available about the population in general, but Judson T. Landis's study of over 500 single and married college students who had been engaged shows that, for a little over a fourth of them, the engagement took place within five months after their first date.[5] By the end of the year, another fifth were engaged. The rest went together for a period of over a year before becoming engaged. Over 20 percent had dated for three years or more before becoming engaged. Remember that these figures deal only with those who did become engaged. Many, of course, go steady for long periods without becoming engaged.

The above discussion of steps leading to engagement assumes that the couple is serious and that the engagement is entered into with intent to marry. One must recognize that in a mobile age where so many contacts are casual and temporary, some men use engagement as a means of persuading the girl to enter into a sexual relationship. In such in-

[4] Paul Popenoe, *Modern Marriage* (New York: The Macmillan Co., 1940), p. 267.

[5] Judson T. Landis and Mary G. Landis, *Building a Successful Marriage*, Fourth Edition (Englewood Cliffs, N. J.: Prentice-Hall, Inc., 1963), p. 224.

stances, the male may have no further intent than this even when the girl is entirely serious about the relationship and fully expects that it will lead to marriage.

Are Engagements Necessary?

The custom of engagement exists. Does it make sense? Authorities in the marriage field think it does. Elopements, most of which involve no engagement, or a short one at best, are one test of the marriage without engagement. How do they turn out?

Popenoe's study of 738 elopements shows that for the most part they were followed by a high rate of unhappy marriages.[6] In nearly half of them, there was parental objection to the marriage. Less than half led to happy marriages. When the motive was pregnancy, only a third were happy. When the motive was economic, or the wish to avoid publicity, over half were happy.

Length of Engagement

Historic studies[7] have shown a high relationship between long engagements and success in marriage, those of two or more years having a high ratio of success, whereas those under six months showing a high rate of marriage failure, with few leading to good marriage adjustment. Whether these findings still have validity is open to some question. As far as the college generation is concerned, they do not consider long engagements necessary or wise. The writer's classes, almost without exception, express a unanimity of opinion in favor of engagements of not more than four to six months.

Their reasoning is based on the fact that there are so many preliminary steps preceding formal engagement that many of the issues once deferred to the engagement period are now faced and disposed of prior to the engagement. Also, many of the intimacies, confidences, and plans once deferred to engagement are now well along prior to the engagement. They seem to feel also that during this preannouncement stage many relationships that would not have weathered the formal engagement period end, and end with less public exposure. To the extent that

6 Paul Popenoe, "A Study of 738 Elopements," *American Sociological Review*, 3:297 ff., February, 1938.

7 Lewis M. Terman and others, *Psychological Factors in Marital Happiness* (New York: McGraw-Hill Book Co., 1938), p. 199; Ernest W. Burgess and Leonard S. Cottrell, *Predicting Success or Failure in Marriage* (Englewood Cliffs, N. J.: Prentice-Hall, Inc., 1939), p. 168; Judson T. Landis and Mary Landis, *Building a Successful Marriage*, Fourth Edition (Englewood Cliffs, N. J.: Prentice-Hall, Inc., 1963), p. 240.

this is true, the length of the engagement ceases to be a primary criterion of the degree of understanding and adjustment.

Today, when young people associate so closely and when considerable physical contact is customary, many authorities are inclined to look upon an engagement of more than a year as producing too much sex strain to be justified, although points of view differ on this subject.[8]

Burgess and Wallin's study of over 500 married couples showed that only a fourth of those married after an engagement of less than three months made good adjustments in marriage; half of them made poor adjustments, the rest only fair.[9] The situation among those who had no engagement also showed a high proportion of maladjustments. With an engagement period of up to two years or over, the proportion of happy marriages greatly increased. In fact, of those who were engaged two years or more, only 10 percent were characterized by poor marital adjustment. Other studies have showed similar results.[10]

It is open to argument whether length of engagement, as such, is the primary factor, or whether people of more steady temperament tend to prolong their engagement; but one thing is certain, a fairly long engagement eliminates a lot of fly-by-night romances that could not have succeeded in marriage.

If a couple has known each other over a long period of time and has had a long period of going steady, a lengthy engagement may be less important than if each has known little about the other's background and if they have gone together only a few months before engagement. The really important thing is not how long the engagement is but what is accomplished during the period. Getting really well acquainted is the most valuable outcome of any engagement, and in nearly all cases getting acquainted takes time.

It is important, too, that a couple be engaged long enough to see whether they can work out patterns of adjustment which will assure the continuing development of a compatible and companionable relationship. A long engagement, however, can do nothing for the couple who are not going in the right direction in their adjustment to each other. They should learn that they never can develop a satisfactory relationship. But a long engagement can give those who are moving in the right direc-

---

[8] Ernest W. Burgess and Paul Wallin find that sexual intercourse is more frequent among couples engaged sixteen months or over than among those of engagements of shorter duration; see their *Engagement and Marriage* (Philadelphia: J. B. Lippincott Co., 1953).

[9] Ernest W. Burgess and Leonard S. Cottrell, *Predicting Success or Failure in Marriage* (Englewood Cliffs, N. J.: Prentice-Hall, Inc., 1939).

[10] A summary of several of these studies appears in Judson T. Landis and Mary G. Landis, *Building a Successful Marriage*, Fourth Edition (Englewood Cliffs, N. J.: Prentice-Hall, Inc., 1963), pp. 293 ff.

tion the opportunity to learn what kinds of adjustment techniques work for them. Both results are equally important—the one in blocking unwise marriages; the other in building assurance that the pair relationship has qualities that will wear well in marriage.

Some young people are inclined to feel that today, when everything is speeded up, marriage can be speeded up too. Such a philosophy is particularly prevalent in wartime. This more than any other factor probably explains the high rate of failure of postwar marriages. Getting acquainted was deferred until after marriage and then the couple found that each had married a strange and incompatible person.

Today, the period of serious association is probably no shorter than in an earlier day. Koller followed the length of going together through three generations, and in all three the serious period of going together covered a median period of a year and a half.[11] The real difference found was that in the earlier generations it was not at all unusual for the couple to have known each other for a lifetime. Today, many start out cold, so that a great deal of time is spent merely getting acquainted with each other's background, personality, and aspirations. This makes time all the more important in preparing the way for a successful marriage.

Disagreements During Engagement

There is considerable evidence that engagements are seldom the smooth-running periods of perfect happiness that young people expect. With growing intimacy and understanding, and with more frequent and less formal contacts, disagreements are common, and actual quarreling may begin.

Burgess and Wallin's study of 1,000 engaged couples was focused upon discovering exactly what does happen during the modern engagement period.[12] Figure 18-1 shows the result of a series of check questions to test extent of agreement. It will be seen that, among the couples studied, agreement on most issues was the rule. On every topic the study covered, some couples disagreed, though the proportion of disagreement varied greatly on different items. As many as one couple in four experienced disagreement on some issues.

The one area in which there was most agreement dealt with dating. Since engagement is primarily a matter of association during dates, this perhaps would be expected. The next highest area of agreement dealt

11 Marvin R. Koller, "Some Changes in Courtship Behavior in Three Generations of Ohio Women," *American Sociological Review*, 16:366-370, 1951.

12 Ernest W. Burgess and Paul Wallin, *Engagement and Marriage* (Philadelphia: J. B. Lippincott Co., 1953), p. 246.

AGREEMENT OF 1000 ENGAGED MEN AND WOMEN IN SELECTED AREAS OF THEIR RELATIONSHIPS

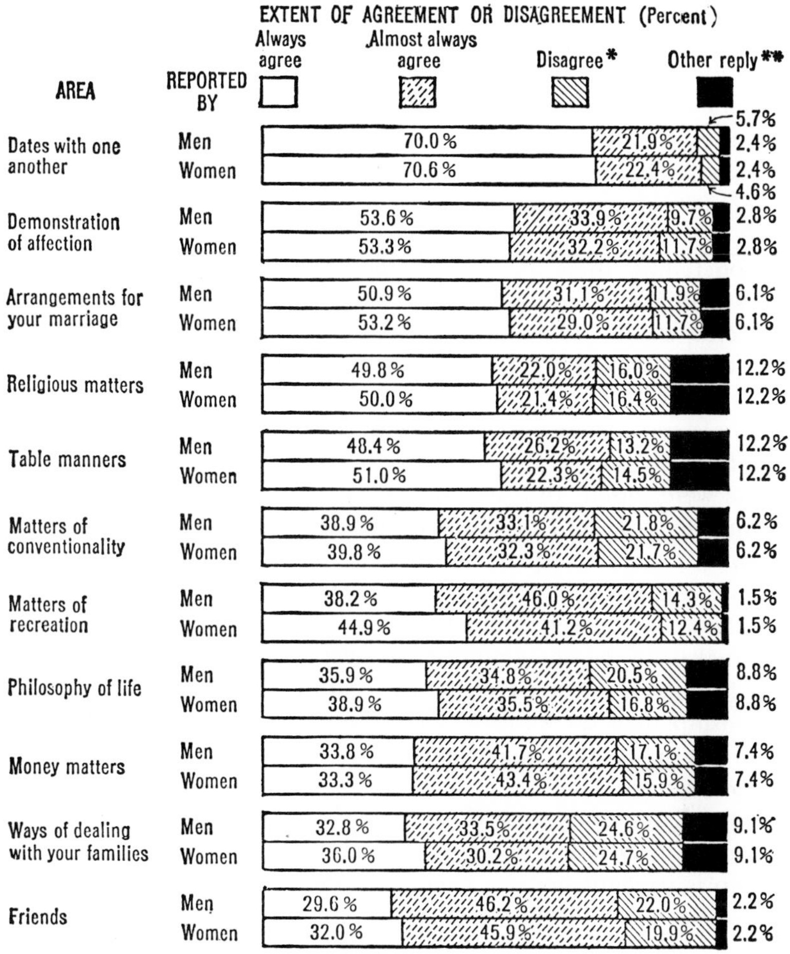

EXTENT OF AGREEMENT OR DISAGREEMENT (Percent)

AREA	REPORTED BY	Always agree □	Almost always agree ▨	Disagree * ▧	Other reply ** ■
Dates with one another	Men	70.0%	21.9%	2.4%	5.7%
	Women	70.6%	22.4%	2.4%	
Demonstration of affection	Men	53.6%	33.9%	9.7%	2.8%
	Women	53.3%	32.2%	11.7%	2.8%
Arrangements for your marriage	Men	50.9%	31.1%	11.9%	6.1%
	Women	53.2%	29.0%	11.7%	6.1%
Religious matters	Men	49.8%	22.0%	16.0%	12.2%
	Women	50.0%	21.4%	16.4%	12.2%
Table manners	Men	48.4%	26.2%	13.2%	12.2%
	Women	51.0%	22.3%	14.5%	12.2%
Matters of conventionality	Men	38.9%	33.1%	21.8%	6.2%
	Women	39.8%	32.3%	21.7%	6.2%
Matters of recreation	Men	38.2%	46.0%	14.3%	1.5%
	Women	44.9%	41.2%	12.4%	1.5%
Philosophy of life	Men	35.9%	34.8%	20.5%	8.8%
	Women	38.9%	35.5%	16.8%	8.8%
Money matters	Men	33.8%	41.7%	17.1%	7.4%
	Women	33.3%	43.4%	15.9%	7.4%
Ways of dealing with your families	Men	32.8%	33.5%	24.6%	9.1%
	Women	36.0%	30.2%	24.7%	9.1%
Friends	Men	29.6%	46.2%	22.0%	2.2%
	Women	32.0%	45.9%	19.9%	2.2%

* Occasionally or more frequently.
** Never discussed and a few cases where a given item was not checked.

SOURCE: Ernest W. Burgess and Paul Wallin, *Engagement and Marriage* (Philadelphia: J. B. Lippincott Co., 1953). Reproduced by permission of the publisher.

FIGURE 18-1————It is rarely possible for two human beings to see eye to eye in all areas of their relationship. This research shows that engaged men and women do not. Relatives, money matters, friends, and philosophy are areas in which a fourth or more of the couples disagree. (Data are for 1,000 engaged men and women.)

with demonstration of affection. The third was "arrangement for marriage." The areas of most frequent disagreement were questions of conventionality, philosophy of life, and ways of dealing with each other's families. This latter indicates that in-law problems actually begin before marriage for at least a fourth of the couples.

In the field of table manners and conventionality, women were such sticklers for etiquette and convention that this frequently became a point of disagreement with the fiancé.

A more detailed analysis of replies showed that only 17 couples out of the 1,000 always agreed in all areas of their relationship. Only 185 always or almost always agreed in all areas of their relationship.

Concluding their analysis of the experience of engaged couples, Burgess and Wallin indicate that about two-thirds of the couples experience some strain. They described the engagement period as one in which the couple attempts to adjust "conflicting differences in the interest of the survival of their relationship."[13]

These researchers also asked whether the couples experienced jealousy often, occasionally, or never. Men are the more jealous sex. Their answers were: often, 16.4 percent; occasionally, 55.1 percent; never, 28.5 percent. Forty percent of the women were never jealous; 49.5 percent, occasionally; only 10.5 percent, often.

This analysis shows that some insecurity is present in most engagements because of previous entanglements of a partner, or because of lack of mutual trust, the one doubting the affection of the other. Men seem to suffer from a greater sense of doubt regarding loyalty in the engagement relationship than do women. The authors conclude that young people should not expect the engagement period today to be "one of continuous bliss and ecstacy."

The disagreements which arise during the engagement period may conclude in a variety of ways. Frequently they are resolved and the relationship is strengthened for having weathered the storm. In other cases, the disagreements as they increase in number begin to plant seeds of serious doubt in the minds of one or both about the desirability of marriage. It was found, in fact, that about half of the men and women studied felt hesitant about the marriage at some time during the engagement period. A fourth of the women and a fifth of the men wished they had never become engaged, and about as many at some time seriously contemplated breaking the engagement.

At such times it is very common for college young people to discuss the advisability of marriage with those in whom they have confidence. Approximately two-thirds of the men and women discussed the advisability of marriage with their respective mothers; over a third, with their

13 *Ibid.*, p. 271.

respective fathers; a fourth, with friends; and a smaller percentage, with other relatives, with doctors, clergymen, etc.[14] Almost half of both men and women at some time during the engagement felt hesitant about marrying the person to whom they were engaged.[15]

About one in four engaged couples, at some time during the relationship, broke off temporarily. Moreover, 16 percent of the men and 23 percent of the women had had previous engagements, and 15 percent of the couples studied, later broke their engagements.[16]

These data indicate quite clearly that among college engagements, at least, there are frequently serious doubts and uncertainties about the desirability of following through to marriage. Burgess and Wallin conclude that the love relationship desired in the American marriage could scarcely be realized without considerable association between men and women before marriage; that there is reason to believe "that various combinations of men and women differ considerably in their probabilities of developing into more or less durable love relationships." Trial and error, they feel, is necessary in order to insure the maximum number of desirable combinations. Engagement has become the final stake in this trial-and-error relationship, and often the relationship proves to be inadequate.

Burgess and Wallin also conclude that one of the serious weaknesses of the engagement period is that it is too often carried on exclusively in an atmosphere of recreation and play, giving an unrealistic picture of what marriage will be like.

How Much to Tell

The very real feeling of interrelatedness of those deeply in love often induces a mood of confession and repentance. During the engagement period, or even before, young people frequently feel a strong urge to confess all their past sins to each other, the girl to test his love, the boy to shed his guilt.

This seems to be a normal phase in the development of love, particularly for the male. Sometimes this way of relieving guilt feelings for past misconduct is an asset, not only to the individual, but to the couple. It may be an indication that the couple has become intimate enough to want to share with each other secrets known to no other. It may also indicate a strong sense of mutual need and trust.

The question of the desirability of confession at such a time is not so simple, however, as it initially appears. One might well ask himself,

[14] *Ibid.*, p. 178.
[15] *Ibid.*, p. 180.
[16] *Ibid.*, p. 136.

"Will the other person have the background to absorb these confessions with understanding, or will it only raise doubts and uncertainty about the advisability of marriage?"

Of course, it all depends upon the kind of thing being confessed and whether or not it has a bearing on the marriage. Certainly if there are factors in one's background that might have a direct or serious bearing on the marriage, the person one intends to marry should know about them.

Judson T. Landis[17] found that all engaged students he studied of both sexes confessed nervous breakdowns, suspected bad hereditary traits, previous marriage, and having a child out of wedlock, although, of course, few had such serious issues in their background. Almost three-fourths of boys who had had sex experience with another girl confessed it; two-thirds of girls with previous sex experience confessed it. Petting experiences were confessed in approximately 60 percent of cases, a higher proportion of boys with experience than of girls with experience confessing.

If one is in doubt as to whether it is the kind of confession that might help or hinder the marriage and whether it actually needs to be made, it is often better to talk to a physician, counselor, minister, or other confidant first. It is useful to get the advice of a third party before taking the risk of revealing matters which may have no significance whatever to the marriage and may actually create an unnecessary stumbling block. It is not wise to confess matters that are of no consequence to the marriage and yet that may be held against one later.

The Premarital Examination

A premarital physical examination is required in many states. Often it is only to check for venereal disease. Sometimes it includes other possible problem areas, but, in general, it should be more extensive than it is. The examination is usually sought immediately before the marriage. A much better practice, for the girl, is for her to visit a doctor, marriage clinic, or specialist in women's problems three months before marriage so that she may benefit by a long period of counsel. In cases where the hymen has to be stretched, or special treatment given, this can be carried on for a period of time before marriage. There is also the advantage of gaining confidence and understanding by discussing the sexual aspect of marriage with someone who is objective and understanding. This has great value for those women who have strong taboos centering on sex teachings and sex behavior. During this period, there is time for the woman to acquire knowledge of contraception from her doctor, to be

[17] Judson T. Landis and Mary G. Landis, *Building a Successful Marriage*, Fourth Edition (Englewood Cliffs, N. J.: Prentice-Hall, Inc., 1963), p. 250.

fitted with a contraceptive device, and to learn how to use it, or to build pregnancy immunity through "the pill."

By starting early the couple will also have time to investigate with a specialist their hereditary backgrounds, possible defects of organic development, and other factors that might have a bearing on successful adjustment in marriage and the rearing of children. Couples should be able to discuss sex matters and attitudes together and with the doctor. They should not hesitate to discuss with a doctor or marriage counselor the psychological as well as the physical aspects of sexual adjustment. They should read books which will give them information as to techniques and attitudes appropriate to the sexual relationship in marriage.

The latter part of the engagement period should, of course, be a period in which the young people enter into a serious discussion of aspirations with regard to children and family. This is the time to understand fully each other's attitudes and interests in children. Some states grant an annulment if one party can prove that the other had decided prior to the marriage not to have children. Although most young people plan to have children, not all do so. The prospective mate has a right to know this beforehand.

A study of two generations shows that the present generation of married college women and wives of college students, much more often than their mothers, discussed children with their prospective husband before marriage[18] (see Figure 18-2). This is desirable and should become universal.

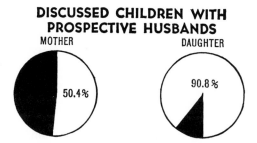

DISCUSSED CHILDREN WITH PROSPECTIVE HUSBANDS

MOTHER   DAUGHTER

50.4%   90.8%

SOURCE: Paul H. Landis, "Marriage Preparation in Two Generations," *Marriage and Family Living*, 8:155-156, November, 1951.

FIGURE 18-2————Between the generations there has been a marked gain in understanding among engaged men and women on this point. Only half of the mother generation discussed the question prior to marriage, almost 91 percent of the daughter generation did.

[18] Paul H. Landis, "Sex Education: The Facts about Two Generations," *The Clearing House*, 24:451-455, April, 1950; also his "Marriage Preparation in Two Generations," *Marriage and Family Living*, 8:155-156, November, 1951.

Premarital Counseling

Although marriage counseling is a new profession, it has a long history as a folk practice. Mothers, grandmothers, older sisters, and friends have always given the girl a few helpful hints on how to handle a man and to meet the intimate emergencies in marriage. In much of their counsel, there was probably as much nonsense as wisdom, and in many instances it was as likely to build suspicion and fear of the male as confidence and anticipation.

Young men, too, have always obtained information somewhere about what is expected of the newly married man, and about the temperament and common responses of women. Here again folk-thinking has not been too sound. In most instances it has been inadequate in giving the man an understanding of female psychology and sex needs.

These time-honored sources are available to young people today, and are no doubt often used. To the extent that the older generation has learned by reading and experience, their advice is sound, but to that extent only. The marriage counselor operates for the most part outside folklore, being guided by research, clinical practice, and wide experience in observing married couples' reactions to difficulties.

Intelligent young people with access to marriage clinics should not hesitate to seek advice there and to put their love under critical examination by counselors experienced in the complexities of human relationships. The counselor is the best person to whom questions can be directed concerning biological and psychological aspects of marriage. The counselor can advise on conflicts and differences that may have led to doubt in the relationship, and on any other problems that may seem important. A counselor does not moralize or condemn. His business is to see the client's problems from the client's viewpoint, to help the client view them objectively, and to assist, when necessary, in working out mutually satisfying solutions.

The marriage counselor can also give advice on practical matters dealing with marriage itself: legal steps in obtaining a license, how much to pay the preacher, etc. In the well-developed marriage clinic, too, there is a medical specialist who gives full time to pelvic examinations, problems of birth control and sterility, and various other psychosexual aspects of the marriage relationship. While one may logically expect that those in charge of clinics believe strongly in their work, and may claim more benefit from it than would their critics, still their claims merit consideration.

The oldest marriage clinic in America, the American Institute of

SOUGHT PREMARITAL ADVICE

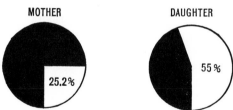

SOURCE: Paul H. Landis, "Marriage Preparation in Two Generations," *Marriage and Family Living*, 8:155-156, November, 1951.

FIGURE 18-3

Family Relations at Los Angeles, has for many years given premarital emotional maturity tests to couples coming for advice previous to marriage. These tests, combined with a thorough physical examination, make up a major part of the premarital counseling. Couples who go through the clinic and who are reassured of their suitability for one another show a high rate of success in marriage.

Dr. Paul Popenoe, the founder, says that not one divorce occurred among couples who came to the Institute for premarital assistance during the first eight years of its existence. This record is outstanding, for the clinic is in the city of Los Angeles where the divorce rate is high.

Marriage fitness tests have been used extensively in the marriage clinic at Pennsylvania State University. Writing a few years after it was established, Clifford Adams, director of the marriage clinic and psychologist, stated:

> . . . hundreds of couples who were tested before marriage at the Marriage Counseling Service are checked periodically after marriage to find how they are making out. Of all the marriages which the service predicted would be successful, not one has yet ended in divorce or separation. Most of the people who went ahead despite the clinic's cautions are already in serious trouble or have been divorced.[19]

While this testimony is convincing, it should not necessarily be interpreted to mean that all divorces would be done away with if all young people, previous to marriage, would go to a premarital clinic for counsel and heed its advice. Since the marriage clinic is a new institution, it is to

[19] Clifford Adams and Vance Packard, *How to Pick a Mate* (New York: E. P. Dutton & Co., Inc., 1946), Preface.

SOURCE OF PREMARITAL ADVICE

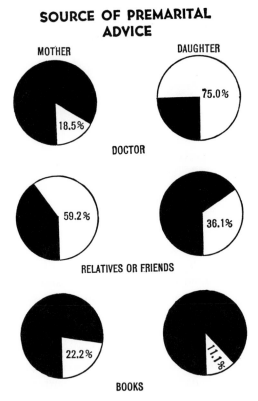

Source: Paul H. Landis, "Marriage Preparation in Two Generations," *Marriage and Family Living*, 8:155-156, November, 1951.

FIGURE 18-4————Of the mother generation only a fourth sought advice; of the married daughters, 55 percent. Of mothers, few sought premarital advice from anyone but relatives and friends. Of the daughters who sought advice, three-fourths consulted a doctor. None of the parent generation sought the advice of a minister or teacher. One in 10 of the daughters consulted a minister; one in 35, a teacher.

be expected that most of those who have used it have been the intelligent and serious persons who are willing to face facts and to follow wise counsel. This may mean that most young people who have used the clinic would have been successful in marriage anyway. There can be no doubt that specialists who have tools and wisdom to bring to their task of counseling can be most helpful to any prospective marriage.

Time to Get Acquainted—An Indispensable Precaution

Of all the simple precautions to assure marriage happiness, the one most obvious and most readily accessible to all is time—time enough to know that the match is a suitable one. Most marriage failures are courtship failures.[20] This point cannot too often be repeated.

The key to success seems to be through acquaintance—being together enough before marriage to know whether or not there is a basis for lifelong companionship and compatibility. Marriage, in order to last, must have wearing qualities. These cannot be tested in short, casual, highly heated whirlwind romances ending in premature marriages. Of course, almost anyone knows of a marriage like this that has succeeded, but research evidence suggests that such marriages are among those lucky accidents in life that befall some people. Most such marriages do not survive.

Figure 18-5,[21] dealing with 526 married couples, gives a characteristic picture of research on this subject. It will be seen that less than a fourth of the "under six months" couples made a good adjustment. (Remember that the couples who divorced quickly are already eliminated, since this is a study of married couples.) Half of these survivors in marriage considered their marriage adjustment poor. The proportion of good adjustments increased with increased length of acquaintance.

Whether people with short get-acquainted periods represent a type of temperament that fails in marriage, or whether these same people, had they prolonged their dating and engagement, would have broken up their relationship, we can only guess. It seems reasonable to suppose that the length of the period is not in itself the only reason for unsuccessful marriages. It could be reason enough, however. The early stages of dating are often very romantic. Marriage at this time might lead a person to expect more of the marriage than any marriage can realize. A lengthened, steady-dating period usually brings about a more reasonable understanding of the person. The halo effect of early romance is diffused with thorough acquaintance. An understanding marriage may result.

---

[20] Dr. Henry Bowman feels that this is so, judging by views expressed in lectures. Burgess and Wallin (*op. cit.*, p. 302) go so far as to suggest that the breakup of engagements probably saves many divorces and that if more engagements were broken there would be fewer divorces.

[21] Burgess and Cottrell, *op. cit.*, p. 164.

RELATION OF HAPPINESS IN MARRIAGE TO LENGTH OF FRIENDSHIP

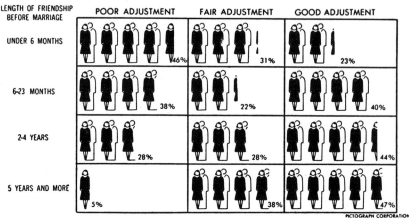

SOURCE: Based on data from Ernest W. Burgess and Leonard S. Cottrell, *Predicting Success or Failure in Marriage* (Copyright, 1939, by Prentice-Hall, Inc., New York). Reproduced by permission of the publisher.

FIGURE 18-5————Short acquaintance before marriage means great risk.

Beware of the Danger Signs!

Time alone will not guarantee a successful marriage. Many people marry who know each other so well already that they have serious misgivings about their compatibility, and yet they move ahead toward marriage and later regret. So this rule must be added: do not ignore the danger signs!

A case comes to mind of a minister's wife who, after 15 years of marriage, had to call it quits. There were two children, a boy and a girl. When she left her husband to prepare for teaching, she took the boy with her and left the daughter with the husband. In leaving the church, she faced great opposition. There was a serious threat to her husband's position in the church; there was great pressure from the bishop to get her to continue, merely to put on a proper front if for no personal reason. She finally told him that even if it wrecked the whole church she could tolerate the marriage no longer; it was a question of breaking up the marriage or going to a mental institution. She admitted she had no one to blame but herself for the 15 years of misery she had endured. During the eight years they were going together his intolerance, tendency to dominate her, his refusal to genuinely accept her as an equal, his coldness, all troubled her greatly. But, he was a good man, he was a Christian, he was a minister. She felt that there must be something wrong with her. The prestige of his work and her desire to share in it, and the service it represented, made a great appeal to her. She said that she hoped that, by some magic, marriage would change the situation with regard to their interpersonal relations; she went ahead into a marriage which almost destroyed her.

It is not enough to become thoroughly acquainted. One must also face the facts of the personal relationship as they are revealed by this thorough acquaintance.

A Canadian girl wrote and asked whether or not she should marry a person she had been going with for some years. She described him and her many reactions to him. Among her comments was, "He has a way of talking which I find rather obnoxious."

Why should a young lady need advice as to whether or not to marry under these circumstances? If she finds certain traits very obnoxious on an occasional date, how is she going to tolerate this man across the table three times a day?

A Levelheaded View of the Engagement Period

For many young people, the engagement period is an endless round of parties, showers, and special gatherings in which there is little time for the real business of preparing for marriage. When doubts and misgivings arise in the minds of such a couple, the possible wisdom of calling the whole thing off is difficult to face. "What would Mama say after that wonderful announcement party?" "What would Uncle George think after practically offering me a partnership in the firm?" "What would our friends think?" "What would people say?" These and a hundred other considerations—plans, presents, and promises—sometimes hurry the couple along into a marriage about which they have serious misgivings. Occasionally even the prospects of eventual divorce seem less terrifying than announcing that it was all a mistake.

Yet many serious affairs, whether or not they are announced engagements, do fold before the final big show. Many others should, judging by the number of divorces that take place during the first year or two of marriage. Why do serious affairs sometimes end? Under what circumstances should an engagement or an affair be terminated or broken? What are the steps in breaking apart? How do couples get over it when it is finally done? These and other questions are serious and common enough to warrant special consideration. The next chapter deals with them.

Problems

1. A young man and woman have dated for six months and have become engaged. He proposes an engagement period of two months. She feels a year is an absolute minmium. Present their discussion and reasons.

2. *Sociodrama:* A young woman visits a marriage counselor and, among other things, brags that she and her fiancé "never disagree on anything." The counselor is dismayed. Continue the discussion emphasizing the questions the counselor might ask.

3. Discuss the advantages of unannounced engagements involving no exchange of rings or pins. What are the problems of such an arrangement?

4. On your campus and among your outside acquaintances, do most engagements lead to marriage? What is the general attitude of your group toward the seriousness of an engagement? For example, do engaged couples date others when separated for a period of time from each other?

5. Jane and Howard have been engaged for close to three years and have planned to marry upon graduation from college next spring. At first they thought the long wait would be unbearable. Now, however, they are a trifle bored with one another but feel that it is only because the engagement has been so long. What would your advice to this couple be?

   a. Marry immediately.

   b. Call it quits.

   c. Take a little vacation from one another.

   d. Continue and see how things turn out.

6. Study the following list of items about which an engaged couple might find themselves in disagreement. Be ready to discuss areas where disagreement would cause you to question the desirability of marriage.

   a. Whether or not to have a large formal wedding ceremony.

   b. Number of children desired.

   c. Whether or not to have children.

   d. Politics.

   e. Religion.

   f. Whether or not "the man runs the family."

   g. What is "good" in music and art.

   h. How children should be disciplined.

   i. Whether to buy a home or spend the money on a long trip.

   j. Leisure-time interests.

7. An engaged couple who are deeply in love ran across a "marriage success" test in a popular magazine. The test, composed by an outstanding man in the field, indicated that their chances for marriage success were very slim. What would your advice to this couple be?

8. Clifford and Madelaine were engaged. While Clifford was stationed overseas he had a brief affair with an English girl. Should he:

   a. Describe the whole affair to his prospective wife?

   b. Let her know there was such an affair?

   c. Say nothing about it?

9. At what time during a couple's relationship should premarital counseling be sought? Why?
10. Are there psychological as well as physical reasons for the premarital physical examination?
11. In general, do you feel that the engagement period of rural couples should tend to be longer or shorter than those of urban couples? Why?
12. Why is it impossible to state a minimum, a maximum, or even an ideal in considering how long all engagements should be?
13. What are your reactions to the idea that couples who are in love can take tests which will tell them whether or not they can succeed in marriage with one another?
14. Among your acquaintances, is the engagement period generally considered:
    a. Important for social reasons?
    b. Important for personal reasons?
    c. Just another custom one must accept?
    d. A waste of time?
15. Do you believe engagements are more important today than, say, one hundred years ago? If so, why?
16. Do you feel that there is such a thing as a "too long" engagement? If so, what are its disadvantages?
17. Under what circumstances, if any, would you consider an engagement period unnecessary?
18. It is probable that during the engagement period most couples come nearest to a "purely romantic" relationship. Should this relationship be protected as much as possible by avoiding issues that might raise arguments and disagreements?
19. Under what circumstances would it be unwise for an individual to confide all his past history to his prospective mate, or do you feel each should tell everything about his past?
20. Are there any advantages to "confessing" to one's mate before marriage?

Selected References

ARTICLES IN BOOKS OF READINGS

BECKER, Howard, and HILL, Reuben (Editors), *Family, Marriage and Parenthood*, Second Edition (Boston: D. C. Heath and Co., 1955).
    1. KUHN, Manford Hinshaw, "The Engagement: Thinking About Marriage," pp. 276-304.
VINCENT, Clark E., *Readings in Marriage Counseling* (New York: Thomas Y. Crowell Co., 1957).
    2. *A Symposium,* "Premarital Sex Relations: The Facts and the Counselor's Role in Relation to the Facts," pp. 104-117.
FISHBEIN, Morris, and KENNEDY, Ruby Jo Reeves, *Modern Marriage and Family Living* (New York: Oxford University Press, 1957).
    3. DUVALL, Evelyn M., "Courtship and Engagement," pp. 144-157.
    4. FISHBEIN, Morris, "Premarital Physical Examination," pp. 167-173.

General References

BEE, Lawrence S., *Marriage and Family Relations* (New York: Harper & Row, Publishers, 1959), Chapter 11.

BOLTON, Charles D., "Mate Selection as the Development of a Relationship," *Marriage and Family Living,* 23:234-240, 1961.

BOSSARD, James S. H., "The Engagement Ring—A Changing Symbol," *New York Times Magazine,* p. 32 ff., September 14, 1958.

BOWMAN, Henry A., *Marriage for Moderns,* Fourth Edition (New York: McGraw-Hill Book Co., 1960), Ch. 5.

BURGESS, Ernest W., and WALLIN, Paul, *Engagement and Marriage* (Philadelphia: J. B. Lippincott Co., 1953), Chs. 5, 10.

CAVAN, Ruth Shonle, *American Marriage* (New York: Thomas Y. Crowell Co., 1959), Ch. 9.

CHRISTENSEN, Harold T., *Marriage Analysis,* Revised Edition (New York: The Ronald Press Co., 1958).

KOLLER, Marvin R., "Some Changes in Courtship Behavior in Three Generations of Ohio Women," *American Sociological Review,* 16:366-370, 1951.

LANDIS, Paul H., "Marriage Preparation in Two Generations," *Marriage and Family Living,* 8:155-156, November, 1951.

MOORE, H. K., "Why Men Drop Women," and "Why Women Drop Men," *Family Life,* 11:4 ff., August, 1951 and 11:4 ff., November, 1951.

MUDD, Emily Hartshorne, *The Practice of Marriage Counseling* (New York: Association Press, 1951).

POPENOE, Paul, "A Study of 738 Elopements," *American Sociological Review,* 3:297 ff., February, 1938.

WALLER, Willard, and HILL, Reuben, *The Family* (New York: Holt, Rinehart & Winston, Inc., 1951), Ch. 12.

19
Broken Engagements

A Birmingham (England) insurance broker is offering insurance against broken engagements. His plan is to cover young Englishmen whose fiancées go to the continent on vacation. Just in case the girl falls for a suave Italian or Frenchman and jilts her English boyfriend, he offers an indemnity up to one thousand pounds.[1]

Perhaps such a monetary reward would be some solace to the broken heart, although hardly adequate for those who were deeply serious about each other.

Engagements at Best Tentative Commitments Today

The casual nature of enagagements today led one college male to remark that, "All the engagement ring does is let you qualify for the finals."[2] At a time when a third to a half of engagements terminate short of marriage, there is much that is tentative about an engagement, no matter how seriously entered into.

Breach-of-promise suits are out of style, as engagement has become a personal matter between two young people. With the vanishing of property considerations in matchmaking, the elimination of the dowery, the passing of elders and marriage brokers from the decisive sphere of influence, and the outmoding of the hope chest, engagement is not a broad contract involving families, their status and possessions, but involving only matters of the heart. These are less substantial than institutional arrangements which take on the character of comprehensive contractual commitments.

[1] *Family Life,* 20:5, January, 1960.
[2] Quoted by James S. H. Bossard, "The Engagement Ring—A Changing Symbol," *New York Times Magazine,* p. 32, September 14, 1958.

Although there may be some loss of status with the breakup of an engagement, it is really more of a thrust at the ego of the persons engaged than at family position. And though public commitments of a sort are in style, at least on college campuses, these commitments have less community implication than the published banns of church and/or state by which public commitment of marriage intent was once made.

The ego slight is still perhaps most severe for the girl, since she is presumably a competitor for the hand of a male, but she has been toughened in most instances by the occasional loss of a desired male in dating. She is less likely to suffer from the "phantom lover" complex, and to become the sainted maiden aunt who can never love again, than women in the day when ladyhood was in style.

With the passing of chivalry and the approach to equality in male-female roles, there is less folk acceptance of the view that the woman has been damaged by the male who has declared his eternal love only, at a later date, to confess "it was all a mistake." Whether the relationship has been between the couple, there is a growing tendency to acknowledge that experiences were mutual, that both were equally responsible for experiences shared and for the ultimate outcome.

Why Serious Affairs Sometimes Fail

What are the most common situations and problems that intrude upon a couple's happiness and cause them to break up?

This problem was investigated extensively among college students at the University of Minnesota some years ago.[3] Here are the most common causes of conflict in serious affairs involving college students:

Cause of conflict	Male affairs (Number 314) percent	Female affairs (Number 582) percent
Jealousy	28.0	23.2
Possessiveness	22.0	23.7
Criticism	21.0	17.9
Irritability arising from emotional tension	19.4	15.3
Dislike of friends	19.1	13.4
Accusations of loss of interest	15.3	14.1
Disagreement about the future	13.1	17.3
Dominance	9.6	8.9
Dependence	3.2	4.3
Exploitation	1.4	3.5

[3] Clifford Kirkpatrick and Theodore Caplow, "Courtship in a Group of Minnesota Students," *American Journal of Sociology*, 51:114-125, September, 1945.

While the issues mentioned cause a lot of grief in serious affairs, these specific reasons were not given as the ones responsible for the breaking up of love affairs. The 71 men in this study who reported broken love affairs had broken 230 affairs in all; the 121 women interviewed accounted for a total of 414 unsuccessful affairs. Here are the reasons given:[4]

Cause of breaking affair	Male affairs (Number 220) percent	Female affairs (Number 414) percent
Parents	5.2	8.6
Friends	3.1	5.8
Subject's interest in another person	15.1	32.2
Partner's interest in another person	29.7	15.3
Mutual loss of interest	46.9	39.1

Much of the dissimilarity between these two lists can probably be accounted for on the basis of specificity. Loss of interest, and interest in another by one or the other or both, which accounts for the termination of about 90 percent of the affairs in the second list are, without doubt, the result of such factors as jealousy, possessiveness, criticism, etc., that rank high in the first list.

Affairs where both lose interest are the easiest to terminate. There is little explaining or rationalizing to do and presumably no one is seriously hurt. Where one causes the breakup because he or she has found another, it is a different matter. Here there is the possibility of the deserted partner suffering jealousy, defeat, humiliation, and other feelings which the love relationship is capable of producing.

Parental influence is often a factor in the girl's reasons, perhaps indicating that parents watch the mate-selection process of the girl more than that of the boy. Would these same types of conflict issues be equally operative in the breakup of noncollege couples or in the breaking of engagements? There has been little attempt to study the noncollege population. Undoubtedly parental influence is often a factor in the termination of affairs among younger teenagers and is likely to be exerted before engagements take place.

What proportion of serious college affairs break up? The study[5] above shows that 71 percent of the serious love affairs of the girls had been broken; 73 percent of those of the men. The median age of the group at the time of the study was twenty-two years.

About what proportion of couples make a go of their affairs up to engagement? Burgess and Wallin's study of 1,000 engagements showed

4 *Ibid.*, p. 123.
5 *Ibid.*

that only 20 to 30 percent of young people have never gone steadily with anyone except their future spouse.[6] Most college students have gone with two or more persons before becoming engaged.

When Should an Engagement Be Broken?

Students of marriage are very strongly of the opinion that many engagements should be broken; probably many more than are, for in most instances the broken engagement forestalls a marriage which, if carried out, would end in unhappiness and divorce. If this logic is sound, an increase in broken engagements might well mean a decrease in divorce.

The average engagement, however, is not without its doubts and conflicts. These alone cannot be reason enough for breaking an engagement. Are there any clues to indicate when a couple should cease their attempts at adjustment and turn instead to new relationships? In any serious affair, whether it involves a ring, a pin, or a promise, the following situations should be considered sure indications that the affair holds little promise of future success:

(1) *When many reforms in the partner are planned-for after marriage:* Changing one's ways—habits, ideas, and values—is a difficult job, one that takes time and effort. It always seems easier to try to change the other person to fit one's own way of life than to make fundamental changes in oneself.

This reluctance to change one's own ways, coupled with the desire to erase the annoying or distasteful habits, attitudes, and manners in the prospective mate, is the cause of many major difficulties in marriage. When one marries, he or she is taking a "person" with a fully developed personality, not a piece of clay that can be molded into any desired form. The man or girl who marries with the expectation of remaking the new spouse into a more desirable person is in for a rude awakening.

Everyone carries into marriage the same patterns and techniques of meeting problems that were used before marriage. The girl who has "played sick" rather than meet the unpleasant issues of life will likely resort to this same escape in marriage, where there are even more issues to be faced. The man who thinks this technique of adjustment will be changed by marriage is fooling himself.

The boy who has used drinking as an escape from problems before marriage will find even more worries to escape after marriage. In times of crisis he is likely to resort again to drinking rather than face and

---

[6] Ernest W. Burgess and Paul Wallin, *Engagement and Marriage* (Philadelphia: J. B. Lippincott Co., 1953), p. 148.

attempt to solve his problems. A girl who thinks she will change this is usually kidding herself.

Irritability, intolerance, moodiness, lack of respect and consideration, placing blame on others rather than shouldering it oneself—these and many other such traits are likely to be magnified rather than cured by marriage.

The writer once counseled a very intelligent couple who failed in marriage because the husband tried to correct the way his wife walked. His nagging became intolerable. Another couple failed in marriage when the husband kept trying to get his wife to correct a slight lisp in her speech which dated back to her childhood and which she probably could not correct. Why should these men have married these girls if they found such traits obnoxious? Why didn't they choose girls they wouldn't have to remake? Many other men would have had no objection to these traits.

One suspects it was not until after marriage that they realized these traits might reflect unfavorably on them in professional circles. Maybe they did object to the traits before marriage and sincerely thought they could change them. It may be that these traits became the object of attack, when more basic matters were involved.

There are exceptions to all rules, but most persons of marriageable age have already formed their basic personality structure and are not likely to be changed much by the pleading or the insistence of even a well-intentioned mate.

Mutual respect is an essential of the marriage relationships. If one finds himself losing it during engagement because of little traits that seem obnoxious, that prove embarrassing in social relationships, or that threaten to reflect unfavorably on one's work, conventions, or reputation, it is time to be wary. If one cannot face these irritations in the short period of companionship during engagement, how can one face them in the day-to-day relationships of marriage?

There are young people available whom one will not need to reform, if one's standards are realistic. If one's standards are so impossibly high that everyone of the opposite sex seems to have many obnoxious traits, then successful marriage is out of the question anyway. If one must do a lot of reforming, it is better to attempt to do it before marriage. Then, the chances are that the marriage will not take place and both will be saved a lot of trouble.

(2) *When the couple recognizes failure in adjusting toward a compatible relationship:* The patterns of adjustment that are established during the serious stage of dating will be the ones carried over into marriage. If roles of dominance and submission are evident then, they will characterize the marriage. If equality is the pattern established, this will likely continue into marriage. If quarreling is the method of adjustment,

rather than discussion and working out of solutions to problems, this will probably carry over into marriage. If one or the other of the pair puts parents, brothers, or sisters first in his emotional attachments, marriage will not cure this. An objective appraisal of the relationship by oneself, or better still by fair-minded friends and relatives who observe the match, will tell a great deal about what the marriage is to be. So, also, will an objective analysis by a marriage counselor or other professional person of wide experience. Such case-history observations are valid measures of the potential marriage, allowing for the margin of error that enters into all such human judgments.[7]

The most extensive study of serious love relationships to date, that by Burgess and Wallin, has related engagement success to later marriage success. The authors work on the assumption that the type of interpersonal relationships begun during the period of going steady and being engaged, will not be radically altered in marriage, and that, therefore, the adjustment made during the engagement is predictive of the kind of adjustment that will be made in the marriage.[8]

Among the engagement factors which were found to offer a basis for forecasting the success of the marriage are: (a) the nature and degree of love of the couple, (b) their temperamental compatibility, (c) their emotional interdependence, dependence, and independence, (d) their common interests, including their attitude toward children, (e) their method of making decisions and the locus of their authority, (f) their adaptability, (g) their vulnerability to adverse factors such as interference by relatives and friends, economic difficulties, etc.[9] This research suggests that the adjustment level and techniques reached during engagement sets a couple's pattern for the marriage and offers a basis for forecasting its success.

On a statistical basis, this study reports a correlation of .50 between engagement history and other engagement factors, and marriage success. The researchers explain the lack of a higher correlation by such factors as the inadequacy of tests of success of engagement, inadequate measures of success in marriage, and by dynamic factors which enter into the relationship in marriage that were not foreseen before marriage.

When one or the other is already sure, during the latter days of serious dating, that the pattern of relationship being worked out is not a satisfactory one, the engagement should be broken. Certainly this does not mean that any couple can agree on every little thing. But it does mean

---

[7] Burgess and Wallin (*ibid.*) find that such judgments have considerable merit in forecasting the outcome of a marriage.

[8] *Ibid.*

[9] *Ibid.*, p. 590-591, 620.

that they should reach compatible terms in the way they approach and handle their differences.

(3) *When one or both lose interest:* Loss of interest is one of the most frequently given reasons for the termination of an engagement or serious affair. As has been previously suggested this explanation is actually only a simple way of indicating any one of a number of things. Dissimilarity of backgrounds, interests, and values generally lead to gradual loss of attraction, as may the more or less serious personality deficiencies or unpleasant personal traits in one or the other—traits which were not discernible or were easily forgiven in the early days of the affair. Loss of interest may merely indicate that the relationship was never intended to lead to marriage—that it was, in fact, only a "grown-up" version of going steady. Many such casual affairs do become serious without the couple's giving up their intention to refrain from marriage. In the case of young people in school or professional training, this is often the case. When the motivation of marriage is lacking, attraction generally eventually dies of its own accord. When the attraction gets out of control and problems of deeper involvement, particularly of a sexual nature, begin to threaten, such couples usually change their plans in favor of marriage or they break up.

The folk expression for the undesirable deep emotional involvement is "getting too serious," by which women mean that the male has begun to demand a sexual relationship, and by which men mean "she wants to get married."

In any case loss of interest should be taken seriously, for if a couple cannot maintain interest in each other in the rather casual and playful relationships of engagement, how long could their interest survive in marriage—facing each other at the breakfast table every morning?

Breaking Up

Occasionally, a couple feel trapped in their relationship with each other. When they say this, they may mean several things—emotional involvement that they find difficult to break, physical attachment where a complete sexual relationship has been established, social entrapment where pregnancy has taken place, or where family and friends and possessions have become involved.

Men more often feel trapped in the serious dating relationship than do women, although Kirkpatrick and Caplow's study shows only 7 percent often felt that way and 23 percent occasionally felt that way.[10] Where

[10] Kirkpatrick and Caplow, *op. cit.*, p. 121.

sex experience is involved, this study suggests that the man more often feels that way than does the woman, since he may feel it would be unfair to terminate the relationship. If an affair has been of long duration the man may feel, too, that it is unjust to drop the woman after having kept her out of the marriage market so long.

The emotional damage of the breakup is, of course, the important thing from the standpoint of facing the future. Unless the relationship terminates by mutual agreement and on the basis of loss of interest, there is likely to be severe readjustment problems for at least one of the mates. Most student reactions indicate that there is considerable emotional turmoil in the breakup of a serious affair.[11] In fact, one suspects that the breakup of love affairs is responsible for the most severe emotional crises facing young people today. A house mother who audited one of the author's classes declared that love affairs were the most serious problems with which she had to deal in her sorority.

Steps in Breaking an Engagement

The buildup of a love relationship is a long and more or less slow process. Breaking one that has reached the point of engagement usually is a slow process, too, rather than a sudden catastrophic act.

In the background of the breakup are such factors as repeated misunderstandings, conflicts, and a growing awareness of differences in background, aspirations, values, and life plans. There may be parental opposition or the opposition of other relatives and friends, coldness due to separations or to a growing awareness of obnoxious, or at least undesirable, personality traits. Perhaps there is also a growing awareness of cultural, economic, religious, or other differences that foreshadow trouble.

Assuming this kind of background in the couple's love development, the five steps through which the breakup goes, according to the most extensive study of it made to date,[12] are: (1) difficulties involving misunderstandings and quarrels, (2) the actual breaking of the engagement which may be an abrupt act or a tapering-off process, (3) the emotional crisis, the severity of which depends somewhat upon the extent to which it has been expected by both parties, (4) the rebound experience which often leads to a new emotional involvement with someone else, (5) a reappraisal of the engagement experience in terms of future behavior. This study finds that the person is often more cautious in making a new commitment, sometimes even cynical concerning the fidelity of the opposite sex.

[11] *Ibid.*
[12] Burgess and Wallin, *op. cit.*, pp. 297-301.

Healing the Broken Heart

In Samoa, where all love affairs tend toward the casual side, the prevailing philosophy is that there is nothing like a new love to cure the pain of the old. The early remarriage of divorced persons in the United States is some indication that the philosophy has some following here.[13] No doubt many people in their early failures in love also follow this philosophy. The phrase "catching him on the rebound" is not entirely myth.

The period of time required "to get over it" varies little between broken engagements and other serious affairs. In both cases the range is from one or two weeks to over two years.[14]

College students studied at the University of Minnesota were asked by Kirkpatrick and Caplow about various "adaptive reactions" in an attempt to get some insight into the emotions and problems that followed the breakup of serious affairs.[15] Findings appear here:[16]

Adaptive behavior	Male affairs (Number 230) percent	Female affairs (Number 414) percent
Frequenting places with common associations	11.3	10.0
Avoiding places with common associations	2.9	3.4
Avoiding meetings	4.7	5.1
Attempting meetings	5.9	4.3
Remembering only unpleasant things	2.3	3.9
Remembering only pleasant things	15.6	15.8
Dreaming about partner	15.5	11.2
Daydreaming	14.3	11.4
Imagining recognition	6.4	7.9
Liking or disliking people because of resemblance	5.5	5.4
Imitating mannerisms	1.8	2.1
Preserving keepsakes	7.0	10.8
Reading over old letters	6.8	8.7

There is considerable evidence here of daydreaming and of thinking about pleasant bygone dating days.

About half of the group, this research shows, got over the affair immediately, but a third of the men and a fifth of the women said it took

[13] Discussed in Chapter 31.

[14] Judson T. Landis, and Mary G. Landis, *Building a Successful Marriage*, Fourth Edition (Englewood Cliffs, N. J.: Prentice-Hall, Inc., 1963), p. 234, Table 5.

[15] Kirkpatrick and Caplow, *op. cit.*

[16] *Ibid.*, p. 125.

them several weeks. Another fifth of the women and 7.7 percent of the men said it took them several months. Five percent of the men and 5.3 percent of the women said it took a year. The real sufferers, 5.3 percent of women and 2.3 percent of the men said it took several years. One may well suppose that some of this group will never get over the broken affair to the point of being able to love and marry.

Getting over an engagement is similar. The time required may range all the way from a week or two to over two years. Judson T. Landis indicates that over two-thirds of college young people get over the emotional effects of a broken engagement in less than six months, and only 12 percent suffer ill effects after a period of two years.[17]

His study of 1,059 students in eleven colleges showed that the typical reaction of the college young person to the breakup of love affairs is to remember the association as a pleasant one. About two-thirds have this reaction.[18] Almost as many soon begin dating somebody else as an aftereffect of the breakup of the engagement. More than a fourth continue to daydream about the lost lover.

Almost a third of the girls preserve keepsakes from the previous love affair; few boys do this. Half of the young people report trying to avoid meeting him or her afterward. About an equal number attempt to meet him or her. Girls are more likely to reread old letters, to remember pleasant associations, frequent places where the couple have been together, daydream, and so forth. It is only rarely that one or the other thinks of suicide.

No doubt the kind of emotional reaction that follows a broken love affair depends somewhat on the way the break is made. There are mean ways to break up, just as there are mean ways to carry out any other social relationship. If the couple discusses the situation reasonably and tries to face a solution together, as adults, the aftereffects should not be too serious. The most tragic affairs, no doubt, are those in which one person is still very deeply attached and wishes to continue the relationship to marriage and the other, seeing no possible future in the situation, breaks it abruptly without discussing the matter with the partner. This is particularly serious for the individual who is left with the feeling that something is seriously wrong with him or her, personally.

The broken affair or engagement also becomes a serious threat to future marriage prospects if the lost partner was idealized to the point that all future affairs pale. The "phantom lover" experience seems to be very rare today, when most young people have had enough experience with dating to know that they have another chance. One suspects that the seriousness with which most breakups are taken is more an indication of

17 Landis and Landis, *op. cit.*, p. 237, Table 6.
18 *Ibid.*

previous experience than it is a measure of love. There are exceptions, of course, but the individual who has dated widely before becoming serious can probably face the future with some optimism. Those with little or no previous dating would be more likely to take the experience seriously and suffer bereavement on its involuntary termination.

Young people who are never again able to let themselves be carried away, after the failure of a love relationship, may well consider a marriage with less love than the "great love" they lost. This is especially true if they are able to bring themselves to see that the "great love" was a product of frustration and that it too would have taken on normal proportions had it not been forcibly terminated.

Some persons approaching spinsterhod or bachelorhood may be trying to duplicate former loves that exists only in their imaginations. Such loves become something heavenly after they are broken off. In all these cases it is the one who did not wish to have the affair broken who finds future love and marriage for himself or herself difficult.

Even for those who get over the breakup with a minimum of pain, there are serious questions left to resolve. "What to do afterward?" is a big question that faces both the man and the girl. Getting back into circulation takes time and effort, deciding whether to date right away, "rest up," or "call it quits" with the opposite sex is also a serious question.

Most of us have heard or known of a person who "married on the rebound"—married the first person to be found after a broken engagement or divorce. Such marriages have very little chance of succeeding for they are seldom based on a solid foundation of long acquaintance and similar backgrounds, attitudes, and plans.

The individual who marries immediately after a broken engagement or divorce usually does so out of loneliness or a desire to prove to himself and others that somebody wants him. Naturally, one's pride and self-confidence get a blow from a broken engagement, but taking someone on the rebound will only add problems to an already confused situation.

The best course to follow is to "slow down." Rejoin the crowd, but don't fling oneself into a mad frenzy of dates and parties. Give oneself a little time to think things over, get him or her out of mind, toss out or put away all the things that act as reminders. When dating does begin again let it be with several persons, thus safeguarding oneself from an engagement or marriage on the rebound by putting off going steady for a while.

In summary, like many a venture of choice, affairs of the heart in our romance-minded culture often come to an untimely and unexpected end. This is undoubtedly as it should be. The opportunity to correct a mistake, once it is recognized, is an important one. The chief difficulty arises when the two people involved do not agree that the time has come to part. Even though not all engagements and serious affairs are of the stuff that promises permanency and happiness, "breaking off" is often a difficult, even heartbreaking business.

Attitudes have changed greatly in the last fifty years on this score. There was a time when the broken engagement was considered, in many circles, grounds for a breach-of-promise suit. The failure of the male, particularly, to carry out a promise to a woman whose time and attention he had commanded was considered a serious insult to her family, to her personal dignity, and a liability to her future. Today, breach-of-promise suits are still possible in some states, but in many they have been outlawed. In either case custom no longer favors such action by the woman. Her dignity today, it is assumed, is best defended not by the law, but by an attitude—real or assumed—of complete indifference to the former love.

But even an appearance of indifference is often difficult to muster at such a time. It may be some consolation, however, to realize that most individuals get over the emotional turmoil in a relatively short period of time and are able to go back into the dating game for another try.

A little thought about appropriate and constructive activities at such a time can do much, it has been found, to shorten the period of bitterness or pain. The total experience is often found to be an asset in the long run.

The evidence of this chapter suggests that the game of love has its brutal and painful aspects. An easy cure would be to revert to age-old custom and let someone else do the mating. The price of individual choice is risk of failure. Individual mate-seeking is an emotionally wasteful and, in rare cases, a tragic process, but as two researchers conclude from their study of college courtship, "Pending the advent of a social engineer who can guide young people directly to their ideal mates, a more or less painful process of selection and rejection—of making and breaking courtships—must take place.[19]

Problems

1. After an engagement of 16 months which of the following discoveries would probably lead you to break your engagement?
   a. He or she has an uncle in a mental institution.
   b. He or she confesses to having had sexual relations with another person at the age of 13.

19 Kirkpatrick and Caplow, *op. cit.*, p. 121.

c. He or she refuses to join your church.

d. He or she suggests not inviting a certain old friend to the wedding because "he wears such odd clothes people would laugh."

e. He or she refuses to establish a home in another community because of parental wishes.

f. He or she still enjoys flirting with casual acquaintances.

g. He or she shows slight tendencies toward characteristics of the other sex.

h. He or she looks down upon the social and economic status of your family.

i. He or she keeps asking questions about your past instead of reassuring you of unqualified devotion.

j. He or she suddenly suggests that you extend your engagement for another six months and that three of these months be spent in separation to test the love.

2. Your close friend is brokenhearted because his girl has just returned their engagement ring. What would your advice to him be?

a. Forget her and start dating Jean who thinks you're attractive.

b. Ask her to give you one more chance.

c. Try to make her jealous by dating other girls.

d. Talk it over with her parents.

e. Spend most of your free time on something else for a little while—reading, outdoor life, traveling.

f. Make sure that some of the other girls know that breaking up was her decision.

g. Decide once and for all that it's better to date than to ever get serious.

3. Do you believe that if a young man begins to tire of his fiancée he should:

a. Tell her outright and break the engagement.

b. Gradually shows his loss of interest.

c. Ask a friend to tell her.

d. Be seen with someone else.

e. Wait for her to break the engagement no matter how long it takes.

f. Initiate the subject deviously even if it takes several weeks to make the point.

Do the views of the boys and girls in the class tend to differ in their choice of alternatives and the arguments by which they support them?

4. List the advantages of a broken engagement over a broken marriage.

5. Bob and Marcy are physically very much attracted to one another. They enjoy the same books and sports, they agree on family size and politics, but Marcy suggests breaking the engagement when she discovers how different are their codes of ethics. Think of a number of situations in which ethics might seriously endanger a marriage.

6. *Sociodrama:* Jim and Kay thought they were "made for each other," but now Kay is suggesting they break their engagement. Let their friendly but serious discussion touch upon some of the situations or discoveries that have brought them to the point of breakup.

7. *Sociodrama:* The wedding is a week away. Most of the gifts have arrived; the wedding gown is finished, the wedding invitations have been sent out, and reservations have even been made for a honeymoon. The young bride-to-be

has just admitted to herself what she has subconsciously known for a long time, that she has been in love with love, not with her fiancé. In a burst of fear and uncertainty she rushes to her parents for advice and comfort.

The drama pictures the attitudes of a levelheaded father, the excited mother, and the very upset daughter.

8. Do you think that if our customs condoned premarital sexual relations, as do the Scandinavian customs, there would be less sexual tension between couples and, consequently, fewer broken engagements?

9. Should a couple refrain from breaking their engagement because of the embarrassment it would cause and the talk it would create?

Selected References

ARTICLES IN BOOKS OF READINGS

CAVAN, Ruth Shonle, *Marriage and the Family in the Modern World: A Book of Readings* (New York: Thomas Y. Crowell Co., 1960).
1. BURGESS, Ernest W., and WALLIN, Paul, "Factors in Broken Engagements," Reading 31.
2. LOOMIS, Bettina, "Breaking an Engagement by Mutual Consent," Reading 32.
3. ————, "How to Untie an Old Beau," Reading 33.

General References

BURGESS, Ernest W., and WALLIN, Paul, *Engagement and Marriage* (Philadelphia: J. B. Lippincott Co., 1953), Chs. 8, 9.
KIRKPATRICK, Clifford, and CAPLOW, Theodore, "Courtship in a Group of Minnesota Students," *American Journal of Sociology*, 51:114-125, September, 1945.
LANDIS, Judson, and LANDIS, Mary G., *Building a Successful Marriage*, Fourth Edition (Englewood Cliffs, N. J.: Prentice-Hall, Inc., 1963), Ch. 14.

20

The Research Score on
Premarital Sex Experience

In more sophisticated sectors of our society, particularly among college youth, there is a growing tendency to question traditional morality in the area of sex behavior. This takes the form of judging the sexual act, not in terms of right and wrong, but rather in terms of whether or not it is a genuine expression of affection. The test becomes a psychological rather than a moral one. The question has changed from "Is it right?" to "Is it right under the circumstances which exist between us?" or "Will it improve our relationship or weaken it?"

While there can be little doubt, from research evidence, that the vast majority of college girls themselves live by a moral guide, an increasing number are willing to grant others the right to live by the psychological test. Perhaps the greatest risk in this kind of atmosphere is that many girls, who have a built-in conscience clearly defining right for themselves, try to embrace the other code and find themselves inflicted with deep psychological wounds. Their rationalizations, their reading of supporting literature from "experts," their "bull" sessions among their peers do not quiet their conscience. They are haunted by the feeling that they have betrayed themselves.

This is by no means a female problem only. The male is more immune from restrictions of morality because few families instill in the male so strict a code, yet there are college men who suffer deeply from having reached beyond the bounds of their internalized moral values. There are also more college men who live by a strict moral code than the popular magazines would lead one to believe.[1]

[1] These observations are based on the reading of student autobiographies in the writer's classes. The autobiographies are written anonymously each semester.

A Broad View of Premarital Sex Experience

An anthropological study by Murdock of 250 societies through-out the world shows that 70 percent permit sexual experimentation before marriage.[2] Even among the 30 percent which place a taboo upon premarital sex relations, the taboo most often applies only to girls. In many of these societies, marriage comes soon after puberty. The prohibition against premarital intercourse is actually, for the most part, a prohibition against prepubertal intercourse. In most societies also the taboo is upper class only.

This study concludes that there is nothing in human societies generally to indicate that a taboo on premarital sex relations has any value to survival of the group. In most societies it is assumed that premarital intercourse has no relationship to postmarital fidelity (all societies seek postmarital fidelity); in other words, it does not seem to interfere with the function of the family institution, once marriage has been entered into.[3]

Where premarital sexual relations are sanctioned, intercourse usually is not extensive or promiscuous. The society recognizes it as a means of preparing for marriage, rather than as a means of indulging in sexual excitement as such.

So much for human experience in the broader perspective. Are there reasons why our society should differ in this matter from the general norm? Does it actually differ?

Reasons for and against Premarital Coitus

The question of premarital coitus is one of the most important issues facing couples today from the beginning of their casual contacts through the engagement period. Numerous reasons for and against premarital coitus are advanced. Kinsey has summarized these arguments as found in the marriage manuals.[4]

REASONS FOR PREMARITAL INTERCOURSE

1. It may satisfy a physiologic need for a sexual outlet.
2. It may become a source of immediate physical and psychological satisfaction.

[2] George P. Murdock, "Sexual Behavior: What Is Acceptable?" *Journal of Social Hygiene*, 36:1-31, 1950.

[3] Evidence that it may do so in American society is presented later in this chapter.

[4] Alfred C. Kinsey and others, *Sexual Behavior in the Human Female* (Philadelphia: W. B. Saunders Co., 1953), pp. 307-309. By permission of Dr. Kinsey.

3. If there is no guilt, it may increase one's ability to function more effectively in other, nonsexual fields.
4. It is more valuable than solitary sexual activity for developing one's capacity to make emotional adjustments with other persons.
5. It may develop one's capacity to make the particular sorts of emotional adjustments which are needed in marital relationships.
6. It may provide training in the sorts of physical techniques that may be involved in marital coitus.
7. It may test the capacities of two persons to make satisfactory sexual adjustments after marriage.
8. It is easier to learn to make emotional and physical adjustments at an earlier age; they are learned with greater difficulty after marriage.
9. Failure in a premarital relationship is socially less disastrous than failure after marriage.
10. Heterosexual experience may prevent the development of a homosexual pattern of behavior.
11. Premarital coitus may lead to marriage.
12. In at least some social groups, an individual may acquire status by fitting into the group pattern for behavior.

REASONS AGAINST PREMARITAL INTERCOURSE

1. The danger for the female of pregnancy.
2. The danger if abortion is used to terminate a pregnancy.
3. The possibility of contracting a venereal disease.
4. The undesirability of a marriage which is forced by a premarital pregnancy.
5. The traumatic effects of coitus which is had under the inadequate circumstances which are supposed to attend most premarital relations.
6. The damage done by the participant's guilt over the infringement of the moral law.
7. The guilt at the loss of virginity, and its subsequent effect on marriage.
8. The fear that males lose respect for and will not marry a female with whom they have had coitus.
9. The damage done when guilt feelings are reawakened after marriage.
10. The guilt resulting from fear of public disapproval.
11. The risk and fear of social difficulties that may follow discovery of the relationship.
12. The risk and fear of legal difficulties that may follow any discovery of the relationship.
13. The possibility that premarital coitus which is satisfactory may delay or prevent altogether the individual from marrying.
14. The possibility that the coitus may make one feel obligated to marry the sexual partner.
15. The possibility that guilt over the coitus may break up an otherwise desirable friendship with the sexual partner.

16. The overemphasis which premarital experience may place on the physical aspects of friendship and marriage.
17. The likelihood that premarital irregularities will lead to later extramarital infidelities, with consequent damage to the marriage.
18. The possibility that the female will be less capable of responding satisfactorily in her marital coitus because of the traumatic effects of premarital experience.
19. The fact that premarital coitus is morally wrong.
20. The principle that abstinence from such activities may develop one's will power.

Is Premarital Sex Experience Usual in the United States?

The general impression is that premarital sexual intercourse is on the increase. Research agrees. Kinsey found that all forms of sex experience showed a marked increase between the generation born in 1890 and that born in the 1900-1910 period.[5] The increase in sex activity among those born since the 1900-1910 decade has not been striking, although the most recent decade of births dealt with was 1920 to 1929. Some other research confirms these findings.[6] One suspects that taboos may not be as strict as they were even a generation or so ago. Yet among the college population, which is no doubt more strict in this matter than the general population, few women have had premarital intercourse. The 1952 study[7] of 1,600 students in eleven universities, to which frequent reference has been made, shows that only about 10 percent of the girls reported having had premarital intercourse. A study[8] of a Florida university group reported similar findings. It is possible, of course, that college girls may not always report this fact accurately.

The Kinsey sample, which deals with large numbers of people with less education, as well as with educated samples, shows a much higher ratio of premarital intercourse. Half of the unmarried women in his sample had had sexual intercourse. Of the unmarried men in his sample, 85 percent had had coitus. The educated group in the Kinsey study of the male had had coitus less often than had the uneducated.[9] Of his sample of college girls less than 20 percent had had sexual relations.

[5] Ibid. Comparisons throughout the book are made by decade of birth.
[6] Lewis M. Terman and others, Psychological Factors in Marital Happiness (New York: McGraw-Hill Book Co., 1938). Terman finds an increase with younger age of couples in his sample.
[7] Judson T. Landis and Mary G. Landis, Building a Successful Marriage, Fourth Edition (Englewood Cliffs, N. J.: Prentice-Hall, Inc., 1963), p. 175.
[8] Winston W. Ehrmann, "Student Co-operation in a Study of Dating Behavior," Marriage and Family Living, 14:4 ff., November, 1952; also his Premarital Dating Behavior (New York: Henry Holt and Co., 1959).
[9] Alfred C. Kinsey and others, Sexual Behavior in the Human Male (Philadelphia: W. B. Saunders Co., 1948).

Data dealing with engaged couples in the higher educational levels show a far higher rate of sexual intercourse previous to marriage than these general statistics present. Burgess and Wallin's study of a thousand engagements reported that about 45 percent of their couples had had premarital coitus.[10] Kanin and Howard, studying 177 wives of college students at a midwest university, show about the same ratio (43.5 percent).[11] This study also reports what other studies have shown regarding the influence of social class and religion as factors: the lower the social class of the wife, the more likely she is to have permitted sexual intercourse before marriage, particularly if she is engaged to an upper-class male. Seriousness about religion is a great deterrent to premarital sexual intercourse. Concerning social class, Kanin and Howard suggest that more than differences in class mores are in operation; the upper-class male is probably exploitive of the lower-class female in a way he is not with one of his own status or above; the lower-class female, lacking other devices of attraction, uses sex to the maximum advantage in winning her man.

The Conflict of Professional Opinion

A few counselors are taking a strong position in favor of premarital sex experience. Walter Stokes,[12] for example, is strong in his belief that the best sexual development is possible through premarital sex experience under emotionally favorable conditions. He believes that in women there is a relationship between the sex response and the development of vaginal musculature. He takes no stock in the idea that we should teach that sex is beautiful and proper, but that there should be no experience with it until after marriage.

He bases his argument largely on clinical evidence. He finds that the young male who comes for counsel previous to marriage boasting that he has never masturbated, or had any sex experience, offers almost hopeless prospects for success in marriage. He goes so far as to say that all of the chaste young men turn out to be impotent to the degree of requiring extensive psychiatric treatment. Dr. Stokes finds, also, that girls who have had no sex experience are more likely to faint during vaginal examination and to otherwise exhibit the tenseness and fear that grow out of lack of sex training and experience.

The big, unanswered question is, of course, would these same types, had they had premarital sex experience, have been any different? Or

---

[10] Ernest W. Burgess and Paul Wallin, *Engagement and Marriage* (Philadelphia: J. B. Lippincott Co., 1953).

[11] Eugene J. Kanin and David H. Howard, "Postmarital Consequences of Premarital Sex Adjustments," *American Sociological Review*, 23:557-562, October, 1958.

[12] See discussion on the Stokes article, *Marriage and Family Living*, 15:39-49, August, 1953.

would the conditioning which led to these negative attitudes toward sex also lead them to the same consequences which he observes had they attempted more intimate forms of sex experience.

He does present limited positive evidence[13] for his position. He indicates that he has worked experimentally with a group of patients who came to him some years ago at the time of their marriage. He has helped these patients train their children without the usual sex inhibitions, and reports that when these youngsters are ready for marriage, he finds an amazing zest for sex enjoyment, greater maturity, and greater sense of responsibility than is usual in young people of their age.

Dr. Albert Ellis,[14] clinical psychologist and counselor in New York City, likewise takes the position that virginity and chastity represent cultural lags in our thinking about marriage preparation. He believes that extreme sexual difficulties in his clients are directly attributable to taboos against premarital sex relations, masturbation, and so forth.

Philosophically, this view has a certain weakness. Social systems have always operated on the assumption that maximum physical satisfaction is rarely or never possible in human relationships—that only through restraint on biological appetite, by restricting it to customary channels of expression, can human society as such exist. The sex impulse is, therefore, always regulated in relation to the goals and objectives of the family itself. Societies are concerned, not with the individual receiving maximum satifaction from the sexual act, but with the establishing of controls which act as a bulwark to the family system.

Most counselors are firmly convinced that conventions must be given a place in appraising premarital sex behavior, and they feel just as certain that, conventions being what they are, premarital chastity is desirable. Among counselors and authors who are strong in their support of the mores are David Mace, Harold T. Christensen, Abraham Stone, and Emily Mudd.[15]

The Logical Case for Chastity

In cultures like those of northwestern Europe and Scandinavia, where the relationships between the sexes are courtship-centered rather than dating-centered, the initiation of sexual intercourse during the premarital period is relatively common.[16] This is possible for two reasons.

---

[13] *Ibid.*, p. 267.

[14] Albert Ellis, *Marriage and Family Living*, 15:242-244, August, 1953, Discussion.

[15] See discussion on the Stokes article, *Marriage and Family Living*, 15:39-49, August, 1953.

[16] In Sweden, about 9 percent of children have been born out of wedlock during recent years; in Denmark, about 10 percent. The proportion ran up to 15 percent in Sweden during the 1920's and 1930's. It is estimated that 50 to 55 percent of first births

First, by limiting association to one male at a time, the girl is assured of being able to legally fix responsibility for paternity. Second, the intent of the couple from the beginning of their serious relationship is marriage. Pregnancy may mark the actual beginning of marriage plans. In a culture like our own where dating is simply a game between a girl and boy, marriage comes late, if ever, in the plans of most couples. It is not until they have settled down to dating one person for a considerable length of time that ideas of a permanent pair relationship even enters into their plans.

Sex activity in the premarital period, therefore, if it comes before the time of serious intentions, is highly hazardous from the standpoint of the girl. In our mobile society with its casual dating, it is difficult for the social system to fix responsibility for paternity. This means that if premarital sex activity were condoned the girl would very likely end up without protection for her child. The age-long expectation of society that the male will provide for the female and helpless young is defeated. Under such circumstances, a society can hardly permit sex relationships during the dating period, and can scarcely sanction it during the engagement period, for dating experience is so extensive in our culture that even the engagement period is a tentative relationship. This is evidenced by the fact that not less than one in three engagements are broken.

Of course, our customs are not so well reasoned out as this argument suggests. The mores rather than any well thought out social policy are the major factor in the control of sex behavior. Sex conduct is based on our Puritanic culture. American morality is sex-centered. Morality has become almost synonymous with being discreet in sex matters. If one inquires or comments about another's morals, he is usually thinking entirely of his sex attitudes and conduct, not of his financial honesty, his truthfulness, his loyalty to persons or causes.

This commonly accepted conception of decency, powerful in itself as a means of controlling sex activity, receives further support from the threat and fear engendered by public opinion. Unlike the Scandinavian

---

in these countries take place prior to 9 months of marriage, and that about 27 percent of births in Holland do. These figures were given the author by population and birth control authorities in the various countries in 1953. For Swedish data on children born out of wedlock, see *Social Sweden* (Stockholm: Social Welfare Board, 1952), pp. 214-218.

A comparison of Norwegian and American college students shows that of Norwegian students 80 percent consider full sex relations proper during engagement. Only about 28 percent of American college students agree. See William Simenson and Gilbert Geis, "Courtship Patterns of Norwegian and American University Students," *Marriage and Family Living*, 18:334-338, November, 1956; see also Harold T. Christensen, "Cultural Relativism and Premarital Sex Norms," *American Sociological Review*, 25:31-39, February, 1960; also Harold T. Christensen and George R. Carpenter, "Value-Behavior Discrepancies Regarding Premarital Coitus in Three Western Cultures," *American Sociological Review*, 27:66-74, February, 1962; also their "Timing Patterns in the Development of Sexual Intimacy," *Marriage and Family Living*, 24:32-35, February, 1962.

TWO SYSTEMS OF PAIR RELATIONSHIPS

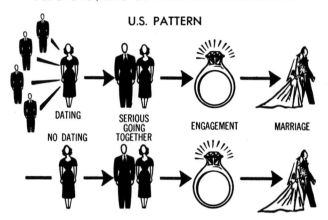

PICTOGRAPH CORPORATION

SOURCE: Paul H. Landis.

FIGURE 20-1————Under the first system of pair relationships premarital coitus carries a much greater risk than under the second. The first kind characterizes the United States; the second, Western Europe and Scandinavia.

peoples, we still make much of the term "illegitimacy"; and the woman who bears a child out of wedlock has more than her own conscience to reckon with. Regardless of the circumstances, she is generally met by a hostile and unsympathetic community.

Fear of pregnancy with all the social stigmas attached represents society's most powerful control over the premarital relationships of its young people. This particular type of control is effective over the males' behavior only indirectly, through its influence on the female. It exposes the woman to great social risk if contraception is faulty. It threatens to ruin her reputation, disrupt her life, and stigmatize an innocent child.

Unreasonable though it is in its harsh and unequal effect upon women, there is here a powerful restraint on sex behavior. In this respect our culture is in striking contrast to the northwestern European culture, and that of Scandinavian countries, in which the unwed mother is referred to merely as an unmarried mother. In these cultures the state is custodian of the child, through welfare guardians.[17] It is the responsibility

17 In 1950 there were 84,393 children in Sweden born out of wedlock, and under the supervision of child-welfare guardians. Paternity had been established for 76,798 or 85.2 percent of these by acknowledgment of the father, and 14.8 by court decision. There were only 7,595 cases in which paternity had not been established; see *Social Sweden, loc. cit.*

of the state to locate the father and give the child his name. The law provides that the child will have equal rights to inheritance with the child of any marriage the father may have. There is no compulsion to marry, but the father assumes the same financial responsibility of parenthood that he would assume if he were married. The child has all the rights he would have if the couple married. The mother has the regular protections of social security available to all mothers in addition to certain extra benefits. This situation permits the equal freedom of men and women to participate in the sex act, both before marriage and in extramarital sexual relationships—a basic necessity in sex equality.

Until 100 percent effective birth control exists, or until adequate provisions are made for the unmarried mother and her child, there is still considerable logic in the existence of premarital sex taboos in our society regardless of the salutary effect premarital intercourse may or may not have on sexual adjustment in marriage.[18]

The fact remains that premarital pregnancy is still a risk to be reckoned with. The illegitimate birth rate has greatly increased over recent decades (see Figure 20-2). In 1940, births out of wedlock accounted for 3.8 percent of all births; in 1961, 5.6 percent. Only one child in 26 was born out of wedlock in 1940; one in 19, in 1961. Either one must assume that a large proportion of unmarried girls voluntarily conceive out of wedlock or that accidental pregnancy is still very much a risk. Vital statistical data show that these pregnancies are not primarily among young and ignorant teenagers. The highest rate of pregnancy is found in the age group 25-29; the next highest, 20-24.

Aside from morality, society has great economic stakes involved. More than a fifth of all these children are cared for on welfare rolls. Where there is no father to assume the economic load, others must bear it: parents, other relatives, persons who adopt, or welfare agencies. One need only compare the load of illegitimate children in this country with that in the Latin American cultures to realize how great the load can become should morality become obsolete.

Effect of Premarital Sex Experience on Engagement

The sharing of sexual experiences, providing they are mutually sought and satisfying, does much to strengthen the close relationship of husband and wife. When intercourse takes place during the engagement period it can be assumed that it does so by mutual agreement. Do mutually sought sexual relations at this time have the same beneficial effects upon the engagement as they have upon a marriage relationship?

In studying couples during the period of their engagement, the most

18 For some evidence on this point turn to p. 393.

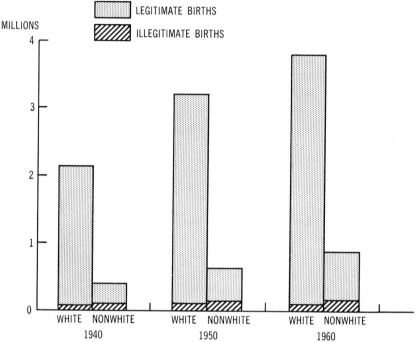

LEGITIMATE AND ILLEGITIMATE BIRTHS
BY RACE, 1940-60

Source: U. S. Public Health Service, National Vital Statistics Division, "Illegitimacy and Dependency," September, 1963.

FIGURE 20-2———Although fear of pregnancy seems to be decreasing among youth, as a deterrent to sexual intercourse out of wedlock, the number of illegitimate births is increasing. In 1940, only one in 26 children was born out of wedlock; now the figure is one in 19. These fatherless children run a quarter of a million a year now, and more than a fifth must be carried on welfare rolls. At present, even the adoption market appears to be more than satisfied. Thus, pregnancy is still a risk of premarital sexual intercourse.

authoritative study[19] to date asked 81 engaged men and 74 engaged women the effect of premarital intercourse on their relationship with each other. Over 90 percent of each group said they thought it strengthened the relationship. Slightly over 5 percent of the women thought it had a weakening effect, but only 1 percent of the men thought so. The others thought that it had no effect at all on their relationship.

[19] Burgess and Wallin, *op. cit.*, p. 372.

These reactions, of course, must be weighed in light of the long-term effects of engagement and marriage; the temporary effect may be to strengthen the relationship, but the long-term effects may be quite diffrent. It is possible too that couples at the time of the interview might have been rationalizing considerably. In any case, it was found that engagement adjustment scores were somewhat higher for the group that was not having intercourse. On the question of whether engaged men and women had had sexual relations with persons other than the spouse, adjustment scores were slightly higher for those who had had no such relations, but there was no significant difference between those who had had sexual relations with the spouse only and with the spouse and others. Nor did frequency of intercourse with the spouse or with others seem to have any relationship to the problem of adjustment. Whether or not they had intercourse at all seems to have been the significant factor.

This study shows further that more couples who had had intercourse than those who had not had intercourse broke their engagements. Although the sample dealing with broken engagements is small (31 cases), it lends support to the view of some doctors and counselors that the male's desire for marriage is lessened when his sex needs are being regularly satisfied outside marriage. This is an important point since sex is generally one of the most powerful incentives to marriage in the male.

Among the reactions most often reported by couples engaging in intercourse were relief of physical tension and confidence that they were going to be married. Among unfavorable feelings most frequently reported were fear of social disapproval, which was mentioned by more than a fifth of both men and women, and fear of pregnancy, which was mentioned by a fourth of men and 26 percent of women. Sixteen percent of women also reported feelings of guilt.

The researchers consider it significant that none of the group, in reporting feelings or justifications that accompanied premarital sex relations, mentioned this as a test of sexual compatibility. They conclude that premarital sex relationships, therefore, are not entered into as a guide to physical compatibility; rather they occur, not with any long-time definite purpose in mind, but as a relief for "frequent and intensive erotic stimulation."

Kirkendall's study has accumulated the case histories of 250 premarital relationships of college students, focusing interest on the quality of the interpersonal relationship which is associated with premarital intercourse.[20] The author of the study concludes that "practically all the premarital coitus in the pre-engagement period takes place under conditions

[20] Lester A. Kirkendall, "Premarital Sex Relations: The Problem and Its Implications," *Pastoral Psychology*, April, 1956; see also his *Premarital Intercourse and Interpersonal Relations* (New York: Julian Press, Inc., 1961).

which, in both the short and the long run, result in more suspicion, distrust, and less ability to set up a good relationship later." Some engaged couples are drawn closer together by coitus during the engagement period, but this study reports other cases where the couple was also drawn closer together by a decision not to have intercourse, indicating that an intimate level of communication may be the main factor in drawing them closer together. Kirkendall concludes that sexual intercourse usually weakens the relationship, and often terminates it.

He finds that motives of men and women differ, and this often leads to misunderstanding. The man usually enters into a sexual relationship merely for the physical thrill, to make himself feel a man, or to accomplish what some of his friends boast about accomplishing. A woman is more likely to enter the relationship to hold the man, or to push him into marriage. After the sexual relationship she may become possessive, show great anxiety to make the relationship permanent, and talk a great deal about marriage. The boastful man begins to feel more sober and sense that he is being pushed or trapped into marriage. Men in this situation are generally much less interested in marriage than are women.

Women generally sense more guilt than do men when they break the moral codes in the sexual area. This also leads them to push the marriage idea. With the loss of virginity, marriageability has been somewhat weakened as far as other prospective mates are concerned. If her violation of the code is discovered she is much more exposed to shame and social censure than is the man, so she feels much less safe. Often the greatest threat to her reputation comes from the man, who may be very indiscreet in boasting about his conquest to friends. This not only threatens the woman's reputation but makes it more likely that other men will expect sex favors if the pair break and she dates them.

Men are not undamaged by casual sexual experience. Many find it hard to settle down when the time comes to marry. Some are forced into marriage before they are ready by a sense of guilt, or because a girl with whom they have had intercourse becomes pregnant, fears she is pregnant, or merely claims to be to force marriage. (Pregnancy can be determined by a one-hour test which can be made by any reliable physician.)

LeMasters feels that sex tends to gloss over serious differences between couples so that these do not appear until after marriage. He believes many couples "neck their way out" of problems before marriage, rather than facing them. Sex thus becomes a confusing force during mate choice.[21]

In talking with engaged couples one frequently hears a young woman say, "My fiancé is always tense and cross before a weekend is over, but

21 E. E. LeMasters, *Modern Courtship and Marriage* (New York: The Macmillan Co., 1957), pp. 195-196.

I'm sure the problem is sex tensions." This may well be. It may be desirable, however, to take a second look at the relationships, and make sure that even the restrained sex play entered into is not an effort to keep from facing real issues, or a device for forcing complete sex relations.

Refraining from sexual intercourse during the engagement period is, of course, often extremely difficult, especially today when close physical contacts are customary.[22] Sexual intercourse, Burgess and Wallin found, is more often entered into by those who have prolonged their engagement 16 months or more.[23] Kinsey finds too that the incidence of premarital coitus increases with delayed marriage. The likelihood of women having an orgasm in premarital intercourse also increases with age. In other words, delay of marriage increases both the incidence of premarital coitus and of orgasmic experience. He finds too that those females who begin coitus early, marry early. Those who attain higher levels of education are more likely to have had premarital coitus by the time of their marriage because of later age of marriage.

Some feel that petting to the point of orgasm may be a part of the natural psychosexual development of this period, a satisfactory substitute for coitus, and a desirable preparation for marriage. It does permit the cultivation of sublimated forms of sex expression in the male and thus prepares him for the more complex and sympathetic part he is often expected to play in the sexual life of the modern married couple. It has the advantage of deferring pregnancy till marriage in cases where couples find it necessary to reduce sexual tension. Use of this outlet depends upon the extent to which intimate petting can be engaged in without guilt, perhaps more than on actual physical factors.

It must be recognized too that most young people have difficulty in petting to the point of orgasm without running considerable risk of actual intercourse. For many couples intercourse occurs, not after mutual agreement, but after mutual stimulation has erased most vestiges of their combined self-control. There are other possible disadvantages to this solution. It frequently brings satisfaction to only the male and, in addition, it is likely to leave some individuals with as great a feeling of guilt as would sexual intercourse.

Effect of Premarital Sex Experience on Sexual Adjustment in Marriage

A rationalization frequently used by young people for justify-premarital sexual relations is the wish to prove their adequacy for the sexual aspects of marriage, and also to prove that they are "physically

22 Ernest W. Burgess and Paul Wallin, *Engagement and Marriage* (Philadelphia: J. B. Lippincott Co., 1953), pp. 386-390.
23 *Ibid.*, Ch. 11.

mated." It is likely that some adolescent girls yield to this argument of the male because although they have no real sex interest they feel they should have. They may fear that they are frigid and cold because they do not feel a sex drive comparable to that of their male partner.

There is abundant evidence that the average woman, especially in her teens or even in her early twenties, has less capacity to respond sexually than she will have later.[24] It is not too likely that the average girl, during a short period of premarital sex experimentation, will develop the capacity to respond sexually to the point of orgasm unless she is much more precocious sexually than the average. Her failure to respond may create anxiety concerning her ability to respond when there is no real ground for such anxiety.

To learn whether or not premarital sexual intercourse affects sexual adequacy in marriage, one sociological study interviewed couples during engagement and again after several years of marriage.[25] This study shows that orgasmic adequacy in marriage is favorably related to premarital sex experience—the more sexual experience the wife has had, the more likely she is to experience a full orgasm in her marital relations. This generalization holds true for both women who had had sexual relations only with their future spouse and those who had had sexual experience with other men as well. These findings correspond to those reported by Terman[26] and Kinsey.[27]

Confirming support for this view is found by Kanin and Howard in studying the degree of sex satifaction on the wedding night and during the honeymoon of 177 wives of married students on a college campus in a midwest university.[28] The more complete their sex activity before marriage, the greater the likelihood of satifaction. Far more of the wives with premarital sexual experience, however, had sex difficulties during the early days of marriage, and of the 14 women who reported long-time difficulties beginning during the first two weeks of their marriage, all had had premarital sexual intercourse. Five of these women reported that they felt like "sex servants." This suggests that the woman who fails to hold the line before marriage, may have no bargaining power at all in restraining her husband after marriage.

In further study of this group, Kanin[29] reports that the upper-class girls reported least frequency of premarital coitus; the middle class, next; and the lower class, greatest frequency. He found that premarital coitus

24 Evidence is presented on pp. 492-497.

25 Ernest W. Burgess and Paul Wallin, *Engagement and Marriage* (Philadelphia: J. B. Lippincott Co., 1953), Ch. 12.

26 Terman and others, *op. cit.*

27 Alfred C. Kinsey and others, *Sexual Behavior in the Human Female* (Philadelphia: W. B. Saunders Co., 1953), p. 383.

28 Kanin and Howard, *op. cit.*

29 Eugene J. Kanin, "Premarital Sex Adjustment, Social Class and Associated Behavior," *Marriage and Family Living*, 22:258-262, August, 1960.

was associated with avoidance of a honeymoon, abbreviated dating histories (couples tended to move quickly into marriage), decrease in the use of premarital counseling, and a decrease in the usual psychological disturbances of the wedding day.

The American Institute of Family Relations collected some 2,000 questionnaires, predominately from among college graduates in the United States. The initial orgasmic response of those women who were virgins at marriage was 28 percent, compared to 39 percent of those who had had experiences of premarital intercourse. The differences vanish quickly with sexual experience in marriage. At the end of the first year, the following results were reported:

| | Percent having orgasm | |
	Virgins	Nonvirgins
Younger wives	67	63
Wives over 30	63	59

These data suggest that even with marriage greatly delayed (into the thirties) orgasmic response is not dependent on the cultivation of early response through premarital sex activity. Popenoe believes that there is evidence here, and in clinical observation as well, that a large part of "premarital sexual experience of young women is neurotic rather than normal."[30]

Confirming this view are Reevy's findings[31] concerning premarital petting and other forms of sexual activity, including sexual intercourse and marriage predictability scores. He summarizes his conclusions thus, "The group with unfavorable marital predictions can be characterized as being more active sexually than the group with favorable marital predictions."

Kinsey makes a strong case for the biological desirability of premarital sex experience, holding that long abstinence, restraint, and avoidance of physical contacts and emotional responses before marriage may well lead to the building of inhibitions which damage the capacity of the organism to respond sexually in marriage.[32] Petting to orgasm, intercourse to orgasm, or even masturbation to orgasm, he believes, help prepare the organism to react physiologically.

Those who masturbate extensively prior to marriage are more likely than others always to have orgasm in marriage,[33] and there is a close

30 Paul Popenoe, "Premarital Experience No Help in Sexual Adjustment after Marriage," *Family Life*, 21:1-2, August, 1961.

31 William R. Reevy, "Premarital Petting Behavior and Marital Happiness Prediction," *Marriage and Family Living*, 21:349-355, November 1959.

32 Alfred C. Kinsey and others, *Sexual Behavior in the Human Female* (Philadelphia: W. B. Saunders Co., 1953), p. 383.

33 *Ibid.*, p. 391.

relationship between the experience of intercourse to the point of orgasm prior to marriage and ability to reach it during the first year of marriage.[34] These findings, of course, may only mean that the highly sexed female is the one who engages in various kinds of sex stimulation prior to marriage.

One of the great faults of the Kinsey work was that he interpreted findings purely from the standpoint of biology. Sociologists have to recognize that moral reality is quite as binding on human beings as are biological impulses. In fact, moral suasion has precedence over biological impulse in human societies everywhere. Man cannot satisfy his sexual desires in defiance of moral codes and go unblemished either in self-conception or reputation.

Sociologists have pursued their study beyond the point of simple physiological response. In a study of the total sexual adjustment scores of 600 men and women in marriage, no relationship, favorable or unfavorable, was found between sexual adjustment scores of husbands and wives and premarital intercourse.[35] It was found, however, that there was a slight favorable relationship to good adjustment where each had had sexual experience with both the future spouse and others. (The sexual adjustment score was based on answers to questions relating to various aspects of the sexual relationship with the marriage partner.) Clearly, ability to achieve an orgasm is not a complete test of the adequacy of the sexual relationship.

On the other hand, even this sociological study concludes that there is no statistical foundation for the belief that premarital intercourse is unfavorable to sexual adjustment in marriage. It recognizes, however, that people who are most likely to suffer from fear, or guilt, and anxiety because of premarital intercourse do not engage in it.

This research carried the investigation one step further in an attempt to relate premarital sex experience to total adjustment in marriage as measured by (1) marital happiness, (2) general marital satisfaction, (3) love, and (4) marriage permanence.

The findings in general agree with those of Terman,[36] Davis,[37] Popenoe,[38] and Locke,[39] that virginity prior to marriage is most favorable to total marriage success.

[34] *Ibid.*, p. 329.
[35] Burgess and Wallin, *op. cit.*
[36] Terman and others, *op. cit.*, pp. 324-330.
[37] Katherine B. Davis, *The Factors in the Sex Life of 2,200 Women* (New York: Harper & Bros., 1939), p. 59.
[38] Popenoe, *op. cit.*
[39] Harvey J. Locke, *Predicting Adjustment in Marriage: A Comparison of a Divorced and a Happily Married Group* (New York: Henry Holt & Co., Inc., 1951), pp. 133-137. Locke found that a higher proportion of the divorced than the successfully married had had premarital sex relations.

This suggests that the total pattern of marriage adjustment is something quite different from sexual adjustment alone. It may well be that secondary reactions to the premarital sexual experience are the decisive ones rather than sexual adjustment as such. Guilt and anxiety, a lack of mutual confidence, a suspicion that the thing may happen again after marriage and establish a pattern of disloyalty—such feelings may be lurking in the background.

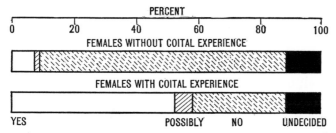

INTENT TO HAVE PREMARITAL COITUS

Source: Alfred C. Kinsey and others, *Sexual Behavior in the Human Female* (Philadelphia: W. B. Saunders Co., 1953). Reproduced by permission of Dr. Kinsey.

FIGURE 20-3————Females without premarital coitus generally are positive that they will not engage in premarital coitus. Almost half of those who have had premarital coitus intend to repeat. The Kinsey research shows that experience in premarital coitus also increases the likelihood of extramarital coitus.

Kinsey finds striking proof that those having had premarital coitus are more likely than others to have premarital coitus again, and also that those having had premarital coitus are much more likely than others to have extramarital relations.[40]

Data relating premarital to extramarital coitus of women show, for example, that those who have had premarital coitus are twice as likely as others to have extramarital coitus. Moreover, a greater proportion of those who had had extramarital coitus than those who had not, thought they would do the same again.[41] This would seem to give some justification to the fear of disloyalty.

On the moral issue, however, there is not too much evidence of a carryover of guilt in Kinsey's data. Only about 31 percent of the unmarried females who had had premarital coitus regretted it afterward. Only

[40] Alfred C. Kinsey and others, *Sexual Behavior in the Human Female* (Philadelphia: W. B. Saunders Co., 1953), Ch. 10, pp. 427-431.
[41] *Ibid.*, Charts pp. 318-319.

23 percent of the married females regretted it. The incidence of regret was not even particularly high among females who had experienced premarital pregnancy. As would be expected, knowing the nature of the human conscience, those who had experienced the greatest amount of coitus over the greatest period of time were least likely to have regrets. Those without religion were less subject to regret than those who were devout.

Again, of course, one is dealing with the group who do have sexual relations, and with their after-adjustments. This is the morally liberated group. Average reactions of all persons to premarital sex experience would undoubtedly be quite different.

These findings may be challenged too on the ground that an expression of "no regret" may not tell the whole story. In fact, Lester Kirkendall, teacher and marriage counselor, in his study of 250 college couples having sexual intercourse shows that many who claim no regret, at the same time tell of experiences of hurt feelings, recriminations, bitterness, distrust, etc.[42] Some boys who report no regret also tell of girls trying to "trap" them into marriage. Even in cases where there is no sense of guilt, there is often a sense of distrust, suspicion, and disrespect, which indicates that the human relationship involved has degenerated because of the sex experience.

Studies by Hillman of inquiries to an advice column of a metropolitan paper indicate that premarital sexual intercourse had brought more problems to the column than any other single factor; 3,371 letters dealt with problems arising from this source. The second most frequent problem arose out of unfaithfulness on the part of the other party. This type of inquiry brought 1,887 letters. Alcoholism was third, with almost as many inquiries.[43]

In the final analysis, the question of premarital sexual relations must be weighed in terms of morality and notions of propriety rather than of biology alone.

Religious and moral convictions are the strong controls on sexual behavior. One may well suspect that when persons who hold these convictions violate sexual mores, they suffer most. Kinsey finds religion the most powerful influence among both men and women in deferring sexual relationships until after marriage[44] (see Figure 20-4). Judson T. Landis found that more than a third of the men in the 11 colleges studied in 1952 gave this as a reason for refraining, and 31 percent of the women concurred. In the Cornell 1940 study, 21 percent of the total group refrained

42 Kirkendall, *op. cit.*

43 Christine H. Hillman, "An Advice Column's Challenge for Family-life Education," *Marriage and Family Living*, 16:51-54, February, 1954.

44 Alfred C. Kinsey and others, *Sexual Behavior in the Human Female* (Philadelphia: W. B. Saunders Co., 1953).

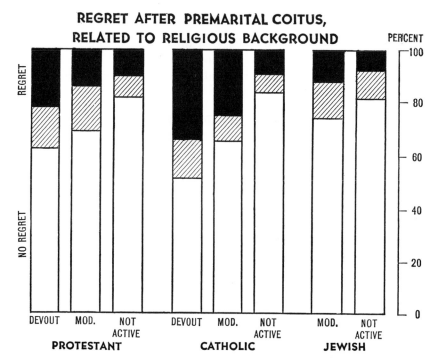

SOURCE: Alfred C. Kinsey and others, *Sexual Behavior in the Human Female* (Philadelphia: W. B. Saunders Co., 1953). Reproduced by permission of Dr. Kinsey.

FIGURE 20-4————The more devout the woman, the greater likelihood of regret following premarital coitus. Intermediate shading indicates some lesser degree of regret. Those of serious Catholic faith most often suffer regret.

for religious reasons.[45] (Both of these groups placed family training far above religious beliefs as a reason for refraining, and more also gave as a reason simply wanting to refrain until after marriage.)

Dedman found religion a strong deterrent to premarital sexual relations,[46] as did also Kanin and Howard.[47] Of engaged couples who were both regular in church attendance, in the latter study only 28 percent had premarital sexual intercourse; of the couples with one regular attender and one nonregular, 48 percent; of the nonregular attenders, 61 percent.

Although American data show very clearly that religion is a great restraint on premarital and extramarital sexual activity, there is no doubt

[45] Landis and Landis, *op. cit.,* p. 175.
[46] Jean Dedman, "The Relationship Between Religious Attitude and Attitude Toward Premarital Sex Relations," *Marriage and Family Living,* 21:171-176, March, 1959.
[47] Kanin and Howard, *op. cit.*

a great difference related to the particular church attended. Chesser's study of over 6,000 marriages in England shows that almost half of the Roman Catholic women had had sexual intercourse before marriage, by far the highest proportion of any religious group studied. Only one-fourth of the Protestant group had had sexual intercourse before marriage, and only one-fifth of the Jewish women.[48]

FACTORS RESTRICTING PREMARITAL COITUS GIVEN BY WOMEN

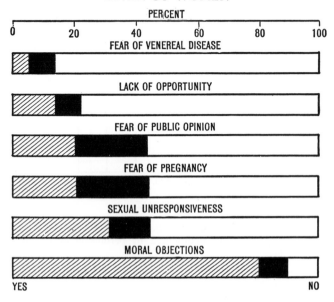

SOURCE: Alfred C. Kinsey and others, *Sexual Behavior in the Human Female* (Philadelphia: W. B. Saunders Co., 1953). Reproduced by permission of Dr. Kinsey.

FIGURE 20-5————Moral factors are the major control; with sexual unresponsiveness, second. Black shading indicates replies falling between "yes" and "no," including data from females with and without coital experience. (Based on total sample, including single and married females.)

It is apparently on the grounds of religion, morals, parental attitudes, and their own conception of their future that most young people refrain from premarital sexual intercourse rather than doing so on the basis of biological considerations. As one girl expressed it in her term paper "I want to have a honeymoon that means something new to me. I don't

48 Eustace Chesser and others, *The Sexual, Marital, and Family Relationships of the English Woman* (New York: Roy Publishers, Inc., 1957).

want it compared with another place, another man. And I never want a husband who could throw it back to me that I was pregnant, that he had to marry me."

Mental Health and Premarital Sexual Relations

Evidence is far too meager to indicate what the lasting influence of premarital sexual relations may be on the personality and mental health of the individuals involved. We do know this—most young people in the United States develop, as they mature, a rather exacting code of right and wrong on sexual matters. These codes are generally centered about religious teachings, but whether they are or not, religious ethics act as nearly inflexible yardsticks by which most persons judge their own behavior and that of others. When one allows himself to act contrary to these codes, society seldom has to punish him; conscience does the job.

In this area there is little or no statistical evidence available. Clinical data is available, however, indicating the results of self-betrayal. An illustrative case from a counselor's experience is described below.

Virginia, daughter of a small-town minister, migrated from her home in Tennessee to a large northern city shortly after her graduation from high school. She lived in a furnished room with a girl friend, became active in church affairs, and obtained steady employment in a clothing store.

George, one of her co-workers, was attracted to Virginia and they dated one another irregularly for a year and a half. There followed a period of six months when they dated one another exclusively, spoke often of marriage, and after considerable urging on George's part had sexual intercourse more or less regularly.

Even though they used a contraceptive device, Virginia became pregnant. After two unsuccessful attempts at abortion by pills, she confided in George who willingly agreed upon an early date for their marriage.

The marriage itself proved to be a generally happy and successful one. When Virginia occasionally became depressed concerning the circumstances of their marriage, George reassured her. None of their friends or acquaintances learned of the untimely conception.

After the birth of the first child, however, Virginia's periods of depression became more numerous and lasting. The climax came when she attempted to enter the date of her marriage and of the birth of her child in her Bible. She found herself incapable of writing the birth, or of inscribing false dates. She began to dwell constantly upon the matter, feeling a deep sense of guilt and unworthiness. She could no longer go to church, associate with her friends, or even feel at ease with her husband.

In the end, a period of intensive professional counseling was necessary merely to enable her to continue even somewhat effectively in her roles as wife and mother. At this time, three years after the birth of her first child, she still experiences periods of dangerous depression in which suicide plans figure vaguely, but persistently.

Not all such cases reach the attention of professional counselors. It is safe to say that, though the percentage of persons so haunted may not be great, the pain and guilt they suffer make their cases highly significant. For every young person who takes lightly the risks involved in premarital sexual intercourse—and the temptation to do so will increase as contraception becomes more dependable—there remains one basic question, "what will the experience mean relative to my own self-respect and mental health?"

Until the moral teachings of most American families undergo very fundamental changes, there will be many young people who suffer as much or more from psychological repercussions as from the potential social consequences of intercourse prior to marriage.

Problems of Premarital Pregnancy

Risk of pregnancy to the girl, and welfare of the child, have been given as the most important social reasons for chastity in a society with dating customs. Is this a real risk? Apparently many girls readily recognize it as a risk for others, but assume they will be smart enough to get by.

In a Kinsey sample of 2,094 single white females, ranging all the way from adolescence to forty years of age, who had had premarital coitus, 476 or 18 percent had become pregnant—almost one in five. Many of this group were not yet married, so the likelihood of even a greater proportion becoming pregnant prior to marriage is, of course, to be taken for granted.

Fifteen percent of those who had become pregnant had been pregnant more than once. While this seems like a high proportion of pregnancies, Kinsey finds that for any given act of intercourse among this group the average is only one pregnancy for each thousand single acts of intercourse. Such statistics are, of course, deceptive. The individual who is highly susceptible to pregnancy is vulnerable, whereas a sterile couple, or near-sterile one, is not at all vulnerable.

There is no doubt that the Kinsey sample was of women who were abnormally sexually active and exposed to pregnancy.[49] Yet the risk is always there. It is, however, diminishing, if young people take the proper precautions. Yet if premarital sex were deliberately planned for, most of it would probably never take place. Youth become overwhelmed by their impulses and at times those with every intention of remaining chaste

[49] For convincing argument and evidence see Judson T. Landis, "The Women Kinsey Studied," *Social Problems*, 1:139-142, April, 1951.

indulge in sexual intercourse. No matter how effective birth control becomes, it will not eliminate premarital pregnancy simply because the required foresight to prevent pregnancy will not be exercised. This is why almost a quarter of a million children are born out of wedlock annually in our contraceptively wise age.

One must assume that in American society premarital pregnancy is rarely if ever desired and planned for. When it results there are three alternatives: (1) marriage, (2) abortion, (3) unmarried motherhood. The third has been discussed. The other two merit consideration.

Marriage is the ideal solution provided the couple are ready for marriage and have favorable attitudes toward life together and toward parenthood. This is a big order where there has been no long period of close association prior to pregnancy. Even where there has been, the very fact of being forced to move the marriage forward in time may be a handicap. Also, if anything goes wrong with the marriage, one partner may be quick to accuse the other of having been responsible. They have both been hurt by being forced to terminate other plans in order to settle down to the responsibilities of homemaking and parenthood. They have suffered some sense of shame and humiliation in being "caught." They may have a feeling of guilt, too. And they may, in fact, because of all of these unfavorable factors, actually have lost their love for each other before they entered into the marriage.

Christensen and Rubenstein have studied the problem of premarital sexual intercourse primarily from the standpoint of the effect of pregnancy on later success in marriage.[50] These studies leave no doubt that premarital pregnancy is a hazard to successful marriage. Premarital pregnancy is associated with an abnormally high divorce rate. They suggest that it may be associated with other unfavorable factors like venereal disease, incurring anxiety and guilt, and inciting social condemnation. Locke's study, which compared backgrounds of divorced and happily married couples, showed a fairly high number of pregnancies previous to marriage among the divorced.[51]

Swedish social workers reported to the 1953 European Study Tour on Marriage and Family, of which the author was leader, that many divorces are caused there by marriage having been entered into because of premarital pregnancies. Yet in Sweden there is no pressure whatever from social workers or public agencies to encourage marriage if the

[50] Harold T. Christensen and Betty B. Rubenstein, "Premarital Pregnancy and Divorce: A Follow-up Study by the Interview Method," *Marriage and Family Living*, 8:114-123, May, 1956; see also Harold T. Christensen and Hanna H. Meissner, "Studies in Child Spacing III—Premarital Pregnancy as a Factor in Divorce," *American Sociological Review*, 18:641-644, December, 1953.

[51] Locke, *op. cit.*, p. 92.

couple involved in the pregnancy do not wish it.[52] This suggests that even where all conditions in the society favor premarital pregnancy, it seems to work to the disadvantage of marriage.

In our culture, even with the strong taboos against premarital pregnancy, marriage counselors do not recommend marriage if the young couple involved are no longer interested in each other.

Abortion is an unpleasant business that offends the moral sense of all but the most callous, yet many girls resort to it to avoid shame for themselves and their child. The death rate for women from illegal abortion is more than twice that for the death rate for women from births. The risk of causing sterility is great, as is the risk of permanent damage or disease to the female organs.

The fear of pregnancy is subject to widespread exploitation. Great quantities of drugs are sold annually for producing an abortion. Until recently, no effective drug could be taken without risk to life. Previous drugs taken for abortion have been entirely worthless, except as they may have given the woman confidence that she was no longer pregnant. In many cases she was not. A gynecologist friend of the author has estimated that as many as half of the abortions carried out by illegitimate practitioners among unmarried girls may involve no pregnancy at all. In Sweden, of 1,200 girls dying of illegal abortions, 100 were not pregnant and of every hundred tested for pregnancy in the clinic of the National League for Sex Education, 40 are not pregnant.[53]

The shock of first intercourse, or the fear and tension that come to one having sexual intercourse outside marriage, often retards menstruation for a considerable period of time. The abortionist exploits the girl's fear and carries out the abortion even when there is no pregnancy.

In cases of pregnancy, the girl is far wiser to seek the counsel of a social worker or a legitimate physician. In most instances she will be directed to an institution offering proper care to her and the child and facilitating its adoption if this is her wish.

In conclusion, much evidence has been considered on the very important topic of sexual behavior during the years previous to marriage. This topic has been much dealt with by research. The biological evidence is not against premarital intercourse. It would seem to slightly favor the

[52] In Holland, pressure is exerted to bring about a marriage in case of premarital pregnancy.

[53] Data given by Elsie Ottesen-Jensen, founder and director of the League, in a lecture to a Marriage and Family Life Student Tour in the Summer of 1953. Unlike the United States, Sweden has legalized abortion for many reasons. For example abortion is legal if the mother contracts German measles during the early period of pregnancy.

position that, considering the physical side only, the exercise of genital musculature is conducive to biological responsiveness.

But the adjustment of two human beings in a close and lasting interpersonal relationship is dependent on so much more than biology that the mere ability to respond to each other sexually is a very small, even though very important, part of the relationship.

There is little evidence that premarital sexual relationships improve the adjustment of a couple prior to engagement. In some instances it appears to do so after engagement, yet even here there are many exceptions. Disrespect may lessen the male's drive to marriage in certain instances. Awkward situations may arise, and data seem to indicate that the likelihood of the engagement breaking will be increased. At least, broken engagements are more often found among those who do than those who do not have coitus.

Evidence available to date suggests that marriages of the chaste are most successful under the culture pattern of the United States. This may merely mean that the conventional are the best marriage risks. Under a different moral order, personal and marital problems resulting from premarital sexual relationships would no doubt be greatly reduced, but the moral system exists and is a reality with which all must reckon. Perhaps the greatest risk in premarital sex relationships is the frequently resulting feeling of self-betrayal and the inner conflicts which this brings.

Problems

1. *Research exercise:* Poll the class or some other student group on the questions, "Do you believe in premarital sexual relations? Why?" According to tabulations:
   a. Does most of your class favor or oppose premarital sexual relations?
   b. Does favorableness to premarital relations tend to be associated with one or the other sex in your group?
   c. What reason is most often given in favor of premarital relations?
   d. What argument is most often given against it?
2. Discuss the institutional changes that would be required if premarital sexual relations were condoned in the United States?
3. In the long run would premarital sexual relations tend to increase or decrease the freedom of young people?
4. As a group do you feel that sexual relations are less objectionable during an engagement than before an engagement?
5. Your friend's fiancée has become pregnant but both agree that had it not happened they would have broken their engagement. What would your advice to him be?
   a. Get out of town.
   b. Take her to an abortionist.

    c. Marry her and try to make it work.

    d. Marry her with the understanding that you will get a divorce when the child is one year old.

    e. Take her to an institution for unwed mothers and put the child up for adoption.

6. A very religious girl, in a moment of excitement, consents to sexual relations with her fiancé and discovers two months later that she is pregnant. List the possible social and psychological consequences if:

    a. They marry after her third month of pregnancy.

    b. They decide not to marry at all.

7. In your opinion how might parents and institutions, such as church and school, best help young people to avoid the dangers of premarital sexual relations?

8. Discuss the statement, "The chief danger of premarital sexual relations is to one's mental health rather than physical well-being."

Selected References

ARTICLES IN BOOKS OF READINGS

FISHBEIN, Morris, and KENNEDY, Ruby Jo Reeves, *Modern Marriage and Family Living* (New York: Oxford University Press, 1957).
    1. STEPHENS, Anna O., Revised by Morris Fishbein, "Premarital Sex Relationships," pp. 158-167.

VINCENT, Clark E., *Readings in Marriage Counseling* (New York: Thomas Y. Crowell Co., 1957).
    2. KIRKENDALL, Lester A., "A Viewpoint on the Premarital Sex Problem," pp. 117-126.

CAVAN, Ruth Shonle, *Marriage and the Family in the Modern World: A Book of Readings* (New York: Thomas Y. Crowell Co., 1960).
    3. PRINCE, Alfred J., and SHIPMAN, Gordon, "Attitudes of College Students Toward Premarital Sex Experience," Reading 39.
    4. KIRKENDALL, Lester A., "Premarital Sex Relations: The Problem and Its Implications," Reading 40.

WINCH, Robert F., and others, *Selected Studies in Marriage and the Family*, Revised Edition (New York: Holt, Rinehart & Winston, Inc., 1962).
    5. CHRISTENSEN, Harold T., and MEISSNER, Hanna H., "Premarital Pregnancy as a Factor in Divorce," pp. 616-621.

GOODE, William J., *Readings on the Family and Society* (Englewod Cliffs, N. J.: Prentice-Hall, Inc., 1964).
    6. HAMBLIN, Robert L. and BLOOD, Robert O., "Premarital Experience and the Wife's Sexual Adjustment," Ch. 13.

CHRISTENSEN, Harold T., *Handbook of Marriage and the Family* (Chicago: Rand McNally & Co., 1964).
    7. EHRMANN, Winston, "Marital and Nonmarital Sexual Behavior," Ch. 15.

General References

BELL, Robert R., and BURKLE, Jack V., "Mother and Daughter Attitudes to Premarital Sexual Behavior," *Marriage and Family Living*, 23:390-393, November, 1962.

BURGESS, Ernest W., and WALLIN, Paul, *Engagement and Marriage* (Philadelphia: J. B. Lippincott Co., 1953), Chs. 11, 12.

CAVAN, Ruth Shonle, *American Marriage* (New York: Thomas Y. Crowell Co., 1959), Ch. 10.

CHRISTENSEN, Harold T., "Child Spacing Analysis via Record Linkage: New Data Plus a Summing Up," *Marriage and Family Living*, 25:272-280, August, 1963.

————, "Studies in Child Spacing: I—Premarital Pregnancy as Measured by the Spacing of the First Birth from Marriage," *American Sociological Review*, 18:53-59, February, 1953.

————, and MEISSNER, Hannah H., "Studies in Child Spacing: III—Premarital Pregnancy as a Factor in Divorce," *American Sociological Review*, 18:641-644, December, 1953.

CLOTHIER, Florence, "The Unmarried Mother of School Age as Seen by a Psychiatrist," *Mental Hygiene*, 39:631-646, October, 1955.

DEDMAN, Jean, "The Relationship Between Religious Attitude and Attitude Toward Premarital Sex Relations," *Marriage and Family Living*, 21:171-176, March, 1959.

DRUCKER, A. J., CHRISTENSEN, H. T., and REMMERS, H. H., "Some Background Factors in Socio-Sexual Modernism," *Marriage and Family Living*, 14:335-337, November, 1952.

DUVALL, Evelyn M., and HILL, Reuben, *When You Marry*, Revised Edition (Boston: D. C. Heath & Co., 1953), Chs. 6, 7.

EHRMANN, Winston W., *Premarital Dating Behavior* (New York: Holt, Rinehart & Winston, Inc., 1959).

————, "Student Co-operation in a Study of Dating Behavior," *Marriage and Family Living*, 14:4ff., November, 1952.

ELLIS, Albert, "Symposium on Premarital Sex Views," *Marriage and Family Living*, 15, August, 1953.

KANIN, Eugene J., "Premarital Sex Adjustment, Social Class, and Associated Behavior," *Marriage and Family Living*, 22:258-262, August, 1960.

————, and HOWARD, David H., "Postmarital Consequences of Premarital Sex Adjustments," *American Sociological Review*, 23:556-562, October, 1948.

KINSEY, Alfred C., and others, *Sexual Behavior in the Human Female* (Philadelphia: W. B. Saunders Co., 1953).

————, *Sexual Behavior in the Human Male* (Philadelphia: W. B. Saunders Co., 1948).

LANDIS, Judson T., and LANDIS, Mary G., *Building a Successful Marriage*, Fourth Edition (Englewood Cliffs, N. J.: Prentice-Hall, Inc., 1963), Ch. 12.

LEMASTERS, E. E., *Modern Courtship and Marriage* (New York: The Macmillan Co., 1957), Ch. 9.

Levy, Dorothy, "A Follow-up Study of Unmarried Mothers," *Social Casework,* 36:27-33, January, 1955.

Murdock, George, "Sexual Behavior, What Is Acceptable?" *Journal of Social Hygiene,* 36:1-31, 1950.

Poffenberger, Thomas, and others, "Premarital Sexual Behavior: A Symposium," *Marriage and Family Living,* 24:254-278, August, 1962.

Reevy, William R., "Premarital Petting Behavior and Marriage Happiness Prediction," *Marriage and Family Living,* 21:345-355, November, 1959.

Social Sweden (Stockholm: Social Welfare Board, 1952).

Vincent, Clark, *Unmarried Mothers* (New York: Free Press of Glencoe, Inc., 1961).

Young, Leontine, *Out of Wedlock* (New York: McGraw-Hill Book Co., 1954).

V
MARRIAGE ADJUSTMENT

21
Marriage Adjustment

"How do they get along together?" "Do they love each other?" "Are they compatible?" are, in our culture, the key questions concerning a married pair.

These are foolish questions in terms of the values of the institutional system of an earlier day in our culture. They are foolish still to one in the traditional joint-family system of India or Pakistan, for example. In East Africa an Indian wife, learning that the writer worked in the field of marriage problems, asked quite seriously, "But what could there be to write about?" She was sincere. In a family system rooted in centuries of tradition, which still outlines a rigid framework of roles, authorities, and values for the man-and-wife relationship as does the Indian family, there is nothing to write about. What happens is taken for granted. Defined institutional relationships are not viewed as individual problems or subjected to analysis.

The goals of social status, economic survival, and offspring are sufficient to justify the marriage relationship quite apart from personal considerations. If a close personal relationship is lacking, there is adequate social and emotional support in the primary group: the large kin group, the tribal group, or the close-knit rural neighborhood. Few lack close ties somewhere in this circle. A dependable confidant is there, a loving friend, a source of constant social support. One is not alone, even if the mate proves distant, hostile, or impersonable.

This is not so in the society created by urban-industrial life, with its great mobility and anonymity. The weaning of the child from the immediate family begins early; often he never has close ties with the larger family. Neighborhoods disintegrate with mobility, and rapid change in the material culture destroys even the familiar childhood locality. The child is launched into the impersonal world of the large high school, the

411

campus, or of industry and must learn to stand alone emotionally, economically, and work out a series of satisfying social relationships.

Our society is one of special interest groups, rather than all-inclusive primary groups. Special interest groups draw only a segment of the personality into their orbit, and even that with reservations. Life is never complete in such relationships. There must still be an all-embracing relationship which the family represented for the individual in childhood. Today this must be sought in marriage. This is why a marriage can be successful by all the old values: satisfactory social status, property, children, and still fail completely.

We who study the pair relationship are increasingly aware that in the marriage system of our culture, failure in the interpersonal relationship of man and wife is responsible for far-reaching human woes. An undeterminable amount of ill health, emotional crises which may lead to the mental institution, alcoholism, and other failures of the adult to measure up to the demands of life have their origin in the pair relationship. Much physical illness is a devious expression of emotional ill health, provoked by a pair relationship which has left one or both partners destitute in love and frustrated to the point of misery.

Very often sanity itself is at stake in the poorly adjusted relationship of man and wife, and these woes are often passed on from parents to children. Unhappy parents, at war with each other, can destroy the security of their children.

Adjustment is not a fictitious norm in the marriage-family system which has emerged in our society—it is the key to married life, almost to adult life itself.

The Honeymoon—The First Big Step in Adjustment

The early days and months of marriage involve a subtle series of interactions by which each partner is trying to reshape the other in his or her own image of what a mate should be. True, this is not always subtle, and it does not necessarily begin after marriage. If the marriage lasts, it will continue and take a decidedly different turn when children are born. The honeymoon is socially provided as a special adjustment period. Popularly looked upon as a time of supreme bliss, it may actually be one of the most strenuous of adjustment periods. There is some truth in novelist Philip Wiley's contention that "Honeymoons Are Hell."[1]

The honeymoon at its best, however, can be an enjoyable and not too strenuous event. Understanding the significance of the honeymoon can

1 *Redbook,* November, 1952.

save a couple months of more difficult adjustment. When the honeymoon is unrealistically planned, however, it can actually become a liability rather than an asset to the new marriage.

The least successful honeymoons, from the standpoint of marital happiness, are those that seek to cram into a week or two all of the activity, adventure, and travel which the couple cannot expect to afford for another five or ten years. Parents are often guilty of encouraging couples to undertake too much. Since the length of the honeymoon trip, and the people and places one visits, are frequently reported in the hometown paper, the honeymoon is often used as a testimony to one's social and economic status rather than one's good sense.

The most desirable honeymoons from the standpoint of all-around happiness are those which are planned for:

1. time for rest
2. time for being alone
3. time to be with others and for doing things in a group

Time for rest: This is of crucial importance. To begin with, if the couple has a large public wedding, they enter the honeymoon period in a state of extreme fatigue. In this condition of nervous and emotional exhaustion, they begin their life together. Regardless of how well acquainted they have become during their engagment period, marriage is bound to raise new situations requiring thought, sensitivity, and tact. Nervous and physical exhaustion make it doubly difficult for the young couple to meet these inevitable circumstances with wisdom and patience. The awkwardness which frequently accompanies this period of initial intimacy is easily exaggerated by fatigue, until the loved one—so familiar only yesterday—may begin to seem strange and more than a little frightening. Research suggests that not more than half of couples can expect early sexual adjustment.[2]

The couple's first venture into sexual relations is apt to be discouraging. Strain, fatigue, and awkwardness often make intercourse difficult or unpleasant for the new wife. The looked-forward-to experience often turns out to be a frightening and completely disillusioning experience. As one young woman commented about her honeymoon, "If I ever see that doctor again, I'm going to give him a piece of my mind for the build-up on sex he gave me." She indicated how awkward and embarrassed she was about sex, even though she was informed and knew what was expected of her. She concluded with, "It was not till weeks later that the wonder of it came to me."

[2] Data are presented in Chapter 24.

Time for being alone: Dating and engagement activities normally lead a couple along a path of steadily growing intimacy. By the time they begin to seriously consider marriage, sexual attraction and desire have already begun to loom as significant factors in their relationship. By the day of the ceremony, this desire for complete fulfillment has generally reached its peak. Yet, sexual fulfillment for the new wife usually is not a simple matter of sexual intercourse. Her greatest satisfaction and happiness may come primarily from the hours of intimate companionship, wooing, and the gradually increasing sexual play that precede intercourse.

When a couple spend their honeymoon in an atmosphere of hectic social activity their opportunities for these periods of gradual sexual preparation are lost. Not only does the sex act itself fall short of expectations but the full meaning of emotional oneness is seldom realized.

Sexual adjustment is not the only justification for planning time to be alone. All during engagement couples oversell themselves to be sure of winning the mate. Now, during the early days of marriage, this idealized mate becomes more and more a real person, both actually and in the eyes of the spouse. The honeymoon should be a time of getting re-acquainted. The new person who emerges from a period of continuous intimacy is likely to be very different in many respects from what was expected. Problems and uncertainties may even be aroused in the process of this awakening and they can seldom be met and solved in a crowd or among relatives and friends.

Time to be with others and for doing things in a group: Before marriage many couples find it difficult to be apart a single moment. They feel that they want to spend every moment of the rest of their lives alone together. Yet, experience shows that honeymoons spent in complete isolation from other people and from all group activities are more than most young people can take.

Many hotels, lodges, and resorts cater especially to honeymoon couples. They provide lengthy meal periods and a variety of activities from which couples may choose and thus live at whatever pace they desire. Such institutions assure the couple the companionship of their age group but of a nonintimate nature.

Whether a couple select such an institution or prefer to make their own arrangements it is important that they consider a number of factors in making the decision:

1. amount of money to be spent
2. length of honeymoon
3. activities both would enjoy
4. amount of travel involved
5. opportunities for rest as well as recreation

Do All Couples Find Adjustment Difficult?

The amount of adjustment that takes place in marriage is determined in considerable part by the amount that takes place previous to marriage. Some couples work out techniques of adjustment during the days preceding marriage and carry the same patterns over. Some couples, it may be supposed, never had major adjustment problems in their relationship from the beginning and do not have them in marriage. There are others who have many problems of adjustment because they should never have married in the first place.

Burgess and Wallin's study[3] of married couples whose engagement periods had been studied when they were in college showed that more than half of husbands and wives were aware of no major adjustment in marriage. Significantly these were for the most part couples who made their adjustments during the engagement period.

Adjustment problems in marital relationships may arise over such factors as sex, social life, religion, economic problems, in-laws, friends, or recreation.[4] They may also develop about problems of temperament, adaptability of habits, and children.[5] All such issues are possible of solution if the couple approach them cooperatively and with a will to succeed. As someone has said, "the only failure in life is failure of purpose."

One of the most comprehensive sociological studies to date finds that a person's adaptability has the most to do with successfully fitting into the marriage relationship. Adaptability is defined as "the person's capacity to change his roles, his attitudes, and his behavior in order to adjust to those of the other person or to a new or modified situation."[6]

Adaptability, it is believed, is determined by the person's "empathy, flexibility, command of appropriate attitudes and roles, and motivation to adjust." By empathy is meant understanding of the other person to the point of recognizing and appreciating his motives. This trait in the marriage relationship, the research shows, is dependent to a great extent upon the husband's and wife's ability to communicate with each other, for understanding to the point of empathy is possible only as they confide, talk, and discuss issues fully.

Flexibility, the study shows, is partly psychogenic, that is, determined by the early years of conditioning. It consists essentially in being able to vary one's responses within a situation. On the matter of motivation to

[3] Ernest W. Burgess and Paul Wallin, *Engagement and Marriage* (Philadelphia: J. B. Lippincott Co., 1953), Ch. 18.

[4] Judson T. Landis, "Length of Time Required to Achieve Adjustment in Marriage," *American Sociological Review*, 11:668 ff., December, 1946.

[5] Burgess and Wallin, *loc. cit.*

[6] *Ibid.*, p. 623.

adapt, findings are to the effect that the couple most in love are most willing to adapt to each other. New situations, crises, and a will to succeed all have a bearing on the person's motive to adapt. It is also reported that associating with an intimate group with similar motives is a strong factor in motivating the individual toward particular kinds of adjustment. For example, the young wife who does not want children may readily and almost unconsciously change her motivation by association with a young married group with babies and with an interest in babies.

The matter of being able to readily command appropriate responses for adapting depends upon the kind of training the person has had and whether or not he is responsive to the wishes of others. One who wishes to adapt learns the kind of responses that will win other people rather than driving them away. Such responses have to be cultivated in marriage.

There are at least three types[7] of decision-making in the marriage relationship: (1) the authoritarian type, in which the decision is handed down by the spouse who assumes the superior role; (2) verbal coercion, whereby one mate forces his opinion upon the other after strong argument; and (3) the democratic type, in which there is mutual discussion with husband and wife each entering into the decision.

Various researches extending over a period of more than thirty years show that the democratic partnerships are the happiest.[8] This, of course, does not mean that other kinds of relationships cannot and do not succeed. Rather, the democratic partnership, probably the hardest of all to practice, brings great rewards to those who succeed with it. It is without doubt among those who try it and fail that the highest divorce rate is found too.[9] Highly individualistic men and women often can settle for nothing short of the ideal.

Wives Adjust More Than Husbands

The ideal of democratic cooperation on the basis of mutuality is as yet merely an ideal. It is seldom fully realized, although it is probable that each generation is approaching nearer to it. There is no precise way

---

[7] Bernard Farber, cited in Burgess and Wallin, op. cit., 643 ff.

[8] Burgess and Wallin, op. cit.; see especially pp. 336-337; see also Judson T. Landis, "A Re-examination of the Role of the Father as an Index of Family Integration," Marriage and Family Living, 24:127 ff., May, 1962.

[9] Alver Hilding Jacobson finds it so in "Conflict of Attitudes Toward Roles of the Husband and Wife in Marriage," American Sociological Review, 17:146-150, April, 1952. Our studies show that divorce rates are highest in families where the democratic philosophy of child training is practiced; see Carol L. Stone and Paul H. Landis, "An Approach to Authority Pattern in Parent-Teenage Relationships," Rural Sociology, 18:233-242, September, 1953; also, Paul H. Landis, The Broken Home in Teenage Adjustments (Pullman, Wash.: Washington Agricultural Experiment Station, April, 1953), Bulletin No. 542.

of knowing exactly how close the average marriage comes to approximating genuine equality. In an earlier section, it was indicated that women still envy the male role, both in this country and Canada, more than men envy the female role. This would seem to be indicative that the male role still has advantages.

In the late 1930's, a study[10] of over 500 marriages showed that in the American marriage at that time the wife was doing the major part of the adjusting. Burgess and Wallin's study of college-educated couples reported[11] that either husband or wife may make most of the adjustments in marriage, or they may adjust equally, but more often both husband and wife agree that the wife has made the greater adjustment. Wives generally fit into marriage more easily than husbands because home, husband, and children are still the central interests in the plans of most women, whereas profession or business are the core interests of the middle-class male.

It may be inevitable that women will adjust somewhat more than men because of the demands of marriage itself. A man rarely changes his vocation or place of residence for the sake of his marriage. A woman must often drop out of the work world entirely and move to the location in which the husband is employed. This puts the major burden of vocational adjustment on her. The woman who has been gainfully employed must shift the entire routine of her life in taking over the management of her home, even though she may continue to work. Whereas she formerly had independence and directed her life to suit her own convenience, she is now required to make this secondary to the interests and work activities of the husband.

Some years ago Hughie Call, writing for *Reader's Digest,* entitled her article "Sheep Come First." A city girl, she had married a sheep rancher in Wyoming. She learned from the rigorous life at a sheep ranch that at lambing time, and at many other times, sheep are much more important than women. The work of many men, even yet, is somewhat like this in that it is very demanding and at times all other things must take second place. This is particularly true of the life of the doctor and perhaps of some other professional men.

When children come into the family the wife faces the most difficult adjustments of all. The man's role is little affected. Being a mother is the most demanding, exacting, and time-consuming task the modern woman faces during her lifetime. To be constantly tied down by the helplessness of the small child is a nerve-testing, exacting routine for many women,

10 Ernest W. Burgess and Leonard S. Cottrell, *Predicting Success or Failure in Marriage* (Englewood Cliffs, N. J.: Prentice-Hall, Inc., 1939), pp. 341-349.
11 Burgess and Wallin, *op. cit.,* Ch. 8.

particularly those who face it with an attitude of frustration, rather than with an attitude of pleasure and pride.

Throughout the entire period of child rearing, the demands on the mother are much more rigorous than those on the father. These demands come from all sides—children, husband, and from various groups in which the children participate. In a real sense, there is a long period in the life of the mother when her soul is not her own. She is in most instances almost completely at the mercy of her family.

This fact makes for more difficult adjustments in the later years, too, when the children leave home and she must develop new roles for herself. The husband continues in his chosen work throughout a lifetime and faces no adjustment crises in his routine activities until the retirement period of old age. The whole lifetime of the married woman is almost inevitably one of continuous adjustment.

Time vs. Technique in Adjustment

Judson T. Landis studied the time it took couples to reach a satisfactory state in six general areas of adjustment—sex, money matters, social activities, in-law relations, religious activities, and mutual friends.[12] Except for the first two areas, which will be discussed in separate chapters, adjustment was satisfactory for two-thirds to three-fourths of the couples from the very beginning. The marriages analyzed had lasted for an average of well over twenty years at the time of the study. A third to a half of those who had not made an early satisfactory adjustment in these four areas never made it. They were still maladjusted.

In about 10 percent of the cases, the adjustment was satisfactory for one spouse, but not for the other at the beginning of their marriage. This, no doubt, reflects differences in values and expectations of men and women as to what the marriage should be.

Does time work the necessary miracle of adjustment? Landis implies that it does for a certain proportion of couples. Burgess and Wallin are positive that time has nothing to do with adjustment. They say:

> The point needs to be made that the passage of time in itself does nothing. Of course, a spouse having endured an unsatisfactory condition may at last come to accept it. But any emphasis on time as a curative factor may result in a laissez-faire attitude toward dealing with an adjustment. . . .
>
> Our review of the interviews of adjustment made in the first three to five years of marriage suggests that adjustments do not happen with the passage of time. They are either made or they are not made.[13]

---

[12] Judson T. Landis, "Length of Time Required to Achieve Adjustment in Marriage," *American Sociological Review*, 11:668 ff., December, 1946.

[13] Burgess and Wallin, *op. cit.*, pp. 617-618.

The decisive factor is whether husband, or wife, or both are adaptable. According to this view, then, technique is all-important. Either during the engagement or in early marriage a couple adopts techniques which lead to a satisfactory working relationship or else they are likely to remain at odds.

The truth probably lies somewhere between these positions. There is no doubt that some couples mature in marriage and become more considerate and understanding in their relationship to the mate. An in-law problem may be cured by time, through death or migration, for example. Time is an important factor in the pair relationship both before and after marriage. Many, no doubt, follow an arbitrary and unyielding pattern after marriage which was already apparent during the engagement. Accommodation or failure are the only alternatives for these people. Time alone will only fix the already established relationship.

The Importance of Early Adjustment

It is important to point out that whether adjustments are made prior to or early in marriage, the earlier the attempts come, the better the chances for the couple. There are many reasons for this. First, during engagement and early marriage most couples are more eager to make their relationship succeed; there is greater motivation to success. Second, they are at a period in life when adjustments come more naturally than they will years later. Third, and perhaps most important of all, is the fact that marriage habits have not yet developed. A new relationship is flexible and capable of easy adjustment. As the marriage pattern becomes increasingly crystallized around certain ways of acting and reacting, the problems involved in changing this pattern become increasingly complex.

One young woman reported, for example, that during her engagement period she observed and became increasingly annoyed at the eating habits of her fiancé. He and members of his family rushed through even the most delicious meals as if they were in a hurry to be done with an unpleasant task. They spoke little during the meal and seemed to resent the intrusion of any unnecessary conversation.

In her own home the evening meal had always been a long, friendly affair to which members of the family looked forward eagerly. It was the one occasion each day for everyone to discuss mutually interesting subjects.

> "This may sound like a trivial difference," she said, "but to me, dinnertime is an important example of what civilized living could be. To Roy, it was merely a way of filling his stomach. I realized that the issue would have to be settled one way or the other eventually and, to be quite frank, I knew that I'd never be happy unless the decision went my way.

"I had seen my sister try to change her husband, who wasn't even so bad as Roy, after they had been married a year or so. He had given her a blank look and replied, 'What do you mean, slow down! Why should I sit here playing with my knife and fork when I could be in the other room reading the paper?' I was determined this would not happen to me.

"In a conversation about a month before we were married, I explained to Roy how much this difference in our eating habits meant to me—how it was very much tied in with an entire philosophy of living. He was not quickly won over, but he was willing to give it a try. We began eating dinner together in restaurants almost every evening. Because we were happy, in love, and full of dreams, we found a lot to talk about and I made a special effort to have ready a couple of really interesting topics of conversation for the dinner table.

"I continued this with conscious effort and forethought through our first few months of marriage. Now, I believe, it is not only an established custom in our house, but an important part of our way of life together."

This example indicates not only one of the common kinds of problems that must be solved but also how a young couple can solve it best early in their relationship.

Questions or differences over in-laws, over child rearing, social life, financial habits, sex attitudes, and in many other such areas can be met similarly during the engagement or early marriage period.

As the example above made clear, the important thing is not just reaching a verbal agreement, but mutually practicing insofar as possible, the agreed-upon behavior. A young man, for example, may be talked into agreeing that his wife rather than his mother should decide questions about his new home, but unless he is willing to act accordingly from the very beginning, there is little hope that he has really been convinced.

In the matter of general marital adjustment, the following rules are practical ones to follow:

1. Work out mutually satisfactory solutions to major differences before marriage.
2. Problems (such as those that might grow out of sexual relations) which cannot be met before marriage should be solved as early in the relationship as possible.
3. Throughout married life, problems and differences should be met and solved as they arise. The longer an unsatisfactory married situation is allowed to persist, the greater the problems involved in changing it.

The scriptural admonition, "Never let the sun go down upon your wrath," is a good motto for marriage.

In-Laws

In parts of India, where the old joint-family system of the Asiatic world is meeting the individualistic nuclear family of the Western World, social workers report that suicides are greatly on the increase among young wives. The bride who has learned Western ways is not happy to become a servant in her husband's household, and be bossed, persecuted, and outrivaled for her husband's affection by the husband's mother and sisters. An ex-governor of Bombay felt the situation was so serious that he proposed a law providing punishment for such in-law persecution.[14] All over India the mother-in-law is proverbially considered a devil. With the joint-family system, and patrilocal residence of the young couple, such a concept of the husband's mother is not surprising.

In the United States, the in-law crisis, if it does not come before marriage, reaches its worst proportions soon after. Each family is appraising the new addition. Parents have a hard time letting go and continue to hope to direct the lives of their young people in a proper and helpful way. As actress Spring Byington said in her TV show, *December Bride,* "When my daughter got married, I made a vow that I'd let her live her own life, even if I had to show her how to do it."[15]

The in-law conflict in the United States is unpredictable since it is a matter of interpersonal relationships and not an institutional arrangement. This is very unlike most cultures in the world where the relationship of in-laws is rather explicitly institutionalized, the culture defining more or less exactly the relative claim that parent family and the adopted family will have on the new members. Usually in the joint-family system, particularly if it is patrilocal, the son's mother has rather comprehensive claims on the new daughter. Until she has born a son, the young wife is expected to have a rating quite like that of the servants in the household, and to be subject to the mother-in-law's command.

As a marriage gets established, parents are in most instances less likely to interfere. They learn that advice is not wanted and will be ignored, or they come to see that the new pair are capable of handling their own affairs. Also, the longer a marriage has existed, the greater likelihood that parents will have died and, therefore, have been removed from the possibility of interference. This, of course, is not by any means always the case. Sometimes when one parent dies the other moves in with the young couple, adding to the problems of adjustment.

In a very real sense every family has its own distinctive way of life.

---

[14] N. P. N. Pillai, *Journal of Family Welfare,* Bombay, March, 1956, p. 90.
[15] *Look,* March 3, 1959.

Marriage adjustments are often intensified because each member of the pair tries to reestablish the way of life of his own childhood family. For this reason, in-laws may get blamed for problems they are only indirectly responsible for causing.

On the other hand, both parental families are judging the new in-law addition by their own standards. It is particularly true that the husband's family is likely to be looking the new daughter-in-law over very carefully, trying to form a judgment as to whether or not she is going to be able to fit their family pattern. The son's relatives are often guilty of trying to make his wife over to fit their pattern. Their ideas of her responsibilities as a wife may be quite different from her own, and, in fact, quite different from what her responsibilities as a wife should be. If they start out to reform her, she may soon find her husband and all his family in agreement as to what she should become to be the good wife.

Actually, the new marriage may require quite a different marriage relationship than that which has been made by either set of parents. Yet it is not unusual for the new wife to find herself hemmed in by their expectations, being gradually forced to conform to their family customs. Undoubtedly, the extent to which the wife is subjected to scrutiny depends on the degree to which premarital acquaintance has been thorough and carried on in close contact with the husband's parents. In such cases much of this adjustment has been made in advance.

Husband's mother more often intrudes: Folklore holds that there are times when any young wife may find it comforting to run home to her mother, instead of establishing from the outset the habit of talking over her problems with her husband. The fact is, however, that the husband's mother is most often the problem character in the modern marriage. One must grant that the attachment between mother and daughter is a very strong one, and that mothers hate to give their daughters in marriage, but they cling even more tenaciously to a son and become a greater nuisance in a son's than in a daughter's marriage.

Two young married women were discussing with each other the problems they had encountered during the first year of their marriage. The one said, "Well, I've learned that it's the husband's mother who gives trouble." The other agreed with considerable emphasis.

One might, of course, expect young women to feel that their husbands' mothers were the greater problem since they would naturally be more tolerant of their own mothers than of the husbands'. But these young women had discovered what research also shows regarding the in-law problem in contemporary marriage relationships. The husband's mother has much more difficulty in letting go than does the wife's mother.

This, perhaps, is not the only factor. The husband's mother identifies the wife's role in marriage and in the family with her own and, therefore, is likely to be very, very critical. The daughter's mother is less likely to be critical of her own daughter, as her own daughter was made after her image and follows housekeeping and marriage patterns which the mother has instilled. She is not likely to interfere so much with the young husband's role, since she has no close identification with the male role.

Duvall analyzed case-history documents of over 1,800 in-law relationships. She found the husband's mother (the wife's mother-in-law) the most trouble-causing personality. Next was the wife's mother, with the husband's sister a close third.[16]

The in-law adjustment is twofold. Not only must the newlyweds reckon with the impact of relatives on the family, but also with their own ties to parents and relatives as they affect the new marriage. Although parental ties are supposed to be fairly well broken by attachment to the new mate prior to marriage, and fully broken in an intimate sense when the marriage is consummated, the break is not always so complete.

Northwestern University sociologist Winch[17] found, in a study of the carry-over of attachments, that the mother is the preferred parent of both husband and wife; that the son is the preferred child; and that the mother-son relationship is the strongest family relationship. He believes that the strong attachment of the son to the mother impedes his mate choice and also his adjustment in marriage. Burgess and Wallin, in their study of engaged and married couples,[18] find that both son and daughter carry over strongest attachments to their mothers.

These and other authorities[19] seem to agree that though both son and daughter carry over close attachments to the mother, the son having been away from home more has emancipated himself more completely from attachments to his mother prior to his marriage. Even though his mother may cling to him more than the wife's mother to her, his prior independence from her and the cultural expectation that he be independent may make his emancipation from his mother as easy, if not easier, than that of the daughter from her mother.

Time and distance factors: About one in ten couples, according to Landis's study, had not worked out a satisfactory adjustment with relatives after more than twenty years of marriage; another 7 percent had taken one to twenty years to do so.[20] If this group is typical, the in-law problem is a difficulty of considerable importance over a long period in one of every five or six marriages. The study does not indicate whether parents

16 Evelyn Duvall, *In-Laws: Pro and Con* (New York: Association Press, 1954).

17 Robert F. Winch, *The Modern Family* (New York: Holt, Rinehart & Winston, Inc., 1952), p. 299.

18 Burgess and Wallin, *op. cit.,* p. 598-599.

19 See Mirra Komarovsky's conclusion in Burgess and Wallin, *op. cit.,* p. 599.

20 Judson T. Landis, "Length of Time Required to Achieve Adjustment in Marriage," *American Sociological Review,* 11:688 ff., December, 1964.

are responsible, or whether the clinging of the husband or wife to a parent is responsible, or whether both situations are responsible. It is probable that in many cases the strong attachment to a parent on the part of one of the mates is a two-way attachment and that the difficulty in the marriage is ultimately resolved only by the death of the parent.

The intrusion of relatives into the new marriage relationship is one which young people in most cultures resent. One of the favorite subjects for jokes in many cultures is the mother-in-law. In many primitive societies a son-in-law is never allowed to look his mother-in-law in the face. These people learned centuries ago what some young couples today have to learn by experience; that is, to keep relatives at a distance.

Actually, the in-law problem may not now be the serious problem it once was. In our mobile society young people usually live in a separate residence, and often in a separate community from their parents.[21] It is very easy to shed the in-laws under these circumstances. Moreover, social security has helped remove the necessity of children caring for the widowed parent in their own home. The new conditions of living have relieved a great deal of strain in the in-law relationship as it affects the couple marrying today. Where it exists, however, the in-law problem can be a serious one because of the individualistic emphases of modern marriage. The young couple are wise to pattern their life after their own wishes rather than after those of relatives.

Positive contribution of in-laws: The in-law relationship has been discussed as a problem. It is not always so. Many married couples do not have in-law problems at all. Duvall's case histories show that in many cases the young wife appreciates the husband's mother as a second mother, loves her and finds her helpful.[22] And the husband sometimes finds the wife's mother a substitute for his real mother who has died, or a second mother if his mother still lives. Many times the in-laws help with the children, take the wife in while the husband is away in military service, and care for her and her children in case of his death or their divorce. Mothers-in-law, and other in-laws have piled up a very good record, but this is less often discussed than is the record of the small proportion who make themselves very troublesome.

Duvall's study also shows that the in-laws sometimes suffer from the neglect, or inconsiderateness of children. Often they do not know quite what role to play with their married children, and later, with the grand-

---

[21] Doubled-up households are becoming very rare in our society of abundance. Since World War II, project housing on low down-payment contracts, has made separate residences possible, as has apartment-house living. By 1947 only 9 percent of households were doubled up; by 1955 the proportion had dropped to 3.5 percent; see Metropolitan Life Insurance Company, "The American Husband," *Statistical Bulletin,* April, 1956, pp. 4-5.

[22] Duvall. *op. cit.*

children. This is a new situation and unique to our type of marriage-family system. Such role-relationships are never left in doubt in the ancient cultures of the world. In the in-law area, as in so many relationships of the married pair in urban industrial society, roles must be worked out through the adjustment process because they are no longer defined by custom.

Disillusionment with Marriage

One of the more significant of all early adjustments is the discovery that marriage is after all primarily a routine way of living. During the early days of marriage there is a preoccupation with the personal feelings and responses of the mate. This is gradually lessened as routine habits are in time established in all successful marriages. Men suffer more from disillusionment than women. Their loss of freedom, new household obligations, and economic responsibilities are a part of the normal cost of marriage. Romance decreases in reality.

Hobart finds some evidence of postmarital disillusionment in both men and women. The disillusionment shows up most in the areas of personal freedom, marital roles, having children, in-law relationships, values of neatness, values on control of money, and attitudes toward divorce. He believes his data show some evidence of a relationship between degree of romanticism prior to marriage and disillusionment.[23]

In marriage the sexual tension of the chaste engagement eases in the satisfying release of sexual relations. The "put on" self of the engagement period becomes the more routine self, with ups and downs of moods and tempers. The painted glamour of the ballroom is balanced by the faded look of dawn in the family bedroom; the exotic odor of perfumes is replaced by the homely smell of the human body and the human habitation.

"Woe unto him or her who cannot understand and accept this 'disillusionment' of marriage," say Levy and Munroe.[24] "The person who must have glamour, who cannot take the disillusionment of settling down, is not ready for marriage."[25] This kind of person, even though he resorts to divorce, will find that a new deal will not help. He has not yet come to accept himself or to know what his own needs are. He will not find them in marriage. "Glamour in marriage cannot be continuous, but

---

[23] Charles W. Hobart, "Disillusionment in Marriage and Romanticism," *Marriage and Family Living*, 20:156-162, May, 1958; see also E. E. LeMasters, "Parenthood as a Crisis," *Marriage and Family Living*, 19:352-355, November, 1957.

[24] John Levy and Ruth Munroe, *The Happy Family* (New York: Alfred A. Knopf, Inc., 1938), p. 67.

[25] *Ibid.*, p. 74.

it needn't be absent."[26] All human beings must learn sooner or later that man is not capable of living at a high pitch of glamorous excitement at all times.

A secretary in her early twenties who possessed certain traits pointing toward spinsterhood made the point well in commenting on the love affair of a very excitable girl who worked in the same office. In appraising this affair, she said, "MY! I should think that would be awfully *strenuous!*"

Certainly married life on a high pitch of continued romantic excitement would be much more strenuous than any human being is constituted to take.

If dating has carried the couple well beyond the first excited stage of love, considerable realism should have entered the relationship before marriage. In such cases disillusionment should not be great. Marriages entered into hastily, and in the overly excited first stages of the pair relationship, may be in for a most painful period of disillusionment.

Some couples sense this risk. During World War II, a young woman who had married the day before her new husband, a young man she had known only briefly, had left for a foreign post with the military, expressed her anxiety over the fact that her husband was writing her an average of 35 letters a week. They were long letters in which he was pouring out his heart in an over-romanticized love.

She was still working in her home county as a home economist with the Agricultural Extension Service, was of a more practical nature, and still felt herself a part of real life. She feared the reality he would have to face when they were able to live together as husband and wife. "I'm no angel," she said. "In his dreams now I seem to be. I'm not sure whether he can accept the discovery or not."

In conclusion, realism and good sense are very important to adjustment during the first months of marriage. Levy and Munroe begin a chapter in a very significant book on marriage with this statement, "Nine-tenths of human misery in the world is sheer nonsense."[27] The authors go on to elaborate man's amazing ability to imagine all kinds of troubles for himself. In this, they consider he has more ingenuity than any other creature on the face of the earth. The book concludes that the "mental cruelty" of the imaginative modern wife is of greater consequence than was the physical cruelty of the Neanderthal caveman to his wife. It also points out that the suffering of a wife today for a mink coat is probably

26 *Ibid.,* p. 77.
27 *Ibid.,* Ch. 2.

more serious than was the suffering of the Neanderthal women who lacked clothing altogether.

The moral of the story is that the modern marriage suffers not so much from lack of fulfillment of physical needs, as from the lack of fulfillment of the thousands of complicated expectations and desires that have been built into young people's personalities through an elaborate process of social conditioning.

These authors, in the tradition of psychiatry, believe that people marry for motives beyond their understanding, mostly nonrational motives, and that whether or not their marriage succeeds is dependent in large part on unconscious factors since human beings are not primarily rational.

There is much to be said for this emphasis in understanding marriage and its adjustments. Many motivations are hidden and people rationalize them in other terms. Each person is conditioned to respond favorably or unfavorably to certain situations and certain traits. Presumably, one marries the kind of person to whom he can respond favorably in most situations. This is the whole idea of dating and engagement, and of getting thoroughly acquainted before marriage. Those who have failed in these respects will soon learn the price. Theirs must be a super effort and determination to make their life together a success in spite of surprising discoveries after marriage.

Problems

1. Ralph and Evelyn are trying to decide how and where to spend their honeymoon. They are young, out-going, and companionable, but neither has a serious hobby. Their list of possible choices has been narrowed down to six. Which of the six would you oppose and why?
   a. Visit Evelyn's aging but lovable grandparents on their little Iowa farm.
   b. Visit Ralph's uncle who owns a dude ranch in New Mexico.
   c. Rent a secluded little island hide-a-way off the Florida coast.
   d. Spend a week in New York City seeing the current plays, buying clothes, seeing all the sights, and if possible, landing a job for Ralph.
   e. Join two other honeymoon couples who are going from Florida to South America on a small yacht.
   f. Spend a more-or-less unscheduled week in Miami.
2. Couples who are happy and report that no adjustments have been necessary are probably:
   a. Well-mated.
   b. Lying.
   c. Delaying the adjustments until a more appropriate time.
   d. So used to adjusting that they are unconscious of doing it.
   e. Unusually successful in their sexual adjustment.

3. In the marriage of your parents or acquaintances, is there any evidence that adjustments are still taking place? Without giving names, describe a situation in which you have observed an adjustment in a marriage that has lasted over five years.

4. List the circumstances under which you would agree to have either your father-in-law or mother-in-law share your home.

5. Married students in the class describe your early relationships with your in-laws. In what areas did problems most often arise?

6. *Research exercise:* Poll the class or some other student group on the question, "In what areas do you anticipate the most numerous adjustments in the early weeks of marriage?"
   a. Diversity of ethical codes.
   b. Recreational interests.
   c. Sexual relations.
   d. Little things such as habits of daily living.
   e. Religious beliefs.
   f. Home management.
   g. Life philosophies.
   h. In-law relationships.

   Tabulate results. Does the class tend to agree on areas of greatest likelihood of difficulty? Do the areas of anticipated adjustment differ according to sex?

7. Do you believe that women usually have to do more adjusting in marriage than do men? That marriage changes their way of life more completely than that of men?

8. *Sociodrama:*
   a. A doting mother whose only son has recently married visits the young couple regularly and explains, "I only want to help out; I know how much a young bride has to do and how many things she has to learn." Tension mounts with each visit and the play opens with the young bride finally telling her mother-in-law how she feels about the situation.
   b. A young bride, after a month of marriage, discusses with an older married sister, her disillusionment with marriage.

Selected References

ARTICLES IN BOOKS OF READINGS

FISHBEIN, Morris, and KENNEDY, Ruby Jo Reeves, *Modern Marriage and Family Living* (New York: Oxford University Press, Inc., 1957).
   1. ARLITT, Ada Hart, "The Wedding and Honeymoon," pp. 177-186.
KLING, Samuel G., and KLING, Esther B., *The Marriage Reader* (New York: Vanguard Press, Inc., 1947).
   2. SANGER, Margaret, "The Honeymoon," pp. 119-128.
LANDIS, Judson T., and LANDIS, Mary G., *Readings in Marriage and the Family* (Englewood Cliffs, N. J.: Prentice-Hall, Inc., 1952).

3. LANDIS, Judson T., "Time Required to Achieve Marriage Adjustment," pp. 169-180.

CAVAN, Ruth Shonle, *Marriage and the Family in the Modern World: A Book of Readings* (New York: Thomas Y. Crowell Co., 1960).

4. BOWMAN, Henry, "Healthy Adult Personality," Reading 49.

5. STONE, Abraham, and LEVINE, Lena, "The Dynamics of the Marital Relationship," Reading 50.

6. DUVALL, Evelyn Millis, "Marriage Makes In-Laws," Reading 88.

7. MARCUS, Peggy, "How to Get Along with In-Laws," Reading 89.

8. NEISSER, Edith G., "What Grandmothers Are For," Reading 90.

CHRISTENSEN, Harold T., *Handbook of Marriage and the Family* (Chicago: Rand McNally & Co., 1964).

9. BERNARD, Jessie, "The Adjustment of Married Mates," Ch. 17.

General References

BEE, Lawrence S., *Marriage and Family Relations* (New York: Harper & Row, Publishers, 1959), Chs. 12, 13.

BOWMAN, Henry A., *Marriage for Moderns*, Fourth Edition (New York: McGraw-Hill Book Co., 1960), Ch. 10.

BURGESS, Ernest W., and WALLIN, Paul, *Engagement and Marriage* (Philadelphia: J. B. Lippincott Co., 1953), Chs. 18, 19.

CAVAN, Ruth Shonle, *American Marriage* (New York: Thomas Y. Crowell Co., 1959), Ch. 12.

DUVALL, Evelyn M., *In-Laws: Pro and Con* (New York: Association Press, 1953).

————, and HILL, Reuben, *Being Married* (New York: Association Press, 1960), Ch. 11.

HOBART, Charles W., "Disillusionment in Marriage and Romanticism," *Marriage and Family Living*, 20:156-162, May, 1958.

KEPHART, William M., *The Family, Society and the Individual*, (Boston: Houghton Mifflin Co., 1961).

KIRKPATRICK, Clifford, *The Family as Process and Institution*, Second Edition (New York: The Ronald Press Co., 1963), Ch. 18.

LANDIS, Judson T., "Length of Time Required to Achieve Adjustment in Marriage," *American Sociological Review*, 11:666-667, December, 1946.

LEMASTER, E. E., *Modern Courtship and Marriage* (New York: The Macmillan Co., 1957), Chs. 11, 12, 15.

LEVY, John, and MUNROE, Ruth, *The Happy Family* (New York: Alfred A. Knopf, Inc., 1938).

MARTINSON, Floyd M., *Marriage and the American Ideal* (New York: Dodd, Mead & Co., 1960).

POPENOE, Paul, *Marriage Is What You Make It* (New York: The Macmillan Co., 1950).

SIRJAMAKI, John, *The American Family in the Twentieth Century* (Cambridge: Harvard University Press, 1953), Ch. 5.

22
Patterns of Adjustment

In any kind of close living or working arrangement between human beings, some way of getting along together must be worked out if the association is to last. Business partners must divide privileges, responsibilities, and work, as well as profits. Roommates in a dormitory must each modify some of their ways if they are to spend a year together. Bachelor girls sharing an apartment must agree on many things, or agree to disagree—on hours for doing certain things, on food, furniture, etc. This necessity is even greater with married couples, for the possible areas of conflict are more numerous than in any of the other pair relationships mentioned.

In all human relationships, whether of individuals or groups, certain interaction processes and adjustment devices are characteristic. The simplest of these is *dominance* and *submission*. This pattern is seen everywhere—in the chicken yard where psychologists have spotted the dominent hen by her ability to outpeck all the others and make them bow to her demands; among the forest animals where the most powerful male wins the female after defeating all comers; among children in their play; among adults in many work and social situations. Once the relationship of dominance and submission has been established, quarreling and conflict cease. The superior need no longer fight to hold his own, for the inferior has already been cowed.

Conflict is another common interaction pattern between persons. At its worst, it aims at annihilating the enemy. In its more gentle forms, it is expressed in quarreling, which is an attempt to annihilate the opponent on the ego level. Where conflict exists, adjustment has not been reached. In fact, conflict is one of the common ways of striving for an adjustment —in war, through defeating the enemy and winning a peace; in marriage, through winning the argument. The difficulty with this device is that someone always has to lose before there can be peace, unless there can be compromise and both can be content to call it a draw.

Accommodation is a sociological term which means about what is meant by the common phrase "agree to disagree." It is settling issues by permanent compromise of differences. Most people can't keep up a fight for a lifetime. Conflict is tiring, even in its mild form of quarreling. There comes a time to call a halt and stake out neutral territory if there is to be any getting along at all.

Competition is another interactive relationship between human beings. It is a common pattern of American life, and to some extent of life almost everywhere. It aims at nothing more than outdoing the other person by superior performance. Modern business is geared to perpetual competition. Success in modern education for the most part is measured by one's ability to outdo his classmates—by landing a little higher toward the "A" side of the normal curve. Men live in a competitive world throughout a lifetime. Women live competitively in school and college. Does competition have a place as an adjustment device in marriage? Many use it.

Cooperation is the goal of adjustment. Instead of outdoing each other, persons in cooperation strive to help each other, to bolster each other. Mutual aid and mutual sharing is the pattern of cooperation. It gives to each the other's strength. The cooperative couple is the adjusted couple.

Each adjustment device is likely to appear in some form in every marriage. The device employed most often and the kind of adjustment arrived at determines the happiness of the marriage.

Dominance and Submission

The story is told of a strapping big lieutenant who married a girl of small stature inclined toward bossiness. After carrying her across the threshold, he took off his pants, handed them to her and commanded her to put them on. She put them on, then protested, "Why, Bill, they're three times too big for me."

His reply was, "Don't forget that."

That is one way to work out a problem of who is to wear the pants in the family. It is not the best way for most marriages, yet throughout history, in the relationships of husbands and wives, dominance and submission have been the most characteristic pattern of man-wife relationships, with the male more often assuming the dominant role.

Life in all social institutions requires that self-interest be minimized for the good of the institution. If the wife, by custom or inclination, surrenders most of her prerogative as an individual at marriage, the male need surrender few of his. This solution to the problems of the marriage can be simple, clear-cut, and remarkably effective if each member of the pair can accept the assigned role. There is little quibbling over issues and little time squandered in family councils.

Many of the peaceful marriages of an earlier day, in which there were never any real quarrels, are explained by this clear distinction in authority in roles of man and wife. The male decided; the female acquiesced. It is little credit to such great-grandparent couples that they never quarreled. If grandpa was the patriarch that most men in his time were, he blew off steam and his wife humbly took it, slipping off in the bedroom to cry, rather than fighting back.

A survey covering 2,596 well-educated families attempted to learn not only who was boss, but also whether or not the couple was happy with the arrangement. Students in three colleges—the University of California, Oklahoma Agriculture and Mechanical College, and Columbia University—were asked by Paul Popenoe of the American Institute of Family Relations to rate couples with whom they were well acquainted and who had been married at least five years, as to (1) who was boss in the family and (2) happiness of the marriage. It was found that men were dominant in 35 percent of the cases; women, in 28 percent; and in 37 percent of the cases there was a democratic partnership. Of the democratic partnerships, almost nine out of ten were found to be happy; of the male-dominated couples almost two-thirds were happy; of the wife-dominated marriages, less than half.

Counselor David Mace emphasizes the point that there are, even today, many patterns of marriage which can succeed. He believes that the marriage in which dominance and submission are the characteristic pattern often has a place, concluding that "there are people who want to be dominated—and not all of them are women."[1]

The democratic ideal, while it is a norm for the urban-industrial marriage, certainly need not be attained by all persons in order for them to be happy. Many couples can and do live together very successfully in a relationship of dominance and submission. It is when one insists on this kind of relationship and the other finds it incompatible, that trouble begins.

Quarreling As an Adjustment Device

It is an unusual couple that has not had some very serious quarrels during their engagement period. Those who do not are probably not well enough acquainted or have failed to be together in enough different situations to learn some of their real differences.

[1] David R. Mace, "Personality Expression and Subordination in Marriage," *Marriage and Family Living*, 15:205-207, August, 1953.

For those who don't have some misunderstandings before marriage, the first real clash after marriage is likely to be unusually disturbing. The chances are that the young couple will wonder how two people so much in love could possibly quarrel so.

Behind the first quarrel is a lot of history. During the romantic days of dating and engagement, both were on their good behavior. Then, too, most of the times when they were together were situations for fun or play. Even on the honeymoon, they were away from everyone they knew and free to play, travel, and do as they pleased. Before marriage, and in the first few days after marriage, life was one big holiday.

During all this time both were probably aware of some little traits or attitudes, some manners or habits, some spendthrifty, extravagant ways, or some friends or relatives that they did not exactly like. But in the grand days of engagement and honeymoon these irritations were overlooked, or passed by, even though there was a feeling all the time that these issues would have to be faced sooner or later.

All goes well during the honeymoon. Then the couple begin their routine life together, and after some very trying event one day the explosion comes. The wife ends up in tears or they both end up pouting and silent. The overly idealistic may conclude they are well on their way to the divorce court. When one considers that this is the first time that either has really let off steam during months of petty irritations, it seems quite the normal thing to do. In any case, most couples do it.

Quarreling near universal: The American Institute of Public Opinion in one of its national surveys asked couples whether or not they had marital disputes. Four out of five couples admitted that they did. The researchers in interpreting these data suggested that they suspected the other fifth either had had some pretty serious marital disputes, or else were still honeymooners, or were people who had passed their golden anniversary and forgotten a great deal.

> Absence of quarrels is too often regarded as a criterion of successful marriage. Usually it means little more than indifference—a superficial placidity attained by shallow people or those whose real interests lie outside the home, or those who, with or without a day of reckoning, habitually bury their antagonism under the thick cotton pad of polite behavior.[2]

Quarreling in marriage is one indication that husband and wife both recognize their equal status in the marriage. The way a young couple handles a quarrel is the thing that tells whether they are building a successful marriage that will result in a cooperative union. The issues about

[2] John Levy and Ruth Munroe, *The Happy Family* (New York: Alfred A. Knopf, Inc., 1938), p. 76.

which a couple quarrels indicate areas where adjustments have to be made. If, after the explosion is over, Ted and Carrie discuss their problems and try to work out a solution, they are taking the first forward step toward successful adjustment.

David Mace[3] states that although a couple is drawn together by such affinities as a need for sexual fulfillment, the need for comradeship—that is, to share a common destiny and to avoid loneliness—and the need for an emotional sense of belonging, it is just as certain that at some point in their relationship hostilities must appear to protect the ego of the individual against too great an encroachment by the other party. This is the only way, he believes, the personality can avoid destruction. Couples must learn where the point of equilibrium is.

Psychiatrist Harold F. Searles[4] has concluded that people become schizophrenic partly by reason of "a long continued . . . unconscious effort on the part of some person or persons . . . to drive him crazy." This can be a family conspiracy, even though unconscious. Better to tell another member of the family "you're crazy" now and then, than to let matters fester to the point where there develops the "unconscious need to drive somebody else crazy so that an unhealthy state of mutual dependence can continue despite anxieties and frustrations."

Mace believes that because of this inevitable hostility, quarreling has a proper and useful place in marriage in that it lets off emotional steam, whereas a mere intellectual interchange on the discussion basis fails to do so. He feels that the couple needs at some time to feel the heat of each other's points of view and needs. To quarrel without either partner giving ground, until emotion is dissipated and they are drawn together by some affinity, most likely sexual need, is likely to be disastrous. No equilibrium is reached and the marriage simply fluctuates back and forth between hostility and attraction. Also for one partner to give in for the sake of peace is not good. In this case the one member becomes the tyrant and the other submits. Mace recognizes that in some marriages this relationship is a satisfactory one, in that there are members of both sexes who prefer the submissive role in marriage.

Discussion of issues is a rational substitute for quarreling and argument. Quarreling is a direct attack on an opponent. It is an attempt to in some measure destroy him. Discussion, by contrast, is an attack on issues to be settled. The one is personal; the other is impersonal. The one leads to chronic nagging and picking; the other brings out issues on which the couple differ, airs them, and tries to work out an intelligent solution. But discussion does not vent hostilities and is not an adequate substitute if there are deep hostilities.

3 David R. Mace, *loc. cit.*
4 *Time*, April, 1959, p. 73.

Advantages of the Quarrel Over Other Reactions to Frustration

Quarreling, like many adjustment devices, though never an ideal relationship is often a better alternative than many others that are likely to be needed if provoking circumstances exist. One is reminded of the old Quaker, with his gentle philosophy of living. The cow has switched him all during the milking and finally dragged her tail through the milk and slapped it around his neck. He jumped to his feet, grabbed her tail and said, "I will not smite thee, I'll not curse thee, but I will twist thy dern tail!"

Situations can reach the point where some kind of action has to be taken or the inner disturbance costs more than venting the emotion externally. The intimate husband and wife relationship requires so much encroachment on the private domain of the other's ego that an explosion may be needed to release tension and establish balance. The explosion clears the air for discussion by venting the emotional pressure. It may open the way for the couple to work out a more clear and understanding relationship, and thus strengthen their relationship with each other.

In the violent quarrel the real issues are more likely to come out than they are under other circumstances. The making-up process often leads to a deeper level of intimacy than existed before, for the sequel is often a confession or admission of mutual guilt and mutual responsibility. People who can quarrel are much less likely to get involved in serious psychological problems than are those whose recourse is sulking, or avoidance. Quarreling is a better adjustment device than brooding, walking out, or running home to mother or to a neighbor. It is better than the neuroses which may develop from constantly ignoring or repressing hostility issues. It is better than escaping in drink, in desertion, in a romance outside the marriage. It is even better, although some authorities disagree, than quietly and passively resigning oneself in religion as an antidote for adjustment.

This is not to say that a couple who can live without a quarrel is not a happier or more perfect pair. There is no doubt that they are. But most couples cannot, at least in the early stages of their marriage, expect to live at this level of perfection. The problems to be worked out are usually too numerous. Quarrels begin with trivialities but they uncover much more. The triviality is the trigger. The built-up hostilities, frustrations, and aggravations are the background for the explosion. As the emotionally charged quarrel breaks loose, and the destructive impulses of one mate are vented on the other, the real issues of the quarrel are likely to be exposed. As the heat of wrath grows, that standard phrase comes forth, "And another thing," and with it an exposure of the vital issues. The issues are no longer trivial, they are the very issues that determine marriage survival or failure.

Compromise not enough: Whether the quarrel leads toward adjustment or carries the marriage toward disaster, will depend on the outcome. Of these there are several possibilities. Compromise is a more logical outcome perhaps than one would expect in a really heated quarrel. Genuine contrition allows the couple to each recognize his faults and ask forgiveness for them. This may bring the partners to a deeper level in understanding of each other's needs, and thus may result in a more perfect love. People who have never had issues to overcome perhaps cannot understand how this can be. This kind of outcome leads to the building of closer marriage relationships and decreased hostilities. It leads to mutual acceptance and increased mutual respect. This is perhaps the finest outcome possible in any kind of human conflict, for it is not merely the peace of compromise that points the way to accommodation (discussed in the next section) but it is a genuine approach to mutual identification and to becoming one in spirit and in aims as well as in flesh. Genuine compromise is, of course, a step forward. And in some marriages, compromise of a purely rational character is necessary. Compromise is not enough, however, where it proves only to be a truce in a cold war. The same hostilities are there if the issues over which the quarrel took place are still there.

If each continues to feel that the other is wrong, that the other is to blame, that the other person is the one who must change, the truce cannot last. It will revive again and continue, and perhaps with each battle the road back to genuine mutual understanding will be made more difficult.

If the result is merely a draw and each recognizes and respects the other person, then the ground is laid for an accommodative relationship in the particular areas of tension.

The quarrel may end in one party or the other being completely cowed. Such a marriage can last. It may be that the wife can recognize and respect her husband and be willing to be subservient to his demands and needs. She may be able psychologically to accept this without neurosis. She (or he) can, however in being cowed, be put on the way toward the development of psychosomatic complaints which are the ego's way of expressing frustration.

In an earlier day, many women, when they had lost all hope of being treated fairly in their marriage, found solace in religion, sufficient solace to retain their sanity. Many today, with less faith but with equal provocation, end up in a mental institution. *The Deseret News Telegram* in a "Confidentially Yours" column by Mary Marker published the account of a woman who found solace in prayer and faith in a marriage where many years of crying had brought no solution. The account goes:

> I never express my needs to my companion but rather to my Heavenly Father. He is our friend and will fill our needs if we trust Him. I have had many things I have wanted badly. Because I knew my husband would be cross and angry if I mentioned them to him, I asked only my Heavenly Father. Many of them came slowly but surely.
>
> Early in my marriage I learned that for peace there had to be a 100 percent husband marriage. So for peace, here I have had to take the mental attitude that I am the hired girl working in his home with no more rights than a hired girl. I talk of only things he is interested in, and when I am with him, I do the things he likes to do.
>
> With this attitude, I can be grateful for all the crumbs he shares with me. To me, the house, furniture, money, children—all things are his and I am fortunate to be able to be in his home that I might care for and be with his children.[5]

One suspects that few psychiatrists would agree with this woman's solution. In fact, it is doubtful that many moderns could accept it for themselves without being victimized by their frustrations to the point of emotional collapse.

In quarreling there is always such a thing as victory without a solution. Certainly the cowed situation that tends to neurotic symptoms proves to be of this character. There may be victories where neither is left cowed but where one is left rebellious, even though silent—more hostile, more deeply determined that in the end he or she must win, must destroy the other or the marriage. If this is the solution, the divorce will take place in the atmosphere of vengeance.

Human nature is highly complicated, and it is most difficult to spell out all types of situations, the hurts, and the solutions that couples arrive at through venting antagonisms. The list of outcomes mentioned must be considered only as suggestions.

Vicarious relief: Idealistically minded critics may well say that mature persons do not use quarreling in the marriage relationship to vent frustrations. But where is one to find a world of such human beings? True, the more mature person learns vicarious ways of venting hostilities, undamaging to others. All can practice in this direction.

The old-fashioned butter churn offered many a mother and grandmother a wonderful relief from the aggravations and frustrations of a dominant and contrary husband. They gritted their teeth and slammed the plunger down. The vigor depended on the extent of their hostility and

[5] Mary Marker, "Confidentially Yours," *The Deseret News Telegram,* Salt Lake City, June 14, 1956.

the depth of their feelings of aggression, which they dared not vent directly on the husband. The result was good—the butter came more quickly, and their feelings were relieved without taking them out on their children.

Some vent hostilities in driving an automobile. A psychiatrist living in the outskirts of the Los Angeles area indicated that he enjoyed the long drive to work through the Los Angeles traffic very much. "It vents my hostilities," he said. Some drivers are dangerous when venting their hostilities while driving through traffic; many seem to get the thrill of combat in dodging traffic, or in speeding, or in outwitting the traffic patrol. This is not a recommended way of relieving one's emotions.

The batting of a ball, the playing of handball, any vigorous physical activity, is for many a wonderful way of easing the spirit of tension and aggression. Perhaps one of the great psychological benefits of hunting and fishing, mountain climbing, and conquest of nature lies here. The revival of interest in these activities in our day, when so many live under heavy social pressure, lies in part in the fact that conquest of nature restores the ego.

Every person needs to learn how to vent hostilities in vicarious, harmless ways, whether this be by pounding the piano keys, or by throwing darts. Thus it is possible to restore one's own ego without destroying another person.

Issues of a Quarrel

Quarreling may occur over any issue that has importance to human beings—money, friends, in-laws, recreation, religion, sex, conventions, honesty, child-training patterns, philosophy of life, politics, etc. It may, in fact, be over nothing at all obvious. In the marriage relationship, where day-to-day contacts are so close, and ego encroachments are risky, often the quarrel is the venting of frustrations accumulated elsewhere. It may be, for the husband, those encountered in his work under the political pressures of the administrative relationships of his position, or under the prodding of a foreman on the job, or under some humiliation he suffers. In these outside situations he has no chance to vent hostility; at home they come out, because there he feels that he is safe, and his feelings must be vented to save his ego. The wife may vent her hostilities on her husband for no other reason than that she has taken all she can take from some neighbor or from her children. The mate is there, the little irritation is the final straw, and the mate is the one on whom the hostilities can be safely vented without their costing too much.

In much of this type of explosion, there is no real intent to destroy the mate, but rather a need to restore the ego, to revive the self in order to save it from the destructive forces which have borne on it too heavily during a particular period of time. With a little picking on the mate, not only is the tension released, but the suppressed ego is revived and made able to face the issues of life again.

Discussion of issues may be more constructive, but it doesn't get at the seat of the problem. Quarreling is a sort of safety valve. Human beings are never perfect—at least not on this side of Jordan! The family is a place where one can explode and express frustrations that have accumulated in the office, during shopping, or in other places where one has to take rebuffs and misunderstandings.

The intimate relationships of man and wife, their very closeness, make the family an easy place for seeking such relief. Such tendencies, however, if allowed to grow, may lead to chronic nagging and dissatisfactions. It is better to work out one's frustrations by kicking at the flat tire, hitting a golf ball, running the lawn mower, shoving the vacuum cleaner, cutting weeds in the garden, or in some other way which does no harm to other human beings. Although quite different, these or similar activities have the same effect in relieving frustration.

A man of an earlier generation, whose independence of spirit had never been bridled, boasted that he wanted a home of his own so that he could spit on the floor whenever he wanted to. He never did spit on the floor, but he was expressing one of the most important values of family life to a man. He may relax and be himself at home in a way that is not possible on the outside. In other groups he is always more or less on his good behavior; his family knows him for what he is.

While this may not always be flattering to the best side of a person, human beings must have some place where they can be off guard. Like it or not, most people are going to be at their worst as well as at their best in the home.

Quarreling and arguments as an habitual pattern, however, can make marriage miserable. Nagging can become a chronic means of letting off tension. As such, it is an extremely bad habit and very difficult to control.

Quarreling and nagging can be reduced somewhat by recognizing certain simple physiological laws. To avoid tension is to reduce the number of conflicts, for much of the conflict in marriage is due to the fact that husband or wife is tense or anxious about some situation outside the marriage. Nerves get taut and the individual is ready to "bite off the head" of whoever happens to be around.

Periods just before meals are often periods of serious tensions since the blood sugar supply of the human body is low and family members are likely to growl like hungry animals. This tense situation before meals can often be avoided by serving orange juice to the children beforehand, or even to the husband, particularly in cases where the meal is to be delayed. Orange juice or some other quick energy food builds up the blood sugar supply and gives quick energy and new stamina.

It is a good rule not to discuss unpleasant issues on an empty stomach. Things take on significance then which could be ironed out simply on a full stomach. Minor quarrels, discussions, and arguments are almost inherent in the marriage relationship. Loss of temper now and then may not be out of line for the quick-tempered person. Human beings are so constituted as to give way when strain becomes too great.

On the other hand, particularly when children enter the marriage, quarreling or even arguing vigorously often gives the children a disquieting sense that there is deep trouble in the family. Couples who must continue to do a certain amount of quarreling and arguing should be particularly careful that it is done in such a way, or at such a time, as not to give the children a sense of insecurity.

Accommodation—The Imperfect Path

Barbara Steel reports asking a friend the secret of her long and happy marriage.[6] The reply was that the friend and her husband discovered early in their marriage "that there was no subject on which we could reach an agreement. And so . . . we've never tried." Hanna Lees, writing for the *Saturday Evening Post,* titled an article "How To Be Happy Though Incompatible," and made a very strong case for her thesis.[7] She declares that men give no thought to the problem of compatibility. Wives may as well face the fact, and a lot of emotional probing won't improve matters at all. She feels that few men give wives the attentions they feel they need, because husbands are preoccupied with other things and take marriage for granted. Almost every marriage, she concludes, has many areas of incompatibility. It is to be expected.

There is much sense in this. Of course, the crux of the matter is: How many areas of incompatibility can be tolerated? And, how serious is the incompatibility to those aspects of the relationship which are most vital?

If the husband is inclined to direct or correct all the wife's moves when she goes bowling, or when they sit at the bridge table, they may find it essential to seek their recreation separately.

The wife may not like the fact that the husband wants an occasional weekend to hunt with his pals, but she comes to recognize that escape into the male subculture provides a type of recreation he needs and likes, and so she accepts it, even though it means that she has to be alone sometimes. At first she may have quarreled about this, then she probably realized that there was no use quarreling about it the rest of her married

6 Reported in *Reader's Digest.*
7 *Saturday Evening Post,* February 16, 1957.

life. Such weekends were important to him and she recognized this fact, even though she would have liked to have it otherwise.

The husband may not like the fact that his wife—say she is a former teacher—takes occasional work as a substitute teacher. Her working inconveniences him. He storms about it at first because his meals are not ready on the days she teaches. She explains that she needs to get out of the home and keep in touch with people and activities that she likes. He grumbles for a while but learns to step aside and let his wife work out this part of her life to suit herself rather than him.

The petty irritations of living are often the worst irritations of all. Dr. Lester Kirkendall, family sociologist at the University of Oregon, tells of a young wife in one of his classes who was irritated almost beyond endurance by the fact that her husband left his socks on the floor. Dr. Kirkendall asked the class of young women what they would do.

"Nail them to the floor," one said. "Put them on his desk," another suggested. And so the answers came—a dozen or more—all of them solutions which would have increased the tension between husband and wife.

Finally one girl, registering a tone of disgust at her classmates' answers, said "They're not very heavy. Pick them up!"

"But," the wife protested, "he's got *no right* to expect me to pick things up!"

A marriage is in for difficulties when either husband or wife insists on living by rights. There are many instances in any human relationship where someone must go the second mile, and there are many second miles to be walked in a successful marriage. It will sometimes be the husband who walks them and sometimes the wife. When both are willing to do this, there is a kind of sharing that raises the marriage relationship to the highest level of happiness.

How much one can give and take very often depends on what the issue symbolizes for him or for her, as the example of the socks so well illustrates. Many women can pick up the socks day after day and, though they dislike it, they take it as part of their work routine and come to accept it. But the wife who protests "he's got no right to expect," etc., has much more at stake than household routine. Ego and status values of great depth are apparently at stake in her case. She no doubt feels herself in servile status picking up socks. If this is so, the giving will probably have to be on the husband's part.

Without doubt, the greater the number of areas of accommodation, the less likelihood there will be of a completely happy marriage. On the other hand, highly individualized persons must often avoid certain areas of difference in order to tolerate marriage at all. The technique of avoidance may not be the best, but in such instances it is the only effective solution.

Although the ideal goal of marriage is cooperation, it is rarely fully realized in the individualistic marriage. There must be some accommodation—ability to tolerate and accept the other person as he is and his activities for what they mean to him. In almost every marriage there are areas in which each partner agrees to accept differences he recognizes but doesn't like. No two human beings can achieve identical interests. One or both yield ground merely to keep peace.

In most marriages there must be some acceptance of the mate in spite of certain incompatibilities. Topics on which the couple can never agree are not discussed. A "keep off" sign is posted over them. It is far better simply to let them lie. There are certain fields of activity which they must avoid together.

Avoidance as a device of accommodation may not meet the ideal of the romantic marriage, yet if couples by avoiding certain subjects, certain issues, certain places, or even each other completely for periodic separate vacations or other breaks and can thus keep the peace, they may find that the most satisfactory way of marriage for them.

In this highly individuated age, many individuals are so completely individual that they cannot submerge their personalities into another. There are vital zones of overlapping, but this is all there ever can be. Those who learn this about themselves and their mate may well find their marriage quite satisfactory, in fact, as satisfactory as any marriage could be for them.

Competition vs. Adjustment

The ego and the love motives in human personality are forever at odds, yet the ego must be preserved from extinction even in marriage. In a society where the game of competition has become the most engrossing activity of life, love is always threatened. In love, one cannot count marks and scores, dollars and cents, honors and distinctions, prizes and awards. These are part of the ego-expressing game. Love cannot be measured in the balance of fair exchange. It gives without asking in return.

The educational and occupational worlds are worlds of competition for survival. Success and status are dependent upon the development of this trait in the personality. In most relationships of adult life in American society, equality assumes competition. Competition involves rivalry—the spirit of excelling and outdoing. This spirit has come to characterize the lives, not only of men, but of women. It is the predominating pattern of school activities from earliest childhood throughout the college years.

Work relationships in industry, relationships in offices, and the vying for social position and standard of living also show this pattern. Admittedly, competition is an invigorating characteristic of a society which has always preached the doctrine of social climbing—a faith of a people who believe that there is room at the top.

Marriage, by contrast, is an institution of close complementary co-operation. Its success or failure depends upon the couple's ability to work together as a team and to get along. Among young people today, each of whom has gone to college and competed both educationally and in the work world, the competitive habit often brings great difficulty to marriage because it is hard not to carry over the competitive spirit into the marriage relationship.

If both continue to work, they may feel they are competing with each other in the amount of income they earn, in the type of expenditures they are able to afford, and in many other aspects of their personal relationship. This is one of the great difficulties faced by the emancipated couple in this age. Instead of being able to bolster the other and strengthen each other's roles in the community and work world, they find themselves trying to detract and run down the mate as a way of maintaining or building up their own status. The wife may envy the husband in his work, if she is confined to the home; if both work, they may feel competitive in seeking status, just as couples who are friendly in school sometimes feel competitive over athletic or social success or grades. This destroys their feeling of security in each other. The wife feels humiliated by the husband's success, or the husband feels outdone by the wife's achievements, be they in social life or the work world.

Rather than being able to share the joy of the partner's achievement, the mate then is likely to suffer from inferiority feelings. Rather than push the mate forward to further success, each tries to draw the other down to his or her own level. Rather than bolstering the husband's or wife's feeling of self-importance, the mate tries to "cut him down to size." Rather than the marriage being a cooperative sharing, it is subjected to the same strain as business life and social life outside the family, where rivalry for position and influence replaces a genial spirit of working together. This is one of the important reasons why every marriage for the well-informed modern couple is a marriage of constant adjustment.

This problem is often presented as one peculiar to the modern wife. It is so only because men have by custom so long been granted authority that the wife gets blamed for her attempt to actually realize equality in the marriage. Something has to give in such marriages, for affection evaporates and the marriage becomes comparable to a business relationship, with the same ruthless driving for success, the same quest for recognition. As love dies, the craving for status and recognition become more desperate. Human nature is so constituted that if one has a full and understanding love, his ego requires little satisfaction in the marriage relationship; without love the ego makes great demands. If the love relationship is lost in marriage, the ego takes on immense dimensions, demanding satisfactions and recognitions that are entirely beyond reasonable expectations.

Paul Popenoe, Director of the American Institute of Family Relations, says that the American male wants a woman who will bolster his ego—give him sympathy, warmth and security, not outdo him. In writing to college-trained women, he has warned that men, even in our sophisticated age, are not interested primarily in women with college degrees. They want a woman in marriage to satisfy emotional needs that cannot be met in the competitive activities of work life. This is no doubt the great appeal of the foreign girl to the American male.[8]

Women, too, in marriage are, in the final analysis, looking for the emotional security that comes from being wanted, loved, and cared for. They crave a sense of belonging. They want this without paying the price of sacrificing their right to be individuals.[9]

The American marriage today sets before men and women the highest ideal of which man has ever dreamed—that of sharing on the basis of complete equality, or recognizing each other as full, complete, and self-sufficient individuals, with rights, privileges, and aspirations to be satisfied both within and outside the marriage. This type of marriage is a much finer relationship than one based on dominance and submission, and yet it is one which is increasingly difficult to attain. This is not because men and women do not realize its merits, but because they are built for a competitive relationship and cannot meet the demands of such a marriage. Consequently, most marriages are a compromise.

The secret of a happy marriage, like a happy romance, is cooperative, self-sacrificing sharing. It is the part of each spouse to bolster, support, and build up the ego of the other. Both men and women seek to satisfy their wish for emotional security in marriage. Both must also find success and recognition to be happy.

Realism in Adjustment Expectations

Throughout this discussion of marriage adjustment, the emphasis has been on the kinds of patterns that make for good adjustment. It must, however, be recognized that marriage today, in its interpersonal relationships, is not a highly standardized institution. It is rather highly individuated and the pattern that is satisfactory for one couple would

[8] For research bearing on this see Chapter 16.

[9] For a discussion of many facets of this problem see Seymour M. Farber and Roger H. L. Wilson (Editors), *The Potential of Woman* (New York: McGraw-Hill Book Co., 1963).

not be satisfactory for another. For the most part, research to date has been drawn from the middle and upper middle classes. There is no doubt that family patterns of the lower classes differ considerably in many respects and that the kinds of adjustment described in many situations in the preceding pages would not be satisfactory for certain couples.

The ideal marriage relationship—the goals for which young people should strive—has been outlined. One should not be discouraged if he does not fully realize the ideal of cooperation. One meets couples who seem to be happiest together after a good spat. They have let off steam and seem closer for it. And there are some wives who seem sure of their husband's love only after he has given them a good beating.

Most such marriages are among couples from national cultures where the expression of violent emotions is sanctioned by customs and where male dominance is still accepted in the culture pattern. The book and film previously cited, *The Quiet Man,* depicted a marriage relationship in which the American male failed to conform to the expectations of Irish culture and lost the respect of both his wife and the community. Only when he became his wife's rough master did he regain a place of respect.

If a couple has found a satisfactory life together along these embattled lines, who is to say that their roles should be revised for the sake of an ideal? Such couples might find peaceful life a monotony. Often the wife who requires such treatment of a husband in order to love him has been punished or severely dominated by her father during her upbringing.

But in the genuine democratic marriage of sharing and cooperation —the ideal of the American family system today—adjustment rather than conflict is the accepted goal. This is for most couples the road to understanding. In general, it is assumed that such a philosophy of adjustment offers a far superior type of human relationship to that which is sometimes attained by means of a beastly struggle for mutual acceptance.

In a definite sense, every family pattern in the United States is different. In fact, some authors talk about family culture, referring to the specific unique characteristics of each individual household. Any young couple should get valuable hints and guides from the foregoing discussion and the research upon which it is based. On the other hand, one should not be anxious about his future if his pattern of life does not exactly fit the norm which this or any other book presents. The important thing is that the pattern of life established create a mutually satisfying family environment and provide a home in which children feel secure. This is a point which has been stressed repeatedly throughout the book and which cannot be overstressed. Human life is not patterned so specifically that any two people can fit into an identical mold, nor would they be happy in doing so if they could.

Husbands and wives cannot, in all situations, see eye to eye and most marriages would be monotonous affairs if they did. Adjustment, after all, is a relative thing. It assumes a working relationship which is satifactory in most respects for the persons involved in it. It need not satify neighbors, friends, even relatives, and it need not satify every criteria of research or of marriage books.

Successful marriage adjustment is not for the overly perfectionistic, nor yet is it for the callous and inconsiderate. The democratic marriage of today offers a sharing between human beings of their strengths and weaknesses and their troubles and anxieties. The way any particular couple work out their life together is their own problem. The institution of marriage no longer standardizes the roles of husbands and wives. In fact, at many points, their roles interchange. The important thing is that the couple work out a way of life that is satisfactory to them. It need not conform to the kind of life their parents found satisfactory or to the norms by which other people live. The important test is that the marriage satisfy a sufficient number of their needs so that their lives run more or less smoothly.

In this age, when marriage adjustment is so much stressed in nearly all women's magazines and in much drama and fiction, couples may develop an overidealistic conception of the perfect marriage relationship. There is much evidence from the study of even the better marriages that marriage cannot satisfy every need and that even at best it is not a perfect institution. The demands of close daily association are rarely met without occasional frictions and the numerous forces which impinge upon the marriage from outside make constantly recurring adjustments almost inevitable.

Couples need to avoid constantly taking their marital temperature and worrying about the state of their relationship together. They need to be realistic and practical about the marriage and recognize what it can and cannot do. Within the family, as in other institutions, there is always the tendency of the individual to want to have life ordered to suit him. However, the institution itself survives only as life is ordered to suit the group. The struggle between these two forces has always gone on in every marriage. It is particularly active today with the recognized equal status of family members. With equality of status becoming socially approved, and men and women becoming more specialized and individualistic, the struggle between individual interests and group interests becomes more evident.

If the central purpose of the couple is to maintain a working relationship together, and to face life's issues together, most of the minor and petty differences will be submerged in the longer and more distant goal. Much divorce today takes place over petty issues, because the couple have not decided in their own minds that their marriage is going to be a success, that it has a future, and that its central purpose will be fulfilled regardless of the many fringe adjustments which must be made in the relationship together.

In conclusion, marriage is a highly individualized institution and patterns of adjustment will vary. Some marriages will have considerable conflict and yet be generally satisfactory; others will reach a high degree of harmony and cooperation. Some spouses can accept, even enjoy a relationship of submission. Some marriages can perhaps survive considerable competition. In an individualistic age most marriages require a certain amount of accommodation. The degree to which a given pattern will be employed will vary with family and ethnic background of the pair as well as with their temperament and disposition.

Problems

1. If one or the other spouse tends toward dominance in marriage, do you think it should be the husband, the wife, or does it matter? Upon what grounds would you justify your position:
   a. Tradition.
   b. Decoy.
   c. Family well-being.
   d. Natural Law.
   e. Economic factors.
   f. Intellectual differences.
   g. Other factors.
   Do the men and women of the class agree? What is the most common justification offered?
2. List several areas of a marriage in which accommodation, rather than adjustment, is likely to occur.
3. Mary and Jarvis are both college graduates with responsible and well-paying jobs in a large, highly competitive, advertising agency. Their jobs rest on their ability to think up schemes for outdoing other firms and outselling other products. They even compete with one another at their job since their salary and prestige depend upon the number and quality of ideas that each submits. How might they guard their private lives from the competitiveness they must feel while on the job?

4. List several situations or personal qualities to which you would refuse to adjust, or even accommodate, in marriage. Does there tend to be consensus among class members on any of these adjustment limitations? Do men's and women's views differ?

5. Describe a situation in which a quarrel might serve as a desirable adjustment device.

6. *Research exercise:* Poll the class or some other student group on the question, "In your own home what pattern of adjustment seemed to prevail?" Tabulate results by sex. What patterns of adjustment are most often found? Do men and women have a different conception of adjustment patterns in their homes?

7. Do you believe that some men, as well as some women, are happier in marriage when they have a mate to dominate them and make decisions for them? If so, how do you explain such personalities?

8. Do you believe that an occasional quarrel is as necessary to a marriage as a pressure valve is to a pressure cooker: that both provide means for letting off steam and keeping the lid from blowing off?

9. Do you believe that competitiveness is on the increase or gradually being reduced in the relationship of the sexes before marriage? After marriage?

10. *Sociodrama:* Stage a quarrel between husband and wife over some common problem such as money, recreation, friends, or religion. At the end let the group discuss the quarrel as an adjustment device. Would another pattern have produced better results?

Selected References

ARTICLES IN BOOKS OF READINGS

KLING, Samuel G., and KLING, Esther B., *The Marriage Reader* (New York: Vanguard Press, Inc., 1947).

    1. TRIDON, André, "Jealousy," pp. 423-431.

BECKER, Howard, and HILL, Reuben (Editors), *Family, Marriage and Parenthood,* Second Edition (Boston: D. C. Heath & Co., 1955).

    2. MOWRER, Harriet R., "Getting Along in Marriage," pp. 341-365.

    3. ————, "Discords in Marriage," pp. 366-392.

LANDIS, Judson T., and LANDIS, Mary G., *Readings in Marriage and the Family* (Englewod Cliffs, N. J.: Prentice-Hall, Inc., 1952).

    4. ROTH, Julius, and PECK, Robert F., "Social Class and Marital Adjustments," pp. 197-199.

CAVAN, Ruth Shonle, *Marriage and the Family in the Modern World: A Book of Readings* (New York: Thomas Y. Crowell Co., 1960).

    5. BOSSARD, James H. S., "Eight Reasons Why Marriages Go Wrong," Reading 62.

    6. JACKSON, Joan K., "Alcoholism and the Family," Reading 64.

General References

BEE, Lawrence S., *Marriage and Family Relations* (New York: Harper & Row, Publishers, 1959), Chs. 15, 16.

CAVAN, Ruth Shonle, *American Marriage* (New York: Thomas Y. Crowell Co., 1959), Ch. 18.

KEPHART, William M., *The Family, Society and the Individual*, (Boston: Houghton Mifflin Co., 1961).

LANDIS, Judson T., and LANDIS, Mary G., *Building a Successful Marriage*, Fourth Edition (Englewood Cliffs, N. J.: Prentice-Hall, Inc., 1963), Ch. 16.

MACE, David R., "Personality Expression and Subordination in Marriage," *Marriage and Family Living*, 15:205-207, August, 1953.

NYE, F. Ivan, and HOFFMAN, Lois Wladis (Editors), *The Employed Mother in America* (Chicago: Rand McNally & Co., 1963), Part 3.

PETERSON, James A., *Education For Marriage*, Second Edition (New York: Charles Scribner's Sons, 1964), Ch. 13.

POPENOE, Paul, *Marriage Is What You Make It* (New York: The Macmillan Co., 1950).

ROSENBAUM, Bernice, "Married Women Alcoholics," *Quarterly Journal of Studies on Alcohol*, 19:79-89, March, 1958.

23

The Issues in Marriage Happiness and Unhappiness

Marriage happiness is not a state which, having once been reached, tends to endure unchanged to the very end. In fact, it is safe to say that marriage constitutes one relationship which, at least in our time and culture, is always either getting better or getting worse. There is no one stage in marriage at which one can say, "This is the stabilizing point; from here on things will always be the same."

There may have been a time when such a theory was warranted. Before mutual adjustment and the goal of maximum happiness became the cornerstones of marriage, it is likely that the early years did determine the interaction patterns of a couple for life. Even those couples who searched eagerly for happiness and failed were probably not too surprised or frustrated, and tended to adjust to their "fate" without undue bitterness. Marriage was a necessary step for most women—how else were they to be provided for? Happiness could seldom be a major consideration in a time when they had few, if any, alternatives to marriage.

Today, divorce is an alternative and women are, in general, more confident of their ability to get along on their own. This means that when a marriage is not actually producing satisfaction and happiness it is less likely to be tolerated. When a marriage does not reach or cannot maintain an acceptable level of happiness, either or both partners are more likely to think in terms of giving up and trying again with a new mate.

This does not mean that couples today work less hard at making their marriages succeed. They probably work harder, for they are more aware than were their great-grandparents that "things can be changed." But few are now willing to continue their efforts when the relationship seems barren of all promise of happiness. They are not so likely to turn their interests and energies into compensating channels.

The modern wife may be no wiser than was her grandmother in how to meet the problems of marriage, but this is to be said in her favor—she is more determined to *solve* the problems rather than *tolerate* them, and she wants a solution that will satisfy herself as well as her husband. Fewer men today than formerly expect or even want complete submission from their wives. They realize that marriage will require adjustments, but they are less likely than their great-grandfathers to expect their wives to do all the adjusting. Both husband and wife want happiness for themselves and for each other.

A Happy Marriage Requires Happy Mates

Happiness, the goal of the modern couple in their marriage, is an intangible quality and yet a real one. People know when they possess it. Many attitudes and values seem to enter into making the happy and the unhappy husband and wife. Psychologist Terman tried to learn the principal traits that characterize the happy and the unhappy husband and wife. Here are the traits he found most indicative:[1]

Happy wives	*Unhappy wives*
have kindly attitude toward others	often have feelings of inferiority
like to help underdogs	tend to be defensive or aggressive
tend to be conventional	are easily annoyed, irritated
are cooperative	often join clubs only to get an office or
have strong urge to save money	recognition in them
are optimistic about life	are extreme in their views
do not take offense easily	are more likely to be neurotic
are less interested in social activities	lose tempers easily
such as dances	are impressed by thrilling situations
like to teach children	seek spectacular activities
put less importance on clothes	want to be on the move; are romance
are systematic homemakers	seekers
do less daydreaming	show little interest in others

[1] Lewis M. Terman and others, *Psychological Factors in Marital Happiness* (New York: McGraw-Hill Book Co., 1938), Ch. 7.

Happy husbands	*Unhappy husbands*
have greater stability	often have feelings of inferiority
are cooperative	compensate by browbeating wife and
get along well with business associates	subordinates
are somewhat extroverted	dislike details
are more conservative in attitudes	are more radical about sex morality
are willing to take initiative	are inclined to be moody
take responsibility easily	are more argumentative
do not get rattled easily	like recreations that take them away
	from home
	are apt to be careless about money

Clearly many of the attitudes and behavior traits mentioned in these lists are rooted in early training. The unfortunate thing about most of them is that one either has them or does not have them by the time one enters marriage. Some of these factors may, of course, relate to the character of the marriage itself. For example, whether or not a husband likes most of his recreation outside the home may depend a great deal on the kind of home his wife provides. The unhappy wife's restlessness, too, may depend on the kind of security and ego satisfaction the husband provides.

Are there qualities which husbands and wives exhibit as partners and mates that bear on the happiness of each other? If so what are the most important of these traits?

In one of its series of polls, The American Institute of Public Opinion asked the public to state what they considered the most important qualities of husbands and wives. The question was worded thus: "What would you say is the most important quality in a good husband (wife)?" Here are the five most frequently given answers:

Qualities men want in a wife	*Married men* *(percent)*	*Single men* *(percent)*
good homemaker, good housekeeper, etc.	47	28
agreeable, good company, pleasant disposition	18	21
faithfulness, loyalty	15	16
cooperative, a partner	13	8
patience, understanding	11	9

Qualities women want in a husband	*Married women* *(percent)*	*Single women* *(percent)*
good provider	42	28
faithfulness, steadiness	22	24
kindness, consideration	20	13
agreeable, good company	14	16
cooperative, a partner	55	1

In this day of restaurants, delicatessens, laundries, apartment houses, it is a little surprising to find that almost half the married men mentioned the old-fashioned quality of being a good homemaker and housekeeper. This, along with good cooking, is about the same standard that their great-grandparents probably would have set. In fact, it is the trait Solomon emphasized centuries ago in his description of the good wife:

> She seeketh wool, and flax, and worketh willing with her hands. She is like the merchants' ships; she bringeth her food from afar. She riseth also while it is yet night, and giveth meat to her household. . . . She perceiveth that her merchandise is good: the candle goeth not out. She layeth her hands to the spindle, and her hands hold the distaff. She is not afraid of the snow for her household; for all her household are clothed. . . . She looketh well to the ways of her household, and eateth not the bread of idleness.[2]

Even in this day of great stress on companionability and compatibility only a small portion of men mention these traits. Married women are quite old-fashioned too in one respect. Almost half of them want the husband to be a good provider, but with them the cooperative partner is even more important. This latter attitude shows that women hold the new concept of marriage in much higher regard than men.

When one compares the standards of single and married men and women, he sees why some adjustment in marriage is necessary. Little more than a fourth of the single men thought of housekeeping and homemaking as of great importance, but almost half of the men with experience in marriage considered it of great importance. Similarly, single women were much less often concerned about marrying a good provider than were married women.

One of the most interesting replies received in this poll was that 19 percent of both single men and women didn't know what qualities they wanted in a mate. This group perhaps will have few adjustment problems. More likely, they will know what they want if they fail to find it in the person whom they marry.

Happiness As a Goal

Is happiness, as such, a realistic goal for marriage? Certainly it is an elusive thing, and probably is more often found by those who do not seek it directly than by those who do. It is a by-product of successful living more often than something one can manufacture by conscious effort. Habits of living and ways of thinking no doubt have a great deal to do with the amount of happiness one realizes in daily life.

2 *Proverbs*, 31:13.

Rather than putting each separate experience to the happiness test, it is better to try to lose oneself in those interests and activities that constitute the normal flow of life. This can bring an all-pervasive sense of contentment and well-being. It must, of course, be recognized that persons differ greatly in temperament and, consequently, in the amount of happiness they are capable of realizing. Some are by nature gloomy and pessimistic; others always see the bright side of situations. General health has a direct bearing on happiness, as do the social situations in which one finds oneself.

While happiness is usually considered the first and most important goal of marriage, some authorities believe that such a view of marriage is a misconception from the outset. Count Hermann Keyserling stresses the fact that "the essential difficulties of life do not end, but rather begin with marriage."[3] He goes on to suggest that marriage assumes above all "an acceptance of responsibility."

These views are not necessarily incompatible with the view that the ultimate goal of marriage is happiness, provided one conceives of happiness as being the natural outgrowth of facing responsibility and measuring up to the essential demands of adult life. Such "measuring up" always involves a degree of suffering, self-denial, and renunciation of personal ambitions for the realization of institutional goals.

One of the writer's colleagues put this succinctly once when commenting on the soberness of a friend who was burdened with a family of two young children, the necessity of paying for a home, and the need to meet the demands of an exacting profession. "He thinks life's tougher than it used to be and is inclined to be a little pessimistic once in a while. All that's wrong with him is that he's grown up. He can't quite get over the fact that he isn't a kid playing around any more." The speaker went on to spell out the same sobering effect of family and financial responsibilities on himself. He had gained enough perspective already to realize that responsibility such as had come his way was the price of mature adulthood.

Interestingly enough, old people in retirement, looking back over their years, pick as happiest not the so-called carefree years of youth, but the busy years of family rearing.[4] Happiness is obviously in part at least a matter of perspective. One's concept of it changes with time and experience.

It is possible that in romanticizing marriage and making happiness the goal of family life, many couples too often fail to realize that mar-

[3] Count Hermann Keyserling, *Book on Marriage* (New York: Harcourt, Brace & Co., 1926).

[4] Judson T. Landis, "What Is the Happiest Period in Life?" *School and Society*, 55:643-645, June 6, 1942.

riage, like any other type of partnership, is bound to encounter some problems and difficulties; that no two human beings, regardless of how intimately they live together, can always see eye to eye on all issues; that marriage like a business partnership brings with it many problems.

The weight the couple, or one member of it, gives to happiness and unhappiness may be a factor in their making proper adjustments in marriage. Some people expect a great deal more satisfaction from marriage than others. If one expects more of marriage than marriage can provide, the satisfaction is less than if marital expectations had been more realistic. The world we live in, with its emphasis on romance in movie, radio, and fiction, has tended to create a fiction of marital happiness that sets a standard frequently beyond possibility of realization.

What Proportion of Marriages Attain Happiness?

Intangible and elusive as the quality "happiness" may be, most husbands and wives today seem to recognize it once it has been attained. It has been found that husbands and wives usually agree in their estimates of their marital happiness, and also that outsiders who know the family well generally agree with the couple in estimating the degree of their happiness.[5] Research has also shown that the happiness ratings of a couple do not change much over short periods of time.

It is significant that happiness ratings generally bear a close relationship to success in marriage and to marital adjustment. Happy marriages are rarely regretted by the couple, whereas unhappy marriages are frequently regretted.

An Illinois study sought to determine just how couples rate their marriages relative to happiness. The 526 couples who replied to the questionnaire were asked to classify their marriages as very happy, happy, average, unhappy, very unhappy. These are their replies:[6]

Happiness rating	Number	Percent
Very happy	224	42.6
Happy	108	20.5
Average	76	14.4
Unhappy	71	13.5
Very unhappy	42	8.0
No reply	5	1.0
Total	526	100.0

[5] Ernest W. Burgess and Leonard S. Cottrell, *Predicting Success or Failure in Marriage* (Englewood Cliffs, N. J.: Prentice-Hall, Inc., 1939), Ch. 3.
[6] *Ibid.*, p. 32.

It will be seen that over 63 percent classified their marriages as either happy or very happy, and that only 21.5 percent classified them as unhappy or very unhappy.

A study at Stanford University of 792 couples living in the urban and semiurban areas of California showed similar results.[7] The group was in the middle and upper middle classes. Each person was asked to fill out a questionnaire independently of husband or wife in the presence of an investigator. Husbands and wives rated themselves as follows:

Happiness ratings	Husbands (percent)	Wives (percent)
Extraordinarily happy	29.5	34.6
Decidedly more happy than average	36.8	35.9
Somewhat more happy than average	16.3	14.7
About average	12.9	9.2
Somewhat less happy than average	2.9	3.0
Decidedly less happy than average	1.6	1.8
Extremely unhappy	0.1	0.8
Total	100.0	100.0

This group had even more happy couples and fewer unhappy couples than did the other study. Women clearly run more toward the extremes in their expression of happiness or unhappiness than do men. It is likely that a wife's happiness is more exclusively dependent on the marriage as such than is that of the husband.

Both of these studies probably give a little brighter picture of marriage than actually exists if all marriages are taken into account. Presumably the most unhappy marriages end in divorce. Neither study included divorced individuals. The California study did, however, include some couples who had visited family clinics and who were, therefore, known to be having trouble with their marriage. In both studies a high proportion of the couples were well educated, and as has been previously shown, success and happiness are realized more often in marriage by those who have gone on to the higher levels of education.

A study of the marital happiness of 17,533 couples as reported by their close friends showed the following:[8]

Rating	Number	Percent
Very happy or happy	10,798	61.6
Average	3,322	18.9
Unhappy, very unhappy, or divorced	3,413	19.5
Total	17,533	100.0

[7] Terman and others, *op. cit.*, p. 78.
[8] Richard Lang, Ph.D. thesis at the University of Chicago, summarized by Burgess and Cottrell, *op. cit.*, p. 139.

At the University of Southern California, a study of 2,080 married men showed that 58 percent were happy; 15 percent, doubtful; 27 percent, unhappy; and that of 2,176 married women, 58 percent were happy, 15 percent doubtful, and 27 percent unhappy.[9] The ratings were by graduate students and were made for educated couples of their acquaintance.

Chesser's study in Great Britain, dealing with over 6,000 women, shows that happy marriages are closely related to happy childhood there, as they are in the United States. Childhood happiness is, of course, dependent largely upon the happiness of the parent's marriage primarily. Happily married women are as much in love with their husbands after marriage as before. They do not regret their marriages and would marry again. The unhappy women's love has diminished since their engagement and first year of marriage. Three-fifths of them would marry different men if they married again, and a third, if they had their choice, would not marry at all. Three-fourths of these women found after marriage that their husbands were not the sort of people they thought they were before marriage. Most of those who were happy found their husbands as they thought they would be prior to marriage.[10]

All of these studies are fairly consistent in showing that approximately 60 percent of marriages are considered very happy or happy by the couples themselves as well as by their friends, and that 15 to 20 percent are considered unhappy or very unhappy. Apparently, then, a fairly high proportion of marriages that last do lead to happiness. It is possible also that some of the couples who at the time of questioning were unhappy may have enjoyed extreme happiness earlier in their marriage.

Of course these statistics omit those marriages that have already terminated in divorce.

Does Happiness Persist Throughout Married Life?

Adjustment to marriage and family life is a progressive thing as has been stressed repeatedly. Better or worse rather than stationary relationships are likely to characterize most human associations. Into every family, factors intrude from the outside. There are relatives, social activities, clubs of one member or the other, friends, children and their problems, obligations to city, church, and school. There are always various influences that infringe upon the family to affect its relationships—economic hazards for which the couple is in no sense responsible, health difficulties of relatives or of the members of the family, tragedy due to

[9] Paul Popenoe and Donna Wicks, "Marital Happiness in Two Generations," *Marital Hygiene*, 21:218-233, 1937.

[10] Eustace Chesser and others, *The Sexual, Marital, and Family Relationship with English Women* (New York: Roy Publishers, Inc., 1957).

the death of near relatives or death within the family, tragedy due to side-line romances. All of these factors—in fact, everything which enters into the experience of one or both members of the pair—affect the marriage relationship in one way or another.

Some of these factors tend to make for greater solidarity. Many couples as they share an increasing number of experiences together, grow closer to each other in understanding, sympathy, and mutual dependence. In other cases, experiences tend to divide the family, to force members further apart, so in every marriage there probably tends to be greater or lesser satisfaction with the marriage partner as time goes on.

Even marriage conflict and divorce are seldom events that happen suddenly. There is usually a long period of increasing friction and conflict prior to the divorce,[11] and even in the best-adjusted families there is often a long history of adjustments, some of which were not wholly pleasant. Marriage, like other relationships, is not always ideal; in fact, it is doubtful whether it is ever ideal. The storybook concept of a couple marrying and living happily ever after is a beautiful illusion. Marriage, like every other human relationship, is a developing, growing, changing affair. The degree of its satisfaction depends upon many factors, not the least of which is the ability of people to find in personal relationships the kinds of responses which satisfy them.

In our day of intimate interpersonal relationships most marriages face the supreme test at some time during their duration. Even happy marriages may approach the point of divorce when certain forces impinge upon the relationship: disloyalty of one mate, financial crisis, in-law crisis, etc.

Burgess and Cottrell's study of happiness in marriage according to years of marriage shows that happiness scores are higher during the first year of marriage. They drop about 10 points during the first six or eight years. After many years of marriage they seem to be somewhat higher again, but not as high on the average as at the beginning.[12]

Lang's study of the happiness of 7,393 couples as reported by friends rather than by the couples themselves finds more couples happy and fewer unhappy during the first two years of marriage than during the later years of marriage.[13] The number of discontented couples, according to the study, slowly increases with the number of years married.

Hamilton's study of 200 married men and 200 married women reports that the first four years of marriage are the happiest.[14]

---

[11] Discussed with data in Chapter 33.
[12] Burgess and Cottrell, *op. cit.*, pp. 246-248.
[13] Lang in Burgess and Cottrell, *op. cit.*, p. 139.
[14] G. V. Hamilton, *A Research in Marriage* (New York: A. & C. Boni, Inc., 1929).

Occupation and the Realization of Happiness

One of the most important and continuous outside forces that impinge on marriage is occupation. Does it have any relationship to happiness? Lang's extensive study has dealt with this problem, classifying the happiness of over 17,500 couples according to the husband's occupation, ratings being made by friends of the couple. Marked variations are observed. Whether these statistics mean that occupation is in part responsible for marital happiness or whether marital happiness is still primarily a value of the upper and middle classes is uncertain. Whatever the meaning one assigns to the differences, they are striking (see Figure 23-1).

A third to almost a half of the marriages in the occupational groups at the top were rated "unhappy" by friends who knew them well, and only 10 to 15 percent of those at the bottom were rated "unhappy." Lang advanced the theory in explanation that (1) occupational groups that are mobile are less happy, (2) groups over which the community exercises less control are less happy.[15] The latter point reminds one of the comment of an early Greek philosopher who observed that a man's troubles begin when he is free to do as he pleases. It will be seen that most of the group shown at the top of the chart move about from place to place a great deal in their occupations, and the communities in which they live exercise little control over them. The traveling salesman is the folklore stereotype of the worker who escapes community control.

At the bottom of the chart are occupational groups which require little migration, and over which the community exercises strict control— the minister, college and high school teachers, college students, administrators.

Popenoe's study of 3,528 marriages, in broad occupational groups, showed that farm marriages were the happiest of those of all occupational groups, over two-thirds of them being happy. At the other extreme were the marriages of unskilled laborers, less than half of which (only 42 percent) were happy.[16] Professional groups ranked next to farmers in happy marriages: semiskilled groups ranked next to the bottom, business groups fell in the middle. The happiness ratings in the study were made by students at the University of California and at Colorado State College of Education. They rated only marriages they knew well, and which had lasted five years or more.

[15] Burgess and Cottrell, *op. cit.*, 139-143.
[16] Paul Popenoe, "Farm Marriages Are the Happiest," *Family Life*, 8:1-2, May, 1947.

HAPPINESS RATING ACCORDING TO HUSBAND'S OCCUPATION

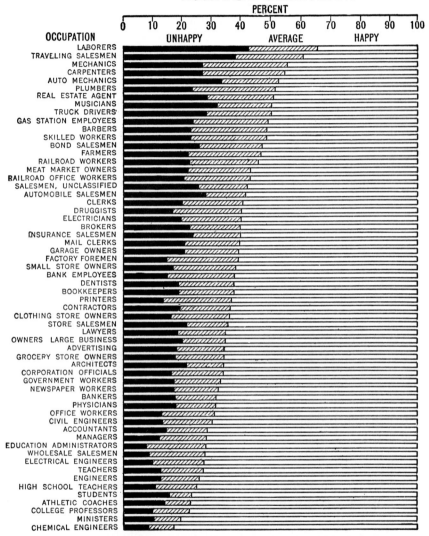

SOURCE: Richard O. Lang in Ernest W. Burgess and Leonard S. Cottrell, *Predicting Success or Failure in Marriage* (Copyright, 1939, Prentice-Hall, Inc., New York). Reproduced by permission of the publisher.

FIGURE 23-1————The results of ratings made by friends of 17,533 marriages, in which the husbands were engaged in the occupations listed in this chart, seem to show that professional men have the happiest marriages, those in the transient occupations have more unhappy marriages.

Burchinal and Chancellor,[17] studying the duration of Iowa marriages, found that among those who divorced, the couples having high economic status stayed together longer than did those having low economic status. In general those of low economic status marry earlier too. Their study further showed an early dissolution of marriages in which both partners were 19 or under.

The evidence of such studies as the above suggests that finding happiness consists in part of finding an occupation in which people either place a value on happiness and find it as a consequence or in which happiness is more nearly an inherent part of the total life pattern. At least it is quite evident that happiness in family life is related to occupation.

Problem Areas on Which Happiness May Hinge

Certain cultural conceptions have much to do with determining differences, the resolving of which husbands and wives consider essential to their happiness and success in marriage. In order to get some idea of what these basic issues are considered to be, the writer asked over 1,100 women—college girls, wives of college students, and the mothers of these two groups, what the five most important things were in making happy and unhappy marriages.[18] This gave a picture of the views of women through two generations, and of both single and married women in the present generation. The answers of these groups were not far different, indicating that the same problems persist and are recognized now, as in the mother generation, and by single as well as by married women. On page 462 are the percentages of women who named the items listed as one of the five most important in marriage.[19]

The most striking fact is that economic and financial problems take first place in the opinions of women, both in their list of factors causing happy and unhappy marriages. Separate chapters are devoted to adjustment to money problems of marriage.

The next most important field has to do with fidelity,[20] general sex-

---

[17] Lee G. Burchinal and Loren E. Chancellor, "Survival Rates Among Religiously Homogamous and Interreligious Marriage," *Agricultural Experiment Station Research Bulletin 512*, December, 1962.

[18] This was not a check list. Women wrote in a blank space the items they considered important.

[19] Paul H. Landis, *Two Generations of Rural and Urban Women Appraise Marital Happiness* (Pullman, Wash.: Washington Agricultural Experiment Station, March, 1951), Bulletin No. 506.

[20] In studies by the Institute for Sex Research, one woman in four, or 26 percent, admitted to having relations with another man or other men during their marriages. Usually it was only once, or occasionally, and often was not premeditated. Only 1.2 percent thought they had become pregnant by another man, and of these only 5 in 32 cases allowed the pregnancy to develop. In most cases, abortions were performed. See Alfred C. Kinsey and others, *Sexual Behavior in the Human Female* (Philadelphia: W. B. Saunders Co., 1953).

Factors producing unhappiness in marriage	*Percent of 1138 women of two generations listing factor*	*Factors producing happiness in marriage*	*Percent of 1071 women of two generations listing factor*
Financial and economic problems	51.9	Lack of financial problems	48.5
Infidelity, unfaithfulness	35.3	Similar social interests	41.7
Personality clashes	34.5	Understanding and considera-	
Vices (drinking, gambling)	32.6	tion	40.5
Religious differences (no		Children	40.1
religion)	28.4	Affection, love, devotion	30.9
Sexual incompatibility	21.3	Agreement on religion	24.7
Lack of understanding and		Sexual compatibility	18.2
consideration	19.3	Lack of personality clashes	16.5
Different social interests	18.9	Confidence and faith (trust)	14.4
Selfishness, wanting own way	16.7	Unselfishness	13.6
Lack of confidence (jealousy)	16.1	Similar education and ability	12.7
Childishness	15.2	Lack of vices	4.0
In-law trouble (relatives inter-		Lack of interference of	
fering)	14.6	relatives	3.1
Differences in education and		Others	68.6
ability	10.6		
Lack of affection	7.2		
Others	59.4		

ual compatibility, affection, and love. If one combines these items in the list, this area of adjustment is mentioned by more women than any other. Asked to mention the one thing most disastrous to marriage, more women listed the problem of infidelity than any other. A separate chapter will be devoted to the area of psychosexual adjustment.

Alcoholism As a Family Problem

The prominence of alcoholism in contemporary society, and its disastrous effect on marriage and family life, make some understanding of it of more than incidental importance. There are more than four and a half million alcoholics in the United States. In fact, we have one of the highest rates of alcoholism in the world, and alcoholism and the excessive use of alcohol short of the disease may well be one of the major problems of marriage adjustment today. For alcoholism is not only a problem in and of itself, but it brings with it many concomitant problems: non-support, infidelity, abuse, lack of companionship, and lost status.[21]

[21] John L. Thomas has stressed such factors in relationship to the problem of alcoholism in the Catholic family. He finds it is not unhappiness that drives the mate to drink. The drinking habit is in itself dangerous for many. See his *The American Catholic Family* (Englewood Cliffs, N. J.: Prentice-Hall, Inc., 1956); see also Albert L. Gordon, *Intermarriage* (Boston: Beacon Press, 1964), Ch. 4.

THE TYPICAL ALCOHOLIC AS FOUND AMONG PATIENTS OF THE CHICAGO ALCOHOLIC TREATMENT CENTER

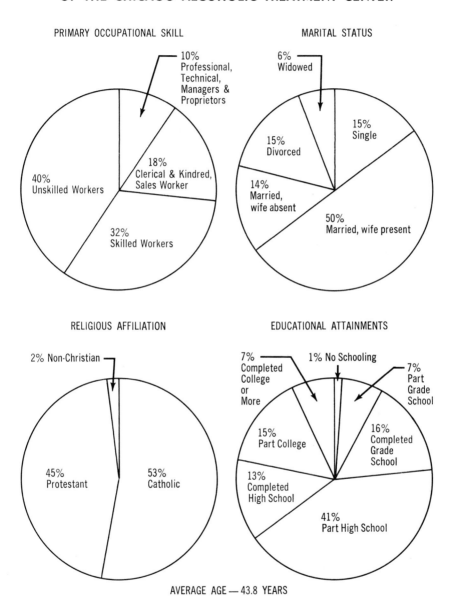

PRIMARY OCCUPATIONAL SKILL

10% Professional, Technical, Managers & Proprietors

18% Clerical & Kindred, Sales Worker

40% Unskilled Workers

32% Skilled Workers

MARITAL STATUS

6% Widowed

15% Single

15% Divorced

14% Married, wife absent

50% Married, wife present

RELIGIOUS AFFILIATION

2% Non-Christian

45% Protestant

53% Catholic

EDUCATIONAL ATTAINMENTS

7% Completed College or More

1% No Schooling

7% Part Grade School

15% Part College

16% Completed Grade School

13% Completed High School

41% Part High School

AVERAGE AGE — 43.8 YEARS

SOURCE: *Chicago's Alcoholic Treatment Center News,* 1:2, September, 1964. By permission of Chicago's Alcoholic Treatment Center.

FIGURE 23-2————Alcoholism disrupts the lives of all family members. It makes for widespread unhappiness.

Alcoholism is basically due to an inadequate psychological constitution, to feelings of inadequacy. Studies of marriage combinations where alcoholism is involved indicate that the wife is not always blameless. In the case of the alcoholic wife, the husband is not always blameless. Research suggests that the wife of the alcoholic husband is often a very difficult person, that there is considerable sense in the expression "she drove him to drink."[22]

There is also evidence that the wife of the alcoholic often gets some kind of deep satisfaction out of his plight. It may be a way of expressing her superiority, or it may be that she gets pleasure in punishing him. Clinicians find that sometimes, even though the alcoholic is cured, the wife is not happy till she creates pressures that make him an alcoholic again. She seems to like his dependence.

One of the tragic effects of alcoholism is on the children. It is particularly likely to build hostilities between the father and the adolescent son.[23]

Joan K. Jackson, psychiatrist, has outlined seven stages in the cumulative pattern of alcoholism. First, there is the stage in which the victim denies the disease.[24] After each drinking bout there is an attempt to define it as normal. The main anxiety at this time is the social disability of drinking behavior. Both husband and wife feel that if it becomes widely known the status of the family will be threatened. This proves to be of greater anxiety to the wife than to the husband. Normal behavior is rationalized by attempting to compare the husband's behavior with that of friends.

The second stage involves an attempt to eliminate the problem. This is done by becoming more isloated socially as the family becomes more drink-centered in consciousness. Drinking tends to become the symbol for all the conflicts between the spouses, as well as between parents and children. The children are shielded from the father's behavior and attempts are made to hide it from the employer by lying. Alienation between spouses increases. The more the wife expresses her hostility, the more the husband tends to drink. Discussions as to what the cause of the problem is and how it can be solved seem to be increasingly unproductive. The wife feels inadequate as a wife, a mother, and as a woman. She begins to feel that she is inadequate to meet her husband's needs. She tends to devaluate herself as part of his drinking process. In spite of all the attempts to reorient values, the drinking continues.

[22] Marian M. Kalashian, "Working with the Wives of Alcoholics in an Out-patient Setting," *Marriage and Family Living*, 20:130-133, May, 1959.
[23] *Ibid.*
[24] Joan K. Jackson, "The Adjustment of the Family to Alcoholism," *Marriage and Family Living*, 18:361-369, November, 1956.

The third stage is disorganization. The attempts of the husband to control his drinking are more sporadic or are entirely given up. The wife begins to adopt a fatalistic attitude. The family shows increasing demoralization. It is no longer possible to conceal from the children the father's behavior. The father has pretty much lost his status in the family. By this time the sexual relationship between the spouses has usually been severely disturbed. They resort now to public agencies for support, which damages self-respect. The wife typically begins to worry about her sanity and finds herself engaging in behavior which is often random and senseless, as she becomes more anxious and hostile. She finds that she has deviated widely from her former self and feels that she is no longer "the real me."

Stage four is usually produced by some subsidiary crisis like an accident or arrest. It requires that some decisive action be taken if the family survives. The wife takes over the husband's role; the husband comes to be ignored and assigned the status of a delinquent child. She begins to recognize her obligations to her children as parallel to her obligations to her husband. As feelings of pity and protectiveness arise, the hostility tends to decrease. The husband's attempts to reenter the family ranks are rebuffed more and more. The wife begins to rationalize the situation so that she does not have to relate his drinking any more to herself or to other family members. She gradually assumes control of the family and regains a sense of worth, worries less about her sanity and begins to try to plan long-time goals for the family. She is helped in this by numerous agencies. Her shame decreases. If she happens to contact Alcoholics Anonymous she gets a new perspective on the drinking problem and, therefore, loses more of the shame and comes to see the problem as an illness. She begins to renew extra-family social contacts. These will be among people who are not disturbed by the drinking problem of her family.

Now comes the period of unemployment, imprisonment, hospitalization. Already other women have usually come into the life of the husband. He may not even hesitate to bring them to his own home. Finally the husband recognizes that he needs help on his problem. The family begins to mobilize itself and try to reinstate him and help him get into contact with agencies which may offer hope and a cure. Roles are reshuffled as an attempt at attitude changes is made. Then there follows the bitter disappointment if treatment fails.

In stage five comes an effort to escape the problem by separating from the husband. This means usually legal separation or divorce for the wife. The husband may accept it passively or resist. In this stage very often the family is threatened by physical violence or actually has experience with it. At this point the husband may actually give up drinking for a short time. This often leaves the wife confused as to what course to pursue. It is very hard for her to seemingly desert him in an hour of crisis. She often resorts to help from public agencies to ease her conscience, or to make it possible for her to live alone.

Stage six brings the reorganization of family life in separate households. The wife must reshuffle her roles, adjust her emotional reactions, work out her feeling of bereavement and go through the other crises that are similar in any divorce action. There is the added problem, however, that the alcoholic may feel that he has to get even with the family for deserting him.

Stage seven is defined as the stage of reorganization of the whole family as a unit. This comes if the husband achieves sobriety with or without separation. Even if there is a complete cure and the restored marriage lasts, there are many role adjustments. The mother has so long been accustomed to managing for the family, to assuming the father and manager role, that numerous role adjustments have to be made. There are also the numerous debts and other obligations that have to be met along with current needs. Children are often unable to accept the father in his restored role. They may carry over deep hostilities or distrust. They may refuse to accept his judgment. The wife, therefore, hesitates to relinquish control in her role as the decision maker. It is very hard for any members of the family to forget the past. The father himself may be more demanding than is justified. He may feel very superior due to the fact that he has overcome his difficulties.

Gradually the memories of the drinking problem fade into the past; its influence remains, however. Whether the wife will be allowed to drink at parties, or whether the children will be allowed to drink, are problems of unusual significance, for here is a husband who knows that to drink again is to again become a victim. If the husband has been restored through Alcoholics Anonymous, he often throws himself so fully into these activities that he neglects the wife and family. Even though the wife is free from alcoholism within her own family, she is not free from alcoholics, since the husband may keep the house full of men he is helping.

In conclusion, when one considers the differences in values of men and women to be reconciled in marriage, the complexities of the world in which the average couple lives, the intimate and demanding nature of the marriage partnership, and the high ideal of adjustment for which the couple strives today, the record of successful adjustment is surprisingly high. Few business partnerships survive for more than a year or two, and many of them end in great bitterness. Seventy percent of all businesses fail in less than five years. The marriage contract is perhaps still the most successful of all human ventures in terms both of its durability and its realizations. When one adds to all the personal complications the forces that impinge on the marriage from without in the modern world, the survival of so many marriages is almost a miracle.

Problems

1. After interviewing the community's oldest couple on their golden wedding anniversary, the newspaper reporter cheerfully asked, "Does all this publicity thrill you? Tell me, are you as happy together today as when you were courting?"

   The old lady snapped back, "Listen young fellow. We're a dozen times happier today than we were when we were young but it isn't the publicity that makes us so. You'd have to be married fifty years before you could understand just how happy we really are and why!"

   What are some of the things that might account for increasing marital happiness with the passage of time?

2. Betty is neither pretty nor witty. She wanted to marry young but she was almost thirty before someone finally proposed. Now she is determined to make her marriage a success by making it happy.

   Her plan is that Bob's income should take care of their everyday needs. Her own income—for she expects to continue working—she calls the "fun fund." It will provide them with two vacations a year, a new car every second year, a show or theater three evenings a week, and funds for entertaining every weekend.

   Betty feels sure that in their old age they will look back upon an unusually happy marriage. What is the logic of Betty's reasoning? What important factors has she failed to consider?

3. Aside from the actual size of their incomes compare the way of life of a judge with that of a man who goes from one selling job to another. What circumstances suggest that the judge's family has a greater chance of realizing a happy life? (Consider such factors as status in community, self-appraisal, security, leisure time, companions, social controls surrounding each, etc.)

4. American wives are frequently criticized for their "refusal to grow up and grow old gracefully." Is this criticism justified in your opinion? What indications are there of its validity or inaccuracy? If true, does it have a bearing on realizing lasting marriage happiness?

5. Which of the following factors would you consider least important to marriage happiness:

   a. Size of income.
   b. Stability of income.
   c. Vocational adventure.
   d. Health.
   e. Community satisfaction.
   f. Job security.

6. Do the older, childless couples of your acquaintance seem:
   a. Less happy?
   b. More happy?
   c. Just as happy as those with families?
7. Most writers in the field of marriage relations argue that conscious effort and planning are more conducive to marriage success than the attitude "if we love one another, we're bound to succeed." Does this mean that couples are more likely to be happy if they make "happiness" an end in itself and keep this goal constantly in mind?
8. Discuss the statement, "Happiness is the by-product of a productive way of life."
9. Much is written about divorce, separation, and marital discord in our times. Has America finally reached the point where most marriages fail to achieve happiness?
10. A young student in a Preparation for Marriage course voiced the following opinion, "Couples should probably postpone parenthood for at least five years, for it is only in early marriage that couples may be said to be happy. After they have the responsibility of children they have to forget about themselves and dedicate their lives to child rearing."

   Do you agree that happiness is bound to fade with the passing years? What does the evidence suggest?
11. How do you explain the fact that stability in occupations is associated with marital happiness?
12. What factors probably account for the apparently high rate of failure and unhappiness among Hollywood marriages?
   a. Instability of income.
   b. Temperament of actors.
   c. Neurosis.
   d. Cultural standards unlike those of United States in general.
   e. Competition to get to the top.
   f. Marriages for publicity only.
   g. Marriage failures are not numerous, just overly publicized.
13. *Sociodrama:* Two young wives discuss the marriage of a mutual acquaintance in such a way as to reveal the grounds upon which a marriage is rated as either happy or unhappy.
14. *Sociodrama:* A mother criticizes her married daughter's decision to postpone parenthood in order to maintain a "happy marriage."

Selected References

ARTICLES IN BOOKS OF READINGS

SUSSMAN, Marvin B., *Sourcebook in Marriage and the Family,* Second Edition (Boston: Houghton Mifflin Co., 1963).
   1. BENSON, Purnell, "The Interests of Happily Married Couples," pp. 139-144.

2. FARIS, Robert E. L., "Interaction of Generations and Family Stability," pp. 376-379.

3. PINEO, Peter C., "Disenchantment in the Later Years of Marriage," pp. 393-401.

4. JACKSON, Joan K., "Adjustment of the Family to Alcoholism," pp. 334-340.

LANDIS, Judson T., and LANDIS, Mary G., *Readings in Marriage and the Family* (Englewood Cliffs, N. J.: Prentice-Hall, Inc., 1952).

5. STRAUS, Robert, "Excessive Drinking and Its Relationship to Marriage," pp. 313-332.

6. BOSSARD, James H. S., "War and the Family," pp. 323-332.

General References

BRAYSHAW, A. Joseph, "Middle-Aged Marriages: Idealism, Realism and the Search for Meaning," *Marriage and Family Living*, 24:358-364, November, 1962.

BURGESS, Ernest W., and COTTRELL, Leonard S., *Predicting Success or Failure in Marriage* (Englewood Cliffs, N. J.: Prentice-Hall, Inc., 1939), Ch. 3.

DAY, Barbara Ruth, "Alcoholism and the Family," *Marriage and Family Living*, 23:253-257, August, 1961.

HATCH, David L., and HATCH, Mary G., "An Unhappy Family," *Marriage and Family Living*, 24:213-223, August, 1962.

JACKSON, Joan K., "The Adjustment of the Family to Alcoholism," *Marriage and Family Living*, 18:361-369, November, 1956.

JELLINEK, E. M., *The Disease Concept of Alcohol* (New Haven: Hillhouse Press, 1960).

KALASHIAN, Marian M., "Working With The Wives of Alcoholics in an Outpatient Setting," *Marriage and Family Living*, 20:130-133, May, 1959.

LANDIS, Judson T., "Some Correlates of Divorce and Nondivorce among the Unhappy Married," *Marriage and Family Living*, 25:178-180, May, 1963.

————, "What Is the Happiest Period of Life?" *School and Society*, 55:643-645, June 6, 1942.

LANDIS, Paul H., *Two Generations of Rural and Urban Women Appraise Marital Happiness* (Pullman, Wash.: Washington Agricultural Experiment Station, March, 1953), Bulletin No. 506.

LeMASTERS, E. E., *Modern Courtship and Marriage* (New York: The Macmillan Co., 1957), Chs. 13, 14.

PINEO, Peter C., "Disenchantment in the Later Years of Marriage," *Marriage and Family Living*, 23:3-11, February, 1961.

POPENOE, Paul, "Farm Marriages Are the Happiest," *Family Life*, 8:1-2, May, 1947.

ROTH, J., and PECK, R. F., "Class and Mobility Factors Related to Marital Adjustment," *American Sociological Review*, 16:478-487, August, 1951.

24
Sexual Adjustment

In nature, sexual adjustment is not a problem. Generally there is no continuity of relationship between mates, although there are exceptions. Some birds and a few animals pair for life. In general, animals do not. Even those birds which mate for life, like geese, confine their sex life to the rhythm of the biological season. Their interest in the opposite sex is for the momentary period, characteristic of sub-human species, when nature calls for sexual expression. Beyond that, the male's responsibility usually ceases and the female's maternal instincts take over the problem of nurturing the young.

It is not so with human beings. Society demands a continuity in the relationship between male and female that is institutionalized everywhere in the world in some form of marriage-family relationship. Numerous social pressures for providing this continuity are to be found, and numerous rules for terminating the pair relationship are also found, for divorce is also a universal phenomenon. Not all pairings of mates can last, but the assumption of all societies is that in adulthood there will be a continuity in the male-female relationship. This is usually a paired relationship, although it may involve multiple mates. Whatever the sanctioned relationship, it is certainly far more than a sexual relationship. In fact, the sexual relationship is made subservient to economic and status relationships. It is also made subservient to the marriage rules of the culture and its sex taboos.

The conditions under which people can marry and under which they can terminate marriage are, however, prescribed. In fact, the institutional aspects of the man-woman relationships are so elaborate in all cultures that the sexual aspects become a relatively incidental matter. For man, sex is not merely a biological fact; it is one of the most significant sociological, psychological, and emotional facts of existence. Human culture makes sex much more than merely a biological act. For man, there is no such thing as mating without emotional connotations.

One of the most unique facts about the human biological mechanism is that both the human male and female seem to be without a decisive, demanding, and conspicuous seasonal period such as one finds through-out animal life, where the coming into heat of the female, or of rut in the male, causes each to aggressively seek to copulate. There is no specific period of rut in the human male and there is serious doubt whether there is a period of heat in the human female. (Evidence pro and con is pre-sented in a later paragraph.) This makes the sex act primarily a factor of social, psychological, and emotional motivation, rather than of bio-logical motivation. This is the basis for a continuing relationship between male and female, a relationship which need not and does not in most of its functioning have any relationship to procreation at all. Prior to mar-riage, if there is sexual intercourse, its timing is determined primarily by the female. After a woman comes to share bed and board, the pro-vider expects to have sexual access, subject to whatever codes and taboos exist in the culture. By virtue of customary regulations of the marriage system, it is assumed that the husband has this right as part of the bargain for supporting a family. The wife must, therefore, give his needs priority over her own feelings. The timing and frequency of sexual intercourse after marriage is determined primarily by the male.[1]

Here again we find a series of circumstances which are unique in nature. The male is capable of copulating with an unaroused and even uninterested female. The sex act in some marriages is performed without the female's interest. Its timing is determined primarily by the male's readiness, as is its consummation by the male's period of response. This pattern is not found elsewhere in nature, but is one established in the adjustment of the human male and female in the institution of marriage where romantic love, economic motives, mutual aid, and many other such values become blended with sexual drives into a highly complex system of motivations.

The human female's accessibility in marriage is to quite an extent a matter of logic, rather than desire. In marriage, sex is expected and cus-tomarily sanctioned. The husband, though nonperiodic, does have regular sexual needs because of the build-up of semen in the glands. Only as he is taught to go through the courting act, to be considerate of the female's feelings, to recognize that her arousal is a part of his obligation, does he sense any need to regard her feelings in the matter at all.

In our culture, where the wife is not only mother but mistress, she is given few of the customary protections by which she may be relieved temporarily from the sexual advances of her husband. Many cultures,

[1] Margaret Mead, *Male and Female* (New York: Mentor Books, 1955), pp. 156-160.

both historic and present, taboo intercourse during pregnancy, during menstruation, and during the period when she is nursing the young—with primitives this may be two or more years—and some taboo it during periods of significant activities demanding the concentrated expenditure of male energy: in periods of battle, when the hunt is on, when fish are to be caught, when artistic products are to be made, when praying needs to be done, etc.

If the female is taught by the culture to be sexually nonassertive, her rewards are not considered important. It is enough that she have children. If she is taught to be assertive, then the male's courting gestures, his ability to arouse and inspire, and finally satisfy, put him to a sexual test. It is under this latter type of marriage philosophy that the concept of sexual adjustment has become a serious consideration. Such it is in the United States today.

No Estrus Phase in the Human Female

The period of heat is marked in apes[2] and in baboons[3] by swelling of the vaginal area and by changes in behavior. In the wild baboon troop, the female in estrus seeks out males of her choice to satisfy her desire, beginning usually with one of lower status and working up in status until her needs have been fully met.

Research among both single and married women fails to show any of the psychological characteristics of an estrus period. That there is a rise in body temperature of a fraction of a point near the time of ovulation (most often falling between the eleventh and fourteenth day from the beginning of menstruation, see Chapter 24) is a well-established biological fact. Benedek finds endocrine and dream reactions at ovulation that give some evidence of an estrus period.[4] But if this is a physiological estrus, overt behavior does not betray it.

Most research finds a slight shift in intensity of sex desire at certain times of the month, but the rise in the curve in any particular research is slight and research of different workers with different groups leaves the whole matter open to question. It is likely that slight statistical differences at different periods in the menstrual month are due to factors of social interaction rather than biology. Research suggests that the time

2 R. M. Yerkes and J. H. Elder, "Estrus Receptivity and Mating in Chimpanzee," *Comparative Psychology Monographs*, 1-39; also J. H. Elder and R. M. Yerkes, "The Sexual Cycle of the Chimpanzee," *Anatomical Record*, 67:119-143, 1936.

3 Sherwood Washburn, Professor of Anthropology at the University of California, in address at Washington State University, Spring, 1959.

4 Therese Benedek, "Psychosexual Functions in Women," in her, *Studies in Psychosomatic Medicine* (New York: The Ronald Press Co., 1952).

of greatest desire is just before or immediately after menstruation, the least likely times for pregnancy to occur.

Landis,[5] studying a sample of 181 college girls, finds that more report increased sexual desire directly before menstruation than at any other time. The second peak is after menstruation. Terman[6] found half of the married women who reported on periods of greater desire placed it either just before or just after menstruation, with about twice as many after as before. Hamilton[7] reported that 81 percent of women he studied recognized greater sexual desire just after menstruation. Davis' study[8] of 868 single women found their period of greatest sexual interest preceding menstruation.

None of the data shows an increase in sexual desire at the time of ovulation, as might logically be expected if nature provides an estrus in the human female. As we have seen, Margaret Mead, from her knowledge of numerous cultures, many of them permitting premarital sexual experience, concludes, as we have seen, that prior to marriage the female controls the timing of the sex act; after marriage, the male.[9] This change would not take place if it were regulated by nature, as in the case of animals where the female is approachable only in times of heat,[10] or as in the case of those animals among which the male is potent only seasonally. Nonbiological factors are operative.

It appears that sexual desire among modern women is largely a function of the psychological climate produced by contact with the male. This seems to be predominantly true both before and after marriage. In marriage, frequency of the male's demands may well determine whether the wife has any desire at all, other than as aroused by her sexual partner. If she has, in most instances it will likely be after menstruation, since with most young couples this is the longest period of abstinence. This being the period of estrogen pickup, many have renewed energy which may also be a factor. Others who suffer considerable discomfort and depression prior to menstruation, and the letdown of the progesterone phase of the after-ovulation period preceding menstruation, may well seek the comfort and loving which sex involves, not from physical desire as such, but for the secondary reasons which are most important

[5] Judson T. Landis, "Physical and Mental-Emotional Changes Accompanying the Menstrual Cycle," *Research Studies of the State College of Washington*, 25:155-167, June, 1957, p. 160.

[6] Lewis M. Terman, *Psychological Factors in Marital Happiness* (New York: McGraw-Hill Book Co., 1938), p. 351.

[7] G. V. Hamilton, *A Research in Marriage* (New York: A. & C. Boni, Inc., 1929).

[8] Katharine B. Davis, *Factors in the Sex Life of Twenty-two Hundred Women* (New York: Harper & Bros., 1929).

[9] Margaret Mead, *loc. cit.*

[10] R. M. Yerkes and J. H. Elder, *op. cit.*

at this time.[11] There is, however, a pickup in energy due to an increased metabolic rate just before menstruation, which is undoubtedly a factor. Finally, premenstrual desire may be in part a rational and planned matter. The wife, knowing that a period of continence lies ahead, if she enjoys the sexual relationship, is interested in intercourse as a means of abbreviating the time until the menstrual flow is over and the rhythm of sex can begin again. Her awareness of her husband's needs may also be a factor in her encouraging his advances and courting; or he may, if he is aware of the coming period of continence, be more aggressive than usual, stimulating both her interest and his own. Thus part of the peak of sexual interest prior to menstruation may be like "banking" sex until the period of deprivation is past.[12]

This kind of speculation illustrates how complicated by conscious, psychological, and biological factors the human sex urge is, and how far it can be removed from a rhythm of nature, if such exists.

The highly socialized character of the sexual experience, its romantic connotations in our culture, its diversity of meaning in the interactions of highly individuated men and women, have apparently largely removed it, for the female, from the level of physical desire and made it secondary to the whole area of sociality and of generalized feeling. The lack of an estrus period in the human male and his recurrent readiness are undoubtedly important factors in this trend of the psychosexual orientation of the female.

Sexual Adjustment As a Goal

Every society faces the problem of resolving the strain involved in the different biological natures and sexual proclivities of male and female. Many societies have accomplished this by denying female sexuality, and leaving not only initiative but satisfaction to the male alone. Polygynous societies, in their favored classes, try to balance male sexual needs with those of the female by providing sufficient wives or concubines so that when one is incapacitated by sickness, pregnancy, or childbirth another will be accessible. The mistress system, where sanctioned by custom, permits a similar male outlet, as does concubinage. The monogamous systems of the world have historically sanctioned prostitution as a device for balancing out the male's greater needs for sexual expression.

[11] Judson T. Landis suggests this as a likely reason for premenstrual sex desire, op. cit.

[12] Many years ago Carl G. Hartman commented on many phases of the sex desire cycle in his book, *The Time Ovulation Cycle in Women* (Baltimore: The Williams & Wilkins Co., 1936).

In polygynous societies, males complain of too many demands from their wives, as each tries to tempt her husband to her bed.[13] In monogamous societies generally it is the male who is perpetually unsatisfied because of deprivation, or because of the monotony of one wife.

The romantic marriage to which Americans aspire has perhaps put a greater strain on both men and women in sexual adjustment than has any other system attempted by man. The wife plays the role of both mistress and wife, attempting to meet the husband's sexual needs fully. The pledge of romantic loyalty compels the husband to confine his advances to the marriage bed. This means that he must make adjustments to incapacities of the wife and deny himself sexual expression at times for the sake of the romantic bond. This is a high ideal, difficult of realization.

What do we know about the sexual needs of modern men and women? What do we know about the degree to which these needs are satisfied in most marriages? What can be said that will help young people in preparing themselves for the sexual relationships of marriage? And finally, what should all young men and women know, not only about their own sexual needs and characteristics, but about those of their potential mates?

The Meaning of Sexual Adjustment

It should be kept in mind that the sexual adjustment of a couple is not synonymous with equality of their sexual desire or frequency of the orgasmic response. Neither does the concept of sexual adjustment involve the regular subordination of one mate's interests to those of the other in their sexual relationship.

Adjustment in this area is basically a matter of the satisfaction of both. One couple may be spoken of as sexually better adjusted than another. The difference between them is not a matter of frequency or intensity of the sex act but the differing degrees to which each couple obtains satisfaction and happiness from whatever relationship they have developed. While one mate might ordinarily find adjustment relatively simple, it is usually impossible for him to do so when his partner finds sex unpleasant or unrewarding. Complete satisfaction comes from the unrestrained sharing of these moments of greatest marital intimacy.

This does not mean however, that both partners must experience similar responses to the sex act. For the male, intercourse brings orgasm and accompanying tension release; for the wife it may bring no physical climax at all but only a feeling of being loved and needed. As long

[13] Margaret Mead, *op. cit.*, p. 161.

as each partner is satisfied with what he or she obtains from the act, their adjustment may be said to be a good one.

Does intensity of sexual desire or frequency of orgasmic response enter into the adjustment process at all? Only indirectly.

When there are marked differences in the desire of the two mates, adjustment is difficult. Whether they desire intercourse only once a month or several times a day is not the point. The significant consideration is whether the frequency of desire in one mate is compatible with desire in the other or whether a mutually acceptable compromise can be worked out.

The desire of the husband—particularly in the early years of marriage—tends to exceed that of the average wife. Good adjustment generally requires that each make some concessions to the needs of the other. The husband withholds his advances when the wife seems genuinely uninterested. The wife must occasionally participate when she does not really desire satisfaction herself.

Equality of orgasmic response seems to have even less bearing on sexual adjustment, providing both mates accept the difference as a relatively unimportant one. Males, as we have observed, experience an orgasm as an inherent part of semen discharge. Wives vary greatly, but it has been found that in the average marriage considerably less than half of the women can expect to always have an orgasm, and during the early months of marriage as many as half of wives experience few if any full responses at all.

What about the relation of submission to sexual adjustment? In an earlier period of American history a couple were assumed to have reached an adjustment (although this expression was probably never used) once the wife had given up any foolish notions or fears she might have and settled down to the expected, though not necessarily pleasant, task of satisfying her husband's sexual needs. Women of that period were taught that the marriage bed was for the indulgence of the husband—usually at the wife's expense. The wife endured it, for it was assumed that the husband had sexual prerogatives.

Today the wife should, and usually does, expect satisfaction in the sexual relationship. Unless she has been hemmed in by taboos and irrational fears in her sex education, she is in most instances capable of as deep a physical and emotional satisfaction in marriage as is her husband, although frequently these reactions are of a very different kind. All modern scientific study shows that the sexual relationship is normal and beneficial alike to both male and female.[14]

14 Marie Stopes, *Married Love,* published in Britain in 1918, first declared woman's right to sensuous enjoyment in the sex act of marriage. The book was long banned in the United States, but has to date sold more than a million copies.

If compatibility of desire and response are not basic, and if submission by one member is not demanded, what then are the factors that contribute to the development of sexual adjustment in marriage? Is it something to work toward, or, like general marital happiness, is it more likely to result if not sought directly?

An answer to these questions calls for an appraisal of the basic factors that contribute to sexual adjustment in marriage. These will not be the same factors as those our great-grandparents' generation would have agreed upon. Times have changed, marriage has changed, and many of the factors which contribute to or detract from a couple's sexual compatibility have also changed. This discussion is, therefore, geared to the modern marriage exhibiting modern expectations for mutual happiness and satisfaction.

The following paragraphs show how basic attitudes affect sexual adjustment in marriage. We shall also consider sexual normalcy and sexual fidelity as factors in this adjustment. In the next chapter attention will be given to the relationship between realistic expectations and sexual adjustment, observing how false information and false conceptions of sex can bring disaster to an otherwise successful marriage.

Healthy Sex Attitudes As a Factor in Sexual Adjustment

Husbands and wives, we have observed, are normally both capable biologically of enjoying the sexual relationship. Inability to perform or respond sexually is in most cases psychological rather than physical. Much literature and clinical experience favor this point of view. This brings up the important problems of acquired attitudes as fundamental factors in sex conditioning.

Current conceptions of sex are many and varied, even within the confines of an average American community. To some people sex is sin; to others it is an activity to be indulged in for procreation only. To some its primary purpose is pleasure. For still others it represents the highest form of human sharing. Even in marriage, sex can mean different things at different times, depending on the total relationship of the pair. Instead of being an experience in sharing and affectional expression, it may turn out to be an experience in male conquest, domination, or exploitation.

There has been a great deal of speculation on the degree to which a child's early conditioning affects his later capacity to give affection and to respond to sexual stimuli. As we observed earlier, much of the Freudian-oriented literature assumes that the child's relationship with the parent of the opposite sex has decided influence on psychosexual development. More likely it is the total family pattern which conditions one's attitude toward members of his own sex, toward the opposite sex, and toward the institution of marriage as such, rather than a particular relationship with a member of the opposite sex within the family. This total influence is so complex that simple generalizations regarding a unilateral factor in determining psychosexual development is likely to lead to more error than insight.

Of this much we can be sure—fundamental attitudes as well as actual behavior patterns basic to a development of the capacity for affection are learned in the family and have much to do with a person's potential psychosexual development. This point was stressed in Chapter 9 and need not be dwelt on at length here.

Tenderness, ability to show affection, and responsiveness are developed in the child by his relationship with the parent. In loving a responsive parent, the child develops a capacity to love others. With expanding contacts, the child develops ability to show affection to others as others show affection to him. In normal development, the mother and other love objects recede into the background as heterosexual love emerges.

The child born in a world without affection is likely to develop without any real capacity for it or any means for expressing it. If he has constantly been rebuffed by his mother and rarely shown affection, he keeps what feelings he has to himself and rarely can relax in the presence of affection. By such a simple process of conditioning, the capacity to love is developed or thwarted in the human being. The child's relationship with the parents is therefore the critical experience in the development of capacity to give and respond to affection in later years. The overstern, unaffectionate parent tends to blight the affectionate nature of the child, and makes it difficult, if not impossible, for him to ever develop a normal pattern for expressing affection. The affectional aspect of the personality is further developed in the relationships of brothers and sisters.

The attitudes a youngster hears expressed in his childhood home are also important in determining his later adjustment in marriage. Even in families where affection and warmth are openly exhibited, sex itself often remains an unmentionable subject, surrounded with mysteries that are suggestive of sin and immorality. It is not enough to shield a youngster from undesirable or frightening experiences in sex. To assure him of healthy attitudes on the subject some positive sex education is necessary. Complete silence is not really neutral. To a child's inquiring mind it is suggestive in itself.

Thus, it is not uncommon for a young person (usually the girl) from even the finest, most conscientious home, to enter marriage with fears and misgivings about the sexual side of the relationship. Such fears are not easily overcome. They produce a tension and hesitancy that encourage withdrawal from even the most tender and considerate of mates. When, as is frequently the case, the young husband is not aware of his wife's attitudes, the situation can quickly become disastrous to sexual adjustment.

Folklore holds that many a marriage has been ruined on the first night of the honeymoon because an impetuous husband failed to sense deep taboos in his wife's attitudes toward sex. The fact that such attitudes result generally from defective training makes them no less significant as realities for her. They provide a background which interprets the normal eagerness of the male as vulgar, animal, and cruel. The initial shock is repeated because the young wife is frequently too frightened or too inhibited to speak of it, and with the repetition, frigidity begins to develop. While this experience is probably not as common today as in our earlier folk culture, it is true that marriage ceremonies do not have the magic power to redraw mental pictures and attitudes concerning sex which have been built up during childhood and adolescence. The marriage ceremony only removes the legal and moral restrictions.

Attitudes of fear and disgust are not the only ones that influence the retarding or blocking of sexual adjustment in marriage, nor are women the exclusive harbingers of faulty attitudes. Below is a listing of some of the most common attitudes that are conducive or detrimental to sound and early sexual adjustment in marriage.

ATTITUDES CONDUCIVE TO SOUND SEXUAL ADJUSTMENT EARLY IN MARRIAGE

1. Sex is a normal, right, and recreative experience as well as a creative experience.
2. Both husband and wife are capable of and have an equal right to sexual gratification.
3. Both husband and wife should be considerate, sympathetic, and patient in sexual relations.
4. Sexual expression is usually more direct in the male, and while he can cultivate some sublimative arts, the male is not to be criticized for his greater preoccupation with sex as a purely physical act.
5. Consistent with physical well-being and mutual interest, there are no restrictions that need be placed upon the sexual expressions of a couple, either upon the method of expression, the frequency of expression, the intensity of expression, or the duration of expression throughout the couple's lifetime.
6. Sex can serve different functions at different times. It can be for pleasure, for comfort, to express love, for relief from tension, for the serious intent of having children, or for rejuvenating a tired body or spirit. It is the closest form of human sharing.

ATTITUDES DETRIMENTAL TO SOUND SEXUAL ADJUSTMENT EARLY IN MARRIAGE

1. When a husband really loves his wife, pleasant conversation and intimacy become much more satisfying to him than sex.
2. Men are like animals in that sex can never acquire any spiritual meaning for them.
3. Women can never get the pleasure from sex that men do; they should accept it, therefore, simply as one of their duties as a wife.
4. Nice girls, because of their higher values and ideals, do not lose themselves in sexual play; they remain patient and reserved, and do not show a great interest in the matter.
5. Only a very vulgar or degenerate man is pleased by experimentation in sex play outside the common pattern.
6. Intercourse is inevitable in marriage, but talking about it before or after is bound to be embarrassing, and detracts from its spiritual quality.
7. In a marriage between modern, enlightened people, the wife who cannot equal her husband in desire or response should consider psychiatric or medical attention, for she must be either physically or emotionally defective.
8. It is a husband's duty to woo his wife from reluctance to eager anticipation before each sex act. The husband who does not or cannot accomplish this, who sometimes becomes impatient or discouraged, is inadequate and failing in his function, for no wife can become interested otherwise.
9. Sex is a private affair. To seek outside help, to get books from the library on the subject, or to talk about "what's wrong" with one's mate is an admission of failure.
10. Once a man has saddled his wife with a house and children he has no right to complain if she loses her interest in sex.

Sexual Normalcy As a Factor in Sexual Adjustment

The sexual relationship of a happily married couple frequently represents one of the most creative and distinctively individualistic and rejuvenating aspects of their life together. In business practices, child rearing, civic activities, and political views they may find it most beneficial to conform to the expected patterns of behavior. In their most intimate relationship, however, even the most conforming couples may discover that the greatest pleasure and satisfaction can be derived by rewriting the rules to fit their own particular needs and wishes.

Custom and nature tend to agree, for example, that in most instances the male should be the aggressor and the female the reluctant or uncertain mate. In many successful mariages, however, the couples have discovered a mutual satisfaction in reversing the roles. This is but one of an endless number of possible variations in what is generally considered the normal sexual pattern.

Young people who hope to make a normal sexual adjustment in marriage must learn to distinguish between behavior that is not normal and behavior that is merely not typical. To label atypical sexual behavior as abnormal is to encourage shock or guilt if such practices should be introduced by an unsuspecting mate.

There is another side to this picture, too. Recognizing the fact that there are sexual attitudes and practices that do spell abnormality can help young people to avoid mates who are incapable of healthy sexual adjustment. It can also help them in understanding and seeking assistance if they discover abnormal traits in themselves or in their marriage partner.

First, as to the nature of atypical sexual behavior and the limits, if any, within which it is desirable in a marriage, young people should realize that the boundaries of typicality are gradually being moved back as American culture develops out of the confining limits of its Puritanical past. Within the life span of many older couples there existed a very narrow pattern of acceptable sexual life. Sexual attitudes were clearly defined around the concepts of male exploitation and female submission. Acceptable sexual behavior of the married couples was also clearly defined. Frequency of intercourse, positions during intercourse, the degree of pleasure one might experience, the amount and nature of initial stimulation, the degree to which one might speak of the relationship—all of these and more were regulated by the unwritten laws of custom.

Today custom permits much greater latitude in sexual expression, but custom is still far behind the limits set by nature and happiness. Many a "broadminded mother" would be shocked at the fun her married daughter gets from the sexual side of marriage and even more shocked at the unheard-of suggestions her son whispers into the ear of his wife. Two very understanding and competent authors make the point of this psychological venturing very well:

> Study of the sex activity of relatively uninhibited happily married couples demonstrates very beautifully both the unorthodox nature of their impulses and the ease with which they are integrated into a "normal" heterosexual pattern. Sometimes the pair will be close and affectionate. Tenderness will pass into a rather solemn passion, a confirmation of their abiding love for each other. At other times their mood will be wholly frivolous. Intercourse then will be just a rattling good time without deeper implications. Or the husband will seek protection and cuddling at his wife's breast. Or he will lie like a girl while she takes possession of his body. At times he will vulgarize the act with smutty words or take a fine pleasure in hurting his wife and forcing her to his will. Or the couple may play at an illicit relationship, acting out a little seduction farce for their own benefit. They will try out

odd positions and experiment with unusual parts of the body. Often, too, intercourse will be a routine satisfaction of a bodily need about as romantic as orange juice, toast, and coffee for breakfast. Our uninhibited happily married couples will take all of these variations and find them good.[15]

The limits within which variations should be practiced are few and simple. First of all they should bring neither physical or emotional harm to either mate. Second, and most important, they should only be indulged in by mutual inclination, for, as we have pointed out, atypical behavior can bring disastrous consequences if not understood or appreciated as normal and legitimate in marriage.

This does not mean that the couple must share similar views of this matter from the outset. Very few do. It is important, however, that the individual who initiates atypical behavior do so only after analyzing the mate's general attitude pattern and then, only gradually and with utmost care, in observing and weighing responses. In this as in all sexual development, the male is the teacher.

Sexual Abnormalities

Abnormalities in sexual attitudes and practices are probably much less frequent but much more disastrous when they do occur. Too little understood but much talked about types of sexual abnormality are frigidity in the female and impotence in the male. Such terms carry with them a great deal of folklore which is often a hindrance to marriage adjustment. A woman is not frigid simply because she may not experience an orgasm in sexual relationships, or does so only on rare occasions. If she is capable of affection and of sharing the sexual relationship without a feeling that it is obnoxious and repulsive, she is not frigid. Frigidity rightly refers only to those few cases in which the psychological and emotional block is such that she cannot accept the sexual relationship and its affectional expressions. Such feelings of repulsion are due to deep-seated psychological problems, sometimes to tragedy, shock, or faulty upbringing, and are problems for mental therapy. Many happily married women rarely or never have an orgasm.

Impotence in the male likewise is a condition of psychological and emotional blocks which make it impossible for him to participate in the sex act. In those rare cases where it exists it is also a problem rooted in emotional conditioning and can be cured only by psychological therapy. Seldom is it biological in origin.

Homosexual tendencies represent a rather common type of sexual

[15] John Levy and Ruth Munroe, *The Happy Family* (New York: Alfred A. Knopf, Inc., 1941), p. 129.

abnormality and in some instances affect marriage relationships. It is fairly well established that such tendencies are not inborn, but are due to conditioning. Just as man is born to hunger, but without any definite notion as to what is fit to eat, so he is born with sex drives. His social experience tells him how they can be satisfied. Appetites of the human being are undiscriminating until trained through certain experiences and through certain satisfactions.

Some cultures have elevated homosexual love to a position far above heterosexual love. The Greeks in the period of their historic glory did so, considering marriage a practical child-rearing arrangement, but homosexual love the true romantic love. Women in the Isle of Lesbos, which lies between Greece and Turkey, elevated love between women to the supreme level. This is the origin of our word *lesbian,* for female homosexual activity. Our culture abhors homosexual behavior and condemns it both by law and custom. The most effective approach to the cure of homosexual tendencies is through some form of psychological therapy.

Confirmed homosexuals usually do not marry, some even fearing to test their sexual adequacy with members of the opposite sex. It is more likely to be the individual who seeks both homosexual and heterosexual outlets who marries.

Other types of abnormality are characterized by fixations of sexual interest upon some inappropriate object, or by the ability to get sexual satisfaction only through visual or auditory experiences. These types of abnormality, while a serious handicap to most relationships, seldom affect marriage since few people characterized by them are interested in marriage.

Sexual Fidelity As a Factor in Sexual Adjustment

Unfaithfulness is seldom found to accompany happiness or sound sexual adjustment in marriage. The crucial question is, however, which of the two comes first and tends most frequently to cause the other? It is easy to understand how one who discovers infidelity in his or her mate is likely to feel bitter, unloved, and thus to lose whatever pleasure he or she might have found in sex. Thus infidelity might logically be said to cause sexual maladjustment. On the other hand, the husband or wife who charges that the mate's infidelity has ruined their marriage may be ignoring an important fact—the mate may have been unhappy with the marriage before an illicit affair could appeal.

There are circumstances, however, where the lines are not so clearly drawn. What about infidelity during a period of prolonged separation, or when one mate is physically unable to meet the other's sexual needs? Are there any circumstances under which infidelity is justified? If not, what about the effects of such a rule on the normal sexual needs of man? If so, what about the effects on marriage?

Since the law forbids but usually ignores adultery, and does not attempt to control extramarital relations except as it makes them a grounds for divorce, in this as in most other areas of marital adjustment the crucial consideration is not an arbitrary rule but an analysis of how the mates involved view the infidelity.

In some marriages, and this was even more true in the past, a husband's obligations are considered to center around providing and caring for his wife and family. Companionship, love, and faithfulness, while desirable, are not considered the crucial demands of marriage. The mistress system is and has been widely found throughout the world. At the other extreme, unfaithfulness may be taken lightly because marriage itself is taken lightly. There are even a few happily married couples who consider extramarital relations as of no importance to the marriage itself.

The marriage vows that couples take (and which most take seriously) reflect the traditional American view that when two individuals marry it is for better or for worse, and for a lifetime. Sexual fidelity is considered not only desirable but obligatory. One does not run out on a mate because of financial problems, sickness, or disability; neither does one break his vow because of disappointment over their sexual life together. The relationship is assumed to be a binding one and the interests of the family are considered to far outweight those of the individual. Most cultures are equally restrictive on married partners.[16]

Many of these traditional views are justified on religious grounds as well as personal considerations, and the general welfare of society lends additional argument to their continuance. In a country such as ours, where the individual family rather than any other institutional agency is held responsible for the care and upbringing of children, there is considerable logic in the widespread rejection of extramarital relations. A more stable family and, consequently, a more stable society are thought to result from the expectations and demands for fidelity placed upon both husbands and wives. Husbands like to feel that the children they support are their own.

What are the facts about fidelity? Do American couples live up to the vows they take, and under what cicumstances do they condone not doing so?

The Kinsey research group found that, of people studied, approximately 26 percent of women and half the men had had extramarital sexual relations. Forty-one percent of the unfaithful wives had had sexual

---

[16] A worldwide survey of 250 societies found that in only five (2 percent) are adulterous relationships sanctioned; see George P. Murdock, "Sexual Behavior, What Is Acceptable," *Journal of Social Hygiene*, 36:1-31, 1950.

experience with only one partner.[17] For almost a third of those who were unfaithful, the act of unfaithfulness had occurred only a few times, often only once. This experience was for many unpremeditated.

The attitude of the younger generation toward extramarital intercourse under special circumstances seems to be more or less one of toleration. A study of the attitudes of 223 engaged men and 215 engaged women toward extramarital relationships showed that approximately half of both men and women would justify extramarital relationships for both men and women under certain circumstances.[18] Women were less tolerant toward extramarital relationships for women than were men.

Over half the men would justify it in case of frigidity in the wife. A fourth of women would justify it in case of their unsatisfactory response from the husband. Twenty percent of men and 16 percent of women would justify it in cases of general dissatisfaction with the spouse. Twenty-three percent of women and 18 percent of men would justify it in case of strong attraction for another person. Almost half thought it would be justified in case of repeated unfaithfulness of the spouse.

The romantic marriage is based on sexual loyalty. It is interesting to observe that most of the reasons recognized as adequate for unfaithfulness are reasons which indicate that mutual sexual responsiveness is not present in the marriage.

One of the real handicaps to restoring confidence between mates in case of marital infidelity is that the offended mate feels disgraced in the eyes of the community. He is made to feel that he is doing less than his duty in tolerating the offense on the part of the spouse. It is more or less expected that a husband or wife will divorce an unfaithful spouse and make him pay the ultimate penalty for disloyalty.

This is the way that American taboos are constituted and to argue that they are irrational is like arguing against any custom. The custom may seem irrational, yet within the framework of a given set of institutions it is rational, however it may look to people with different social institutions and different taboos. The very fact that society holds the attitudes it does makes a sexual offense outside marriage not merely a sexual offense, but also an offense against social values which the community holds. This is why the community refuses to permit the wife or husband who is innocent in the situation to ignore it.

From the standpoint of the adjustment of the pair, of course, the important thing is the reason for the offense. Is it momentary sexual hunger

17 Alfred C. Kinsey and others, *Sexual Behavior in the Human Female* (Philadelphia: W. B. Saunders Co., 1953). Because of the nature of the Kinsey sample, incidence of infidelity reported is probably higher than average.

18 Ernest W. Burgess and Paul Wallin, *Engagement and Marriage* (Philadelphia: J. B. Lippincott Co., 1953), pp. 400-402.

during a period of absence? Is it a means of defying the mate? Is it due to certain frustrations that the individual is trying to escape? Is it simply a moment of venturing or a quest for variety? Does the offending person still actually love the mate and wish to maintain the marriage?

Often the husband and wife themselves do not know the answer to these questions. By visiting a marriage counselor, a psychiatrist, or discussing the problem with a person who approaches the situation not as one of guilt, but as one in human relationships, they may learn the answer. In so doing, they may reestablish a relationship with each other without suffering the serious damage which often results from blindly following the dictates of custom.

Monogamy is so constituted, and the taboos of society are so complicated, that any variation from monogamy is bound to bring its problems, whether it is handled frankly or whether it is concealed. Often, when it is concealed, a feeling of guilt results and devious behavior may develop in the marriage causing problems that are not ever directly associated with the feelings of guilt. Unfortunately, the violations of monogamy must be taken much more seriously than they might deserve were standards more lenient. One of the most sensible discussions of this problem, from a clinical point of view as well as from common sense points of view, is that by John Levy and Ruth Munroe in *The Happy Family*.

In conclusion, it has been observed that in every area of life which contributes to sexual adjustment it is attitudes, rather than actual physical characteristics or behavior, that are most significant.

While sexual adjustment is a highly personal matter, coming to no two couples in exactly the same way, it is true that the chance a couple has for an early and satisfactory adjustment is greatly affected by whether or not they go into marriage with their eyes open and their facts straight. In the next chapter, therefore, will be presented a detailed discussion of realistic expectations as factors in sexual adjustment.

Problems

1. Helen and Tom are the pride of their community—gay and very much in love after six years of marriage. Tom is called the "perfect husband"— thoughtful, considerate, and proud of his wife. And who could want a better wife than Helen? She is pretty, efficient, and devoted. Only her closest friends know that sexual relations have never given her pleasure, and they

admire her for never having hurt Tom by mentioning this fact. What would you say about Helen?

   a. She has shown more realism in her sexual expectations than most women.

   b. She is reasonable and has therefore made a satisfactory sexual adjustment.

   c. She has cheated herself and her husband by not telling him of her problem.

   d. Her sexual life could probably be improved.

2. What relationship do you believe exists between a happy marriage and sexual adjustment? Would you say that happiness in marriage:

   a. Is the result of satisfactory sexual adjustment?

   b. Produces satisfactory sexual adjusment?

   c. Is not closely related to satisfactory sexual adjustment?

   d. Is neither cause nor effect but is generally associated with satisfactory sexual adjustment?

   e. Is primarily a matter of attitude rather than of physical satisfaction as such?

3. In a popular book which promises to teach its readers *How to Achieve Sex Happiness in Marriage,* approximately three-fourths of the writing is devoted to discussions of techniques in sex. About one-fourth of it is devoted to helping the reader form healthy general attitudes toward sex in marriage. In your opinion, which of the two areas, technique or attitudes, is responsible for most of the problems that trouble sexually unadjusted couples?

4. In almost every American city one may see burlesque theaters crowded with men who enjoy the sexually suggestive skits and jokes and the semi-nude female performers. Are these audiences made up mostly of:

   a. Sexually abnormal men?

   b. Sexually immature men?

   c. Sex-starved men?

   d. Men who are probably normal?

Upon what grounds do you base your opinion?

5. A happily married woman who feels that the sexual adjustment she and her husband have made is a good one suddenly notices her husband reading books on sex techniques. Later he begins to initiate certain new and somewhat unconventional sexual practices into their relationship. In your opinion should she:

   a. Talk about it with a psychiatrist?

   b. Let her husband know she is worried about him?

   c. Read the books with her husband?

   d. Reexamine his background for a hint of some sexual abnormality?

   e. Accept his behavior as natural?

6. For what specific reasons is sexual fidelity generally considered basic to sexual adjustment?

7. Are there any circumstances under which you consider sexual infidelity justifiable in a happy marriage?

8. *Sociodrama:* Two mothers discuss the attitudes toward sex their fifteen-year-old daughters are learning from their high school course in preparation for marriage. One mother favors the course; the other is shocked by it.

9. What do you know about the nature and extent of homosexuality? As a class, or through a committee, study this problem in America today. Discuss it along the following lines:
   a. What are believed to be its causes?
   b. Is there a cure?
   c. What is our legal and social treatment for the homosexual?
   d. Is a slight homosexual tendency dangerous?
   e. What better program and/or attitude might be adopted with reference to homosexuals?
10. In your opinion, if a couple begins to talk together and joke about their sexual relations are they apt to detract from its spiritual quality and reduce it to a mere physical act?

Selected References

ARTICLES IN BOOKS OF READINGS

VINCENT, Clark E., *Readings in Marriage Counseling* (New York: Thomas Y. Crowell Co., 1957).
   1. STOKES, Walter R., "A Marriage Counseling Case: the Married Virgin," pp. 256-270.
   2. ELLIS, Albert, "Marriage Counseling with Couples Indicating Sexual Incompatibility," pp. 270-279.
   3. STONE, Abraham, and LEVINE, Lena, "Group Therapy in Sexual Maladjustment," pp. 342-355.
CAVAN, Ruth Shonle, *Marriage and the Family in the Modern World: A Book of Readings* (New York: Thomas Y. Crowell Co., 1960).
   4. Family Service Association of America, "Why Marriages Fail: Infidelity," Reading 63.
COSER, Rose Laub, *The Family: Its Structure and Function,* (New York: St Martin's Press, Inc., 1964).
   5. FOOTE, Nelson N., "Sex as Play," pp. 184-191.

General References

BOWMAN, Henry A., *Marriage for Moderns,* Fourth Edition (New York: McGraw-Hill Book Co., 1960), Ch. 11.
BROWN, Fred, and KEMPTON, Rudolph T., *Sex Questions and Answers* (New York: McGraw-Hill Book Co., 1950).
BURGESS, Ernest W., and WALLIN, Paul, *Engagement and Marriage* (Philadelphia: J. B. Lippincott Co., 1953), Ch. 6.
KINSEY, Alfred C., and others, *Sexual Behavior of the Human Female* (Philadelphia: W. B. Saunders Co., 1953).

LANDIS, Judson T., POFFENBERGER, Thomas, and POFFENBERGER, Shirley, "The Effect of First Pregnancy Upon the Sexual Adjustment of 212 Couples," *American Sociological Review*, 15:767 ff., December, 1950.

LEMASTERS, E. E., *Modern Courtship and Marriage* (New York: The Macmillan Co., 1957), Chs. 17, 18.

LEUBA, Clarence, *Ethics in Sex Conduct* (New York: Association Press, 1948).

LEVINE, Lena, and GILMAN, Mildred, *The Doctor Tells the Bride and Groom*, Revised Edition (New York: Planned Parenthood Federation of America, 1953).

————, *Frigidity* (New York: Planned Parenthood Federation of America, 1952).

LEVY, John, and MUNROE, Ruth, *The Happy Family* (New York: Alfred A. Knopf, Inc., 1941).

MEAD, Margaret, *Male and Female* (New York: William Morrow & Co., Inc., 1949), Ch. 14.

MURDOCK, George P., "Sexual Behavior, What Is Acceptable," *Journal of Social Hygiene*, 36:1-31, 1950.

NOVAK, Emil, *The Woman Asks the Doctor* (Baltimore: The Williams & Wilkins Co., 1944).

SCHEINFELD, Amram, *Women and Men* (New York: Harcourt, Brace & Co., Inc., 1943).

STONE, Abraham, and LEVINE, Lena, "Group Therapy in Sexual Maladjustment," Reprint of the Marriage Counseling Service of the Margaret Sanger Research Bureau, New York.

25
Realistic Sex Expectations

Knowing what to expect of sex in marriage can do much to help young people over the first difficult hurdles in their life together. For some, expectations need to be toned down—movies and fiction and campus "bull" sessions have led them to expect more than the average marriage is capable of giving. For others, expectations need to be raised—they expect so little or fear so much that they are bound to relegate sex to a negative position or one of insignificance. There are even those who would hope for a sexless marriage. For a large number of young people, however, what is needed most is simply some facts—facts that will help them develop a realistic pattern of sexual relations, facts that will encourage them, reassure them, guide them, inform them of what they can expect in the all-important partnership they hope to enter.

Although our culture is one in which sex is more talked about, and used more extensively in entertainment and advertising than in almost any other part of the world, sex ignorance is appalling. The masses do not have a scientific sex vocabulary. Otherwise informed leaders are often grossly ignorant of the facts of human biology and psychology where sex is concerned. For example, McHugh and Moskin studied the attitudes and information of ministers in the area of sex.[1] They found most of them grossly ignorant, uninformed, and incompetent as counselors. Less than 15 percent are actually competent to counsel, and 50 percent still preach that sex is evil. Their study of 451 young ministers concerning their information about sexual reproduction showed that 35 percent did not know the period of greatest likelihood of pregnancy and almost half thought menstruation cleared the womb of the unfertilized ovum. Almost

[1] G. McHugh and J. Robert Moskin, "What Ministers Are Learning about Sex," *Look*, November 25, 1958, pp. 79-86.

three-fourths considered a woman slightly ill when menstruating. Forty percent thought a woman's sex interest ceased at menopause.

It is very likely that many doctors would not score much higher on some of the psychological and emotional aspects of sex as it affects the marriage relationship.

Sexual Intercourse

Preparation: The male is responsive to a wide range of psychic and physical stimuli. The female may require considerable love play, called "foreplay" in counseling literature. In this the male is normally the aggressor; the female, the pursued. Love play in marriage is likely to be bypassed by the husband. If it is, he need not be surprised that his wife often cannot share the sexual act to the fullest. Mutual sexual enjoyment usually requires that the act of courting be maintained in marriage. The courting consists of stimulating the more sensitive zones of the female's body. This brings about the flow of lubricating fluids in the vaginal tract, preparing her for the sex act. It also stimulates lubricating fluids in the male. This, with the psychological readiness, is complete readiness for the sex act.

The sex act: The sex act involves stimulation with increasing ecstasy until one or both reach a climax, which is a series of spasmodic contractions. In the male, climax is accompanied by the discharge of a tablespoon or two of seminal fluids carrying the sperm. In the female there is no such discharge with the spasmodic contractions, but there may be a sucking motion in the uterus which can help draw the sperm up through the opening of the cervix, thus increasing the likelihood that the sperm will reach the Fallopian tubes and meet the egg cell. To reach a climax usually requires that both participate in spontaneous rhythmic motions.

Between married people any form of foreplay or stimulation that proves exciting and any physical position for the sex act that they wish to assume is normal and proper. The usual face to face position with the male surmounting the female is a matter of local custom, far from the universal position, as human cultures go, and no more moral than any other position spontaneously assumed and mutually enjoyed. Anthropologists find the customary position of our culture far from universal.

Afterplay: The male usually is relaxed and ready for sleep on the concluding of the sex act. The wife usually desires further courting play, petting, etc., in an atmosphere of "delicious langour" in which she senses great tenderness for the male. This is a time for strengthening the love bond, and often for close confessions of differences and for patching up difficulties that have entered their life. This is called the period of afterplay.

The Importance of Spontaneity

Margaret Mead has stated as a principle that the more a crea-ture thinks "the less he may copulate, unless copulation and thought are skillfully integrated at each level."[2] She goes on to elaborate this view, indicating that in cultures where goods are considered to be limited, the expenditure of energy in sex is likely to be conceived as a loss from productivity.

She believes that the sexual functioning of the male is most effective when it is most automatic, a response to simple signals such as the ex-posure of the female, her gestures, etc., and that the complications of sex by conceptions of romantic love, theories, moral qualms, and other abstractions complicate the sexual functioning of the particular group or social class involved.

She finds that in the upper-class groups these inhibitions are likely to be most common, and that in such groups numerous indirect culturally conditioned practices for stimulating the male are invented. Among the lower classes such stimulations are not found and are not needed. The male's approach to sex is direct, uninhibited, and automatic.

Length of Time Required for Sexual Adjustment

Among those whose expectations need to be deflated are the "enlightened youth" who feel sure that they have a "head start" toward sexual adjustment merely because they recognize that such an adjustment will be necessary. As one young man explained to his friend, "Marian and I have taken all the courses and read all the books. We know just what kind of things have to be worked out, so it's not likely to take us more than a week or two to overcome any of the problems we're likely to experience."

This young man may have been correct. For a few the adjustment does come easily, and certainly being well informed can be a great asset. But sexual adjustment is much more than knowing the right answers. It involves one's most deeply rooted attitudes and habits, one's values, and when everything else is settled, it frequently requires time, practice, and patience. Just what are the facts about time and sexual adjustment?

A study of this question by Judson T. Landis has revealed that sex is the one zone in which couples least often experience adjustment from the beginning. His study deals with 409 couples who were the parents of

[2] Margaret Mead, *Male and Female* (New York: Mentor Books, 1955), pp. 158-164.

college students at Michigan State, and compares the periods of time they required to make adjustments in their sexual relationships. It will be seen from Figure 25-1 that few more than half agreed that sex relations had been satisfactory from the beginning; in another 12 percent of cases, one member had thought the relationship unsatisfactory. At the far extreme are 12.5 percent who never made an adjustment in sex relations, and yet they were still married at the time of the study.

TIME IT TOOK 409 COUPLES TO ACHIEVE SEXUAL ADJUSTMENT

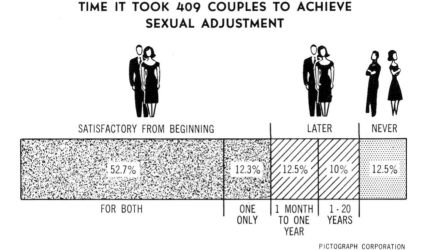

PICTOGRAPH CORPORATION

Source: Judson T. Landis, "Length of Time Required to Achieve Adjustment in Marriage," *American Sociological Review*, 11:668 ff., December, 1946.

FIGURE 25-1————Note that only half of the couples made a satisfactory adjustment at the beginning.

The current generation, with less prudishness and more realistic sex education, should expect to do much better, but most couples must anticipate a delay in achieving sexual adjustment and must not assume that they will realize complete satisfaction at the outset.

Problems of sexual adjustment have by no means disappeared in the new generation. Kinsey reported that adjustment problems appeared at some time during the marriage in two-thirds of the relationships he studied.[3] Our study of marital happiness of two generations indicates that more young married women than their mothers considered sex

[3] Alfred C. Kinsey and others, *Sexual Behavior in the Human Female* (Philadelphia: W. B. Saunders Co., 1953).

adjustment an important factor in happiness (see Table 25-1).[4] While we have no way of knowing the extent to which this view reflects difficulties in the younger generation's own experience, we assume that it probably does.

TABLE 25-1————Percent of two generations listing sexual compatibility as one of five factors most important to marriage happiness; and sexual incompatibility, in unhappy marriage

	SEXUAL COMPATIBILITY IN HAPPY MARRIAGE		SEXUAL INCOMPATIBILITY IN UNHAPPY MARRIAGE	
	Number	Percent	Number	Percent
Mothers	83	16.1	90	16.7
Single Daughters	74	16.6	113	23.2
Married Daughters	38	35.2	39	35.1

If so, why? Sex education, at the college level particularly, has led the new generation of women to expect completeness in their sexual life. Literature given to newlyweds also stresses the possibility of women's full participation in sex experience. This literature often gives rather elaborate information on physical positions to be taken in sex relations and other intimate details of sex functions.

It is possible that the new generation, in their self-conscious effort to achieve completeness in sex relations in marriage, may hinder rather than help sexual adjustment.

The overemphasis on sex in modern marriage is another factor. Because of women's great hopes for complete sexual relations, many are dissatisfied with the adjustment they are able to make. It is possible that many seek divorce on grounds of sexual incompatibility who in another generation would have been content because their expectations were more modest.

It is possible also that this group is still recently enough married to be in the early stages of sexual adjustment characterized by the early years of married life. It is also possible that some of this group have faced difficulties imposed by the new patterns of sexual intercourse introduced to the marriage by their husbands' experience during military duty abroad. Doctors report that new techniques of sexual intercourse learned abroad have violated many wives' codes of propriety and produced shock in the marriage relationship. Here the problem is one of taboos, for, as we have seen, customary position varies in different cultures of the world.

[4] Paul H. Landis, *Two Generations of Rural and Urban Women Appraise Marital Happiness* (Pullman, Wash.: Washington Agricultural Experiment Station, March, 1951), Bulletin No. 524.

Whatever the cause, the problem of sexual adjustment seems to be one that unduly preoccupied the thinking of the newly married group here compared to the other two groups studied.

Those who do not achieve sexual adjustment after a few months of marriage should seek the advice of a family clinic, or of an understanding physician. To enjoy the sexual relationship in marriage is the normal heritage of both men and women. Those who are lacking in health, or who have been shocked by punishment when a child, for exploring sex organs, or who for other reasons have thwarting attitudes, who are emotionally too deeply attached to parents, or else are lacking in the basic knowledge of how to participate in the physical act—these may fail to achieve it. There is a cure for many of these cases.

Unrealistic expectations concerning the length of time adjustment may require are very serious, but probably not so common as other types of misconceptions that may affect the adjustment process. Many young people enter marriage with no ideas, or only false ideas, about what the physical and psychological responses of each mate are likely to be. What is a realistic expectation?

Orgasmic Reactions Among American Women

In only half of the marriages of young couples can it be expected that the wife will experience an orgasm during the honeymoon and the first four weeks of marriage. In a fourth of the cases, it will take from a month to a year.[5] Whether biology alone is responsible for the fairly high proportion of married women in our culture who are slow to experience an orgasm is, of course, an unsettled question. It is known that the female has a much less localized sex interest than the male. Most virgins have little or no localized sex desire and most women who achieve it do so only after experience in marriage. Sex feeling is much more diffused throughout the body of the female and more closely related to affection and general emotional satisfaction.

With the male, sex can often be isolated from love feelings. No doubt the same thing is possible for many females, but as the female is trained in the middle and upper classes of our society, emotional factors are highly important to sexual responsiveness.

Some authors today believe that practically all women could develop orgasmic adequacy if training from childhood was adequate and there were no shocks or other developmental factors to interfere with normal

5 Kinsey's data suggest this, in Alfred C. Kinsey and others, *Sexual Behavior in the Human Female* (Philadelphia: W. B. Saunders Co., 1953); see also Eugene J. Kanin and David H. Howard, "Postmarital Consequences of Premarital Sex Adjustments," *American Sociological Review*, 23:556-562, October, 1958.

TOTAL SEXUAL OUTLET IN MALES AND FEMALES

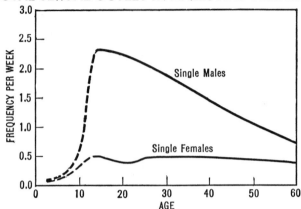

SOURCE: Alfred C. Kinsey and others, *Sexual Behavior in the Human Female* (Philadelphia: W. B. Saunders Co., 1953). Reproduced by permission of Dr. Kinsey.

FIGURE 25-2————Striking differences in sex activity are indicated at all ages of life. (Lines show median frequency of orgasm in total sexual outlet. Dotted lines represent estimates for the prepubertal period.)

maturation. These authorities are inclined to blame sexual maladjustment almost exclusively upon the psychic factors, which have deep roots in the childhood development, or which grow out of the ignorant blundering of the male during the early period of marriage. Some counselors believe that skillful counseling and direction can cure most of these cases.[6] In this age of counseling and optimism concerning female sexual adequacy, it is probable that these views overstate the case.

Kinsey and his co-workers found that about 50 percent of wives experience an orgasm at least once during the first month of marriage and that about 75 percent do so by the end of the first year. This rises to above 80 percent by the fifth year and to a peak of almost 90 percent by fifteen years of marriage.[7] These data refer not to regular orgasm but to having had the experience at least once.

There is of course great variation. Some wives have multiple orgasms during a single act of intercourse; others have an orgasm only once or a few times in a lifetime. Approximately 10 percent of married females in Kinsey's sample had never reached an orgasm at any time in their marital coitus. About 75 percent had responded at least once in the first five years of their marriage. Generally speaking, the older a woman (up to age

[6] See, for example, Oliver M. Butterfield, *Love Problems of Adolescents* (New York: Emerson Books, Inc., 1941), p. 45.

[7] Kinsey, *op. cit.*, p. 349.

forty), the greater the likelihood of her having an orgasm. The peak period in women's experience seems to be age 31 to 40. Lack of orgasm is very common in the younger marriage group. For example, between the ages of 31 and 40, 90 percent of females had reached an orgasm at least once; whereas, among the married females 16 to 20 years of age, only 71 percent had done so. After 40, the incidence declined somewhat.

The Kinsey researchers found that 70 to 77 percent of coital experiences in marriage produce an orgasm for the wife. The incidence is much less in the early years of marriage than in the later years, ranging from an average of only 63 percent in the first year of marriage to 85 percent in the twentieth year of marriage. The exact findings are as follows:[8]

Year of Marriage	Percent of coital experience producing orgasms in the wife
first	63
fifth	71
tenth	77
fifteenth	81
twentieth	85

The figures need some interpretation. During the early years of marriage, coitus is more frequent and is engaged in for the sake of the husband, whether or not it brings satisfaction to the wife. These are his most active years, sexually speaking, while at the same time the wife is most heavily burdened by pregnancy and the care of small children. In the later years of marriage, the husband's sexual needs have diminished and more nearly equal those of the wife. The wife loses her fear of unwanted pregnancy and may participate in sexual activity without this inhibiting fear. Also she is in a period of life when family burdens are light.

In the average marriage, somewhat less than 40 percent of women can expect to always have an orgasm. The proportion will be considerably lower than this for those with lower education levels and considerably higher for those with higher education levels. The proportion will be somewhat less during the early years of marriage and somewhat higher in the later years, according to the Kinsey findings.[9]

The Significance of Orgasmic Response

It cannot be emphasized too often that orgasms cannot be taken as the sole criterion for determining the degree of satisfaction which a female may derive from sexual activity. Considerable pleasure may be found in sexual

[8] *Ibid.*, p. 375.

[9] Judson T. Landis finds that the Kinsey sample of women was probably a very highly sexed group, and that therefore norms for women in general would be much lower; see his "The Women Kinsey Studied," *Social Problems*, 1:139-142, April, 1954.

arousal which does not proceed to the point of orgasm, and in the social aspects of a sexual relationship. Whether or not she herself reaches orgasm, many a female finds satisfaction in knowing that her husband or other sexual partner has enjoyed the contact, and in realizing that she has contributed to the male's pleasure. We have histories of persons who have been married for a great many years, in the course of which the wife never responded to the point of orgasm, but the marriage had been maintained because of the high quality of the other adjustments in the home.

So Kinsey and colleagues conclude from their studies. Whether one is concerned with general marital adjustment or with sexual adjustment alone, the facts seem to indicate that the purely physical aspect of sex is being greatly overemphasized today.

No two women will respond exactly alike. For some the orgasm is a muscular spasm of almost epileptic proportions; for others it is nothing more than a relaxing sigh. For still others it does not exist at all, and yet they enjoy the close contact of the sexual embrace and feel content in helping the husband satisfy his needs.

The ability to respond is more often a matter of psychology than physiology. In women, sexual response is likely to be identified with a whole complex of attitudes centering about genital functions. The woman who dreads menstruation and who dreads pregnancy may also find sexual response difficult. The woman who has welcomed menstruation as a normal function and who is eager for childbearing and motherhood is more likely to make a good sexual adjustment.

A man usually experiences a physical ejaculation and the accompanying orgasm in sexual intercourse. There is no evidence to indicate that all women can reach an explosive climax. The female has no organ of sexual sensation fully comparable in importance to the male organ. In many women, there is no developed clitoris and even in those who have a developed clitoris, the organ in no way corresponds in size or area of sensitivity to that of the male. Generally speaking, the woman's sensation awaits development by the male sex organ.

In many societies all that is expected of women is that they be passively receptive. Whole societies can ignore the climax as a part of female response, Mead[10] finds. She also finds that in some societies, as in Samoa, where males have an elaborate repertoire for stimulating the female, some women cannot respond to sexual stimulation. Mead states the probability that an undeveloped clitoris, lack of tone in vaginal muscles, poor general health, or other weaknesses may be factors. Even though the female probably has more sensitive erogenous zones capable of sexual stimulation and orgasm than the male, as a matter of fact sexual response

[10] Margaret Mead, *Male and Female* (New York: William Morrow & Co., Inc., 1949), pp. 164-170.

is less universal than among males. Responsive sexuality in the female is a learned reaction.

The American Institute of Family Relations has found, among wives coming to the clinic for help, that a lack of tonus in the pubococcygeus muscle is a key factor in lack of female response. By teaching them to strengthen this muscle through exercise, they are able to improve response in many instances. Maxine Davis, in her book, *Sexual Responsibility in Marriage*, claims that "orgasm adequacy" is less rare than once thought, if women can be taught to use the "magic muscle." Even she, however, recognizes that too much emphasis has been placed on the orgasm leaving "everybody expecting too much." She recognizes that for some women the orgasm is very mild; for some, almost as intense as labor pains.

In the current popular conception of sex, the test of marriage seems to be the ability of husband and wife to realize a mutually satisfying physical climax in their sexual relationship. The suggestion that such coordination is not always necessary and often even impossible is difficult for most young couples to believe at a time when so many doctors, psychiatrists, counselors, and writers have emphasized the physical aspects of sex.

Orgasm Not the Only Test of Sexual Adjustment

Sex, as an expression of love and mutual regard in marriage, as a thing which encompasses the personalities of husband and wife, is a symbol of their oneness, even the key to it. As a mere mechanical process to be judged by the intensity and coordination of physical release alone, it is no more significant than such release among creatures of the barnyard. By making the perfection of this mechanical process the goal of sexual life in marriage, many marriages are found wanting. Yet it is known that there are and always have been happy and otherwise successful marriages that have failed to reach this physical goal, just as there have been many marriages that were sexually perfect that have ended in the divorce court.

Because of the current narrow and unrealistic concept of sex, some men and women fear to marry. Others go through married life with unnecessary feelings of personal guilt, frustration, and failure. Dr. Nadina Kavinoky, gynecologist and past president of the National Council on Family Relations, believes that the fear of inability to measure up to this standard has given us frigidity, impotence, and many other marriage problems.[11] Dr. Edward A. Strecker, psychiatrist, agrees.[12] He believes

11 Nadina Kavinoky, "Premarital Examination," *Western Journal of Surgery, Obstetrics, and Gynecology,* 51:315, October, 1943.

12 Edward A. Strecker, "A Doctor Looks at Marital Infidelity," *This Week Magazine,* June 8, 1952, p. 22.

that the physical rewards of the perfect sexual relationship have been too greatly emphasized by his own profession as well as in fiction and so-called scientific literature.

Much of this current misconception of what sex in marriage should be is centered on the kind of sexual satisfaction a woman should receive. It is popularly believed that she is inadequate, or that her husband is, if she fails regularly to achieve an explosive physical climax. This belief persists in spite of the contradictory nature of the facts concerning orgasmic response which were presented above.

Realistic expectations are important to marital adjustment for a marriage cannot long survive in an atmosphere of failure and frustration. Too many marriages crumble under the weight of sexual disappointment that would have been unnecessary had the couple but known the facts.

A young divorcée still thinks with tenderness about a marriage that broke up because of this striving to reach an impossible goal. She confided to the author:

> We would have been the happiest couple in the world if, somehow, we could have forgotten all the "stuff" we ever heard or read on the subject of sex. My happiest moments were when we were together. I loved to feel his nearness and wanted nothing more than to satisfy his every wish. But he was sure that I should get the same excitement out of sex that he did. We never relaxed and enjoyed the intimate life that could have been ours; instead we searched for a kind of mutual ecstacy that was forever out of reach. Our sex life became a time of tension and awkward experimentation that left us more and more upset and dissatisfied. After a while, I lost the simple but deep happiness I had known in our intimate life, and from there on our marriage seemed of little value or meaning to either of us.

While very different from the explosive climax promised in most books, this couple might have been content with their sex life had they not expected so much from the physical side alone. The pleasure the wife received from mere intimacy and joy of giving herself to her husband was amply rewarding in itself. Many happily married wives share this woman's feeling of joy in giving themselves to their husbands, a joy which often fully compensates for their own lack of physical excitement.

Does this mean sexual satisfaction is unimportant for most wives? Certainly not. A marriage, to succeed, must have sexual satisfaction. But many wives do not need peaks of sexual excitement. They are quite content with the simple intimacies—the nearness of a husband, the protectiveness and security that his body gives, the curling of a foot around the ankle, the touch of a loving hand on a soft breast, a kiss.

The woman who has not expected too much and who is not guilt-ridden and frustrated by her inability to match her husband's sexual desire can nevertheless establish a completely happy marriage which leaves none of her husband's needs unsatisfied.

Dr. Kavinoky believes that the pendulum in sex teaching has swung to the extreme of a "narrow physical concept of the act."[13] She believes that it is time we consider sex "in its relationship to the entire life of the two people concerned." She is less concerned about a specific organic reaction to the sexual relationship than that the couple find in it adventure, excitement, release from tension, contentment, unity and spiritual oneness, and in times of sorrow or trouble, even comfort and consolation.

If the concept of sex can be expanded to include this breadth of oneness—this is in fact the pledge couples take in marriage—less anxiety in young people concerning their failure to consciously attain certain specific organic reactions will be created. In removing anxiety, it will be possible for more of them to relax and find genuine physical satisfaction. This will also permit those who fail to do so to live happily without guilt.

Technique Is Not Enough

This does not mean that physical techniques are never important. They are, and couples should try to adjust to each other's needs by discussing them frankly and, when necessary, even seeking help from a doctor or counselor. But the first criterion of success should always be whether the two people themselves are happy in their sexual life. If the wife finds that a physical climax in some sort of complete and explosive form is necessary to her satisfaction, and her husband is, through faulty timing or techniques, unable to achieve this condition, she may be frustrated and unhappy. A good marriage counselor or doctor can sometimes offer help to the couple in attuning their responses. The importance of such an adjustment cannot be dismissed lightly. Often it is only a matter of faulty sex education that is to blame. The husband may not realize that courting prior to the sex act is often essential to her response. Or the wife may not understand her own sensitivities and her powers of bringing the greatest degree of pleasure to both her husband and herself.

Techniques are not of first importance. More often what may be required for harmony is not refinement of technique, but rather, "a mutual generosity of body and soul.[14] Many will obtain the explosive reaction by preliminary love play and improved timing; others, with the best love play, will never reach it, but with proper attitudes can find pleasure in the intimacy and sharing that can come to all happily married people.

Love and trust constantly expressed are great satisfactions in them-

[13] Kavinoky, *op. cit.*
[14] Simone de Beauvoir, *The Second Sex*, edited and translated by H. M. Parshley (New York: Alfred A. Knopf, Inc., 1953), p. 402.

selves. Despite Hemingway's classic description, the earth need not always move in the ecstasy of sexual love.

Two final facts should be mentioned in connection with sexual adjustment and the orgasmic response of the female. First, such an ability has no necessary connection with her capacity for becoming pregnant.[15] Second, neither is the capacity to respond with orgasm affected by menopause and cessation of capacity to reproduce, as many generally well-informed people suppose it to be. Many women experience an upsurge when the fear of pregnancy is gone.

Dr. Chesser's study of sexual adjustment among English women and their happiness in marriage showed that one-half of the happiest women had a great deal of satisfaction in sexual intercourse; only one-tenth of the unhappy women did. On the other hand, it must be pointed out that half of the happily married women did not get a great deal of satisfaction out of the sexual relationship as such.[16]

Burgess and Wallin report guilt feelings among men whose wives did not respond to orgasm.[17] This they suspected was a middle-class norm which had not yet affected the lower classes. Bettelheim[18] states that "today the boy wants his girl to prove him a man by her 'orgastic experience'." In trying to have one for him she becomes anxious and often ends up pretending.

Ruth Cavan[19] has stressed the fact that "anxiety and intense effort to achieve only add to difficulty," and goes on to state that the "great concern with . . . lack of orgasm . . . is not limited to the wife's feelings of deprivation, but may become a contentious subject leading to lack of satisfaction . . . for both husband and wife."

Bettelheim blames the "alarming rise in homosexuality" to such factors in the relationships of husbands and wives."[20]

Religion and Sex Activity in Marriage

Wallin has studied the degree of religiosity as it relates to sexual gratification.[21] He finds that religion apparently is a sublimating factor in women's sex-marriage relationships, for low sexual gratification

---

[15] A recent study does express the view that orgasm may set up a sucking motion in the uterus and aid in pregnancy, but this action is not necessary to pregnancy; see John F. Oliven, *Sexual Hygiene and Pathology* (Philadelphia: J. B. Lippincott Co., 1955).

[16] Eustace Chesser and others, *The Sexual, Marital and Family Relationships of English Women* (New York: Roy Publishers, Inc., 1957).

[17] Ernest W. Burgess and Paul Wallin, *Engagement and Marriage* (Philadelphia: J. B. Lippincott Co., 1953).

[18] Bruno Bettelheim, "Growing Up Female," *Harper's*, 225:120-128, October, 1962.

[19] Ruth Cavan, *The American Family*, Third Edition (New York: Thomas Y. Crowell Co., 1963), p. 397.

[20] Bettelheim, *op. cit.*

[21] Paul Wallin, "Religiosity, Sexual Gratification, and Marital Satisfaction," *American Sociological Review*, 22:300-305, June, 1957.

scores of religious women depreciate their overall marital satisfaction scores less than do low sexual gratification scores of the nonreligious. This relationship is not clear in the case of men.

Frequency of Coitus in American Marriages

Sexual intercourse (coitus) is a recurrent need for both men and women. How often the need recurs differs vastly with persons, with mates, with age, and seems to differ somewhat with occupational groups. Terman, studying psychological factors in marital happiness of 792 couples, found that husbands on the average wanted coitus somewhat more frequently than wives (see Figure 25-3).

PREFERRED FREQUENCY OF INTERCOURSE

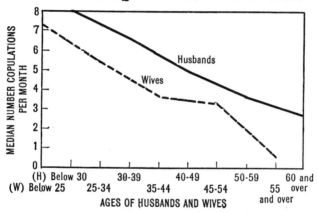

SOURCE: By permission from Lewis M. Terman and others, *Psychological Factors in Marital Happiness* (Copyright, 1938, McGraw-Hill Book Co.).

FIGURE 25-3————At all ages the wife's preferred frequency averaged less than the husband's. Such averages, of course, do not depict the wide range of individual differences in both men and women. (Data are for 792 married couples.)

To summarize briefly Terman's findings according to the way his married couples matched up sexually, the following table is given, showing what proportion of wives and husbands were satisfied with the frequency of their sexual relations:

	Wives (percent)	Husbands (percent)
Too frequent intercourse	24	3
Just the right amount	53	54
Too little intercourse	22	44

Frequency is largely determined by the biological rhythms of the couple, particularly of the male. The buildup of seminal fluids, along with psychological stimulation operate here. Sexual appetite is, of course, variable with amount of activity and with degree of restraint and self-control. Frequency is not a matter of morals in the view of most married people today. It is a recreative activity without being an intentional act of procreation, except on rare occasions. The norm of younger people is two or three times weekly, but variations up and down from this norm are to be expected.

The degree of resulting stimulation—the extent to which the couple feel tired and irritated or rejuvenated and more energetic—is the practical measure of desired frequency. Usually the husband is more eager and must temper his demands to the wife's tolerance; otherwise she becomes fatigued, irritable, and may in time dread his approaches. If the wife is the more eager, too great demands may lead the husband to the point of impotence, since the male usually must take the initiative in order to feel psychologically safe.

It is very likely that the degree of sexual satisfaction in coitus will depend on the degree of mutuality. In this there appears to have been some improvement in recent generations, possibly due in part to the male's increased recognition of the need for restraint in order to meet the wife's norm. Of wives in the Kinsey research born before 1900, marital coitus had a frequency of 3.2 per week; of those born after 1900, the frequency was 2.6.[22] This research also finds a greater variety of techniques and more foreplay among couples at the later period;[23] also that more wives responded to orgasm—37 percent of those born prior to 1900 and 42 percent of those born later.[24]

All of these findings would seem to point toward greater mutuality in the sexual aspect of marriage and to greater satisfaction of sexual needs.

Some couples desire sexual relations once a month, or even less. At the other extreme are sxual athletes who desire intercourse three or more times daily. Happy are they if married to a mate with similar desire frequency. The average for couples in the United States seems to range between ten and fifteen times a month. In other words the cycle of the usual marriage is one to three times a week.

Figure 25-3 shows the average difference in desire for intercourse of couples of different ages. It will be seen that the men at all ages feel the need for coitus more often than the wives. These data are, of course,

22 Alfred C. Kinsey and others, *Sexual Behavior in the Human Female*, (Philadelphia: W. B. Saunders Co., 1953), Table 97, p. 397.
23 *Ibid.*, pp. 360-366.
24 *Ibid.*, pp. 380-381.

averages. In some couples the wife is more strongly sexed. Kinsey's data show the range of extremes more variable in women than in men.

At the beginning of marriage, intercourse daily is not unusual, with a gradual tapering off as the novelty of it passes, until the couple adjusts to their normal cycle of needs. After this point there is a slow decline in frequency until the late fifties. From then on coitus may continue until old age with declining frequency, depending on the physical energy and psychological outlook of the pair.

Studies of the great biologist Raymond Pearl and some later studies suggest that sexual intercourse is most frequent among farmers, second among people in the business classes, and least frequent among those in the professions. Such differences might well be explained in terms of diversity of interest, habits of living, physical energy, variety of other recreational outlets, psychic stimulation outside the marriage, etc., rather than by differences in biological drives.

The Duration of Sexual Activity Among American Couples

Many young people are inclined to think that sexual attraction and sexual drives are characteristic phenomena of youth but have no significance in the later years of married life. This notion of American folklore is very persistent. It is also completely inaccurate. Although youth is the more highly romantic age, and although, for the young male particularly, sexual drives may seem overwhelming, the facts are that sexual attraction and interest in sexual intercourse persist throughout most of the years of married life.

Kinsey's data deal with large samples of both males and females in the later years of life. The young male reaches his maximum capacity during the teens, having on the average an orgasm approximating two and half times per week during this age period. His sex activities decline consistently thereafter. But at 60 years of age he still averages about one orgasm every three weeks. At age 60, only 5 percent of males, he finds, are inactive; at 70, only 30 percent. Some are still active at 80 or older.[25]

The average female during the early teens has little capacity for sexual responsiveness. Even at twenty, her median orgasm is about one every three weeks. She reaches her peak of orgasmic response—about one every two weeks—at around thirty years of age, and remains near this level till past fifty. At age sixty her capacity to respond by orgasm remains almost as high as it was at age 20.

There are, of course, marked differences in individual capacity to

[25] *Ibid.*, pp. 231-235.

respond sexually. But the fact remains that sex is a more permanent bond in marriage than the average young person is inclined to think, and it does constitute a life-long adjustment in the marital relationship.

Contraception and Sexual Adjustment

Today few couples share the attitude of helplessness or indifference that characterized their ancestors' views on limiting family size.

In that earlier generation, a sexually active couple might well expect a large family unless they were both willing to consciously repress their sexual desires. Modern Americans are eager for many of the good things in life, and they realize that the financial burden of a large family puts many of their other goals completely out of reach. At the same time, few happily married couples are willing to sacrifice any of the pleasure and contentment they might obtain from indulging in sexual intercourse as frequently as they desire.

Young men and women entering marriage today have several choices open to them. Their sexual adjustment in marriage will depend considerably on how they face the facts about childbearing, contraceptive practices, and the significance of family planning upon marital happiness. Realistic plans and expectations in this area are basic to all-around marital adjustment as well as sexual compatibility.

A basic fact to be considered is that the widespread acceptance of the principle of family limitation has done much to bring a new pleasure in marital relations to many couples.[26] The anxiety brought about by concern over too large a family or health problems associated with frequent pregnancy can now be largely eliminated. Effective family planning has made it possible for husbands and wives to enter into sexual relations in a spirit of confidence and lightheartedness that has been beneficial to both.

The average couple who expect to enjoy the highest standard of living within their reach and who also hope to make a healthful sexual adjustment must generally accept the necessity of limiting their family's size. This requires agreement upon some method of birth control. Superficially this seems to be an area where the facts concerning the effectiveness of various techniques would be the only factors to be considered. Actually, however, both personal and religious considerations frequently enter in.

A marriage clinic, with its expert medical advisor, or doctor, is the

---

[26] Confidence in contraceptives has been found to be related to good marital adjustment according to studies of the Milbank Memorial Fund (see *Milbank Memorial Fund Quarterly,* July, 1952); see also Judson T. Landis, Thomas Poffenberger, and Shirley Poffenberger, "The Effect of First Pregnancy upon the Sexual Adjustment of 212 Couples," *American Sociological Review,* 15:767 ff., December, 1950.

best source of advice on the latest and best methods of family limitation. A later chapter deals with problems of child spacing.

The Biology of Reproduction

This is not the place for an extensive discussion of human physiology. Presumably most young people will have made some study of human physiology before they study a book of this kind. On the other hand, there are always those who have had no training even in the fundamentals of reproduction. To enter marriage in such a state of ignorance can bring serious consequences in the fields of sexual and general adjustment. The following figures represent a simple summary of the matter.

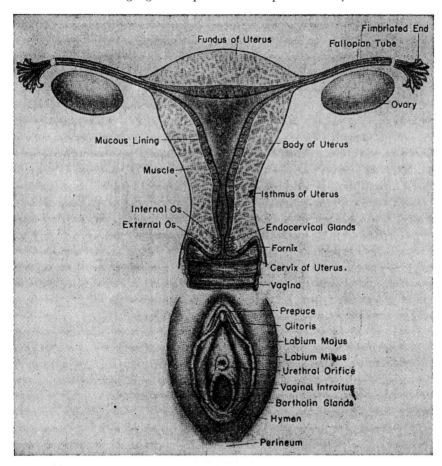

SOURCE: C. L. Anderson, *Physical and Emotional Aspects of Marriage* (St. Louis: C. V. Mosby Co., 1953). Reproduced by permission of the publisher and Dr. Anderson.

FIGURE 25-4————Diagrammatic view of the female reproductive system.

Figure 25-4 gives a detailed frontal view of the female reproductive system, with a cross-section view in the lower part of the diagram. The point of deposit of semen' by the male is in the vaginal tract near the cervix. The sperm must be sucked in or swim through the cervical opening and travel up through the uterus to the Fallopian tube to reach the ovum. The ovum, or egg, and sperm can meet only during a short period of the month, usually seven or eight hours.[27]

The second diagram (Fig. 25-5) shows the male reproductive organs. Millions of sperm are manufactured daily in the testicles which lie outside the body in the scrotum,[28] are stored in the seminiferous tubules, and dis-

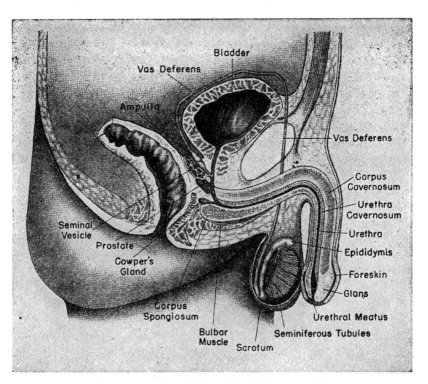

Source: C. L. Anderson, *Physical and Emotional Aspects of Marriage* (St. Louis: C. V. Mosby Co., 1953). Reproduced by permission of the publisher and Dr. Anderson.

FIGURE 25-5————Diagrammatic view of the male reproductive system.

[27] Charles H. Best and Norman B. Taylor, *The Living Body: A Text in Human Physiology*, Fourth Edition (New York: Holt, Rinehart & Winston, Inc., 1958). p. 657; also Edmund J. Farris, *Human Ovulation and Fertility* (Philadelphia: J. B. Lippincott Co., 1956).

[28] Sperm require storage in a temperature lower than normal body temperature.

charged through the penis at the time of the male orgasm in sexual intercourse. In normal sexual intercourse millions are deposited, along with fluids from the cowper's gland and prostate gland, in the upper end of the vaginal vestibule of the female.

Problems

1. It has been stated that, with reference to their sexual expectations, "American women have gone from one extreme to another. They used to expect nothing; now they expect everything. Of the two extremes, today's is probably the more dangerous."
2. What are your reactions to the proposal that it would be desirable for each young couple to set a time limit of, say one year, in which to achieve sexual adjustment? During the year they would read about sex, patiently experiment, and seek help if necessary. At the end of the period they might reasonably say that they had done everything possible and, if they still feel dissatisfied, they should seek a divorce.
3. What would your advice be to a woman who has experienced no orgasm by her third year of marriage?
    a. Visit her doctor.
    b. Visit a psychiatrist.
    c. Keep trying.
    d. Discuss the matter with her husband.
    e. Accept the fact gracefully and recognize that she need not match her husband in orgasmic response.
    f. Some other alternative.
    Defend your choice.
4. Most couples with children believe that their marriage is a happier one than it would have been had they remained childless. Why then is some form of birth control often considered important to marital happiness?
5. What stand does the Catholic Church take on birth control? What are the arguments in favor of this position? Is it possible for sincere Catholics to control the size of their family within the framework of their religious belief?
6. Sexual relations, even in happy marriages, are thought by most young people to cease by middle age. It is difficult for many to realize that older people could find one another sexually interesting and attractive. In general, what are the facts concerning duration and frequency of sexual activity among older couples?
7. While no class is a typical cross section of young people, your class nevertheless represents various levels of opinion and knowledge. Poll the class on their sex knowledge as it was prior to reading this chapter with the following statements.
    Before reading this chapter I believed that:
    a. Sexual adjustment was generally a matter of (1) hours, (2) days, (3) weeks, (4) several months, (5) a year or so, (6) a lifetime.

    b. Most women experience an orgasm (1) generally, as do men, (2) almost always, (3) about half the time, (4) occasionally, (5) very seldom.

    c. In order for both mates to be happy, the wife (1) must experience an orgasm, (2) should experience an orgasm occasionally, (3) need never experience an orgasm.

    d. The average young couple engages in sexual relations (1) nightly, (2) almost every night, (3) about once a week, (4) infrequently.

    e. That sexual relations between most couples tends to cease (1) after the first 5 years of marriage, (2) after about 12 years, (3) in middle age, (4) after menopause, (5) when the couple become very old.

In analyzing the results of this poll consider the degree to which the answers (*a*) agree with the facts in the chapter, (*b*) differ by sex.

Selected References

ARTICLES IN BOOKS OF READINGS

FISHBEIN, Morris, and KENNEDY, Ruby Jo Reeves, *Modern Marriage and Family Living* (New York: Oxford University Press, 1957).

    1. DICKINSON, Robert L., "Anatomy and Physiology of the Sex Organs," pp. 187-203.

    2. KELLY, G. Lombard, "Technique of Marriage Relations," pp. 204-214.

    3. ENGLISH, O. Spurgeon, "Sexual Adjustment in Marriage," pp. 215-231.

CAVAN, Ruth Shonle, *Marriage and the Family in the Modern World: A Book of Readings* (New York: Thomas Y. Crowell Co., 1960).

    4. LANDIS, Paul H., "Don't Expect Too Much of Sex in Marriage," Reading 51.

KLING, Samuel G., and KLING, Esther B., *The Marriage Reader* (New York: The Vanguard Press, Inc., 1947).

    5. WALKER, Kenneth, "The Nature of the Sexual Impulse and of the Sexual Act," pp. 129-141.

    6. EVERETT, Millard S., "The Anatomy and Physiology of Sex," pp. 142-157.

    7. WRIGHT, Helena B., "The Perfect Sex Act," pp. 176-185.

    8. HIMES, Norman E., "Positions in Coitus," pp. 186-190.

    9. ELLIS, Havelock, "The Play Function of Sex," pp. 191-201.

    10. GUYOT, Jules, "A Ritual for Married Lovers," pp. 202-212.

    11. STOPES, Marie Carmichael, "The Frigid Wife," pp. 228-235.

    12. ————, "Undersexed Husbands," pp. 236-246.

KRICH, A. M. (Editor), *Women: The Variety and Meaning of Their Sexual Experience* (New York: Dell Publishing Co., 1954).

    13. MEAD, Margaret, "Potency and Receptivity," pp. 111-135.

————, *Men: the Variety and Meaning of Their Sexual Experience* (New York: Dell Publishing Co., 1954).

    14. MENNINGER, Karl A., "Impotence and Frigidity," Ch. 4.

    15. WALKER, Kenneth, "The Art of Love," Ch. 13.

General References

BEE, Lawrence S., *Marriage and Family Relations* (New York: Harper & Row, Publishers, 1959), Ch. 4.

BENEDEK, Therese, "Psychosexual Functions in Women," *Studies in Psychosomatic Medicine* (New York: The Ronald Press Co., 1952).

CAVAN, Ruth Shonle, *American Marriage* (New York: Thomas Y. Crowell Co., 1959), Ch. 13 by Ida M. Brechtel.

CHESSER, Eustace, and others. *The Sexual, Marital and Family Relationship with English Women* (New York: Roy Publishers, Inc., 1957).

KEPHART, William M., *The Family, Society and the Individual* (Boston: Houghton Mifflin Co., 1961).

LANDIS, Judson T., and LANDIS, Mary G., *Building a Successful Marriage*, Fourth Edition (Englewood Cliffs, N. J.: Prentice-Hall, Inc., 1963), Ch. 17.

PETERSON, James A., *Education for Marriage*, Second Edition (New York: Charles Scribner's Sons, 1964), Ch. 16.

WALLIN, Paul, "Religiosity, Sexual Gratification, and Marital Satisfaction," *American Sociological Review*, 22:300-305, June, 1957.

26
Harmonizing Économic Values

Thorstein Veblen, brilliant iconoclastic economist, saw material goods as a means to status. This theory he enlarges upon in one of the most cutting satires in social science literature, his *Theory of the Leisure Class*. Leisure itself is the key to social status: it testifies that here is a man who lives with little work; he has plenty. His wealth is spent in costly publicity-gaining activities—at the races, golfing, hunting, gaming, and in lavish entertainment of the "right" people. Conspicuous consumption (lavish spending in ways that are apparent to others) is another device of status-seeking, as is conspicuous philanthropy.

Veblen saw this pattern affecting not only the wealthy but all who imitate them, or nearly everyone in our culture. He saw deeply into the mainsprings of human nature in the area of economic motivation. However, the motivations he saw operating in our economic life seem to the writer more typical of nonindustrial civilizations, where there is no middle class, than of modern American society. The writer's travels have led him to conclude that the American, in spite of his supposed greed and moneymindedness, is less driven to conspicuous consumption than many peoples of the world. Yet the use of goods for status does operate here, and is a factor in the relationships of men and women. The Veblen views point up the fact that the adjustment struggle centering about money in marriage is of much deeper significance than monetary values as such. Money is at the roots of status seeking in the value systems of men and women, and what money means to a particular individual must be understood in this broader framework.

Economic Adjustments after Marriage Rather Than Before

The property problem in the institutional marriage systems of the world is negotiated in advance of marriage by the families concerned. Economic values, as we have seen, are critical in mate choice where elders are in control of matchmaking. Property and family status are the criteria of appropriate mate choice, not personal characteristics of bride or groom. In our propertyless concept of mate choice, however, love and companionability are what count. Property matters are considered later. Consequently, as has been discovered by researchers, a major problem after marriage, one rivaling or equaling the problem of sex adjustment itself, is that of money matters.[1]

Money, or more broadly, economic values have become the symbol of innumerable needs and satisfactions, and because they have, money values become the supreme issues in many aspects of husband-wife adjustment in the marriage. The real problem of the modern marriage is not merely how money shall be earned or how it shall be spent, but rather the kind of values in life which the couple seek to obtain through its use. Differences in ideas concerning the use of money in the marriage are symbolic of basic differences in personal values and aspirations, for money actually has a place in the personal values of everyone, and the ends the individual pursues with money are symbolic of his total value system.

The rural-born person with a background of thrift and practicality may, for example, experience real satisfaction and boast at length about the bargain-counter purchase of a dress at a fourth its regular price. In this person's scheme of values, such a purchase represents a shrewd and wise way of overcoming economic limitations and of actually achieving success and status. Many of today's urban dwellers, those reared in a luxurious environment and those who aspire to a higher social status, are likely, by contrast, to achieve satisfaction through buying a garment that is conspicuously expensive or that bears the most exclusive shop's label.

Value Differences of Men and Women

A *Fortune* poll some years ago asked men and women to indicate which sex they though was the more extravagant. A majority of both men and women felt that women are the more extravagant. Undoubtedly,

[1] See data in the latter part of Chapter 23; also see Judson T. Landis, "Length of Time Required to Achieve Adjustment in Marriage," *American Sociological Review*, 11:688 ff., December, 1946.

this feeling is the basis of much of the conflict between men and women over economic values.

Probably the reason women have gained the reputation of being more extravagant is that they do such a high proportion of the spending. It usually falls to the wife's lot to do most of the day-to-day shopping.

Far too often the male role becomes that of supercritic of all the purchases. Frequently, he does not mean to be a critic; he merely wants to know what is going on. When he notices new drapes at the living room windows, he immediately asks, "Where did these come from?" The wife, if she is sensitive, may anticipate the next question, "What did they cost?" When beefsteak appears on his table the husband asks, "Where did you get this steak?" perhaps meaning, "It's a fine piece of meat. Go there more often." Or he may mean, "We're buying more steak than we can afford," or "Steak like this costs more than we can afford." In either case, the wife has the feeling he is questioning her judgment. If the steak happens to be a tough one, he is likely to growl, "Where'd you get that piece of leather?" Immediately he implies that her judgment in purchasing meat is not to be trusted.

So the interactions centering about the wife's role as consumer-purchaser in the marriage go on. In this role she is inclined to receive little praise and a great deal of blame unless the husband too has absorbed a large measure of the commonly held attitude that you've got to "put on" to "get on" in this world.

When it comes to the big purchases, like the family car, a home, life insurance, or investments, the great male sallies forth with omnipotent wisdom. Women's judgment is not appreciated in such circumstances. They don't know the business world. When the husband pulls a big boner, which he is as likely to do as not, he prefers to live above censure, but if called upon to justify his move he rationalizes that one must, in investment ventures, expect to make some mistakes; that the man who does not venture never has anything.

At the nonthrifty extreme are those husbands who are always out for a quick deal which promises to bring the family immediately to the luxury plane. It may be the horses that fascinate them, the stock market, the commodity market, the long shot in a business venture, or any one of the thousands of deals that bait the speculation-minded with a gambler's hope of quick success. Certainly some wives are guilty of this, too, but generally speaking the man is the culprit and the patient, or impatient, wife protests, guided by the sound evidence of past example.

It is difficult even yet for the male to recognize that one of the most influential newspaper financial columnists and authors on income tax matters today is a woman (Sylvia Porter)—a married woman. For years she used only her initials in order not to betray the fact that she is a woman. It was feared that she would have no readers if it were known that she was a woman.

Women, the bargain hunters: Women, much more than men, are bargain hunters when it comes to shopping. Considering their time of no value, they are inclined to do a great deal of footwork, and sometimes drive the family automobile a considerable distance to "save" a few cents. They work on the philosophy that anyone can get an article at the full price, but that it takes a shrewd woman indeed to find a bargain. At some social levels, there is prestige as well as personal satisfaction in such achievement, particularly if it is learned that some unwitting friend or neighbor paid two cents more for the same article. In certain instances, bargain hunting becomes such a fascinating game that sale items are bought in excess and the total outlay far exceeds the savings. If purchases are confined to the actual need, however, there is a saving. The farm woman's bargain counters are the sales catalogs of Sears Roebuck, Montgomery Ward, and other mail-order houses. Here (more comfortably than at the urban bargain counter), they search for the discount items that will add to their convenience, home appearance, or dress.

Men, the discount seekers: There are many exceptions, but generally women do not believe in arguing the seller down in price. They feel guilty in trying to do so. Prhaps they feel it is giving the impression they can't afford the article. Verbal bargaining is the realm in which the male shines. He wants to do his shopping in a hurry and without unnecessary footwork. He is aware that nothing is saved by driving the car about hunting for the cheapest article in town, but he likes the game of beating the seller down. He knows there is a 30 to 50 percent markup on various articles he buys and has no compunctions about talking the seller out of a slice of his cut. He will argue that the markup is for time customers, to cover worthless trade-ins, that such items are not moving anymore—anything to bring the seller to his terms. And he is always ready for a chance to gloat about his bargain and to strut his success before his less brazen neighbor who was sucker enough to pay the full price. Buying wholesale, too, has become a great American game.

Merging roles: One suspects that, with the entry into the work world by women, the traditional clashes between husbands and wives over economic values have been modified somewhat. Both husbands and wives may be getting greater insight into the buying roles that have traditionally belonged to the other sex. Where both work, both often shop together in the supermarket. While the wife is filling her shopping cart with canned goods, the husband is over at the cooler selecting the steak or roast that strikes his fancy, or his purse. And where both earn, they are more likely to talk over investments and plan them together.

The wife who has had experience in earning also may realize as clearly as does the man how much labor goes into earning the money for a particular expenditure. Such wives' standards of value may in time become similar to those of the husband in spite of differential values dominating the childhood training of boy and girl.

The old division of labor within the household tends to break down, too, as sex roles become modified to fit modern economic roles. Where both husband and wife work, the hard and fast line no longer exists in their domestic world. Even the care of small children is shared by the husband in a way that would have shamed the masculine male of a few generations ago.

TABLE 26-1————Percent of 202 middle-class and 341 lower-class fathers in Tampa, Florida, who usually did or shared economic activity listed*

Task	Middle-class fathers (percent)	Lower-class fathers (percent)
Earns money for the family	98	98
Shops for the family's new car	92	87
Pays the bills	79	77
Provides the children's spending money	75	78
Selects large household equipment	71	66
Plans savings for the family	73	63
Shops for furniture and other homefurnishings	65	62
Goes to the store for groceries	39	45
Shops for clothes for family members	21	29

* Abstracted from Johannis, footnote below.

The division of labor in economic activities for over 500 middle- and lower-class urban families (Tampa, Florida, 1953) is shown in Table 26-1.[2] It will be seen that the father in most families is an income producer. He usually buys the new car, and in three-fourths of families he usually makes or shares decisions involving large expenditures or savings. His taking over or sharing the buying of groceries and clothes is less frequent, although today he often plays this economic role too.

While it is assumed that the disappearance of rigid lines of division of labor have for many couples eased the friction and increased the co-operative spirit of the household, all is not peace. The very fact that roles are no longer strictly defined, and the division of labor is no longer clear, is the basis for many a family argument.

Where division of labor is fixed, each accepts his place and carries out his appointed task. Where there is no real division of labor, the marriage

2 Theodore B. Johannis, Jr., based on data presented in a paper before the Research Section, National Council on Family Relations, Oakland, California, July 9, 1954.

must define each new work situation for itself. This calls for the maximum of tolerance, good humor, and cooperation. It also calls for a great deal of good sense.

So the problem is ramified into hundreds of struggles between husbands and wives in their attempts to define a satisfactory division of labor and a compatible scheme of economic values. Maximum adjustability is required if marriage is to be a truly cooperative economic venture.

Conflict Over Property Ownership vs. Comforts

In the rural economy of an earlier day—and some of those values still survive—the accumulation of possessions was symbolic of a person's accomplishments. The contrasting urban value is to "live well" whether one actually owns anything in the way of tangible assets or not. There is a world of difference in the two approaches to life, and where the two meet in marriage, as they often do, a major compromise is required.

The roots of the first series of values, so deeply imbedded in history, persist and merit a brief examination. In an agricultural economy a man's character and accomplishments were measured by the time he went into the field in the morning, the acres and fertile land he acquired, the success of his crops, and the size of his flocks and herds. Woman was a helpmate in these achievements and shared a sense of accomplishment and respect in them. She also acquired success and respect in a domain of her own. The successful agrarian housewife was respected for the good bread she baked, her pies or cakes, doughnuts, chicken noodles, or for some other specific art in which she excelled her neighbors. For her homemaking and general ability to carry her share of the farm load, she received unspoken but deeply felt gratitude from her husband and respect from neighbors.

The new world of wages and salaries, and the new setting of urban industrial civilization, have shifted emphasis from the desire to accumulate possessions or to achieve in domestic spheres where accomplishment was once significant. The new values of the masses now center in earning, in order to spend for a higher level of living. This means greater comfort, greater leisure, even greater luxury. The quest for security in land, home, and other real property has receded into the background. Women's domestic arts now have to compete with the processed products of the great factory, with its packaged cake mix, pie crust, and factory-cured ham.

The economic world is no longer family-centered, nor are economic values so clear-cut in the personalities of either man or wife. The comfort-minded and the possessions-minded are merely two points of view among many contrasting types of value systems around which personalities are oriented today.

Investment in Male and Female Subcultures

Gain made by investment of money for long term goals of family security has been largely in the area of the male subculture. Many wives think that when they spend money for something they want they are making an investment, some even consider this saving. These ideas shock the investment-minded husband.

While these weaknesses in the female subculture may bring arguments and misunderstanding in early married life, they can be serious indeed in later life if the wife is left with property which must be managed if she is to remain independent and live in the comfort which her husband's management of money may have provided.

Because women are the more durable of the species, women inherit much of the wealth in houses, farms, livestock, lands, stocks, bonds, life insurance and cash, which the couple has laid by for the rainy day. It has usually been the husband's investment and money management which has led to such an estate having been accumulated. Suddenly, usually without prior training on the part of the wife for the responsibility, it is hers to use, manage and, if she has the capacity, to multiply until such time as it is passed on to the children and grandchildren, or to whatever charity she may choose as an alternative to passing on the inheritance to her descendants.

Albert E. Schwabacher, Jr.,[3] has commented with the wisdom of wide experience of an investment banker on the weakness of widows. He expresses the view that women probably own half the property, but control only about 20 percent, since most husbands and estate planners leave it in such a form that control is provided for through pensions, etc. But when they are left free to control their money, they usually turn to professional managers, most of whom are men.

As a manager of money, he has found women with real understanding of money and property management are rare. Only a few are informed, intelligent and competent in this area of operation. He finds that with many, discussing their business with them is a waste of time. Often he finds that they appraise investment situations strictly in personal terms and by impulse. "Buy Aunt Sally Candy Company Stock!" Ask her why and her answer, "I like the candy." The fact that the stock makes no money, makes no difference. "Don't buy any Safeway Stock." Ask her why, "A Safeway clerk was rude to me."

He finds many want to sell a good stock—one that should be kept—

---

[3] Albert E. Schwabacher, Jr., "The Repository of Wealth," in Seymour M. Farber and Roger H. L. Wilson (Editors), *The Potential of Woman* (New York: McGraw-Hill Book Co., 1963), pp. 241-254.

on impulse; that others want to keep a stock that has no future "because my departed husband bought it."

As a manager of money, he feels that the female subculture is weak in not teaching women the principle of risk involved in investment— to invest in a capitalistic economy means risk, the possibility of losing. A capitalistic society is always short of risk capital and women tend to hoard wealth, or have it managed too conservatively so that much of it is of little use in expanding the economy.

The Need of Both Men and Women to Feel Productive

One of the principal roads to personal satisfaction and high social standing in our culture is still through productivity. The wealthy in America have failed to fit Thorstein Veblen's picture of the leisure class. They have not, in fact, been a leisure class; they have been among the most productive individuals in the economic system; for here a man's measure is still, in part, his ability to contribute something worthwhile to the creative wealth of mankind.

Being productive brings a feeling of importance and the admiration of others. The desire to feel important and to be admired explains in large part the acquisition of wealth and property throughout history. The flocks and herds, the apartment houses and factories, the finery and gadgets, and particularly the material comforts and luxuries, are means. Possession shows the world that this man or woman, or this man and woman together, have been able to get ahead in the highly competitive struggle for success.

The urban worker employed by others, particularly the wage worker, has found it difficult to take as much satisfaction from productivity as the self-employed man usually has and does today. In fact, the tendency of the labor union movement, and of labor union philosophy, has been to play down production and play up income received for production. Slowdowns and other devices have tended to make the worker feel that to produce more than the man working at his elbow is disloyal to labor and tends, in the long run, to reduce the number of jobs available for workers. This value, of course, is in direct contrast to the old rural value under which a man's productive effort was a measure of his character, almost of his religion.

This need to feel productive is still to some extent characteristic of the great majority of Americans, but there is evidence that it varies greatly among individuals and can be cultivated or largely destroyed by early training. The average male exhibits it more consistently than does the average female. In most communities, however, as has been stressed, a man

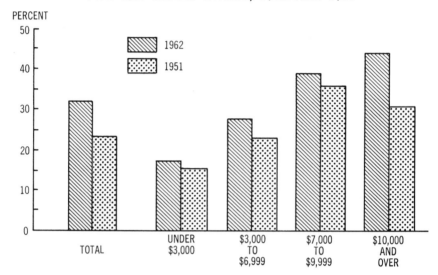

WORKING WIVES AS PERCENT OF HUSBAND-WIFE
FAMILIES, BY FAMILY INCOME
IN CONSTANT (1962) DOLLARS,
FOR THE UNITED STATES, 1962 AND 1951

SOURCE: U. S. Department of Commerce, Bureau of the Census, *Consumer Income,*
Series P-60, No. 41, October 21, 1963, p. 10.

FIGURE 26-1————Observe that the great increase in working wives during
the last decade has been among those in the highest income bracket. More
than economic motive operates here. The need to feel significant is likely an
important factor among the better qualified, particularly after the short period
of childbearing is over. In 1962 wives in the paid labor force as a percent of
husband-wife families in the under-$3,000 group was only 17 percent; in the
$10,000-and-over group, 44 percent.

is still judged and judges himself primarily in terms of his productivity.
"Poor Jones," for example, "is just a flop!" This is the community's
verdict because Jones has not been able to make more than a bare living
from his grocery store. The community judges Jones by his business
success, not by his success as a father, a husband, or a human being. He
may be happy and well adjusted, but until he makes his business a prosperous one he is likely to remain a failure in the eyes of his neighbors.

Smith, on the other hand, may have ulcers or suffer from high blood
pressure and constant worry, but among his acquaintances he is known
as a "go-getter," because he has put himself—his time, money, energy,
and perhaps his health—into achieving vocational success.

This difference in values, or in the emphasis upon values, is no serious problem on a national or even community-wide basis. Such differences, in fact, tend to complement one another and both extremes can find satisfaction in our culture, as well as in our economy. A real problem does arise, however, when such differences clash head-on in marriage. Clashes of this kind are not uncommon, since the value of personal productivity is much more strongly emphasized in the rearing of boys than of girls.

Women judge themselves and one another more consistently in terms of consumption. The location of one's residence, the size of one's TV set, the number of one's labor-saving electrical gadgets, rather than what one can produce, determine one's success and status in the community.

In many marriages, then, the husband is largely production-oriented, the wife, consumption-oriented. When an adjustment is not reached, or when funds do not allow for the satisfaction of both, a clash almost inevitably results. In farm families of the past, women usually shared their husbands' value scheme. Today the likelihood of differences is much greater.

Overemphasis on productivity: The well-known practice of the farmer building a good barn or hog house before considering a new house for the family is often ridiculed, but the farmer is production-minded. He makes his living from the barn and hog house. Without them he feels he cannot afford the new house, running water, or the bathtub. It takes a rurally reared woman of the old school to have sympathy with such standards, and if one is to read meaning into the extensive migration of girls from farming areas immediately after high school, one must surmise that a decreasing proportion of farm girls are willing to sacrifice their comfort to a production philosophy of farm living.

It is characteristic of the older generation of farm families to become so production-minded that even when they can afford the higher level of consumption that would spell comfort for parents and children, they continue to draw all their satisfaction from producing, living on in the same old inconvenient way. This is often a point of conflict between parents and teenagers in the farm family. The teenager becomes ashamed of his home and living conditions and tries to make his voice heard in getting the home improved so that he will not feel embarrassed when bringing his friends into it.

The vice of overproduction-mindedness is not entirely one of the rural male. The struggling small-town and urban businessman, particularly in the eyes of a consumption-minded wife, may also be guilty of wanting to plow everything back into the business. He justifies this in terms of greater comfort and wealth in the future. The wife often wants her cake now.

Then there is the aspiring professional man who feels disposed to plow all family surplus into his further training rather than permit the wife to raise the level of family living. Legitimate as such a goal is, wives and husbands may not see eye to eye, and of course there are no doubt many husbands who are too willing to sacrifice interests of the marriage to their own ambitions. At least there are often legitimate points of difference between husbands and wives centering on the philosophy of the utilization of money as an investment in future productivity rather than as an investment to improve the family level of living.

In thinking of production-mindedness and consumption-mindedness, one finds striking examples of types in the movie colony. John Barrymore made millions, but lived it up in wine, women, and song, and ended up in debt, with even his household goods confiscated by creditors. That is consumption to the limit. Walt Disney's daughter, in writing about her distinguished father, told how at home there was never much ready cash. Beyond the necessary living, everything was going into her dad's latest project: a new cartoon series, Disneyland, etc. Production-mindedness is in evidence here. Rockefeller taught his sons the same lesson, as did also Henry Ford.

Woman's Need for Productive Outlets

Much is written today of the failure of competent women to live up to their promise, of their great readiness to settle down into an early marriage, childbearing, and domesticity.[4] Much is written also of the fact that many find later along in life that they settled for too little. They find life boring, domesticity less satisfying than they had hoped, and yet find themselves unprepared for the kind of creative work roles they might have had and found satisfying had they pursued education to its conclusion. They awake too late to the fact that the last 30 to 40 years are important ones, those years after children are no longer dependent.

Friedan declares, "If women do not put forth, finally, that effort to become all that they have in them to become, they will forfeit their own humanity."[5] She has discovered since writing the *Feminine Mystique* that

[4] Seymour M. Farber and Roger H. L. Wilson (Editors), *The Potential of Woman* (New York: McGraw-Hill Book Co., 1963) deals with many aspects of this subject. Betty Friedan in her best-selling *The Feminine Mystique*, made much of it. Margaret Mead in lectures on college campuses has been critical of this pattern of female performance; see her views in *U. S. News & World Report*, June 6, 1960. Rosemary Park, president of Barnard, warns girls of the need to be able to use the last 40 years of their lives; see Terry Ferrer, "Rosemary Park: New President of Barnard," *Saturday Review*, April 20, 1963, pp. 66-68.

[5] Friedan, *op. cit.*, p. 324.

a surprising number of women have found a new fourth dimension of productivity that makes their lives complete.[6]

The woman's need for productive outlets is one which many husbands, busy in their own work or creative hobbies, fail to appreciate when their wives insist on working outside the family. For many women housework alone does not provide sufficient recognition and creative satifaction to justify their existence to themselves. In order to live the full and complete lives which they desire, and in order to avoid the neurotic developments which come from a feeling of uselessness, they must seek activity in outside employment. This explains why women today, by and large, are more willing to engage in gainful employment than men are to have them do so. Polls of young people show that many more girls than boys think girls should work before marriage and also after marriage.[7] This difference in viewpoint can become an issue in marriage and is an area where an adjustment must definitely be worked out.

For some women the home alone is not enough and cannot be. The job means a great deal as an escape from the monotony of home and as a way of expressing the need to achieve and create. Previous to the time that children are born, particularly, the average young wife can escape loneliness and monotony only by being given an opportunity to work and to secure the recognition that comes with earning. The husband who blocks his wife in her work endeavor is inviting trouble for himself, for her, and for the whole family. Research confirms this view.[8]

Those women who are able to find a sense of productivity in the household activities alone, and in the rearing of their families, are happy indeed. The ability of a woman to do so depends, no doubt, on a number of factors. The conception of what a wife should be, what she may do, and how she may act is usually learned in early life as a youngster observes her mother and absorbs her mother's attitudes concerning a wife's role. These early impressions are very strong and frequently account entirely for the later attitudes and behavior of the grown girl. They are not incapable of modification, however. Other women whom the child admires, a school curriculum emphasizing career training rather than preparation for a domestic life, or a husband who gives little credit and recognition for housework—any or all of these help account for the over-

[6] "Woman, the Fourth Dimension," a special issue of the *Ladies Home Journal*, June, 1964.

[7] Howard M. Bell, *Youth Tell Their Story* (Washington, D. C.: American Council on Education, 1938); *Youth and the World of Work* (Lansing: Social Research Service, Michigan State College, 1949); also *Purdue Opinion Poll for Young People*, 15:4a, February, 1956.

[8] Ernest W. Burgess and Leonard S. Cottrell, *Predicting Failure or Success in Marriage* (Englewood Cliffs, N. J.: Prentice-Hall, Inc., 1939), pp. 266 ff., find that if a woman wishes to work, it is an asset to good adjustment in marriage that she work.

whelming personal need of many wives and mothers to find work outside the home.

In the end a large proportion of women must find a place outside the home to feel content. Family life is a transient experience, largely over by age 40. Then, if not sooner, most women need new outlets. For the woman who completed school early and is inadequately trained, this offers serious problems. Most women may need to return to school to brush up or to improve skills of information. These necessary adjustments also require the sympathy and understanding of the husband. Such adjustments cannot be appraised primarily in terms of increased earning power, but rather in terms of increased self-esteem for the wife who may no longer feel useful.

Husband appreciation needed: At all stages of their married life the appreciation of the husband is needed. The appreciation which he gives the wife in her domestic roles is frequently the deciding factor, as well as his recognition of the savings occurring to the household from the labor contribution she makes. Often, in fact, the husband is far too little aware of her very great economic contribution and is quick to criticize and slow to praise her for her part in making the family an economic success.[9]

In the early years of marriage husbands and wives alike generally exert considerable influence over the role attitudes of their mates. The man who marries a working girl and takes her out of her earning role, for example, can do much to make her transition to housewife and mother an easy and unregretted one if he greets each of her domestic efforts with praise and real appreciation. The young wife, wanting very much the recognition of her husband, generally enjoys the cultivation of qualities and abilities which he admires. If, on the other hand, he challenges every expenditure, asks her to justify every bill, and rarely if ever expresses any appreciation for her thrift and saving or her long hours of regular work in providing for a comfortable home, she can take little pleasure or pride in her new wife-homemaker role.

The need for recognition of the homemaker role is particularly acute in urban homes, in cases where the wife does not continue in gainful employment. Farm women still take great pride in their productive activity within the household, recounting at every opportunity the number of quarts of this and that they have canned, the glasses of jelly made, the pickles and preserves, and the stone jars of sauerkraut and pickles in their basement. One reason they can do so is that their husbands and their communities rate this productive role favorably.

---

[9] Some estimates place her economic contribution through domestic activities at $7,000 to $8,000 per year.

The Strain of Overconsumption

If one must place primary blame on the American husband for overemphasizing productivity for himself and tending to deny the right of productivity to his wife, the primary blame for the painful overconsumption that plagues so many couples in this day of high-pressure advertising and time contracts must be placed on the modern overshopping wife.

Actually one should not speak of placing blame in either case. Both men and women, in economic values as in everything else, are what they are taught, or rather conditioned to be, for much learning of attitudes and values is acquired very subtly in men's and women's own unique and different worlds.

The woman who cannot achieve distinction and prestige by earning, or through a sense of productivity in some other way, must seek it through consumption. How else may she find a place in the sun? So she buys to help the family put on front. This paves the way into influential circles and gives the proper social boost to the husband's position, or so she rationalizes.

The average urban wife takes comparatively little pride in the kind of productive activity that goes on in the home. Her satisfactions, therefore, have to be derived largely from the kind of consumption in which the family can engage. The well-furnished home and well-dressed children are a means to a feeling of recognition and importance for her. To the extent that this is true, her personal satisfactions among her neighbors and relatives is dependent on the amount of money she can spend for the improvement of the level of living in the family. It is her source of pride and personal satisfaction. What the husband considers extravagant may be for her, necessity, basic to satisfying her need for feeling important.

This all goes to say that the expenditure of money is not always the same to the man as to the woman, and one has difficulty in understanding the other unless he tries to appreciate what the motivation may be. The motivation may not be too evident. In fact, one must assume that the economic activities of both men and women are deeply fraught with significance in terms of the recognition they bring to their personalities of the individuals involved.

One hears less today than in prewar days about the underworked and overshopping housewife, but no doubt she is in many cicles still present, making marriage adjustment quite difficult, particularly for those husbands whose training built into them a wide streak of thrift. Such husbands must recognize that the cure for such a wife is some other outlet for personal recognition.

Actually today the pressure on all sides is to encourage the new couple to overstrain their economic resources in an effort to match the pace of friends, fellow workers, or neighbors. The luxury goal of living is evidenced in the whole trend of American invention. Once a particular invention, whether it be a gadget or an automobile, has reached a stage of relative mechanical perfection, the manufacturers compete in terms of beauty and ornamentation. In fact, this becomes the final level of appeal in modern advertising, for here there is no satiation point. There is a limit, for example, to the amount of horsepower that is desirable in an automobile engine. That limit may have been reached or even exceeded in the present state of highway development. But when the automobile market becomes highly competitive, the major emphasis shifts to styling and design. In this realm there is no limit to the creative imagination of man. One new model can follow another year after year by simply changing the styling. This keeps up the hunger to buy and puts competition of new-car ownership strictly on the basis of prestige rather than utility. If only automobiles were involved the matter might be quite simple, but the luxury-ornamentation motive is no less characteristic there than in dress, spectacles, bathtubs (colored, round, and square, as well as rectangular), and in almost every other item of daily use.

The American standard of living has risen so precipitously that young couples in many instances are able to begin married life on or near the level of comfort which their parents achieved only after years of struggle and thrift. Aspirations for a high level of living, in fact for an increasingly high level of living, are a part of the American heritage. The common laborer shares it along with the middle and upper classes. An open-class system sets no limits to human aspirations. There is no standard by which one knows when he has reached a satisfactory level and can rest content in his achievements.

Modern business is sales-minded and uses every possible means of contact and communication to whet desire and raise aspirations—the display window, the talking mannequin, the demonstration, psuedo and real scientific opinion, high pressure salesmen, advertising by press, radio, and television. There is no end to what a couple can want, for new models, styles, and even new products are flashed before them in a never-ending stream.

To make it all easy, and nearly painless, there is the generous time contract by which the couple may mortgage their income for two to three years ahead even with readily consumable goods to say nothing of twenty to forty year mortgage contracts or the life-long insurance contracts. One can mortgage any share of his future income he chooses years before it is earned.

Somewhere early in the marriage the couple must learn, if they have not before, that the sky is not the limit. Similar philosophies on the use of credit and limitations on it are highly important in keeping down marital friction in this area. The male who believes in operating on a strictly cash basis, and who is worried half to death about any debt, is in for strenuous times if he has unwittingly married a girl from a family that has always had its money bargained-for months or years in advance.

The emphasis of urban life, as has been observed, centers more and more upon conspicuous consumption. Status is gained to a considerable extent by giving an appearance of prosperity. Dress, cars, living quarters, leisure-time pursuits, country club memberships, foreign travel, and a thousand and one other items for which people spend, enhance their standing and prestige. In a world of casual contacts, superficial appearances count. In small rural groups, everyone knows whether or not the person has the wherewithal to spend as he does; in large urban aggregates one may get by on appearances. No one knows whether Mrs. Smith's diamond has been or ever will be paid for. It is even reported that, in large cities, when television came in, numerous couples who could not afford a television set put up an aerial to gain TV status in the anonymous communities where they lived.

"Keeping ahead of the Joneses" is a favorite American game, and no doubt explains some of our remarkable progress as a nation toward new and better things. This spirit keeps the family on its toes, too, but it can readily become a vice, particularly for those young housewives whose aspirations far exceed their husband's earning power. In many marriages, basic conflicts in values of husband and wife center on consumption standards and values. Such conflicts are almost inevitable in many marriages today.

The Two-Income Family

We have spoken at length about the need for a feeling of productivity as a motive for the outside employment of housewives. What about the simple consideration of "making ends meet"?

According to one woman who has successfully combined a career with motherhood, the questions of women's rights, individual development, and so on, are no longer the crucial considerations. Among young married women today it has become simply a "matter of bookkeeping."[10] "Under present circumstances, a single pay envelope will not meet the needs of a white-collar family. It is as simple as that."

It should be added, however, that the justification for working to supplement income, while sometimes easier to understand, is no greater

[10] Nancy Barr Mavity, "The Two-Income Family," *Harper's Magazine*, 203:57-63, December, 1951.

than working to satisfy personality needs. The woman who "works out" in order to keep up payments on the new car, but who worries over neglecting her children, is probably doing herself and her family greater harm than if the car were allowed to revert to the creditors. At the same time, the wife who because of unjustifiable guilt feelings or because of uncertainty about her role, forces herself to stay at home full time and pass up opportunities for an interesting job is inviting frustration and bitterness that can easily undo many of the advantages of being a full-time wife and mother.

Mutual Role Acceptance Basic to Marital Adjustment

Whether the young bride becomes a full-time housewife, combines her new role with a part-time job, or devotes her daytime interests and energies to a full-fledged career is not the point. The important consideration to marital adjustment is whether husband and wife agree on the course of action taken and are mutually satisfied with the kind of family life it entails.

The wife who does not work outside the home, for example, has no right to expect the same amount of sharing of her domestic duties as has the wife who works the same length of day as her husband in gainful employment, yet she may do so. The husband whose wife works may expect the same leisure and attention at home as though his wife were not working, and be negative toward any suggestion that he share the housework or care of the children. There are no set rules to follow. The husband in this instance is trying to live by the division of labor that may have existed in his parental home, not realizing that he hasn't established the same sort of family.

The choice of several possible roles is not the exclusive right of wives. Husbands, too, must decide whether or not they will divorce themselves completely from housework, household interests, and child-rearing activities. A good marital adjustment is seldom achieved unless husband and wife can genuinely accept whatever role the former decides to assume.

Whether or not she decides to work outside the home full- or part-time, the average wife soon discovers that, in our culture, the husband's work activities usually take precedence over her own. There are numerous exceptions, but they are exceptional, nevertheless. A "good wife" is still expected to look up to her husband in the matter of making a living and to show an interest in his productive activities. If she fails to do so before marriage, she is likely to lose her man in spite of her personal attractiveness. A wife who fails to develop an interest in her husband's work, investments, and other productive efforts, and to grow in knowledge and understanding of such activity is bargaining for a lonesome future.

He may or may not leave her, but he will find much of his conversation, companionship, and true friendship in quarters where there are men or women who appreciate the things that are vital to him. The most vital interests of most successful males are centered on productivity. If their work is uninteresting, it may be hobbies or avocations that give life zest for them.

This does not mean that a wife should lose her own interests and hobbies and become a drudge of the home. Far from it. To be the wife most men want she must keep alert, informed, have her own vital and stimulating interests, and understand his world of activity and meaning, also.

This takes the young wife through one step after another of adjusting to the husband's world. In spite of romantic considerations, most wives must learn early in marriage to share a great deal of their husband's time with his job. Many professional men and others ambitious to get ahead in their work are inclined to spend longer hours with their profession or business than they should, sometimes to the unnecessary neglect of the wife. Some employers also are inconsiderate of their employees, requiring a great deal of overtime work. With men, work tends to come first, although every man should realize that marriage takes time and that the wife's interests must be given consideration.

The very demanding, possessive woman had better marry a man who has no deep male recreational or occupational interests. Otherwise, either he, or she, or both are likely to be unhappy in marriage. For example, she should never marry a doctor. She will either succeed in ruining him as a doctor and as a man, or she will have to suffer from seeing him devote a great deal of his interests and time to his profession. Similarly, if she wants a great deal of attention, she should not marry an ambitious college professor, or, in fact, any individual who expects to seriously pursue a highly competitive vocation. She may actually succeed in shaping him to her will, but if she does, his career will be ruined. Few men can forgive a woman for being so demanding.

So also for the male who marries a woman who has her heart set on a vocation and who insists on confining her to the home after marriage. He will have on his hands a person disillusioned with marriage as soon as she realizes that the marriage has robbed her of satisfactions which mean more to her than housekeeping or even marital romance.

Most wives recognize that a great deal of a man's time and energy will be consumed in work; most of them are willing to have the attention of their husband in the family for only a limited portion of the time, recognizing that the husband's devotion to his occupation is essential to the family's economic well-being. But there are some wives who are too demanding to make such adjustments.

In the case of a few highly intellectual individuals, it seems to be possible to have a marriage that permits each member to continue very much the independent life he has lived, before marriage, each continuing with his own work, associations, etc., and the couple knowing, well before they marry, that their married life will make demands on only a relatively small part of their time and attention. Such couples usually do not plan to have children, and each plans to retain a high degree of individual self-interest within marriage. The average marriage, however, cannot be of this character.

For most couples, give-and-take to a degree never required of them before is necessary in the early weeks and months of marriage. The blending of two distinct personalities into one way of living is for most people something more of a task than they expected. But it can be done by those who are determined to succeed.

The adjustments of the early years of marriage, even under the companionship family, are generally more demanding of the wife than the husband. This is why, as we have seen in an earlier chapter, a girl looking forward to marriage must have a great deal in the way of character and courage to succeed. It is the wife's way of life that is usually reshaped to fit the husband's. This will probably be true as long as men earn the living in most families.

While most couples follow in the traditional pattern, the significant issue is not that they do so but that they do so willingly and with a mutual respect for whatever role the other takes in the home as well as in the world of work.

In summary, it is possible to do no more than point up a few of the thousands of ways in which economic values become a factor in marriage interaction today. These are enough, however, to show that economic values and habits become the issues in marriage adjustment at many points and that in our day of individuated personalities the economic area is one which seldom takes care of itself automatically. Some plain talk and logical planning are often necessary to avoid major difficulty.

The following chapter provides information which may at points offer help in arriving at a logical program in certain major areas.

Problems

1. Describe specific American traditions or customs, and specific instances from American education and advertisements that seem to produce differences in values held by men and women.

2. Modern society has greatly increased the number of areas in which women may play productive roles. Why then is the modern wife likely to feel less productive than the wife of two generations past?

3. Is it possible to educate women away from the need they feel to be productive? Describe a way of life in which feminine productiveness is frowned upon. Why would such a role be unacceptable to most American women today?

4. *Sociodrama:* A young doctor and his wife have come to live in a new community. The wife realizes how important it is to make the "right" impression in order to gain standing in the community. In order to make this impression she is willing to spend all their savings and mortgages most of their future earnings in possessions. The husband is beginning to be concerned about the fact that they have no children, no real savings, no money for relaxation and adventure. Dramatize a discussion or argument between them in which their values are pictured, in which the dangers of overconsumption are suggested, and in which the arguments for the wife's point of view are presented.

5. If a young couple agree that the wife shall work for a limited time, are there any rules they should agree upon as to how her income shall and shall not be spent?

6. Marilyn was a graduate student in interior decoration with a "brilliant career awaiting her," when she fell in love with Mike. Mike is not a tyrant but he firmly believes that a home can be happy only when the wife devotes herself full time to her roles as wife and mother. He believes that she should channel her professional talents into her own home and forget about the career that might have been. Still, she feels that life would never be complete without a little success in the competitive world outside marriage. Would you advise her to:
   a. Forget about marriage; Mike is unreasonable?
   b. Postpone marriage a few years in order to further her interests?
   c. Marry and try to forget the career?
   d. Some other alternative?
   In weighing and discussing each alternative, consider its possible risks as well as its advantages.

7. Describe several common customs or practices that illustrate the "consumption-mindedness" of modern Americans.

8. Poll the class on the problem: If, upon marrying, you were able to live in a comfortably but simply furnished apartment and save one hundred dollars a month would you prefer to:
   a. Save the $100 without specific purpose?
   b. Use the $100 for recreation?
   c. Buy a car?
   d. Invest the money?
   e. Begin having children?
   f. Buy furniture?
   g. Buy a home or property?
   h. Travel and have some adventure?

 i. Use the $100 for attractive wardrobes, eating out, and entertaining?

 j. Divide it in half and let each mate spend $50 as he chooses?

9. After tabulating the anonymously submitted data do you find that:

 a. Most students tend to agree on economic values?

 b. Students differ according to sex?

10. If no agreement can be reached on how to spend the family's income, how should the dilemma be solved and why?

 a. Husband's values prevail?

 b. Wife's values prevail?

 c. Some other arrangement?

Discuss.

Selected References

ARTICLES IN BOOKS OF READINGS

KLING, Samuel G., and KLING, Esther B., *The Marriage Reader* (New York: The Vanguard Press, Inc., 1947).

 1. ROOSEVELT, Eleanor, "Should Wives Work?" pp. 440-448.

CAVAN, Ruth Shonle, *Marriage and the Family in the Modern World: A Book of Readings* (New York: Thomas Y. Crowell Co., 1960).

 2. BIGELOW, Howard F., "The Ebb and Flow of Finances in the Family Life Cycle," Reading 9.

 3. AGAN, Tessie, "Housing and the Family Life Cycle," Reading 10.

 4. DUFFIN, B. Keith, "Career as a Lifetime Choice," Reading 52.

 5. FELDMAN, Frances Lomas, "A New Look at the Family and Its Money," Reading 59.

General References

BOWMAN, Henry A., *Marriage for Moderns,* Fourth Edition (New York: Mc-Graw-Hill Book Co., 1960), Ch. 12.

DUVALL, Evelyn M., and HILL, Reuben, *Being Married* (New York: Association Press, 1960), Ch. 13.

FARBER, Seymour M., and WILSON, Roger H. L. (Editors), *The Potential of Woman* (New York: McGraw-Hill Book Co., 1963), Parts 3, 4, 5.

GOODE, William J., "Economic Factors and Marital Stability," *American Sociological Review,* 16:802-812, December, 1951.

Ladies Home Journal, June, 1964. This is a special issue devoted to "Woman in the Fourth Dimension."

LANDIS, Judson T., "Length of Time Required to Achieve Adjustment in Marriage," *American Sociological Review,* 11:688 ff., December, 1946.

MAVITY, Nancy Barr, "The Two-Income Family," *Harper's Magazine,* 203:57-63, December, 1951.

NEISSER, Edith G., "Emotional and Social Values Attached to Money," *Marriage and Family Living,* 22:132-138, May, 1960.

SPRINGER, John L., *Make the Most of Your Income* (Englewood Cliffs, N. J.: Prentice-Hall, Inc., 1961).

U.S. Department of Labor, Women's Bureau, *American Women,* Report of the President's Commission on the Status of Women, Washington, D. C., 1963.

27
Finance Management

Most young couples in the early years of their marriage, when they are struggling to get ahead, look forward to a day when they can have about anything they want. That day probably will never come, for wants will most likely multiply more rapidly than resources. One of the most certain things about the money aspect of marriage is that there will never be enough money. Wise management will be necessary if even a substantial portion of wants of all family members are to be met. The word wants is used advisedly; most families in the United States have their needs met quite adequately. Wants are as flexible as human aspirations, and tend to grow Veblian fashion, as members of the family use money to keep pace with the demands of their social circle; the husband with other men in the male subculture—business, club life, recreation; the wife with other women, primarily in the female subculture —clothes, beauty care, household furniture and equipment, club life, etc.; and as children grow, each with his age group in toys, appropriate clothes and gadgets from the cowboy outfit to the first dress suit of the budding adolescent.

A few years ago *Life* carried an editorial based on a study by William H. Whyte, Jr., for the *Wall Street Journal*. It was entitled "Is Thrift Un-American?" and described the spending habits of 83 young couples with incomes of $5,000 to $7,500. He found typically that their incomes were "hocked" far in advance, so they never had cash. For example, he found of a $500 gross monthly income, only about $45 remains after all commitments for the month are met: time contracts, food and lunch money set-asides, but no savings. The system is to have oneself committed to regular monthly payments for all major items. In buying, cost is disregarded. The question asked is "What is the monthly payment?" There is more concern in the fact that it is $12.73 a month than in the total price. And there seems to be a complete disregard of the fact that 12 to 18 percent interest piles up. In big expenditures like automobiles, Whyte finds that buyers take dealer "packs" without even calculating the total amount, and often end up suckers.[1] Not only has Yankee thrift vanished, but so has Yankee shrewdness, he suggests.

His sampling of the $13,000 to $17,000 junior-executive group shows a similar pattern of being committed far in advance, carrying a large amount of debt in as many as 15 different loans. Saving, he concludes, is no longer identified with morality.

Happiness—A Question of Dollars and Sense

In the average family, the difference between success or failure in money matters is largely a matter of money sense, no matter what the income level. One can always be in debt regardless of salary, and with the possible exception of the very lowest income group, savings are usually possible. Barring major illness or other such misfortune, success is simply a matter of money management.

There is no significant or consistent relationship between the amount of income and marital happiness.[2] The economic security of the family, as measured by the proportion of the income being saved, has been found to bear an association with poor and good adjustment in marriage, as does regularity of employment and income.[3] This may mean that the desire or ability to save is an index to a certain type of character which adjusts well in marriage. It is more definitely established that occupation and steadiness of income are related to successful adjustment in marriage. Managerial and professional occupations where income is regular show greater happiness scores than the less regular income occupations.[4]

The couple who plan the wise use of available funds and concern themselves with savings for future security are acting wisely from the standpoint of making a success of marriage. Such prudence may not provide much money for "keeping ahead of the parade," but the atmosphere of thrift and thoughtfulness that it entails has been found to be anything but detrimental to marriage. In fact, an economic struggle during a couple's early years together represents a wholesome atmosphere for a successful marriage if carried out without resentment or feelings of frus-

---

[1] This situation became so bad that the government entered the field, requiring that actual interest rates be shown and that the cost of the car be made known, to protect the gullible buyer.

[2] Ernest W. Burgess and Leonard S. Cottrell, *Predicting Success or Failure in Marriage* (Englewood Cliffs, N. J.: Prentice-Hall, Inc., 1939), p. 404.

[3] *Ibid.*

[4] *Ibid.*, Ch. 9, pp. 398-401. Refer again to Figure 23-1.

tration. There is a great likelihood of success where both husband and wife are willing to go through a period of very modest living in order that they may eventually achieve the things they want in their family life.

Money Management

Advice is always cheap, yet in the field of money management it is always in demand. By and large, the American family's success at money management falls far short of an ideal standard. Loan sharks by the dozens flourish in every city. Other finance agencies with greater respectability but equally excessive hidden interest rates abound in cities, states, and even on a nationwide scale. Installment financing is usually offered at more than twice a normal bank rate of interest.

In the field of life insurance and investments, the average couple are "babes in the woods" with little or no knowledge to help them in judging when they are or are not buying wisely. In the daily purchases of the household, many wives have too little knowledge to provide a sound basis for wise purchases of furniture, fabrics, and nutritious foods. A great deal of consumer education is needed.

Although one cannot assume that wise money management would ease all the family tensions that arise over money matters today, it undoubtedly would help. Not all prospective housewives can take a broad course in home economics, nor can all men be trained in money management, but some money sense is essential to successful home management.

The average white young man who makes it through college will earn about $9,800 for his family. It will be less at the beginning, more as he climbs (see Figure 27-1). To have more to meet the luxury needs, either his wife must earn or he must learn to save and invest wisely to increase his income later on as family responsibilities increase. There are only two ways to obtain income: (1) earn it as a reward for services performed, (2) add value to investments.

A Picture of Family Income

A realistic conception of probable earning power is important to success in marriage. In the modern world, income is closely related to the schooling of the family head (Figure 27-1). This is inevitable since a high level of training is the prerequisite to both the better paying and more stable occupations. Whites with less than grade school education have a median income level of under $4,000; those with 8th-grade schooling, of over $5,000; high school graduates, of close to $7,000; and

MEDIAN FAMILY INCOME BY YEARS OF SCHOOL COMPLETED AND BY RACE, UNITED STATES, 1963

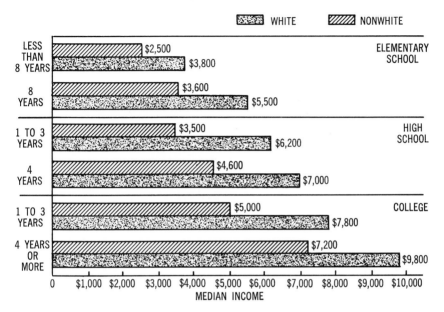

SOURCE: U. S. Department of Commerce, Bureau of the Census, "Current Population Reports," *Consumer Income*, Series P-60, No. 43, September 29, 1964, Figure 4.

FIGURE 27-1————Education and race are factors in family income. Among both whites and nonwhites, the more schooling, the higher the family income. At current wage and salary rates a college graduate will provide $375,000 to $425,000 income for his family during his working lifetime, depending on his race; a high school graduate, $275,000 to $325,000; a grade school graduate, only $200,000 to $250,000. Schooling is also the most important gateway to occupational security.

college graduates, of almost $10,000. Nonwhite families receive substantially less income than white families at all levels of education, but among them also, more training brings a higher median level of income.

The occupation decided on will also have a direct bearing on earnings. Most of the college trained seek positions at the professional and managerial levels. These salaried fields are now the best paid, providing the highest median income which in each field exceeds $9,000 (see Figure 27-2). More important still to the security of family life, they provide regularity of income.

MEDIAN INCOME BY OCCUPATION,
U.S. FAMILIES AND PERSONS, 1963

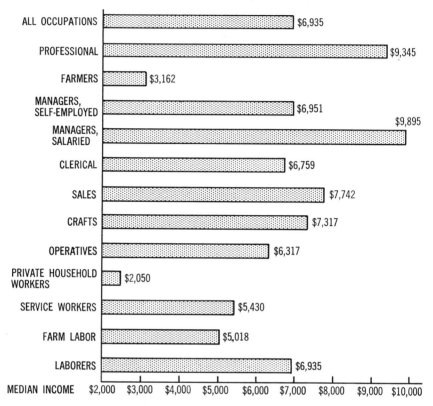

ALL OCCUPATIONS	$6,935
PROFESSIONAL	$9,345
FARMERS	$3,162
MANAGERS, SELF-EMPLOYED	$6,951
MANAGERS, SALARIED	$9,895
CLERICAL	$6,759
SALES	$7,742
CRAFTS	$7,317
OPERATIVES	$6,317
PRIVATE HOUSEHOLD WORKERS	$2,050
SERVICE WORKERS	$5,430
FARM LABOR	$5,018
LABORERS	$6,935

MEDIAN INCOME $2,000 $3,000 $4,000 $5,000 $6,000 $7,000 $8,000 $9,000 $10,000

SOURCE: U. S. Department of Commerce, Bureau of the Census, "Income of Families and Persons at Record High in 1963," *Consumer Income*, Series P-60, No. 42, June 12, 1964.

FIGURE 27-2

The Cost of Money

Whether or not a young couple of average or above average income will be economically secure at age 45 or still living beyond their income will depend in considerable part on their learning early in their married life, or before, the cost of money.

Money used for *investment debt* is cheap money. It is used in the purchase of tangible assets which have permanent value and which often increase in value with the passage of time. Investment capital is usually to be had at a simple rate of interest of around 6 percent. Land, a home, a business are examples of investment debt.

Money borrowed on *consumer debt* is high-priced money. It is used for consumable items which perish with the using, and the value of which rapidly diminishes with the passage of time. Cars, refrigerators, washing machines, furniture, clothes, boats are examples of consumer debt.

Investment debt is financed by *simple interest,* that is, interest on the unpaid balance. In other words, the amount of interest declines with each payment on the principle. Consumer debt is financed by *discount interest,* or *hard interest,* that is, interest which is charged on the whole amount for the whole period of the loan. The interest is charged in advance and does not decline as monthly payments are made, so it is actually almost twice the simple-interest rate. Actual interest rates range usually from 10 to 35 percent on consumer debt.

Money is made by the use of borrowed money for investment debt in assets which will increase in value. The borrower pays, say 6 percent simple interest, expecting with the passage of time that his investment will grow in value far beyond the purchase price and accumulated interest.

Agreement on Who Is to Handle Family Spending

A seemingly simple, but frequently contentious aspect of money management is the handling and the spending of the family income. In every marriage an early decision must be made concerning who shall handle the money and how it shall be handled. With some couples, the question does not come out in the open. Circumstances seem to decide the answer before it ever becomes an issue. With others there is a good deal of experimentation and sometimes quite a contest develops before a mutually satisfactory arrangement can be reached. There are at least five possible methods of handling money: (1) the husband may control all the spending; (2) the wife may control all expenditures; (3) the husband may control the income but give his wife an allowance for meeting household expenses, her own personal needs, and the needs of the children; (4) the husband and wife may have separate incomes and bank accounts, each one controlling his own funds, and each agreeing to meet certain of the family's financial obligations; (5) the husband and wife may maintain a joint bank account, each drawing upon it at will.

This question appears on the surface to be one of simple expediency. It is that, but it is much more, too. The decision reached influences how the family shall live and also has an effect upon attitudes and interrelationships of family members. Problems of domination, submission, insecurity, inferiority feelings, and many others are frequently created or exaggerated by the circumstances surrounding the spending of the family income.

This suggests that the way money is handled and who handles it is laden with psychological and personal values, not just with the monetary ones. Money is a device through which subtle struggles for power and dominance in the marriage relationship may be waged.

The following case, reported by a family relations counselor, illustrates a characteristic difficulty as well as the importance of reaching a mutually satisfactory decision:

> Jim and Gertrude married during their senior year in college. Jim was receiving veterans' schooling benefits and Gertrude had a part-time typing job. Their combined incomes allowed for few luxuries and only by careful planning were they able to finish their schooling without outside assistance.
>
> At first, they handled the money together, both planning and worrying about making ends meet. After a few months, however, a budget was worked out and Gertrude took over the routine jobs of bill paying, grocery buying, etc. Since there was no "extra money," no question or argument ever arose as to how any of their income *should* be spent.
>
> After graduation, Jim obtained an excellent position with a local insurance office. His income rose steadily and, by mutual agreement, they invested in a new car and began the accumulation of household furnishings. Gertrude maintained her position as the family money manager and as Jim's pay increased she regularly revamped their budget to allow for larger expenditures on furniture and appliances.
>
> When Jim occasionally complained about his own lack of spending money or about the absence of extra cash for unplanned-for expenditures—magazines, books, records, or a show—Gertrude would reassure him that after next month, "when the TV set is payed-off, we'll have plenty for extras."
>
> Months passed but the day when there would be plenty for extras was always a month or two away. Jim finally exploded over a situation in which he, a man earning $5,000 a year, should "have to borrow from somebody every time I want a pack of cigarettes or a cup of coffee!"
>
> Gertrude, in turn, felt accused and unappreciated for her hours of budget planning. For several months the atmosphere remained bitter and the problem unsolved. Sometimes Jim handled all of the money himself, but bills went unpaid and insufficient funds were being put aside for groceries and living expenses. Then Gertrude took over and the old problems reappeared.
>
> In their third year, they reached the point of considering divorce because of the constant bickering and frustration over money. A friend induced them to take their problems to a local family relations clinic. They did, and after several weeks of "talking things over" with a counselor they began to understand one another's values and wishes in money matters. After months of effort they finally reached a solution in which both could find satisfaction. Only by giving up a few of the furnishings that Gertrude had set her heart on was Jim able to carry sufficient money in his pocket to regain his sense of confidence and pride in himself as a successful money-earner. Gertrude continued to handle most of the routine spending, but whenever the ques-

tion of a new purchase of any significance arose, they talked over its desirability and the effect it would have upon their regular way of life.

This is but one of an endless number of possible situations which can grow out of money handling. Because of the importance money plays in the satisfaction of our needs and wishes, it is desirable that every couple face personality needs, as well as economic considerations, in deciding who shall handle the money and how. There is no one best answer. The policy adopted by one couple is bound to differ from that of others even in the same income group.

It may be said, however, that in general a mutually acceptable routine plan for money spending is more conducive to happiness than the policy of meeting each month's financial demands as if they were a new experience. Money matters can become the foremost issue in every family discussion. To allow this is to invite poor management as well as hard feelings. To prevent it, however, demands mutual concern, give and take, and a real desire to make money a tool of happy family life rather than the family's master.

Since financial patterns are a matter which must vary among families, no one system can be given to suit all needs. There are, however, certain basic considerations in financial planning which should help most couples in working out a program suited to their own needs.

Financial Planning

Every family, regardless of the amount of its income, has to face the problem of dividing up that income according to the use that will be made of it. This may be done according to plan or simply by deciding what one wants and spending the money without any systematic plan, but in either case it will be divided up in some way in an attempt to meet the needs of the family.

To develop a family budget requires, first, an estimate of income; second, an estimate of various kinds of expenses which the family wishes to undertake for a given period of time; and third, a plan for dividing this income among these various expenditures. Usually involved is a cash record of the expenditures so that it is possible to know whether or not the plan of the family budget has been carried out.

Even though each family is in some respects unique in its patterns, knowing what the norm for large numbers of couples is can often be helpful in developing a satisfactory pattern. Both the British and the American Institute of Public Opinion asked this question, "In some families the wife manages most of the money, while in others the husband does. Who manages most of the money in your household?"

	Husband (percent)	Wife (percent)	Both (percent)
Great Britain (all families)	22	54	24
United States (all families)	29	32	39
Professional and business families	30	26	44
White-collar workers	29	32	39
Farmers	37	16	47
Manual workers	24	42	34

The amount of income determines not only the amount there is to be spent, but also determines the ratio of income that can be spent for different things. Generally speaking, the smaller the income, the greater the proportion spent for food, clothing, and the necessities of life; the larger the income, the smaller the proportion spent for necessities and the greater the proportion spent for comforts, luxuries, and savings.

By developing a family budget, it is usually possible to make money go further in obtaining the things that are most important to the family. It also has the advantage of making all members of the family plan together for the use of money to be spent. Thus, neither partner is so likely to blame the other if the money runs short.

No family should become a slave to the family budget, even though they may plan out in advance each year or each month the amount they are going to spend for a given class of items. Such exact accounting has certain advantages, but it may, like any other exact scheme, become a source of irritation and conflict. Some people can probably do better without any written budget at all, but families should give some thought to the way they will spend their income in order to get the most satisfaction from it.

Frequently the difficulties over a family budget come not in planning how to spend the money, but rather in trying to keep an exact accounting of what each penny was spent for. At least keeping such an account will show where the seepages are. Many couples are amazed to discover how these small expenditures mount into many dollars.

The expenditures for every family are in most respects quite standard, at least for major items, which usually fall into the following categories: food, shelter (which may be broken down into rent, or, if the person owns property, taxes and so on), clothing, transportation, operating expenses (under which come the costs of keeping up the home, heat, light, electricity, telephone, and so forth), benevolences, and recreation (under which may come expenditures for personal items, vacations, candy, tobacco, and so forth), education (under which comes the purchase of books, papers, and magazines), and savings (under which come life insurance, the fund for emergencies, and other investments).

The amount that can be allotted to these various items depends, first, upon the amount of income the family has to divide, and second, upon the interests of the members of the family.

The American Institute of Family Relations (Los Angeles) has worked out a practical guide sheet to help couples in setting up a spending plan and in anticipating major items of expense. Here is their outline:

STEPS IN SETTING UP A SPENDING PLAN

1. Decide for what you want to plan: The most important thing you want to accomplish; things of lesser importance, but desirable.
2. Decide for how long you want to plan. (Six months, a year, etc.)
3. List the income from all sources that can be depended upon each month.
4. Next set down the various fixed expenses, placing the amount of each under the month when it must be paid.
5. Then calculate the amount which must be set aside each month to meet these fixed expenses which occur less often than monthly (insurance, taxes, etc.).
6. Set up some sort of reserve fund to take care of these expenses. This might be done by:
   a. Having a separate envelope for each of these items and placing the specified sum in each, each month.
   b. Adding together the monthly allowances for the various items to make up a reserve fund which must be set aside as a whole each month. This can go into a temporary savings fund or account, or into the checking account provided it is not used for purposes other than those decided upon.
7. Subtract the total of the fixed expenses for each month, from the income for each month. This difference is what is available for the less predictable expenses or those that can be adjusted or varied.
8. Out of this, set aside first a small sum to take care of small unexpected demands or miscalculations. If it is not needed it can be used for some special pleasure or item.
9. Make an estimate of the amount needed for each of the variable expenses. For this, one can go for information to:
   a. His own past experience.
   b. What he considers essential, or his own standards.
   c. The experiences of others.
   d. Studies of how others spend.
   e. Scientific information.
   f. Suggested divisions of the budget.
   g. "Standard" budgets.
10. Make adjustments until the total of all of these expenses for the month does not exceed the sum available for the variable expenses for that month. Where there are larger expenses which do not occur monthly (larger items of clothing, Christmas gifts, etc.) make some provisions for accumulating the

necessary amount through additions to the reserve fund mentioned above, a separate fund, or the like.

11. Select some method for keeping a record of what is spent.

12. Decide who is to be responsible for keeping the record of expenditures, paying the bills, and being responsible for the business maangement of the household—or which person is to be responsible for which things.

13. Try out the plan for a month, keeping a record of expenditures. Make any adjustments that seem necessary, then try it out again. Continue this until a satisfactory plan is developed.

14. When the budget is running smoothly, simplify the work of account-keeping as much as possible.'

15. Measure the success of the plan frequently in terms of what you hoped to accomplish with it.

16. Strive continually to maximize the satisfactions possible from the income available through:

   a. Independence and originality in choice making.

   b. Careful buying.

   c. Intelligent using.

FIXED EXPENSES

Taxes: (state, federal) personal, income, automobile, real estate, assessments.
Insurance: life, accident, health, automobile, and other property.
Licenses: car, business, etc.
Fixed payments for medical or hospital care.
Union or professional dues or fees.
Rent, after a decision is made.
Minimum charges for utilities; telephone.
Tuition: fees, special lessons, books and equipment.
Newspapers and magazines if on a yearly subscription basis.
Installment payments and interest on debts.
Obligations for the support of others.
Pledges made to church or to civic organizations.
Savings: war bonds, savings accounts, investments.
Reserve fund: A fund set aside to take care of larger expenses occurring less often than monthly.

VARIABLE EXPENSES

Food
   meals at home, lunches, other meals away from home, entertaining
Clothing

outer garments	materials	cleaning and pressing
underwear	dressmaker, tailor	laundry (if not under
footwear	clothing repair	*Household Operation*)
hats, accessories		

Personal Care
barber and beauty parlor services, shaving supplies and equipment, cosmetics, toilet articles, dental supplies

Housing
rent, if not already determined; improvements, repairs, and depreciation on owned home.

Furnishings and Equipment

furniture, rugs, carpets	kitchenware
draperies, curtains, shades	cleaning and laundry equipment
silver, china, glass	lamps, fixtures, vases
linen, bedding	clocks, etc.

Household Operation
utilities, fuel, refrigeration, laundry, household service, household supplies, small equipment, stamps and stationery (if not taken from *Personal Allowance*)

Transportation
car, train, bus fare; running expenses of automobile; car repairs and upkeep

Health
doctor, dentist, hospital, medical supplies, devices or equipment

Education
books, technical journals, supplies, tuition and special lessons until a fixed expense, miscellaneous school expenses

Recreation
travel, vacation, sports, hobbies, musical instruments, music, records, toys, club and organization dues, books, magazines, lectures, concerts, opera, theater, movies, dances, meals out, entertaining, prizes, races

Gifts
to members of the family
to others: wedding, shower, baby, birthday, Christmas, etc.; flowers for funerals
to community welfare: Community Chest, church, Red Cross, etc.

Personal Allowance or Spending Money
An amount allocated to each member of the family for pocket or spending money. In the case of children this might be gradually increased as an educative measure to provide for additional items as school supplies, lunches, clothing, etc.

Estimating the Cost of Children

Family planning has come with urban industrial civilization. Because children are a heavy drain on the family budget, their numbers are limited in most families and the couple tries to save up for the extra cost. In agricultural societies, by contrast, children are workers and are desired in part for the contribution they will make to the family income.

What does a child cost? The initial cost will depend a great deal on the level of living of the couple, their income and standard of medical care. The upbringing will vary with the same conditions. To provide couples with a standard for planning, the Metropolitan Life Insurance Company once estimated the cost of rearing a child from birth until he is eighteen years of age, for the family with an annual wage of $2,500, at $7,763. This was on the basis of price levels prevailing in 1935-1936, the cost being divided as shown in Table 27-1. Data are also given for a higher income family where the cost totals $16,337. These depression-period costs are approximately doubled today.

TABLE 27-1————The cost of rearing a child

Items of Expense	Family of $2,500 Income	Family of $5,000 to $10,000 Income
Cost of being born	$ 300	$ 750
Food	2,272	3,628
Clothing	710	1,697
Shelter	2,648	5,774
Education	82	283
Medical care	297	846
Transportation and recreation	1,127	2,787
Sundries	327	572
Total	$7,763	$16,337

A current study of costs per child from birth to wedding places the cost between $11,000 and $12,000 for farm families to as high as $30,000 for city and suburban families who send their children to private schools.[5] Birth costs now range from $500 to $1,000, care costs through the 8th grade average $14,000, high school costs are approximately $7,000, college costs approximately $8,000, and marriage costs the parent family from $1,000 to $1,500. These costs vary with income level of the family, with sex of the child, and are at best rough approximations. They do indicate, however, that before he is established in a home of his own the child will represent a substantial investment for the parent.

The cost of rearing a child to maturity, regardless of price levels, may be calculated roughly as requiring three years of the father's income. One child will take three years of the father's earnings; three, nine years, etc. (see Figure 27-3).

Three Major Economic Issues

Three major issues face the newlywed couple, each involving very important financial considerations and each fraught with serious consequences to the success of the marriage. They are (1) life insurance, (2)

[5] These cost figures were developed by T. J. Mayo in "The High Cost of Parenthood," *This Week*, September 27, 1965, pp. 26-27.

COST OF A CHILD
IN YEARS OF FATHER'S INCOME

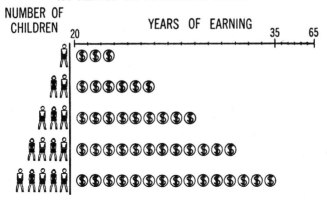

SOURCE: Based on estimates from Metropolitan Life Insurance Company, *Statistical Bulletin*.

FIGURE 27-3————Each child in the average family requires 3 years of the father's income for his rearing.

housing, and (3) installment buying. The way these matters are handled has a great deal to do with the couple's financial security and with the long-run success of their joint effort to become a successful economic unit. Let us consider each of these items briefly.

Life Insurance

The young are relatively propertyless, yet they have major responsibilities once children become dependent upon them. This means that in case of the untimely death of the breadwinner, they will have no estate, unless it is provided for by life insurance. By the mere passing of a physical examination and paying of a premium on a policy, an estate of considerable value can be had immediately, the amount of the estate depending on the amount of insurance purchased.

This is the only kind of estate that may be had for a small outlay of cash. It is, therefore, the only kind of estate that the young marriage can afford. Even so, unless wisdom is used, even this estate will be too small to provide for the emergency of death of the family earner. Where investment funds are limited, as they are in the average young marriage, the goal should be to buy the maximum protection for the least cash outlay.

Assuming that the couple will soon have three dependent children, that the husband is earning $6,000 per year, that the couple has the average number of debts and the average standard of living for the beginner in the professions, adequate protection would seem to call for an insurance policy that would replace three or four years of his income if he should die. In other words, he should think of providing an insurance estate with a minimum value of $20,000 to $25,000. This would help pay off pressing debts, in case of his death, and give the family security while the wife was getting back into the work world. If the husband is covered by Social Security and is paying in the maximum contribution (on $4,800), the insurance load can be cut in half since income from this source will carry about half the family burdens of the family with a $6,000-per-year income.

To be able to afford this much insurance requires that the young man spend his insurance dollar where it will buy the most protection. A look at the chart will show quickly where the greatest protection lies for the least cost-term insurance.

The shorter the term for which he buys insurance, the less it will cost, since the risk of death goes up each year, and therefore, the cost of coverage increases slightly with each year of age.

Unfortunately, in certain instances, life insurance is sold for the benefit of the insurance salesman or broker rather than for the customer. This is certainly the case when young couples of low income are sold high-priced endowment policies which net the agent the greatest commission. Often these policies appeal to uninformed young people because an endowment policy pays something back while they are living. The salesman calls when the announcement of the birth of their baby appears in the local paper. At this time, couples uninformed about insurance will do well to make sure that they are dealing with a reliable and well-informed agent, of whom there are many today. Endowment policies should be bought only by those who are in a position to save money. In an endowment policy, a person is buying not only insurance but a savings plan which returns only 3 or 4 percent interest on money deposited beyond the cost of insurance—a return that is little if any more than he can get from government bonds.

There is no objection to the endowment or other type savings policy for the prosperous, but the beginning family usually cannot afford a 3 percent return investment. If it is bought it is usually at the expense of an adequate protective coverage for dependents. Some are talked into these policies, being told that insurance will cost them a much higher rate later on in life. This is true enough, but they will also be earning more and will have a shorter term to go until they collect by death. The facts are, that the average couple will have very little need for heavy insurance coverage after age 40 to 45, for their children will have passed the age of dependency. Besides, by then the shrewd couple will have built an inheritance of other business or property assets to protect each other.

Some are intrigued into buying high cost endowment policies by the thought that they will get all their money back in 20 years, or whatever the period of maturity may be. One never gets his insurance money back unless he dies before his time. At around age 25 it costs about $6.00 per year to insure a young man. This rate is based on the actuarial tables which show the likelihood of death in a given million, or other large unit of people in this age group. This goes to pay death claims. Some will die in their 25th year, some even the day after the policy is written in a large group, others the 26th year, but some will still be living at 100 years of age. Company rates collect enough to pay off every person's inheritors at his death, regardless of his age, and to retain a profit. On endowment policies, one does not get his insurance back. He gets the extra money back which he invested, plus accumulated compounded interest.

Assuming that a young couple can afford, say $150 per year for life insurance, the choice is clear. For this $150 they can buy around $25,000 renewable term insurance, or at the other extreme, they can buy a 20-year endowment policy worth around $3,000. If they choose the latter the widow may not have enough left to pay the doctor and funeral expenses, to say nothing of providing for herself and the children during the transition back to a normal life.

For a brief graphic comparison of the more common types of policies, see Figures 27-4 to 27-7. The most ideal type of insurance for the young couple who can afford a little more than the average beginner is the type depicted in Figure 27-7. Here one is getting a small amount of permanent insurance. Onto this is attached a reducing term rider, which greatly increases his protection at very low cost for the term in life when his load of dependents is greatest.

Much insurance today is carried through group plans rather than on a personal basis. The military; federal, state, and local government employees; public institutions; business corporations; and many other employers have group plans under which employees are covered, usually at advantageous rates. Often the employer shares part or all the cost. In the teaching field, the Carnegie Foundation has established the Teachers Insurance and Annuity Association[6] which is nonprofit. A legal reserve life insurance company, incorporated in New York State and operating without agents, this company, in addition to funding the retirement plans

[6] Address: 730 Third Avenue, New York, N. Y.

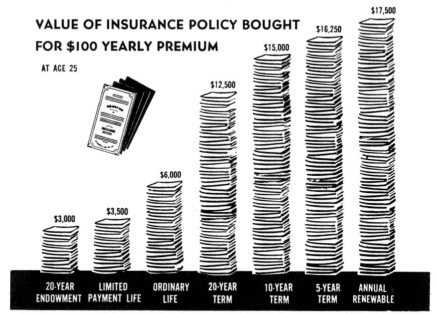

VALUE OF INSURANCE POLICY BOUGHT
FOR $100 YEARLY PREMIUM

AT AGE 25

Source: Paul H. Landis.   PICTOGRAPH CORPORATION

FIGURE 27-4————Different kinds of insurance policies give different kinds of
values. Insurance can give two principal values: (1) protection against risk and
(2) savings. Renewable term policies give maximum protection against risk for
those with little to spend from present income; that at the bottom gives least
protection, but maximum savings. Which is the more appropriate for the young
married man with a child and with low income? Why?

of colleges and universities, also issues specially designed life insurance
policies for college staff members. Here the teacher pays standard rates
but at the close of each year, when the profits are known, refunds are
made. Most industries have group plans at very favorable rates.

The need of the young couple for life insurance is depicted statistically in Figure 27-8 which shows the chance of a child's being orphaned
now compared to his chance at the beginning of the century.[7] The
chances are much less now than then, but still there is sufficient likelihood
of the father dying before the child has reached eighteen to justify carrying a reasonable amount of protective coverage.

[7] Metropolitan Life Insurance Company, "Family Responsibilities Increasing," *Statistical Bulletin*, 40:3-5, April, 1959.

COMPARISON OF NET PREMIUMS FOR $1,000 INSURANCE

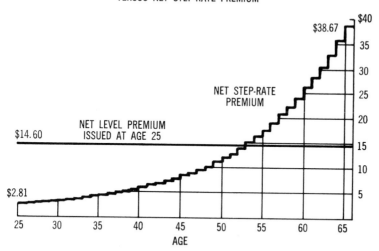

NET LEVEL PREMIUM FOR
STRAIGHT LIFE POLICY ISSUED AT AGE 25
VERSUS NET STEP-RATE PREMIUM

Source: Jerome B. Cohen, *Decade of Decision* (New York: Institute of Life Insurance, 1958), p. 11.

FIGURE 27-5————The cost of a *straight life* insurance policy is level through-out a person's lifetime. The amount he pays depends on the age at which the policy is taken, the younger the age, the less the death risk and the less he pays per year. Of course, he pays a larger sum years before death. In this kind of policy he pays far more in the younger ages than it costs to cover the risk of his death—in the chart above, he pays in excess of cost until he is into his fifties.

Term policies step up each year in cost, but in the younger ages rates are very low because death risk is low. A five-year term policy, for example, taken at age 25 costs what it costs to cover death risk between the years 25 and 30 only. This is why term insurance offers maximum coverage at very low costs for the young family, providing the wife and children an immediate estate in case of the death of the husband.

Home Ownership

In acquiring home ownership debt, the couple is in the area of simple interest money and investment use of credit. Not only are homes looked upon as investment debt in credit circles, they are considered the safest of all debts. For this reason, home finance is the cheapest in the marketplace of money. In fact, the bulk of insurance company loans,

TWENTY-YEAR ENDOWMENT

ISSUED AT AGE 25
$1,000 VALUE

SOURCE: Jerome B. Cohen, *Decade of Decision* (New York: Institute of Life Insurance, 1958), p. 16.

FIGURE 27-6————The *endowment policy* insurance offers a minimum amount of protection for the money and the maximum amount of savings. A 20-year endowment policy for $1,000 pays $1,000 at the end of 20 years because the buyer has paid in a small amount for insurance and a large amount for savings which draw interest at a low rate. If cashed at the end of 20 years, insurance ceases. This kind of policy is not recommended for the young family in that premiums are so high that it is impossible to create an adequate estate for those dependent on the father's income.

FAMILY INCOME POLICY
PROTECTION VALUES

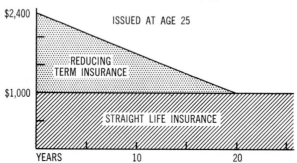

SOURCE: Jerome B. Cohen, *Decade of Decision* (New York: Institute of Life Insurance, 1958), p. 20.

FIGURE 27-7————This policy combines *straight life* insurance—giving a small amount of permanent insurance—with a *reducing term* of almost two-and-a-half times the value of the straight life insurance. The reducing term is very cheap since it declines in value with increased age and cuts off entirely before death risks become great. This policy costs slightly more than term insurance. For those who have bought costly insurance policies before marriage, adding the declining term rider to the existing policy offers a good solution to the problem of providing a maximum estate while children are most dependent.

CHANCES IN 1,000 THAT A NEWBORN CHILD WILL BE ORPHANED BEFORE ATTAINING AGE 18

Mortality Experience of White Population, United States, 1900-02 and 1956

☐ 1900-02   ■ 1956

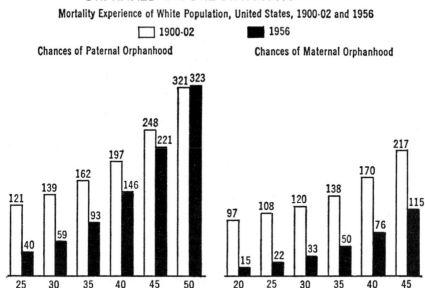

Chances of Paternal Orphanhood   Chances of Maternal Orphanhood

AGE OF FATHER AT BIRTH OF CHILD   AGE OF MOTHER AT BIRTH OF CHILD

SOURCE: Metropolitan Life Insurance Company, "Family Responsibilities Increasing," *Statistical Bulletin*, 40:3-5, April, 1959.

FIGURE 27-8————Although the chances of death of a parent have greatly decreased, there is still sufficient risk that the breadwinner will be taken to justify purchase of insurance on a basis which will assure maximum protection for the young couple without property, rather than provide for savings in old age. (Study Figure 27-4 and see that $100 a year can buy $17,500 worth of protection, or $3,000 worth of protection plus the investment feature.)

much labor union retirement fund money, and much bank capital is invested in homes. And throughout the nation are numerous savings and loan associations which use most of their capital in home finance. Those with federal charters, guarantee the money deposited by investors on the same basis as deposits are insured in banks with federal charters.

Home ownership should be an aspiration of most young couples, and separate living quarters, even though a renfed house or apartment, are almost a necessary beginning today when a rather complete economic break from the parental family is expected at marriage.

Whether one can buy a home depends very much on the kind of credit arrangements that can be made, the down payment, and the interest rates. Homes are almost always bought on credit, and ordinarily in the younger years should be. This kind of debt is creative, in that homes, with a little work by the couple in improving them, usually increase in value.

The general standard is that one can buy a home valued at twice his annual income and not be overreaching himself. In other words the $5,000-a-year man can safely buy a $10,000 home. He may go higher if he gets low interest, and a low down payment.

The importance of housing to the success of marriage and family life has never been adequately studied, but certainly living arrangements have much to do with the personal relations of husband and wife and of parents and children. Living with in-laws results in congested living arrangements, a lack of privacy, and other such factors, as well as in a tendency of relatives to interfere with the couple's adjustment to each other.

In Great Britain during the war, when family members were forced to live in one room because of the heating problem, many families found it necessary to impose the rule of silence on the family. Only by this means could they tolerate the close and congested living that was forced upon them.

One only has to investigate the matter casually in Europe to know the terrible strain and frustration of inadequate housing. In France, Holland, and Germany, for example, into the 1950's, people who had more than an average of one and a half rooms per family member were required to take in an additional family. Many young people could not marry because they were unable to find housing. Some married and had to live apart a good deal of the time. Even in Sweden and Denmark, where such rules of combining households were not in force, many of the same problems of housing shortage existed, hindering marriage and increasing unmarried motherhood and other problems.

TABLE 27-2————Home ownership of nonfarm families in the United States by income*

Family Income	Home Owning (percent)	Rent Paying (percent)	Neither (percent)
Under $1,000	48	40	12
$1,000-$1,999	44	49	7
$2,000-$2,999	39	56	5
$3,000-$3,999	54	45	1
$4,000-$4,999	55	43	2
$5,000-$7,499	63	36	1
$7,500 and over	76	23	1
Average	54	42	4

* In this table, families include single persons too. (Federal Reserve Board, 1952.)

Low-cost government-insured bank loans have been a major factor in the development of private family housing in the United States since World War II. It has made possible extensive home ownership even during a period of high building costs. Over half of American nonfarm families now own their own homes (see Table 27-2). Home ownership is certainly a factor in family stability, both from a psychological and mobility standpoint.

Undoubtedly some young couples have overextended themselves economically in order to acquire a new home, or too high-priced a home, but there are others who would have been much further ahead had they bought rather than paid high rental rates. When can one afford to buy a home?

It is not necessary to be rich to buy a home but usually a down payment of about one-tenth of the price of the house is required (more liberal terms have been granted to veterans). A rough standard by which one may judge what amount he should pay for his home in relation to his earnings is the following:

If income is	Family can afford a home costing
$ 2,500	$ 5,000 to $ 6,250
5,000	10,000 to 12,500
10,000	20,000 to 25,000

In financing a home one should usually expect to pay an interest rate of 5 to 6 percent on the unpaid balance. This means that a family with a $5,000 income wishing to buy a $10,000 home should be able to make a down payment of $1,000 (10 percent). If the contract were for twenty years, the payments at 6 percent interest would be $64.53 per month. In addition there would be taxes and insurance to pay, the rates for which would vary with the community. And there would be the cost of upkeep, the amount of which will depend on whether the property is new or old, and on the degree to which husband and wife are handy with paint and brush. On a twenty-five-year contract the mortgage payments would be reduced to $58.05 per month.

The Chicago Metropolitan Home Builders' Association has set up the following even more specific table to help persons determine how much of a family's monthly income may be invested safely in a home. It is not contradictory to the preceding—in fact, it agrees quite closely with that standard, but does spell it out in greater detail. Here are monthly payments on a home that families of different monthly incomes can handle ranging from the safe side to the risky side:

Monthly income after taxes	Safely	Probably	Risky
$200	$ 58	$ 66	$ 75
250	64	72	83
300	68	78	91
350	74	84	100
400	78	90	109
450	82	96	118
500	86	102	127
550	89	108	135
600	92	112	142
650	96	118	149
700	99	124	156
750	101	130	161
800	103	136	168

Installment Credit

Here we enter the world of hard-interest money, or discount interest. Rates usually range upward from 10 percent, with the average in the 15 to 20 percent range. Can one get ahead paying a fifth of his income for the use of money? This is a question to which few young families today give serious thought.

Interest is the wolf at the door in many families. A heavy interest load is usually the result of living ahead of one's income. An interest load of modest proportions is often justified in the interests of a better standard of living, particularly when it deals with assets of permanent value like a home or real estate. On such items of permanent value, minimum interest rates are paid—usually 6 percent on the unpaid balance. Although the interest will reduce the money left for current expenditures, the average family is usually justified in paying such a rate on the use of money for such purchases, for they actually are acquiring ownership and have the satisfaction of a residence which they may improve and manage as they choose. As long as the purchase is not far out of line with the earning ratios given above, there should be little difficulty with such an interest load.

The American family is time-contract-minded. The merits of this philosophy of economics is widely debated, and of course, even from the standpoint of the individual family, there are two sides to the question. There is no doubt that a young couple can get off to a quicker start by buying on contract to the full extent of their credit. But they burden themselves with an interest load which reduces their capacity to buy for one or two years ahead, particularly if they load themselves with contracts with excessive interest rates. Yet in periods of inflation part of the excess interest is offset by price rises in goods over a two-year period.

Most time contracts on consumable goods carry excessive and often hidden charges. In fact, carrying charges on installment contracts are usually twice as high as represented in most cases, for the interest is charged on the full amount of the contract for the full period. With monthly payments on a contract running for a year, half the loan is paid by the midyear. Thus a contract that charges 9 percent interest on the full amount for the full year is really charging 18 percent. Automobile finance contracts which are represented at 6 percent usually collect interest on the full balance at the beginning of the contract, so the actual rate is nearer to 12 percent.

The standard contract terms for time payments on a $100 balance from one of the largest and most reputable mail-order houses are: monthly payment, $9.00; added for easy payments, $10.00 (or 10 percent). Payments begin one month after the contract is taken, so at the end of ten months the buyer will have repaid $99.00 of the cash cost of the purchase, or all but $1.00 of the total. Yet he paid at the beginning a full 10 percent interest on $100 for a full year. If we examine the deal further, we find that after six months he has paid back $54, or more than half the balance on the cash price. Considering this and the fact that practically all the principal has been repaid by the end of ten months, the real carrying charge paid is around 23 percent.

Companies selling on installment contracts do not, of course, consider the carrying charge on installment contracts an interest charge, except in certain representations to the buyer. Actually, it is not an interest charge. The carrying charge must cover, not only interest, but also loss on merchandise which is never paid for, loss on items repossessed and sold at a large discount, the cost of paper work, record keeping, and collection.

Many couples justify purchases with high carrying charges in terms of immediate comfort, convenience, or necessity. There are no doubt instances where such added costs are justified, but to make installment buying a habit in family living is to sell oneself short in making the most of the income. In cases where quick credit is needed, those who, after a period of thrift and saving, have established sound credit, can always borrow on a straight bank loan at 6 to 8 percent simple interest on the unpaid balance. This is the thrifty way to use both credit and debt.

There Will Never Be Enough Money

As was stated at the outset, one of the most certain facts that any young couple must face in planning for their economic future is that they will never have enough money to meet all their needs. A nationwide survey of attitudes on this point by the office of Public Opinion Research of Princeton showed that most Americans are not satisfied with the amount of money they make. The less than a third who felt that they were more or less satisfied with their incomes were not necessarily the most prosperous; in fact, they were more likely to be farmers and businessmen who were self-employed and felt that they controlled their own economic future.

The most dissatisfied group of all was the professional group, where income is generally fairly adequate but where aspirations for an improved level of living are apparently extremely high. Another finding of opinion polls is that people who define happiness in terms of making money actually are not as likely to achieve happiness as those who consider love, family, and wisdom the essentials in life. It seems to be true, in fact, that those who choose wisdom above riches, as did King Solomon, achieve more contentment in the long run than those who put money first.

Probably the greatest worry of the American family is in making ends meet. This struggle between the amount of money the family makes and the number of things they want suggests that perhaps the majority of American families never really learn to live within their incomes.

The family with a $2,500 income is sure its members would have everything they wanted with $5,000; but the family with the $5,000 income is just as certain, and perhaps even more so, that it could meet all its needs with $7,500 or $10,000. Yet Spectorsky's study of "exurbanites"[8] —the high-pressure New York advertisers and promoters who live in the lavish mansions with acreages out beyond the suburbs—shows that not only are they living high on the hog, but they are also so deeply in debt that the $40,000 man must look forward to moving up another $10,000 to $20,000 a year to ever get out, and the man already up there is as badly or worse off.

In summary, the secret of happy family life from the standpoint of its economic adjustment would seem to be largely a matter of limiting desires to one's ability to pay. The worry over unmet bills can become chronic in those families which are constantly living beyond their income. The habit of thrift, of cautious and wise spending, probably has no relationship whatever to amount of income earned. These habits either are or are not deeply ingrained in the training of the child and in the philosophy of the individual as he learns to use money. Those who are thrifty can save, even on a small income, and can limit their expenditures to their prospective income. Those who are of extravagant habit and

---

[8] A. C. Spectorsky, *The Exurbanites* (Philadelphia: J. B. Lippincott Co., 1955).

who see no virtue in saving seldom realize a secure and prosperous living on any amount of income. This has been shown repeatedly in the lives of sons of American millionaires, who in many instances have been able to run through their parent's acquisition of millions in a matter of years and end up in poverty.

Money is the road to purchasing many of the satisfactions that make life worthwhile, but whether it actually does so is a matter of judgment, taste, values, and buying habits, much more than the amount of money the family handles.

Problems

1. Discuss this statement with reference to marriage happiness, "Dollars alone are not enough. You've got to have dollars and sense."
2. Lawrence earns a comfortable income but he and Jane are only recently married and there are a hundred ways in which each "extra" dollar could be spent. When Lawrence handles the money, he and Jane have a lot of fun but at the end of the month there are always bills he forgot to pay. When Jane handles the money, the bills get paid and they are able to buy some of the extra things they want—furniture, records, etc., but Lawrence feels that they have no fun and resents the fact that he is given an allowance like a child. What alternative method of money management might you suggest that would satisfy the economic-psychological needs of both Lawrence and Jane?
3. Poll the class on the questions, "What income are you likely to receive in the occupation you plan to enter? Do you believe that it will be more or less than ample for your needs and wishes?" Tabulate and discuss the class expectations with regard to future income. Do the expectations of the group seem to be realistic?
4. A marriage counselor advised a childless couple after their fifth year of marriage, "If you wait until you can afford to have children, you'll never have them." How accurate do you consider his observation? What merit is there in estimating the cost of children?
5. *a.* Nat and Alice are twenty-eight and twenty-six respectively. They have two children, aged two months and two years and plan to have one more after a few years. Nat has a relatively secure position and Alice has a temporary half-time job. Their combined incomes total $6,700 a year before taxes. What type of insurance and what amount would you advise them to buy?
   b. With a saving of only $1,000 would you advise Nat and Alice to consider buying a house? If so, what price-range should they consider? Under their circumstances what are the advantages, or disadvantages, of apartment living?
6. What is the appeal of installment buying? Under what circumstances is it justified? Some couples argue that it helps in budgeting if almost everything is bought on the installment plan. In what way is this true? What argument is there against it?

7. One occasionally hears of people with fabulous incomes who are sued for indebtedness. How can this situation be explained in the case of honest, well-meaning people?

8. *Sociodrama:* A young man and wife who have not yet begun their family disagree on how the income should be handled. The play opens as the husband suggests, "Let's pay all the bills at the beginning of each month; put the rest in a big purse and trust one another to draw from it wisely. We'll save whatever is left over each month."

Selected References

ARTICLES IN BOOKS OF READINGS

BECKER, Howard, and HILL, Reuben (Editors), *Family, Marriage and Parenthood,* Second Edition (Boston: D. C. Heath & Co., 1955).
    1. BIGELOW, Howard F., "Financing the Marriage," pp. 393-420.
    2. REIMER, Svend, "Designing the Family Home," pp. 493-531.
LANDIS, Judson T., and LANDIS, Mary G., *Readings in Marriage and the Family* (Englewood Cliffs, N. J.: Prentice-Hall, Inc., 1952).
    3. CYRUS, Della, "Problems of the Modern Home-maker-Mother," pp. 392-402.
KLING, Samuel G., and KLING, Esther B., *The Marriage Reader* (New York: Vanguard Press, Inc., 1947).
    4. GROVES, Gladys Hoagland, "Family Finances," pp. 449-483.
FISHBEIN, Morris, and KENNEDY, Ruby Jo Reeves, *Modern Marriage and Family Living* (New York: Oxford University Press, 1957).
    5. BIGELOW, Howard F., "Home Management and Finance," pp. 288-310.

General References

ANDERSON, Odin W., and FELDMAN, Jacob J., *Family Medical Costs and Voluntary Health Insurance: A Nationwide Survey* (New York: McGraw-Hill Book Co., 1956).
CAVAN, Ruth Shonle, *American Marriage* (New York: Thomas Y. Crowell Co., 1959), Chs. 14, 15 by Doris E. Pullman.
COHEN, Jerome B., *Decade of Decision* (New York: Institute of Life Insurance, Educational Division, 1958.)
LEMASTERS, E. E., *Modern Courtship and Marriage* (New York: The Macmillan Co., 1957), Chs. 19, 20.
MARGOLIUS, Sidney, *How to Finance Your Home* (New York: Public Affairs Pamphlets, 1964), No. 360.
MATTESON, William J., and HARWOOD, E. C., *Life Insurance from the Buyer's Point of View* (Great Barrington, Mass.: American Institute of Economic Research), annual revisions.

Ross, Irwin, "When You Borrow, When You Buy—Watch Those Interest Rates," *Reader's Digest,* November, 1963, pp 157-165.

SCHWABACHER, Albert E., Jr., "The Repository of Wealth," in Seymour M. FARBER and Roger H. L. WILSON (Editors), *The Potential of Woman* (New York: McGraw-Hill Book Co., 1963), pp. 241-254.

The Women's Division of the Institute of Life Insurance, 448 Madison Avenue, New York 22, publishes certain free materials of value to the average couple; for example, *The Money Manager* (a work-sheet for a family budget); *A Discussion of Family Money; How Budgets Work and What They Do* (Informal Study No. 3).

VI
PARENTHOOD

28
Family Planning

The scriptural admonition to the early patriarchs to "multiply and replenish the earth" has in our day been replaced by the sociological admonition to beware of the "population explosion." With the nations of the earth struggling for space and with large sectors of the more densely populated areas of the globe already suffering from hunger and malnutrition, the survival struggle is not one of enough children to replace the dying adult generation, but rather one of too many surviving children.

With the reduction of the death rate, and in industrial nations, the control of the birth rate, children have a high value in the scheme of marriage for most couples. But quality is more emphasized than quantity, and nurture more than numbers. Sex is no longer viewed primarily for procreation, but rather as a key factor in satisfactory interpersonal relations of the married pair. Only rarely is the sex act engaged in today with the goal of offspring in mind. Yet, when couples want children and learn they cannot have them, the situation is seldom one of incidental concern.

Problems of conception, heredity, sterility, and child spacing are real ones. Some anticipation of them, and knowledge of them is important.

How Life Begins

Each girl is born with a lifetime supply of many thousands of immature eggs in her ovaries. During her fertile lifetime only some 400 to 500 eggs will ripen, at the rate of one per twenty-eight days. About the twelfth day after the beginning of menstruation, an egg cell is released from an ovary and floats into the opening of the Fallopian tube. Its capacity to survive in the tube is limited, perhaps to a maximum of eight hours. To be fertilized, the thick wall of the cell must be penetrated during this period by the male sperm cell. If it is met in the tube by male sperm, which have been discharged into the vagina and have swum up through the uterus and into the Fallopian tube, the fertilized egg then begins to divide and to move down into the uterus (or womb). Here it attaches itself to a spot on the wall that is fully lined with bloodfilled tissues to cushion the egg and nourish it.

One ovulation occurs, normally every 28 days, from one ovary or the other. This will usually be between the tenth and sixteenth day. During most of the ovulations that take place in the woman's fertile life cycle, no sperm will be there to meet the egg, or even if they are there, they may not succeed in penetrating its wall. As a consequence, rather than the womb performing its function of nursing the egg, the microscopic-sized unfertilized egg floats on through and is discharged. Since the blood-filled uterine wall is unused, some fourteen to sixteen days later it breaks down and passes out in the menstrual flow.

After the cessation of the flow, the rebuilding of the womb lining begins again preparatory to another ovulation, which takes place, as is mentioned above, about the twelfth day after the beginning of menstruation.

There is a slight rise in temperature near the time of ovulation. The temperature change is due to hormone changes and often does not conform exactly to the period of ovulation. Some women feel the egg burst through the wall of the ovary, with a sharp cutting pain (called *mittelschmerz*) but most are not aware of the time of ovulation.

In sexual intercourse, approximately a tablespoon of semen, containing some 500 millions of sperm, is deposited in the upper part of the vaginal tract, near the *cervix,* or neck of the *womb* or *uterus.* The cervix is a strong muscle with an opening that is normally very small, but which can stretch to permit the passage of the baby at birth. Vaginal fluids are hostile to sperm, but if pregnancy is to result, some sperm must swim rather quickly through this tiny opening (or be sucked through with the orgasmic contractions of the uterus) and travel the long distance up through the womb to meet the female ovum in the Fallopian tube. The five-inch journey of the sperm has been likened to a man's five-mile swim upstream. If the egg meets the sperm, and one finally breaks through its tough wall, the egg is fertilized. The fertilized egg becomes the *zygote,* and as cell division proceeds, the *embryo,* which after birth becomes the child.

The point at which the zygote becomes attached to the uterine wall develops into the umbilical cord and provides the nutritional contact between mother and child. Here the blood streams of mother and child flow side by side, permitting nutrition to pass through the thin wall by osmosis from the mother's blood stream to the embryo's, and permitting the embryo's wastes to pass into the mother's blood stream.

In the womb the embryo grows the normal nine months (known as the *gestation period*), when contractions in the uterus warn the mother that the birth of the child is imminent. [For an excellent film showing all these processes, see *Human Reproduction.*]

Heredity in Family Planning

Many young people enter marriage with groundless fears about their heredity. Others who enter marriage with hereditary defects should be concerned about them, but are not. The field of heredity is a highly technical one and only a competent eugenist can give adequate advice on specific problems. In case of doubt, a couple should consult such a person prior to marriage. If questions arise after marriage, he should be consulted about them at that time.

Suffice it here to give some general advice. Each of us brings to marriage the hereditary traits of our line of ancestry. When two young people mate, the hereditary traits which they possess through their lines of ancestry, and these traits alone, determine the hereditary characteristics of their offspring.

The marriage of close relatives has been condemned in most primitive and modern societies. Yet the question comes up frequently as to whether cousins can marry. In the Arab culture cousin marriage is still extensive. The difficulty of cousin marriages arises out of the simple fact that all human strains carry certain undesirable and usually hidden traits in the germ plasma. These pathological genes are recessive. When two recessive genes combine they produce an individual with the undesirable trait. The likelihood of relatives combining the recessive genes is many-fold greater than of nonrelatives doing so. Cousins, therefore, have a greater chance of producing offspring with genetic abnormalities than do people with completely different blood lines.

A study of 106 first-cousin marriages showed that while there was little ill effect prior to birth, insofar as spontaneous abortions and still-births were concerned, damage began to appear after birth and increased with age.[1] The death rate was three times that of marriages outside the

[1] Herman M. Slatis, Raymond H. Reis, and Robert E. Hoene in the *American Journal of Human Genetics*, December, 1958, summarized in *Family Life*, 19:2-4, March, 1959.

bloodline, and abnormalities were twice as numerous—major abnormalities, even much more than twice as numerous.[2]

Human heredity is a highly complex problem.[3] Those with serious hereditary defects in the family need to marry wisely, if at all, unless they choose to be sterilized. One of the most important considerations is to marry outside a line that carries the same type of defect. For example, diabetes is one of the most common hereditary diseases.[4] Diabetics should not marry into families that are diabetic, since this recessive trait is likely to produce the defective pancreas which predisposes to diabetes.[5] Schizophrenia is believed to be in part due to recessive genes which create a predisposition to the disease. In some cases epilepsy, hypertension, and coronary disease seem to be the result of an hereditary predisposition.[6] Manic-depressive psychosis is more definitely hereditary. Huntington's Chorea (deteriorating brain disease with onset of middle age) is definitely hereditary and dominant. Dwarfism is hereditary and muscular dystrophy is a group of hereditary disorders, of which one of the most severe forms is sex linked. Hemophilia and color blindness are sex-linked hereditary defects (carried by mother line but appearing in male line). There are numerous other less common diseases which are known to be of genetic origin.

Young people with families characterized by unique hereditary diseases and young people considering mates whose families harbor these diseases should seek information through a human genetics study center.

It is wise to make the contact through one's doctor. Here are the institutions with the major human heredity clinics in the United States and Canada:

United States

Bowman Gray School of Medicine, Winston-Salem, N.C.

Children's Memorial Hospital, Chicago, Ill.

Dight Institute, University of Minnesota, Minneapolis, Minn.

Johns Hopkins University Medical School, Baltimore, Md.

Medical College of Virginia, Richmond, Va.

[2] For study of a line degenerated by inbreeding see Carl Mydans, "Far-Off Exiles of Tristan," *Life*, July 12, 1963, pp. 72-78.

[3] Recent discoveries in the chemistry of the genes show that heredity is far more complicated than even the specialists had dreamed. The geneticists' horizon has widened greatly.

[4] Diabetes seems to be a combination of several hereditary factors and not a simple gene trait.

[5] Ray C. Anderson, "The Influence of Heredity on Family Health," *Marriage and Family Living*, 19:136-141, May, 1957; also see C. Nash Herndon, "Medical Genetics and Marriage Counseling," *Marriage and Family Living*, 16:207-210, August, 1954; and Curt Stern, *Principles of Human Genetics* (San Francisco: W. H. Freeman & Co., Publishers, 1949.)

[6] Like diabetes, they may be a combination of hereditary, predisposing, and developmental factors.

Minnesota Dept. of Health, University of Minnesota Campus,
   Minneapolis, Minn.
New York State Psychiatric Institute, New York 32, N.Y.
Tulane University Medical School, New Orleans, La.
University of Chicago, Dept. of Zoology, Chicago, Ill.
University of Michigan, Ann Arbor, Mich.
University of North Carolina, Chapel Hill, N.C.
University of Oklahoma, Norman, Okla.
University of Texas, Austin, Tex.
University of Utah, Salt Lake City, Utah
University of Washington Medical School, Seattle, Wash.
Western Reserve University, Dept. of Biology, Cleveland, Ohio

Canada

Children's Hospital, Winnipeg, Manitoba
Children's Memorial Hospital, Montreal, Quebec
Hospital for Sick Children, Toronto, Ontario
McGill University, Toronto, Ontario
University of Alberta, Edmonton, Alberta
University of British Columbia, Vancouver, British Columbia

It is an interesting fact that length of life and susceptibility to many kinds of disease tend to run in families because of inheritance of physical structure, even though the disease itself is not hereditary. The physical structure of the type which falls an easy victim to certain diseases such as tuberculosis tends to be passed on from generation to generation. It is for this reason that diseases which in themselves are not hereditary tend to recur generation after generation in some families.

If both families have a history of tuberculosis, diabetes, mental deficiency or mental illness, the couple, even though normal, is taking a considerable risk, since the physical structures which tend to succumb to these conditions are more likely to be passed on to the offspring than when only one member of the pair has a family history showing such defects.

If of definitely unsound heredity, man or wife should consider being sterilized. This will in no way affect their physical capability in marital relations and removes the fear that they will bring seriously defective offspring into the world. States having laws permitting sterilization in case of seriously defective heredity are shown in Table 28-1. To January 1, 1964, in the United States, 63,678 eugenic sterilizations had been reported, most of them because of mental illness or mental deficiency. These figures, of course, do not include voluntary sterilizations which are sought by men and women for fixing the size of their families. The Scripps Foundation for Population Research estimates that these run around 110,000 per year. This is another problem and is discussed later in the chapter.

TABLE 28-1————Sterilizations performed under U. S. state sterilization statutes to January 1, 1964; based on reports from state authorities and superintendents of state institutions.

| | CUMULATIVE TOTALS* | | | | | |
| State | Mentally ill | Mentally deficient | Others† | Grand total | | |
	(total)	(total)	(total)	(total)	(male)	(female)
Alabama‡		224		224	129	95
Arizona	24	6		30	10	20
California	11,758	7,542	808	20,108	10,152	9,956
Connecticut	414	143		557	46	511
Delaware	278	641	26	945	468	477
Georgia	2,531	744	9	3,284	1,474	1,810
Idaho	12	25	1	38	8	30
Indiana	667	1,751	6	2,424	1,167	1,257
Iowa	843	963	104	1,910	545	1,365
Kansas	2,063	856	113	3,032	1,763	1,269
Maine	22	234	70	326	46	280
Michigan	440	2,927	419	3,786	991	2,795
Minnesota	418	1,930	2	2,350	519	1,831
Mississippi	602	67	14	683	160	523
Montana	42	214		256	72	184
Nebraska	165	728	9	902	423	479
New Hampshire	248	379	52	679	152	527
New York‡	41		1	42	1	41
North Carolina	1,566	4,385	346	6,297	1,072	5,225
North Dakota	379	634	36	1,049	397	652
Oklahoma	306	250		556	122	434
Oregon	871	1,343	127	2,341	888	1,453
South Carolina	114	162	1	277	22	255
South Dakota	23	748	18	789	283	506
Utah	112	660		772	354	418
Vermont	14	211	28	253	83	170
Virginia	3,529	3,466	167	7,162	2,779	4,383
Washington‡	403	276	6	685	184	501
West Virginia	23	52	23	98	15	83
Wisconsin	9	1,813	1	1,823	391	1,432
Totals	27,917	33,374	2,387	63,678	24,716	38,962

SOURCE: Association for Voluntary Sterilization, Inc., February, 1964.

* Cumulative totals represent the number of sterilizations performed since each state law was enacted.

† Certain of the laws are available to classes other than the mentally deficient and mentally ill, for example, the epileptic.

‡ Alabama law, enacted in 1919, has been inoperative since 1935 when State Supreme Court rendered an adverse opinion regarding broader sterilization legislation then pending. New York law, enacted in 1912, was declared unconstitutional in 1918 on the ground that it denied equal protection of the law to the noninstitutionalized. Washington law, enacted in 1909, was declared unconstitutional in 1942 due to technical deficiencies.

The Problem of Sterility

Some 10 to 15 percent of marriages throughout the world are sterile; at least, this proportion never bear children throughout their married life. This is the conclusion of The First World Congress on Human Infertility, held in New York City in May, 1953, with 1,300 physicians from fifty-three nations in attendance.[7] It is assumed that most of the sterility is involuntary. United States Census data show that childlessness ranges from 9 percent of rural marriages in the United States to over 17 percent in urban marriages. Certain marriages, of course, are voluntarily childless.

Of the Kinsey Institute for Sex Research sample of women, 20 percent of marriages proved infertile.[8] Women who married youngest proved to be the most fertile, in that they became pregnant most often and in a higher percentage of cases. Of those who married before the age of 21, pregnancy occurred among 90 percent and they averaged 3.5 pregnancies. Of those who married between 21 and 25, pregnancy occurred among 86 percent and averaged 2.8 pregnancies. Of those who delayed the marriage until after age 30, the Institute reports that not more than half became pregnant, although the researchers admit that their sample of this age group is rather small. They do cite the confirming evidence, however, that after age 30 very few women in any of the samples become pregnant, even those who had previously demonstrated their fertility. From age 46 on there is only one chance in 500 of a woman becoming pregnant.

Throughout history sterility has been considered a tragedy. It has quite universally been looked upon as a defect in the wife. In our times, however, the problem of barrenness has taken a new turn. Absolute sterility is thought to characterize only a small percentage of the childless marriages and where it exists it is now recognized that the husband is as often responsible as the wife.

In general the treatment of infertile husbands is less successful than the treatment of sterile wives. Hormone and drug treatments have for the most part proved disappointing. A recent development is the use of pituitary hormone to bring about ovulation in women who do not ovulate.[9] The hormone, at first taken from the glands of the dead, is now extracted from the urine of postmenopausal women. The drug (Pergonal, for gonad) often causes ova to break out of both egg sacs at once so that nearly half who become pregnant have twins. A few have quadruplets.

[7] For a brief summary of this conference see Abraham Stone, "World Conference on Human Infertility," *Marriage and Family Living*, 15:231-233, August, 1953.

[8] Paul H. Gebhard and others, *Pregnancy, Birth and Abortion* (New York: Harper & Bros. and Paul B. Hoeber, Inc., 1958).

[9] Isabella Taves, "New Adventures in Female Fertility," *Look*, May 19, 1964, p. 91 ff.

Various medical and surgical techniques have been developed to treat sterility. Knowledge of them may be obtained from doctors, specialists, and clinics. It is, however, important to know that the likelihood of barrenness on the part of the woman seems to increase somewhat with delay of pregnancy; each year pregnancy becomes more difficult. This leads some practicing gynecologists to advise the young woman with an underdeveloped uterus or other symptoms which might indicate difficulty in becoming pregnant to have her first pregnancy early in the marriage.

That emotions can affect fertility is becoming well established.[10] The Margaret Sanger Research Bureau in New York City studied 500 cases of sterile couples. Of these, 122 couples were found to be sterile because of psychological tensions.[11] Once the tensions were removed by counseling and reassurance, they became pregnant. Only five of the 122 needed psychotherapy. It may well be that this is nature's way of keeping the nervous mother from conceiving offspring who would be damaged during development by her extreme stress. As is shown in a later paragraph, extreme nervous tension of the mother can produce a child who is neurotic at birth.

Alternatives to Natural Conception

In many cultures of the world, perhaps in most of them historically, a fertility ceremonial has been institutionalized. This may consist of a sanctioned period of license, in which mating with others than the spouse is more or less taken for granted. There is a survival of these practices in many advanced cultures today. In the West German Catholic areas, for example, especially in the Rhineland, Swabia, and Bavaria, there is an annual ceremony called the *Karneval*. (In rural areas it is called *die Fastnacht*.) It is a Mardi Gras type of celebration, with riotous parties and a carnival atmosphere that takes over the community. Drinking and carousing are the order of the day. It is said that the spouse who would attempt to sue the mate on grounds of infidelity which occurred during Bavaria's carnival time would be laughed out of court.[12]

Such practices are a boon to the spouse of an infertile mate, but they are hardly an acceptable solution to this problem in our society.

Artificial insemination now offers scientific help to the apparently sterile couple. In cases where both husband and wife are fertile but conception fails to take place, instrumental insemination using the husband's semen is often successful.

[10] "Emotions Affect Fertility," *Science News Letter*, 61: p. 308, June 14, 1952.
[11] *Family Life*, 16:5, February 6, 1956.
[12] *Time*, February 27, 1956, p. 35.

Artificial insemination is far past the experimental stage. Thousands of artificial inseminations have been successfully carried out. It is, however, according to some authorities, still hazardous to the marriage. Husbands rarely suggest artificial insemination. It is usually initiated by the wife. Even when his consent is willingly given, and in spite of the fact that he is present when the act of insemination is performed, the husband often becomes a victim of jealousies and suspicions, feeling that the wife has been disloyal. It should not be undertaken, using a donor's semen, without being discussed fully.

The emotional impact of artificial insemination is found by Farris to be less serious than these warnings suggest. He reports, for example, that there may be the same emotional complications in the case of adoption, when there is resentment against the adoption agent. Artificial insemination does meet the desire of the couple to experience pregnancy, and promises 50 percent heredity, which gives promise of a closer tie than does adoption. It also protects the husband's pride, in that no one but he and his wife know the child is not his. He also finds that couples he studied who had a child by artificial insemination would unanimously agree to have another.[13]

Student attitudes generally favor artificial insemination by the husband but not by a donor. Vernon and Broadway, studying attitudes toward artificial insemination, both by donors and by husbands at Central Michigan College, reported a great preference for adoption over artificial insemination by any means.[14] Only 73.5 percent would approve artificial insemination using the husband's semen, compared to 90 percent studied by Greenberg at Colorado, and only 17 percent would approve it by a donor compared to 52 percent at Colorado studied by Greenberg. Religious reasons were among those given for condemning artificial insemination. The more conservative attitudes, as would be expected, were among the Catholics. Whether a difference in the classroom atmosphere in which artificial insemination was discussed is the real variable here, or regional differences, or whether students are actually becoming more conservative in this matter is debatable (Greenberg's study was made earlier). It seems unlikely that the statistical differences found represent real differences in attitudes.

The legitimacy status, and inheritance rights of the child sired by the donor's semen are in question. So far most courts have ruled such

---

[13] Edmund J. Farris, *Human Ovulation and Fertility* (Philadelphia: J. B. Lippincott Co., 1956).

[14] Glenn M. Vernon and Jack A. Broadway, "Attitudes Toward Artificial Insemination and the Variables Associated Therewith," *Marriage and Family Living*, 21:43-47, February, 1959; also Joseph H. Greenberg, "Social Variables in Acceptance or Rejection of Artificial Insemination," *American Sociological Review*, 16:86-91, February, 1951.

children illegitimate unless the husband adopts the child. Some courts have ruled that the act of siring a child by such means is adultery.[15]

These problems will no doubt vanish with time, and the increased use of artificial insemination. Scientists are already advocating sperm banks for eugenics reasons, particularly as a protection of human stock from possible radiation damage. A seminal Fort Knox through deep-frozen semen[16] was recommended by Nobel Prize winner, Hermann J. Muller to the American Institute of Biological Sciences. So far the preservation of human sperm has not been achieved with the same degree of success as has been the case with cattle-sperm storage. It is, however, at least in the area of practical possibility.

Prenatal Influence—Myths vs. Science

The "old wives' tales" about the baby's harelip being caused by the mother's being frightened by a rabbit is not so far from the truth as was once supposed. Experiments with animals show that damage to lip and palate can be caused by drug injection or severe emotional stress, which has the effect of releasing chemicals into the blood stream. Two variables determine the degree of damage to the embryo: (1) time of influence—it must be when the jaws and lips are being formed, (2) extent of influence—it must reach a degree of intensity for damage to result.

Study of harelip and cleft palates among human beings shows that most persons with these defects were born to mothers who experienced the damaging influence between the sixth and eighth weeks, the time when jaw structures form in the human embryo.

Such research has led to a reevaluation of the arbitrary opinions regarding the possibility of the mother's health, nervous stability, and emotional experiences affecting the child. Instead of writing all prenatal influences off as old wives' tales, research is now trying to assess the specific effect of the prenatal environment on the unborn child. Briefly, for this is too highly complex a subject to present in any detail, evidence to date suggests the following:

1. PRENATAL MARKING

The idea that if a mother is scared by a snake the child will have the print of a snake on its back; or by a rabbit, and the harelip will result; and many other such folk myths are strictly myth. Extreme fright at a time when given embryo structures are forming can, however, create developmental damage.[17]

[15] For a sample case, see "Test-tube Test Case," *Time*, December 27, 1954, p. 52.
[16] "Frozen Fatherhood," *Time*, Sept. 8, 1961, p. 68.
[17] "Link Cleft Palate with Stress in Early Pregnancy," *Science News Letter*, 20:217 ff., October 6, 1956; see also Sylvia Brody, *Patterns of Mothering*, (New York: International Universities Press, Inc., 1956).

2. PRENATAL CHEMICAL DAMAGE

Certain chemicals injected into the body can affect the development of the embryo, as experiments with animals have clearly demonstrated. X-rays and radiation can damage an embryo. There is considerable opinion that women should avoid x-ray and fluoroscopic examination during the first half of the month while the mature egg is forming.[18] Cigarette smoking by the mother, while it will not produce a yellow baby as folk myth holds, may cause premature births.[19]

3. PRENATAL NUTRITIONAL DAMAGE

Lack of vitamins may damage the embryo. During the stress of war, when carbohydrates were burned up by mothers in excessive amounts, babies were born light in weight but of normal length, since mineral elements that form bone structure were not consumed in excess.[20]

4. PRENATAL DISEASE DAMAGE

High fever diseases of the mother, particularly German measles (which may explain as much as 30 percent of cerebral palsy), but even chickenpox and diabetes, may also damage the embryo, causing deformity or mental retardation.[21] This is so well recognized as a hazard during the first three months of pregnancy that, in Sweden, having German measles is legal grounds for abortion as a eugenics measure.[22]

An untreated syphilitic mother can transmit syphilis to the child during the embryonic stage. Although the blood streams of the mother and the fetus are separate, syphilis can pass through the placenta wall by osmosis, just as do food and waste materials.

5. PRENATAL EMOTIONAL DAMAGE

Extreme emotion causes release of chemicals into the blood stream, which can very decidedly affect the embryo, just as can externally injected chemicals.[23]

Dr. Sontag's studies show such effects in mothers undergoing extreme emo-

18 *Children Limited,* 7:18, May, 1958.

19 Winea J. Simpson of Loma Linda, California, studied 7,500 women in three San Bernardino hospitals. Premature births increased with number of cigarettes smoked daily. *American Journal of Obstetrics and Gynecology,* Vol. 17, April, 1957. The U.S. Public Health Service report on *Smoking and Health,* p. 343, finds that babies of women who smoked during pregnancy are lighter in weight. They also find that smokers have a significantly greater number of premature deliveries.

20 For a summary of this significant research see Lester W. Sontag, "War and the Fetal-Maternal Relationship," *Marriage and Family Living,* 6:3-4, 1944.

21 "Dangers before Birth," *Time,* June 10, 1959, p. 76.

22 *Social Sweden* (Stockholm: Social Welfare Board, 1952).

23 Gladys D. Schultz, "The Uninsulated Child," *Ladies Home Journal,* June, 1956, p. 61-62; see also Sontag, *loc. cit.*

tional stress. Fetal activity is greatly increased, too, and the fetal movements last far beyond the stress of the mother, causing it to burn up excessive carbohydrates. Infants born to mothers undergoing extreme emotional stress are hyperactive after birth, want to be fed frequently, and have frequent bowel movements. They are in a real sense born neurotic.

Ashley-Montagu's research confirms the fact of the neurotic child being born to the extremely nervous mother. He also summarizes other research confirming this view.[24]

In the animal field, breeders have long recognized the necessity of a calm gestation period, particularly for captive wild animals like foxes and mink. Perhaps with continued research we will have equal insight into the effect of maternal temperament on prenatal environment.

6. PRENATAL DAMAGE FROM RH FACTOR

Intrauterine damage to the fetus due to the clash of the mother's and the child's blood is rather rare now,[25] but it once resulted in jaundice, anemia, and stillbirth of the baby, as well as accounting for about 10 percent of cerebral palsy cases. (It now accounts for less than 3 percent.) Rh incompatibility (named for its discovery in Rhesus monkeys) of mother and fetus occurs when one parent is Rh positive and the other, Rh negative. Pregnancy in this situation sets up antibodies in the mother's blood which are injurious to the child. The buildup of antibodies is very slow, however, and rarely affects a child until the second or third pregnancy. If one child is affected, all subsequent children will be, as there is no correction for the mother. Transfusions today can correct the live-born child's difficulty, and induced early delivery reduces the infant's late-pregnancy exposure. The statistical chances of danger to the child today are not more than one in 20 to 25.

The Risks of Youthful Pregnancy

Ashley-Montagu[26] has found in his extensive research, that full female maturity for purposes of reproduction is reached only very slowly, and not until years after puberty. Pregnancy before full biological maturity is risk laden. Here are the main risks which he finds exist:

1. There is a high death rate among children born to young mothers.
2. There is a high death rate among young mothers themselves during or following childbirth.

[24] M. F. Ashley-Montagu and Gertrude Schweitzer, "There Is Prenatal Influence," *Ladies Home Journal,* 71:43 ff., February, 1954; for animal experiments see William S. Kroeger, "Influence of Prenatal Maternal Anxiety on Emotionality of Young Rats," *Science,* 125:698, April 12, 1957; see also, William S. Kroeger, "Baby May Be Neurotic if Mother Is Disturbed," *Science News Letter,* 63:376, June 20, 1953.

[25] The Rh negative factor is found in 15 percent of white people, 7 percent of Negroes, and 1 percent of Chinese and Japanese.

[26] M. F. Ashley-Montagu, *The Reproductive Development of the Female with Special Reference to the Period of Adolescent Sterility* (New York: Julian Press, Inc., 1958).

3. Spontaneous abortions are high among young mothers.
4. The stillbirth rate is high among young mothers.
5. Toxemia is more frequent among the younger mothers.

Ashley-Montagu, surveying the evidence, concluded that we should not only discourage young marriages, but that where young people in their teens do marry, they should delay the first pregnancy for several years.

Hazards of Birth and Birth Timing

Birth damage to children is extensive. Dr. Meyer A. Perlstein's research in the area of cerebral palsy, which affects one child in every 215 born in the United States, suggests that about 3 percent is caused by forceps delivery, but that 60 percent is due to brain hemorrhage and contusions during a difficult natural delivery,[27] and to oxygen starvation.[28] Illness of the mother during pregnancy, notably German measles, anemia, and diabetes may account for 30 percent, and the Rh factor about 3 percent. Childhood injuries account for the rest.

Premature births are another problem of great significance. About half of the infant deaths are among this group. Extremely careful handling is necessary not only to save life but to protect the premature from brain damage due to bile pigments which the liver cannot handle, and from blindness due to an excess of oxygen in the incubator. The excess of bile pigment usually requires blood transfusion.

About 12 percent of births are delayed about two weeks beyond due date, and 4 percent are delayed three weeks. Research by Dr. Mitchell J. Nechtow has found the death rate of the latter group three times that of normal term babies.[29] His explanation is that the placenta may shrink, causing the baby to live off its own tissues, thus losing weight. Difficulty of delivery also increases, with more frequent breach births and use of forceps and Caesarean sections, all of which bring risk of injury.

Multiple Births

Although the likelihood of multiple births is seldom a matter for anxiety in our culture, there are few questions of a biological nature that are of greater interest to young people looking forward to marriage. In fact, throughout much of human history and, among most cultures,

[27] This makes all the more risky the practice of delaying births until the doctor comes, etc., described in the latter part of this chapter; see "Cruelty in the Maternity Hospital," *Ladies Home Journal*, November, 1957; May, 1958.

[28] For a part of Perlstein's work, see "Against Cerebral Palsy," *Time*, December 16, 1957, p. 39.

[29] See "Premature and Past Due," *Time*, April 20, 1959, p. 77.

twins have assumed a unique significance as omens of either good or of bad luck. Some peoples have put them to death to protect the group from evil; others, which accept them as good omens, have elevated them to enviable places in the group. In our sophisticated culture, superstitions concerning twins have disappeared, but twins have nonetheless held a place in humor, folklore, and particularly in scientific study.

Identical twins begin with a single ovum which has been fertilized by a single sperm and which later divides to form two embryos, each having the same pattern of genes and therefore the same common inherited characteristics. They are, of course, of the same sex. If the egg divides late after fertilization, the twins may be mirror images of each other rather than identical images; that is, their hair will part on opposite sides, one will be left-handed and the other right-handed, etc.

The handwriting and fingerprints of identical twins are very similar. Their skin is so identical that skin grafts can be made on each other's bodies interchangeably and without difficulty.

Numerous studies of identical twins show that they have the same general characteristics of temperament, interest, and even hereditary weaknesses. Researchers[30] find few twins in the list of distinguished persons. There seems to be frequent intellectual retardation among them. Premature birth may be a factor. Some think a factor of retardation is speech-caused. The twins are able to communicate with each other and do not have to learn to do so through normal vocabulary.

In America, a twin occurs about once in every 84 births. The common notion that twins tend to run in families is true, both the male and the female of certain families tending to carry the twinning characteristic.

Identical twins make up only 25 percent of twins born in the United States. Nonidentical twins make up the rest. Nonidentical twins are born of two different eggs which have been fertilized by two different sperms. The fertilization may even take place in different acts of intercourse, even by different males, as has been proved in tests of paternity. Such twins may be of either sex and are no more alike in hereditary than siblings born separately.

A rural myth of long standing holds that twins are sterile. This is not the case. They are actually more fertile than average, in that twinning tends to be hereditary. The sterility myth apparently originates from the "free martin" situation in cattle. In the case of mixed-sex twins, the female is almost always sterile in cattle. The reason seems to be that the placenta surrounding the calves is very thin in cattle, permitting the male sex hormone to dominate the female's sexual development and making it sterile.

[30] Frank Sandon so concludes after studying thousands of records of English twins, *Eugenics Review*, July, 1958.

The Control of Pregnancy

As has been observed in an earlier chapter, the young wife to-day has almost complete control over the decision to bear or not to bear children. In historic societies there was little choice. It was taken for granted that girls would marry and bear children; this was the custom, and a woman's only means of obtaining protection and economic security was through marriage and childbearing.

The ability to control conception is at the very heart of the companionship marriage, and is a prerequisite to the maximum happiness of the romantic marriage. For the welfare of the children, too, child spacing is considered an essential in providing the maximum social and economic advantages. Effective timing and spacing of children is for the most part a problem of medical technology. Most couples will have consulted a physician or visited a clinic prior to marriage, ideally three months before. Methods of conception control will have been provided so that the marriage insofar as is possible is protected from unwanted pregnancy.

Thanks to the increasing alarm centering about the threat of over-population to the welfare of great areas of the world, major attention has recently been directed to the control of fertility. Even the Catholic Church has weakened its stand to the point that many leaders and laymen are critical of the Church's position and to where the Church hierarchy is considering changing its stand. At least attitudes have modified enough so that the Catholic Church is no longer disposed to force its position on non-Catholics, thus hampering official bodies and medical research, as in the past.

Such significant strides have been made that it is now possible, either by chemical or by mechanical means, to control conception 100 percent. "The pill" has been used by millions without harmful effects, and it is completely effective. There have been the usual alarms about possible side effects, but none have been proven to have substantial foundation. The pill in general usage consists of ovarian hormones of the kinds which appear in the mother's bloodstream on pregnancy to terminate ovulation. The pill does this when taken daily for 20 days each month, beginning the day after menstruation ceases. When the pill is no longer used, fertility returns. In fact, some infertile women conceive after taking the pill for a term and then stopping.

Other chemical approaches are in the making, some promising to make the wife sterile for periods as long as a year. Still others are in the making to produce temporary sterility in the male.

Devices can also be inserted into the uterus by the physician and left for long periods of time and have proved, under experiments to date, to be 100 percent conception proof. No ill effects are reported in experimental cases where the devices have been left in for up to four years. They are noncorrosive plastic, and shape and size seem not to be important except as a factor in their remaining in the uterus.

The best source of information for young couples who plan to defer pregnancy for a time after marriage is the Planned Parenthood Federation of America which has offices in most large cities. Clinics of this group are prepared to give helpful information to those planning marriage as well as to the married.

The Rhythm Method of Timing Conception

The rhythm method is based on the assumption that a couple may determine quite exactly the time of ovulation and by avoiding sexual intercourse then, avoid conception.

The rhythm method, although usually identified with spacing births or limiting births, is of equal importance in achieving pregnancy. It depends for its effectiveness upon accuracy in determining the time of ovulation.

Edmund J. Farris has reported research which casts considerable doubt on existing theories about the specific period of ovulation. He finds that in 90 percent of the cases, ovulation takes place between the 10th and 16th days from the beginning of the menstrual flow, and that in the majority it takes place between the 11th and 14th days, the 12th day being the most common. He is very doubtful that the ovum can be fertilized later than 8 hours after its rupture from the egg sac or that sperm cells are potent for more than 24 hours after ejaculation.

He recommends that women who wish to establish the time of ovulation either for purposes of birth control or conception determine the midpoint of the cycle and subtract two days from this number. This is the time of most likely ovulation. The earliest possible day of fertility then would be two days before this date and the latest five days afterward. He believes that the temperature method of determining ovulation is not reliable in more than half the cases.[31]

Farris has indicated that to assure conception it is desirable to refrain from sexual intercourse for at least five days prior to ovulation to assure maximum development of the husband's sperm.[32] Then at the period when ovulation is expected, the couple should have sexual intercourse daily for three days before the midcycle day.

[31] Edmund J. Farris, *Human Ovulation and Fertility* (Philadelphia: J. B. Lippincott Co., 1956).
[32] *Ibid.*

As a means of birth control, the "safe period" is the only means approved by the Catholic Church, and even this method is approved with reservations by some of the Church leaders. For limiting offspring it is highly ineffective (see data below).

A careful mathematical analysis of the reliability of the "safe period" has been made by André J. DeBethune. He finds that even if the fertile period is no longer than 12 hours, a couple who wish to space children two years apart are limited statistically to two acts of coitus per mentrual cycle. Those who expect to space children by four years are limited to one act of coitus per cycle. His data and his logic are most convincing. He concluded his analysis with the observation, "It is not surprising that the rhythm method has become a source of mental torture to many couples."[33]

A Rating of Birth Control Methods

Time,[34] reporting particularly on the latest intrauterine devices for contraception, places these devices on a parallel with the pill in effectiveness. (The risk is that they may slip out of the uterus. A tail is now attached to some of the devices so the woman can check. The risk with the pill is that they may not be taken regularly.) *Time* concludes that:

If 100 wives use:	Number of pregnancies per year
nothing	90
rhythm	40
diaphram and condom	2 to 20
intrauterine devices	1
pill	1

Sterilization for Family Limitation

Vasectomy involves the tying off and cutting of the vas deferens, an operation of approximately seven minutes duration, involving an incision into the scrotum. Usually the male can return to work and renew sexual intercourse within a day or so after the operation. Ligation or salpingotomy involves opening the abdominal cavity of the female to tie and cut the Fallopian tubes. Since this involves surgery of considerable seriousness, it is usually not used in this country except when the

---

[33] André J. DeBethune "Child Spacing: the Mathematical Probabilities," *Science,* 142:1629-1634, December 27, 1963.
[34] *Time,* July 31, 1964, pp. 48-49.

abdominal cavity is opened for other reasons or when serious medical reasons exist. In Catholic countries like Puerto Rico, it has been used extensively by women, who usually give as their reason, "one confession is sufficient," whereas with birth control, repeated confessions are necessary.

Vasectomy is being promoted by the government of India as one of the principal means of population control, some states giving a payment to the male submitting to the operation, and some also a reward payment to the recruiter. By March, 1964, some half million persons had been sterilized there in public clinics alone. Although this method of family limitation has not been widely used in the United States, its use is greatly on the increase. Neither vasectomy or ligation are illegal in the United States, and the male operation is so economical in terms of discomfort and cost (as low as $50) that it offers a final solution to the problem of unwanted pregnancies for couples choosing to use it. The Association for Voluntary Sterilization is promoting voluntary sterilization throughout the world and has estimated that over 110,000 sterilizations take place within the United States annually.

Some recent studies have given answers to some of the physical, psychosocial, and marital implications of the operation. Landis and Poffenberger[35] studied 2,007 vasectomy records of physicians and obtained follow-up questionnaires from 330 of the men. Most couples appraised the results as beneficial to their sexual life and to their marriage; almost none regretted it. Greater frequency of sexual intercourse was reported by most couples. The principal motive for the couple's joint decision to have the operation was their desire to fix the size of their families, even though most of the couples did not have large families. They had small families and wanted to keep them that way.

In considering this form of family limitation, the young couple with a small family is taking one risk which is not common to other forms of birth control. The operation on neither the male nor female is easily reversible. They must reckon with the likelihood that no matter how badly they may want children in the future, or in a future marriage, they will be unable to do so. In many cases the tubes can be repaired and fertility restored. Various studies of small samples report varying results. And it is likely that ways to tie off the tubes of both male and female may be found which will make correction possible in a large proportion of cases. But at present, couples should view this method as having a high degree of finality.

For couples who are sure they have arrived at the family size they

[35] Judson T. Landis and Thomas Poffenberger, "Population Control—The Vasectomy," a paper read before the annual meeting of the American Sociological Society, Los Angeles, California, August 29, 1963.

wish, sterilization offers an easy solution to their problem. As a device for national policy in population control among impoverished urban groups and in isolated pockets of rural poverty, this method offers great hope if it should receive adequate backing and promotion. In the summer of 1964, The Association for Voluntary Sterilization began a pilot project for the Kentucky mountain region, for which funds had been donated by a New York businessman to pay for 300 sterilizations. Other projects were planned for selected Florida counties.

Abortion

Throughout countries where birth control is extensively practiced, particularly where groups promoting it are legally permitted to operate, as in the Scandinavian countries, Holland (in Holland the Society for Anticonception was initiated more than seventy-five years ago), and in many parts of the United States, effective contraception is considered a deterrent to abortion.[36]

From a social and health standpoint, contraception is much less costly than induced abortion. Nevertheless, abortion is a major problem in the United States and is much more common among the married than among the unmarried.

Of all the pregnancies among married women studied by the Kinsey group, only 66 percent resulted in birth of the child; 17 percent ended in miscarriage; 17 percent, in induced abortions.[37] Their data show that the most frequent patron of the abortionist, then, is not the unmarried girl, nor the widow or divorcée, but the wife. The younger the wife, the higher the proportion of miscarriages and of abortions. Women who start having abortions under twenty also tend to have abortions later. A married woman under 20 who has an induced abortion will have an average of 2.4 abortions in her married lifetime, according to these research data. The lower they are on the socioeconomic ladder, the greater the abortion rate by wives.

Devoutness in religion is inversely related to the abortion rate. The devout have few abortions; those who lack devoutness have relatively more.

There is something hopeful in these data, if generations are compared. Young wives are having fewer induced abortions than did their mothers. In fact, since the depression years of the 1930's, abortions have been on the decline. The researchers conclude that young wives today

---

36 *Social Sweden* (Stockholm: Social Welfare Board, 1953), pp. 320 ff., also *The National League for Sex Education* (Stockholm, 1949).

37 Paul H. Gebhard and others, *Pregnancy, Birth and Abortion* (New York: Harper & Bros. and Paul B. Hoeber, Inc., 1958).

are more eager for motherhood than any wives this nation has seen in years. They are not afraid of pregnancy; they have less to do with the abortionist than the preceding generation.

Another factor must, however, be taken into account. Contraception has become more widely known and more effective over the years shown in this study. Effective contraception is without doubt the most effective preventive for abortion. Sweden considers it so.[38] In Japan, where abortion rates have been unusually high and effective in holding down population growth, promotion of contraception is now considered the method for reducing abortion.

PREGNANCIES IN MARRIAGE TERMINATED BY INDUCED ABORTION*

Year†	Percent
1925	23.6
1930	24.3
1935	18.3
1940	13.5
1945	12.3
1950	10.4

* *Source:* Paul H. Gebhard and others, *Pregnancy, Birth and Abortion* (New York: Harper & Bros. and Paul B. Hoeber, Inc., 1958), p. 205.
† Year given is mid-point of decade

Induced abortion, except for medical reasons (to save the life of the mother), is illegal in the United States. The only way an abortion can be obtained for any other reason either by the unmarried or married, is to patronize a practitioner who operates in secret and who must always operate outside hospitals. This greatly increases the risk. It is an important factor in producing sterility. The psychological risks are, however, the greater ones (see Table 28-2).

We have already suggested that a high percentage of abortions among the unmarried are performed on women who are not pregnant. Frequently women who have been divorced or separated from their husbands also cease menstruation due to nervous tension and anxiety and immediately fear they are pregnant. These women are also easy victims for the abortionist, as are married women who fear pregnancy and who fail to go to a reliable physician for a pregnancy test before visiting an abortionist.

A very simple test is used to determine pregnancy now which gives a conclusive answer in one hour.

38 *Social Sweden* (Stockholm: Social Welfare Board, 1953).

Child Spacing

The problem of spacing children is one which must depend largely upon the couple's own desires. An early study of maternal and child development by Dr. R. W. Woodbury, in 1915, recommended that children be spaced at least two years apart for the sake of the health of the mother. More recent research and medical opinion suggests that the nearer the children can be spaced, the better for the health of the mother.

This new view is based on the fact that, beyond age twenty, child-bearing becomes slightly more difficult each year. By spacing children close together, the wife can complete her family during the years when childbirth is easiest. The short nursing period of today makes such a schedule of childbearing practical from the standpoint of nursing the child.

From the standpoint of social development of children, also, there is something to be said in favor of having children as close together as possible. It provides a play group of similar ages in the home. Of course, it takes a sturdy mother to effectively handle and care for two or three very small children at the same time, particularly if the family does not have the financial resources to hire help with housework and child care.

Coitus During Pregnancy

There is much folklore about the possibility or impossibility of sexual intercourse during pregnancy. Actually, pregnancy usually does not reduce interest in sexual intercourse until the later phases. In fact, the wife's desire may actually increase during the early stages of pregnancy. During the final stages, particularly the last two weeks to a month, when the neck of the uterus is likely to be somewhat open and the nearly full-grown embryo may be expanding the uterus down into the vaginal canal, intercourse is not wise, at least intercourse by deep penetration of the vagina (see Figure 28-1).

The folk belief that having sexual intercourse during pregnancy will make the child oversexed is strictly myth, as is also the notion that intercourse will make the delivery easier.

After childbirth, intercourse may begin as soon as the wife feels ready for it. Unless there has been surgical damage, she is usually ready in three to six weeks. The need for contraception by those who wish to space children will be greater after pregnancy than before. Because of the dilation of the cervix a new pregnancy is often very easy following childbirth. The myth that a nursing mother cannot become pregnant has no basis in fact.

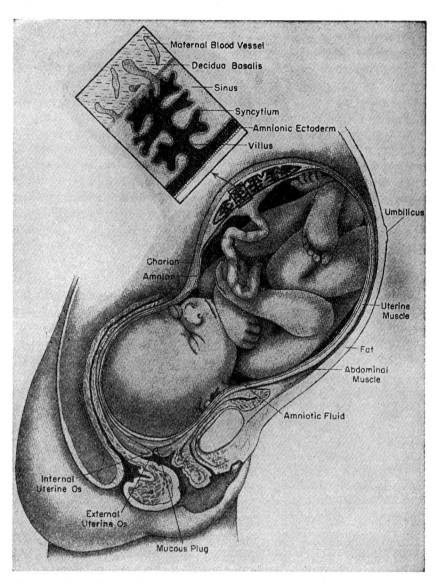

Labels on figure:
Maternal Blood Vessel
Decidua Basalis
Sinus
Syncytium
Amnionic Ectoderm
Villus
Umbilicus
Chorion
Amnion
Uterine Muscle
Fat
Abdominal Muscle
Amniotic Fluid
Internal Uterine Os
External Uterine Os
Mucous Plug

Source: C. L. Anderson, *Physical and Emotional Aspects of Marriage* (St. Louis: C. V. Mosby Co., 1953). Reproduced by permission of the publisher and Dr. Anderson.

FIGURE 28-1———Fetus just prior to birth. The magnified section shows the sinuses in which the mother's blood circulates. Only the thick lining of the sinuses separates the maternal blood stream from that of the fetus.

TABLE 28-2————Unfavorable consequences of illegal operative abortion reported by white nonprison females and males by marital status at event*

| Unfavorable consequences | FEMALE REPORT | | | | MALE REPORT |
	Pre-marital (percent)	Marital (percent)	Post-marital (percent)	Total (percent)	Total (percent)
None	67.7	81.8	78.4	74.2	86.6
Mild physical	4.1	2.0	2.7	3.2	3.2
Moderate physical	7.7	5.4	6.8	6.8	2.5
Severe physical	6.4	6.8	6.8	6.6	2.8
Psychological	13.6	4.1	5.4	9.0	4.2
Social	3.6	0	0	1.8	1.1
Legal	0	0	0	0	0
Total	103.1	100.1	100.1	101.6	100.0
Number abortions, consequences known	220	148	74	442	283
Number abortions, consequences unknown	92	363	36	491	406

* *Source:* Paul H. Gebhard and others, *Pregnancy, Birth and Abortion* (New York: Harper & Bros. and Paul B. Hoeber, Inc., 1958), p. 205.

Psychological Adjustments to Pregnancy

Folklore and old wives' tales persist in giving the young wife a picture of what pregnancy may be expected to be. The symptoms are so familiar that the woman who does not have her morning nausea, often accompanied by vomiting and symptoms of dizziness, considers herself almost abnormal. The motion picture has perpetuated folklore by having the young husband act most solicitously of her well-being when the young wife announces that they are going to have a baby.

The particular symptoms of pregnancy are, in part, a matter of custom and culture. This is well demonstrated in Margaret Mead's analysis of the extent of nausea that exists among women in various cultures.[39] In cultures where the nausea feeling is considered the universal experience of pregnant women, practically all women have it; in societies which ignore the phenomenon, nausea is rare, although it may be felt by some women. She explains this by the fact that nausea and even vomiting, are biological capacities of the organism, but that a culture may elaborate

[39] Margaret Mead, in A. M. Krich (Editor), *Women: The Variety and Meaning of Their Sexual Experience* (New York: Dell Publishing Co., Inc., 1954).

these to the point where they become important and customary. Or the culture may neglect, ignore, or even frown on such reactions so that they are not so frequently in the consciousness of the pregnant woman.

She also finds that cultural expectations very much affect the reaction of the woman to the menstrual period. In some cultures where pain is glorified, women may almost all feel severe symptoms during the menstrual period. In cultures where menstrual pain is ignored, the woman may simply rub her body with stinging nettles to obscure a real feeling of menstrual pain and go about her day, attempting to ignore it completely.

One sees in the recent trend of American history a tendency to ignore the symptoms of both pregnancy and menstruation. In an earlier day, when the delicate woman was worshiped in the culture, it was assumed that women would play the delicate part. The attention-getting device of morning sickness and of menstrual pain was a considerable asset in the social situation.

This is not to deny that pain may exist in both situations—it does often exist. But it is evident that during recent years both types of pain have either been greatly on the decrease or else greater absence of fear and the pleasures of active participation in the stream of life by the pregnant woman or the menstruating woman have made these traditional pains less evident. Certainly a part of the change is a change in taboos, because practically all of the things that women were not supposed to do in previous generations during menstruation or pregnancy are now done by the average woman. The penalties the old wives' tales held to be the consequences for such action have not been visited upon women of this generation. No doubt certain new inventions, like Kotex and Tampax, have been in part responsible for the changed role of women during menstruation, but certainly the basic change has been that in attitudes and taboos.

Some women do have nausea and vomiting and a great deal of discomfort during pregnancy. A few are even confined to bed for considerable periods of time in order to avoid miscarriage. For many healthy young women, however, none of these symptoms appear at all. In fact, a woman is more likely than not to feel better during pregnancy than at any other time. This may be due to the release of certain hormones which prepare the uterus, particularly, but the entire physiological system to some extent, for handling the fetus.

Sex Life During Pregnancy

Judson T. Landis and co-workers at the University of California, asked a group of 212 wives who had completed their first pregnancy the question, "What effect, if any, did pregnancy have upon your sexual adjustment?"[40] Husbands and wives generally agreed as to the answer. Their answers were:

Effect	Husbands (percent)	Wives (percent)
No effect	58	58
Unfavorable	28	25
Favorable	19	17

Of those who indicated that the effect had been favorable, most had had poor sexual adjustment previous to conception. Of those who reported an unfavorable effect, a considerable proportion had had a good adjustment before pregnancy.

In general, husbands and wives reported a decrease in sexual desire with the duration of the pregnancy. Toward the end of the pregnancy, many women were found to lose interest in sexual contact, or found it painful. Others quit because of doctors' advice for fear of hurting the baby.

A significant effect of pregnancy is the decreasing of the husband's desire. About 10 percent felt "it didn't seem right" or that they didn't enjoy intercourse. Almost all the wives felt that their husbands were more considerate of them and exhibited more sensitivity concerning their feelings during the pregnancy than before.

Childbirth

Childbirth is another field in which much has been done to banish superstition and needless fear. One of the most influential factors has been the publication by the late Grantly Dick Read of his world-famous book, *Childbirth Without Fear*. This book's spontaneous acceptance by modern women, who had been reared on the old wives' tales of childbirth in painful travail, has been one of the marvels of changing family life in the postwar generation. Young mothers, particularly, have approached doctors and hospitals with requests for childbirth following this procedure. Classes teaching women the way to cooperate with nature have become popular, and the entire birth process has come to be looked upon as a challenge rather than something to be dreaded.

Dr. Read, in 1953, to see how his theories worked out in a state of nature, carried his research on childbirth into Africa. In a new book, *No Time For Fear*, he reports that among Bushmen, Basutos, Hottentots, and Masai, from 95 to 98 percent go through childbirth with no pain.

[40] Judson T. Landis, Thomas Poffenberger, and Shirley Poffenberger, "The Effects of First Pregnancy Upon the Sexual Adjustment of 212 Couples," *American Sociological Review*, 15:766-772, December, 1950.

Confirming evidence that fear is an inhibiting factor in the birth process and induces pain was discovered among adulterous women, some of whom struggled in painful labor two or three days. Dr. Read reports that when persuaded to confess their adultery, they would suddenly relax and release the child.

The essence of the Read philosophy is that the mother approach childbirth in pleasant anticipation and without fear. She is expected to understand natural muscle reactions that take place during childbirth and to take certain exercises which make it possible for her to cooperate with nature. Read believed from his experience with women in childbirth that too many modern women, fearing the process and considering it an ordeal, tensed themselves with fear and fought the natural muscle spasms, thus making childbirth much more difficult than nature intended.

This view of childbirth represents a remarkable step forward in the removal of psychological inhibitions from womanhood—in correcting the age-long traditions and taboos that are centered about the weaknesses, frailties, pains, and miseries of woman. From time immemorial, among the literate portion of mankind, childbirth has been looked upon as one of woman's great tortures. Childbirth has been called travail, which means painful—excruciating, racking pain. Old wives' tales have elaborated this pain in teaching the young girl about her function as a mother. The entire psychological preparation has been to condition the expectant mother for this excruciating ordeal.

Women in the community have acquired status by telling their friends, and this often in the presence of young girls, how "hard" a particular birth was. In rural folklore, it has been a competitive game to be able to endure a particularly painful, long, and trying first childbirth. Let no one doubt that these pains were actually suffered. One who is prepared psychologically to fear an experience can often realize very great pain, even though a substantial part of it may be imaginary, just as one can get scared badly in an isolated lonely house or graveyard, hear all kinds of fantastic sounds and even see ghosts, if he has adequate psychological preparation.

The Read theory of natural childbirth proposed the thesis that childbirth can, when intellectual, physical, and emotional preparation is adequate, be a highly satisfactory and rewarding experience, one of the finest experiences that comes to a woman. He proposed that prospective mothers attend classes and be prepared psychologically for childbirth, that they develop a mind-set which would make childbirth the normal event which nature intended. Women thus prepared for childbirth experience it without fear and go through delivery with comparatively little pain.

The psychological and emotional effects of this approach to childbirth have been revolutionary.[41] The nonanesthetized mother is allowed the emotional joy of knowing when the baby comes from her body. She hears its first cry. She may watch the doctor cut the umbilical cord.

In this modern theory of childbirth, the father is often a participant in welcoming the child into the world and in sharing the mother's joy. He may have attended classes for expectant fathers and been psychologically prepared for the experience of fatherhood. He may have been taught to diaper a baby and to give it a bath, as well as some of the fundamental principles of parental psychology.

The mere fact that the expectant mother and the expectant father participate in a group looking forward to the same event intensifies their interest in parenthood, and gives them the information which makes the experience a welcome one rather than one of awkwardness and fear. Instead of being guided entirely by folklore passed on largely within the family, they are guided by the best scientific knowledge of child care and child psychology. Instead of feeling that childbirth is more or less an accident for which they feel half shameful, they look forward to parenthood with pride and satisfaction.

Such psychological preparation is supremely important to parenthood today when there are so many conflicting aspirations to make both prospective parents rather dread the experience of parenthood. It may help the new parents to realize that the psychological and emotional values of parenthood outweigh those of monetary achievement or other ambitions, goals, and aspirations which the culture prizes so highly.

Hospital experience where natural childbirth and where preparation for childbirth are standard procedures give convincing evidence that these procedures reduce the tension of labor, shorten labor, and in general make for a more favorable total childbirth situation.[42]

The "Birthsuit"

The most revolutionary development in the childbirth field is that centering around a pressurized birthsuit. Professor O. S. Heyns at the University of Witwatersrand, South Africa, has been using the suit for some years to reduce the pain of labor and to minimize risks of complication of mother and child.[43]

41 For an excellent discussion of the significance of this movement and also for contrasting case histories of women who approach childbirth with fear and women who approach it after adequate education, see Frederick W. Goodrich, Jr., "Natural Childbirth," in A. M. Krich (Editor), op. cit., pp. 149-170.

42 See Herbert Thoms and Robert H. Wyatt, "One Thousand Consecutive Deliveries Under a Training for Childbirth Program," American Journal of Obstetrics and Gynecology, 61:205-209, January, 1951; also Herbert Thoms, Training for Childbirth (New York: McGraw-Hill Book Co., 1950).

43 Ora Mendels, "A Revolution in Childbirth?" Ladies Home Journal, Winter, 1963, p. 40.

The mother sits in the suit with her arms free. She can regulate the pressure in the suit. Regulation of pressure keeps the uterus in a normal position, avoiding the painful muscle spasm in the uterus. Painful labor, shock, and mental distress are eliminated. Reports say that 90 percent of women who used it got relief from labor pains or eliminated them completely. Labor time has been cut by half in most instances. Chances of brain damage, cerebral palsy, and mental deficiency in, or stillbirth of the child are greatly reduced. It is estimated that fetal distress is cut 80 percent.

The most amazing aspect of the method is that babies are superior in tone and behavior from the beginning. Researchers feel that the level of mental ability is substantially increased in that there is no longer damaging oxygen deprivation during birth. Use of the pressure suit keeps up the free flow of blood to the fetus, thus keeping up the oxygen supply. It is even recommended that the suit be used for half-hour daily periods during the latter stages of pregnancy to increase the oxygen saturation of fetal blood.

These beginnings would seem to promise something revolutionary in the fields of technological improvement over nature in childbirth.

The Hospital Situation

Along with the Read plan for childbirth another movement of great significance has developed, that of rooming-in, or the Cornelian Corner in Detroit. With the development of the modern hospital, the practice of partially isolating the infant from the mother during the period of her stay in the hospital had become more or less customary. Now, rooming-in, or the Cornelian Corner, provides that the child be placed with the mother a great deal during her period in the hospital; that she nestle and cuddle it, give it affection, and nurse it. It is believed that the basis is laid here for a more secure personality, in addition to the satisfaction and comfort given to both mother and child.

The conditions of childbirth itself change to some extent with changing social outlooks. It is possible in some hospitals now to have the husband present in the delivery room at birth. This trend has been speeded by the exposure of occasional mistreatment of women in the delivery room of hospitals. Many mothers have been critical of the cold and inhospitable atmosphere, feeling that nurses and doctors considered them a nuisance because they were not sick persons.[44]

There has developed, too, the idea that infant care should follow a natural rather than a rigorously controlled schedule, such as was so cus-

[44] "Cruelty in the Maternity Hospital," *Ladies Home Journal*, November, 1957; May, 1958.

tomary in child rearing a decade ago. It is now believed that the baby's cries are true indications of his needs ("demand feeding") and that his expressed needs should determine the adult's routine in handling him— rather than routine being placed first and the new-born infant being made to fit it. Early toilet training is condemned, along with punishment for delinquencies in toilet functions at any age.

Armed with the latest reliable information in this area, couples today enter the period of child rearing with much less anxiety and much greater assurance than was customary in an earlier day.

Problems

1. Few couples consider it necessary to have more than the conventional physical examination prior to marriage. Under what circumstances would an analysis of one's physical heredity seem warranted?
2. A happily married couple who want children have failed to have any by the end of their third year of marriage. Which of the following courses of action would you advise, and why?
   a. Consult a marriage counselor.
   b. Consult a psychiatrist.
   c. Consult a doctor.
   d. Consider adoption.
   e. Concentrate on keeping their marriage a happy one in spite of their failure.
3. *Sociodrama:* A young woman whose husband is sterile seeks the counsel of her doctor (this doctor may be either male or female) on whether and how she and her husband may have a family. Through a question-and-answer type discussion the two of them consider the advantages and disadvantages (physical, psychological, etc.) of such alternatives as: (a) adoption, (b) artificial insemination, (c) remaining childless.
4. What do we know about the effect of prenatal conditions on a child? For example:
   a. Can a child be physically "marked" as a result of traumatic experiences happening to its mother during pregnancy?
   b. Can a child be physically affected by certain physical conditions of its mother during pregnancy?
   c. Can a child be psychologically affected as a result of traumatic experiences happening to its mother during pregnancy?
5. Is there any way in which an individual can increase his or her chances of bearing twins in marriage?
6. What are the various common techniques for controlling pregnancy? Which method seems to be the most effective? Are any of them 100 percent effective? What are the psychological advantages and disadvantages of birth-control devices?

7. Giving birth out of wedlock to an unwanted child can bring tragedy to many people: to the couple whose life plans must be changed, to the infant who is unwanted, and to the families of the girl and boy involved. Why then is abortion unlawful? Are there any circumstances under which abortion is legal? Do you think the grounds for legal abortion should be broadened?

8. *Sociodrama:* A young mother whose children are one and three years old respectively is sorry that she followed the advice of her pediatrician in spacing her children. Her old sister whose two children are now six and eight defends the pediatrician's advice. Show how both have good arguments for their positions.

9. In what way is our culture, rather than nature, responsible for many of the pains and problems of pregnancy and childbirth?

10. Describe the physical and psychological arguments in favor of the "rooming-in" maternity wards that are now increasing in American hospitals.

Selected References

ARTICLES IN BOOKS OF READINGS

FISHBEIN, Morris, and KENNEDY, Ruby Jo Reeves, *Modern Marriage and Family Living* (New York: Oxford University Press, 1957).

1. SPENCER, Warren P., "Heredity: Facts and Fallacies," pp. 341-356.
2. DAVIS, M. Edward, "Ovulation and Fertility," pp. 357-367.
3. NELSON, Janet Fowler, "Preparing For A Baby," pp. 368-377.
4. POTTER, Edith L., "Pregnancy," pp. 378-386.
5. GREENHILL, J. P., "The Birth of the Baby," pp. 387-400.
6. GUTTMACHER, Alan F., "Abortions," pp. 401-413.
7. BROOKS, Lee M., and BROOKS, Evelyn C., "Adoption: Some Legal and Social Procedures," pp. 442-456.

KLING, Samuel G., and KLING, Esther B., *The Marriage Reader* (New York: Vanguard Press, Inc., 1947).

8. STONE, Hannah M., and STONE, Abraham, "Health in Marriage," pp. 247-269.
9. POPENOE, Paul, "The Truth About Sterility," pp. 303-310.

LANDIS, Judson T., and LANDIS, Mary G., *Readings in Marriage and the Family* (Englewood Cliffs, N. J.: Prentice-Hall, Inc., 1952).

10. STERN, Curt, "The Rh Blood Factors," pp. 221-227.
11. LANDIS, Judson T., POFFENBERGER, Thomas, and POFFENBERGER, Shirley, "Effects of First Pregnancy on Sex Adjustments," pp. 228-234.
12. GREENBERG, Joseph H., "Artificial Insemination," pp. 234-237.
13. ROPER, Elmo, "Birth Control, The Fortune Survey," pp. 247-248.
14. BARTEMEIER, Leo H., "The Practical Application of Basic Mental Hygiene Principles by the Cornelian Corner," pp. 257-260.
15. LEVY, David M., "Maternal Over-Protection and Rejection," pp. 269-274.

BECKER, Howard, and HILL, Reuben (Editors), *Family, Marriage and Parenthood,* Second Edition (Boston: D. C. Heath & Co., 1955).

   16. GORDON, Edgar S., "Taking Physical Factors into Account," pp. 305-340.

   17. OWEN, Ray D., "Heredity and the Family," pp. 421-438.

   18. GENTRY, Elizabeth, "Caring for Mother and Child Before and After," pp. 439-453.

KRICH, A. M. (Editor), *Women: the Variety and Meaning of Their Sexual Experience* (New York: Dell Publishing Co., Inc., 1954).

   19. GOODRICH, Frederick W., Jr. "Natural Childbirth," pp. 149-170.

WINCH, Robert F., and others, *Selected Studies in Marriage and the Family,* Revised Edition (New York: Holt, Rinehart & Winston, Inc., 1962).

   20. FERREIRA, Antonio J., "The Pregnant Woman's Emotional Attitude and Its Reflection on the Newborn," pp. 203-212.

KRICH, A. M. (Editor), *Men: The Variety and Meaning of Their Sexual Experience* (New York: Dell Publishing Co., Inc., 1954).

   21. MARSHALL, F. H. A., "Physiology of Reproduction," Ch. 6.

CAVAN, Ruth Shonle, *Marriage and the Family in the Modern World: A Book of Readings* (New York: Thomas Y. Crowell Co., 1960).

   22. PULFORD, G. S., "The Rh Factor," Reading 74.

   23. MACE, David R., "Should You Have a Baby the First Year?" Reading 77.

General References

ANDERSON, Ray C., "The Influence of Heredity on Family Health," *Marriage and Family Living,* 19:136-141, May, 1957.

ASHLEY-MONTAGU, M. F., and SCHWEITZER, Gertrude, "There Is Prenatal Influence," *Ladies Home Journal,* 71:43 ff., February, 1954.

BOWMAN, Henry A., *Marriage for Moderns,* Fourth Edition (New York: McGraw-Hill Book Co., 1960), Ch. 13.

CAVAN, Ruth Shonle, *American Marriage* (New York: Thomas Y. Crowell Co., 1959), Ch. 19 by David M. FULCOMER, and Ch. 20 by Ida M. BRECHTEL.

"Cruelty in the Maternity Hospital," *Ladies Home Journal,* November, 1957; May, 1958.

"Family Planning in Modern Societies," symposium, *Marriage and Family Living,* Vol. 25, February, 1963. This issue covers family-planning practices in various countries of the world.

FARRIS, Edmund J., *Human Ovulation and Fertility* (Philadelphia: J. B. Lippincott Co., 1956).

FREEDMAN, Ronald, and others, *Family Planning, Sterility and Population Growth* (New York: McGraw-Hill Book Co., 1959).

GEBHARD, Paul H., and others, *Pregnancy, Birth and Abortion* (New York: Harper Bros. & Paul B. Hoeber, Inc., 1958).

GILBERT, Margaret Shea, *Biography of the Unborn* (Baltimore: The Williams & Wilkins Co., 1938).

GUTTMACHER, Alan F., *Birth Control* (New York: Ballantine Books, Inc., 1961), paperback.

————, *New Facts about Birth Control* (New York: Public Affairs Pamphlets).

HERNDON, C. Nash, "Medical Genetics and Marriage Counseling," *Marriage and Family Living,* 16:207-210, August, 1954.

HILL, Reuben, and others, *The Family and Population Control* (Chapel Hill: University of North Carolina Press, 1959).

KROEGER, William S., "Influence of Prenatal Maternal Anxiety on Emotionality of Young Rats," *Science,* 125:698, April 12, 1957.

LANDIS, Judson T., POFFENBERGER, Thomas, and POFFENBERGER, Shirley, "The Effects of First Pregnancy Upon the Sexual Adjustment of 212 Couples," *American Sociological Review,* 15:767-772, December, 1950.

LANDIS, Paul H., *Population Problems,* Revised Edition (New York: American Book Co., 1954).

LEMASTERS, E. E., *Modern Courtship and Marriage* (New York: The Macmillan Co., 1957), Ch. 24.

MEAD, MARGARET, *Male and Female* (New York: William Morrow & Co., Inc., 1949), Ch. 11.

POFFENBERGER, Shirley, POFFENBERGER, Thomas, and LANDIS, Judson T., "Intent Toward Conception and Pregnancy Experience," *American Sociological Review,* 17:616-620, October, 1952.

————, "Vasectomy as a Preferred Method of Birth Control," *Marriage and Family Living,* 25:326-330, August, 1963.

READ, Grantley Dick, *Childbirth Without Fear* (New York: Harper & Bros., 1944).

ROGERS, David A., and others, "Sociophysiological Characteristics of Patients Obtaining Vasectomies from Urologists," *Marriage and Family Living,* 25:331-335, August, 1963.

SCHEINFELD, Amram, *The Basic Facts of Human Heredity* (New York: Washington Square Press, Inc., 1961), paperback.

SCHELLEN, A. M. C. M., *Artificial Insemination in the Human* (Princeton: Elsevier Press, Inc., 1957).

SCHULTZ, Gladys D., "The Uninsulated Child," *Ladies Home Journal,* June, 1956, pp. 61-62.

SHEEHAN, Robert, "The Birth-Control Pill," *Fortune,* April, 1958, p. 154 ff.

Social Sweden (Stockholm: Social Welfare Board, 1953).

SPOCK, Benjamin, *The Pocketbook of Baby and Child Care* (New York: Pocket Books, Inc., 1946).

STERN, Curt, *Principles of Human Genetics* (San Francisco: W. H. Freeman & Co., Publishers, 1949).

STONE, Abraham, "World Conference on Human Infertility," *Marriage and Family Living,* 15:231-233, August, 1953.

VELLAY, Pierre, *Childbirth without Pain,* Translated from the French by Denise Lloyd (New York: E. P. Dutton & Co., Inc., 1960).

YOUNG, Leontine, *Out of Wedlock* (New York: McGraw-Hill Book Co, 1954).

29
Parenthood

In the United States the death rate is at an all-time low; it now takes less than 2.5 children per family to replace our population. Childbearing in such a culture has become an incidental function, immensely significant, but involving only a brief portion of the life span of the parents. The emphasis is on quality of nurture, the conditions of life, and the learning and development that can be offered. This is the challenge of parenthood today and it takes well-trained, mature couples who know far more than how to exercise their procreative functions. Unless a mother is much more than a mother, unless she lives broadly and builds her life into the activities of the community and uses her creative talent to improve the socioeconomic and political order, she does not meet the real challenge of motherhood in the broadest sense, nor does she meet the needs of her husband most fully and become a contented, happy person herself.

This may seem like an extreme statement and yet the boredom of modern women, their psychoneurotic ailments are of such immense proportion that we know there is great frustrations in the lives of a large number of urban women. It is a safe speculation that, for many of these women, the problem is that they have tied themselves down to a limited marriage-family routine only to find later on that their lives are filled with idleness and boredom, that they are frustrated and defeated. Such a woman picks on her husband, and criticizes him for the ego satisfactions he receives because her life by comparison seems poverty stricken.

There is no more futile philosophy in life than that which places motherhood above everything else, makes the woman a breeder, and makes breeding, generation after generation, woman's main function in life. Procreation demands most of a woman's energy under this futile philosophy, which is found in exaggerated form in India. What is the point in bringing new generations into the world only to produce more hungry children?

Parenthood is very much more an individual matter with us. It is not taken for granted as in the institutional family. In the small family, parents choose to have children and influence their destiny in a way never true of the joint-family system—in which there is the impact of many personalities. In the small family, parents create the emotional environment that surrounds the child. Their period of monopoly is short, however, and greater freedom follows, more freedom than young people have under other systems. This means that the parent must not only love, but must have an intelligent understanding of the world into which the child will move when he begins to venture out into secondary groups that are certain to present many problems of choice.

In past generations parenthood was looked upon as so natural and inevitable a part of life that it required little if any special training or preparation. There was also widespread acceptance of the belief that some special "instinct," particularly in women, could be counted upon to guide the young couple in caring for and rearing their children. Current scientific views have discarded the notion of a maternal instinct. Being a successful parent is now considered an art and a science, rather than a matter of chance.

No single relationship in life has greater and more lasting significance than that between parent and child. The connection is more than one of blood; there are deep ties of emotion and lasting marks of influence that affect both throughout their lives. No experience can cause so much growth in one's own personality as that of parenthood, and certainly no single circumstance in the life of the child is so fateful as his relationship with his parents. Ashley-Montagu[1] sees the development of every human being as a loving person who is capable of realizing himself in cooperative relationships with others as the great challenge to our society and especially to motherhood.

What are the basic issues of parenthood? What questions must young people face in preparing themselves for the lifelong effects of the assumption of the responsibilities of parenthood?

The following chapters do not pretend to substitute for a course in child development, nor can they summarize all of the significant information young couples should consider. They are designed, rather, to point up a few of the basic issues and to give some insight into problems of parenthood in the modern world.

1 M.F. Ashley-Montagu, *Education and Human Relations* (New York: Grove Press, Inc., 1958).

Is Parenthood Necessary to Marital Happiness?

Happy couples who want no children have been found to be the exception rather than the rule. A study[2] of over 500 married couples showed that a desire for children is very closely associated with successful adjustments in marriage (see Figure 29-1).

DESIRE FOR CHILDREN AND MARITAL ADJUSTMENT

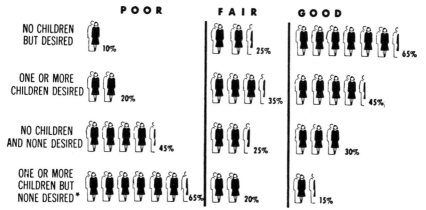

* Not desired by husband, or wife, or both.

SOURCE: Based on the data from Ernest W. Burgess and Leonard S. Cottrell, *Predicting Success or Failure in Marriage* (Copyright, 1939, by Prentice-Hall, Inc., New York). Reproduced by permission of the publisher.

FIGURE 29-1————Results are for 526 middle-class couples.

It will be seen that poor adjustments were few among couples who had no children but who wanted children. Good adjustments were high among this group. The group which had one or more children and desired them, also showed a high percent of good adjustments. But those who had children that were not desired showed the greatest proportion of poor adjustments, and very few of these couples showed good adjustment.

This study, like others, shows that it is not necessary that children be born to the marriage, but that the attitude of the couple must be favorable to them if the marriage is to have high prospects of success.

[2] Ernest W. Burgess and Leonard S. Cottrell, *Predicting Success or Failure in Marriage* (Englewood Cliffs, N. J.: Prentice-Hall, Inc., 1939).

America has perhaps passed the period when any substantial number of women hope to live without plans for children in their life. The feminist movement of the early part of the century and the quick emancipation of women from domestic life, led many female rebels to cherish a life of independence and one free from the responsibilities of children. Fifty years ago scarcely half of American women who were college graduates married, and the birth rate among college women who did marry was very low.

Marriage has more recently become the style even among the college group. This is partly because more women are going to college and partly because college is considered a proper preparation for marriage. In the past, it was more or less a disgrace for a college woman to marry. It was assumed that she was wasting her education if she settled for marriage after having spent four years in college.

During and following World War II, veterans, many of whom were married and had children, began flooding American college campuses. The old myth about the scholar being a voluntary eunuch in a cloistered cell largely disappeared from the American mind. College campuses became accustomed to fathers and mothers attending the same classes while another veteran's wife, who was not in school, acted as baby-sitter.

The place of children in the values of a people, the place they occupy in their social institutions, the way they are treated, and the way their personalities are formed are perhaps the most significant indices of a people's, and a particular person's, scheme of values. It may well be that in the new generation there are fewer unwanted children than in earlier decades because of the higher value placed on children and because parenthood is more often voluntary rather than the result of biological accident.

Is Parenthood a Cure for Unsuccessful Marriage?

Well-meaning people sometimes advise couples who are in difficulty in their marriage to have a baby, assuring them that this will likely make their marriage a success. There is no scientific opinion to support this view, and the risks of bringing a child into a situation of tension are great indeed. Research and clinical observations indicate that a home in which there is severe tension between parents is the worst possible situation in which a child can be placed. Prenatal damage may result.[3] The additional work and worry accompanying the birth of a child is more likely to add problems to the already difficult situation.

Much research, too, has shown that there is a close relationship be-

[3] See pp. 575-576.

tween the happiness of the parental home and the happiness of the child.[4] Unhappily wed people usually have a negative attitude toward children, which may account in part for the failure of children in such homes to obtain happiness. Unhappiness as a parental attitude frequently leads to a lack of harmony in the parent-child relationship also.[5]

Differentials in the divorce rate of couples with and without children are not as great as folklore holds. Although divorce is more frequent among the childless in the early years of marriage, there is no difference in the rate after thirteen years of marriage. Even the differences in rates which exist in the early years of marriage are probably not explained by the presence or absence of children as such.[6]

Young couples who find they are not happy will seldom become so simply by having children. If they cannot work out techniques of adjustment during the relatively simple childless period of family life, there is little likelihood that they will be able to face the complicated adjustments that are involved as the family grows.

The only circumstance under which the birth of a child could be expected to save a failing marriage is that in which childlessness itself is at the root of the marital discord. When an otherwise compatible couple begin to find life meaningless and empty, but feel, for example, that they cannot yet afford the children they both want, they must frequently reexamine their values and ambitions in order to save their marriage. As one counselor advised a group of newlyweds, "Young couples who are determined to get somewhere in this world will probably never feel that they have reached the place where they can afford children. At some point they must merely decide to compromise ambition for the sake of their own happiness."

All the evidence points up the conclusion that only those couples who genuinely want children should have them, and that only those couples who are well adjusted in marriage should plan to have children.

Timing Parenthood

A few years ago research among college students indicated a desire to delay children until the marriage was well established financially and in terms of companionability.[7] Today young couples seem to be more

[4] Burgess and Cottrell, *op. cit.;* also Lewis M. Terman and others, *Psychological Factors in Marital Happiness* (New York: McGraw-Hill Book Co., 1938).

[5] Paul Wallin and Howard M. Vollmer, "Marital Happiness of Parents and Their Children's Attitude Toward Them," *American Sociological Review,* 18:424-431, August, 1953.

[6] Paul H. Jacobson, "Differentials in Divorce by Duration of Marriage and Size of Family," *American Sociological Review,* 15:235-244, April, 1950.

[7] William S. Bernard, "Student Attitudes on Marriage and the Family," *American Sociological Review,* 3:354-361, 1938.

parent-minded early in marriage.[8] There is a desire "to have children while we are young enough to enjoy them," "to get the childbearing part of marriage over with early," and "to have the experience and see what it is like."

Actually, today, family building begins early in marriage for the average couple. Before they are married two years nearly one out of two couples have a child.[9] By the end of the fifth year, three-fourths have a child. For the average mother, childbearing is ended during the twenty-ninth year of age.

The question of the best time to start a family is one which is likely to trouble every young couple as they plan their life together. The question has no universal answer. There are, however, some general principles that can be mentioned. It is safer from the standpoint of the wife's health and life to have the first child while she is still in the twenties. With the low maternal death rates of today, however, one need not consider having a child somewhat later as being a serious risk. Life-conserving techniques improve from year to year. Financial considerations and the status of the couple's marital adjustment are more often the issues which need to be faced, rather than the health risk. Sterility, however, does increase with age.

What do we know about the effects of early childbearing upon happiness, adjustment, and economic well-being?

There is some evidence that having a child during the first year of marriage interferes somewhat with the happiness of the couple.[10] This would seem to agree with the popular opinion that the couple should be alone during the first year or so of their marriage and not have the interference of a third member. It is assumed that a period of adjustment to marriage and to the community is desirable before confinement. Marriage books and clinicians usually advise a delay of a year or two to permit time for adjustments in the marriage and in social and community relationship.

Some couples fear that the pregnancy and the child will in some measure interfere with their love life. Studies of marriage happiness show that the happiest years are those early in marriage before children come.[11] Old people looking back on life, however, indicate the years when the

8 Metropolitan Life Insurance Company, "Family Building in the Early Years of Marriage," *Statistical Bulletin*, 36:406, November, 1955.

9 *Ibid.*

10 *Ibid.*; see also Harold T. Christensen and Robert E. Philbrick, "Family Size as a Factor of Marital Adjustment of College Students," *American Sociological Review*, 17:306-312, June, 1952.

11 Burgess and Cottrell, *op. cit.*, pp. 246-248.

children were growing up in the family as their happiest in terms of total life satisfactions.[12]

Some of the early births are a result of marriages forced by pregnancy, which no doubt is a factor in discounting happiness. Evidence shows that the highest rate of failure in marriage is among those who become pregnant premaritally.[13] Happiness ratings for those who become pregnant early in the marriage are lower than for those who become pregnant after a year or more of marriage.

There are however arguments in favor of having a baby fairly early in the marriage provided the wife is physiologically mature.[14] The belief of some that children should be delayed in order to improve the conditions of the young couple's home is often not a reasonable one in terms of their past standards of living. Many young people now start marriage with a home in which a fairly high level of comfort has already been obtained. The longer the couple is together in a pair relationship, the greater the difficulty in breaking the established routine and the habits in order to make room for a third party.

The companionship marriage, which emphasizes the partnership role of husband and wife, is in fact the one most likely to suffer severe problems of readjustment of husband-wife relations. The more traditional family system had no place for marriages in which the role of wife was distinct from the roles of housekeeper and mother. Where a high level of companionship has been established by the couple in their marriage, the coming of the small child, with its rigorous demands on the mother and the requirement that the entire routine of the couple be disturbed, is often very serious.

One English statesman, in commenting on the problems of the contemporary family, observed that the main trouble with the modern companionship marriage is that couples get to be so companionable that they have no place for children in their lives. This foreboding has certainly not been justified in the United States. Having many children has been the trend. Margaret Mead[15] has criticized the young wife for wanting to be a

[12] Judson T. Landis, "Social-Psychological Factors of Aging," *Social Forces*, 20:468-470, May, 1942.

[13] Christensen has made extensive studies in this area. For representative results see Harold T. Christensen and Betty B. Rubenstein, "Premarital Pregnancy and Divorce: A Follow-up Study by the Interview Method," *Marriage and Family Living*, 8:114-123, May, 1956; see also Harold T. Christensen, "Child Spacing Analysis via Record Linkage," *Marriage and Family Living*, 25:272-280, August, 1963.

[14] See David R. Mace's statement on this problem as presented in "Should You Have a Baby the First Year," *Woman's Home Companion*, 76:38 ff., December, 1949. David Mace, now a professor in the United States, developed the program for marriage counseling in England.

[15] *U. S. News & World Report*, June 6, 1960.

mother to the neglect of her obligations as a wife. She fears the trend toward overdomesticity which draws the young male into the safe shelter of the home, thus curbing his creative, venturesome outlook.

Nursing the Infant

In primitive societies, if the mother is not biologically adequate for the task of nursing, the child dies, unless some substitute mother is found. Wet-nursing has been common in many cultures to provide for this emergency. With the modern family, bottle feeding is a new substitute for the biologically inadequate mother. This even brings the father into the picture in a new way.[16]

Contemporary research on breast feeding, or lack of it, has led to some important conclusions. The isolation of the infant from the mother, as is done in many modern hospitals, is proved to be wrong. Research by Ashley-Montagu confirms the fact that the child should be allowed to nurse from the beginning.[17] Research by Dr. Paul G. Gyorgy, professor of pediatrics at the University of Pennsylvania, shows that the colostrum which is in the mother's breast prior to the flow of milk is necessary to the growth of micro-organisms important to the infant which give it resistance to disease.[18] Cow's milk has only 1/13 to 1/15 the amount of fortification against disease as has human milk.

Ashley-Montagu's research shows that, for the mother, the sucking of the infant immediately after birth sets up contractions in the uterus which help to constrict blood vessels, guard against post-partum hemorrhages, and cause the immediate detachment of the afterbirth, and its ejection. This immediate nursing of the infant is nature's way of getting the uterus to return to normal size. The contractions in the uterus produced by nursing last as much as 20 minutes after the infant ceases sucking. Where nursing is delayed as much as 20 hours or more, blood oozes into the uterine cavity, causing irregular spasmodic contractions. The mother whose baby has nursed immediately will not suffer afterbirth pains and will return more quickly to her nonpregnant condition.

What is known as the "let-down reflex" in the mother may start the milk flowing even before the infant begins sucking. There is a definite erotic feeling in connection with this reflex that is a factor in the emotional bond between mother and child.[19]

16 Margaret Mead, "Changing Patterns of Parent-Child Relations in an Urban Culture," *International Journal of Psychoanalysis*, 38:369-378, November-December, 1957.

17 M. F. Ashley-Montagu, *Anthropology and Human Nature* (Boston: Porter Sargent, Publisher, 1957), p. 20.

18 *Ibid.*

19 Newton Niles, "The Influence of the Let-down Reflex in Breast Feeding in the Mother-Child Relationship," *Marriage and Family Living*, 20:18-20, February, 1958.

The contractions of the uterus which accompany nursing and continue even beyond the completion of the breast feeding seem to be of the same character as those experienced during orgasm in the sexual act. The nursing reaction, therefore, not only brings close contact with the child but also brings deep emotional and physical satisfaction to the mother. In many primitive cultures, nursing extends beyond a two-year period; in some as long as four or five years, perhaps accounting in part for the built-in security of the child.[20]

The Baby in the Family

The coming of the first child into the family calls for numerous readjustments in the habits of the parents. Much of the routine of family life must be centered around the child. Times of rising and retiring, sleep habits, recreational habits, the time spent outside the home—all these things have to be viewed from a new angle when young people face the responsibilities of parenthood.

The first baby is one of the most significant educational experiences in the life of any person. This is especially true now because an increasing number of young people have had no experience with babies, even in their parental home. Their first experience comes with their own first baby. Unfortunately, the average couple today faces this turning point in their lives with little more to guide them than folklore.

The modern hospital and physician have relieved the family of most of the responsibility for childbirth. The care of the mother prior to the birth of the child is also left in the hands of the physician. The real problem begins when the young mother returns home from the hospital after a few days of confinement.

One of the first things the young parent has to learn is that a baby is quite a different physiological mechanism. The heart beats around 135 times a minute, rather than 72 times, as in the adult. The infant breathes 35 times a minute instead of 16. Although much more susceptible to dietary upsets than an adult, he recovers from fevers and many diseases, and from injuries, much more quickly than will the adult. His temperature-adjusting mechanism is much more flexible, permitting quick adjustments to hot and cold. This is true to a considerable extent throughout childhood. And the abounding energy of the young child and older child is unmatched in the adult. Growth and development are very rapid; so also is the repair of damage to tissue.

[20] Refer back to Chapter 9 for a further discussion of this topic.

Emotional Adjustments of Parenthood

The coming of the first baby quite frequently creates emotional problems centering around the relationships between husband and wife. This may occur immediately after the child's birth or come when it is a few weeks old and the couple begins to sense the change parenthood has brought into their lives. Often the wife goes through a honeymoon period with the baby, a time in which the husband is likely to feel sadly neglected. In some cases the mother from that point on makes the child, rather than the husband, the emotional center of her life. The wife who relegates the husband to the position of merely earning the money, giving all her attention and emotional life to the child, cannot expect to continue to have a satisfactory home life.

There are other cases where the wife resents the coming of the child because his birth means sudden and unwanted termination of her career, her independence, or some other special status she enjoys. The wife may also fear that the coming of the child will interfere with the relationship between husband and wife.

No matter how much the baby is wanted or how happy the couple may be on its arrival, the home life or the husband-wife relationship will never be the same. Babies are in their own innocent way tyrants in the home. As Levy and Munroe have so well expressed it:

> No matter how going a concern a marriage may be, the advent of children causes severe strain between parents. Newborn babies cannot be taken in their stride; they have none. Their very physical disorganization sets the pace for their influence on marriage ties. Children are as disturbing to marriage as their own physical eccentricities. Any orderly, smooth, satisfactory relationship carefully worked out between husband and wife is broken up the very first night the child is home from the hospital. The inability of a child to do anything for itself means that demands are made on parents which create a new relationship between husband and wife. Their time and energy are no longer their own for companionship or intimacy. The little tyrant need only raise its voice a tiny bit to break up the parents' closest embrace. The warmth of the adult relationship is forever being disturbed by the child's demands for physical attention. At any hour of the night the newborn youngster can separate husband and wife without repaying them for their loss with even a friendly smile. The child's physical requirements have the right-of-way over their feelings toward each other and toward the child. No matter how much one or both of them may resent this intrusion, their only choice is to obey the child's call and sacrifice their own need for each other. Babies are tyrants.[21]

[21] John Levy and Ruth Munroe, *The Happy Family* (New York: Alfred A. Knopf, Inc.. 1938), p. 243.

On the other hand, children always bring to the home a new focus of interest which is usually of decided advantage. They also bring new responsibilities which may intensify the loyalty of parents to each other and intensify their loyalty to the family itself.

LeMasters has made a case-history study of the adjustments of 46 couples to the coming of the first child.[22] Of this group, 38 couples, or 83 percent, reported "extensive" or "severe" crisis in adjusting to the first child. This was a joint rating of the parents. LeMasters concludes that adding a child to the urban middle-class married couple constitutes a crisis event.

Most of these couples actually wanted and planned for the child, so this was not a case of unwanted children, and most of them considered their marriages good marriages, so it was not a matter of husband-wife conflicts. Much of the difficulty was a romanticized, rather than a realistic conception of what parenthood and babies were like. Mothers had not anticipated the loss of sleep, chronic tiredness and exhaustion, the confinement to the home, the curtailment of social contacts, the drain on income, the isolation, the washing and ironing, the seven-day-and-night week, the worry over the child and their ability to meet its demands adequately, etc., that are a part of parenthood. Women with professional work experience suffered a crisis in every case.

Fathers added to these adjustments the decline in sex interest of the wife, the loss of her earnings, putting a greater burden upon him, and worry about future pregnancies and income. LeMasters reports that the husbands quickly became "disenchanted" with the parental role.

He concludes that there is a great deficiency in preparing young people for the parent role in our culture. They anticipate with great hope the mate role, but not the parent role. The first child destroys the pair role relationship and creates the triangle relationship. The husband no longer has priority in the wife's interests and attentions. The first child painfully forces the couple to take the last step into the adult world.

Most of the group LeMasters studied eventually made the transition into successful parenthood, even though the transition was painful. And most felt it was worth what it cost.

In many cities, infant-care classes are offered for prospective mothers and fathers. These are valuable, not only in that they help young people gain confidence in handling and caring for a baby, but also they place the couple with other parents who are enthusiastic about parenthood.

    [22] E. E. LeMasters, "Parenthood as a Crisis," *Marriage and Family Living*, 19:352-355, November, 1957. This research was confirmed by findings of Everett D. Dyer, "Parenthood as Crisis: A Re-study," *Marriage and Family Living*, 25:196-201, May, 1963.

The Growth of the Parent

One of the rather surprising things the young couple has to learn when the first baby comes is that the role of the mother in the family is quite different from that of the wife, and that the role of the father is quite different from that of the husband. The coming of the child, in fact, calls for a recasting of attitudes of the parents toward each other.

Dorothy Canfield Fisher, the novelist, once discussed the topic "How Children Educate Their Parents" in *Progressive Education.* She says:

> Most mothers and fathers at the beginning of their career as mothers and fathers are immature, egotistical, raw, spoiled children, whom society has not been able to "educate" in any real sense of the word; at whom life has not been able to get, through the thick barrier of protection set up around the young; in whom the most careful training has been able only to plant the barest germs of what we know as "character." Their ideal of life, expressed or subconscious, is the childish, shallow unrewarding one of doing as they like, and leaving somebody else to take the consequences. They have been (I speak of course only of the majority of cases) cherished more or less wisely, protected more or less wisely, protected more or less completely, looked out for by their families. In the back of their minds has always been the feeling that if things got too bad, or difficulties too steep, or the water too deep, one could always fall back on the older generation.

She then goes on to show how being a mother or father puts many young people on their own resources for the first time, and she concludes, "The great majority of ordinary human beings would be unbearable if they had no children to bring them up."

The proper emotional attitude of the parent is all-essential in providing the child with a proper atmosphere for development. The infant at birth has a capacity to learn but no knowledge, emotions but no orientation of them around persons or things. Experience, the social traditions, moral beliefs of parents and other social groups must be acquired. The mind is plastic, highly impressionable, capable from the outset of receiving an almost unlimited number of impressions. This plasticity of mind and receptivity of the nervous system makes possible the cultivation of his emotional life and the passing on to the child of the experiences of the race.

The family atmosphere surrounding the child in early infancy and childhood is the most important single factor in personality development for he absorbs the atmosphere of the life about him. Impressions and attitudes resulting from these early experiences carry over through the individual's lifetime, affecting many other relationships. The relationships between the parent and the child are important factors in the happiness of the child as he grows to adulthood and to his later success in marriage.

Critical Periods in Child Development

Psychologists have done considerable research in animal psychology in the area that has come to be called *critical periods*.[23] These are periods when optimal learning of skills, and the development of emotional and social traits are characteristic. We have already discussed (Chapter 5) the fixing of sex role identification at the two ½-year age. After this, the child's identification with his sex role becomes so fixed that change is almost impossible.

Imprinting takes place in animals and birds during the critical period of socialization at a rapid rate and soon becomes irreversible and self-enforcing. With ducklings and lambs, for example, imprinting takes the form of early close attachment to the mother, normally; but if man or some other animal is substituted during this critical period, they will follow him instead, and very soon they will always thereafter ignore their own species.

We have seen (Chapter 6) how emotional starvation in early infancy may destroy the child. Spitz finds that if emotional deprivation starts late, in the third quarter of the first year, a condition develops which resembles depression in the adult. If the deprivation lasts no longer than 3 months, reestablishment of development is possible. If it lasts longer than 5 months, no improvement is shown after restoration of social contacts.

Dr. Spock believes that the stage in childhood development between five months and three years is analogous to the imprinting observed with certain animals.[24] It is at about five months that the baby begins to discriminate between familiar and strange people. From this time on through three years of age, he needs a familiar figure for love, comfort, approval, play, gentle kidding, and curbing. Dr. Spock feels that this is the critical time of socialization, when the child gets his self-image which builds in him a sense of being a good or bad person, of a world that is hostile or loving. After three, he believes, the child can be left by the mother in the care of a reliable substitute without anxiety being provoked.

[23] René A. Spitz, "The Role of Ecological Factors in Emotional Development in Infancy," *Child Development*, Society for Research in Child Development, Inc., Purdue University, 20:145-155, 1949.

[24] Benjamin Spock, "When Mothers Work," *Ladies Home Journal*, March, 1963, p. 142 ff.

The Second Baby

The following is the actual experience of a young couple, the father with a Ph.D. in sociology, the mother with an MA in psychology:

> Well, we seem to have weathered the worst of it; not without scars, however. Five weeks have passed and things are beginning to seem almost normal again. Our problem came from the least expected source—not the baby, but our two-year-old, Sue. After two days of angelic behavior she hit the baby with a toy truck, grabbed her bottle and finished it off and the battle was on. Since then she has kept us under a more or less constant trial by fire— up late at night, at any and all hours of the night and at 5:30 or 6:00 every morning; temper tantrums; whining ill-humor, and all of the other horrible things that a child of mine "just wouldn't do." At the first signs of what was happening we hastily read all the books we should have read six months ago on the peculiarities of the two-year-old and sibling jealousy. Bill ended up playing mama to the baby, while I became a 24-hour-a-day mama to a very babylike Sue.
>
> Within the last couple of days she has begun to get sick of me, which is the sign I've been waiting for, and to return to much of her former independent activity. If this is really about the end of it, I guess we've gotten off fairly easy, although the weeks since it began seem much more nearly like four months.

At the time the second child is conceived, or soon after, preparation of the first child for the sibling's coming is highly important. This will be a momentous event in the life of the firstborn. He has had a world in which the affection of parents has been his exclusively. He cannot share his rights, privileges, and attention with an intruder without a great deal of adjustment.

Parents need to begin early by telling the child he is to have a brother or sister playmate and helping him to look forward to the coming of the baby with happy anticipation. This also will be a time for a new step in the sex education of the child. If he is old enough, he is certain to ask where babies come from, how they grow, who brings them, or some similar question which opens the way to explain that the baby grows inside the mother. When he asks how it gets out, the question must be answered by a simple statement such as, "through the birth canal," or "it comes out through a very special place that opens at that time." It is important that questions be answered honestly, up to the level of the child's understanding.

When the mother returns from the hospital, full attention should be given to the lonely child who has been left at home, and not to showing off the new baby. As much attention must be given to him in the days following as is possible, to avoid jealousy and the development of aggression of the child toward the new baby. Even then a perfect relationship should not be taken for granted.

Family Size: Is It Important?

The size of the average family has diminished greatly in the last few generations. This can be accounted for, in part, by improved means of birth control and by economic changes produced by the transition from a rural to an urban culture. Attitudes and values too have changed.

What is the "ideal" family size in the eyes of modern couples? Why do they feel as they do on this matter, and what are the results in family well-being and personal happiness?

The study of engaged couples previously cited showed that two children was the number most commonly desired by men and women.[25] Over two-thirds of both engaged men and women desired very much to have children. Approximately 6 percent objected mildly or very mildly to having children. The above study was made in the metropolitan area of Chicago where urban values were reflected. No doubt in rural areas the desire for children might be even stronger. In fact, there is much evidence in rural sociological literature and research that farm life is family-centered and that a desire for children is practically universal.[26] The relatively high farm birth rate is also an indication of the high rating of children in the farm marriage.

Various youth surveys over a period of two decades show that few young people expect no children.[27] The norm is two to four, the average being fractionally higher during the postwar decade than during the depression decade of the 1930's.

There is some evidence that family size is a matter in part of family tradition, for there seems to be a definite family-size relationship running through the generations. Those children who come from large families tend to have large families. This is more true if the mother comes from a large family than if the father does, although it holds true somewhat for both. It seems also to hold for all social classes.[28]

25 Burgess and Wallin, *op. cit.*, Ch. 13.

26 Data are summarized in Paul H. Landis, *Rural Life in Process,* Revised Edition (New York: McGraw-Hill Book Co., 1948), Chs. 4, 21.

27 Summarized in Paul H. Landis, *Adolescence and Youth,* Revised Edition (New York: McGraw-Hill Book Co., 1952), Ch. 16.

28 For a summary of findings on this point and analysis of original data dealing with 1,482 families see J. Berent, "Family Size of Two Successive Generations," *Milbank Memorial Fund Quarterly,* 31:39-50, January, 1953.

The most profound influence today in size of family is education. Census data on size of family by education shows that those with least education have the largest families; those with the most education, the smallest families. High school and college graduates tend to have small families (see Figure 29-2).

NUMBER OF CHILDREN EVER BORN PER 1000 WOMEN 15-24, AND EVER MARRIED STANDARDIZED FOR AGE

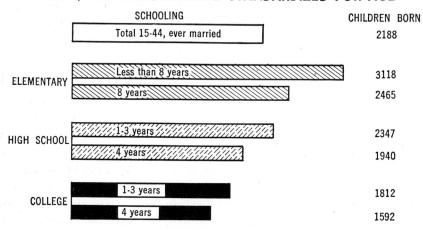

SOURCE: U. S. Department of Commerce, Bureau of the Census, "Fertility of the Population: March, 1957," *Special Reports,* Series P-20, No. 84, August 8, 1958.

FIGURE 29-2————Education tends to decrease the size of family. A part of this is due to the later age of marriage of the educated; more important, no doubt, is motive and aspirational differences of those with different educational attainments. Since World War II the birth rate of the college educated has risen faster than that of other groups. Subsidy of college marriage through veterans assistance programs was a factor in this trend.

One must recognize, of course, that this association between education and size of family is a two-way relationship. Parents with large numbers of children are able to give them less education and, therefore, the large family pattern persists.[29] Families with small numbers of children can educate their children, so the small-family pattern persists.

Even within our most conservative groups there is a decline in the family with increased education. A study of the Mormons, for example,

[29] Paul H. Landis, *Parent Teenage Relationships in Large and Small Families* (Pullman, Wash.: Washington Agricultural Experiment Station, April, 1954), Bulletin No. 549.

shows this is true. Although the Mormons in 1950 still tended to have larger-than-average families, those with the most education were decreasing their families most.[30]

Studies of the effect of number of children on marital happiness shows that, in general, happiness tends to decrease with an increase in the size of the family.[31] Ability of the couple to plan and control the size of the family seems to be an important factor in happiness.[32]

The number of children a couple should plan and the time at which they should plan to have them, are a highly individuated aspect of marriage, as are so many other adjustments and decisions. Moreover, a couple may well change their views on the number of children they want as the marriage progresses, and unless they are 100 percent successful in the practice of contraception, the time of the first birth, child spacing, and even the number of children they will have will not be fully in their control.

It is, however, important to understand that the size of the couple's family will have a decisive effect on the character of their family life and the nature of their children's environment. This has long been known with regard to the only child, but an increasing body of research now indicates that this is so for families of all sizes—that is, families of all sizes have their characteristic interaction pattern.

The Size of Family and Characteristic Interaction Patterns

An intensive study of 100 large families by Bossard and his co-workers led them to a comparison of large families with the general small-family systems and to the development of some interesting hypotheses concerning the characteristics of each.[33]

The researchers found that in the small family, planning is one of the basic characteristics, along with the spacing of children and a strong emphasis on child rearing. Educational aspirations are high; the quest for

[30] Lowery Nelson, "Education and the Changing Size of Mormon Families," *Rural Sociology*, 17:335-342, December, 1952.

[31] For a concise summary of studies on this problem and original data, see Harold T. Christensen and Robert E. Philbrick, "Family Size as a Factor in Marital Adjustment of College Couples," *American Sociological Review*, 17:306-312, June, 1952.

[32] *Ibid.*; also Robert B. Reed, "Social and Psychological Factors Affecting Fertility. VIII: The Interrelationship of Marital Adjustment, Fertility Control and the Size of Family," *The Milbank Memorial Fund Quarterly*, 25:383-425, October, 1947.

[33] James H. S. Bossard and Winnogene Pratt Sanger, "The Large Family System," *American Sociological Review*, 17:3-9, February, 1952; also James H. S. Bossard and Eleanor Stoker Boll, *The Large Family System* (Philadelphia: University of Pennsylvania Press, 1956).

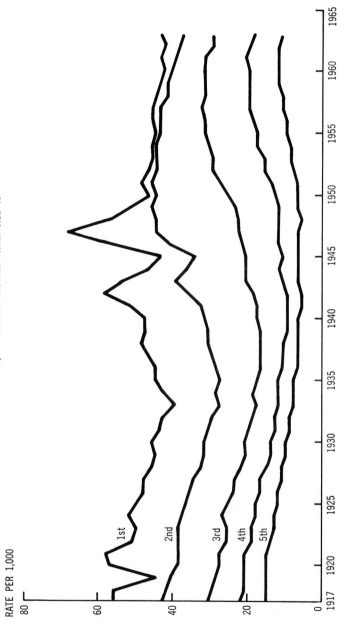

BIRTH RATES BY ORDER OF BIRTH, UNITED STATES, 1917-1963

BIRTHS PER 1,000 MARRIED WOMEN UNDER AGE 45

RATE PER 1,000

SOURCE: Metropolitan Life Insurance Company, *Statistical Bulletin,* 44:3-5, October, 1963.

FIGURE 29-3———Families of three or more children have greatly increased. Twice as many women are having four children as at the beginning of World War II. The proportion of women having five children is equal to that of the later 1920's. Size of status is conscious and deliberate, pointing toward a career for the child. Parenthood is intensive, with a great deal of professional care being given the child. In many cases, both parents are working; often the mother has a career-oriented personality. Family life is generally democratic, with the child having a voice in the family discussions. The full development of the child is the objective of the family atmosphere, so that the pattern is essentially one of cooperation, with the parent being conscious of numerous problems of child psychology. The parent is always comparing his child with other children in the social group. There is great pressure on the child to measure up and great anxiety on the part of parents if the child fails to measure up. There is little discipline from siblings, and little direct interaction between the child and other children. The child's resentments, because of his limited contacts, are directed against a few persons—often the parents. The same is true of his affections. In most conflict situations, it is two against one rather than there being a large group in the conflicting unit. In the small-family pattern, it may be one parent and child against the other parent—a struggle, in effect, between the parents for the favor of the child.

Summarizing the characteristics of the small family, Bossard and Sanger say:

> The small family rests upon the ideas of planning, individualization, democratic co-operation, social isolation and intensive pressures. The small family system is the quality system, chiefly at the middle-class level. Its driving force is one of ambition, in an open class system; its social justification, if one may thus speak of it, is that it represents an adjustment to a rapidly changing society, with its train of attendant insecurities.

These writers find that the large family is different in almost every respect, and that it produces entirely different personality types. Involved in the birth rate itself is a different philosophy of life. Where the large family is intentional, the desire for it is usually a desire of husband or wife, rather than of both. In nonplanned large families, children are accepted as a product of fate.

The large family provides an environment in which there is a constant readjustment to the vicissitudes of life. Things are always happening in the large family, and there must be a constant shifting of roles, statuses, and responsibilities of various members of the group to meet these emergencies. The family group is the unit of first concern in the large family, whereas in the small family the individual is the unit of concern. In the large family, each person's wishes are always subservient to those of the rest of the group. Sleeping arrangements, dress, dates, every aspect of living is limited by the economic resources, crowded conditions, and constant pressure of family members upon each other. The large family is more rigidly organized within, and therefore tends to be more authoritarian, with one or more persons being dominant. A greater degree of executive direction and arbitrary control is necessary. This control is usually by the father or mother, but sometimes by an older sibling. Authoritarianism is almost an inevitable part of the large-family system. This, the writers suggest, is probably why the early family was authoritarian in character compared to the democracy of the small, modern family.

This research also finds that in the large family there is a great deal more specialization of roles among family members. One girl may be a household drudge, a son may be a father substitute. One child may be a gadabout, one a whiner, another a tattletale, and so forth. Obviously such specialized roles cannot be played in the small family. The young child in the large family has fewer choices of roles, as many roles are already taken by the time he appears on the scene.

In the large family, parents and children are likely to be less demanding in attitude, and less tolerant of neurotic tendencies of members than in the small family. It is impossible for the child in the large family to receive the much-emphasized individual attention so characteristic of family philosophy in small families. The crowded space of the home, it is believed, tends to lead young people to want to leave home early and to marry early.

The writer has been able to test some of these interesting hypotheses further with a group of more than 4,300 high school seniors and 1,424 college students.[34] This study gives statistical confirmation to many of the differences suggested by the Bossard and Sanger series of case studies.

In the writer's study, also, it was found that the large family (large families, those with 6 or more children) does tend to be authoritarian, the small family democratic (Figure 29-4). The small family was found to be much more education-oriented than the large family. Even those representatives of large families who finished high school and went to college were less academically oriented, had lower educational aspirations, and were less successful in their school performance. Those from large families were more certain they knew the vocation they wanted to go into, which probably indicated a limited range of choice rather than actual preparation for a wide range of choice.

The pattern of dissolving the family differed, too. Marriage in the large family is characteristically terminated by death rather than divorce, which confirms the previous researcher's claim of greater individuation of personality in small families. In the writer's sample, only 6 percent of

[34] Paul H. Landis, *Parent Teenage Relationships in Large and Small Families* (Pullman, Wash.: Washington Agricultural Experiment Station, April, 1954), Bulletin No. 549.

HIGH SCHOOL SENIORS IN FAMILY PATTERNS

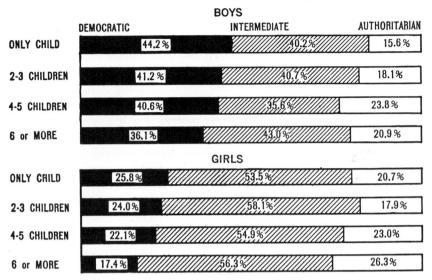

SOURCE: Paul H. Landis, *Parent Teenage Relationships in Large and Small Families* (Pullman, Wash.: Washington Agricultural Experiment Station, April, 1954), Bulletin No. 549.

FIGURE 29-4————The larger the family the more authoritarian it tends to be. Data are for 4,377 high school seniors in the state of Washington and show the percentages of these young people living under family administrative patterns by size of family.

homes in families of six or more children were broken by divorce, and 16 percent by death. In the broken, only-child families, 11.5 percent had been broken by divorce, 10 percent by death. There was a 50-50 chance of divorce and death in the broken two- and three-child families.

Much evidence was found of economic pressure and home crowding in the large family. This is inevitable in a society where wages and salaries are based on individual performance alone, with no subsidy being made by industry or government for children.

Our most striking finding, and one which, to the writer's knowledge, has not been previously discovered in the analysis of family behavior by size, is that the boy from a large family adjusts well; girls from large families do not. In fact, girls from large families have more problems of adjustment in senior high school and college years than others. They are more often friendless or have few friends, and seldom exercise leadership. Girls from the small family, particularly from the only-child family, are far superior in their adjustments as measured by number of friendships, number of activities, and leadership roles at this period in life to those from large families, and in fact have a more prominent place in leadership than any other group.

Historically, this may not have been true. Formerly the girl's life was submerged in the family. The modern girl who finishes high school, and particularly the girl who goes to college, is venturing far out into the individualistic world of contemporary life. She is sampling competitive values that were once the privilege of the male only. Her training in the individualistic family, under the small-family pattern, has led to the maximum of independence and self-sufficiency, and she has, therefore, formed her personality more appropriately for living in an individualistic society. The girl in the large family, by contrast, has had her personality so submerged in the family that she is not particularly well fitted for the adjustments of our highly individualistic teenage world.

It may well be that the personality deficiencies of the teenage girl in the large family are due largely to the fact that she has been tied down with being an assistant mother or house-keeper to younger children. This is often the case with the older girl in the large family. She is thus hindered from making the plunge into her peer group at the puberty period. This may be for the girl what the psychologists call a "critical period"[35] it must either be done then or she can never feel at home with her peers. In any case, we know that she tends to develop a feeling of friendlessness.

There is much evidence from our study of teenagers that boys are never as submerged in the family as are girls and are seldom so completely subject to authoritarian patterns, regardless of family size.[36] This is probably a factor in the adjustability of the boy by type of family background. The boy in the only-child family probably suffers from over-mothering, making his adjustment outside the family difficult. He is also an only rival of his father for his mother's affection.

The problems faced by teenagers of large families tend to be largely external in nature—schooling, living space, money, and vocational problems. The only child suffers more from problems that are introspective in character. He more often has problems in his relationships with family members, with his age mates, and in boy-girl relations. He also tends to have more problems in the area of morals and religion.

Elder and Bowerman[37] studied the effect of family size and com-

[35] For a discussion of this concept see J. P. Scott, "Critical Periods in Behavioral Development," *Science*, 138:949-956, November 30, 1962.

[36] Paul H. Landis and Carol L. Stone, *The Relationship of Parental Authority Patterns to Teenage Adjustment* (Pullman, Wash.: Washington Agricultural Experiment Station, September, 1952), Bulletin No. 538; also Carol Larson Stone and Paul H. Landis, "An Approach to Authority Patterns in Parent-Teenage Relations," *Rural Sociology*, 18:233-242, September, 1953.

[37] Glen H. Elder, Jr. and Charles E. Bowerman, "Family Structure and Child-rearing Patterns: The Effect of Family Size and Sex Composition," *American Sociological Review*, 28:891-905, December, 1963.

position on child-rearing patterns with a sample of 1,261 Protestant seventh-grade pupils. They found that with the increase in family size, the lower-class girl was more likely to perceive of her father being in the authoritarian role, and of both parents being less communicative, more controlling and given more to physical punishment and less to praise than was the case in the smaller family.

Among the boys, it was in the middle-class family that authoritarian traits more clearly emerged as the family pattern with increase in size: more physical punishment, more parental dominance, less communication.

Hawkes and his colleagues found that the small-family environment did not have a detrimental effect on the personalities of children they studied—a fifth-grade group. They found no evidence favoring the beneficial effects of the large family. Generally speaking, they concluded, children from the small family probably fare better psychologically than those from larger families.[38]

These studies suggest that the pattern of life of the family, and the personality formation of children, will be very much affected by the size of the family a young couple has. The evidence is sufficient to suggest that there is no one pattern that may be considered ideal. One cannot accept the folklore notion that a large family is ideal for the adjustment of the child because brothers and sisters knock the rough spots off personality. The large family seems to hold no disadvantage for the boy in his later adjustments, but is a decided handicap for the girl. We must also modify current conception about the only child, particularly in cases involving the girl, if results of the above study are found to be generally characteristic. She adjusts better in many of her social relationships than do girls from families with more than one child.

Finally, families of all size types have their characteristic problems in marriage relationships as well as in parent-child relationships.

Sib Relationships

There probably never was a family with more than one child in which a certain amount of jealousy, rivalry, and bickering, or at least hidden suffering, did not take place in the relationship between children.

One of the earliest accounts of family relationships known to man is the bitter jealousy between Cain and Abel, which led to murder. Joseph's relationship with his brothers is one of the most widely known accounts of the interplay of family relationships in a large patriarchal family— their envy of his coat of many colors given him by a doting father, their sale of him into bondage, his later forgiveness, when as a member of Pharaoh's household he was able to save them from famine. The Cinder-

[38] Glenn R. Hawkes, Lee Burchinal, and Bruce Gardener, "Size of Family and Discipline of Children," *Marriage and Family Living*, 20:65-68, February, 1958.

ella story and numerous other tales of fiction and fact, as well as historical ·
biography, tells of the struggles, rivalries, jealousies, resentments, as well
as the magnanimity of human relationships between brothers and sisters
in the family.

These relationships constantly change and require growth and insight
on the part of the parent as well as on the part of the children within the
family. The nature of the sib relationship is of lifelong importance. The
larger the family, the more likely that each individual will come to be
typed for the particular roles he plays and the interactions he has with
brothers and sisters. The oldest child often has the role of boss, the youngest child being the whiner or the baby. Others play these unique roles,
depending upon their age, physical strength, looks, emotional adjustment,
particular relationships with parents or with another brother or sister.

Jessie Bernard, who has studied the literature on sib relationships
thoroughly, concludes her review of research with this significant statement:

> If, standing on a crowded street corner, we could see all the adults about
> us in terms of their sib relationships, we would see not the seemingly inde-
> pendent, self-resourceful individuals who pass before us, but rebellious little
> sisters fighting against parental discrimination, resentful little brothers hat-
> ing older sisters whose superiority in age and maturity frustrated their male
> egos, jealous older sister resenting the attention bestowed on little sisters,
> sisters of all ages envying the privileges of brothers of all ages. Most of us,
> on becoming closely acquainted with men and women of apparent maturity,
> have found that in certain aspects of their personalities they are still much
> under the influence of brother or sister, still smarting under childhood pat-
> terns. It does not matter that they are now successful in their own right;
> they must still convince brother or sister of their success. One man's whole
> life is spent in achieving goals which his sister unconsciously set for him
> years ago; he must prove to her that he can do it. One woman's life is
> shattered because of her ambivalent attitude of hatred and love for a brother
> who dominated her childhood.[39]

Each human being is an individual developing along his own lines,
according to his own pattern, but part of his shaping as an individual
depends upon how he relates himself to his brothers and sisters in the
family. Parents cannot hope that children will be alike in temperament,
disposition, or lovability, or that each will be able to accept the other
fully. Some children will live under the shadow of a brother or sister for
a lifetime, even though they are far separated by marriage. Others carry
in their personalities the experience of dominance or submission which
was established early in life by a relationship with a brother or a sister.

[39] Jesse Bernard, *American Family Behavior* (New York: Harper & Bros., 1942),
p. 312.

This may affect their choice of a mate. Still others will carry a long resentment against a sib, always fighting against anyone who interferes with their development because they are still subconsciously fighting a dominating brother or sister.

The writer in reading autobiographies of thousands of college students finds various relationships between brothers and sisters vividly described as a deterministic force in the development of the personalities of young people. Take, for example, the young person who has suffered from an overshadowing relationship with a domineering or brilliant brother or sister and who has literally shaped his life in the sib's image. Some describe how painful and discouraging such a relationship is as they continue to live under this shadow, even when they go to school, being faced by their teachers all the way from grade school to college with the record of an older brother or sister who happened to achieve perfectionistic standards. Such a person may never get over the feeling of inferiority and hostility this constant unfavorable comparison has brought.

Parents can do much to keep down the bitterness and rivalries between children in the family, but wisdom and understanding and a great deal of patience are required. The best book which has come to the writer's attention for giving insight and removing anxiety of parents in the little rivalries and difficulties that normally develop in the family is that by Edith G. Neisser, *Brothers and Sisters* (New York: Harper & Bros., 1951).

Adoption

Because of the low death rate of parents today, there are comparatively few orphan children available for adoption. Most children for adoption are born out of wedlock. Of these, there are almost a quarter million born yearly.

To secure a child for adoption through an agency, hopeful foster parents must submit to the most careful social-work investigation which will appraise not only, or even primarily, their economic resources, but their emotional resources and the success of the adjustment of their marriage. Reliable adoption agencies today are legitimately concerned with whether or not the home is going to be adequate in meeting the social, psychological, and emotional needs of the child. In fact, children placed in homes of adopted parents probably have a better opportunity for an ideal home environment than the child which comes by birth. But all has not gone well.

Novelist Pearl S. Buck, writing for the *Women's Home Companion*,[40] made one of the most serious indictments of the adoption situation yet

---

[40] Pearl S. Buck, "The Children Waiting," *Woman's Home Companion*, September, 1955, pp. 33 ff.

made. Her investigation of orphanages, social-work agencies, and other charitable institutions handling children indicates that vested interests create the situation of so many couples wanting children who cannot be had. Agencies will not release children in their custody. They have vested interest in keeping the institutions operating. They handle sums of money left as legacies and gifts. These funds require a cause. Caretakers, cooks, placement agents, nuns, superintendents, deaconesses, teachers, and social workers are dependent on the institutions for their living and for their work.

Many religious groups have orphanages, as do fraternal organizations. They have vested interest in maintaining them; they solicit funds for their maintenance. They do not seek to have the child released for adoption. Many religious groups have restrictions on who can adopt, often requiring that the foster parents be of their own religion. Adoption across religious lines is prohibited by law in several states and is quite generally looked down upon by placement agencies everywhere, making it very difficult for the mixed Protestant-Catholic marriage, for example, to adopt a child. Miss Buck quotes a Pennsylvania physician who discusses his shock in learning that there are 62,000 institutionalized children in that state. The main reason for their remaining in institutions, he found, was the religious factor.

While it must be recognized that orphans are rather few in our culture compared to those in underdeveloped areas of the world, there are, nevertheless, large numbers of children for adoption who have little chance of escaping the custodial care of the institution in which they have been placed.

The public reaction to the difficulty of adoption has been to bypass the recognized agencies of placement. In fact, Pearl Buck herself says that, knowing what she does about adoption agencies, if she were unable to get a child she would go to the "grey" market and get one by the usual channel of doctor or lawyer, or others who give babies to foster parents with good intent. She indicated that she would prefer working through a good social agency, but if that failed she would use this other channel. Others who have looked into the adoption situation have said that even if they had to go to the black market they would get a child that way rather than go childless, and some even go so far as to indicate they would go to the grey market in preference to the adoption agency.

Actually, the cost of getting a child through the grey market (through the lawyer or the doctor who represents the girl having her baby out of wedlock) is much cheaper than getting it through the standard agencies. Most of the agencies charge costs of placement.[41] Many doctors or lawyers

41 Elizabeth I. Lynch and Alice E. Mertz, "Adoptive Placement of Infants Directly from the Hospital," *Social Casework*, 36:450-457, December, 1955.

require only the cost of their services—in the case of the doctor the cost of the pregnancy and delivery, and perhaps of the hospital, if a hospital is used. The lawyer's fee is the cost of legal counsel and adoption papers.

Vincent has studied adoption in relation to the type of doctor to whom the girl goes, if she has the baby delivered rather than seeking an abortion. Of unorthodox adoption, many are arranged by doctors and lawyers.[42] An increasing number of agencies, like the Salvation Army, are adopting directly. Many hospitals now are adopting directly, rather than going through the complicated channels of agencies and risking that the child will never be adopted at all.

Lynch and Mertz in a study of direct placement conclude very positively that the best adjustment and physical development of babies comes where they are adopted directly from the hospital at the age of 3 to 10 days.[43] These authors feel that this is due to the fact that only in this way can the child from the beginning get the affection and love which all children need. They advise the following precautions. If these are met, they feel direct adoption is safe:

1. Adoptive parents are eager for the child.
2. The prenatal records of the mother are complete, and show no difficulties.
3. The delivery was normal.
4. The child at birth is in good health.

Ernest and Francis Cady, in their excellent book *How to Adopt a Child*,[44] report that half the adoptions today are independent, that is, arranged directly by the physician, attorney, or other persons who bypass the child-placement agencies. In some states as many as three-fourths are placed through the grey market, which is no more costly than the voluntary contributions, fees, and so on of the usual adoption agency (ranging from $500 to $1000). [The black market is quite a different matter. Almost any price may be charged. The difference between the black market and the grey market lies in the motivation, the black-market operator being in the business for profit rather than trying to recover fees for helping a girl who became pregnant out of wedlock.][45]

The Cadys point out that many people bypass the agencies because of the rather forbidding atmosphere of the placement agency and its per-

42 Clark E. Vincent, "The Adoption Market and the Unwed Mother's Baby," *Marriage and Family Living*, 18:124-127, May, 1956.

43 Lynch and Mertz, *op. cit.*

44 Ernest Cady and Francis Cady, *How to Adopt a Child* (New York: William Morrow & Co., Inc., 1956).

45 Although children for adoption are more plentiful now than at any time since World War II, due to the increasing out-of-wedlock birth rate, black markets still flourish. In mid-1964 the U. S. Congress started a nation-wide investigation into this racket. They reported fees for babies running as high as $7,500. A million-dollar racket in baby placement was reported. (Associated Press release, June 18, 1964).

sonnel, their lack of warmth, and their apparent lack of genuine interest in the prospective foster parent. They find also that agencies do not look too favorably on applications of people who quibble about fees or gifts expected by the orphanage.

It is not unusual for parents after adopting a child to have a pregnancy. This seems to indicate that in many instances the tenseness and anxiety of a couple desiring children is a factor in hindering pregnancy. Once they are relaxed and enjoy the atmosphere of a complete family, conception takes place.[46]

It is now generally believed that the sound procedure in handling an adopted child is to make his adoption clear to him from the time he is able to first understand it. The parent can conscientiously take the position that the child is more wanted and that his family has been more carefully selected, than that of the average baby born to its own parents. By frank handling of the situation, without overdoing it, the child will develop normally, and naturally without any anxiety about the situation whatever—probably, in fact, with less anxiety, than many children who feel insecure with their natural parents. Many of these children at times daydream that they are adopted and, of course, in their case the connotation is undesirable.

In conclusion, parenthood has come to be considered one of the most serious undertakings in life, and certainly the one fraught with the most far-reaching consequences to the next generation. The need to be informed and to accept the task as a challenge is important to success.

The small family has made increasingly rigorous demands on the mother because of the very high value placed on child care and training. The training of the child has, in fact, become the most exacting obligation of her life. In this respect her job is more demanding than in the large family, where the physical needs of the child are preeminent, but where his training may be guided largely by folklore.

Problems of child training in the new family system are the topic of the following chapter.

Problems

1. Childlessness in marriage may result from physical or emotional factors, sterility, voluntary control of pregnancy, continued delaying of parenthood, or the conviction of one mate that children are undesirable. Under which of

[46] Refer again to p. 572.

these circumstances do you think a childless marriage will most likely remain happy? Under which circumstances is the marriage most likely to be doomed?

2. Cases X and Y below are taken from a marriage counselor's file. In the first of the two cases the counselor advised the couple to seriously consider having a child; in the second, he discouraged parenthood. After studying the cases discuss:

   a. Why the counselor advised as he did.

   b. Whether or not his advice seems justified.

   c. What the future of the two marriages will probably be if the couples follow the counselor's advice.

   d. What the future of the two marriages will be if the couples do not follow the counselor's advice relative to having a child.

   Case X: Wife and husband, aged 26 and 30, respectively. Married six years. Report that, while still compatible and in love, marriage seems to be losing its joy. Both feel despondent, and sad. Wife reported, "We just don't have anything to stay married for or even to stay alive for, for that matter." Couple childless because their financial circumstances would not, as husband put it, "allow us to raise the children with the advantages we would want them to have."

   Case Y: Wife and husband aged 25 and 27 respectively. Married three years, during which they have separated briefly twice but have not considered divorce because of religious convictions of wife. Report that, while they occasionally enjoy things together, marriage has lost much of its meaning. Wife wants to continue working but husband disapproves of a wife's earning money. Husband thinks wife would "settle down" if she had a child. Wife is unsure but tends to think that the way to save their marriage is for both of them to work and make money "so we can start having some fun again."

3. *Sociodrama:* A wealthy but conservative young wheat grower sells his farm, moves to New York, and later becomes engaged to a young office worker. Dramatize a scene in which they disagree about how long they should wait before having their first child. Let their backgrounds, role conceptions, and values determine the arguments they present.

4. A man and his wife in looking back at their early months with their two children admit that:

   "Actually they were both very much alike—neither cried excessively, neither was sick or unusually demanding, both followed much the same sleeping and eating schedules. Why then," they wonder, "did the first seem like such a terrible problem? How could it have so disrupted our lives and spoiled our relationship when the second seemed so angelic and undemanding?" How would you explain the difference in the way they felt about the two infants who acted so much alike?

5. Do you consider the role of the mother or that of the father more important in child rearing? Do you believe it is unnecessary, rather silly, or very important for men to be formally prepared for their roles as fathers? Why?

6. In terms of social and psychological (rather than economic) advantages, what size family do you consider ideal? What, if any, are the advantages of growing

up in a very large family? What, if any, are the advantages of being an only child or one of two children?

7. When couples are unable to have children, adoption is considered by many to be a desirable alternative. Why should couples be urged to think long and hard about the disadvantages of adoption when childlessness is their only alternative.

Selected References

ARTICLES IN BOOKS OF READINGS

FISHBEIN, Morris, and KENNEDY, Ruby Jo Reeves, *Modern Marriage and Family Living* (New York: Oxford University Press, 1957).
   1. KROGMAN, Wilton M., "The Physical Growth of the Child," pp. 417-425.
   2. HURLOCK, Elizabeth B., "Child Development," pp. 426-441.
BECKER, Howard, and HILL, Reuben (Editors), *Family, Marriage and Parenthood,* Second Edition (Boston: D. C. Heath & Co., 1955).
   3. TAYLOR, Katherine Whiteside, "The Opportunities of Parenthood," pp. 454-492.
   4. WOOFTER, T. J., "Larger or Smaller Families for America?" pp. 743-772.
SUSSMAN, Marvin B., *Sourcebook in Marriage and the Family,* Second Edition (Boston: Houghton Mifflin Co., 1963).
   5. FREEDMAN, Deborah S., and others, "Size of Family and Preference for Children of Each Sex," pp. 198-201.
   6. LeMASTERS, E. E., "Parenthood as a Crisis," pp. 194-197.
KRICH, A. M. (Editor), *Men: The Variety and Meaning of Their Sexual Experience* (New York: Dell Publishing Co., 1954).
   7. BENEDEK, Therese, "The Meaning of Fatherhood," Ch. 7.
CAVAN, Ruth Shonle, *Marriage and the Family in the Modern World: A Book of Readings* (New York: Thomas Y. Crowell Co., 1960).
   8. *Changing Times, The Kiplinger Magazine,* "If You Want to Adopt a Baby," Reading 79.
   9. POLLAK, Gertrude K., "Some Principles of Positive Parent-Child Relationships," Reading 80.

General References

Adopted Break Silence, The (Philadelphia: Life History Study Center, 1954).
ASHLEY-MONTAGU, M. F., *Anthropology and Human Nature* (Boston: Porter Sargent, Publisher, 1957), p. 20.
BEE, Lawrence S., *Marriage and Family Relations* (New York: Harper & Row, Publishers, 1959), Ch. 14.
BLANTON, Smiley, *Love or Perish* (New York: Simon and Schuster, Inc., 1955).

BOSSARD, James H. S., and SANGER, Winnogene Pratt, "The Large Family System," *American Sociological Review*, 17:3-9, February, 1952.

BOWERMAN, Charles, and IRISH, Donald P., "Some Relationships of Stepchildren to Their Parents," *Marriage and Family Living*, 24:113-121, May, 1962.

BROOKS, Lee M., and BROOKS, Evelyn C., *Adventuring in Adoption* (Chapel Hill: The University of North Carolina Press, 1939).

BUCK, Pearl, "The Children Waiting," *Woman's Home Companion*, pp. 33 ff., September, 1955.

BURGESS, Ernest W., and WALLIN, Paul, *Engagement and Marriage* (Philadelphia: J. B. Lippincott Co., 1953), Ch. 21.

CADY, Ernest, and CADY, Francis, *How To Adopt a Child* (New York: William Morrow & Co., 1956).

CHRISTENSEN, Harold T., "Rural-Urban Differences in the Spacing of First Births from Marriage: A Repeat Study," *Rural Sociology*, 18:60, March, 1953.

————, and PHILBRICK, Robert E., "Family Size as a Factor in the Marital Adjustments of College Couples," *American Sociological Review*, 17:306-312, June, 1952.

HAWKES, Glenn R., BURCHINAL, Lee, and GARDNER, Bruce, "Size of Family and Discipline of Children," *Marriage and Family Living*, 20:65-68, February, 1958.

KIRK, H. David, "A Dilemma of Adoptive Parenthood: Incongruous Role Obligations," *Marriage and Family Living*, 21:316-326, November, 1959.

LANDIS, Paul H., *Parent Teenage Relationships in Large and Small Families* (Pullman, Wash.: Washington Agricultural Experiment Station, April, 1954), Bulletin No. 549.

LeMASTERS, E. E., "Parenthood as a Crisis," *Marriage and Family Living*, 19:352-355, November, 1957.

LEVY, John, and MUNROE, Ruth, *The Happy Family* (New York: Alfred A. Knopf, Inc., 1938).

LOCKRIDGE, Rances, *Adopting a Child* (New York: Greenberg, 1947).

LYNCH, Elizabeth I., and MERTZ, Alice E., "Adoptive Placement of Infants Directly from the Hospital," *Social Casework*, 36:450-457, December, 1955.

MEAD, Margaret, "Changing Patterns of Parent-Child Relations in an Urban Culture," *International Journal of Psychoanalysis*, 28:369-378, November-December, 1957.

————, *A Creative Life for Your Children* (Washington, D. C.: U. S. Department of Health, Education, and Welfare, 1962).

NILES, Newton, "The Influence of the Let-down Reflex in Breast Feeding in the Mother-Child Relationship," *Marriage and Family Living*, 20:18-20, February, 1958.

ORLANSKY, H., "Infant Care and Personality," *Psychological Bulletin*, 462:1-48, 1949.

SCOTT, J. P., "Critical Periods in Behavioral Development," *Science*, 138:945-958, November 30, 1962.

SPOCK, Benjamin, *The Pocketbook of Baby and Child Care* (New York: Pocket Books, Inc., 1946).

VINCENT, Clark E., "The Adoption Market and the Unwed Mother's Baby," *Marriage and Family Living*, 18:124-127, May, 1956.

——, "Unwed Mothers and the Adoption Market: Psychological and Familial Factors," *Marriage and Family Living*, 22:112-118, May, 1960.

WALLIN, Paul, and VOLLMER, Howard M., "Marital Happiness of Parents and Their Children's Attitude Toward Them," *American Sociological Review*, 18:424-431, August, 1953.

Young parents will find many helpful pamphlets available on parenthood and child care: Public Affairs Pamphlets, 381 Park Avenue South, New York 16, publishes a series of some 20 pamphlets in this field; Science Research Associates, 228 S. Wabash Ave., Chicago 4, publishes a series on various phases of child training. The U. S. Children's Bureau, Department of Health, Education and Welfare, Washington, D. C. also publishes helpful pamphlets.

30

Child-Training Patterns

Cultures have different ways of rearing children, and the end product in adulthood is very different. Englishmen, Germans, Japanese, Frenchmen, Tahitians, etc., are made by the way infants and children are handled. The product may be a stern, unaffectionate administrator, an overly disciplined military type, or it may be an affectionate, home-loving, domestically oriented type who loves and is loved by the opposite sex.

The differences in training begin at birth. Tight wrapping in swaddling clothes may be customary; there the child lies bound hand and foot for two to three days. Being tucked in beside the mother's warm body and given the breast immediately may be the custom, or it may be separated by a glass cage in the hospital, comforted by the sounds of an artificial heart beating out the pulse-like rhythm to which he was accustomed in the womb.

Such patterns of child care vitally affect what the child is to become as a man, emotionally. Yet even in our scientific age, we take care of and train the child more by folklore than by convincing scientific knowledge. We do not yet know a fraction of what should be known for best preparing a child for adulthood in a modern urban industrial world, with its characteristic pattern of secondary groups and anonymous contacts; but we know a great deal more than we are able to practice. If we were able to "do" as well as we "know" for children, adulthood adjustments would be enormously improved in one generation.

The Theological vs. Psychological Conception of Human Nature

Our culture is rooted in a theological conception which held that human nature is evil, that the child is born in sin, and that before he can be good his nature must be changed. A maxim of parental training of an earlier day held that the child is by nature willful, sinful, and carnal, that before goodness could even begin to be built, his will had to be broken. "Spare the rod and spoil the child" was one expression of this philosophy in practice.

Scientific study of human nature leaves no basis for such a psychology of childhood. Gesell, who has spent a lifetime in child-study research, declares "The intrinsic charm and goodness of childhood still constitute the best guarantee of the perfectability of mankind."[1] He further observes, "The most ameliorative force . . . is an intensified conservation of the development of infants and children."[2]

Here we see an expression of the current scientific view: that human nature is to be accepted, cultivated, developed, and brought to its full potentialities. It is not to be destroyed. Good and bad are in the training system, not in the nature of the child.

Psychologist Maslow has condemned the system of child training which employs fear, punishment, loss of love, and threat of abandonment. He finds that children and adults who feel safe, loved, and respected, were trained by positive rather than negative methods. They were taught to please, to make others happy; they were taught truth, logic, justice, consistency, right, and duty. Their personalities were not built in an atmosphere of anxiety, fear, insecurity, guilt, shame, but in one where reality, fair play, fitness, beauty, and rightness were stressed.

Maslow sees positive building of human nature, not negative and suppressive tactics, as the route to desirable character. Rather than seeing child-parent relationships as a chance primarily to make mistakes, as a set of problems, he sees them as "a pleasure and a delight, a great opportunity to enjoy."[3]

Early Impressionability

A baby does not wait until his hair is long enough to cut, his first teeth have appeared, or his first sentences have been lisped to his admiring parents before he begins to learn. From the earliest days of an infant's life, his personality is being shaped. Psychologists now believe that his sense of belonging, which is basic to the way he responds to other people throughout his lifetime, is established by relationships with those closest to him, usually the mother, during the first two or three years of life. If a mother by affection and care makes her child feel that he is

[1] Arnold Gesell and Frances L. Ilg, *The Child from Five to Ten* (New York: Harper & Row, Publishers, 1946), p. 453.

[2] *Ibid.*, p. 454.

[3] A. H. Maslow, *Motivation and Personality* (New York: Harper & Row, Publishers, 1954), pp. 376-378.

wanted, and important to her, he acquires a sense of security which carries over to other relationships. If, on the other hand, she is irritable or hostile and makes him feel that he is unwanted, he develops a sense of insecurity which is difficult to eradicate in later years.

In Chapter 9, dealing with love, we discussed, with considerable case material, the importance of the emotional climate to the development and even to the physical survival of the child. We also introduced the concept of "critical period" which psychologists recognize in the growth of the child. Research[4] suggests that the critical period for socialization comes from six weeks to six months, and the beginning of the critical period for emotional disturbance is at about seven months. There are also optimum periods for development of particular skills and for establishing particular controls.

The most wholesome attitude for parents is one of affection without overindulgence. They should be firm and consistent but at the same time tolerant and reasonable. To achieve such a balance is by no means easy in an individualistic age when the right of the parent to seek his own ends is taken for granted. An astute analyst of American family behavior concluded that one of the major problems of the modern family is that of harmonizing the needs of women for achievement and self-realization with the needs of young children for almost continuous attention.[5]

A balance between a cold, harsh attitude toward the child and an over-indulgent attitude, wherein the parent is trying to satisfy his own emotions rather than seeing that the child is given normal affection and care, is difficult to achieve. Yet it is between these two extremes that a secure, happy child takes his first unconscious steps in forming a personality that will fit the family and larger social groups.

Parental Authority in Child Training

The question of the amount of authority that should be exercised by parents over the child is unsolved. Customs vary from age to age and practices vary from family to family. Some parents may rule with an iron hand, others exercise almost no control, believing that complete independence from the beginning is essential.

The American philosophy of child training, for instance, is in direct contrast at many points to that of certain European and English societies. In France and England the visitor gets the impression that children are reared by tea-time etiquette and are made young adults from the very

4 J. P. Scott, "Critical Periods in Behavioral Development," *Science*, 138:949-957, November, 1962.
5 J. K. Folsom, *The Family in Democratic Society* (New York: John Wiley & Sons, Inc., 1943).

beginning. The French child meets his schoolmate on the street and shakes hands with him as an adult would do. An English boy will ask his boyfriend in for tea in midafternoon. Adult standards of etiquette and behavior seem to prevail. British training methods are still stern,[6] perhaps a carry-over from the day when the British upper-class male was trained to rule the empire.

In the United States, children are seldom thought of or treated as miniature adults. They are credited with different standards, values, and interests. They are treated as children and adults are very much surprised if they do not act as such. Scandinavian cultures conceive of childhood in much the same way. The world of a child is believed to be a world of play and independent activity. He is not expected to live entirely, or even primarily, by the manners, codes, and restraints of adults, or to share in their responsibilities and problems. He is to have a warm and affectionate relationship with parents, but otherwise live in a child's world.

His attachment to parents is emotional and affectional, whereas the child in European society tends to be reared in an attitude of respect, honor, and obedience to parents, much as in the patriarchal family of America some generations ago.

There is no one proper and right way to rear children, and practices must vary to suit the particular culture in which the child is to live. A study of the home life of 158 children in Milwaukee, Wisconsin, suggests that there is a great variety of practices and ways of doing things in families even within the United States and that good adjustment is associated with no particular technique.[7] Some of the factors that are generally associated with good adjustment, however, are "love and affection, being wanted, being appreciated, being trusted, being accepted as a person, being looked upon with respect as individuals."

It must always be kept in mind, too, that personality formation is a continuous and never-ending process, that it goes on throughout childhood and the teen years into adulthood, and that forces outside the family have their part in it.

Where is the proper balance of authority and freedom? This is always a problem. The parent who extends too much freedom places too much

---

[6] *Time* reports a great deal of cruelty to children still. Caning is heavily used in home and school. A recent Gallup poll, they report, showed that 70 percent of British men and 76 percent of British women urge the flogging of young criminals. A British doctor is reported to have said "Instead of feeling a sense of horror on hearing of some father brutally belting his son, many people instinctively think that the little bastard probably deserved it." They report that the National Society for Prevention of Cruelty to Animals was founded in 1824; 58 years later some protection for children came into law. The penalty for mistreating a child is $70.00; an animal, $140. See also Eleanor Wintour, "Bringing Up Children: The American vs. the British Way," *Harper's Magazine*, 229:58-63, August, 1964.

[7] Irving W. Stout and Grace Langdon, "A Study of the Home Life of the Well-Adjusted Children," *Journal of Educational Sociology*, 23:442-460.

decision in the hands of the immature child. The child becomes like a rat in a maze. Psychologists are able to construct such complicated mazes that the animals lose their mind trying to reach the food at the end of the maze. A child can suffer great confusion and strain if forced to make decisions only adults have the background to make.

At the other extreme, the excessive demands of overly authoritarian parents frequently drive young people to revolt. This is particularly true in communities where other youngsters enjoy greater freedom of activity. Children in a democratic society, with their freedom of contact outside of the home and their experience in the school system, are prone to be extremely critical of a harsh disciplinary pattern in the home. It is at this point that the break so often comes between immigrant parents and their children. The parents in this group have been taught to value obedience for its own sake; their youngsters, who are absorbing the values of the new community, feel that they are entitled to a complete hearing and an equal voice in decisions affecting them.

In earlier years, when rigorous discipline was the basis for authority in both home and school, youth revolted by running away from home. Many found themselves in serious trouble when they finally escaped parental authority simply because they had never had any experience in making decisions for themselves. The world of freedom outside the home was for them a world of confusion. In many cases the standards of good and bad given them at home were so arbitrary and unreasonable that adjustment to the world outside was a long and uncertain process.

This does not mean, as stated above, that "freedom unlimited," is the right answer. A youngster who is confronted with too many choices too soon in life is in an equally difficult situation.

Some modern parents tend to overemphasize the strength of the child, pushing him into independence at too early an age and putting him into competition with the adult for authority in the home. The child may have the rest of the family "buffaloed" by the time he is two. This, of course, is the individualistic American family carried to its extreme.

Without the training and experience to use it sensibly, freedom can be more of a liability than an asset in the young person's life. Every child wants the recognition and affection that comes from pleasing others but when no guidance is given as to how he can succeed—that is, what kind of behavior will be rewarded—then he, like any adult, is only frustrated by the many choices open to him.

Discipline Is Necessary

All experts in child psychology recognize the need for discipline in the child's experience. There are wide differences of opinion as to its purpose, its nature, and methods of applying it. By discipline is meant outside direction of the child. This involves, as does all control, (1) teaching which will direct the child in his choices, and (2) guidance and correction. The goal of discipline is to make him fit into the social group with which he must live and work as an adult member of society.

No society has a place for the individual who ignores all authority. Those who fail to recognize the authority of the law find themselves outcasts or in institutions for the delinquent and criminal. Those who fail to accept the ethical or religious standards and customs of their group may find themselves in moral confusion. Those who fail to recognize that every game has to be played according to its rules find themselves maladjusted in many situations, at odds with their fellows, and in discord with the general tenor of social life.

The child who has never known authority is of all children most unhappy. Adulthood assumes a willingness to recognize the rights and wishes of others, and to assume one's share of the load of human responsibilities. The child who grows up without ever having recognized that every human being has obligations to others is not ready to face the compulsory restrictions of an adult society happily.

Margaret Mead, anthropologist, has described the experience of children of the Manus tribe, primitives on the Island of New Guinea.[8] There, children are allowed to grow up with almost no restriction by parents or elders, carefree and with their every wish indulged by the adults of the group. In adolescence they are initiated into adulthood, a state in which men and women everywhere have to recognize social control and assume their share of the world's duties. These young people enter adulthood sorrowfully and always look back upon their childhood as the happy period of their lives.

The child psychologist of today believes that childhood should be happy, but he also knows that happiness and discipline can and should go hand-in-hand; that they are, in fact, complementary rather than inconsistent. He knows that a child can be happy and at the same time be prepared best for adulthood by receiving direction from adults, discipline if you will, along with as much freedom to choose and decide for himself as his age, experience, and sense of responsibility permit.

The amount of adult direction required by a two-year-old is much greater than that needed by a child of ten. His physical health must be supervised more completely, his habit formation more constantly supervised, and his regard for others' rights developed.

At no age in life is blind obedience to be expected. It is possible for parents to gain respect for their position of authority and for their greater

[8] Margaret Mead, *Growing Up in New Guinea* (New York: William Morrow & Co., Inc., 1935); also her, *From the South Seas* (New York: William Morrow & Co., Inc., 1939).

experience through a system of family management which is entirely democratic. This is not accomplished by laying down rules. Youngsters even in their earliest years can be taught cooperation best not by a demanding parent but by a home atmosphere in which cooperation among family members is given freely and taken for granted in return. Too few parents fully realize that it is what they themselves do in interpersonal relationships that determines what their children will do. Advice and admonitions have been found to be of little positive value in themselves.

Children of all ages have the right to expect an explanation of the "why" behind their parents' requests. In the democratic home there is no place for the attitude. "Do it because I said so—I'm older and I know best." This does not mean that each time we request something of a child a full explanation should automatically be given. Children frequently become downright bored with parents who are too eager to talk to them and treat them as little adults. It does mean that, upon request, we should be willing and able to justify our stand with reason rather than emotion.

Discipline Without Punishment

Many parents cannot reconcile the idea of a need for discipline of children and modern theories that the child should not be punished. The late Ellsworth Faris, sociologist, differentiates the two and makes a strong case for discipline without punishment. He defines punishment as "the intentional inflicting of suffering administered by authority on one who has been guilty of offense."[9] He ably defends the thesis that discipline without punishment is feasible and more effective than discipline achieved by punishment.

He begins his defense by citing his early observations among natives of the Belgian Congo rain forest who never punish children. He indicates that critics were inclined to look upon his observations as being inaccurate, but reports that since that time all anthropologists have come to recognize that punishment of children is unknown among preliterate people everywhere. The children are taught the taboos, inhibitions, rituals, and customs of tribal life. They are well disciplined but they are not subjected to punishment.

Our logic for punishment, he believes, is to deter the offender from future transgression and to deter others by publicizing his punishment. This is particularly true in the field of penal practice with adults.

In applying his theory of discipline to the child, Faris indicated that the child must have its full measure of love. When language begins,

[9] Ellsworth Faris, *Discipline Without Punishment* (pamphlet) (Salt Lake City: University of Utah Press, 1952).

discipline takes on new meaning for the child. If, for example, he picks up objects which he should not have, they should be taken away from him with "affectionate inflexibility accompanied by gentle tones." In this way he learns that some things are for grownups and not for him. Close bonds are maintained between child and parent which should never be broken.

Punishment in any form tends to weaken this bond. He should not be given his own way, but by "loving, gentle compulsion be required to do what he is expected to do and do it on time." There should be no violation of the intimacy and trust which exists between child and parent. In the childhood stage, when he is no longer a toddler, praise should be added to the love-and-fun relationship between child and parent. Expressions of approval soon become important factors in discipline. The parent, by rewarding certain conduct with approval, makes the child eager to repeat the conduct and thus win approval again. The never-ending thirst of children for affection and admiration is a parent's most valuable ally in drawing out the best in a child.

The later stage of boyhood or girlhood brings the need not only for love, fun, and praise, but for membership. There is a desire to belong to the group, to be accepted and appreciated by his age mates. Organized games become very important and the child is eager for the first time to play by rules. Now is the time when abstract moral precepts can be taught "in cozy, intimate moments, when only two are present, the child and one parent." Faris believed that moral teaching should be divorced from particular offenses, and that an offense should not be reproved until a day or two afterwards when there is no tendency on the part of the child to want to justify what he did.

The next stage is adolescence. All the teaching that the parent can effectively do has been done before this stage is reached. Those who have done the job well need have little anxiety about the future. Those who have failed can do very little at this time to undo the effects of their serious mistakes.

In concluding his statement of child-training theory, Faris indicated that discipline is essential and that any method of producing it is better than no discipline at all, but reaffirms his thesis that discipline without punishment is possible and effective. In summarizing his views, Dr. Faris states:

> The rearing of children is not a science and can never be; it is rather an art, for no two situations are identical. But scientific principles must guide the method, whether these principles are learned systematically or transmitted by tradition.
>
> The young parent can lovingly overpower the runabout, define the objects for the child, give a due measure of love, fun, and praise, avoid produc-

ing a sense of guilt, never reprove what has been done accidentally, and, if it is thought important make disobedience impossible by substituting polite requests for arbitrary or semi-military commands. There is a strong close intimate bond between parent and child, given—not acquired—and this precious bond can be kept unbroken. The child's very conception of himself is wholly within the power of the parents in the early years.

The subject here discussed is controversial, highly controversial. Many have argued the point with me and have contended that discipline without punishment is inferior to the method which visits every offense with its appropriate penalty. This can be argued and I have tried to argue it here. But when I am told that discipline without punishment is not possible, then I insist that there is no argument. It has been done and is being done, and successfully.

Not only is the example of the millions of preliterate children in Africa and the islands of the sea before us but many of my own students have tried this better way and have been successful.

And if I may be pardoned for a more personal reference I will say that I have fourteen (14) grandchildren, ages from two to thirteen, all of whom are, so far, well disciplined but none of whom have been punished in any manner.[10]

Recognition of Growing Independence

Even though authority and discipline must enter into the child's world, it is equally important that discipline leave room for growing individuality. As the youngster passes from infancy into childhood the parent must accept his growing need for independence. With each passing year the normal child develops new interests and an ever-increasing belief in himself and his own power and wisdom. He challenges his parents' opinions and authority, not because he is bad, but because he is developing a normal confidence in his own opinions—a confidence which is necessary in adults but often resented in children. Parents who do not understand the genesis of this growing assertiveness are inclined to "clamp down" before the teenager gets completely out of hand. Clamping down is their way of saying "look, you are only a child, now act like one," but to the young person it is an open challenge and may represent the beginning of real disciplinary problems.

The Conflict in American Child-Training Practices

In child rearing, as in many of our other practices, Americans are going none too gracefully through a difficult period of transition. The way ahead is rather clearly indicated by the kind of people and country

10 *Ibid.*

we have become. Still we are held back from embracing the new and more appropriate patterns wholeheartedly by the powerful carry-over of yesteryears' contradictory practices. Within a single community, or even a single family, child-training patterns will be found to vary from those of strict adherence to the "traditional way" to an absolute conviction that "practically everything my mother did was wrong."

But, as has been observed, social and economic changes brought new customs in mate seeking and marriage, so they are bringing a new philosophy of family life and child training. Since the practices of the past are in conflict with modern thinking at so many points, it is assumed that time and the gradual processes of reeducation will ultimately bring about consistency of practice among American families.

Parents who still cling tenaciously to yesterday's methods generally do so out of a certain distress at the new and revolutionary, or because they have linked their child-training philosophy with religious convictions and justified their practices on moral grounds rather than by their practical results. Those who feel a strong attachment to the methods their own parents or grandparents used need to understand that, while suited to the world and values of yesterday, the authoritarian pattern does not adequately prepare young people for life in modern times.

The goal of yesterday's training system was to make of the child a working member of the household at as early an age as possible. This meant that he was taught to work. He began with simple chores and each year was given an increasing share of the household work load. With work playing so important a part in the child's life, discipline was necessarily strong. A heavy hand was needed to channel youthful energies away from play into routine duties.

Except on farms, and even there to a lesser extent than in the past, children are no longer valued in terms of their ability to make an immediate contribution to the family's economic well-being. Child labor legislation has eliminated children from industry and greatly limited the number of jobs in which young teenagers can be gainfully employed. Custom and school pressure further limit the work demands parents can make on their children. The type of discipline which was necessary when children were workers is pointless now that their chief activities are centered around school and play.

Other adults are skeptical of the newer pattern because it seems to produce a more casual parent-child relationship. They remember the strong emphasis of the past upon the obligations of children to their parents and they fear that when these obligations are no longer stressed family loyalty and unity will vanish. It is true that the commandment, "Honor thy father and thy mother" was a basic one in generations past, often repeated to the child by parents, grandparents, aunt, and uncle, in fact by all of the elders. Honor and obedience were the criteria of good child training. Disobedience was looked upon as a cardinal sin.

Religious leaders as well as educators of the past lent their full support to the commandment. In orthodox theological terms, this philosophy took the form of an admonition to parents to "break the child's will," it being held that the child was almost worthless until his carnal nature was destroyed by discipline and punishment, his will broken, and submission to authority achieved. Only then could he attain to grace and become a submissive member of the church, community, and family.

What is the present situation? Is there justification for the doubts some parents have concerning the loyalty and social attitudes of young people trained according to today's more permissive pattern?

Although the relationship between parent and child in the democratic family does tend to be more casual (less ritualistic and formalized), it is actually a closer and more mutually satisfying one than existed in the past.[11] The loyalty which young people give their families is much more likely to be given freely; their sense of obligation much more likely to grow out of real respect rather than parent-instilled fear. When the break with parents comes, as it inevitably must if the young person is to become a self-directing adult with a family of his own, it is less likely to be the cruel and complete break that it once was. In the old-fashioned American family, far too often father and son either came to physical or verbal blows, leading to an abrupt and unqualified break. This assertion of independence by the son was looked upon not as natural but as a direct challenge to the father's position of supreme authority. The son was sometimes ordered out of the home and told never to return. The old revival song, "Oh, Where Is My Wandering Boy Tonight?" grew out of this characteristic break in family relations.

In the modern family, parents accept each new step the child takes toward independence as not only inevitable but completely desirable. They visualize for their son or daughter, not a life of submission but one of independence, self-respect, creativity, and ambition. To cultivate these qualities, greater rather than lesser freedom of thought, choice, and behavior are permitted.

The democratic system of child training has emerged with urban industrial development. It is in direct contrast to the older system of child training at almost every point, and the clash of the two explains the frequent conflict of values of young husbands and wives as they face the task of child training.

[11] Paul H. Landis and Carol L. Stone, *The Relationship of Parental Authority Patterns to Teenage Adjustments* (Pullman, Wash.: Washington Agricultural Experiment Station, September, 1952), Bulletin No. 538; also Stone and Landis, "An Approach to Authority Patterns in Parent-Teenage Relationships," *Rural Sociology*, 18:233-242, September, 1953.

The democratic family can best be differentiated from the authoritarian family of the past by recognizing its focal point. In almost every aspect of its pattern of living the modern home is child-centered rather than adult-centered. It assumes that the needs of the child are paramount to those of the father and mother. Parents do not consider that their children "owe" them anything—either love, respect, gratitude, or repayment for their own work and worry in the child's behalf. They hope, however, that by their own attitude of unselfish devotion they can arouse and develop similar attitudes in their offspring.

Even legal statutes recognize the paramount obligation of parent to child, for the state is willing to investigate where there is evidence of neglect or mistreatment of the child, and even to remove the child from the parent. This is a striking contrast to early agrarian cultures, in some of which the child could be stoned to death for disobedience to parents. No question was ever raised then about the parents' right to demand obedience. Now it is assumed that the child has to become an independent and self-sufficient adult. It is taken for granted that sometime during his youth he will become almost entirely weaned from the family and lose practically all sense of obligation to it.

This is true in the emotional sense to a degree; it is even more true in the economic sense. The Social Security Act, by providing through the state, means of support for the old when they are no longer able to care for themselves, partially removes the burden of personal obligation to parents for economic support. In a wage economy, it is enough for most young people to carry the support of their own children. The obligation is now to the new generation, not to the old.

Because the democratic family is dedicated to the development of independence and individualism, rather than conformity and submission, it tends to be guidance-centered, rather than discipline-centered. This does not mean that discipline is absent in the family; it is rather a discipline achieved by cooperation and mutual understanding. It operates by discussion and explanation, by pointing out a better way when error is committed, by giving the child sufficient freedom to make mistakes and gain experience from them, to choose and, eventually, through trial and error, choose wisely. Punishment as such is gradually disappearing as a disciplinary concept. Physical punishment has been done away with to a considerable extent. Sharing and working together, rather than honor and obedience, have become the bonds.

With individualism rather than familism as the goal, it is the dream of most parents that their child will become a creative, independent, self-sufficient person, able to play a highly individualized role in a specialized social order. For this reason a parent cannot stamp his own pattern and philosophy upon the child. He shares the training function with many other institutions. He encourages initiative in the child, smiles upon evidence of independence, even welcomes a certain amount of revolt, for he knows that only through such independence and originality can greatness be achieved.

The democratic parent does not expect a period of sowing wild oats and complete teenage rebellion. He expects the child to gradually achieve independence and to be ready for the freedom that inevitably comes in the teens. With the recognition of increasing maturity, the parental hand is gradually withdrawn and the child is given greater opportunities to exercise his own judgment within the areas and limits which the parents consider safe. The way he behaves when not in the custody of parents is the final test of the training system employed.

Problems

1. Most child-training authorities agree with Father Flanagan's observation that, "There is no such thing as a bad boy." Why then is discipline considered essential in training children?
2. In using the word "discipline," people often mean very different things. Give a definition and example of at least two different usages.
3. Hill Street is a busy thoroughfare lined with middle-class homes. In the nine-hundred block there are three houses on the north side of the street and in each there is a child under two years of age. These youngsters frequently play together on one of their lawns while their mothers sit together talking and watching them play. The children, of course, are too young to know about the dangers of the traffic on Hill Street so they frequently venture out toward the exciting highway. When this happens the mothers react in very different ways.

    Analyze the typical behavior of each mother described below, and discuss it in terms of:

    a. Effectiveness in controlling child's behavior.
    b. Effectiveness in controlling child's future behavior.
    c. Effect of behavior on child-mother relationship.
    d. Theory that seems to lie behind mother's action.

    Mother A: Runs after child, screaming "Don't!" Grabs child and spanks it. Repeats this if child goes out again.

    Mother B: Sees her child wandering in general direction of street and calls out in frightening voice "Don't you go out there. If you do a big car will hit you and kill you." If child continues, mother pulls her back to middle of lawn. Repeats this ritual if child starts out again.

    Mother C: Sees her child wandering toward street and says nothing. When child reaches a certain point, mother calls pleasantly, "Mary," to get her attention. If child does not return, mother goes out and takes her hand and watches the cars. If child wants to go nearer street, mother picks her up and carries her back to center of lawn without saying anything. Repeats this action whenever necessary.

4. Read pages 253-260, entitled "Discipline," in Dr. Benjamin Spock's *The Pocketbook of Baby and Child Care*. What are Dr. Spock's views on punishment? Do you think he is correct in his evaluation of its effectiveness?

5. Two very healthy, high-spirited, inquisitive young boys are handled in two very different ways. Both are described by their parents as "difficult to manage."

One is encouraged in his inquisitiveness, urged ahead in all physical activity, and given maximum freedom within the limits of health and safety. The other boy's parents try to curtail his excesses by discouraging his constant questions, and trying to channel his interests into reading. They do not punish him physically, but rebuke him frequently for his tactlessness and forwardness, and remind him that, "where choices are concerned, we know what is best." Which boy is most likely to:

a. Be an unmanageable adult?

b. Respect his parents most?

c. Develop unsocial energy outlets?

d. Develop a distaste for reading?

e. Be most successful as an adult in terms of leadership and achievement?

6. A well-meaning young mother has read that "permissiveness" is the best method in child rearing. She feels that she should do what the authorities say is best for the child but secretly she feels that a good spanking is what her child needs most. What are the dangers of attempting to administer a system of discipline in which one does not sincerely believe? What course would you advise this parent to follow?

7. *Sociodrama:* The scene opens a moment after Mary's twelve-year-old daughter, Jean, has rushed out of the room screaming at her mother, "I hate you! I hate you! I hate you! You're the meanest person I know!"

Mary's mother-in-law, who has witnessed the scene, says, "Call that child back and punish her on the spot. She can't be allowed to talk to you that way. Why, when I was a child. . . ."

Mary interrupts, "I'll do nothing of the sort, Mother. You probably felt just as Jean does many times when you were young and it would have been better if you hadn't been punished for expressing what you felt."

Let the drama picture the two philosophies of discipline held by the two women. Try to show both philosophies in sympathetic light.

Selected References

ARTICLES IN BOOKS OF READINGS

Sussman, Marvin B., *Sourcebook in Marriage and the Family* (Boston: Houghton Mifflin Co., 1955).

    1. Littman, Richard A., "Social-Class Differences in Child Rearing: A Third Community," pp. 231-240.

2. HOFFMAN, Lois Wladis, "Effects of Maternal Employment on the Child," pp. 241-247.

3. RAINWATER, Lee, and others, "The Inner Life and Outer World of the Workingman's Wife," pp. 173-185.

4. RODMAN, Hayman, "On Understanding Lower-Class Behavior," pp. 186-193.

5. WOLFENSTEIN, Martha, "Trends in Infant Care," pp. 202-209.

6. SEWELL, William H., "Infant Training and the Personality of the Child," pp. 207-217.

LANDIS, Judson T., and LANDIS, Mary G., *Readings in Marriage and the Family* (Englewood Cliffs, N. J.: Prentice-Hall, Inc., 1952).

7. DALE, Martha Ericson, "Child-Rearing and Social Status," pp. 260-263.

VINCENT, Clark E., *Readings in Marriage Counseling* (New York: Thomas Y. Crowell Co., 1957).

8. KIRKENDALL, Lester A., "Helping Parents Become Better Sex Educators," pp. 80-88.

WINCH, Robert F., and others, *Selected Studies in Marriage and the Family*, Revised Edition (New York: Holt, Rinehart & Winston, Inc., 1962).

9. KOHN, Melvin, "Social Class and Parental Values," pp. 304-321.

CHRISTENSEN, Harold T., *Handbook of Marriage and the Family* (Chicago: Rand McNally & Co., 1964).

10. DAGER, Edward Z., "Socialization and Personality Development," Ch. 18.

General References

BACMEISTER, Rhoda W., *Your Child and Other People* (Boston: Little, Brown and Co., 1950).

BARUCH, Dorothy Walter, *New Ways of Discipline* (New York: McGraw-Hill Book Co., 1949).

BECK, Lester R., *Human Growth* (New York: Harcourt, Brace & World, Inc., 1949).

BIBBY, Cyril, *Sex Education. A Guide for Parents, Teachers, and Youth Leaders* (New York: Emerson Books, Inc., 1946).

BIESTER, Lillian L., GRIFFITHS, William, and PEARCE, N. O., *Units in Personal Health and Human Relations* (Minneapolis: University of Minnesota Press, 1947).

BLANTON, Smiley, *Love or Perish* (New York: Simon and Schuster, Inc., 1955).

BOSSARD, James H. S., *The Sociology of Child Development*, Third Edition (New York: Harper & Row, Publishers, 1960).

————, and BOLL, Eleanor S., *The Large Family System* (Philadelphia: University of Pennsylvania Press, 1956).

CAVAN, Ruth Shonle, *The American Family*, Third Edition (New York: Thomas Y. Crowell Co., 1963), Ch. 18.

Child Study Association of America, *Parents' Questions*, Revised Edition (New York: Harper & Bros., 1947).

CROW, Lester, and CROW, Alice, *Sex Education for the Growing Family* (Boston: Christopher Publishing House, 1959).

DRIVER, Helen (Editor), *Sex Guidance for Your Child* (Madison, Wis.: Monona Publications, 1960).

ECKERT, Ralph, *Sex Attitudes in the Home* (New York: Association Press, 1956).

FAEGRE, Marion L., and ANDERSON, John E., *Child Care and Training* (Minneapolis: The University of Minnesota Press, 1947).

FARIS, Ellsworth, *Discipline Without Punishment* (pamphlet) (Salt Lake City: University of Utah Press, 1952).

GESELL, Arnold, and ILG, Frances L., *The Child From Five to Ten* (New York: Harper & Row, Publishers, 1946), p. 453.

GRUENBERG, Sidonie M., *We the Parents* (New York: Harper and Bros., 1939).

HYMES, James L., *How to Tell Your Child About Sex* (New York: Public Affairs Pamphlets), No. N.L. 149.

JENKINS, Gladys Gardner, *These Are Your Children* (Chicago: Scott, Foresman & Co., 1952).

KELL, Leone, and ALDOUS, Joan, "Trends in Child Care over Three Generations," *Marriage and Family Living,* 22:176-177, May, 1960.

LANDIS, Judson T., "Experiences of 500 Children with Adult Sexual Deviation," *The Psychiatric Quarterly Supplement,* Part I, 30:91-109.

————, "The Nondelinquent Child and the Sexual Deviant," *Research Studies of the State College of Washington,* 22:92-101, March, 1955.

LANDIS, Paul H., and STONE, Carol L., *The Relationship of Parental Authority Patterns to Teenage Adjustments* (Pullman, Wash: Washington Agricultural Experiment Station, September, 1952), Bulletin 538.

LEMASTERS, E. E., *Modern Courtship and Marriage* (New York: The Macmillan Co., 1957), Ch. 25.

McCORD, William, *Origins of Crime* (New York: Columbia University Press, 1959).

MASLOW, A. H., *Motivation and Personality* (New York: Harper & Row, Publishers, 1954).

MEAD, Margaret, *A Creative Life for Your Children* (Washington, D. C.: U. S. Department of Health, Education, and Welfare, 1962).

————, *From the South Seas* (New York: William Morrow & Co., Inc., 1939).

————, *Growing Up in New Guinea* (New York: William Morrow & Co., Inc., 1935).

NEISSER, Edith, *Brothers and Sisters* (New York: Harper & Bros., 1951).

NIMKOFF, Meyer F., *Marriage and the Family* (Boston: Houghton Mifflin Co., 1947), Ch. 16.

NYE, F. Ivan, and HOFFMAN, Lois Wladis (Editors), *The Employed Mother in America* (Chicago: Rand McNally & Co., 1963), Part 2.

SHULTZ, Gladys Denny, and HILL, Lee Forrest, *Your Baby, The Complete Baby Book for Mothers and Fathers* (New York: Doubleday & Co., Inc., 1948).

SMART, Mollie Stevens, *Babe in a House* (New York: Charles Scribner's Sons, 1950).

SPOCK, Benjamin, *The Common Sense Book of Baby and Child Care* (New York: Duell, Sloan & Pearce, Inc., 1946).

————, *The Pocketbook of Baby and Child Care* (New York: Pocket Books, Inc., 1946).

STRAIN, FRANCES BRUCE, *New Patterns in Sex Teaching* (New York: Appleton-Century-Crofts, Inc., 1951).

————, *The Normal Sex Interests of Children* (New York: Appleton-Century-Crofts, Inc., 1948).

TENNEY, H. Kent., *Let's Talk About Your Baby,* Revised Edition (Minneapolis: The University of Minnesota Press, 1947).

U. S. Department of Labor, *Your Child from One to Six* (Washington, D. C.: U. S. Department of Labor), Children's Bureau Publication 30.

For sources for purchasing inexpensive pamphlets on child training see the publishers in the note at the end of the General References of Chapter 29.

31
The Democratic Family

With all the freedom that has been given the modern child, there is still evidence that many people grow from childhood to maturity without the kind of socialization and character development that makes them acceptable adults. Is the democratic pattern of child training to be blamed? Or is the guilty factor rather a carry-over in many families of authoritarian patterns in a world where they no longer fit? Are the delinquents by and large from homes where too much freedom has been given, or too little and too late?

Perhaps a fully convincing answer to this question cannot be given, but certainly a great deal of logical and inferential evidence supports the young parents' faith in democratic methods of family administration.

The Modern Family Is a Launching Platform into an Individualistic World

Anthropologist Margaret Mead has likened the American family to a launching platform from which young people are cast out to live independent and self-sufficient lives in an anonymous world of impersonal contacts. It is this fact of modern life that makes the democratic family training pattern have significance in our mobile, highly urbanized social system.

The final test, therefore, of the democratic family pattern comes in the teen years when the young person is on the threshold of adulthood. How do those reared in democratic and authoritarian families compare as they face this transition which determines whether or not they are ready for an independent and self-sufficient adulthood, such as is required in contemporary culture? The evidence is strongly in favor of the democratic family insofar as parent-teenager relationships are concerned, and insofar as the adjustment of teenagers to the peer group, church, community, and school and in social relations is concerned.

Our studies of more than 4,300 seniors in high school show that the teenager in the democratic family has fewer problems than the one reared in an authoritarian family.[1] He feels more ready to enter the world as an independent person, and yet he is more closely attached to his parents. He has less of a sense of rebellion against parents. The bond is one welded out of mutual respect, and of close emotional ties, rather than being one of honor and obedience.

The Democratic Pattern and Parental Patience

To many, the idea of handling young children democratically is overwhelming because of the tremendous drain on patience that such a system implies. To command obedience and to force it by virtue of greater physical strength seems to be much the easier course.

Little research has been done on this problem, but Blood's very suggestive study indicates that this popular assumption may have some foundation in fact.[2] This study of forty couples shows that the permissive pattern does disrupt parents' lives more. The children are inclined to be more noisy, to encroach on the parents' privacy from morning to night. The parents also need to be more alert in controlling the children's activities in order to protect them from harm and to protect the family possessions from damage.

In general, the living quarters of permissive parents were more cluttered from the activities of the children, and the parents had to supervise the picking up of toys or, more frequently do it themselves. In homes where the pattern of discipline was strict, the children expected little freedom and conformed more or less to the rigid controls of their parents.

In the permissive homes the ideal was to give the children a chance to grow and learn. In the authoritarian homes the virtues of obedience, honesty, courtesy, and neatness were emphasized. The democratic parents were inclined to use the living room as a place to which the children had full access, making the comfort of guests secondary.

The developmental parent, as Blood states, works on the assumption that in the long run the independence he gives, and the sacrifices he

---

[1] Paul H. Landis and Carol L. Stone, *The Relationship of Parental Authority Patterns to Teenage Adjustments* (Pullman, Wash.: Washington Agricultural Experiment Station, September, 1952), Bulletin No. 538; also Carol L. Stone and Paul H. Landis, "An Approach to Authority Patterns in Parent-Teenage Relationships," *Rural Sociology,* 18:233-242, September, 1953.

[2] Robert O. Blood, Jr., "Consequences of Permissiveness for Parents of Young Children," *Marriage and Family Living,* 15:209-212, August, 1953.

makes for his children in early childhood, will make them more self-sufficient later on and perhaps more self-directive, requiring a total of less time and worry on his part.

Blood suggests that those who do not genuinely believe in the permissive home may find the regime of such a home too strenuous, for he finds that the permissive home demands not only a certain philosophy but rugged furniture and willingness on the part of parents to sacrifice the comfort and appearance of the home to the interests of the child.

The Ultimate Test of Effective Discipline

The way the child acts when the parent is absent is the true test of whether the parent's disciplinary patterns have been internalized. Until the child is self-disciplined, the goal of discipline remains unattained. It seems likely that in the authoritarian disciplinary system this goal is often unattainable.

In the farm home of yesteryear, children were taught never to play with matches and were severely punished if ever caught with them. The usual consequence was that when parents were out doing the chores or visiting neighbors, the child set the lace curtains on fire, built a fire under the bed with waste paper, or set fire to shavings in the woodshed or elsewhere.

In the democratic family, children are as fascinated by matches as children ever were. Parents let them start the fire when a picnic fire is being lighted or when kindling in the fireplace is ready to be ignited. They light the candles on the birthday cake and the Christmas altar. Not having been taught never to play with matches, and having had experience in the correct use of matches, child-started family fires no longer occur with regularity. The child internalizes mature standards with regard to matches.

Blind obedience is the lowest possible standard of discipline. It can be enforced because parents are physically stronger, but what does enforcement accomplish? If it succeeds, it destroys the child. Initiative, inventiveness, experimentation are the way to learning. Curb these and growth is curbed. Permit them to develop under an atmosphere of guidance and unlimited growth is possible.

Dr. John Anderson, director of the University of Minnesota Child Welfare Research Station, in an address many years ago in Los Angeles made the point strikingly clear. "The world is always waiting for the executive in the $100,000 class. Positions are never filled. There are always plenty of people to fill the routine factory jobs where others make all the decisions. These masses are trained to obedience."

Another test of the ultimate effect of the training pattern is the ease and confidence with which the child makes the transition toward adulthood during the teen years. The writer has given considerable attention to this problem and is convinced from his research and that of others that in contemporary American culture the democratic family pattern proves superior.

RESPONSES OF TEENAGERS BY FAMILY PATTERN TO QUESTION:

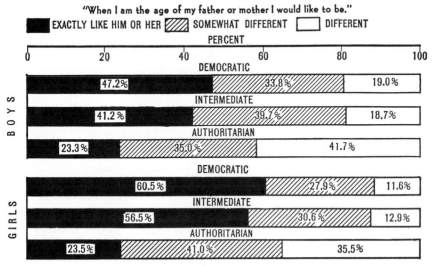

SOURCE: Paul H. Landis and Carol L. Stone, *The Relationship of Parental Authority Patterns to Teenage Adjustments* (Pullman, Wash.: Washington Agricultural Experiment Station, September, 1952), Bulletin No. 538.

FIGURE 31-1————The democratic family does not stress honor and obedience, but as young people stand on the threshold of adulthood, those reared under the democratic pattern are more desirous of emulating parents than those reared in authoritarian homes, and pesumably come closer to obeying the spirit of the Fourth Commandment: "Honor thy father and thy mother. . . ."

One way to test the extent to which the child has internalized the values and standards of his parents is the extent to which he wishes to emulate the parent in their life patterns. Figure 31-1 shows in striking contrast, by type of authority, the comparative desires of 4,310 high school seniors to emulate their parents. Those in authoritarian families[3] in few

[3] Families were classified into the three administrative types on the basis of young people's responses to a lengthy questionnaire which dealt with all aspects of their adjustment. Relationships within the home as checked by teenagers were used in classifying families, a scale following the Guttman technique being employed in the classification. In other words, young people themselves were not asked to classify their homes into authority types by direct questions.

cases considered their parents' lives as ones they wished to follow. Those in democratic families often wished to pattern after parents and less than a fifth of the boys and little more than a tenth of the girls wished to be entirely different. This is striking testimony to the stronger influence of parent over child in the democratic family. Elder also found that adolescents more often model their roles after parents who are democratic than after those who are either authoritarian or permissive.[4]

A second index of comparative adjustment of the democratically reared and authoritarian reared child is shown in Table 31-1, which summarizes responses of 4,310 high school seniors to a check list of 250 adjustment problems. These problems are classified by area. It will be seen that in all areas, and in total problems, the more democratic the family, the fewer the problems checked.

TABLE 31-1————Average number of problems checked by 4,310 high school seniors living in democratic, intermediate, and authoritarian families*

			FAMILY ADMINISTRATIVE PATTERNS		
Problem areas	Number of problems checked	Sex	Democratic (av. problems checked)	Intermediate (av. problems checked)	Authoritarian (av. problems checked)
Personal	33	boys	3.5	3.6	4.4
		girls	4.2	4.5	5.1
Family	63	boys	2.9	3.3	5.1
		girls	3.2	3.9	6.5
Social	30	boys	1.8	1.9	2.5
		girls	1.9	2.4	2.7
Boy-girl relations	34	boys	2.0	2.2	2.7
		girls	2.2	2.6	3.0
School	30	boys	2.2	2.4	3.0
		girls	2.2	2.5	3.0
Vocational	30	boys	2.9	2.9	3.4
		girls	2.6	3.1	3.2
Morals, religion	30	boys	2.2	2.4	2.5
		girls	2.4	2.9	3.0
All problems	250	boys	17.5	18.7	23.6
		girls	18.7	21.9	26.5

* Landis and Stone, *op. cit.*

These are but a few aspects of the problem studied but they illustrate the kind of conclusions which were found in almost every aspect of teenage adjustments and relationships.

Rose finds, from an analysis of 183 male and 206 female University of

[4] Glen H. Elder, Jr., "Parental Power Legitimation and Its Effects on the Adolescent," *Sociometry*, 26:50-65, March, 1963.

Minnesota students, that the transition of the adolescent to maturity seems to be made much more easily by those who have secure family relationships. He advances the hypothesis that difficult family relationships, particularly when their origin is in relationship to the mother, cause the adolescent to withdraw from the family before he is fully socialized and/or emotionally mature. He is, therefore, likely to be less able to accept adult roles than is the youth whose family relationships are more congenial.[5]

The home atmosphere—relationship of parents to each other, and relationship of father to child, and above all, of mother to child—is the key factor in juvenile delinquency. A long-time study of delinquent children, begun in the 1930's and following them into adult life, indicates that where the home provides the wrong environment, community efforts, social-work programs, and counseling show little results in improvement.[6] The absent father, or the cruel, neglectful one, tends to produce criminalty in the child. Mothers who are absent, passive, cruel, rejecting, or neglectful tend to produce criminal sons. A quarreling home, with or without affection, produces delinquents, as do also lack of discipline and erratic punitive discipline. A firm but kindly discipline is preventive. The treatment of the young delinquent is primarily a problem of working with the family, so McCord concludes in summarizing results of this study which follows the group up through the year 1955.

The Glueck study of delinquency rated overstrict and erratic discipline high as the factor predictive of delinquency.[7]

Conflicting Conceptions of Parent Roles and Goals in Child Training by Social Class

The democratic pattern, no matter how appropriate to an individualistic society, is by no means universal. In every community and from one social class to another one may find in practice different philosophies of child training. Kohn and Carroll[8] found that "to the middle-class parents, it is of primary importance that a child be able to decide for him-

[5] Arnold M. Rose, "Acceptance of Adult Roles and Separation from the Family," *Marriage and Family Living*, 21:120-126, May, 1959.

[6] William McCord, *Origins of Crime* (New York: Columbia University Press, 1959). This is a report of the Cambridge-Somerville Youth Study begun in the early 1930's with 650 boys—a group of 325 delinquents and a matched control group. The one was subject to all the reform efforts which money and social-work knowledge could provide. Reform for the most part failed utterly, yet it was probably the most extensive and costly project of this nature ever attempted in this country.

[7] Eleanor T. Glueck, "Spotting Potential Delinquents; It Can Be Done," *Federal Probation*, September, 1956, p: 9.

[8] Melvin L. Kohn and Eleanor E. Carroll, "Social Class and the Allocation of Parental Responsibilities," *Sociometry*, 23:372-392, December, 1960.

self how to act, and that he have personal resources to act on these decisions—to working-class parents . . . it is of primary importance that the child act reputably, that he not transgress the proper rules."

A survey of over four hundred mothers in Chicago, for example, gave a revealing picture of how differently the traditional and modern group conceive their role as mothers and the goals to be achieved in child training.[9]

Those who held the traditional concept considered their functions to be those of (1) keeping house, (2) taking care of the child's physical needs, (3) training him to regularity, (4) disciplining him and teaching him obedience and goodness.

Mothers with a modern conception of parenthood considered their function to be a developmental one. They felt that they should (1) train the child for self-reliance and citizenship, (2) see to his emotional well-being, (3) help him develop socially, (4) provide for his mental growth, (5) guide him with understanding, (6) give him love and affection, (7) be calm, cheerful, growing persons themselves.

The first group of mothers thought the child should be judged by whether or not he (1) was neat and clean, (2) was obedient and respectful of adults, (3) pleased adults, (4) respected property, (5) was religious, (6) worked well, (7) fitted into the family program.

The second group of mothers felt they were succeeding as mothers if the child (1) was healthy and well, (2) shared and cooperated with others, (3) was happy and contented, (4) loved and confided in his parents, (5) was eager to learn, (6) was growing as a person.

Obviously these concepts of motherhood are far apart in practice and basic philosophy, yet they are both current in the American scene. The first is more common among the lower classes; the second, among the middle and upper classes; the first, among the uneducated; the second, among the educated; the first, among large families; the second, among small families.[10]

The husband's role as father is also changing. As shorter working hours provide for greater interaction between father and child, the role of fatherhood becomes an increasingly important one. He is no longer primarily the stern disciplinarian.

True, many fathers today still conceive of their function in terms of the traditional pattern. Like their fathers before them, they willingly leave child rearing to their wives, but consider themselves the final au-

---

[9] Evelyn Millis Duvall, "Conceptions of Parenthood," *American Journal of Sociology*, 52:193-203, 1946.

[10] For research on some of these points, see Paul H. Landis and Carol L. Stone, *op. cit.*; also Paul H. Landis, *Parent Teen-Age Relationships in Large and Small Families* (Pullman, Wash.: Washington Agricultural Experiment Station, April, 1954), Bulletin No. 549.

thority in any uncertain situation or in circumstances where the mother's methods prove inadequate. The traditional father's chief function in their eyes is that of providing for the physical well-being of the family. They enter into the world of their children primarily as a disciplinarian. Their attitude toward their children is likely to be one of impatient tolerance rather than understanding companionship. They do not pretend to understand the child or his special needs and do not feel that such understanding is their responsibility. They, like the old-fashioned mother, are inclined to judge children in terms of the children's effect upon their own lives, reputations, and comfort. They believe children are properly handled if they are obedient, respectful, and useful.

The father with the modern concept of parenthood willingly accepts a much more complex and involved role for himself. He is likely to differentiate very little between the mother's duties in child training and those he himself accepts. He is concerned about each step in his child's development and assumes that he can and must play an important part in it. He considers himself less the disciplinarian and more the companion of his children. He is likely to plan his hours with them, not around ritualized activities, but around play, hobbies, and other enjoyable pursuits.

While the mother in most modern families must of necessity still take chief responsibility for the actual rearing of the children, present-day fathers generally desire to play as active a part as their time and energy permit. When working hours are long, this may mean that their chief influence over their children is an indirect one—the result of plans and policies agreed upon by husband and wife in late evening talks and put into practice by the wife. Whenever possible, however, most modern couples agree that every effort should be made to provide situations in which father and child can develop an intimate and companionable relationship. Some young men even consider the amount of leisure time for family life a major factor in the selection of a vocation or a particular job.

Food, clothing, and shelter are still major responsibilities of the father, but more and more young couples are coming to accept the view that these alone are not enough. Children need the influence of the father as well as of the mother in their development, and the special kind of companionship that he can provide is often far more important to them than new clothing or a better house.

Although the more favored socioeconomic classes have likely acquired an improved philosophy of child rearing, and may more often practice a democratic type of family administration, some believe that during infancy and early childhood parents of the lower classes are more permissive than are parents of the middle classes.

Dale's study shows that in the middle class (which social-class experts often refer to as the frustrated class) fewer children are breast-fed than in the other social classes.[11] In this class, too, three times as many children were thumb suckers as in the other social classes. It was found that the middle class tends to train its children in bowel and bladder control earlier than do the other classes. In general, the disciplinary pattern throughout childhood was found to be more rigid in the middle than in the lower classes. This study was conducted some time ago with small samples and by personal interviews in which 48 middle-class mothers and 52 lower-class mothers were studied. The middle-class group was selected from nursery schools and child-study groups. The families of both social classes had only normal children. The author expresses the belief that the disciplinary regime employed by the middle class tends to condition the child toward frustration and anxiety. The lower-class infant, by contrast, is permitted a more natural and spontaneous development.

While these results may be taken as suggestive, they should not be accepted as conclusive. The culture has shifted from the view that the infant and the child should be handled by the cold Watsonian techniques of an earlier generation to the view that a warm "rooming-in," "self-demand" feeding, and permissive pattern are the only safe ones.

The new approach is derived, somewhat at least, from the Freudian notion that discomfort and denial lead to frustration and frustration to a neurotic condition. The new method, like the old, must be taken on faith and the outcome observed in the development of the child.

Child Rearing in Modern Rural America

The greatest progress in the modernization of child rearing has understandably been among the more enlightened couples of urban residence. High school and, more particularly, college-trained parents have generally to some extent, been exposed to the research findings and the social and psychological theories that lie behind the newer methods. Information is diffused among the lower classes in urban areas through popular magazines, P.T.A. organizations, parent-teacher contacts, free clinics, and the wide dispersion of leaflets and booklets from child-guidance agencies.

Rural parents who have a high school or college education and whose farms are somewhat mechanized also tend to employ newer techniques in child training. But in most rural areas, especially among the poorer and more isolated farm families, one may find child-training patterns that differ in few respects from those of one hundred years ago. Much of this is explained by their isolation, but one must also understand that on such farms life is a rigorous economic struggle in which the child has a place as a worker. Many farm parents still expect their children to do an adult's

[11] Martha Ericson Dale, "Child-Rearing and Social Status," *The American Journal of Sociology,* 52:191-192, 1946.

work without giving them the privileges that adolescents and youth in town and city families expect. Where high school education is nearly universal, these patterns are weakening, and farm young people are gaining the freedom and independence of other young people.

Importance of Agreement on the Training Pattern to Be Employed

No matter what the pattern of child training adopted, the important essential is that parents agree on it. This is so not only because inconsistency breeds uncertainty and insecurity in the child, but also because differences in philosophy of child training are often basic factors in the marital conflict of husband and wife. This is particularly true today when there has been a rapid transition in American culture away from the authoritarian pattern to the democratic pattern for family living.

The modern college-trained wife, and even many of the high school trained ones, have had some experience in nurseries or in nursery schools and know the importance of the democratic pattern of family administration to the proper development of the child. By and large, women are more likely to favor the democratic pattern than are the men. The male, having grown up without special training for parenthood, is inclined to revert to the family patterns which were practiced in his own home. Many times these patterns were authoritarian in nature, and the father proceeds to handle his children in the same manner as his parents handled him.

This situation produces conflict between husband and wife and leaves the child uncertain as to what is expected of him. The one parent operates on the philosophy that kindness, catering to the child's needs, and making him an equal partner in the family relationship is important to the development of the young personality. The other assumes that such efforts amount to nothing more than pampering and spoiling the child. The one assumes, for example, that crying indicates discomfort and need and that the baby should be picked up and patted until he belches; the other believes he should be allowed to cry it out and not be pampered and petted lest he become a demanding tyrant. With the older child, the one operates under the old ordering-and-forbidding technique, which has come down from time immemorial; the other believes in consideration for the child's wishes and approves of reasoning with him and attempting to understand him. The one believes in punishment; the other believes in correction by nonpunitive methods. The husband is more likely to tend toward a harsh extreme in the handling of the child, which the mother considers to be frightening and shocking. In such extreme cases, neither parent has any sympathy toward the approach of the other in child care.

In such families, the husband should visit nurseries and nursery schools to learn how children are properly handled, or he should read some of the better books on child development to know the outcome of different systems of family pattern, or he should retire from the administrative situation entirely, leaving it to the better-trained wife. Certainly unless one or he other can change, the marriage is in for turmoil, as well as the children being in for a rough time in their critical developmental years.

While teaching veterans after World War II, the writer advised all men in his classes to spend at least two days at the college nursery school observing how children were handled there. They were warned that unless they did this they were likely to be at odds with their wives on the matter of child training, and that they would be wrong. Most of them took this advice, were appreciative of it, and profited by it. This has become established course procedure.

Young wives with just a smattering of information on permissive child rearing are often attracted to the method without understanding its full implications or recognizing the degree of thought and effort it requires. Above all it should be understood that this is not a "do nothing" approach. It does not mean that the mother can stand aside and let the child raise itself, so to speak. Slapping a youngster's hands, or shouting "No!" everytime he does something wrong is much easier, in fact, than calmly and repeatedly restraining him until he understands and accepts certain limits to his behavior. Patience, tact, and the ability to see the world as your child must see it are important prerequisites to success in permissive child rearing. All parents ought to get down on their hands and knees occasionally and see how different the world looks to a child who cannot even see what's on the table.

There is much more to the theory behind modern practices than can be set forth in this chapter. All young couples owe it to themselves and to their unborn children to look into the literature in this field before attempting parenthood. "Gentle discipline" can easily deteriorate into "no discipline at all"; and a great deal of behavior which may be lastingly detrimental to the young person is often countenanced in the name of "progressive child training."

Sense of Destiny

There can be little doubt that the family sets the pattern of creativity and adventure in the child.[12] There can also be little doubt that the family is the major influence in the aspiration level of the child.[13]

[12] For some thinking on this subject see Margaret Mead, *A Creative Life for Your Children* (Washington, D. C.: U. S. Department of Health, Education, and Welfare, 1962); also T. F. James, "New Route to Excellence," *This Week Magazine*, April 26, 1964, pp. 4-5.

[13] Robert E. L. Faris, "Ability Dimensions in Human Society," *American Sociological Review*, 26:835-842, December, 1961.

Whether he expects great things or the mediocre of himself is determined in large part by parental expectations and their method of expression.

The internalization of self-control and of high aspirations is the ultimate in discipline. Achieving it is an art which few parents realize to the full.

Good Sense in Child Training

It is important to caution, as has been done at many points in this book, that children are highly individualistic creatures. Parents wish them to be. They do not fit at every point the patterns of development that are standardized according to the norms of this or other books. Every child has his own distinct problems of growing up and of making adjustments to the family, to brothers and sisters, to his own age group, and to adults outside the family. These adjustments may not follow in the exact order the parents think they should, and they may not all be made without pain on the part of the child and considerable anxiety on the part of the parent. Life is not abnormal when this is so. A lot of trial and error goes into the formation of a personality. As one psychiatrist has put it "all children have difficulties."[14]

While parents may learn a great deal from reading and studying, they should not be afraid to use their own good sense in meeting situations and in helping the child with his adjustments. Their good sense can be improved, of course, by reading, but they should not hesitate to use judgment in the light of their best understanding of the situation. They also need to have confidence that growth itself will work wonders in the experience of the child. The adjustment that he finds so difficult to make at a particular time in his development, may be made almost automatically and as a matter of course as he acquires a little more age and experience. Time itself will cure many of his problems.

Neither do parents need to have great anxiety that some serious period of maladjustment in the child's early life is going to maim him permanently as a human being. This mythology of an earlier period in genetic psychology has been pretty well exploded. Personality is a constantly growing and developing affair. Many of the mistakes of the past can be corrected and many of the wounds that have been suffered through rather severe periods of maladjustment can be healed by time. The child's confidence and assurance can be rebuilt as his path into the future is plotted with greater certainty.

Human growth and development are most amazing phenomena and very interesting to watch. The parent, if he is not overly anxious, will see in his child's growth and maturation the fascinating and miracle-working power of nature as it transforms the personality with age and experience.

[14] John Levy and Ruth S. Munroe, *The Happy Family* (New York: Alfred A. Knopf, Inc., 1938), p. 28.

A few parental blunders are not going to ruin a child. These are merely some of the bumps he experiences in growing up. It is the long-persistent, seemingly incurable situations in the environment that work the damage, not the little day-to-day ups and downs that are characteristic of the normal experience of childhood.

Problems

1. A young man leaves his home in a small town and moves into a dormitory of a large state university located in a metropolis. Describe the adjustments that face this young man and discuss the way he will react to them if he is:
   a. The product of a highly authoritarian training pattern.
   b. The product of a democratic training pattern.
2. What type of personality is best suited to parenthood in a democratic family? Describe common traits that would be assets to parents adhering to the democratic pattern. Describe traits that would handicap the practice of modern child-rearing techniques.
3. Describe several aspects of the childhood training patterns in typical middle-class and lower-class homes: Consider the differing degrees of emphasis put on toilet training and, a little later, on training in manners and early formal learning. Which training pattern do you consider superior? Why?
4. In what respects do the training patterns of rural America still differ from those common in urban centers?
5. When conscientious parents find themselves disagreeing on disciplinary philosophy and techniques, which course of action is best? Discuss advantages and disadvantages of:
   a. Leaving the discipline entirely in the hands of one parent.
   b. Getting an authoritative handbook on child rearing and doing exactly as it advises.
   c. Reading books on child discipline and consulting a specialist in the field.
   d. Leaving the discipline in the hands of one parent until an agreement on techniques and philosophy can be reached.
6. *Sociodrama:* Two young wives, both of whom consider themselves "modern" in their child-rearing practices, find that they disagree on some very basic principles. One argues that modern theory "teaches you to keep your hands off and let nature take its course." The other feels that modern practices call for "greater thought, patience, and hard work for the parent than ever before."
7. Does the democratic pattern of family living require that young people have a voice equal to that of their parents in family matters?
8. List on the blackboard several of the traits and characteristics which are admired and encouraged in young people in authoritarian homes. Make another list of youthful traits that are most admired by democratic parents. With these traits in mind, discuss the probable adult personality which would emerge from each training pattern.

Selected References

ARTICLES IN BOOKS OF READINGS

SUSSMAN, Marvin B., *Sourcebook in Marriage and the Family*, Second Edition (Boston: Houghton Mifflin Co., 1963).
1. DAVIS, W. Allison, "Child Rearing in the Class Structure of American Society," pp. 225-231.
2. ABERLE, David F., and NAEGELE, Kaspar D., "Middle-Class Fathers' Occupational Role and Attitudes Toward Children," pp. 217-225.

CAVAN, Ruth Shonle, *Marriage and the Family in the Modern World: A Book of Readings* (New York: Thomas Y. Crowell Co., 1960).
3. JONES, Alma H., "How to Hold a Family Council," Reading 84.

General References

BLOOD, Robert O., Jr., "Consequence of Permissiveness for Parents of Young Children," *Marriage and Family Living*, 15:209-212, August, 1953.

BOSSARD, James H. S., *The Sociology of Child Development*, Third Edition (New York: Harper & Row, Publishers, 1960).

DALE, Martha Ericson, "Child-Rearing and Social Status," *The American Journal of Sociology*, 52:191-192, 1946.

DUVALL, Evelyn Millis, "Conceptions of Parenthood," *American Journal of Sociology*, 52:193-203, 1946.

FAEGRE, Marion L., and ANDERSON, John E., *Child Care and Training* (Minneapolis: The University of Minnesota Press, 1947).

GESELL, Arnold, and ILG, Frances L., *The Child From Five to Ten* (New York: Harper & Row, Publishers, 1946).

LANDIS, Paul H., and STONE, Carol L., *The Relationship of Parental Authority Patterns to Teenage Adjustments* (Pullman, Wash.: Washington Agricultural Experiment Station, September, 1952), Bulletin No. 538.

MARTINSON, Floyd M., *Marriage and the American Ideal* (New York: Dodd, Mead & Co., 1960), Ch. 25.

MASLOW, A. H., *Motivation and Personality* (New York: Harper & Row, Publishers, 1954).

NEISSER, Edith, *Brothers and Sisters* (New York: Harper & Bros., 1951).

NYE, F. Ivan, and HOFFMAN, Lois Wladis (Editors), *The Employed Mother in America* (Chicago: Rand McNally & Co., 1963), Part 2.

READ, Katherine H., *The Nursery School* (Philadelphia: W. B. Saunders Co., 1950).

SLOCUM, Walter L., and STONE, Carol L., "Family Culture Patterns and Delinquent Type Behavior," *Marriage and Family Living*, 25:202-208, May, 1963.

VII
MARRIAGE PROBLEMS

32

The Unmarried Adult

There is little doubt that a great number of people who marry, should remain single. They are not adapted to marriage, and bring failure to themselves and involve others in their failure. There are also, no doubt, people who should marry, but who for one reason or another do not.

Although our culture identifies personal happiness with marriage, a study[1] of mental health in the nation showed that for women the home is a great source of distress, and that mothers have a great number of problems with their children. These things trouble them much more than they trouble husbands. One in seven families seek outside help, and one in four confess they have felt the need of it.

Even so, the married are more satisfied, all in all, with their lives than are the single; but single women are happier and more active in working out their problems than are bachelor males. The unhappiest group of all are the widows and widowers.

The Changing Status of the Unmarried

Even the happiest of married persons will generally admit that in our society today there are some convincing arguments in favor of bachelorhood for both men and women. This does not mean they wish they were single; it does indicate that the status of single people has changed greatly in most communities.

According to one young bachelor woman:

It's among girls like me that you find the world's happiest, as well as the most unhappy, people. The girl who isn't married, but wishes she were,

[1] Gerald Gurin, Joseph Veroff, and Sheila Feld, *Americans View Their Mental Health* (New York: Basic Books, Inc., Publishers, 1960).

is the saddest of all, but those of us who willingly pass up marriage generally do so because we have found that life can be wonderfully complete without it.

I think that it's mostly the way the community feels about single people that makes our lot today so much better than in the past. Unmarried women with some talent and ambition have an almost limitless number of fascinating jobs to choose from; and, unlike working women of fifty years ago, we are not automatically made the subordinates of men in our field.

There has been a change, too, in the social acceptability of the unmarried. I belong to just as many clubs, get invited out to group affairs, and have as large a circle of friends of both sexes as do most of my married sisters. I dress better than they do, look younger, read more books, and see more plays. I'm less tired, just as healthy, and have a wonderful feeling of independence and self-direction. Even married men do not look down on us. In fact, unless one becomes the proverbial "old maid" I think they greatly respect us. As for married women, I've seen the shadow of envy in their eyes more than once.

In urban areas, particularly, the lot of the bachelor man may be even better than that described by the single girl above, for the sex ratio is generally such that the eligible male is greatly in demand. If he happens to have sufficient income, the bachelor suffers little domestic inconvenience because of his bachelorhood. Special laundry and dry cleaning services, dwelling places with homelike atmosphere and efficient maid service, restaurants that invite comparison with any home-cooked meal are but a few of the factors that make most bachelors think twice before entering marriage.

With industrialization and greater occupational specialization there has been a considerable increase in the number of jobs for which a single person can qualify. Among these jobs many have developed that favor or even demand the employment of the single rather than the married. And as single persons of both sexes became economically respectable, their social status also improves.

Today, most communities actually depend upon their especially capable bachelors to carry out certain important functions. This is particularly true among women's professions and occurs not because married women are less capable, but because they generally are able to devote less of their time and energy than the work demands. The stigma which was once attached to the word, "spinster," has almost entirely disappeared. In fact, the word "spinster" itself is no longer commonly used to describe most unmarried women. Only in the unsophisticated rural areas does one hear it applied to a bachelor girl in any but a humorous way.

Even with the greater social acceptance of the single person today, there are nonetheless psychological problems to be faced by the single. Those women who lack opportunity to marry cannot avoid feeling "what's wrong with me," Maurice J. Karpf, marriage counselor in Beverly Hills,

California, indicates that this is the question asked by young women past twenty who come to him for counsel.[2] They also want to know where to meet suitable men and also how to act on dates to be effective in achieving marriage.

Martinson challenges the belief that married girls are necessarily happier. His study of married and single girls graduating from high school during the years of 1945-1949 shows the single girls more self-reliant, getting along better with family and friends, making a better use of their talents, and being less frustrated than the married group.[3] The age factor may be significant here, as all had married within four years of leaving high school. Martinson's study of males who married within four years after leaving high school shows greater maladjustment among them than among the single males.[4]

An anonymous "bachelor girl," writing for *Family Weekly Magazine*,[5] outlined her advantages as a bachelor girl but admitted that she, rather than her bachelor brother, was the object of pity, sympathy, and wishes that she might soon find a mate. "Poor Alice," her neighbors call her. Such folk attitudes are to be deplored in a culture which should rate productivity and human improvement far above marrying and procreating. Marriage is not a must. Many people now marrying would be better off single. And some very marriageable women may well leave a deeper imprint on human history in choosing to pass marriage by for other values.

Social Reasons for Failure to Marry

There are a number of factors which help explain the poor marital prospects of many men and women. Knowing what these factors are can be of help in planning one's strategy for marriage. Some of these factors are social; some are personal in origin.

Mobility: Many males do not marry or defer it because they fear they cannot bear the heavy economic responsibility of marriage. In the United States, moreover, a considerable proportion of males are highly mobile. Construction and other such jobs often require temporary residence or seasonal work. The logging industry used to be such an industry, although many loggers now do marry and many logging companies establish temporary residences for couples rather than barracks for single men.

[2] Maurice J. Karpf, "Counseling the Unmarried Female Adult—Single, Widowed, Divorced," a paper delivered before the Marriage Counseling Section, National Council of Family Relations, Oakland, California, July 9, 1954.

[3] Floyd M. Martinson, "Ego Deficiency as a Factor in Marriage," *American Sociological Review*, 20:161-164, April, 1955.

[4] Floyd M. Martinson, "Ego Deficiency as a Factor in Marriage—A Male Sample," *Marriage and Family Living*, 21:48-52, February, 1959.

[5] August 25, 1957.

The highly mobile worker, although he may not lack interest in marriage and may have none of the abnormalities which make marriage undesirable, is often reluctant to take on the responsibilities of supporting a wife and family. Women may also be hesitant about accepting a proposal of marriage from the worker who frequently changes residences, because most women desire a certain amount of stability for themselves and their children after marriage.

In many instances, there is no desire on the part of the mobile worker to permanently defer marriage, but high pay is the reward of the kind of jobs he seeks and he often assumes that some day he will acquire enough to be willing to settle down to a less exciting and more routine, even though lower paying job. Actually, the kind of life that goes on at the construction camp leads many to spend money about as fast as it is earned in gambling, drinking sprees, etc., so workers may never lay by a nest egg for marriage.

Uneven sex ratio: The problem of failure to marry in many communities is a matter of uneven sex ratio. The situation in this country is not as serious as in most European countries. In Germany, France, and Russia, for example, there are millions of women with no chance of marriage. In those countries war casualties have been such that there are insufficient men of marriageable age in the population.

In the mid-1940's the United States for the first time became a nation with a low male sex ratio. Previously there had been more males than females in the population. This situation will become more critical in the years ahead if we continue to bar immigrants from our shores, for in any normal population women tend to outnumber men because of their greater length of life. Age differential of men and women in marriage also exaggerates the unfavorable sex ratio. The average male is two years older than his bride. With each year of age death eliminates some from the marriage market.

The real difficulty in America is that caused by migration. In rural areas most occupations are male occupations. Opportunities for women are extremely few. By contrast, in most cities there is more work opportunity for women than for men. This is particularly true in such cities as Washington, D. C., with its large population of government clerical and office workers, and in wealthy Palo Alto, California, with its large domestic class. A few heavy-industry cities of the Great Lakes area are dominantly male in population. Most metropolitan communities have a considerable excess of females in the marriageable ages because of work opportunities and social attractiveness; in large cities there are, per 100, ten to twelve more women than men in the most marriageable ages (refer again to Figure 8-1 in Chapter 8). And within the city there are barriers to the intermingling of single men and women. Women tend to congregate in the residential apartments of the white-collar and professional classes; men in the heavy-industry sections. The two worlds seldom meet, and when they do, they often find their differences too great to make for compatibility.

In most large cities the better residential apartment areas are crowded with young bachelor women who have little chance of meeting marriageable men. At the same time, there are many young men in the industrial sections with poorer housing who have little contact with eligible young women. These men do not appear particularly attractive to white-collar girls who are able to earn a good wage as secretary or office worker and share expenses in a beautiful apartment house with another bachelor girl. Many girls prefer their life of bachelorhood to settling for a husband who represents a different level of living and of aspiration from their own.

The isolation of the sexes in war is another unavoidable factor. It has greatest impact on the generation of girls the same age as the military men being separated from civilian life. If long removed, when they return these men often marry someone considerably younger rather than one of their own age group. The man in his late twenties usually marries someone about five years younger than himself, whereas, had he married in his early twenties, he would probably have married someone not more than two years younger than himself.

Once a woman becomes established in a white-collar job, she is, for the most part, in a one-sex world. The principal professional positions available to women are teaching, nursing, library work, welfare, charity, and religious work. In none of these, with the possible exception of nursing —and nurses are preponderantly in the older age groups—is there much contact with males. In business and industry, her chances are probably somewhat better.

Men and women who are seriously interested in marriage should face these facts concerning sex distribution in the population and use them to their own advantage. In a sense, the eligible young farmer or farmhand who wants to marry but sees few prospects in his community has no one to blame but himself. The same is true of the career girl in a large city.

In most cases, all that is needed is an awareness of the facts and a willingness to do something besides daydream about them. There are places in every city where young men and women can meet and get acquainted in a wholesome atmosphere. Church activities, community recreational centers, special talent and hobby groups, even schools provide ways and means for getting acquainted.

In rural areas—especially in isolated farming, ranching, or mining centers—the task of wife-finding may be a more formidable one. Marriage is, however, one of the most important goals in life to most people. It may necessitate frequent trips to the churches or recreational centers of nearby towns or cities. In extreme cases it may even involve a change in job location or a complete change of jobs for a period of time. A successful marriage is, however, worth considerable effort and inconvenience.

A false sense of obligation: Others who are unmarried against their own wishes frequently are so because of a genuine or a false sense of obligation to dependent or sick parents or other relatives. Often no one else is willing to assume this burden and the young woman carries it until Providence finally removes the handicap by death of the relative. She may no longer be marriageable, or at least may no longer be in contact with men who are marriageable. This is by no means a problem exclusively of the girl in the family; however, she more often assumes the burden of dependents in the family than does the boy.

Sometimes the feeling of great obligation to parents is an emotional bond rather than an economic obligation. In cases where there is too great emotional attachments to parents, the young woman may feel guilty for even thinking of falling in love with anyone else. In such cases, psychiatric help is needed to be able to make the transfer from parents to members of the opposite sex.

In some cases the girl's sense of social obligation is little more than a strong feeling that she must fulfill her parents' aspirations for her. This may require finishing college or graduate school, may require entering a vocation, or fulfilling some other requirement. In such cases, where the girl faces the choice of marriage or fulfilling her parents' aspirations, she has a right to ask herself whether she really holds these aspirations for herself and whether they are realistic for her in the light of her interests and abilities, or whether the parents are wanting her to help fill out for them a life which they have found inadequate in some particular respect. Parents sometimes project unrealistic aspirations on their children and hinder marriage when the time has come to marry. In such cases, the counsel of others is more to be trusted than that of parents.

Ruth Reed, in her book *The Single Woman,* gives reports of her interviews with single women who feel that they delayed marriage too long and with too little reason. Some felt that they had been too particular, or their parents had, about the person they dated. They felt that these impossibly idealistic standards had kept them from marriage.

Others rejected a good marriage opportunity because either they or their parents felt that finishing college at the time was the all-important thing and that marriage should wait. A second opportunity did not come. Still others never seemed to be able to fall in love with a man of the social and economic level they had attained because of their education and training. They fell in love with men who came from the social and economic level they had been reared in and could not bring themselves to marry on that level because it would lower their present standard of living.

Personality Traits of Bachelor Men and Women

The female: Studies of unmarried women seeking help at the American Institute of Family Relations in Los Angeles, over a period of twenty-nine years, deal with approximately five hundred cases.[6] These women considered their main problems: shyness, feelings of inferiority, rejection or fear of it, and moods. All wanted to marry, as might be expected of unmarried women contacting the Institute, yet 30 percent were having no dates and 40 percent had dates only occasionally. Almost all complained that they could not get a man or hold a man. Very few believed their problem lay in parent domination, yet counseling revealed this was one of their most important problems. The group was short on hobbies, yet they were for the most part well-educated, professional women, holding excellent jobs. Few were trying to solve their own problem of finding a mate. Many refused to continue counseling.

Benton reports that most unmarried women coming to the clinic for counseling are having difficulty getting along with men because of their infantile tactics in human relations; they do not know how to meet men on a level of "satifying equality."[7] They ask anxiously, "what's wrong with me," or say, "I'll do exactly as you say, but if it doesn't work, you're to blame." Some know all the answers, boss men around and the counselor as well. Some have no feeling that they need to change. Some see nothing satisfying in homemaking.

H. K. Moore asked 100 summer-session students to describe unmarried women over thirty whom they knew and married women of similar age.[8] From these descriptions the researcher drew up a check list of 104 items. This list of items was given to 174 summer-session students and they were asked to check items that applied to one married woman they knew. On a duplicate check list they were asked to check traits of a spinster they knew. Three distinct aspects of personality were covered with the following findings: (1) *Personal appearance.* The spinsters were more likely to have an extremely homely face, to be masculine in manner or appearance, to have a physical handicap and to seldom smile. The two groups differed little, if any, in general neatness of dress, appearance, hairdo, body shape, or size. (2) *Social acceptability.* The spinsters were more aggressive, unsocial, inward-looking, stubborn, stingy, and unmagnetic than were the married women. (3) *Behavior, activities, tendencies.* The

---

[6] Donald Powell Wilson, "The Woman Who Has Not Married," *Family Life,* 18:1-2, October, 1958.

[7] Margaret Benton, "The Woman Who Wants to Marry," *Family Life,* 15:3-5, November, 1955.

[8] H. K. Moore at Arkansas A & M College. Reported in "The Wife and the Spinster," *Family Life,* 11:14, May, 1950.

spinsters were more given to compensation, moodiness, rigidity, and to academic activities.

Another aspect of the study was concerned with relationships with men. The spinsters were inclined to want more in the way of a mate than they could get in terms of their attractiveness and bargaining power. They had a bad technique of mate attraction, either being too anxious or too repellent to advances. The spinsters more often came from a family that was mother-dominated, where parents were peculiar or overprotective, or from homes where there was unhappiness.

A second study of 184 unmarried women (most of them nurses) over thirty-five years of age asked them to indicate why they had not married.[9] Of the group, 72 stated that it was because marriage would compete with their desire for a career; 42 stated that they had had no opportunity to meet suitable individuals of the opposite sex; 29 stated that marriage competed with other values they held; 22 stated that they felt inadequate to meet the demands for personal involvement required in marriage. A few had passed marriage up because of lack of interest in the opposite sex, inability to find a suitable mate, or hereditary or health defects.

A third exhaustive comparison of 30 single and 30 married women ages 30 to 40, with the sample matched for race, religion, absence of physical defects, and education (all had a college degree), found that the single group had had less heterosexual activity during the years 16 to 25, were more likely to fall at the extremes of high or low self-esteem compared to married women, who were about in the center of the continuum on self-esteem, and tended to have had more of a sense of "obligations" to others at age 25 (a few cases of extreme sense of obligation of single girls was responsible for most of this latter difference).[10] One may well argue that the results here are not typical of the population, and this is undoubtedly true. Yet one cannot deny that the results are highly suggestive and at many points agree with one's own observations.

Some of the personality traits and personal values described were obviously present in these women during earlier years when marriage would normally take place. One may suspect that some of the others are the results of delaying marriage or at least that they had become exaggerated with delayed marriage.

[9] Earl Lomon Koos, *Marriage* (New York: Holt, Rinehart & Winston, Inc., 1953), Table 7, p. 373. Three-fourths of the group studied by Koos was made up of nurses seeking graduate degrees, which may explain why more than half of them gave careers or other values as a reason for not marrying. It may also explain why so many had not had an opportunity to meet marriageable men, particularly since the study was made in Rochester, New York, a metropolitan community with a sex ratio unfavorable to marriage opportunity for women.

[10] Richard H. Klemer, "Factors of Personality and Experience which Differentiate Single from Married Women," *Marriage and Family Living*, 16:41-44, February, 1954.

It is known, for example, that the college-trained, and particularly those who complete graduate work, marry less often than women at large. This is undoubtedly, in part, a matter of the less marriageable pursuing education to the higher levels, but education in and of itself may build restraints in the personality, reduce emotional responsiveness, and increase the tendency to be critical and perfectionistic, all of which hinder marriage. Application to an exacting work routine or profession may do the same thing, so that time itself works a hardening process in those who do not continue dating and developing their affectional nature.

With increased competence of the girl in education, in professional and other work achievement, the number of eligible males is greatly reduced, for men by and large do not like to marry above themselves in education, income, or ability. The male ego is a delicate thing, cultivated as such by our culture with its historic worship of the male character. Then, too, the competent male is shamefully desirous of being coddled, pampered, and admired by his wife. It is difficult for the male to reverse this role.

In short, the more competent a woman becomes, no matter what her graces, the fewer the men who are willing to live under her shadow. Of course, this is a serious weakness in men, but one which must be reckoned with.

The male: What about the bachelor man? Does he tend to be as happy, healthy, and well adjusted as those who marry?

There is substantial evidence that, on the average, those males who do not marry are deficient biologically. Note in Table 32-1 that in the more vigorous years of life single males have a death rate running as high as twice that of married males. During the years from 35 to 44 the death rate of bachelors is more than twice that of married males. It remains higher at all ages. The differential death rate of single females is not as great, but is higher than for married women in all age groups.

As to personal and social characteristics, a hundred adults, most of them women, were asked to describe the bachelors (unmarried men over thirty-five) they knew well, indicating why they thought these men were or were not marriageable.[11] The group gave a detailed sketch of 185 bachelors. Of these bachelors 120 were classed as unmarriageable; 57, marriageable; and 8, doubtful.

All the men described were educated and in the respectable part of the population. The analysis showed that most of them were either so much in love with themselves or with their mothers that there was no place for a wife in their life. Many were homosexuals, had developed a

[11] Study by Paul Popenoe, reported by him in "The Old Bachelor," *Family Life,* 15:1-2, May. 1953.

TABLE 32-1————Death rates by marital status, age, and sex: United States*

AGE AND SEX	SINGLE	EVER MARRIED
Male, 20 years and over	*1963 (est.)*	*1963 (est.)*
20-24 years	2.1	1.5
25-34 years	3.6	1.6
35-44 years	7.6	3.5
45-54 years	15.9	9.2
55-64 years	29.7	22.1
65-74 years	68.3	49.2
75 years and over	126.3	117.5
Female, 20 years and over		
20-24 years	0.8	0.6
25-34 years	2.2	0.9
35-44 years	4.7	2.2
45-54 years	7.3	5.1
55-64 years	12.2	11.6
65-74 years	29.4	28.7
75 years and over	107.9	93.0

* Data based on a 10-percent sample of deaths. Rates per 1,000 population in specified group. From National Center for Health Statistics, *Monthly Vital Statistics Report*, Vol. 12, No. 13, July 31, 1964, Table 8.

taste for a variety of superficial relations with women, or could not accept a woman on a basis of equality. Some were alcoholics.

This study dealt mostly with men in urban situations. It is not likely that so high a proportion of unmarriageables would be found among men in isolated farming and ranching regions, barring the hobo and other migrant workers. Even among completely normal men, however, prolonged isolation frequently results in eccentricities that make marriage difficult or impossible.

Since the male has a strong sex drive to marry, one must expect to find among the voluntary bachelors a high proportion of those who are incapable of a normal emotional or sexual relationship. Few marriageable men actually delay marriage until the age of bachelorhood—at thirty-five, only twelve in a hundred are unmarried. Of these, about ten will never marry. This means that most men who delay marriage past thirty-five are deficient sexually, in emotional development, have physical handicaps or disfiguration, or have very severe emotional problems.

The reason sometimes cited by students of marriage for the failure of some men to marry is their fear of sexual impotency. In America, where so much emphasis is placed upon sex as an important factor in marriage, some males actually develop a fear that they may be impotent and cannot meet the demands of marriage. This abnormality may go back to child-hood. One of the Freudian premises was that an emotional crisis may develop in the relationship of the infant to the mother in the very early days of their association, making him cling to her with emotional ties that cause sex functioning to be difficult if not impossible later in life. How much of this is myth and how much is science, of course, is still a matter of speculation, but suffice it to say here that some men actually do have psychological blocks to sexual activity which may make it impossible for them to participate in the sex act. Others only fear that they may not be able to do so and this in itself may become an inhibiting factor.[12] Some find a safer haven in homosexuality.

Some Considerations in Contemplating Voluntary Bachelorhood

Young men and women who contemplate bachelorhood owe it to themselves—particularly to their future well-being—to consider what the decision is likely to entail. While they are young, many consider being single a decided social advantage. The attention and affection of one's regular dates seem to more than compensate for marriage and involve none of the responsibilities of marriage. It is easy to imagine that this state can be prolonged indefinitely.

Some young people, fresh out of school or professional training, become so absorbed in their careers that marriage seems relatively unimportant. With a minimum sexual and emotional satisfaction from dating, they are able to lose themselves completely in their work. With women, particularly, in whom the sex drive is generally less demanding than in men, this occupational satisfaction can make marriage seem unnecessary, even undesirable.

But the decisions which seem right in youth may prove to be all wrong in later years. Difficult though it may be, it is important for all young people to try to determine in advance what their future needs may be. The kind of companionship and emotional satisfaction that can be had from dates may be satisfactory for a few years, but even in cases where the dating years can be indefinitely prolonged (and this is not common), this kind of superficial relationship seldom remains fully satisfying. The excitement of a "big date" or the thrills of "necking" or "petting" are a part of youth. With constant repetition their fascination wears away. After their youth has passed, most men and women need the more or less

---

[12] For a study of various problems of the unmarried, see Laura Hutton, "The Unmarried," in A. M. Krich (Editor), *Women: The Variety and Meaning of Their Sexual Experience* (New York: Dell Publishing Co., Inc., 1954).

constant affection, sexual satisfaction, and companionship that is only afforded by a permanent relationship.

Marriage for the purpose of having a family may have little appeal to a young person. Many who have only recently escaped the responsibilities of living in their parental household are not eager to take up these and other responsibilities in a home of their own. Children, in the eyes of a young adult, are often little more than a nuisance. In these years, crammed full of recreation, work, friends, and new experiences, it is difficult to imagine that children could ever be a vital part of one's feeling of completeness, yet most adults feel that they are.

Even the profession, which seems so absorbing in one's youth, seldom remains a completely satisfying outlet for emotions and energies for a lifetime. One occasionally reads of people who live satisfying lives completely dedicated to their work, but they are the exceptions. Few can survive for long on such a limited emotional diet.

But when the fun and advantages of being single begin to wear thin, isn't there time enough to reverse one's decision and give matrimony a try? Unfortunately, it is not so simple. Biology or natural law has little to do with it, but the period for mating and marrying in our culture is a relatively short one for most persons, particularly women.

Woman's bargaining position is the greatest in youth when she is most fair and attractive to the male sex. In our culture sheer physical attractiveness is a major factor in mate selection, regardless of what we may say about the advantages of brilliant conversation, wittiness, prestige, etc. A review of Figure 17-2 will remind one how rapidly the statistical chances of marriage decline for the average woman in our culture. Note that by age thirty the single woman's chances of marriage have dropped to less than fifty-fifty. Even if she is one of the lucky 50 percent, the chances are she will have to marry a secondhand husband. The woman of thirty must expect to marry a man from five to ten years older than she; at least that is the way it works out on the average.[13]

Of men thirty-five to forty, practically all the eligible ones have been married. Therefore, her main chance of marriage at age thirty or older is of marrying a widowed or divorced man. The statistical chances of success or failure of marriage to the widowed man are not known, but it is known that the divorced man is a considerably higher risk in marriage than the man who has never married. In fact, the divorced man is about a 50 percent greater risk in marriage than the single man.

The longer one delays marriage, the greater the likelihood that the

13 U. S. Department of Commerce, Bureau of the Census, "Marital Status, Number of Times Married, and Duration of Present Marital Status, April, 1948," Series P-20, No. 23, March 4, 1949; see also Paul H. Landis, "Sequential Marriage," *Journal of Home Economics*, 42:625-628, October, 1950.

person married will have been married before. This is, of course, because most marriageable persons have been married prior to age thirty-five and to be eligible again must have been widowed or divorced.

Figure 32-1[14] shows the proportion of each age group marrying which is single, divorced, or widowed. During the years thirty-five to forty-five,

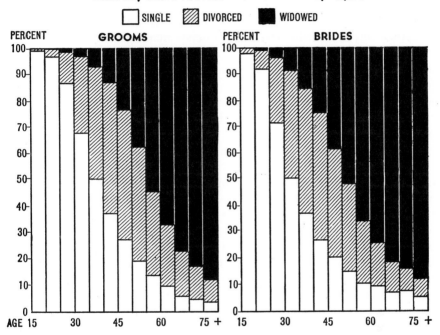

PREVIOUS MARITAL STATUS OF GROOMS AND BRIDES, MARRIAGES IN 14 STATES, 1950

☐ SINGLE   ▨ DIVORCED   ■ WIDOWED

Source: Metropolitan Life Insurance Company, *Statistical Bulletin*, June, 1953.

FIGURE 32-1————Most of those who marry late in life marry a second-hand spouse.

the divorced make up the highest proportion of those marrying. After forty-five, the overwhelming proportion, and this increases with age, is the widowed. Above sixty-five, more than four in five marriages are of widowed persons.

One may argue that the values of mate selection in our culture are spurious, based too much on the male worship of adolescent female beauty

[14] Metropolitan Life Insurance Company, "Current Patterns of Marriage and Re-marriage," *Statistical Bulletin*, 34:6-8, June, 1953.

and freshness, rather than on substantial companionable characteristics of maturity. This may be right. Actually, why should a woman's chances of marriage decline when she has lost her "sweet-sixteen" look if she has become more competent, companionable, and interesting because of training, work experience, or travel? Men may be far too much interested in physical attraction in mate selection. There is still much evidence that, in an age when happy companionship is a major goal of marriage, the more mature, experienced woman is a more dependable and satisfying wife. There is also evidence that intelligent, college-trained women more often succeed in marriage than do noncollege-trained women.

Also, why should the woman who delays marriage be plagued by inferences that she has not married because she did not have the chance? Many college-trained women spurn attractive offers of marriage because they feel a need to express their creative energies in a competitive work world. The entire educational system is designed to shape women for careers. They should not be blamed for choosing them. Yet traditions persist.

With many women in their twenties, the question of marriage is not simply a question of weighing one's chances of actually realizing marriage. Often there are other drives so fundamental that she cannot take a chance of their being frustrated by marriage. The young woman who wishes to travel, who wishes to achieve competitive success in some type of career, who has very strong creative drives that must be fulfilled, has no choice but to follow the direction of drives if she is to achieve any degree of satisfaction in her life. She must pursue these other drives to the point where they are at least fulfilled to some extent before she can even safely consider marriage. There is some evidence that the driving career woman is often neurotic, and tries through occupational climbing to satisfy very basic wants. Whether experience in a career builds these characteristics into the personality or whether careers select a type is debatable.

Some Should Not Marry

The need to have children, a secure source of affection, and consistent sexual satisfaction are strong arguments in favor of marriage. This does not mean, however, that marriage should be the choice of all young people. In spite of the desirability of marriage for most people, far too many persons attempt marraige in the United States. A higher proportion of persons in the United States marry than is the case in most other modern nations, or than married in our own nation's past; they marry younger than elsewhere and also younger than they once did in the United States. Over 90 percent of both men and women marry at some period in their lives. There are many, of course, who should not marry.

One must assume that a substantial proportion of those who do not marry in the United States today are the feebleminded, the mentally ill, the crippled, the physically handicapped, or those who suffer from chronic ill health.

The Social Security Act has made it possible for some of these groups to marry. The physically handicapped can live with a minimum of work. The blind and the crippled, for example, are now supported, in part, by the Social Security Act.

People with defective strains in the bloodstream may, through sterilization, marry without penalizing the next generation and, therefore, without social condemnation. In many cases defectives may enjoy the marriage relationship, even though they may not be able to have children or to carry out some of the activities which other couples take for granted as a part of married life.

It is not those who are physically or mentally deficient, however, with whom this chapter is primarily concerned, but rather with those who are physically normal and of sound mind who for some reason fail to achieve marriage at the usual age of marriage.

The high death rate of bachelor males is some evidence that many men who should not marry, from a biological standpoint, do not. The evidence that the right women are marrying and that those who should stay single are doing so is much less clear.

Adjustment to the Single State

The foregoing pages have provided some insight into the experiences, motives, and social situations explaining the fact that a considerable number of marriageable people, particularly women, do not achieve marriage at the usual time, and in some instances do not achieve it at all. Certainly there should be greater tolerance in our culture for those who fall short of marriage or who, for some reason—social, personal, genetic, or otherwise—choose not to marry.

To fail to marry is much less often a tragedy than to marry unwisely. This obvious fact should be considerable consolation to those who have failed to marry but who feel deprived, even though they may have made a fair adjustment to life in other aspects of their total life organization.

Acceptance of any state and a will to make the most of it is the first step in successful adjustment and a prerequisite to happiness. A sense of being socially useful and productive is, no doubt, a source of great satisfaction for many single people, particularly those in the service occupations. A useful, even if not a completely full life, can be had outside marriage.

The temptation to seek love and sex outside marriage in an illicit relationship may be great where there is a strong desire to love and be loved. In Europe, some women are even arguing for the right to have children by artificial insemination. In Scandinavian cultures many have children out of wedlock and take advantage of the very liberal provisions of the society for the unwed mother and her child.

Our society still frowns upon the kind of sexual activities that are available to single men and provides for no direct sex outlets for the single woman. It provides no institutions, or for that matter attitudes, favorable to the unwed mother or her child.

One of the great difficulties of the unmarried woman's state is that she is likely to be tempted to various love affairs which almost always involve complications. She may have great difficulty in accepting her single state and in trying to make the mental and social adjustments it requires. This may lead her to venture in various love affairs such as those with married men or those of a clandestine nature, where sex is the motivation on the part of the male. Such ventures may prove to be an outlet for meeting physical sex needs, but they are very unlikely to meet the emotional needs.

In case of ties with the married man there is a frustrating of love because their relationship cannot be consummated in marriage and cooperative childbearing. There is always a sense of guilt, if the woman involved has a conscience, that she may be infringing upon or even breaking up a marriage which involves a wife, and in many cases, children. She is challenging the taboos of our society which consider any such interference a threat to the stability of the family structure.

There are, no doubt, many women who have so conditioned themselves to ignore conscience and social propriety that they are able to engage in such affairs without any serious feeling of personal disorganization. The great majority, however, cannot. The unscrupulous single person in our culture can be a threat to marriage and the family, in that he or she can be responsible for love triangles that destroy marriages of others.

Fortunate, of course, are those single women who have no conscious sex drive. These women find their sex drives very easy to sublimate, because in a real sense they have never felt a sexual urge in any concrete way. They find it easy to engage in sublimative activities which seem to give them emotional satisfaction and a good orientation to their work and social relationships.

Women with maternal yearnings often engage in socially sanctioned, sublimated outlets in our culture such as nursing, medicine, and social welfare work, particularly child welfare work. Teaching, too, particularly in the primary grades, and some forms of religious service offer an opportunity for the cultivation of the sentiments of love and tenderness which usually find expression in family life. Those who keep these sentiments alive sometimes marry widowers in later life.

Except for those who may have psychological inhibitions to sex activity, leading to impotence, the average single male finds sexual outlets much more readily than the single female. Prostitution caters to his needs, and even though it is outlawed, it still exists.

Clandestine sexual affairs, of a noncommercial nature, are also much more available to him without fear of serious social censure than they are to the unmarried woman. He does not share the risk of pregnancy in such affairs and can readily avoid social condemnation for them. He does run the risk of venereal disease, is always threatened by the temptation to homosexuality, and may, of course, suffer a great deal from sexual hunger and tensions.

In summary, the universal need of human beings for affection, companionship, and sexual fulfillment are likely to be serious lacks in the single person's life. To meet them in a clandestine way is risky, both physically and socially. The safe social course is through sublimation by way of socially sanctioned channels of service.

A single person should accept full responsibility for his state, and recognize that it has many advantages along with its disadvantages. One only has to look at the divorce columns of the daily paper to guess the amount of misery that the unwise or ill-advised marriage brings.

Problems

1. Many people in our society reach adulthood without having developed the necessary attributes for success in marriage. These people are called the "unmarriageables." List several of the traits which may distinguish them from the average man or woman. Are most unmarriageables so classified because of inherited or acquired characteristics?
2. Which sex runs the greater risk of not being able to find a mate if marriage is delayed? What circumstances seem to explain this situation best?
3. Robert is 28 and a full-time hired worker on a large western wheat ranch, located seventy miles from a small city. His wages are relatively high and since his room and board are free he hopes to have saved enough for a substantial down payment on his own ranch before he is 30.

   Although marriage just now is impossible, because of his working arrangements, he hopes to find a wife before he buys his ranch. His prospects are not encouraging, however. The unmarried women in the scattered farming communities are all too young. The single ones of marriageable age have migrated to the city and are not eager to return. Robert goes to the city once or twice a month but has no way of meeting likely marriage prospects once he is there.

What would your advice to him be?

4. For many generations we have placed a high evaluation on the type of devotion which would cause a young person to delay or renounce his own chances for marriage in order to care for his parents. Today, pensions, Social Security, and other impersonal arrangements give such young people freedom to marry. Still, this transition from personal to social responsibility is not without its critics.

Which method of caring for the aged do you prefer? Consider such factors as:

a. The responsibilities of religious youth.

b. The dignity of the aged.

c. The proper sphere of government.

d. The importance of marrying while young.

5. Two social-science students recently conducted a little study to discover attitudes toward unmarried women. The young man of the team introduced his fellow student (a woman of 27) to a large number of his acquaintances. In half of the cases he mentioned before the formal introduction that "my friend is a spinster." In the other half he said "my friend is a bachelor girl."

They found that when the word "spinster" was used it was greeted with expressions of mild sympathy or mirth. Interest in meeting the "spinster" was not high. When the woman was referred to as a "bachelor girl," neither sympathy nor mirth was registered and interest in meeting her was generally high.

a. What connotations does "bachelor girl" or "bachelor woman" carry that "spinster" lacks?

b. Why would a male consider a "bachelor girl" more interesting to meet than a "spinster"?

c. Would your reaction have been similar to that of the majority had you been included in this little study?

6. Explain this observation, "It is the motives that lie behind not marrying rather than spinsterhood or bachelorhood as such that determine whether or not an individual will make a healthy adjustment to his unmarried state."

7. Lillian is an attractive widow of thirty-two. Her friends refer to her lovingly but accurately as "lighthearted and a little scatterbrained." She has a child of seven and because her first marriage was such a happy one she is now considering a second marriage, but is having difficulty deciding among three candidates:

Tom is forty. He has never been married because most women annoy him. He is independently wealthy and has spent most of his adult life and fortune in traveling and collecting rare glass and china for his apartment, which he refers to as "my museum."

James is a bachelor, too. He is forty-three and has put off marriage because of his determination to make something of himself. He came from a poor family and has devoted himself exclusively, first to his education, and then to reaching the top in his profession. He is still a little uncertain as to whether he is "really at the top," and this worries him, but he is certain that if he doesn't marry soon his prospects will begin to fade.

Ross is divorced after nine stormy years of marriage to a woman whose only ambition was "to own the biggest house in town." He decided that they could never harmonize their values. To Ross "an income big enough to live comfortably on is plenty for me. Any extra time and energy I have I'd rather put into enjoying what I have than acquiring more."

What do you believe are the assets and liabilities of each of these men? Considering what you know about Lillian, which man seems to be best suited to her temperament and way of life?

Selected References

ARTICLES IN BOOKS OF READINGS

Krich, A. M. (Editor), *Women: the Variety and Meaning of Their Sexual Experience* (New York: Dell Publishing Co., Inc., 1954).
  1. Hutton, Laura, "The Unmarried," pp. 189-219.
  2. Groves, Ernest R., "Sex Psychology of the Unmarried Adult," Ch. 8.
Vincent, Clark E., *Readings in Marriage Counseling* (New York: Thomas Y. Crowell Co., 1957).
  3. Karpf, Maurice J., "Counseling with the Unmarried Woman—The Singleton, the Widow, and the Divorcee," pp. 289-297.
Cavan, Ruth Shonle, *Marriage and the Family in the Modern World: A Book of Readings* (New York: Thomas Y. Crowell Co., 1960).
  4. Panzer, Martin, "No World for a Single," Reading 5.
  5. Reed, Ruth, "Women and Single Life," Reading 34.

General References

The Abortionist, Dr. X, as told to Lucy Freeman (New York: Doubleday & Co., Inc., 1962).

Benton, Margaret, "The Woman Who Wants to Marry," *Family Life,* 15:3-4, November, 1955.

Doty, Carol M., and Hoeflin, Ruth M., "A Description of Thirty-five Unmarried Graduate Women," *Journal of Marriage and Family Living,* 26:91-95, February, 1964.

Duvall, Evelyn M., and Hill, Reuben, *When You Marry,* Revised Edition (Boston: D. C. Heath & Co., 1953), Ch. 8.

Gleason, George, *Single Young Adults in the Church* (New York: Association Press, 1952).

KLEMER, Richard H., "Factors of Personality and Experience Which Differentiate Single from Married Women," *Marriage and Family Living*, 16:41-44, February, 1954).

————, *A Man for Every Woman* (New York: The Macmillan Co., 1959).

Koos, Earl Lomon, *Marriage* (New York: Holt, Rinehart & Winston, Inc., 1953), Ch. 19.

LANDIS, Paul H., "Sequential Marriage," *Journal of Home Economics*, 42:625-628, October, 1950.

LEUBA, Clarence, *Ethics in Sex Conduct* (New York: Association Press, 1948).

MOORE, H. K., "The Wife and the Spinster," *Family Life*, 11:14, May, 1950.

POPENOE, Paul, "The Old Bachelor," *Family Life*, 15:102, May, 1953.

REED, Ruth, *The Single Woman* (New York: The Macmillan Co., 1942).

SCHEINFELD, Amram, *Women and Men* (New York: Harcourt, Brace & Co., Inc., 1943), Ch. 16.

SMITH, M. B., *The Single Woman of Today* (New York: Philosophical Library, Inc., 1952).

VINCENT, Clark E., "Unwed Mothers and the Adoption Market: Psychological and Familial Factors," *Marriage and Family Living*, 22:112-118, May, 1960.

WILSON, Donald P., "The Woman Who Has Not Married," *Family Life*, 18:1-2, October, 1958.

YOUNG, Leontine, *Out of Wedlock* (New York: McGraw-Hill Book Co., 1954).

33

The Second Half of Life

All the world's a stage,
And all the men and women merely players.
They have their exits and their entrances;
And one man in his time plays many parts,
His acts being seven ages. At first the infant,
Mewling and puking in the nurse's arms.
And then the whining school-boy, with his satchel
And shining morning face, creeping like snail
Unwillingly to school. And then the lover,
Sighing like furnace, with a woeful ballad
Made to his mistress' eyebrow. Then a soldier,
Full of strange oaths and bearded like the pard;
Jealous in honour, sudden and quick in quarrel,
Seeking the bubble reputation
Even in the cannon's mouth. And then the justice,
In fair round belly with good capon lined,
With eyes severe and beard of formal cut,
Full of wise saws and modern instances;
And so he plays his part. The sixth age shifts
Into the lean and slipper'd pantaloon,
With spectacles on nose and pouch on side;
His youthful hose, well saved, a world too wide
For his shrunk shank; and his big manly voice,
Turning again toward childish treble, pipes
And whistles in his sound. Last scene of all,
That ends this strange eventful history,
Is second childishness, and mere oblivion,
Sans teeth, sans eyes, sans taste, sans everything.

SHAKESPEARE, *As You Like It*

The Long View

Youth has a short-term look at life. This is natural and almost inevitable. The immediate problems ahead are mate choice, marriage, early-marriage adjustment, and then parenthood. These are the pressing problems. These are the problems to which this book is directed. But it would be short-sighted not to take a brief look at the longer span of life.

Today for the first time in human history, the more favored parts of the world offer youth a span of life after the above stages of the life cycle have passed which is almost twice as long as the mate choice and parenthood stage. College young people can expect to live to be somewhere between 85 and 100 years old. The statistical chances will depend partly on the longevity which they have inherited and partly on progress made in extending life during the coming decades.

In less than 30 years, their family will have gone, and the couple will be alone together. Many will already be grandparents before they are 45, and most, before they are 50. After their children go, they can expect to live 30 to 50 more years, a period of time equal to or exceeding that from their birth to the loss of their family through the maturing of their children.

At his present stage in life, the college youth can see the problems his parents now experience. But the far-seeing youth may well consider too that the preparation he now makes for life, must be for long life and not for a life that will be extinguished even before children grow up, as it so often was in earlier generations and still is now in the underdeveloped countries. If he would live life fully in the latter half of life, his preparation now must be broadly based, his aspirations exceeding those of home and family.

This long look is particularly necessary for the college girl. Marriage, motherhood, domesticity are too much with us as the cultural compulsive of the contemporary college campus. This has been stressed at various points. Now it is important to reiterate that studies of women who have arrived at motherhood show quite clearly that motherhood alone is far from enough to make the woman's life complete. Even before child rearing has been completed, many find in themselves a discontent which calls for the use of talents, for a fulfilling work challenge.[1] And when children leave, most women have to seek meaning for the second half of the life span yet remaining.

The broadest preparation is needed to face the long stretch of life in

---

[1] See several studies in Seymour M. Farber and Roger H. L. Wilson (Editors), *The Potential of Woman* (New York: McGraw-Hill Book Co., 1963); see particularly, Part III, "The Roles of Woman," and Part IV, "The Consequences of Equality."

our day and generation. Great flexibility in plans and purposes is also essential. Life for both men and women is one long series of adjustments, but this is particularly true of the life of modern college women.

The Life Cycle of Marriage

Marriage has its natural beginning in dating and its natural end in the death of husband or wife. Where it is terminated in this manner there are five stages which the pair normally experience during their lifetime together. Each stage is unique; each demands its special adjustments.

The first is going together, which is marked by increased intimacy between a man and woman and during which each tries to understand the social, emotional, and intellectual traits of the other. The second stage—a relatively short one, generally—is the period of marriage prior to the arrival of children in the home, the stage in which husband and wife are adjusting to each other as mates. The third stage is that of parenthood, in which the child or children enter the marriage bringing new interests and arousing deeper emotions. The living habits, recreational interests, and home routine of parents must be modified to a greater or lesser degree because of the presence and constant demands of the ever-dependent child in the family.

In the modern family of from one to three children, childbearing will likely be over in five to eight years after the date of marriage. Statistically speaking, according to Census data, in the average United States marriage childbearing is over by age 29. This short period, when small children keep the mother more or less restricted to the home with a rigid domestic routine, is such a distinct break from the freedom of girlhood which preceded it that it requires considerable adjustment. For the woman who planned to work after marriage, it is also a trying period; this is the period when it is most essential that she give her full attention to babies.

The wife may console herself with the fact that it is a five- to eight-year period for her rather than a 25-year period as it was formerly. If she can adjust to the rigid routine it imposes, it may be one of the happiest periods of her life. It should be, for no period is more deterministic in the personality formation of the child. Her happiness with her child, as well as her full emotional acceptance of it, is basic.

In the democratic family, the life of the young husband is also greatly changed by the coming of children. Since he is no longer content to leave all of child rearing to his wife, he frequently begins to replace many of his habitual leisure-time pursuits with new ones—helping his wife with the physical care of an infant, romping with his toddlers, or spending evenings and weekends in companionship with his growing youngsters. This is the norm under the new concept of parenthood.

The next 20 years is given to the care of children who each year become more self-sufficient and, therefore, less demanding of their parents' time and attention. This period need not last 20 years, for in less time in most small families the children will be through high school and away from home at work or in college. The oldest may even be married and have homes of their own. Grandparenthood is not unusual by the early forties.

INCREASE IN AVERAGE TIME SPAN
FROM CRADLE TO GRAVE

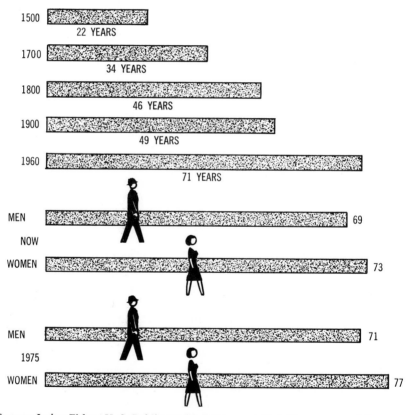

SOURCE: Irving Fisher, U. S. Public Health Service and U. S. Department of Commerce, Bureau of the Census. 1975 projection by the Metropolitan Life Insurance Company.

FIGURE 33-1————The increase of average length of life in 450 years. The child-rearing span is but a fraction, enabling a mother to begin a new career during the "empty-nest" period of family life.

If the average wife finds domestic life less than fully satisfying she may, after her children are well along in school, enter the work world herself, at least on a part-time basis. If she has hobbies or club interests, she will probably spend an increasing amount of time in them. The husband too may begin again the cultivation of old or new interests that do not involve his children. This will help prepare both parents for the next stage, which for many requires the most difficult adjustments of all.

The next stage is often referred to as the "empty nest," or more technically, as the postparental period. The children leave home and the couple is again alone. The final stage is widowhood, for rarely do both members die at the same time.

Marriage, for most couples, passes so rapidly and naturally from one of these stages to another that the problems or pleasures shift before they realize it. In Figure 33-2, the various stages of the typical four- or five-member family of today are shown. It is assumed that the family is unbroken by divorce or death until the years when death normally takes one member of the pair, usually the husband, since women live longer and the husband is usually the older.

Glick's calculation of the life cycle for the average family for 1950 shows the median age for husband and wife at marriage is 22.8 years. The last child comes at 28.8 years, making the childbearing period only 6 years. Marriage of the last child comes at age 50; death of one spouse at 64; death of the other spouse at age 72.[2] This will greatly increase in the lifetime of the present college students.

The first three stages have been covered in preceding chapters of this book. Here brief attention will be given to the last two stages.

The Empty Nest

The empty-nest stage comes at about the time when the average couple are most likely to be experiencing some of the emotional upsets brought on by the climactic period of beginning old age (the late forties or early fifties). For the wife there are the physiological changes of menopause, for the husband the first awareness of youth past, opportunities gone by, ambitions unfulfillable. If the couple lost their outside interests when the children were small and occupied most of their time and concern, then the period of the empty nest will be extremely difficult. But this is the time for outside interests, hobbies, companionship, and for all the other things that the couple have dreamed about during the busy days of hard work and constant parenthood. At this stage in the

---

2 Paul C. Glick, "The Life Cycle of the Family," *Marriage and Family Living,* 17:3-9, February, 1955.

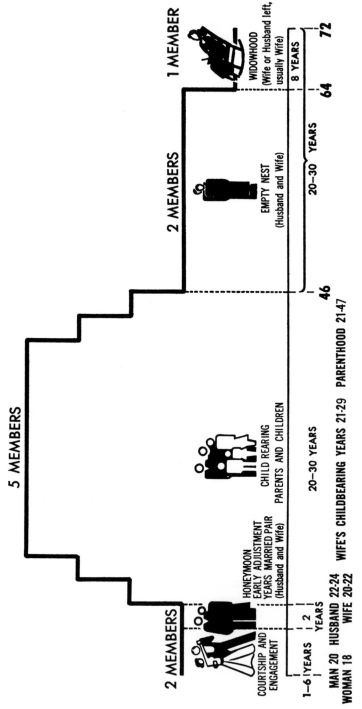

LIFE CYCLE OF THE PAIR RELATIONSHIP
(FAMILY WITH THREE CHILDREN)

5 MEMBERS

2 MEMBERS

COURTSHIP AND
ENGAGEMENT

HONEYMOON
EARLY ADJUSTMENT
YEARS
(Husband and Wife)

1–6 YEARS | 2 YEARS

MAN 20 HUSBAND 22-24 WIFE'S CHILDBEARING YEARS 21-29 PARENTHOOD 21-47
WOMAN 18 WIFE 20-22

CHILD REARING
PARENTS AND CHILDREN

20–30 YEARS

2 MEMBERS

EMPTY NEST
(Husband and Wife)

20–30 YEARS

1 MEMBER

WIDOWHOOD
(Wife or Husband left,
usually Wife)

8 YEARS

46   64   72

SOURCE: Paul H. Landis.

FIGURE 33-2———Childbearing for most wives ends by the 29th year. Child rearing is over by about age 47, requiring only about a third of the life cycle of modern women. As the life span increases, the time after the responsibilities of parenthood have terminated may well become almost half of an average lifetime.

modern marriage cycle, many couples whose work, lives, and affections have centered largely around the children and their needs for attention and development find themselves suddenly without a focus for their emotions and a meaning for their industry.

Often they have lost intimate contact with each other, their lives having long since settled into an unimaginative routine. Suddenly, the future looks bleak and barren, both from an emotional standpoint and from the standpoint of meaningful motivation. Ambition seems to peter out once ambitions for the children are satisfied, particularly if the couple has enough substance to feel more or less secure for the years ahead.

The children become wrapped up in their own lives and interests, and for the parents there suddenly appears a great emotional void, particularly if there are no grandchildren close at hand around whom the middle-aged parents can build a new affectional relationship. Axelson, studying 199 wives in the empty-nest period, found an increase in loneliness a characteristic of the period. He found them with greater concern about health and in need of more outside contacts.[3] He did not find it a period of more severe adjustments than other periods in life.

The wife, if she is unable to anchor her new-found freedom in some vigorous and inspiring activity outside the home—a new job or some very meaningful nonremunerative activity—may turn her attention to her pains and become consumed with neurotic anxieties, particularly if the time of the children leaving home coincides with the menopause, when she may naturally be highly nervous, introspective, self-condemning, periodically depressed, sometimes melancholic, and more or less anxious, not only about life, but about all her relationships with others.

Life becomes rudderless and the future has no vital focal point. Whenever this is true, the couple become vulnerable to many inner tensions and the tendency is to blame these tensions upon the mate rather than upon the fact that the couple have lost hold on their mutual life.

In many instances, the couple have been so far apart and so well-fenced-off from each other, in so far as intimate communication is concerned, that it seems almost impossible to break down the barriers and reinstate the close, intimate level of communication they had in the earlier days of their marriage. Yet at this time in life, perhaps even more than in the earlier years, they need an intimate level of communication.

If they fail to reestablish it, they must substitute ego drives and plunge into more vigorous work activities, money making, or other forms of achievement to compensate for the lack of a relaxing and satisfying love based on a very intimate relationship with each other.

If they have the energy to achieve, they are able to again capture the

3 Leland J. Axelson, "Personal Adjustment in the Postparental Period," *Marriage and Family Living*, 22:66-68, February, 1960.

feeling that they are moving ahead instead of backward—that tomorrow can be brighter than yesterday, in spite of the fact that the children are no longer in their immediate lives and that they have lost a vital love for each other. Gradually, as grandchildren come and they are able to establish contact with them, the grandchildren become the center of emotional focus and interest, which gives them a grasp on the future, again in a close family relationship.

One must grant, however, that even when the adjustment is good, it is seldom achieved without many rough moments and without a considerable amount of anxiety. Our culture worships youth, not age; it looks upon the days of dating, marriage, and child rearing as the fair days of life. The more leisurely period of the last third of life is looked upon by all age groups as a period which cannot be attractive.

Our culture has no philosophy sanctioning retirement. The compulsive force of the culture provides satisfaction only in driving forward. In this atmosphere few can drop the competitive spirit in late middle age and find full satisfaction in nonproductive activities. It is more satisfying, particularly for the male, to drive himself forward, even at the risk of sudden death by a heart attack in the vulnerable 50- to 55-year age period. In some cultures which revere retirement, leisure, and hobbies such as characterize the late period of life, the cultural compulsion is quite different.

This is a serious deficiency in American culture, and one which an individual couple can scarcely deal with fully unless they are unusually imaginative and unusually successful in ordering their life for the full period, rather than for the period prior to fifty.

This is the time when renewed interest in one's spouse is essential. It is a tragedy when the life husband and wife have built together with their children terminates in divorce at the beginning of the empty-nest period. They are just reaching the time when they could belong to each other in a fuller sense than ever before. But too many marriages do break at this point through climacteric divorces.

The wife is absorbed in the emotional adjustments of menopause, or is consumed with lonesomeness over the children's departure from home and community. She neglects the husband, or is callous to his feelings of loss and loneliness which may be as strong as her own. The husband at this time is particularly susceptible to the romantic lure of a younger woman who may seem to promise him his lost youth and a new lease on life. He may even plunge into an adolescent love affair with all the violence and emotional turmoil of a sixteen-year-old in his first throes of puppy love.

This experience of middle age provokes the saying "There's no fool like an old fool." Unless the wife shows unusual wisdom, or unless social restraints of the community are strong, this affair of the late forties or fifties may actually break the marriage, for in some cases the husband learns too late that he is not as young as he thought he was. For the ventures of a new sex experience, of which he tires quickly, he has sacrificed a companion who could share the wisdom and understanding of his years. With that sacrifice he has lost the lifetime continuity of experience which they share in each other and in their families.

For those parents whose deep emotional attachments to children make it hard to let their children go when they reach the age of maturity, who want to feel indispensable to their children and to continue habits of doing things for them, who miss deeply the companionship of their children, this is the time for developing a new kind of maturity. The years ahead demand a maximum amount of social and psychological preparation at this time.

The opportunity to live a new life, unhampered by exacting home routines, should be welcomed by the wife. Greater freedom for travel and for companionship with her husband is made possible. Wise parents can remind themselves, too, that what has been a loss for them at this stage has been a gain from the standpoint of their children. The ability of the children to get away from home when they marry and to be free from the domination of the parents and in-laws is undoubtedly an advantage to the modern young couple. This may be slight consolation to those experiencing the loneliness of the empty nest, but should be acknowledged none the less. Both man and wife throughout the passing years should keep outside interests alive and try to be ready for this difficult stage.

Arnold M. Rose, studying factors associated with life satisfaction among middle-class women, found that their happiness is very much dependent on whether they are able to assume a new central role to take the place of the declining homemaker role. Earning an income, engaging in organizations, and other such roles seem to be adequate substitutes.[4]

The Menopause Crisis

More has been written about this period in the life of woman than about almost any other period, because it is viewed as a period of crisis. On the biological level, radical glandular change comes with the decline in importance of the ovaries and the sex hormones they release throughout the body. The cessation of menstruation and of ovulation is the physical mark that the woman's period of fertility is ended.

[4] Arnold M. Rose, "Factors Associated with the Life Satisfaction of Middle-Class, Middle-Aged Persons," *Marriage and Family Living*, 17:15-19, February, 1955.

Fertility terminates before fifty in most women (the average age in the United States is 49). Physiologically this is a great advantage, since pregnancy, and particularly childbearing, are rather exhausting biological activities. They make greater demands on the female than are justified after she is past age fifty. In fact, most women conclude childbearing before they reach thirty.

In the Kinsey studies, some women began menopause as early as age 33; half had begun by age 46.[5] However, as far as the practical problem of pregnancy is concerned, this research shows that many women are incapable of pregnancy many months or even years before there is any evidence of menopause. The average age of menopause in one sample studied was forty-seven years. The average age of last pregnancy for this group was five and one-half years earlier. Of course, the main factor here may be contraception. In some cases, women of these ages have already had the Fallopian tubes tied off to prevent pregnancy or had surgical operations which made them sterile. Another factor in decreased rate of pregnancy in older years is decreased frequency of sexual intercourse and, therefore, a lower rate of exposure.

Bernard's study in Germany of more than 5,000 women found menstrual disorders much more frequent among women who smoked. Premature menopause seems also to be produced by smoking: 20 percent for smokers, compared to 2 percent for women in the general population. It would appear that cigarette smoking has pretty direct effects on the physiology of the female.[6]

During the menopause period emotional crisis may occur. Certain hormones are dwindling away and the whole biological system is reconstituting itself for the declining phase of life. Some women suffer great anxiety, tension, and neurosis because of the organic changes that are going on. In the most extreme cases, this strain manifests itself in *involutional melancholia,* a mental disease characterized by an extreme emotional drop. The victim is overcome with the feeling that life is hopeless, that it has lost its meaning, that there is nothing to live for. Often the tortured woman experiences an overwhelming sense of guilt. The form it takes will depend somewhat on the areas in which the woman's conscience has been particularly acute. If she has had serious doubts as to whether or not she has handled the children correctly, been too severe with them, or too lax, or if they are involved in mistakes which she feels are her fault, her guilt may make her feel she has completely failed as a mother. She may even feel certain that she has passed on biological deficiencies to her offspring.

[5] Alfred C. Kinsey and others, *Sexual Behavior in the Human Female* (Philadelphia: W. B. Saunders Co., 1953).

[6] *Family Life,* 17:3, August, 1957.

Often such doubts and the guilt have no basis in reality. She may have been a model parent and still the doubts assail her. Her moroseness may become so great at this time that she courts the idea of suicide, and she may actually be in danger, at the depths of the *involutional melancholia* phase, of taking her own life as a way out. Everything seems so futile that it seems a logical choice for her. The full span of these feelings usually does not exceed two years, and the very intense drop in emotions may cover only a short period of time.

Today medicine has come to the aid of the woman in middle life and is able to help most avoid severe crisis. Even those who drop into a severe crisis may often be helped by various medical techniques. To avoid the development of severe tensions, sex hormones in various combinations are used with increasing effectiveness. Testosterone (the male sex hormone) is frequently given to the woman at this period to help her maintain a more even hormone balance. In some cases a balance of male and female hormones are used with effectiveness.

The tranquilizing drugs have also come to the rescue of many women to ease tension and feelings of despair. The release from tension by these drugs, their pacifying effect is often enough to carry the woman through the crisis.

In cases where a woman of middle age has dropped into the pit of *involutional melancholia,* various types of therapy are effective. The most decisive, and the one most easily administered, is shock therapy which seems to destroy the depressive pattern long enough so that the woman can live with a reasonable degree of happiness and peace until she goes through the worst of the menopausal phase. Whether or not such therapy is wise is still a matter of considerable debate. Whether permanent damage is done to the brain is a matter of speculation. The alternative, however, is an expensive and torturous period of psychological help of one kind or another, which may or may not be effective in relieving the immediate symptoms. Likely as not, before the psychotherapy has relieved the distress, the woman will have already moved through the crisis period and be rallying by virtue of the completion of the physiological cycle.

Bossard and Boll, from studies of case materials dealing with brothers or sisters, think they find a period of crisis for women in the late forties or early fifties.[7] They attribute this to the loss of children, to the inadequacy of the husband to meet his wife's sexual needs, and to emotional factors of menopause. They also find evidence of the fifties being a crisis period for married men. The crisis seems to center around occupational rather than sexual matters. One type of problem occurs among men who have fulfilled their promise to some degree, only to find that their

[7] James H. S. Bossard and Eleanor Stoker Boll, "Marital Unhappiness in the Life Cycle," *Marriage and Family Living,* 17:10-14, February, 1955.

wives have not kept pace with the upward climb. Another group are men who have failed occupationally. These husbands seem to find some comfort in self-pity and developing animosity toward their wives. Many women seem to lose their sexual inhibitions at about this time, and become more interested in sex now when their mate is declining in sexual interest.[8]

This same study of the marital life cycle finds that a low point in marital happiness is reached in the late forties and early fifties for women, and in the fifties for men.

Widowhood

If the marriage bridges the dangerous menopause period, as most marriages do, in spite of difficulties which beset them, it ultimately enters the final stage of widowhood. Because of the publicity given to divorce, one gains the impression that most families are broken by divorce; yet more are still broken by death than by divorce. Eventually death comes to take one member of the pair. It is generally the husband who is taken, the wife who is widowed.

The chances of widowhood by death of the spouse are two-thirds greater for the wife than for the husband.[9] The exact chances of widowhood, based on the difference in age between husband and wife, have been calculated by the Metropolitan Life Insurance Company (see Figure 33-3). There is a 50-50 chance of the wife's being left when the husband is five years younger than the wife. Where the husband is twenty years older, the statistical chance is 90 in 100 of the wife surviving.

Most women still have a good many years ahead of them when their husbands die. Three-fourths of the women widowed at age 50 will live another 20 years. More than half of the women widowed at 65 will live another 15 years, and considerably more than half of the wives widowed at 70 will live another 10 years.

Each year thousands of women enter widowhood. While widowhood is concentrated in old age, great numbers also are widowed each year in the ages under 50 (see Figure 33-4). Over 4,000 wives with husbands under 25 years of age become widows annually. The number increases rapidly for each later age period. If one takes a group of women and a group of men of equal ages, he finds that the death rate for men is higher in every age group from birth through old age. In case of widowhood in the years

[8] *Ibid.*

[9] Metropolitan Life Insurance Company, "Widowhood and Its Duration," *Statistical Bulletin*, 34:1-3, September, 1953.

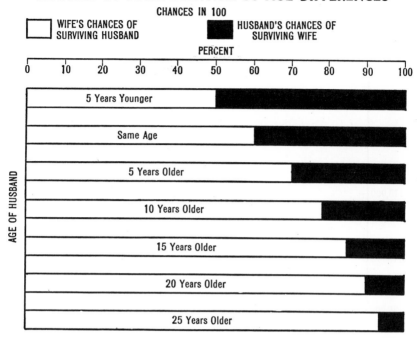

CHANCES OF MATE SURVIVAL BY AGE DIFFERENCES

CHANCES IN 100

WIFE'S CHANCES OF SURVIVING HUSBAND   HUSBAND'S CHANCES OF SURVIVING WIFE

PERCENT

Source: Metropolitan Life Insurance Company, *Statistical Bulletin*, September, 1953.

FIGURE 33-3————The longer life of women, and the fact that they are usually the younger member of the pair, means from a few to many years of widow-hood for the wife in the average marriage.

20 to 40, children under 18 are likely to be left with the surviving wife. At all ages widowed women in the population exceed widowed men by more than three to one. In the retirement years there are more than four and a half million widowed women, but less than half a million widowed men (see Figure 33-5).

This excess of widowed women is explained not only by the fact that men usually marry women younger than themselves and that women live longer, but also by the fact that men more frequently remarry.

Fortunately, because of the increased length of life during the twentieth century in America, the problem of widowhood and orphanhood is only a fraction of what it was a few generations ago. Each year, thanks to science applied in the fields of diet, sanitation, and medical care, fewer homes are broken prematurely by death.

WIVES ENTERING WIDOWHOOD ANNUALLY, 1948

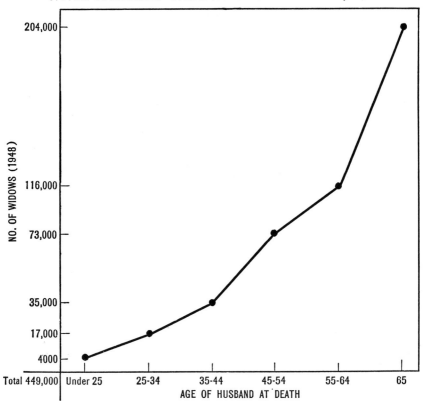

SOURCE: Metropolitan Life Insurance Company, *Statistical Bulletin,* May, 1951.

FIGURE 33-4————Almost a half million women enter widowhood annually. Although the majority are in the older age group, many are in the age group when dependent children may require support and care.

Adjustments to Widowhood

What are some of the adjustments called for in homes broken by death of husband or wife? This is an important question, for even now it is estimated that a quarter of all American marriages are broken by the death of one partner at any given time.

Death is an extreme shock, since it may come suddenly and without previous warning. In the case of divorce there has usually been a long history of expectation prior to the final break. In the case of death there is frequently a close attachment of members of the family so that the

WIDOWED MEN AND WOMEN

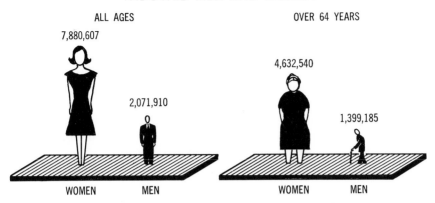

ALL AGES

7,880,607

2,071,910

WOMEN MEN

OVER 64 YEARS

4,632,540

1,399,185

WOMEN MEN

SOURCE: U. S. Department of Commerce, Bureau of the Census, "Marital Status of the Population: 1960," *Supplemental Reports,* PC(S1)-39, December 28, 1962.

FIGURE 33-5————Sex ratio of widowed persons over 65. The wife usually survives. Among the elderly, the widowed spouse is usually the wife. At all ages widowed women are much in the majority.

emotional shock is much greater; in the case of divorce there has probably been a long period of bickering, quarreling, and conflict, so that the break is likely to be less of a shock, even to the children. It is in part for this reason that an overwhelming loneliness is likely to follow the death of husband or wife.

The death of a young bride or groom soon after marriage is extremely serious because the young couple have never been able to realize their plans as a family. On the other hand, the tragedy is probably much more severe from the standpoint of human adjustment for those who have been married many years. Death then removes the person around whom a married lifetime of habits, attitudes, and mutual dependencies have centered.

Added to the complications of bereavement in the case of widowhood of the wife is the matter of economic responsibility. In most homes the husband has almost complete charge of business affairs, aside from those of buying consumer goods for the family. The wife ordinarily knows little about real estate titles, mortgages, contracts, stocks and bonds, and other accounts.[10]

The widow who knows nothing of handling financial affairs may

[10] See Albert E. Schwabacher, Jr., "The Repository of Wealth," in Seymour M. Farber and Roger H. L. Wilson (Editors), *The Potential of Woman* (New York: McGraw-Hill Book Co., 1963).

easily become the victim of fraudulent schemes fostered by unscrupulous people who try to acquire her inherited property or life insurance benefits.

Women as a consequence of outliving their husbands control a great deal of the inherited wealth of the United States, are beneficiaries of 80 percent of life insurance policies, and in the majority of cases actually live to collect the life insurance. They inherit the family estate—lands, houses for rental, etc.—when their husbands die, and they have the problem of managing it. They inherit stocks and bonds and acquire other managerial obligations that add to the normal difficulties of bereavement even though such inheritances do give financial security.

The practical-minded wife should at all times know something about the business and financial activities of the husband if she is going to be able to take over economic responsibilities in case of sudden necessity. Most wives prefer to put away the evil day and give no thought to it, and yet a realistic appreciation of crisis situations helps one to prepare for them, and gives fortitude to meet them. Economic security for the wife, if the husband should be taken, is dependent on such foresight.

The very young widow is seldom confronted with the handling of affairs of an estate, involving stocks, bonds, mortgages, and other accumulated wealth. Nor do wives of most middle- and lower-class men face these problems. For almost all widows, however, there are two big problems, both closely related: (1) money, and (2) finding a job.

The problems are greatest when there are children to be cared for. They are further complicated if the wife lives in a community where there is little work, or if she lacks training or work experience. There is also for the young widow with children the pressing problem of where to live. To live alone is costly and often lonely, but to live with relatives also has its undesirable aspects.

To remarry may be an easy solution, if the opportunity comes. But in many communities the wife is considered to be lacking in respect for her dead husband if she remarries soon. (Husbands are not supposed to refrain from marriage out of respect for a departed wife. It is assumed that a man must have thought well of his former marriage to try it soon again.)

Even in remarriage, there are unexpected adjustments. New habits are required to live with a different mate, and experiences of the previous marriage cannot safely be projected into the new marriage, or reviewed with the new mate. A whole new set of interests and friends may be required.[11]

[11] Marion Langer, *Learning to Live as a Widow* (New York: Julian Messner, 1957); also, Louis Zalk, *How to Be a Successful Widow* (New York: Fleet Publishing Corp., 1957); and Ernest Osborne, *When You Lose a Loved One* (New York: Public Affairs Pamphlets), No. 269.

As to the social and psychological adjustments of widowhood, in the younger years the problem is largely one of taking care of children and, if the surviving spouse overcomes bereavement,[12] of seeking a new marriage. For the older woman, difficulties in securing employment and in making an adjustment to the work world may be great. The possibility of remarriage is slight.

Widowhood in the early years of married life brings the constant advances of predatory males, who think because the woman is no longer a virgin she is easily approachable sexually. The older woman is likely to be spared this problem, but at the same time may feel a serious lack of affection and attention by others.

Today, many marriages are terminated short of their natural life cycle by divorce. Marriages so terminating have their own problems and these are the subject of the following chapter.

In summary, we have considered in this chapter the relatively brief duration of the childbearing period of modern couples, and the adjustments they must face after family life is over, the empty nest with its threat of loneliness, and the added problems, for the wife, of the physiological menopause. We have also considered the last stage in the life span, widowhood, when one or the other is left alone after years of marriage. Most often it is the wife who is left, for women have greater longevity.

Problems

1. The childbearing period in the modern small family is seldom over five to ten years in length. Even when there are more than two children they are generally spaced within so few years as to keep the period relatively short.
   a. Give arguments in favor of having all of one's children within the space of a few years in early marriage.
   b. What might the advantages to parents and children be if a couple delayed the birth of their third child until almost middle age?
   c. What reasons do you think enter into most couples' decisions not to have another child later in life?
2. Lynn has four children, aged 8, 11, 15, and 17. She prides herself on what she terms "my old-fashioned notion that children come first." She has politely turned down every invitation to join Smade City's various clubs and community activities. She busies herself at home and does not miss the friends she

[12] For one of the best summaries of studies revealing the nature of the bereavement experience, see Willard Waller and Reuben Hill, *The Family: A Dynamic Interpretation* (New York: Holt, Rinehart & Winston, Inc., 1951).

has gradually lost track of in her self-imposed isolation. "I love my children," she insists. "They are my vocation, my avocation, my life."

Jess, three years her junior, also has four children, aged 4, 7, 11 and 13, and is sure her maternal love is no less than Lynn's. "I'm just a different kind of mother," Jess explains, "and only time can prove whether Lynn's philosophy is really any better than mine." While her older children are in school, Jess sends her four-year-old to a nursery four afternoons a week. "I think this arrangement is good for him and good for me," Jess explains. During this free time Jess paints in a garage-studio in her back yard. Three evenings a week Jess hires a baby-sitter so that she and her husband may attend their bridge club, work in the Little Theatre group, and participate in political and civic affairs.

In your opinion which of these two women:

a. Most nearly represents your conception of an ideal mother?

b. Holds the "healthier" attitude toward her role as mother?

c. Is probably the better wife?

d. Will rear better-adjusted children?

e. Will most likely enjoy a successful and rewarding old age?

Why?

3. What specific habits and activities would you encourage in order to improve the adjustment of an individual to the empty-nest stage of marriage?

4. *Sociodrama:* The groom's mother visits the bride's mother a week after the young couple have left on their honeymoon trip. She greets her friend with tear-stained eyes and the drama might begin something like this:

"Well, Helen, what now? Our youngsters have outgrown us; what is left for women like you and me?"

The bride's mother might reply, "Don't you ever repeat this to my daughter, but this has been one of the happiest weeks of my life and, frankly, I'm getting ready to really enjoy a lot of things I've been missing out on. . . ."

Go on from here to present a picture of the empty-nest stage of marriage as seen by two different types of women.

5. Would you measure an individual's devotion to his or her mate by the length of his bereavement after the other's death? Explain.

6. A man of 54 married just one year after the death of his wife only to find that in so doing he had alienated the affection of his son, aged 27.

"I'm ashamed of you, Dad," the son insisted. "If you had really loved Mother you could never have done this, at least not so soon."

a. Explain the son's argument. Is it justified?

b. Does an early remarriage usually reflect on one's love for his former mate?

c. Justify the father's action from his point of view.

Selected References

ARTICLES IN BOOKS OF READINGS

KRICH, A. M. (Editor), *Women: the Variety and Meaning of Their Sexual Experience* (New York: Dell Publishing Co., 1954).

    1. Novak, Emil, "Menopause: 'the Change of Life'," pp. 274-285.

Sussman, Marvin B., *Sourcebook in Marriage and the Family,* Revised Edition (Boston: Houghton Mifflin Co., 1963).

    2. Simmons, Leo William, "Social Participation of the Aged in Different Cultures," pp. 419-425.

    3. Burgess, Ernest W., "Family Living in the Later Decades," pp. 425-431.

    4. Dinkel, Robert M., "Attitudes of Children Toward Supporting Aged Parents," pp. 402-410.

    5. Pineo, Peter C., "Disenchantment in the Later Years of Marriage," pp. 393-401.

Becker, Howard, and Hill, Reuben (Editors), *Family, Marriage and Parenthood,* Second Edition (Boston: D. C. Heath & Co., 1955).

    6. Eliot, Thomas D., "Handling Family Strains and Shocks," pp. 616-640.

    7. ————, "Bereavement: Inevitable but Not Insurmountable," pp. 641-668.

Landis, Judson T., and Landis, Mary G., *Readings in Marriage and the Family* (Englewood Cliffs, N. J.: Prentice-Hall, Inc., 1952).

    8. Glick, Paul C., "The Family Cycle," pp. 32-36.

    9. Anderson, W. A., "Spacing of Births in Graduates' Families," pp. 215-218.

Winch, Robert F., and others, *Selected Studies in Marriage and the Family,* Revised Edition (New York: Holt, Rinehart & Winston, Inc., 1962).

    10. Sweetser, Dorrian Apple, "The Social Structures of Grandparenthood," pp. 388-396.

    11. Cavan, Ruth Shonle, "Family Tensions Between the Old and Middle-Aged," pp. 407-412.

    12. Schorr, Alvin L., "Current Practices in Filial Responsibility," pp. 417-436.

Krich, A. M. (Editor), *Men: The Variety and Meaning of Their Sexual Experience* (New York: Dell Publishing Co., 1954).

    13. Maranon, Gregorio, "Climacteric: The Critical Age in the Male," Ch. 12.

Cavan, Ruth Shonle, *Marriage and the Family in the Modern World: A Book of Readings* (New York: Thomas Y. Crowell Co., 1960).

    14. Bigelow, Howard F., "The Ebb and Flow of Finances in the Family Life Cycle," Reading 9.

    15. Agan, Tessie, "Housing and the Family Life Cycle," Reading 10.

    16. Metropolitan Life Insurance Company, "Increased Chances for a Golden Wedding," Reading 11.

    17. Eliot, Thomas D., "Adjusting to the Death of a Loved One," Reading 70.

    18. Neisser, Edith G., "What Grandmothers Are For," Reading 90.

General References

Axelson, Leland J., "Personal Adjustments in the Postparental Period," *Marriage and Family Living,* 22:66-68, February, 1960.

BOSSARD, James H. S., and BOLL, Eleanor S., "Marital Unhappiness in the Life Cycle," *Marriage and Family Living*, 17:10-14, February, 1955.

BRAYSHAW, A. Joseph, "Middle-Aged Marriages: Idealism, Realism and the Search for Meaning," *Marriages and Family Living*, 24:358-363, November, 1952.

CAVAN, Ruth Shonle, *The American Family* (New York: Thomas Y. Crowell Co., 1963), Ch. 19.

GLICK, Paul C., "The Life Cycle of the Family," *Marriage and Family Living*, 17:3-9, February, 1955.

HAMBLEN, E. C., *Facts About the Change of Life* (Springfield: Charles C Thomas, Publisher, 1949).

ILGENFRITZ, Marjorie P., "Mothers on Their Own—Widows and Divorcees," *Marriage and Family Living*, 23:38-41, February, 1961.

JACOBSON, Paul H., "Differentials in Divorce by Duration of Marriage and Size of Family," *American Sociological Review*, 15:235-244, April, 1950.

KOOS, Earl Lomon, *Marriage* (New York: Holt, Rinehart & Winston, Inc., 1953), Ch. 18.

LANDIS, Paul H., *Social Problems: Unfulfilled Welfare Aspirations in Nation and World* (Philadelphia: J. B. Lippincott Co., 1959), Ch. 35.

LANGER, Marion, *Learning to Live as a Widow* (New York: Julian Messner, 1957).

LAWTON, George, and STEWART, Maxwell S., *When You Grow Older* (New York: Public Affairs Pamphlets), No. 131.

MEAD, Margaret, *Male and Female* (New York: William Morrow & Co., 1949), Ch. 17.

Metropolitan Life Insurance Company, "Widowhood and Its Duration," *Statistical Bulletin*, 24:1-2, September, 1953.

OSBORNE, Ernest, *When You Lose a Loved One* (New York: Public Affairs Pamphlets), No. 269.

PINEO, Peter C., "Disenchantment in the Later Years of Marriage," *Marriage and Family Living*, 23:3-11, February, 1961.

WALLER, Willard, and HILL, Reuben, *The Family* (New York: Holt, Rinehart & Winston, Inc., 1951), Ch. 22.

ZALK, Louis, *How to Be a Successful Widow* (New York: Fleet Publishing Corp., 1957).

34

When Marriage Fails

A marriage-family system which holds happiness as the goal of marriage must of necessity tolerate the breaking of marriages in which this goal is not realized. Otherwise, it forever condemns a certain number of couples to a life of misery together. Were our expectations for marriage different, our philosophy of divorce would also be different. In fact, that of the institutional family of earlier days was different. It did not place happiness as the major goal of marriage, and made little use of divorce.

The Changing Philosophy of Divorce

It is because of this change of philosophy that divorce in most circles is no longer considered a sin, but is rather looked upon as a means of adjustment—a necessary means under our family philosophy. Divorce is the ultimate adjustment and to be resorted to only if all other devices of adjustment fail.

Consequently, the rigorous condemnation of divorce a few generations ago no longer exists. Many states have liberal divorce provisions. One state (New York) still clings to the old-fashioned requirement— divorce for adultery only—but regardless of state law, the general public, even including religious bodies, is more tolerant of divorce than in previous generations. They are more tolerant because there is at least a vague understanding of the social forces which make modern marriage quite a different institution from that of the past and give divorce a different meaning than it had in previous generations.

There is general recognition that the bonds of love are the basic bonds of the modern family; that the ties of common property, of common work, and a large family no longer exist for many couples. There is also a general recognition that the day when a woman was safe only in the bosom of her family has passed. She is often more secure economically, and more emotionally at ease, freed of an unsatisfactory marriage. There are even cases where, through divorce, she may assure her children a better future than within an unsatisfactory and tumultuous marriage. This fact is recognized in public policy under the Social Security Act, which makes no distinction between widowhood by death and widowhood by divorce where the welfare of dependent children is involved. Even before that act was passed many states had mothers' pension laws which similarly made no distinction.

The emerging philosophy also holds that a person who has failed to find happiness in marriage should be made free to seek it again in another marriage if he chooses to do so. While this philosophy is not accepted by all religious groups, or by all elements in the population, it is law and is a prevailing sentiment which is becoming increasingly accepted with each passing decade.

Because divorce is not only a common, but in some cases, a necessary form of adjustment, both from the standpoint of the couple and of their children, it must be discussed in a book, such as this one, designed for helping young people develop a philosophy of marriage and parenthood that will lead to success. The fact that some will fail cannot in realism be ignored. It is important that all understand the divorce process as it affects the couple involved as well as their child or children. Recent research and clinical experience provide insight into this very common phenomenon of our time.

Extent of Divorce

General statistics are a very poor index of whether any given individual or couple are likely to end up in the divorce court. Studies by Judson T. Landis[1] indicate very clearly that divorces, like permanent marriages, run in families. There are many families that have never had a divorce as far back as memory or geneologies carry them. There are other family lines that are highly divorce prone.

Landis studied the ancestors of 1,977 college students and found this to be strikingly so. Taking the students' own parents and aunts and uncles he related the divorces of this generation to whether or not the students' grandparents had been divorced. In the group of parents and aunts and uncles, there were 13,255 persons. Where there had been no divorces in the grandparent generation, only 14.6 percent of parents and aunts and

[1] Judson T. Landis, "The Pattern of Divorce in Three Generations," *Social Forces*, 34:213-216, March, 1956.

uncles had been divorced; where one set of grandparents had been divorced, 23.7 percent had been divorced; where both sets of grandparents had divorced, 38 percent had been divorced.

To get a more accurate picture of divorce than that given by general rates, one must also know the racial group being referred to. Glick[2] has shown that disrupted marriages are three times as high among nonwhites as among whites. Two-thirds of disrupted white marriages are broken by divorce, whereas only one-third of disrupted nonwhite marriages are broken by divorce. Among nonwhites the separation ratio is very high. The disrupted marriages of the nonwhite are three times as likely to have dependent children as are the disrupted marriages of the white.

The long-term national trend of divorce has been upward. Of marriages taking place in 1900, only about one in twelve were ultimately terminated by divorce rather than death; of those taking place in 1922, about one in eight so ended (see Figure 34-1). It is assumed that of current marriages almost one in four will eventually terminate in divorce.

OF EVERY FOUR MARRIAGES ONE WILL END IN DIVORCE

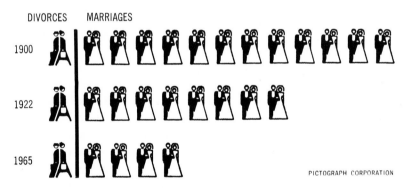

PICTOGRAPH CORPORATION

FIGURE 34-1————"Until Death Do Us Part," is the marriage vow taken by all. But in our nation the divorce court with increasing frequency does the parting. Sociologists believe that the divorce rate will continue to rise.

Clearly the traditional goal of marriage, "until death do us part," is now held in less esteem than is the happiness of the marriage partners. When the choice is one of living unhappily together or of divorce, the second alternative is now more frequently chosen.

The practice of annulment, which evades many of the embarrassing and difficult processes of divorce, is also on the increase, particularly

2 Paul C. Glick, "Marriage Instability: Variations by Size of Place and Religion," *The Milbank Memorial Fund Quarterly*, 41:43-55, January, 1963.

where divorce is made difficult by law. Leander B. Faber, of the New York Supreme Court, discussing annulment in the *Woman's Home Companion,* in September, 1945, indicated that he used to hear only one annulment case for every fifty divorces, but that in 1945 he was hearing one annulment for every three divorces. Once the annulments were primarily among youngsters under legal marriage age; now an increasing number of annulment suits are brought by people who have been married five to ten years, and several of whom are even parents of children. Faber reported that many seek annulments who would have weak grounds for divorce under the law, or who would avoid divorce because their religion forbids it.

The most common grounds for requesting annulment, he reported, are fraud and duress—the latter on the grounds of pressure having been exerted by the girl's family, or on grounds of lack of capacity to understand the nature of marriage. In four out of five cases the action is for fraud, the ground being that the husband or wife had a secret determination never to have children.

This new trend, which opens up avenues of escape from marriage for those who, for one of a great number of reasons, have found it unsatisfactory, is a strong indication that the companionship marriage cannot and will not be held together by legal requirements alone. Its bonds are personal rather than institutional.

In the United States now some 450,000 children are from homes broken by divorce, and the proportion of broken homes where children are involved is increasing.[3] In 1960, 57 percent of homes broken by divorce had children under 18. The average number of children per family was 1.18.[4] Even large families are not immune to divorce and annulment. A special analysis of data gathered by the Census of 1959 shows the number of families of different sizes involved in divorce (see Figure 34-2). Only-child families are more exposed to divorce, but a substantial number of families of all sizes are affected.

Burgess and Wallin, in their study of engagement, found that of 913 engaged men and 911 engaged women, approximately two-thirds thought that the couple should divorce if they ceased to be in love. Over two-thirds of the group, however, felt that their attitude would be changed on this matter of divorce if there were children in the family.[5] Even when there are children involved there is increased public tolerance because divorce in many cases is the only means of removing the child from an environment of damaging conflict.

[3] U. S. Department of Health, Education and Welfare, "Trends in Divorce and Family Disruption," *Indicators,* Washington, D. C., September, 1963.

[4] *Ibid.*

[5] Ernest W. Burgess and Paul Wallin, *Engagement and Marriage* (Philadelphia: J. B. Lippincott Co., 1953), pp. 394-396.

DIVORCES AND ANNULMENTS BY NUMBER
CHILDREN REPORTED: DIVORCE-REGISTRATION AREA,
TOTAL OF 16 REPORTING STATES, 1959

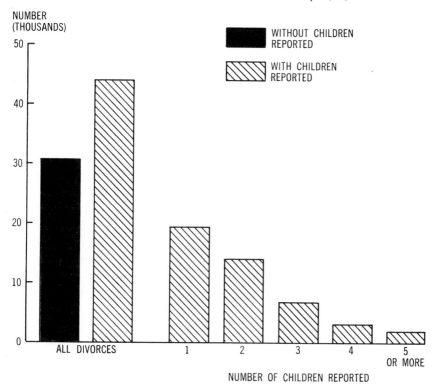

Source: U. S. Public Health Service, National Vital Statistics Division, "Trends in Divorce and Family Disruption," September, 1963, Chart 5.

FIGURE 34-2————Some 460,000 children in the nation under 18 years of age have lived through the divorce or separation of their parents. Over half of all divorces today are in families with dependent children. More divorced families have only one child, but all size families are affected.

Divorce by Occupation

Divorce is an escape device of the lower socioeconomic and lower educational classes more than of the more prosperous and better educated classes.[6] Desertion is even more so. Divorce is also an escape for those who marry too young, more than for others.[7]

[6] Glick's study shows this, as have many others; see Paul C. Glick, *American Families* (New York: John Wiley & Sons, Inc., 1958), p. 147 ff.

[7] *Ibid.,* Table 72, p. 112.

Using occupational categories, Monahan studied couples involved in divorce in the state of Iowa.[8] Employing vital statistics data for the state, he found, as did Lang,[9] that marriage problems are very closely related to socioeconomic status. The divorce measure, like the happiness measure used by Lang, shows that generally the higher the occupational level the lower the divorce rate. His divorce data for the year 1953 show ratio to employed males in the various occupational categories. Although labor constituted less than 10 percent of the population, they had almost one-third of the divorces. Professional people had less than half the divorces that would be expected on the basis of their ratio of population. Owners and officials had a few more than one-third of the expected divorces.

Divorce—A Legal Farce

Divorce is a legal action. Only the law can "put asunder" those whom the church or the law have joined together. Every divorce must, therefore, present to the court a legal cause. In New York state this must be adultery, so an adultery scene must be arranged in cases where a couple wants a divorce for other reasons. From a strictly legal standpoint, the court case is almost always a farce, not only because false reasons are given for the action, but because the couple usually agrees to the divorce in advance, rather than one party bringing grievance against the other as is presumed by law.

The usual legal grounds for divorce vary only slightly from year to year with proportions being about those shown in Figure 34-3.

There are marked variations among the states regarding legal grounds for divorces. The East and South are conservative with regard to permitting divorces and have low divorce rates. The West, acknowledging more grounds for divorce, has a high divorce rate. This high rate is explained in part by the fact that Easterners go west to take advantage of the ease of Western divorce laws, and also by the fact that residents of the West resort to divorce as a solution to marriage problems more often than those of other regions. The West lacks an established tradition; community pressures are weaker than in longer-settled areas where people have lived together for three or four generations. Its people are more mobile; there is less attachment to place. Its people are often far removed from the claims of kinship, many having left all relatives behind in moving west. It is less bothered by attitudes of the institutional family which persist more tenaciously in the deep South and the conservative East.

Florida has since 1935 drawn part of the divorce trade by shortening

---

[8] Thomas P. Monahan, "Divorce by Occupational Level," *Marriage and Family Living*, 17:322-324, November, 1955.

[9] Refer back to Figure 23-1, p. 460.

REASONS GIVEN IN COURT FOR WANTING DIVORCE

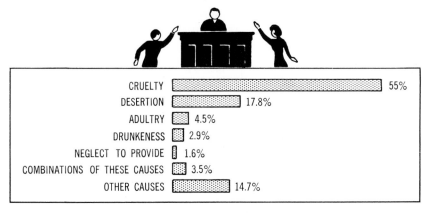

SOURCE: Paul Jacobson, *American Marriage and Divorce* (New York: Holt, Rinehart, & Winston, 1959), p. 123.

FIGURE 34-3————Which of these reasons do you think might be honest ones? Do you think couples always know themselves why they seek a divorce?

its residence requirements, as has also Arkansas. And now, in a day of jetting between continents, Paris, Havana, Mexico, and the Virgin Islands offer easy escapes from marriage.

Ernest R. Mowrer, sociologist at the University of Chicago, has studied broken families to get at the real reasons for divorce and desertion.[10] His studies make it strikingly clear that a great deal of rationalization enters into the court reason for obtaining a divorce. For example, in 295 divorces where desertion was given as the legal grounds, he found that in 40.2 percent of the cases financial tension was the actual cause for the desertion. In 13.2 percent of the cases, the party forsook the mate for another. In 10.9 percent of the cases, dissatisfaction with home or married life was the real reason. In 10.5 percent of the cases, infidelity was the real cause. In other cases, drink, cruelty, and irregular habits were found to be the cause.

In the case of 156 divorces granted on legal grounds of cruelty, he found that 45 percent were in reality brought on by financial tensions; 28.6 percent by drink; 14.6 percent by jealousy and infidelity. Excluding New York state, divorce on the grounds of adultery seems to most nearly represent the facts. In ninety-six cases he found that all but 8 percent had actually been involved in illicit sexual intercourse.

[10] Ernest R. Mowrer, "The Variance Between Legal and Natural Causes for Divorce," *Social Forces*, 2:388-392, March, 1924.

Harmsworth and Minnis have made an extensive analysis, through contact with lawyers in the state of Idaho, of the statutory and the non-statutory causes of divorce. They find great contradiction between the real and the legal causes. Lawyers admit that they tend to substitute for the real cause broad categories which are least likely to be challenged by the court. Extreme cruelty seems to be one of those causes which is least likely to be challenged, and is therefore extensivly used. This means that even statutory causes are abused as far as integrity is concerned.[11]

Divorce—A Social Process

People abroad get the impression that divorce in the United States is a very casual experience. It is not so. It usually builds up slowly. There is a revival of hope and return to despair; a period of good adjustment and a glimpse of happiness, then a slipping back. Often this goes on until misery is so great that temporary separations are necessary. Love may revive only to be followed with disillusionment and near despair. For most couples there is a long time lapse between the first consideration of divorce and the decree (see Table 34-1).

TABLE 34-1————Time from first serious consideration of divorce to decree*

Time (in months)	Percent	Cumulative percent
0- 5	6	6
6-11	15	21
12-23	30	51
24-35	23	74
36-47	17	91
Not known	15	
Total	425	

Median = 23.8 months

* William J. Goode, After Divorce (New York: Free Press of Glencoe, Inc., 1956), p. 137.

Under the companionship-family social system, divorce is a social process which in outline is not unlike the process of dating, courtship, engagement, and marriage. It is, in fact, those processes in reverse. Instead of a series of experiences creating greater intimacy and involvement and culminating in marriage, divorce is a series of experiences beginning with

[11] Harry C. Harmsworth and Nhyra S. Minnis, "Non-Statutory Causes of Divorce: The Lawyer's Point of View," Marriage and Family Living, 17:316-321, November, 1955.

the initial frictions and climaxing in emotional indifference or even violent animosities.

Tension may arise over any factors that have meaning in the lives of the husband and wife. It may arise over so little a thing as orderliness, especially if one person is meticulous and the other is naturally careless. It most often arises over money, since money has so much meaning in American culture. It may arise over misunderstandings about sex. The tensions may exist over social relationships, especially if one member likes social activity and the other shuns the crowd. It may arise over such trivial things as the way the mate spends his leisure time or the kind of recreation he indulges in.

Almost anything in the human relationship may be exaggerated to a place of major importance and become the primary source of tension once it becomes a focus of difference. Many couples cannot analyze fully the source of their tensions. Such tensions, whatever their cause, and whether or not their cause is recognized by the individuals themselves, are at the basis of the divorce.

The late Willard Waller once traced the various steps through which the couple goes in approaching divorce.[12] The first stage is a disturbance in the love life of the pair. This eventually leads to the point where friction is so intense that the possibility of divorce is first mentioned.

The next stage is that in which husband or wife tells some outside person or persons of their difficulty. This immediately puts the marriage on a different basis, since the couple has lost face with other people. Usually this does not end the marriage; it goes on in a matter-of-fact way, discussions taking place as to the proper course of action.

Finally, there comes the stage when the husband and wife definitely decide to make a break. This is followed by a separation, which is followed later by the divorce action itself. The divorce does not end the relationship. There is still the important period of mental conflict, during which both individuals are confronted with the problem of reconstructing their lives to fit the new situation.

There is also the problem of emotional readjustment. Waller has stated that, in his studies of divorce cases, he had yet to find a divorce which was not followed by a serious form of bereavement, along with problems of loneliness, sex tensions, and problems of lowered income and social standing among friends. In many cases the bereavement following divorce for one or sometimes for both parties is much more serious than bereavement (grief and shock) following the death of a mate. Death is always classed among the inevitable occurrences of life. The shock of death

---

[12] Willard Waller and Reuben Hill, *The Family: A Dynamic Interpretation* (New York: Holt, Rinehart & Winston, Inc., 1951), p. 540.

may be more sudden, but it can be charged to Providence, to accident, or to natural causes, and one can absolve himself of blame. But in the case of divorce, there is always the knowledge that it might have been avoided and always the background of disappointed happiness against which to project it.

This early analysis of Waller's, based on the case history analysis of thirty-three couples involved in divorce, shows great insight. Much of it is still irrefutable. It does, however, need some modification and elaboration to suit current conditions.

First, it should be stressed that the divorce process may be arrested at any step, and adjustment turned toward better rather than worse relationships. This is particularly true today when more specialists are available for counsel and where many ministers, teachers, and others are sufficiently informed to help a couple in conflict gain insight into their problems, thus helping to solve them. Waller's basic thesis that marriage relationships are dynamic, always tending either to get better or worse at any stage of the relationship, is probably more true now than when he made the observation. Only among couples who adhere religiously to a custom-dictated pattern can marriage in our time be a fixed state, if indeed it can be there.

Second, bereavement and shock do not inevitably follow divorce today. Some find in it genuine and complete relief from tension. Greater public tolerance may be a factor here, although it is doubtful that the shock reaction was ever universal. Locke's more recent case histories[13] show that in many instances there is no shock at all. He also suggests the probability that where there is emotional trauma, it may be eased by early remarriage.

Even more recently, Goode[14] has studied one hundred urban mothers who have been divorced. He finds that there is no consistent traumatic pattern following divorce. Half of the subjects studied indicated an attitude of indifference toward the former spouse.

Divorce in the Marriage Cycle

Generally speaking, the longer the marriage survives, the less likelihood that it will ever end in divorce. The divorce rate is highest during the first few years of marriage, when major adjustments must be made

---

[13] Ernest W. Burgess and Harvey J. Locke, *The American Family*, Third Edition (New York: American Book Co., 1963), pp. 451-460.

[14] William J. Goode, "Problems in Postdivorce Adjustment," *American Sociological Review*, 14:394-400, June, 1949.

or the marriage declared a failure. The peak in number of divorces comes in the third year of marriage and drops sharply after the seventh year.[15] (see Figure 34-4).

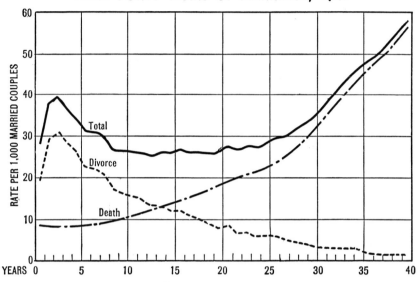

MARRIAGES BROKEN BY DEATH AND DIVORCE, FIRST FORTY YEARS OF MARRIAGE, 1947

SOURCE: Metropolitan Life Insurance Company, *Statistical Bulletin*, November, 1949.

FIGURE 34-4———The first three years of adjustment bring the most divorces. After the third year, rates gradually decline throughout the lifetime of the couple, with the exception of a slight rise in the 21st year. Dissolution by death increases with the passing of time.

In about three-fourth of all cases, the wife initiates the divorce action. In most cases, collusion is involved; the couple agreeing that she is most likely to succeed in obtaining a decree. Most divorce cases are uncontested, indicating that there has been prior agreement as to obtaining a divorce. It must, however, be granted that women use divorce as a solution to marriage problems more often than men do. The wife's happiness, success, mental health, and general well-being is much more identified with success of the marriage than is that of the husband. He may use out-

[15] Paul H. Jacobson, "Differentials in Divorce by Duration of Marriage and Size of Family," *American Sociological Review*, 15:238-239, April, 1950.

side recreation, work, an extramarital love affair, or even desertion as an escape much more readily than she. He becomes the overt offender against the marriage. She requests the divorce on the grounds of his offense.

Remarriage As a Postdivorce Adjustment

One of the serious problems the divorced woman faces, and in this respect she is more suspect than is the widow, is that insecure wives consider her a competitor for their husbands.[16] In some respects the suspicions of these wives are justified, for although students of the family, until recently, were inclined to think of the divorced person as one who pines away the lonely years with little chance of remarriage, statistical studies of the last decade show this view to be an erroneous one.[17]

It is known now that the chances of remarriage after divorce are much higher than: (1) the chance of eventual marriage for single persons of the same age group, and (2) the chances of remarriage after widowhood for given ages (see Figure 34-5). At age 30, the chances of remarriage for a divorced woman are 94 in 100; for the widowed woman, only 60 in 100; and for the spinster, only 48 in 100. At age 30, the divorced man's chances of remarriage are 96 in 100; the widowed male's chances of remarriage, 92 in 100; and the bachelor's chances of marriage, only 67 in 100.[18]

The new data also show that marriage and remarriage rates drop with increased age for all groups and for both sexes, both the remarriage and marriage rates dropping faster for females than males, but that throughout life the divorced person continues to have much better chances of marriage than the other groups. For example, at age 40, the divorced woman has 65 chances in 100 of remarriage; the widowed woman, only 29 chances in 100 of remarriage; and the single woman, only 16 chances in 100 of marriage. Or to approach it differently, a spinster of 30 has ap-

[16] Maurice J. Karpf reports that in his counseling experience the divorced woman is particularly aware of this attitude on the part of wives; see "Counseling the Unmarried Female Adult—Single, Widowed, Divorced," a paper delivered before the marriage-counseling section, National Council on Family Relations, Oakland, California, July 9, 1954.

[17] The most comprehensive analysis of Census data is that of Paul H. Jacobson, *American Marriage and Divorce* (New York: Holt, Rinehart & Winston, Inc., 1959). For a detailed analysis of Iowa data see Thomas P. Monahan, "The Duration of Marriage to Divorce: Second Marriages and Migratory Types," *Marriage and Family Living*, 21:134-138, May, 1959; also his, "The Changing Nature and Instability of Remarriage," *Eugenics Quarterly*, Vol. 5, June, 1958.

[18] Metropolitan Life Insurance Company, "The Chances of Remarriage for the Widowed and Divorced," *Statistical Bulletin*, May, 1945, pp. 1-3; data are from records in 22 states and the District of Columbia and are, therefore, extensive and conclusive; see also Paul H. Jacobson, *American Marriage and Divorce* (New York: Holt, Rinehart & Winston, Inc., 1959); Jacobson compares remarriage rates at age 25 and finds them higher for the divorced than the single or the widowed; see Chapter 6.

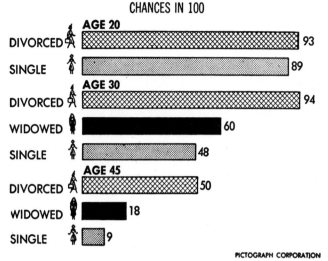

CHANCES OF MARRIAGE FOR SINGLE, DIVORCED, AND WIDOWED WOMEN
CHANCES IN 100

PICTOGRAPH CORPORATION

SOURCE: Based on data from Metropolitan Life Insurance Company, *Statistical Bulletin.* Chart by Paul H. Landis, "Sequential Marriage," *Journal of Home Economics,* 42:625-628, October, 1950.

FIGURE 34-5————At all ages, the divorced woman's chances of marriage are greatest. The divorced man also is more likely to marry than the single or widowed man.

proximately a fifty-fifty chance of marriage; the widow of 33 has a similar chance; but the divorcee of 45 has a fifty-fifty chance of remarriage.

How soon does remarriage take place? There are as yet no specific and comprehensive data on this subject, but data for a five-year interval indicate that remarriage after divorce usually comes within the first five years. Glick[19] made estimates from large samples and concludes that of those divorced in the five years preceding the 1948 Bureau of the Census survey, all but one-fourth had remarried. Of those who had been divorced five to fourteen years, only about one-seventh had not remarried. While Glick advises caution in the acceptance of his data, he suspects that the estimates may be low in that unattached adults tend to be missed in sample Census surveys and a certain proportion of divorced persons fail to report themselves as divorced.

19 P. C. Glick, "First Marriages and Remarriages," *American Sociological Review,* 14:726-734, December, 1949.

Using the same series of data, Glick found that approximately one-half of the men and three-fourths of the women who had lost their spouses by death during the preceding five years had not remarried. Of those losing their spouses by death during the five- to fourteen-year period preceding the survey, about one-third of the men and two-thirds of the women had not remarried.

A special study of remarriages during the early 1950's shows that over a third of divorced persons who had married had done so within a year or less. Almost another fourth married within the second year (see Table 34-2). Of widowed males a fourth married within the year, but less than a fifth of widowed females did.

TABLE 34-2————Period of divorce or widowhood prior to remarriage for widowed men and women who remarried*

Years since divorced	Males (percent)	Females (percent)
One year or less	34.4	34.3
2	18.4	19.4
3	10.7	12.7
4	10.4	6.1
5-9	12.2	14.5
10 and over	7.4	8.8
not reported	6.5	4.2
	100.0	100.0

Years since widowed	Males (percent)	Females (percent)
One year or less	25.7	19.0
2	17.1	23.2
3	10.5	7.0
4	7.6	4.9
5-9	22.9	23.2
10 and over	13.3	14.1
not reported	2.9	8.6
	100.0	100.0

* "Demographic Characteristics of Recently Married Persons, United States, April, 1953," *Vital Statistics-Special Reports,* Vol. 39, No. 3, Oct. 12, 1954. Data are for persons in the United States who remarried between Jan., 1950 and April, 1953.

Jacobson[20] in a similar analysis concludes that of divorced women, a third remarry within a year; almost half within two years and two-thirds

[20] Paul H. Jacobson, *American Marriage and Divorce* (New York: Holt, Rinehart & Winston, Inc., 1959), pp. 67-71.

within five years. Men are not quite so quick to take on new marriage responsibilities, but three in five, he finds, remarry within five years.

The above is clear evidence that divorced persons remarry much more quickly than the widowed. The fact that such a high proportion remarry so quickly makes one suspect that students of the family have discounted too heavily the notion of the man in the street that some divorces take place so that one or both parties may be free to marry a person already selected. Even behind such divorces there is often a long period of tension, where one spouse or the other has attempted to escape by forming a love relationship outside the marriage. The male is most often the offender in such cases.

Success of Remarriage After Divorce or Widowhood

It is known that marriages now are about four times as likely to be broken by divorce as in 1890, but what of remarriages? Until recently little has been known, except from scattered studies of small samples, concerning the success of remarriage. Studies of Popenoe[21] and others[22] give the impression that remarriage is less often successful than original marriages. Locke's comparison[23] of a small sample of happily married and divorced persons led to the tentative hypothesis that divorced women are approximately as good a risk in remarriage as single women; divorced men are not so good a risk. These findings give an erroneous picture of the general situation.

Studies by the Bureau of the Census[24] with a sample practically nationwide in scope present for the first time convincing evidence that remarriages do not work out so well as first marriages. In 1948, 20 percent of the divorced and 18 percent of the married persons whose spouses were absent had been married before. Only 13 percent of widowed persons and of married persons living with their spouses had been previously married. For 19.2 percent of divorced men, this was at least the second break; for 21.2 percent of divorced women, the same. While there is no way of knowing what proportion of the first marriages were broken by death and what proportion by divorce, the evidence suggests that second marriages are

21 Paul Popenoe, "Divorce and Remarriage from a Eugenic Point of View," *Social Forces*, 12:48-51, October, 1933.

22 H. Hart and E. B. Hart, *Personality and the Family* (Boston: D. C. Heath & Co., 1935), p. 109.

23 H. J. Locke and W. J. Klausner, "Prediction of Marital Adjustment of Divorced Persons in Subsequent Marriages," *Research Studies of the State College of Washington*, 16:30-32, March, 1948.

24 U. S. Department of Commerce, Bureau of the Census, "Marital Status, Number of Times Married, and Duration of Present Marital Status, April, 1948," Series P-20, No. 23, March 4, 1949.

about 50 percent more risky than first marriages, and the woman in her second or subsequent marriage is a somewhat poorer risk than the man. Specifically, the remarried woman is, according to these data, a 10 percent poorer risk than the remarried man.

Monahan's study of Iowa data, where statewide statistics are available, shows that not only are second marriages of shorter duration than first marriages but that the oftener the divorced person remarries, the shorter the average duration of the marriage is (see Figure 34-6). His data also prove conclusively that it is the remarried divorced person who accounts for the high divorce statistics among those with one or more previous marriages.[25]

DIVORCES PER 100 MARRIAGES BY PRIOR MARITAL STATUS, IOWA DATA 1953-1955

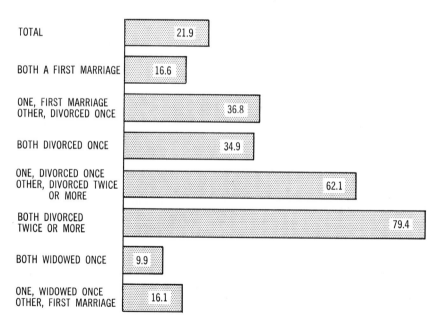

SOURCE: Thomas P. Monahan, "The Changing Nature and Instability of Remarriage," *Eugenics Quarterly*, June, 1958.

FIGURE 34-6————Note how divorce experience pyramids toward repeated divorce. The widowed are very stable in remarriage.

[25] Thomas P. Monahan, "The Duration of Marriage to Divorce: Second Marriages and Migratory Types," *Marriage and Family Living*, 21:134-138, May, 1959.

A special study of marriages in the District of Columbia, relating duration to previous marital history, presents striking evidence on the greater risk of remarriages (see Figure 34-8). Where both partners had been married previously, marriages had lasted less than half as long prior to divorce or separation as those in which couples were ending their first marriage. Note also the briefer duration of marriages in which the wife had been married before than of those in which the husband had been married previously. This is further indication that a previously married wife is a greater marriage risk than a previously married husband.

REMARRIAGES BY MARITAL STATUS OF BRIDE AND GROOM, BY AGE: 28 STATES, 1959

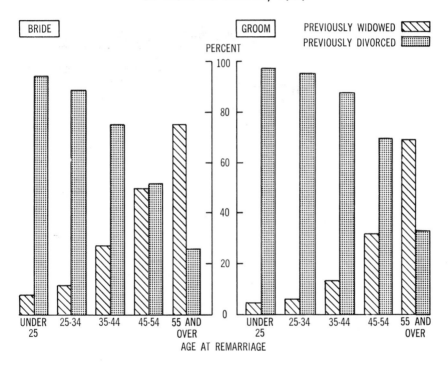

SOURCE: U. S. Public Health Service, National Vital Statistics Division, "Trends in Divorce and Family Disruption," September, 1963, Chart 6.

FIGURE 34-7————People taking a second-hand spouse in the younger ages will find that most of those who are eligible are among the divorced; in the older ages, among the widowed. Almost all the eligibles under 25 years of age are among the divorced group. For evidence on the risk involved with a previously married individual, male or female, see evidence on pp. 717-721.

Goode's study of divorced women shows that most of those who had remarried felt their second marriage was better than the first, and that their situation for themselves and children would have been worse had they not divorced. These marriages were, however, in their beginning.[26]

MEDIAN DURATION OF MARRIAGE BY FIRST MARRIAGE AND REMARRIAGE OF SPOUSE, DISTRICT OF COLUMBIA, 1957

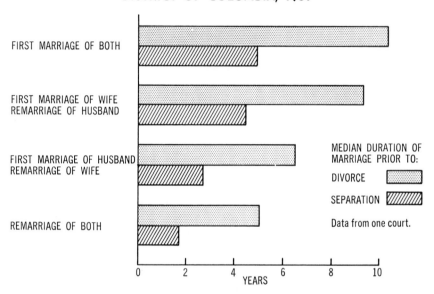

SOURCE: U. S. Public Health Service, National Vital Statistics Division, "Trends in Divorce and Family Disruption," September, 1963, Chart 4.

FIGURE 34-8————The more experience an individual has had with previous marriage breaks, the greater the likelihood of a short marriage. First marriages last longest, remarriages of males next; remarriages of females are very fragile. Where both of the pair are remarrying, the new marriage has a low median duration.

One may be reckoning here with a considerable amount of the kind of rationalization that enters into situations requiring self-justification.

A certain proportion of divorcees remarry each other. Some years ago Popenoe[27] studied the success of 200 cases of the remarriage of divorced

26 William H. Goode, *After Divorce* (New York: Free Press of Glencoe, Inc., 1956).
27 Paul Popenoe, "Remarriage of Divorcees to Each Other," *American Sociological Review*, 3:695-699, October, 1938.

persons to each other. Of these, he found 48 percent happy, 15 percent doubtful, and 37 percent definitely unhappy. The unhappy ones usually resorted to divorce again very quickly.

These data indicate that remarriage is for many a successful post-divorce adjustment. Some no doubt gain maturity and insight into their own personalities and into the nature of marriage itself from their first experience as well as from their period of widowhood following divorce. This makes it possible for them to find happiness in a new relationship. On the other hand, the facts also show clearly that those who have been through divorce once, more readily seek this solution to marriage problems than those who have not been previously married.

Divorce and the Child

Society has ceased to be very greatly concerned about the divorce of man and wife but dares not view so lightly the effects on children. One cannot, however, ignore the evidence that perpetual marital conflict may be much worse for the child than divorce itself. There is in many cases a great damage to children in continuing a marriage in which an established pattern of antagonistic relationship exists.

One of the most convincing analyses on this point is that by Plant.[28] Writing for judges involved in the legal processes of the divorce courts, he stated that in many cases divorce is the best possible solution for the child. He found that ten times as many children were sent to the Essex County, New York, Juvenile Clinic from separated parents as from divorced parents. Less disturbance was shown in the lives of children of divorced parents than in those of separated parents. He believed the divorce court, in granting the decree and in assigning the child to one parent, making whatever financial arrangements are necessary, is often doing the most that can be done to remedy the situation from the standpoint of the welfare of the child. Divorce is not an ideal solution, but is the only one possible in certain instances. In such cases, it comes as a great relief to the child.

There has been much publicity of the fact that children of divorced homes make up an undue proportion of delinquents. As a consequence of such reports, the public generally blames divorce for these problems. Actually, this kind of thinking is erroneous. Divorce itself is simply the legal incident in the conflict of marriage partners.

Far from being the cause for children's problems, divorce is often the solution. The damage to the child was done long before the divorce de-

---

[28] James S. Plant, "The Psychiatrist Views Children of Divorced Parents," *Law and Contemporary Problems,* 10:807-818, Summer, 1944.

cree was sought and might have been avoided had the divorce come sooner. The damage to the child comes from perpetual conflict and bickering between parents; from his being used as a pawn in their conflict. Those who work with children's problems and with courts of domestic relations observe that parents in conflict are rarely fair to the child. Each parent will try to influence the child against the other parent. In some cases, one parent will use the child as an excuse for holding the marriage together. Without any regard for his feelings or interests, a parent may pour out his miseries and condemnations of the other parent into the innocent child's ears. It is this kind of atmosphere that creates children's problems, not divorce as such.

Judge Paul W. Alexander, of Toledo, Ohio, who has presided over 30,000 divorces and who on alternate days presides over the juvenile court, has observed that during some years as many as 40 percent of couples with children who come for divorces have been to the juvenile court previously with their children's problems.[29] Certainly this is striking evidence that problems of delinquency appear before the divorce. To interpret problems of juvenile delinquency among the children of divorced parents as being due to the divorce is unsound thinking.

There is an increasing body of evidence that divorce in and of itself is not seriously harmful to children. The aftereffects depend a great deal on the kind of relationship that preceded the breakup. There is the strong likelihood in many instances that the effects on the child might have been more disastrous had the divorce not taken place. Burchinal,[30] in one of the most refined pieces of research to date, compared five types of family groups in their effects on some 1,500 young people in grades seven through eleven: unbroken families, mothers only, mother and stepfather, both parents remarried, and fathers and stepmothers.

For the most part, he finds no differences in personality and social relationship scores. He concludes that the broken family, and even the

[29] Paul W. Alexander, "A Therapeutic Approach," *Conference on Divorce* (Chicago: University of Chicago Law School, February 29, 1952). Numerous other recent studies have supported the view that it is the tension that precedes divorce rather than the divorce itself that does the damage. See such studies as F. Ivan Nye, "Child Adjustments in Broken and in Unhappy Unbroken Homes," *Marriage and Family Living*, 19:356-361, November, 1957; Judson T. Landis, "A Comparison of Children of Divorced Parents and Children of Happy or Unhappy Nondivorced Parents on Parent-Child Relationships, Dating, Maturation, and Sex and Marriage Attitudes," a paper read before the National Council on Family Relations, Minneapolis, Minn., August 27, 1955; Paul H. Landis, *The Broken Home in Teenage Adjustment* (Pullman, Wash.: Washington Agricultural Experiment Station, June, 1953), Bulletin No. 542.

[30] Lee G. Burchinal, "Characteristics of Adolescents from Unbroken, Broken, and Reconstituted Families," *Marriage and Family Living*, 26:44-50, February, 1964; see also F. Ivan Nye, *op. cit.;* also Judson T. Landis, *op. cit.;* also Judson T. Landis, "A Comparison of Children from Divorced and Nondivorced Unhappy Marriages," *Coordinator*, 11:61-65, July, 1962.

reconstituted family, where remarriage of a parent or parents takes place, "was not the overwhelming influential factor in the children's lives that many thought it to be."

Perhaps the social adjustment process is far different today, even for children, than it was in an earlier day when divorce was a more definite challenge to the mores. Greater tolerance has no doubt permeated both community and school.

One of the more damaging results of this kind of logic is the persistence of intolerance toward parents who seek divorce. It is assumed that such parents, in the act of seeking divorce, are doing their children great damage. Quite to the contrary, conscientious parents who are in bitter and perpetual conflict beyond their control or understanding are doing their children a great injustice if they fail to get a divorce. They deserve greater public tolerance.

Judson T. Landis has found that the effect of divorce on the child varies greatly with the age of the child at the time of divorce—it is less

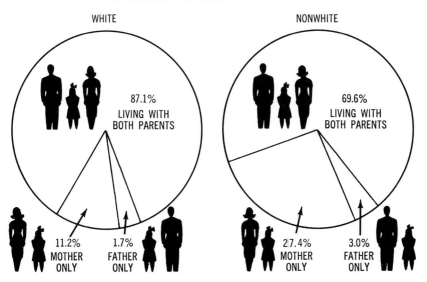

CHILDREN IN BROKEN FAMILIES

WHITE

87.1% LIVING WITH BOTH PARENTS

11.2% MOTHER ONLY

1.7% FATHER ONLY

NONWHITE

69.6% LIVING WITH BOTH PARENTS

27.4% MOTHER ONLY

3.0% FATHER ONLY

* See also Paul C. Glick, "Marriage Instability: Variations by Size of Place and Religion," *The Milbank Memorial Fund Quarterly*, 41:43-55, January, 1963.

SOURCE: U. S. Department of Commerce, Bureau of the Census, *Current Population Reports: Population Characteristics*, Series P-20, No. 112, December 29, 1961, p. 13.

FIGURE 34-9————Distribution, by race, of children under 18 living with one parent.

traumatic for younger children—and how the child viewed the parent relationship prior to the divorce—those who considered the home happy suffered more trauma.[31]

Bernard[32] studied attitudes of men and women toward children acquired through remarriage. Almost two-thirds of divorced men and 56 percent of divorced women were affectionate toward children acquired. Only about 5 percent of divorced men and 7 percent of divorced women rejected them. About a third neither rejected nor were affectionate.

A Therapeutic Approach to Divorce

There is much discussion today of a therapeutic approach to divorce. Pioneer of this approach has been Paul W. Alexander, Judge of the Court of Common Pleas in Lucas County, Ohio. Today he is chairman of the interprofessional commission on Marriage and Divorce Laws which holds that we should develop socialized divorce procedures to terminate the divorce fraud now perpetuated by law. This commission recommends that a case-work approach to divorce be instituted to replace the present system of a spouse bringing legal charges against the mate. Judge Alexander has presided over enough divorce cases and cases in the juvenile court to know the many ins-and-outs of the psychology of marriage conflict and of the legal deviations of the divorce procedures.

He has now a staff of some eighty people who cooperate with him in studying and trying to find wise solutions for divorce cases. If there is a child under fourteen in the family the case must be investigated by one of these workers before divorce comes to court. If there are no children, the investigation is permissive. The aim of the divorce proceeding is to make it helpful rather than harmful.

Judge Alexander believes that we should try to do away with legal grounds for divorce. As long as there are legal grounds for divorce, courts will probably continue to pit one party against the other in a bitter emotional battle that may be largely of the court's making. Each divorce case, he believes, should be approached with the question, "What is best for the individuals concerned?" If a child is affected, "What is best for the child?" Divorce will then proceed without public trial in line with evidence presented. The judge, with the investigators' evidence at hand, is in a position to apply the greatest scientific insight into the problems involved.

Psychiatrist Lawrence S. Kubie recommends that custody of children

---

[31] Judson T. Landis, "The Trauma of Children Where Parents Divorce," *Marriage and Family Living*, 22:7-13, February, 1960.

[32] Jessie Bernard, *Remarriage* (New York: Holt, Rinehart & Winston, Inc., 1956), p. 111.

suffering from the divorce of their parents be relegated to a committee. Parents would agree on custody arrangements, as is now usually the case, but would select a committee composed of a pediatrician, a child psychologist, an educator, and a lawyer or clergyman who would arbitrate disagreements between parents rather than have custody disputes thrown into court. Another child specialist would serve as an "adult ally" for the child, winning his confidence and keeping informed on the child's feelings about the custody relationships. This ally would report to the committee.

Although this sounds like a cumbersome arrangement, a growing number of parents are using it and finding it better than a court for settling custody disputes and for holding down quarrels about custody. It also relieves the courts of a heavy burden.[33]

To What Extent Can the Divorce Court Become Therapeutic?

The question is often raised whether or not a divorce court, to which people come as a final resort, is a place where marriages can be repaired. Obviously, this is not the ideal place. Many couples by this time are beyond the point where their marriages can be repaired.

On the other hand, divorce-court proceedings should generally become much less formal, patterned after the juvenile court. They would justify themselves even if they effected no reconciliations, because they could more intelligently grant custody of children, better assure support of wife and of children, and carry out the divorce procedure with less social and psychological damage to all parties concerned.

Many socially minded judges today, uninformed in psychological and sociological techniques, proceed to work on the assumption that all marriages should be saved. Their counseling is preaching, motivated by a desire to save all marriages or merely to see their own narrow philosophy in practice.

Those who work with people in trouble must realize that to save marriages is not the first or the main objective of counseling. Tradition would have it so; those who consider divorce a sin would have it so; but those who are looking for the best means of adjusting personality problems must always look upon divorce as possibly the nearest thing to an ideal solution that can be found—both for the couple and for the child. It may not be, but the divorce judge must accept the possibility as likely in approaching the case.

[33] See "Domestic Relations: Custody by Committee?" *Time*, September 18, 1964, pp. 67-68.

Some psychiatrists even conclude, from their counseling experience, that many couples who come to them for counsel about nervous problems are not aware that marriage is at the basis of their difficulty. This must be pointed out to them before they can find any peace in their inner life, or be relieved of their disturbance.[34]

Marriage should never be saved simply because marriage is an institution that we regard highly. Marriage should be saved only when it is to the benefit of both partners, and when it is to the benefit of the child if children are involved. Often it must be dissolved in the interests of one or all.

In many instances, exploring marriage difficulties early brings relief. As people understand themselves and their problems they may find that their problems diminish in severity. This is why divorce courts are and must, even when reformed, be in harmony with prevailing marriage philosophies and be places of last resort in which only final therapeutic measures are tried.

Community Action to Ease Marital Conflict

Not all communities can have marriage counselors. Oklahoma City had none, but decided a few years ago that something must be done about divorce. A counseling center was established in which volunteer professional people agreed to counsel free. This family clinic was started in 1947. By 1953, 250 estranged couples had brought their troubles to the clinic; 225 of the couples had been reconciled and the home maintained.[35]

Other Oklahoma communities have followed the pattern of the Oklahoma City group and have established clinics with volunteer counselors made up of doctors, lawyers, judges, teachers, ministers, and business men serving on the panel of counselors. A group of these volunteer counselors sit as a panel listening to the difficulties of the husband and wife and then offer their counsel based on common sense and good judgment. The fine thing about this experiment is that it works. It is a wonderful stopgap measure, until such time as enough people are prepared in the field of marriage counseling to handle it on a professional basis.

An organization called Divorces Anonymous now exists for mutual help and understanding and many churches now have "divorce clubs" to

34 See Thomas M. French, "Contributions to a Therapeutic Solution to the Divorce Problem: Psychiatry," in *Conference on Divorce* (Chicago: University of Chicago Law School, February 29, 1952); see also Aaron L. Rutledge, "Should the Marriage Counselor Ever Recommend Divorce?" *Marriage and Family Living*, 25:319-325, August, 1963.

35 The work of this group was reported in *Lifetime Living*, December, 1953, and reprinted in *Reader's Digest* under the title, "Ganging Up on Divorce," February, 1954, pp. 147-150.

try to give religious support to the many who feel shame and stigma and yet who are religiously inclined.[36] Many divorced persons need the church to help them find new purpose in life.

In conclusion, while divorce is not to be condoned as an easy solution to superficial marriage problems, society has come to recognize it, legally and extralegally, as the ultimate solution where marriage difficulties arise from deep-seated psychological and emotional problems. When such difficulties are established by professional counsel, the quicker the divorce the better, even when children are involved. Divorce is looked upon by the social scientist as therapeutic when it is used in this connection. It can only be condemned when used casually. In such instances it solves no problems, but leads to a series of necessary new adjustments which place the unstable person in a more vulnerable situation than he was in before.

Problems

1. Which of these philosophies do you consider most desirable in a young bride or groom?
   a. "I said it and I meant it, 'until death do us part.' I shall never never consider divorce."
   b. "If things don't work out well, there is always the divorce court."
   c. "I believe in this marriage and I'll do my best to make it a happy one. If my best isn't good enough, however, I won't let pride or pressure frighten me of divorce."
2. Dividing the class into two opposing groups discuss divorce as: (a) an indication that marriage is taken less seriously than in the past, (b) an indication that marriage is taken more seriously than in the past.
3. Upon what legal grounds are most divorces obtained? Compare these reasons with the actual grounds as shown by special studies.
4. Divorce, unlike death, is a separation usually preceded by tension and antagonism. Why, then, are so many divorces accompanied by tears and a period similar to bereavement?
5. Charles and Hana have read about the undesirable effect divorce has on children. They no longer love one another; seldom ever speak, and Charles, who is deeply in love with another woman, spends most of his time in town to escape Hana's bitter tears. They have agreed, however, that until their children, five and seven, are fully grown, they will not consider separation.
   a. How wise do you consider their decision?
   b. What might the effect of their relationship be on the two children?

[36] See Thomas J. Fleming, "The Divorced Ones," *This Week Magazine,* January 26, 1964.

    c. Do you think their two children might profit if Charles and Hana obtained a divorce?

6. Compare the motives and justifications for divorce and remarriage among average people with the motives and justification in such cases as Tommy Manville's and certain Hollywood personalities'.

7. Considering the statistical evidence, would you say that a marriage ending in divorce tends to embitter most individuals against the institution of marriage?

8. Marriage is, after all, a relationship between two people that is capable of producing intense and lifelong misery as well as happiness. Do you think that it is justifiable for any individual judge to have the power to deny a divorce to an unhappy couple? Discuss.

9. Upon what grounds may divorces be obtained in your state? In what ways could divorce laws be improved?

10. *Sociodrama:* A young divorcée returns to her parents' home but receives a rather cool reception. The drama might open with the observation of one of her parents: "Now, you've been bitten once, I hope you don't expect to try marriage again. You just aren't the type!"

    "Nonsense!" The girl might reply. "This has been sad, but it has also been the best thing that ever happened to me."

    Go on to picture the therapeutic results of the divorce.

Selected References

ARTICLES IN BOOKS OF READINGS

WINCH, Robert F., and others, *Selected Studies in Marriage and the Family,* Revised Edition (New York: Holt, Rinehart & Winston, Inc., 1962).
    1. CHRISTENSEN, Harold T., and MEISSNER, Hanna H., "Premarital Pregnancy as a Factor in Divorce," pp. 616-621.

SUSSMAN, Marvin B., *Sourcebook in Marriage and the Family,* Second Edition (Boston: Houghton Mifflin Co., 1963).
    2. BERNARD, Jessie, "The Institutionalization of Remarriage," pp. 464-470.
    3. NIMKOFF, M. F., "Contributions to a Therapeutic Solution to the Divorce Problem: Sociology," pp. 450-453.
    4. GOODE, William J., "Social Engineering and Divorce Problem," pp. 454-459.
    5. NYE, F. Ivan, "Child Adjustment in Broken and in Unhappy Unbroken Homes," pp. 248-254.
    6. JACKSON, Joan K., "Adjustment of the Family to Alcoholism," pp. 334-340.

BECKER, Howard, and HILL, Reuben (Editors), *Family, Marriage and Parenthood,* Second Edition (Boston: D. C. Heath & Co., 1955).
    7. ELLIOTT, Mabel A., "The Scope and Meaning of Divorce," pp. 669-708.

VINCENT, Clark E., *Readings in Marriage Counseling* (New York: Thomas Y. Crowell Co., 1957).

8. HARPER, Robert A., "Failure in Marriage Counseling," pp. 197-203.

9. BERKOWITZ, Sidney J., "An Approach to the Treatment of Marital Discord," pp. 203-213.

LANDIS, Judson T., and LANDIS, Mary G., *Readings in Marriage and the Family* (Englewood Cliffs, N. J.: Prentice-Hall, Inc., 1952).

10. SMITH, William C., "The Stepmother," pp. 306-310.

11. ————, "The Stepchild," pp. 310-313.

12. DAVIS, Kingsley, "Statistical Perspective on Divorce," pp. 333-338.

13. JACOBSON, Paul H., "Divorce and Size of Family," pp. 339-341.

14. DAVIS, Kingsley, "Children of Divorce," pp. 351-360.

15. ALEXANDER, Paul W., "A Therapeutic Approach to the Problem of Divorce," pp. 360-374.

FISHBEIN, Morris, and KENNEDY, Ruby Jo Reeves, *Modern Marriage and Family Living* (New York: Oxford University Press, 1957).

16. SMITH, William Carlson, "Remarriage and the Stepchild," pp. 457-475.

CAVAN, Ruth Shonle, *Marriage and the Family in the Modern World: A Book of Readings* (New York: Thomas Y. Crowell Co., 1960).

17. CAVAN, Ruth Shonle, "Legal Regulation of Marriage," Reading 41.

18. LEOPOLD, Alice K., "Marriage and Divorce Laws," Reading 42.

19. GOODE, William J., "Divorce as an Escape Mechanism," Reading 66.

20. PLOSCOWE, Morris, "Is There a Right Amount of Alimony?" Reading 67.

21. BERNARD, Jessie, "Remarriage of the Widowed and the Divorced," Reading 68.

22. PLANT, James S., "The Psychiatrist Views Children of Divorced Parents," Reading 85.

23. PLOSCOWE, Morris, "Who Gets the Children?" Reading 86.

24. POLOLSKY, Edward, "The Emotional Problems of the Stepchild," Reading 87.

General References

BEE, Lawrence S., *Marriage and Family Relations* (New York: Harper & Row, Publishers, 1959), Ch. 17.

BERNARD, Jessie, *Remarriage* (New York: Holt, Rinehart & Winston, Inc., 1956).

CAVAN, Ruth Shonle, *American Marriage* (New York: Thomas Y. Crowell Co., 1959), Ch. 17.

CHRISTENSEN, Harold T., and MEISSNER, Hanna H., "Studies in Child Spacing: III—Premarital Pregnancy As a Factor in Divorce," *American Sociological Review,* 18:641-644, December, 1953.

Conference on Divorce, a symposium (Chicago: University of Chicago Law School, February 29, 1952).

GLICK, Paul C., "First Marriages and Remarriages," *American Sociological Review,* 14:726-734, December, 1949.

GOODE, William J., *After Divorce* (New York: The Free Press of Glencoe, Inc., 1956).

————, "Problems in Postdivorce Adjustment," *American Sociological Review,* 14:392-401, June, 1949.

HAUSSAMEN, Florence, and GUITAR, Mary Anne, *The Divorce Handbook* (New York: G. P. Putnam's Sons, 1960).

ILGENFRITZ, Marjorie P., "Mothers on Their Own—Widows and Divorcees," *Marriage and Family Living,* 23:38-41, February, 1961.

JACOBSON, Paul H., *American Marriage and Divorce* (New York: Holt, Rinehart & Winston, Inc., 1959).

KEPHART, William M., *The Family, Society and the Individual* (Boston: Houghton Mifflin Co., 1961), Part 7.

KIRKPATRICK, Clifford, *The Family as Process and Institution,* Revised Edition (New York: The Ronald Press Co., 1963), Chs. 21, 22.

LANDIS, Judson T., "The Trauma of Children When Parents Divorce," *Marriage and Family Living,* 22:7-12, February, 1960.

LANTZ, Herman R., and SNYDER, Eloise C., *Marriage* (New York: John Wiley & Sons, Inc., 1962).

LEMASTERS, E. E., *Modern Courtship and Marriage* (New York: The Macmillan Co., 1957), Ch. 26.

MONAHAN, Thomas P., "Divorce by Occupational Level," *Marriage and Family Living,* 17:233-234, November, 1955.

————, "The Duration of Marriage to Divorce: Second Marriages and Migratory Types," *Marriage and Family Living,* 21:134-138, May, 1959.

MUDD, Emily Hartshorne, *The Practice of Marriage Counseling* (New York: Association Press, 1951).

RUTLEDGE, Aaron L., "Should the Marriage Counselor Ever Recommend Divorce?" *Marriage and Family Living,* 25:319-325, August, 1963.

35

Better Marriages

The present-day belief that every man's life can be perhaps indefinitely improved is relatively new to human
thinking and is largely a product of Western culture. Historically, peoples
have looked backward to a golden age long past, rather than forward toward a brighter tomorrow. American culture is especially optimistic about
tomorrow, particularly with regard to the materialistic aspects of civilization. The new model has so often been demonstrated to be an improvement that technological change has come to be identified with
improvement in level of living.

The belief that man can improve himself has not been so readily accepted with respect to human relationships. It has, however, an increasing
number of followers. The pessimist sees in all change a threat to human
adjustment and sees in everything new the symptoms of moral decay. One
cannot deny that every change, mechanical and otherwise, is a challenge
to adjustment, nor that serious problems have generally accompanied the
rapid changes of the modern era. One may even grant that it is difficult,
if not possible, to prove that human adjustment is at a higher level than
in the past or that happiness is more often realized now than yesterday.

Certainly such appraisals are primarily a matter of value judgment
based on arbitrary standards. They may also be a matter of faith. This
is particularly true with regard to appraising marriage. One approaching
this institution from the viewpoint that marriage is a sacrament and that
social order demands an authoritarian orientation will obviously reach
a different conclusion from one appraising it from the standpoint of its
adequacy in meeting human needs. The first view inevitably places the
contemporary institution in a decadent position because of the nearly
universal practice of birth control, the emphasis on sensual enjoyment
and personal happiness, the ideal of equality of the sexes, and the ideal of
a democratic relationship between parents and children.

The second approach, which appraises marriage in terms of meeting human needs as they are expressed in contemporary culture, views each of these developments as signs of improvement.

This book began by expressing faith in the latter point of view and presented evidence in support of it. It is logical and consistent, therefore, to express faith in the future improvement of marriage and to point out forces which are working and can be made to work in this direction.

Family-Life Education

The educational system has made great strides in reorienting the school curriculum away from purely academic subjects and toward a new focus—the functional demands of adult life. Today, the average high school and college student can be prepared to step into a job and perform efficiently from the first day on. Potential teachers gain experience vicariously through books and class lectures and directly through class projects and a supervised cadet practice-teaching program. Potential lawyers study actual cases, prepare briefs, and debate cases before their fellow students.

Although marriage has always occupied a high place in the lives of most men and women, there has been little thought of any formal preparation for the roles of husband and wife and parent. The case for marriage education has never been adequately demonstrated objectively, but certain studies suggest there is a definite benefit. Moses' study of students and married alumni shows that they do feel that they gain insight and learn to solve problems as a consequence of their training in marriage.[1]

Unlike their ancestors of only a few generations back, young couples today do not live and raise their children under the watchful eye and helping hand of a large, interdependent family group. The couple today are on their own from the very beginning, and the beginning, as has been pointed out, comes earlier in life today than it once did. They must generally learn by trial and error all that was learned by experience in the larger family of yesterday. Many a young man and wife have never even seen, much less cared for, a newborn child until they are handed their own at the hospital. The physical care, the training, and the discipline of most children are in the hands of young couples who are little more than children themselves.

The acknowledgment of this situation—more specifically, the recognition of its significance—has led to the development of books and courses in marriage and the family for the public school. Popular reaction has ranged from approval to indifference to outright opposition. Those who

[1] Virginia Musick Moses, "A Study of Learning Derived from a Functional Course in Marriage and Family Relationships," *Marriage and Family Living*, 18:204-208, August, 1956.

are favorable to the innovation tend to recognize the complexity and uniqueness of present-day family life. Those who are indifferent hold a narrow concept of the place of marriage in the life of the individual. Those who are openly antagonistic are generally the very traditional or the unduly prudish who doubt that anything so intimate and sacred as marriage could be prepared for in advance. The fact that sex must inevitably be discussed in such a course makes it taboo in the minds of some school administrators and parents.

Fortunately, such courses are proving to be the best possible evidence in favor of increased family-life education. Young people are learning and convincing their parents, in turn, that marriage and marital relations are not untouchable subjects. Scattered studies of marriages which followed some kind of preparatory courses indicate, too, that in marriage, as in the less intimate areas of life, youth can profit by the wisdom and experience of others.

Once it is admitted that marriage is the most exacting of all contracts, and family life the most demanding of all interpersonal relationships, there is no alternative but to place preparation for marriage and family high on the list of basic educational requirements. Family-life education not only gives tools and techniques for successful living, it helps to build favorable attitudes toward marriage and family and at the same time gives young people a better understanding of themselves, the opposite sex, and of children.

One of its aims is to help young people approach marriage and family living realistically. This requires the debunking of many popular, overly romanticized conceptions, as well as providing information concerning those things which can make marriage a success or failure. Family-life education in helping to develop an understanding of the opposite sex and the interaction patterns of marriage makes for greater marriage competence. The very fact that it helps young people to be objective and to rise above the folklore can be in itself a thing of great value.

Most colleges now teach a general marriage course and a course in the history of the family, as well as various courses in child psychology and child development. Unfortunately, these courses are still taken primarily by women, even though men are in as great need of some of them as are women.

One of the interesting developments in this field has been the tendency for the content to become increasingly functional; that is, directed at the specific problems which young people face in their adjustments to the opposite sex during the premarital period and during the early years of marriage. This book has attempted to carry out such an approach. Courses following this pattern have become more or less universal in American colleges.

The greatest handicap in the development of this approach to date is the lack of sufficient research material to provide an adequate guide on all points, but an increasing amount of sociological and psychological research is in the making. So far, social science has barely scratched the surface in understanding the significant factors in the complex relationship that is marriage. Research and clinical experience, however, are building up an increasing body of data, on the basis of which generalizations concerning premarital relationships and postmarital adjustments between the sexes can be inferred.

Family-life education needs to be extended in the high school to provide both boys and girls with opportunity to observe nursery schools in operation, to observe the care of small babies, and to learn more about parenthood and child training.

One of the barriers to popular acceptance of broad courses in preparation for marriage, particularly on the elementary and high school level, is that they are frequently equated with sex education courses. Many parents are still frightened or suspicious of group teaching in this delicate area.

Sex education has an important place in these courses because of its importance in marriage, but it is not the only, not even the primary, purpose of the course. Combating folklore notions of mate finding and marriage adjustment, and instilling some appreciation of the full possibilities of marriage and family life—these are more often the basic goals.

But what about this controversy over sex education? Does it have a place in the classroom, or is it a subject that can only create unnecessary problems? Should it be left alone or to the discretion of parents?

Sex Education

Historically, marriage has had as its primary function the bearing and rearing of children. It was justified primarily as an economic arrangement which provided for a fair distribution of the burdens of caring for society's dependent members—women and children.

Today, women have proven that they are no longer society's helpless dependents and schools have taken much of the responsibility for the rearing of children away from parents. Still marriage and family living persist with even increased popularity, so one has to conclude that the primary function of marriage has shifted.

The evidence as pointed out in preceding chapters indicates that the new function of marriage is personal, rather than social in origin. Men and women marry and live in such a way as to satisfy their own wishes and needs, rather than the customs and dictates of society.

High on the list of personal needs which marriage now seeks to satisfy are those of intimacy, companionship, and love. These needs, as has been observed, derive their fulfillment in large part from the sexual relations of man and wife. This elevates sex to a position of new importance in marriage. Unlike their ancestors, most couples now consider satisfactory relations in this area a necessary part of marriage and unsatisfactory relations as ample justification for divorce.

With this new concept of the significance of sex, it is natural that those who are concerned with improving American marriages should also be concerned with improving the sex life of American couples. The preoccupation of some scientists and writers with this aspect of marriage does not represent, as some believe, an exaggeration of its importance. They are being guided by evidence which has suggested that couples who make a mutually satisfactory sexual adjustment are frequently able to make better adjustment in other areas of their life together.

Early sex education, which is the means by which many hope to effect an ultimate improvement in marriage, is gaining increased acceptance on the elementary and secondary level of the public school system. Were it practical to delay this formal education until later adolescence, the program would probably arouse much less opposition. Many parents feel that beginning instruction in this area in the lower grades is either unnecessary or dangerous. They argue that it may only arouse questions and curiosity that would otherwise have never existed. The fact is, however, that formal or otherwise, sex education does begin in a child's early years. Questions are inevitable, and the natural curiosity of children is a powerful asset in opening the way for presenting wholesome facts and building normal attitudes. During the first six years of a child's life, he inevitably begins to wonder about such obvious and fascinating matters as "where babies come from." How this and similar questions are handled—the atmosphere in which they are discussed, the individual answering them, the facts or fictions that are passed along—can have a serious and lasting effect upon a young person's attitudes toward sex, marriage, and parenthood.

Assuming that sex education is in itself desirable, one still may question the desirability of putting it into the hands of the school. The fact that this is being done represents realism, rather than any ideal arrangement. Ideally, most agree, the intimate, unrestricted atmosphere of the home is the place for sex education. Realistically, however, most concede that too few parents are willing or able to accept the responsibilities of this task.

Parents, by and large, are poor teachers, except as they pass on tradition more or less unconsciously to their children. In the field of sex, traditional wisdom is certainly far from sufficient in this age. There is no doubt that the average teenager of today makes more moral decisions than his

RECEIVED FIRST SEX
INFORMATION BEFORE AGE 13

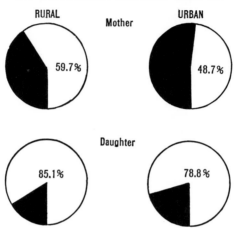

SOURCE: Paul H. Landis, "Marriage Preparation in Two Generations," *Marriage and Family Living*, November, 1951.

FIGURE 35-1———Sex information in the preadolescent period is important to sound emotional development. This chart compares two generations of women —mothers and their daughters. Preadolescents today receive more sex education than did their mothers a generation ago.

great-grandparents made in a lifetime. With unchaperoned dating, automobiles, and other means of mobility, practically every young person has to face, at a very immature age, the problem of whether or not to engage in sexual intercourse, often in a highly tense emotional situation. The only way he can cope with social pressures and his own biological drives is to have been adequately informed concerning his own nature, the nature of the opposite sex, and the facts of sex and reproduction themselves.

It is foolish to assume, as some do, that because one has married, had children and raised them, he is therefore able to prepare his own youngsters to do the job well when their time comes. Many lack the vocabulary; others lack general information, and in relying upon only their own experiences may actually pass on false or distorted ideas. Some are still so timid or inhibited that they unwittingly create an atmosphere of tension and uncertainty around the topic; others are so disappointed or disgusted that they cannot speak without bitterness. A few even try to protect their youngsters by giving them half-truths or actual fables about sex that must some day be unlearned either by better teaching or unfortunately more often, by shocking experience.

The program which leaders in family-life education hope to initiate is one demanding the cooperation of both parents and the school. Since much of a youngster's basic sex knowledge is generall acquired long before he enters school, it is hoped that all parents can be trained or helped to effectively supervise these first steps at least. With this accomplished, the schools' more general program of sex education will become a vastly less complicated task, for, as one third-grade teacher put it, "Right now my chief problem is not in teaching youngsters the facts of life; but in helping them outgrow the fiction their parents fed them in reference to the facts."

The most severe critics of family-life education are to be found in communities where the training of youth in this field has not been tried. In communities where it has been tried, fears vanish, for the results are favorable. Even in the area of sex education, the most feared aspect of such courses, the results are reassuring. In Pittsburgh, for example, four years after a course in sex education had been instituted, pregnancies among 60,000 public and parochial school girls declined by more than one-half. In Wisconsin, where social hygiene courses have been given for twenty years, illegitimacy rates have fallen 18 percent, while they have risen 2 percent in surrounding states. Wisconsin also had the lowest syphilis rate of any state in the union among returning veterans of World War II. The divorce rate in that state, too, has shown less increase than in most other states (only three have a better record).[2] A statewide program of sex education in Oregon has been more recently introduced with favorable results.

There is little doubt that education is, in part, the answer to better marriage and family life. Unfortunately, public administrators too often fear condemnation from public opinion which would favor rather than condemn. The Oregon film experiment indicates how few are the critics of an adequate program of sex education.

The Oregon film, developed by the Brown Trust Fund under the direction of Dr. Beck, psychologist of the University of Oregon, deals frankly with the problem of sex in a movie aimed at school children on the sixth-grade level. This film has been shown in every kind of community in Oregon. It is always presented first to the parent-teacher group, where a questionnaire is handed out and reactions obtained. In communities of all kinds, less than 2 percent of the parent-teacher group have criticized the film; more than 98 percent have fully approved it. When the

---

2 This summary of results of various programs is taken from "Effects of Education for Family Life," *Family Life*, 16:1-2, February 1, 1954. For a critical evaluation on a college marriage course, see Judson T. Landis, "An Evaluation of Marriage Education," *Marriage and Family Living*, 10:81 ff., 1948.

problem of sex education is approached in this manner, the superin-
tendent or principal has evidence with which to combat the inevitable,
though increasingly few, critics of innovation.

RECEIVED SEX INFORMATION
FROM SPECIFIC SOURCE

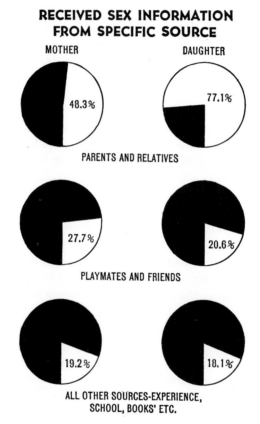

MOTHER   DAUGHTER

48.3%   77.1%

PARENTS AND RELATIVES

27.7%   20.6%

PLAYMATES AND FRIENDS

19.2%   18.1%

ALL OTHER SOURCES-EXPERIENCE,
SCHOOL, BOOKS' ETC.

SOURCE: Paul H. Landis, "Marriage Preparation in Two Generations," *Marriage and Family Living*, November, 1951.

FIGURE 35-2————The daughter generation more often received sex information from adult sources.

A study of Proffenberger discusses, among other things, the great
need for sex education. Anonymous questions put in a question box by
eighth-grade girls in a marriage and family-life course indicate a shocking
lack of sex education. About half of the girls asked questions about sexual
intercourse using vernacular terms.[3]

[3] Thomas Poffenberger, "Family Life Education in a Scientific Age," *Marriage and Family Living*, 21:150-154, May, 1959.

Hillman's study of correspondence with an advice column shows that more informational inquiries center around sex than around any other single topic. Second were queries about birth control. This would seem to indicate a great deficiency in the sex education in the typical person writing such a source for information.[4]

The Parents' Duty

It is inexcusable for any college student to grow up today unable to answer the sex questions of his youngsters. The time has long since passed when there is any justification for the young father's or mother's awkwardness in answering the child's first sex question, which usually is, "Where do babies come from?" or some variation of this question.

In the past, fathers, particularly, have been embarrassed and evaded this question, immediately throwing sex into the zone of superstition and wonder for the child. The parent who answers this question frankly and wisely will be asked the other questions that bother the child as he matures. Similarly, the teacher who answers the child's first sex questions honestly and frankly will be asked other questions. Those who do not answer frankly will be avoided later. The child will turn instead to his uninformed or half-informed age mates and between them they will think out answers or speculate on reasons. The results cannot help but be unfortunate; often they are dangerous. Children and young people must have answers to their questions concerning life. Parents who relinquish their teaching role have lost a valuable opportunity to serve their child and his future well-being.

The modern nursery school opens up the way for sex education for those relatively few small children who are able to attend. The special training of the personnel and the special facilities of the nursery are conducive to early and effective training of a completely informal nature. Youngsters of both sexes use the same toilet facilities at the same time. This is a particularly effective method of casually introducing an only child to the physiology of the opposite sex—a point of natural curiosity among children, generally preceding their first interest in sex as such. The nursery school teacher who is prepared for this common curiosity finds that it leads quite naturally and without emotional overtones to a number of other basic questions which form the groundwork for early sex information.

This situation is, of course, easily reproduced in the home of parents who do not harbor outmoded ideas of modesty or shame. Brothers and

[4] Christine H. Hillman, "An Advice Column's Challenge for Family-Life Education," *Marriage and Family Living,* 16:51-54, February, 1954.

sisters should be allowed, from the very beginning, to see one another nude. Starting this practice early forestalls the undue curiosity that would otherwise build up and keeps the situation so informal as to make it unnoticed and, therefore, unembarrassing. Where there is only one child, parents themselves can bathe or dress with the youngster occasionally during his early years and casually answer the questions he generally asks.

Premarital and Marriage Counseling

Modern society has had to develop many substitutes for the intimate local groups of an earlier day. Premarital and marriage counseling is one of these. In the large family and close-knit neighborhood of an earlier generation, young people had the benefit of not only folklore but of adult counsel in their mate selection and premarital arrangements. Their courtship period was carried out in a milieu of adult opinion. If trouble developed with the marriage, they could appeal to adult wisdom in whatever source merited their confidence. In a day of great mobility and anonymity, these sources of counseling are seldom available; when available, they are often not dependable. Many need to consult a specialist in the field of marriage relationships.

A new profession of marriage counselors has arisen to work with (1) couples seeking premarital counsel, and (2) couples seeking help in adjusting to the problems of their marriage.

In several of the large cities, and on a few university campuses, marriage counseling clinics have been established. In other instances, counselors operate on a fee basis as private practitioners, in the same way as doctors of medicine or psychiatrists do. Marriage counseling is a new and growing field. Those concerned with learning the address of reliable clinics or of practitioners who belong to the American Association of Marriage Counselors should address their office (27 Woodcliff Drive, Madison, N. J.) for advice on where a reliable counselor can be contacted.

As yet, most communities have no qualified specialist in this field. Some doctors, ministers, and college teachers have sufficient training and insight to be of assistance to those contemplating marriage or experiencing difficulty in their marriage. Such persons have often made a reputation in the community and may be sought for counsel.

The professional marriage counselor performs the role of a trained and sympathetic auditor before whom persons needing advice, previous to marriage or after marriage, can state their problems, anxieties, and perhaps their hopes and dreams. In premarital advising the counselor will usually employ tests designed to appraise the temperament and interests of the individual or the pair. He is also guided by the subject's statements in the interview. One of his main functions is to help the counselee objectify his problems and analyze and understand himself in relationship to the love experience that has created his problem or anxiety.

One of the aims of professional counseling is to discover the unmarriageable person or incompatible pair before marriage. Research gives some clues here. In fact, tests of some reliability are now available for predicting the success or failure of a marriage.[5] Greater development can be expected in this field, but aside from this, counseling can be of great value in helping young people understand themselves and each other prior to marriage. Objectivity at this stage when change is easy involves little personal and social damage.

There are, as yet, no devices by which success or failure in marriage can be predicted with finality. Two methods of study have been attempted. The one is statistical. It analyzes the backgrounds of successfully married and unsuccessfully married couples and compiles the common factors in the background of each, using this as the basis for predicting the outcome of marriages between persons with similar backgrounds. This method was launched by Burgess and Cottrell in their pioneer study, *Predicting Success and Failure in Marriage,* and by Terman and his colleagues in their pioneer study, *Psychological Factors in Marital Happiness.*

On the basis of such studies, certain measuring devices have been developed. They usually take the form of a scale with a series of questions about the person's background, attitudes, and experiences. Answers, when scored, give some index of the individual's likelihood of succeeding in marriage. These scales are one of the techniques used in premarital counseling. Other counselors use standardized personality tests or emotional tests of various sorts which give a general personality inventory. These are used as aids to predicting success or failure in marriage.

The second method of predicting the outcome of a marriage venture is the case-history method which tries to analyze in detail the characteristics of the relationship between the couple prior to their marriage. This technique is the one developed extensively by Burgess and Wallin in their case-history analysis of 1,000 engaged couples. In this they tried to learn whether the type of relationship that develops between the engaged couple during their courtship interactions throws any light upon their future interactions as marriage partners. They find a correlation of .50, indicating that there is considerable relationship between the adjustment

---

5 For a brief summary of traits found to be of predictive value in indicating the probable outcome of a marriage, see E. W. Burgess and Harvey J. Locke, *The Family,* Second Edition (New York: American Book Co., 1953), pp. 408-429. An earlier and more comprehensive summary is found in Clifford Kirkpatrick, *What Science Says About Happiness in Marriage* (Minneapolis: Burgess Publishing Co., 1947).

techniques developed in courtship and the later success of the marriage.[6]

Marriage counseling is such a new field that few married couples ever seek advice or help until they are in serious trouble. Even more seek the divorce lawyer rather than the counselor. The person (or couple) who comes to the counselor usually comes only when he senses that his marriage has got beyond his own control and understanding.

Even the informed person who knows about the marriage counselor hesitates to come admitting that he is in trouble. For some there is a feeling of shame in airing their troubles before an outsider. For others, it is difficult to realize that the counselor is a professional person who will neither condemn, place blame, or censure, but whose sole business it is to understand and help. He never passes judgment or takes sides. He is not shocked by personal revelations.

The counselor's role appears on the surface to be a passive one. He listens but says little. He expresses few, if any, opinions and seems both unimpressed and disinterested. Actually, upon closer scrutiny, he is found to be active in a subtle way; he encourages freedom in expression of hostilities and anxieties, and in so doing he allows the troubled individual to relieve tensions that may be blocking his way to understanding and happiness. His job is to help the individual objectify his problems, take them out and handle them, look them over, talk about them and then decide for himself the best solution.

The counselor, when it is possible, gets both husband and wife together to air their petty or serious grievances against each other. When expressed before a third party, grievances often shrink in importance and appear in less dramatic proportions. By such means the counselor hopes the individuals concerned will become sufficiently understanding of themselves to take positive steps.

These positive steps may lead toward the dissolution of the marriage or may lead to a rebuilding of it.[7] The outcome is not the counselor's responsibility, and he does not assume responsibility for it. All he hopes to do is to provide the environment in which the contending parties can see their relationship and appraise it in such a way as to make an intelligent and unemotional decision.

Often the counselor, in leading the couple to see what the facts of their marriage are, helps to release the pressure and opens the way to seeing the positive aspects of their marriage. The couple may, after the experience, come to look upon their marriage relationship in terms of its

[6] For the best summary in the literature on problems of predicting and forecasting success in marriage, see E. W. Burgess and Paul Wallin, *Engagement and Marriage* (Philadelphia: J. B. Lippincott Co., 1953), Chs. 16, 17.

[7] Aaron L. Rutledge, "Should the Marriage Counselor Ever Recommend Divorce?" *Marriage and Family Living*, 25:319-325, August, 1963.

reality, rather than in terms of what they formerly thought the marriage ideal was, and in so doing conclude that it is a finer relationship than any other they can possibly conceive for themselves. "The first step toward a happier marriage is freedom to value the relationship as it is."[8]

The problems which people in marital trouble bring to the counselor are the same kinds of problems any person in psychological stress experiences. The essence of the situation is learning to relate onself to other people—in marriage counseling, the other person concerned is usually the mate.

The whole field of premarital and marriage counseling is in its infancy, and there are very few well-trained persons practicing in the field. It is, however, one of the devices by which it is hoped that some of the rough spots in modern marriage may be smoothed out.

Social Policies to Improve Marriage

The demands an industrial society makes on marriage are so far different from those made by the agricultural society of an earlier day that adaptations in the institutional structure are needed to make marriage and family life more effective in meeting human needs. Certain of these adaptations must be made at the governmental policy level.

Marriage subsidy: Some countries have tried the general subsidy of marriage, as did Hitler in the pre-World War II days by advancing loans, a fourth of which were cancelled on the birth of each child. The only national social policy focused primarily upon marriage and family responsibilities in the United States is the family allowances for military personnel and for veterans completing their education. The effect of these programs has been to help make marriage and normal family life possible at an earlier age than would otherwise have been the case.

Although such a program has not been considered on a national scale, there is something to be said for the subsidizing of marriages among the more able civilian college group. An increasing proportion of the population is going to college. The need for professionally trained persons in many fields far exceeds the supply and will for some years to come. It is in the eugenic interest of a society to encourage at least a normal birth rate among its more educated members. It is to the advantage of society, as well as the individual, to encourage marriage and childbearing during the twenties when schooling is still in progress, rather than delaying it until the chances of finding suitable mates and having children are seriously jeopardized by advancing age.

More needs to be done through social policy to relieve the mother of

8 John Levy and Ruth Munroe, *The Happy Family* (New York: Alfred A. Knopf, Inc., 1938), p. 177.

the restrictive burdens of child care. The demands of modern society are such that many intelligent and highly competent women cannot be happy devoting all their time to housekeeping and child care. There is no reason why our urban industrial society cannot do a great deal more than has been done to make it possible for the average wife and mother to work full- or part-time without neglecting her children.

Public nurseries, nursery schools, kindergartens, and child-care centers, along with income tax deductions for child care for the married, working mothers would give women opportunities for greater freedom, self-expression, and a feeling of greater family and social usefulness than many now enjoy.

Medical care: Although attempts of the Congress to introduce compulsory health insurance as a part of the Social Security Act have been defeated each time so far, and although socialized medicine is taboo with the American Medical Association with its powerful lobby and propaganda machine, some such measures will have to be devised to reach the level of family health and psychological security needed by the American family. Private insurance plans have grown by leaps and bounds, indicating the public interest in protection, but few of these plans are fully adequate. A major operation or long sickness can wreck the finances of most families in a short time.

Our system of private medicine stresses cure rather than prevention. We lock the barn after the horse is stolen. Had education been left on the same basis as medical care, we would still be a nation of ignorance. Thanks to socialized education, we are the best-educated people on earth. Although any kind of public protection of family health is fought by the organized medical profession, the evidence of greater protection for family health is all in favor of socialized medicine. The lowest general death rates in the world, the lowest maternal death rates, and the lowest infant death rates are to be found in countries having socialized medicine, not in the United States. In fact, our record is shameful by comparison.

Here are infant death rates of a few countries having socialized medicine, compared with our own:

Country	Infant death rate
United States	25.3
Sweden	15.3
The Netherlands	15.3
Norway	17.9
Denmark	20.1
New Zealand	20.3
Australia	20.4
England and Wales	21.4

Annual wage: The annual wage for industrial workers is full of promise for greater happiness in marriage. Research has shown that regularity of income is associated with successful marriage.[9] The industrial classes, which now show the greatest amount of unhappiness in marriage,[10] might well enjoy a higher level of marital happiness with a regularity of income that would provide for greater stability and permit more meaningful planning.

Family allowances: In the economic field, too, the family allowance systems now in effect in practically every other major industrial nation represent a means of bringing about greater equality between the sexes. This system is also conducive to a greater feeling of economic security and to greater marital stability. Family allowances, paid from taxation, usually are paid to the mother, giving her a new sense of independence and equality. The family allowance also gives her vocation a new dignity. By providing a regular guarantee for the minimum support of all children, it places marriage on a safer foundation.

In Canada, for example, all mothers receive a monthly allowance for each child from birth to age sixteen (provided the child remains in school). The average per family is $16.63 per month, $6.69 per child. Allowances are from taxation.[11] All political parties in Canada now agree on the value of this program, according to the Ministry of National Health and Welfare.[12] It provides children with better food, shelter, health, care, and education than would have been possible otherwise. The program is the best truant officer, too, since the child must attend school for the mother to get payment. This expenditure of funds, which is constantly turned over in the purchase of consumable goods, keeps the economy primed with spending power.

In an agrarian society, security is in the land, and all members of the family, as workers, increase that security. In an industrial society, a man and wife's only security is in their own earning power. Marriage is permitted only when the couple can become self-sustaining; children are approved only when the couple can support them, and yet industrial society has placed numerous hazards of insecurity before the couple and the parent. The economic disadvantage of having children in an industrial society is clearly shown by data presented in Figure 8-2 (see p. 161). Democratic industrial society must, through such social policies as those suggested above, make life safer for marriage and the family.

[9] Ernest W. Burgess and Leonard S. Cottrell, *Predicting Success or Failure in Marriage* (Englewood Cliffs, N. J.: Prentice-Hall, Inc., 1939), pp. 416 ff.

[10] Refer again to Figure 23-1 on page 460.

[11] Bernice Madison, "Canadian Family Allowances and Their Major Social Implications," *Journal of Marriage and Family Living*, 26:134-141, May, 1964.

[12] Before allowances came into effect, a 1943 Gallup poll showed 49 percent favorable; in a 1955 poll, 90 percent favorable. *Ibid.*

Population control: The time has come when complete control of fertility is possible, yet we have many lower-class families, particularly among the nonwhites, who are propagating themselves into the third generation on relief. There is little hope of successfully attacking poverty or raising the standard of living of this great dispossessed group in the city slums and rural poverty pockets except by bringing fertility under control.

Children in all families, the privileged and underprivileged alike, should be the voluntary issue of the family. This can be only as we develop a national policy of birth control which seeks aggressively to make parenthood voluntary. It will require a system of birth control clinics throughout underprivileged rural areas and slum sections where such programs can be promoted as an end toward raising the standard of living and economic and educational aspirations.

The Future of Marriage

Throughout this chapter, attention has been called to various devices which have been developed by social science to aid in mate selection and marriage adjustment. To the extent that these devices help create a more realistic attitude of mind and a more realistic understanding of marriage, they are fraught with great possibilities.

Perhaps the gradual trend of young people, particularly college-trained young people, to be more realistic about the whole matter of mate selection and marriage is the most hopeful sign for the future. The fact that young people today are interested in studying marriage, serious about its purpose, and concerned about its outcome, is salutary.

Those who enter marriage with serious purpose and who put the success of marriage above numerous petty little difficulties and adjustments have already risen above the factors that defeat most marriages. Serious young people today no longer approach marriage as an experiment with the general notion that if it doesn't work they can try again. Informed young people know that this kind of trial and error is very expensive in terms of one's emotional life, economic future, reputation, and social relationships. The greatest hope of marriage education is that it will help young people to defer marriage until they are certain they are ready to assume its responsibilities and assume them finally and without question—that they will put the success of the marriage above everything else and, in so doing, not be detracted from its ultimate purpose by petty difficulties, emotional upsets, and temporary sexual tensions or other distractions which are inevitable in any marriage relationship.

To the extent that they enter marriage with a determination to work out a way of life together, they are well on their road to success. This does not mean that life must return to the stoic philosophy of enduring a futile marriage. It does, however, mean that positive and final attitudes of mind concerning the marriage relationship are factors in building it toward success. The greatest threat to any venture is a hesitant and unsure attitude of mind. This attitude can drive a husband or wife to neurosis and can drive marriage to the rocks. The greatest failure in life "is the failure of purpose." Those with a purpose to move forward and to succeed can override obstacles such as readily defeat the weak-hearted.

Those with high purpose do not throw a marriage overboard because of temporary difficulties and adjustments or because the mate may become temporarily infatuated with another in a period of absence. Those with high purpose do not allow minor upsets in their interpersonal relationship to poison the whole family atmosphere so that it destroys the life of children and the security of the family.

In the emphasis on happiness, today, many fail to be realistic and to learn that even happiness has its price, perhaps the most exacting price of all human values—the price of duty, of obligation, of meeting requirements, and of keeping pledges, the price of maintaining loyalties and of experiencing sacrifice. It does not come without its price and it does not come for the direct seeking—it is the reward of a life of unfailing purpose, the counterpart of a mature approach to situations and to life itself.

Without some measure of these personal qualities, there can be no real happiness and no real permanence in marriage. With these, marriage can persist and happiness be found. It will be greater at some times than at others. At times, it may be overshadowed by tension, sorrow, or other crises, but those who fight through these periods will again come into an area of sunshine and happiness, if not the bliss of their first romance.

In conclusion, the companionship marriage, built on an individualistic basis, promises human beings much—perhaps too much. But accompanied with realistic good sense it can bring more than the authoritarian marriage of an earlier day ever brought. Its rewards are only for those who pay the price, however. Marriage happiness is no more a storybook affair today than it ever was. It involves sickness and health, a sense of obligation, a will to persist, and a determination to succeed. And, on the negative side, it must rise above a feeling that one needs to run to a divorce court or a divorce judge every time there is a little rift in the personal relationship. Numerous persons who have divorced could have found a much more satisfactory life and greater happiness in their marriage than they found either in the loneliness which followed divorce or in the second marriage which may have followed the breakup of their first.

Many, no doubt, settle for a much less satisfactory marriage the second time, because they approach marriage with greater realism, knowing from the divorce experience that they expected too much in their first relationship. Others shift from marriage to marriage because they never grow up to the mature state of mind which recognizes that life is full of responsibilities, they never find what they want in life because they do not have within themselves the qualities of perseverance, determination, and good will essential to success in the most demanding venture which human beings undertake—that of marriage and of parenthood.

Problems

1. List and discuss various attitudes and skills which might be taught to young people in courses in family-life education.
2. Which goals do you believe should be uppermost in such courses—teaching specific homemaking skills or developing specific homemaking and family-oriented attitudes?
3. At what grade level do you believe sex education should begin in school?
4. What are the chief arguments presented by some parents in opposition to sex education at any level in public schools? How might these arguments best be met?
5. Ideally, should sex education be handled chiefly by the home or the school? Why?
6. Discuss the views presented in the following conversation.

   One mother, "I'm opposed to sex education in or out of school. I believe that young men and women should be given the necessary facts when they're old enough to need them, not before." She adds, "All of this fuss about chilren being 'naturally curious' is just poppy-cock. Why my eleven-year-old daughter has never once asked a question having to do with sex, reproduction, or the like."

   Her companion answers, "If I had an eleven-year-old daughter who hadn't asked about anything associated with sex, I would not brag; I'd be alarmed."
7. A respected marriage counselor in a New York community was recently sued for a divorce. As a result he lost many of his clients who seemed to feel, as one woman put it, "If he can't make a success of his own marriage, how can others have faith in him?" Among those who remained with him was a young husband who answered this charge with, "My physician is often sick, but this does not reflect upon his professional skill."

   What would your reaction have been to this divorce had you been a client? Justify your position.
8. In the West Haven Marriage and Family Relations Clinic there are two marriage counselors using very different techniques in their counseling. Of the two, Dr. Robell is the more popular. He is generous with his advice and not at all reluctant to suggest specific action as a cure for a couple's problems.

Dr. Murry seldom gives advice. His chief goal seems to be getting man and wife, or an engaged couple, into the clinic together. Once there, Dr. Murry speaks only enough to keep the two of them going in their conversation together about their differences.

a. Upon what principle is Dr. Murry operating?

b. Why is Dr. Robell more popular?

c. Which counselor do you believe is the more successful in helping couples work out solutions to their problems?

Selected References

ARTICLES IN BOOKS OF READINGS

BECKER, Howard, and HILL, Reuben (Editors), *Family, Marriage and Parenthood,* Second Edition (Boston: D. C. Heath & Co., 1955).

1. HILL, Reuben, "Plans for Strengthening Family Life," pp. 773-806.

VINCENT, Clark E., *Readings in Marriage Counseling* (New York: Thomas Y. Crowell Co., 1957).

2. STONE, Abraham, "Marriage Education and Marriage Counseling in the United States," pp. 12-19.

3. BOWMAN, Henry A., "Collegiate Education for Marriage and Family Living," pp. 19-29.

4. MACE, David R., "What Is a Marriage Counselor?" pp. 29-35.

LANDIS, Judson T., and LANDIS, Mary G., *Readings in Marriage and the Family* (Englewood Cliffs, N. J.: Prentice-Hall, Inc., 1952).

5. MUDD, Emily Hartshorne, and PRESTON, Malcolm C., "The Contemporary Status of Marriage Counseling," pp. 439-445.

6. COTTRELL, Leonard S., "The Present Status and Future Orientation of Research on the Family," pp. 445-453.

FISHBEIN, Morris, and KENNEDY, Ruby Jo Reeves, *Modern Marriage and Family Living* (New York: Oxford University Press, 1957).

7. MANWILLER, Charles E., "Sex Education and the Child," pp. 476-483.

8. BOSSARD, James H. S., "The Family Council," pp. 510-522.

SUSSMAN, Marvin B., *Sourcebook in Marriage and the Family,* Second Edition (Boston: Houghton Mifflin Co., 1963).

9. BURCHINAL, Lee G., "Research in Young Marriage: Implications for Family Life Education," pp. 508-529.

10. COTTRELL, Leonard S., "New Directions for Research on the American Family," pp. 548-554.

CAVAN, Ruth Shonle, *Marriage and the Family in the Modern World: A Book of Readings* (New York: Thomas Y. Crowell Co., 1960).

11. BRANGWIN, Lorna C., "Marriage Counseling," Reading 93.

CHRISTENSEN, Harold T., *Handbook of Marriage and the Family* (Chicago: Rand McNally & Co., 1964).

12. BROWN, Muriel C., "Organizational Programs to Strengthen the Family," Ch. 20.

13. KERCKHOFF, Richard K., "Family Life Education in America," Ch. 21.
14. LESLIE, Gerald R., "The Field of Marriage Counseling," Ch. 22.
15. KEPHART, William M., "Legal and Procedural Aspects of Marriage and Divorce," Ch. 23.
16. CHRISTENSEN, Harold T., "The Intrusion of Values," Ch. 24.

General References

BEE, Lawrence S., *Marriage and Family Relations* (New York: Harper & Row, Publishers, 1959), Ch. 18.

BURGESS, Ernest W., and WALLIN, Paul, *Engagement and Marriage* (Philadelphia: J. B. Lippincott Co., 1953), Chs. 16, 17, 22.

CAVAN, Ruth Shonle, *American Marriage* (New York: Thomas Y. Crowell Co., 1959), Ch. 22.

CUBER, John F., *Marriage Counseling Practice* (New York: Appleton-Century-Crofts, 1948).

DAGER, Edward Z., HARPER, Glenn A., and WHITEHURST, Robert N., "Family Life Education in Public High Schools: A Survey Report in Indiana," *Marriage and Family Living*, 24:365-370, November, 1962.

DYER, Dorothy, "A Comparative Study Relating Marital Happiness to University Courses Helpful in Marital Adjustment," *Marriage and Family Living*, 12:230-234, August, 1959.

ELIOT, Thomas D., "Sex Instruction in the Norwegian Culture," *Social Problems*, 1:44-48, October, 1953.

FARBER, Bernard, *Family: Organization and Interaction* (San Francisco: Chandler Publishing Co., 1964), Ch. 7.

FOSTER, Robert G., "How a Marriage Counselor Handles a Case," *Marriage and Family Living*, 16:139-142.

KIRKPATRICK, Clifford, *The Family As Process and Institution*, Revised Edition (New York: The Ronald Press Co., 1963), Ch. 23.

LANDIS, Judson T., and LANDIS, Mary G., *Readings in Marriage* (Englewood Cliffs, N. J.: Prentice-Hall, Inc., 1952), Ch. 16.

LANTZ, Herman R., and SNYDER, Eloise C., *Marriage* (New York: John Wiley & Sons, Inc., 1962).

LEVY, John, and MUNROE, Ruth, *The Happy Family* (New York: Alfred A. Knopf, Inc., 1938).

MACE, David R., "What Is a Marriage Counselor?" *Marriage and Family Living*, 16:135-138.

MOSES, Virginia Musick, "A Study of Learning Derived from a Functional Course in Marriage and Family Relationships," *Marriage and Family Living*, 18:204-208, August, 1956.

MUDD, Emily Hartshorne, *The Practice of Marriage Counseling* (New York: Association Press, 1951).

MYRDAL, Alva, *Nation and Family* (New York: Harper and Bros., 1941).

NIMKOFF, Myer F., *Marriage and the Family* (Boston: Houghton Mifflin Co., 1947), Ch. 20.

OGBURN, W. F., and NIMKOFF, M. F., *Technology and the Changing Family* (Boston: Houghton Mifflin Co., 1955).

POFFENBERGER, Thomas, "Family Life Education in a Scientific Age," *Marriage and Family Living*, 21:150-154, May, 1959.

TURNER, Bernadette F., "Common Characteristics of Persons Seeking Professional Marriage Counseling," *Marriage and Family Living*, 16:143-144.

APPENDIX A

Motion Picture Films[*]

This bibliography is only a suggestion. Film users should examine the latest annual edition and quarterly supplements of *Educational Film Guide,* a catalog of some 10,000 films published by the H. W. Wilson Co., New York. The *Guide,* a standard reference book, is available in most college and public libraries.

Part I: Introductory

Communication and Interaction in Three Families (Kinesis 80 min). Film documentation of nonverbal communication observed in three families during their daily activities and explanation of the three behavior patterns expressed in their methods of communication and interaction.

Marriage Today (McGraw 22 min). Two couples are the protagonists of this film, two couples who have made their marriage work through clear analysis of their mutual aims and through cooperation. Neither of these marriages is perfect for there are bound to be conflicts. But these people have their ideals and goals in true perspective and they are willing to work together to reach them.

Our Changing Family Life (McGraw 22 min). A farm family in 1880 is shown as a closely integrated unit—economically, culturally, emotionally. Members of the three generations living under one roof contribute to the family life accord-ing to a well-established pattern. Religion and recreation, in addition to the sharing of work, play important roles in holding the family together as an insti-tution. Since 1880, industrial expansion, the growth of cities and the political and economic emancipation of women have radically changed the traditional pattern of family life. We see how the farm family has become less important as an economic and social unit, how the roles of husband and wife in the urban family have shifted, and how the companionship of marriage has become even more important in today's impersonal urban society.

The Family (USA/Du Art Film Laboratories, Inc. 20 min). Explains how daily problems confronting a family are solved when each member understands the needs and desires of others and the family faces its problems together.

[*] Full names and addresses of distributors appear at the end of this list.

The Good Earth (MGM/TFC 18 min). Excerpts from the feature film based upon Pearl Buck's novel, showing marriage customs in China, status of women in Chinese peasant households, their roles as wives and workers, and the importance of bearing children.

Part II: Male and Female, Predispositions and Roles

As Boys Grow (Medical Arts Productions 16 min). A coach working with a group of boys develops a situation in which he explains various aspects of puberty in boys and girls and the processes of human reproduction.

Molly Grows Up (Medical Arts Productions 15 min). Factual data on normal menstruation for encouraging a healthy and wholesome attitude toward this biological function. A typical 13-year-old girl gets reassurance from mother, older sister, and the school nurse.

Physical Aspects of Puberty (McGraw 19 min). This film is an animated description of the development of the primary and secondary sex characteristics in boys and girls during adolescence. Normal variations in development can have social repercussions, and behavior problems that seem emotional are often based on the rate of physical growth.

Social-Sex Attitudes in Adolescence (McGraw 22 min). The life stories of a young married couple are presented and contrasted from the aspects of their sex education and sex adjustments in adolescence. The importance of personal experiences and the influence of parents and friends are seen in their struggle to achieve mature social-sex adjustment. The film focuses clearly on the desirable aspects of the problems handled.

Your Body During Adolescence (McGraw 10 min). What puberty means and how it affects the body is the theme of this film. Using animation, the film shows the seven glands that regulate human life and growth. Then follows a description of the reproductive organs with a complete and detailed explanation of their function and use.

Part III: Preface to Mate Choice

Mental Mechanisms (CNFB/McGraw). Five films portraying through case studies different individual problems and their roots in early childhood and family relationships. Titles and running times of the individual films are:

> *Breakdown* (40 min)
> *Feeling of Hostility* (27 min)
> *Feeling of Rejection* (23 min)
> *Feelings of Depression* (30 min)
> *Over-dependency* (32 min)

Family Circles (CNFB/McGraw 31 min). Portrays, through three dramatized situations, the interplay between home and school influences and shows how family attitudes affect children's success in school.

Preface to Life (USPHS 29 min). Parental influence on a child's developing personality, illustrated by a series of episodes showing the effects of an overly solicitous mother and an overly demanding father. In contrast, the healthy child-hood resulting when both parents accept their child as an individual is portrayed.

Roots of Happiness (International Film Bureau 24 min). One Puerto Rican family where four children are being raised in an atmosphere of love, mutual understanding, and happiness is contrasted with another family where there is strife, shouting, and hatred.

The Quiet One (Contemporary Films, Inc. 1 hour, 7 min). "The Quiet One" is Donald Peters, an emotionally sick boy who lives in New York's Harlem. For-saken by his parents, unloved by his cranky grandmother, friendless and alone, he skips school and eventually gets into trouble. Donald, now 10, is taken to an unusual school for delinquent boys: the Wiltwyck School at Esopus, New York. It is a long time before the staff is able to break through the boy's wall of bitter-ness and isolation. Finally, Donald becomes attached to one counselor, and this is the turning point toward recovery and rehabilitation. There are setbacks, including a crisis which causes the boy to run away. The shock of nearly being hit by a train helps Donald cut the ties to his past. The film, deeply moving, has been widely acclaimed for its content and its exceptionally fine photography and narration.

Age of Turmoil (McGraw 20 min). Adolescent development series. Case histories of teenagers and their problems. Eternal hunger, bragging, roughhous-ing, primping, daydreaming, endless telephoning, etc., as symptoms of a stage that must be tolerated.

Are You Ready For Marriage? (Coronet 15 min). A marriage counselor gives a practical check list of criteria for engagement and marriage to a young couple who are planning to marry.

Choosing for Happiness (McGraw 14 min). "Is he right for me?" is Eve's first question when she meets a new boy, and somewhere in the passing weeks each one fails to measure up. As she sets about changing him for his own good, he drifts away, leaving her hurt and puzzled. Gaining Eve's confidence, Mary, her cousin, suggests that for Eve, as for everyone, self-analysis must come first, that she must accept the possibility of making certain changes in herself and fewer demands on other people.

How Do You Know It's Love? (Coronet 13 min). The picture introduces Jack and Nora, who enjoy dating each other but are confused about their feel-ings toward each other. A double date with a more mature engaged couple and Nora's heart-to-heart talk with her understanding mother give them valuable guideposts by which to measure their attraction. The film explains that love is something learned through experiences with parents and friends, rather than a trap into which one "falls." An excellent printed guide accompanies the film.

How Much Affection? (McGraw 20 min). How much affection should there be between a couple who is going steady? How far can young people go in pet-ting and still stay within the bounds of social mores and personal standards? The carefully presented drama of this film sets the stage for constructive and frank discussion of these and related questions of vital importance to young people today.

Is This Love? (McGraw 14 min). The film contrasts the romances of two college roommates. One girl, impulsive and emotional, is resentful of any persuasion to delay her marriage. The other girl hesitates to consider marriage until she has solid proof of her love through successive stages of dating, courtship, going steady, and engagement. The film ends with open-end questions leading to evaluation of the two romances and of their respective chances for success in marriage.

Parents Are People Too (McGraw 15 min). Illustrates ways in which adolescent resentment toward authority is aroused, and suggests means, particularly family discussions, which can serve to overcome some family-argument situations.

Part IV: Mate Choice

It Takes All Kinds (McGraw 20 min). The right marriage partner need not be one's exact counterpart, but for a happy marriage, two personalities must complement each other. The traits that identify personalities are not difficult to discover; most people in a moment of stress will reveal them quite clearly. As the film points out, the successful marriages will be those where the partners choose each other with care, with a sure knowledge of each other, and then accept them for what they are, not what they might wish the other to be.

One Love—Conflicting Faiths (Methodist Publishing House 27 min). The story of a Protestant-Catholic Marriage.

The Meaning of Engagement (Coronet 13 min). Explains the functions of the engagement period as being the development of psychological unity, learning to know each other, and planning for the future.

This Charming Couple (McGraw 19 min). Portrays through dramatized situations a young married couple and the reasons for their failure to achieve marital happiness.

When Should I Marry? (McGraw 19 min). A young couple, eager to marry but urged by their parents to delay, ask a minister's advice. He describes the experiences of two other couples who married at an early age. From this description, he is able to summarize some practical points that should be of help to all young people in answering the question of when to marry.

While the River Waits (Academy Pictures Corporation 18 min). Tells how one unmarried mother was helped by the Florence Crittendon Home to solve her problem.

Part V: Marriage Adjustment

Families First (NY Com 17 min). Contrasts two middle-class families and shows the results of tensions and frustrations in one and of affection and harmonious relationship in the other.

Home Management: Why Budget (YAF 11 min). Importance of budgeting income and expenses and explanation of budget methods for individuals and for families.

Jealousy (McGraw 14 min). The problem of jealousy—a young wife, reluctant to give up acting for the role of a housewife, imagines her husband's long business hours to mean unfaithfulness.

Marriage Is a Partnership (Coronet 15 min). Raises and discusses some of the major problems that arise during the early married years and emphasizes that marriage is a partnership.

Marriage Today (McGraw 22 min.) Some answers to problems raised in *This Charming Couple.* The ideals and goals of adult love; how two couples make their marriages work through analysis of mutual aims and cooperation in striving to achieve them.

Your Family Budget (Coronet 10 min). Explains the planning and operation of a family budget and its importance to family living.

Who's Right? (McGraw 18 min). The film questions the soundness of and analyzes a marriage where one is driven by the desire to boss and rule, the other, by the desire to acquire and possess things.

Who's Boss? (McGraw 16 min). Compromises and adustments are necessary in maintaining a happy marriage relationship. This film emphasizes the need to think of oneself as a member of a partnership first and as an individual secondarily. It shows how patience, love, and understanding help achieve a good balance where neither is boss, but both are partners.

Part VI: Parenthood

FAMILY PLANNING

A Planned Parenthood Story (Mayo 18 min). Deals with the need for planning the size of a family and spacing the birth of children. Tells of the services of the Planned Parenthood Federation of America.

Human Heredity (Brown Trust 18 min). Basic facts and concepts pertaining to human heredity; union of egg and sperm; determination of sex and physical characteristics by chromosomes and genes; cultural influence on sex attitudes and roles, using animation. Open ending.

Heredity and Prenatal Development (McGraw 20 min). Discusses cell growth and heredity, describes fertilization of ovum and traces development of fetus until delivery, considers development of physical functions of new-born, and stresses connection between physical and emotional sensitivity.

CHILDBIRTH

Labor and Childbirth (Medical Films 17 min). This film is prepared for showing to parents during the time they are attending a program of education for childbirth and preparation of the mothers for labor and delivery conducted by nurses and doctors trained in that specialty. A nurse or doctor familiar with the films and able to interpret the incidents of labor and delivery which it portrays should be present.

Childbirth: Normal Delivery (Medical Films 16 min). Gives a close-up of the actual birth of a baby. Photographed under medical supervision. Distribution restricted to medical schools, hospitals, nursing and educational institutions, and lectures or showings under medical supervision.

Natural Childbirth (Wesminster/XWN 18390). A 12-inch long-playing record by Dr. Grantly Dick Read. Documentary recording of a woman giving birth to a baby by the Read Method of natural childbirth. Instructions to patient by Dr. Read and his wife and comments of the patient on her sensations and reactions to her first experience in childbearing.

CHILD CARE

Doctor Spock (McGraw 26 min). Dr. Spock's book on child care is the book by which many families throughout the nation are rearing their children. This film shows Dr. Spock at work in his clinic in Philadelphia. Consultation and research work go hand in hand here to find the best answers to all kinds of problems in the care and training of babies and children.

Baby Sitter (YAF 14 min). Outlines the training needed for the job and points out the responsibilities of both parents and sitters.

Martha Belongs (Wisconsin State Board of Health 12 min). Emphasizes the early contacts of a baby with her own family and the need of an infant to have opportunities to develop at her own pace and to have freedom for exercise. Points up natural opportunities for sex education of older children in the family.

CHILD DEVELOPMENT

Life with Baby (McGraw 18 min). With candid-camera sequences photographed through a one-way vision dome, this film shows how children grow. Observing youngsters of different ages, the film reveals the patterns of normal child development. Under the direction of Dr. Arnold Gesell, The Yale University Child Development Clinic has been able to establish definite standards of development for children up to six years of age.

Life with Junior (McGraw 18 min). Capturing the spirit and inquisitive exuberance of the nation's small-fry, this delightful film presents a typical day in the life of a ten-year-old. Such common problems as acceptance of the new brother, and Junior's refusal to eat are pictured in sequences made in cooperation with the Child Study Association of America.

Sibling Relations and Personality (McGraw 22 min). Observation of personality manifestations among children in the family of five children under varying conditions where conflicts develop; ways for parents to meet the problem raised.

Discipline During Adolescence (McGraw 16 min). This film is addressed to the age-old question of how much discipline is good for adolescents. Results of both too little and too much parental control are dramatized in a typical family setting.

Family Affairs (Mental Health Film Board 31 min). An adolescent's defiance of his parents brings to the surface the husband's long-smoldering resentment of his wife's domination. As the parents receive professional family counseling, typical interviews are presented in detail.

Preface to a Life (USPHS 29 min). Parental influence on a child's developing personality, illustrated by a series of episodes showing the effects of an overly solicitous mother and an overly demanding father. In contrast, the healthy child-hood resulting when both parents accept their child as an individual is portrayed.

Ages and Stages Series (McGraw). This series of films is designed to show child growth, year by year, from two to fifteen years. They present a wealth of valuable information about the age levels dealt with, illustrating positive parent-child relationships, and stressing that each age level has its own values in the child's life, in addition to being a stepping-stone to adulthood.

> *From Sociable Six to Noisy Nine* (22 min)
> *From Ten to Twelve* (26 min)
> *Frustrating Fours and Fascinating Fives* (22 min)
> *He Acts His Age* (13 min)
> *The Teens* (26 min)
> *Terrible Twos and Trusting Threes* (20 min)

Child Development Series (McGraw). Keyed to the problems of the normal child, these nine films analyze the many developmental patterns of infancy and childhood, providing parents with the understanding needed to help children achieve a happy, well-balanced maturity.

> *Child Care and Development* (17 min)
> *Children's Emotions* (22 min)
> *Children's Fantasies* (21 min)
> *Children's Play* (27 min)
> *Heredity and Prenatal Development* (21 min)
> *Principles of Development* (17 min)
> *Sibling Relations and Personality* (22 min)
> *Sibling Rivalries and Parents* (11 min)
> *Social Development* (16 min)

Studies of Normal Personality Development (N.Y.U. Film Library). Series includes the following films:

> *Balloons*
> *Finger Painting*
> *Frustration Play Techniques*
> *Meeting Emotional Needs in Childhood: The Groundwork of Democracy*
> *Pay Attention*
> *Preschool Incidents (No. 1) When Should Grown-ups Help?*
> *Preschool Incidents (No. 2) and Then Ice Cream*
> *This Is Robert*

Made under normal nursery school conditions, the films document the prob-lems faced by children in growing up and learning to fit into family, school, and community.

SEX EDUCATION

Growing Girls (EBF 13 min). Represents the physiological aspects of men-struation.

Human Beginnings (Assn 22 min). Designed to help children of primary school age develop healthy attitudes toward a new baby brother or sister and to clarify their feelings about this important event. The film opens in a classroom, where a sympathetic teacher helps the youngsters express, through art materials, their ideas and anxieties about birth. Little Tommy then tells the story of his new baby sister taking the audience to his home and to the hospital. Although intended for showing in elementary schools, the picture is even more valuable as an eye-opener for adults, helping them better understand the child's misconceptions and emotional needs.

Human Growth (Brown 19 min). A mixed group of 7th graders in a class situation view and discuss an animated film which traces human growth and development of the organism from mating through pregnancy and birth, then from infancy through childhood and adolescence to adulthood. Differences in male and female structural development are emphasized.

Part VII: Marriage Problems

Courtship to Courthouse (RKO/McGraw 15 min). Popularized presentation of the divorce problem in the United States in 1948. One of the "This is America" series.

In Time of Trouble (McGraw 14 min). Presents a marriage problem through an interview between a minister acting as a counselor and a woman of his parish. The woman is worried over her husband's growing tendency to drink, a reaction to her domination.

Marriage and Divorce (MOT/McGraw 15 min). Surveys the problems of broken homes and the increasing divorce rate (1949) in terms of present-day family living.

The Steps of Age (International Film Bureau 25 min). Mrs. Potter, 62, faces crucial problems as she embarks upon the last quarter of her life. The film portrays her confusion, her fears, and her far-from-easy struggle to understand herself. As she climbs a long stairway (symbolizing life's continuing challenges), she relives three episodes from the past: her husband's stubborn battle against retirement, her own unhappy relationship with her daughter and her grandchild, her pitiful attempts to find work. The picture suggests that people need to begin early in life to handle well the situations which come with increasing age.

Directory of Distributors

Academy Pictures Corporation, 1022 Forbes Street, Pittsburgh 19, Pa.

Assn—Association Films, Inc., 347 Madison Ave., New York 17, N. Y.

Brown—E. C. Brown Trust, 220 Southwest Adler St., Portland 4, Ore.

CNFB—Canadian National Film Board, 1270 Avenue of the Americas, New York 20, N. Y. (Films listed in this bibliography distributed by McGraw-Hill Book Company.)

Contemporary Films, Inc., 267 West 25th St., New York 1, N. Y.

Coronet—Coronet Instructional Films, 65 East South Water Street, Chicago 1, Illinois

EBF—Encyclopaedia Britannica Films, Inc., 1150 Wilmette Ave., Wilmette, Ill.

International Film Bureau, 332 South Michigan Ave., Chicago 4, Ill.

Kinesis—Kinesis, Inc., 566 Commercial St., San Francisco 11, Calif.

Mayo—Mayo-Video, 50 West 57th St., New York 19, N. Y.

McGraw—McGraw-Hill Book Company, Text-Film Department, 330 West 42d St., New York 36, N. Y.

Medical Films, Inc., 116 Natona Street, San Francisco 5, Calif.

Methodist Publishing House, P. O. Box 871, Nashville, Tenn.

MGM—Metro-Goldwyn-Mayer, Hollywood, Calif. (Films listed in this bibliography distributed by Teaching Film Custodians, Inc.)

MOT—March of Time, Inc., New York, N. Y. (Films listed in this bibliography distributed by McGraw-Hill Book Company.)

NY Com—New York State Department of Commerce, 112 State St., Albany 7, N. Y.

NYU—New York University Film Library, 26 Washington Place, New York 3, N. Y.

RKO—RKO Radio Pictures, Inc., New York, N. Y. (Films listed in this bibliography distributed by McGraw-Hill Book Company.)

TFC—Teaching Film Custodians, Inc., 25 West 43rd St., New York 36, N. Y.

USA—U. S. Department of the Army, Washington 25, D. C. (Films listed in this bibliography distributed for civilian use by Du Art Film Laboratories, Inc., 245 West 55th St., New York 19, N. Y.)

USPHS—U. S. Public Health Service, Department of Health, Education and Welfare, Washington 25, D. C.

UWF—United World Films, Inc., 1445 Park Ave., New York 29, N. Y.

Wisconsin State Board of Health, 1 West Wilson Street, Madison 2, Wis.

YAF—Young America Films, Inc., 18 East 41st St., New York 17, N. Y.

APPENDIX B

Autobiographical Term Paper

On each topic trace your background, and show how each trait or characteristic is likely to affect you as a marriage partner and parent.

I. LOVE

A. Affection: Can you give and receive affection? Is love or hostility the dominant trait of your personality? Relate to family background. Relate to marriageability and parenthood.

B. Romantic love: (1) On separate sheets of paper, chart your completed love affairs; love, attraction, indifference, dislike (page 204 of text for pattern). . . . (2) Chart course of your emotions after breakup of love affairs using the same curve—love, attraction, indifference, dislike (text page 204). . . .

II. WORK DUTY PATTERNS

What is your balance between work and pleasure? Can you pursue goals to their conclusion? Are you willing to assume the obligations of caring for others, particularly children? Is your orientation primarily toward consumption or production; acquiring goods or display? Relate to the past and the future.

III. PSYCHOLOGICAL PATTERNS

A. Ego needs: Are you essentially ego-centered or love-centered? Why?
B. Basic emotions: What is your dominant emotion, love, hate, fear, anxiety, etc.? Completing statements like the following will be helpful, "I hate most deeply"; "I fear most deeply"; "I am most anxious about"; etc.
C. Approach: Is your approach to people and to life essentially negative or positive?

D. Psychosexual orientation: Here consider the physical, psychological, and moral orientation of your personality. Is your personality in this area primarily guilt-centered, pleasure-centered, love-centered? Are your attitudes those of disgust or wholesome anticipation?

IV. LIFE GOALS

Dominant aspirations: What do you want most in life? Wealth? Happiness? Learning? What influences built this goal? How will it affect your mate choice and the development of your family life?

V. ROLE ORIENTATION

Male and female grow up under different subcultures. Do you accept the role of your sex or protest it? What do you expect in the way of behavior of the person you marry? Do you anticipate a role of equality or the traditional male-female pattern of roles? Can you readily compromise your role expectations for a member of the opposite sex whom you expect to marry? If you are already engaged, what role changes do you expect of your future spouse?

VI. SIB POSITION

What is your place among brothers and sisters? How has this affected your personality as it relates to your marriageability? If an only child, how has this affected your adjustments to the opposite sex?

VII. CONVENTIONALITY

Are you a rebel or an easily institutionalized person? Do you regard conventions such as control married people important? Does marriage make sense in the obligations and vows it imposes? Do you want children in marriage? Do you consider a similar religion important to your marriage? Were there family ceremonial occasions in your parental family which you plan to reproduce in your family?

Specifications:

1. Paper should range between 2,000 and 5,000 words.
2. Place name on a face sheet, which will be keyed and removed before papers are read to assure anonymity.
3. Papers will be held in complete confidence for two years when the file will be available to marriage classes.

AUTHOR INDEX

SUBJECT INDEX

Abortion
  during premarital pregnancy, 402-404
  extent of, 583-584
  trend of, 584
  unfavorable consequences of, 583-587
Accommodation in marriage, 440-442
Adjustment
  after breaking engagement, 375
  during engagement, 335-355
  during honeymoon, 412-414
  to marriage, 411-449
  to marriage by age of marriage, 320-325
  of mixed marriages, 278-305
  to parenthood, 606-607
  patterns of, in marriage, 430-449
  of religious and nonreligious mates,
    281-283
  in remarriage, 717-718
  sexual, in marriage, 470-511
  time required for, in marriage, 418-419
  to unmarried adulthood, 677-679
Adolescent
  homosexual stage of, 58, 87
  preoccupation of, with his body, 86-88
  sterility, 52-53
Adoption, 621-624
Age
  and chances of widowhood, 696
  chronological vs. maturity, 325-326
  differences in, at marriage, 30, 311-312
  factor in mate selection and marriage
    success, 311-312, 320-341
  for marriage, 13, 320-325
  and risk of spinsterhood, 337-339
  and sex activity, 496
  statistics on, and marriage success, 320-
    325
  statistics on, of marriage, 13, 30, 323
  of women in work world, 167
Alcoholism, 239-240, 462-464

American Association of Marriage Coun-
    selors
  address of, 740
  see also Counseling
Artificial insemination, 572-574
Attitudes
  toward pregnancy, 587-589
  toward romantic love, 194-195
  toward sex, 477-481
Authoritarianism
  by community and sex, 124
  in family by size, 617
  see also Discipline
Authority in child training, 124, 617, 631-
    637
Authority pattern in families of teenage
    boys and girls, 124, 617

Baby
  second, 610-611
  see also Child; Children
Bachelor
  death rates of, 28, 672
  personality traits of, 669-671
  risks of becoming, 399-400
  see also Unmarried adult
Birth
  hazards of, 577
  Read method of, 589-591
Birth control, 579-583
Birth suit, 591-592
Bride
  age of, 30
  chances of being, by age, 351-354
  see also Wife; Widowhood
Broken engagements, see Engagement
Broken homes
  statistics on children in, 707, 721-724
  see also Widowhood; Divorce